EXPLORER'S GUIDE

MAINE

EXPLORER'S GUIDE

MAINE

EIGHTEENTH EDITION

Including the Coast & Islands

CHRISTINA TREE & NANCY ENGLISH

THE COUNTRYMAN PRESS
A division of W. W. Norton & Company
Independent Publishers Since 1923

For lifelong explorers Liam, Tim, and Christopher Davis —C. T.

To Emma, with thanks and appreciation —N. E.

Maps by Erin Greb Cartography © The Countryman Press
Book design by Chris Welch
Manufacturing by Versa Press

The Countryman Press
www.countrymanpress.com

A division of W. W. Norton & Company, Inc.
500 Fifth Avenue, New York, NY 10110
www.wwnorton.com

ISBN: 978-1-58157-330-5 (pbk.)

10 9 8 7 6 5 4 3 2 1

EXPLORE WITH US!

We have been fine-tuning *Explorer's Guide Maine* for more than 30 years, a period in which lodging, dining, and shopping opportunities have more than quadrupled in the state. As we have expanded our guide, we have also been increasingly selective, making recommendations based on years of conscientious research and personal experience. We describe the state by locally defined regions, giving you Maine's communities, not simply her most popular destinations. With this guide you'll feel confident to venture beyond the tourist towns, along roads less traveled, to places of special hospitality and charm.

WHAT'S WHERE In the beginning of the book you'll find an alphabetical listing of special highlights and important information that you may want to reference quickly. You'll find advice on everything from where to buy the best local lobster to where to write or call for camping reservations and park information.

LODGING We've selected lodging places for mention in this book based on their merit alone; we do not charge innkeepers to be listed. The authors personally check as many bed & breakfasts, farms, sporting lodges, and inns as possible.

PRICES Please don't hold us or the respective innkeepers responsible for the rates listed as of press time in 2016. Some changes are inevitable. The 8 percent state rooms and meals tax should be added to all prices unless we specifically state that it's included in a price. We've tried to note when a gratuity is added, as it often is in high-end accommodations, but it's always wise to check before booking.

SMOKING Maine B&Bs, inns, and restaurants are now generally smoke-free, but many lodging places still reserve some rooms for smokers, and some restaurants still offer a

KEY TO SYMBOLS

- ✪ **Authors' favorites.** These are the places we think have the best to offer in each region, whether that means great food, outstanding rooms, beautiful scenery, or overall appeal.
- ♂ **Weddings.** The wedding-ring symbol appears next to lodging venues that specialize in weddings.
- ❧ **Special value.** The blue-ribbon symbol appears next to selected lodging and restaurants that combine quality and moderate prices.
- ❦ **Pets.** The dog-paw symbol appears next to venues that accept pets.
- ✎ **Child-friendly.** The crayon symbol appears next to lodging, restaurants, activities, and shops of special interest or appeal to youngsters.
- ♿ **Handicapped access.** The wheelchair symbol appears next to lodging, restaurants, and attractions that are partially or completely handicapped-accessible.
- ((ψ)) **Wireless Internet.** The wireless symbol appears next to public spaces, restaurants, and attractions that offer wireless Internet access.

smoking area in their outdoor seating. If this is important to you, be sure to ask when making reservations.

RESTAURANTS In most sections please note a distinction between *Dining Out* and *Eating Out*. By their nature, restaurants included in the *Eating Out* group are generally inexpensive.

We would appreciate any comments or corrections. Please write to:

Explorer's Guide Editor
The Countryman Press
A division of W. W. Norton & Company
500 Fifth Avenue
New York, NY 10110

For more info, go to: maineguidebook.com.

You can also email info@maineguidebook.com or tree.christina@gmail.com.

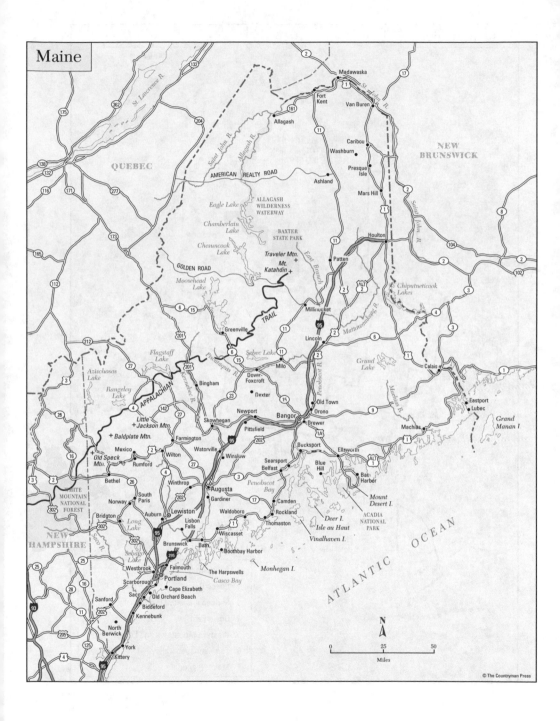

Maine

QUEBEC

NEW BRUNSWICK

AMERICAN REALTY ROAD

ALLAGASH WILDERNESS WATERWAY

BAXTER STATE PARK

GOLDEN ROAD

Traveler Mtn.
Mt. Katahdin

TRAIL

APPALACHIAN

WHITE MOUNTAIN NATIONAL FOREST

NEW HAMPSHIRE

ACADIA NATIONAL PARK

ATLANTIC OCEAN

N

0   25   50

Miles

© The Countryman Press

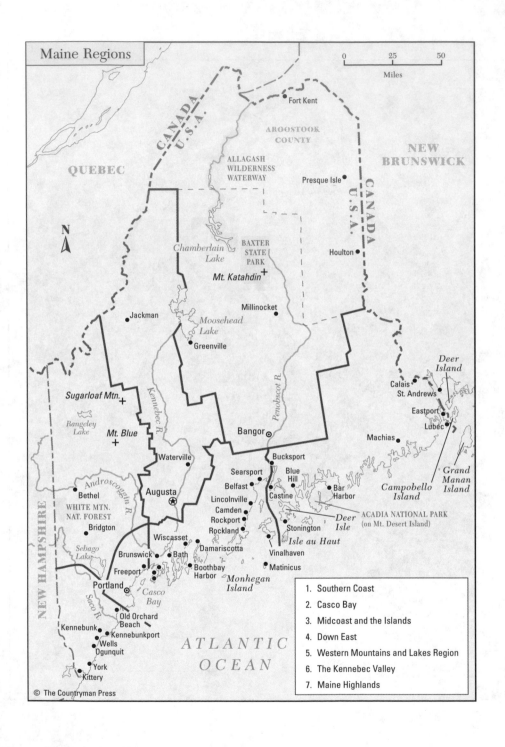

Maine Regions

0   25   50
Miles

CANADA
U.S.A.

Fort Kent

AROOSTOOK
COUNTY

NEW
BRUNSWICK

QUEBEC

ALLAGASH
WILDERNESS
WATERWAY

Presque Isle

CANADA
U.S.A.

N

Chamberlain
Lake

BAXTER
STATE
PARK

Houlton

Mt. Katahdin

Jackman

Moosehead
Lake

Millinocket

Greenville

Penobscot R.

Deer
Island

Calais
St. Andrews

Sugarloaf Mtn.

Kennebec R.

Eastport

Rangeley
Lake

Mt. Blue

Bangor

Lubec

Machias

Grand
Manan
Island

Waterville

Androscoggin R.

Bucksport

Searsport

Blue
Hill

Campobello
Island

Bethel

WHITE MTN.
NAT. FOREST

Augusta

Belfast

Bar
Harbor

Lincolnville

Castine

ACADIA NATIONAL PARK
(on Mt. Desert Island)

Bridgton

Camden
Rockport

Deer
Isle

Sebago
Lake

Wiscasset

Rockland

Stonington

NEW HAMPSHIRE

Brunswick

Bath

Damariscotta

Isle au Haut

Freeport

Boothbay
Harbor

Vinalhaven

Portland

Casco
Bay

Monhegan
Island

Matinicus

Saco R.

Old Orchard
Beach

ATLANTIC

Kennebunk

Kennebunkport

OCEAN

Wells
Ogunquit

York

Kittery

© The Countryman Press

1. Southern Coast

2. Casco Bay

3. Midcoast and the Islands

4. Down East

5. Western Mountains and Lakes Region

6. The Kennebec Valley

7. Maine Highlands

CONTENTS

MAPS

INTRODUCTION

He who rides and keeps the beaten track studies the fences chiefly.
—Henry David Thoreau, *The Maine Woods*, 1853

Over the past 36 years *Explorer's Guide Maine* has introduced hundreds of thousands of people to many Maines.

When this book initially appeared, it was the first 20th-century guidebook to describe New England's largest state region by region, rather than to focus only on the most touristed communities, listed alphabetically. From the start, we critiqued places to stay and eat as well as everything to see and to do—based on merit rather than money (no one pays to be included).

The big news, however, isn't that *Explorer's Guide Maine* was first but that readers constantly tell us that it remains the best Maine guidebook—that despite current competition, this "Maine Bible" gets better with each edition. Our publisher tells us it's still the best-selling guide to the state. While the number of Maine guidebooks has multiplied, we remain proud of the depth and scope of this one. With each edition we strive not only to update details, but also to simplify the format and sharpen the word pictures that describe each area.

We like to think of this book as the ultimate Maine search engine.

Back in 1981, this didn't seem like a tall order. Chris's three sons—ages 3, 6, and 8—helped her research reasonably priced rental cottages, ice cream stands, and beaches. The guide, however, quickly grew as inns, B&Bs, and other lodging options proliferated, as did things to do and see, dining venues, and shopping options. The book also soon included all the parts of Maine in which a visitor can find commercial lodging, from Kittery to Caribou and from the White Mountains to the islands of Monhegan and Matinicus, not to mention all of Rt. 1 from Kittery to Fort Kent. After the first couple of editions it became obvious that no one person could explore this immense and richly textured state during one season.

We now describe more than 500 places to stay, ranging from campgrounds to grand old resorts and including farms as well as B&Bs, inns, and off-the-grid sporting camps—in all corners of the state and in all price ranges. We have also checked out a similar number of places to dine and to eat (we make a distinction between dining and eating), and of course we have to include *Selective Shopping*.

This book's introductory section, "What's Where in Maine," is a quick-reference directory to a vast array of information about the state. The remainder of the book describes Maine region by region.

Note that "off-season" prices are often substantially lower than those in July and August—except in ski-resort areas, when winter is high season. September is dependably sparkling and frequently warm. Early October in Maine is just as spectacular as it is in New Hampshire and Vermont, with magnificent mountains rising from inland lakes as well as the golds and reds set against coastal blue. Be aware that the inland ski resorts of Sunday River near Bethel and the Sugarloaf area are "off-season" all summer as well as fall.

Maine is almost as big as the other five New England states combined, but her residents add up to less than half the population of Greater Boston. That means there is plenty of room for all who look to her for renewal—both residents and out-of-staters.

It's our hope that, although this book should help visitors and Maine residents alike enjoy the state's resort towns, it will be particularly useful for those who explore off the beaten track.

The Authors

Chris was born in Hawaii and bred in Manhattan, came to New England to attend Mount Holyoke College, and has been living in Massachusetts since she began to work for the *Boston Globe* in 1968. She is addicted to many Maines. As a toddler she learned to swim in the Ogunquit River and later watched her sons do the same in Monhegan's icy waters—and then learn to sail at summer camp in Raymond and paddle canoes on the Saco River and down the St. John. Her number two son was married on Little Cranberry Island off Mount Desert. She has skied Sugarloaf, Sunday River, and Saddleback, dogsledded and cross-country skied between North Woods sporting camps and "huts," llama trekked and camped in Evans Notch, sea kayaked off points from Portland to Pembroke, and sailed whenever possible on Penobscot Bay. She values her Boston vantage point, far enough away to give her the perspective on what it means to be a visitor, yet near enough to comfortably and continuously explore Maine.

Born in New York City and raised in northeastern Vermont, Nancy has spent most of her adult life in Portland, Maine. She has heard the cry of a bobcat at night in Vermont, listened to the calls of loons on Maine lakes, and watched a red-tailed hawk pluck a pigeon for dinner from her Portland backyard. She was the restaurant reviewer for the *Maine Sunday Telegram* for more than six years. Her travel writing started in the 1970s while still an undergraduate at Vassar College, with articles in *Vermont Life* magazine. She wrote *Chow Maine*, a guide to the best restaurants, cafés, lobster shacks, and markets on the Maine coast. Working on this edition of *Explorer's Guide Maine* took her inland, to great restaurants far from the summer crowds—although some of them are the favorites of year-round tourists, like the Oxford House Inn in Fryeburg. Traveling in Maine is a pastime she shares with many other Mainers, who have their own seasonal traditions, from eating a lobster roll at Harraseeket Lunch every summer to fly-fishing in the North Maine Woods every fall.

We are frequently asked how we manage to keep up with Maine's constant changes, and the answer is: Only with the help of the many kind and knowledgeable people along the road (for this edition Chris logged more than 8,000 Maine miles) and to those kind enough to read and comment on our updates. Chris owes special thanks to old friends and local experts like Carol Lord of York, Richard Moseley of Harpswell, Tom Church in Georgetown, Bobby and Sherry Weare in Damariscotta, Joan Yeaton in Addison, Joyce Morrell and Jan Meiners on Campobello, and Russell Walters of Northern Outdoors. Special thanks to John Willard of The Birches in Rockwood for flying me around the North Woods. Finally, thanks to the world's most helpful, talented, and long-suffering husband and companion on the road, former *Boston Globe* travel editor William A. Davis.

In the interest of transparency, along the road lodging payments varied from full to discounts to comps; the comps came from the New Brunswick Office of Tourism and from Maine lodging places with which we were already familiar and felt comfortable recommending. No way can we afford to travel the state as thoroughly as we do without the help of innkeepers, many of whom—over the years—have become friends and local sources. We do try to stop at every lodging place en route to recheck. Check out **mainemeanderings.wordpress.com**.

Nancy wishes to thank all the many people willing to speak to her. Thanks for extensive assistance from Jessica Donahue, director of marketing and promotions at the Greater Bangor Convention & Visitors Bureau, who polished the Bangor chapter like a gem. Karen Arel of the Ogunquit Chamber of Commerce and assistants at the Greater Portland Convention and Visitors Bureau were also generous with advice. For help in Rangeley, staff at the Rangeley Chamber of Commerce deserve many thanks. In western regions, Nancy thanks innkeepers and restaurateurs at the Oxford House Inn and other area B&Bs. Along the coast the help has

TOURISM IN MAINE

We are fascinated by Maine's history in general and her tourism history in particular. It seems ironic that back in the 1920s "motor touring" was hailed as a big improvement over train and steamer travel because it meant you no longer had to go where everyone else did—over routes prescribed by railroad tracks and steamboat schedules. In Maine cars seem, however, to have had precisely the opposite effect. Now 90 percent of the state's visitors follow the coastal tourist route faithfully, as though their wheels were grooved to Rt. 1.

Worse still, it's as though many tourists are on a train making only express stops—at rush hour. At least half of those who follow Rt. 1 stop, stay, and eat in all the same places—Kennebunkport, Boothbay or Camden, and Bar Harbor, for example—in August.

Tourism has always been driven by images. In the 1840s Thomas Cole, Frederic Church (both of whom sketched and painted scenes of Mount Desert), and lesser-known artists began projecting Maine as a romantic, remote destination in the many papers, magazines, and children's books of the decade. While Henry David Thoreau's *The Maine Woods* was not published until 1864, many of its chapters appeared as magazine articles years earlier (Thoreau first climbed Katahdin in 1846), and in 1853 *Atlantic Monthly* editor James Russell Lowell visited and wrote about Moosehead Lake.

After the Civil War, Maine tourism boomed. Via railroad and steamboat, residents of cities throughout the East and Midwest streamed into the Pine Tree State, most toting guidebooks, many published by rail and steamboat lines to boost business. "Sports" in search of big game and big fish patronized "sporting camps" throughout the North Woods. Thanks to the rise in popularity of fly-fishing and easily maneuverable canoes, women were able to share in North Woods soft adventure. Splendid lakeside hotels were built on the Rangeleys and Moosehead, and farms took in boarders throughout the Western Lakes region. Along the coast and on dozens of islands, hotels of every size were built, most by Maine natives. Blue-collar workers came by trolley to religious camp meetings, and the wealthy built themselves elaborate summer "cottages" on islands and around Bar Harbor, Camden, and Boothbay Harbor. Developments

STATE OF MAINE STEAMER

been generous. Thanks go to Melanie Graten at the Bar Harbor Chamber of Commerce, Caroline Sulzer and David Walker of Surry, and all the friendly people in Downeast Maine who took time from their busy schedule to answer questions. Thanks to volunteers everywhere who answer so many questions so patiently! And all the chambers of commerce of Maine are staffed with courteous and generous people who have contributed many details to this book.

Kate O'Halloran deserves a special bow for enabling the comparison of Word documents. Thanks also are due to Emma English, Nancy's daughter, who has provided details of

THE CLAREMONT HOTEL, SOUTHWEST HARBOR, IN AN 1885 PAINTING BY XANTHUS SMITH

and sophisticated landscaping transformed much of the previously ignored sandy Southern Coast.

Although it's difficult to document, it's safe to say that Maine attracted the same number of visitors in the summer of 1900 that it did in 2000. This picture altered little for another decade. Then came World War I, coinciding with the proliferation of the Model A.

The 1922 founding of the Maine Publicity Bureau (the present Maine Tourism Association), we suspect, reflects the panic of hoteliers (founder Hiram Ricker himself owned three of the state's grandest hotels: the Mount Kineo House, the Poland Spring House, and the Samoset). Over the next few years these hotels went the way of passenger service, and "motorists" stuck to motor courts and motels along Rt. 1 and a limited number of inland roads.

By the late 1960s, when Chris began writing about Maine, much of the state had all but dropped off the tourist map; in the decades since, she has chronicled the reawakening of most of the old resort areas. Whale-watching and whitewater rafting, skiing and snowmobiling, windjamming and kayaking, outlet shopping, and the renewed popularity of country inns and B&Bs have all contributed to this reawakening. Maine is, after all, magnificent. It was just a matter of time.

Recently the extent of waterside (both coastal and inland) walks open to the public has dramatically increased. It's interesting to note that this phenomenon of preserving and maintaining outstanding landscapes—from Ogunquit's Marginal Way to the core of what's now Acadia National Park—was also an offshoot of Maine's first tourism boom. In this 18th edition we note the dramatic growth of coastal trails way Down East in Washington County and the ever-increasing ways of exploring the North Woods.

meals and perceptions about inns that make descriptions come alive, while clocking many miles on travels through Maine.

Both authors are deeply grateful to the entire staff at Countryman Press for their combined efforts in producing this big book, implementing the many changes—maps, photos, and format as well as myriad facts—with each new edition. Many publishers do not permit this degree of flexibility with updates.

Maine is a truly special place, and to fully appreciate it you need to know a little more about it. Consider this section your orientation—everything from can't-miss experiences to local know-how. But first, a bit of history.

You can experience Maine's rich history through the places that still recall or dramatize it. For traces of early-17th-century settlement, see our descriptions of **Phippsburg**, **Pemaquid**, and **Augusta**. The French and Indian Wars (1675–1760), in which Maine was more involved than most of New England, are recalled in the reconstructed English **Fort William Henry** at Pemaquid and in historical markers scattered around **Castine** (Baron de Saint Castine, a young French nobleman married to a Penobscot Indian princess, controlled the coastal area we now call Down East). A striking house built in 1760 on **Kittery Point** (see "Kittery and the Yorks") and exhibits in the **Kittery Historical and Naval Museum** evoke Sir William Pepperrell, credited with having captured the fortress at Louisburg from the French. The nonprofit **Museums of York** in **York Village** (oldyork .org) evokes Maine's brief, peaceful colonial period.

In the **Burnham Tavern** at Machias you learn that townspeople captured a British man-of-war on June 1, 1775, the first naval engagement of the Revolution. Other reminders of the Revolution are less triumphant: At the Cathedral Pines in **Eustis** and spotted along Rt. 202 in the **Upper Kennebec Valley**, historical markers tell the poignant saga of Colonel Benedict Arnold's ill-fated 1775 attempt to capture Quebec. Worse: Markers at **Fort George** in a multimedia presentation at **The Castine Historical Society** detail the ways in which a substantial patriot fleet utterly disgraced itself there. Maine's brush with the British didn't end with the Revolution: The **Barracks Museum** in Eastport tells of British occupation again in 1814.

Climb the 103 steps of the **Portland Observatory** (built in 1807) and hear how Portland ranked second among New England ports, its tonnage based on lumber, the resource that fueled fortunes like those that built the amazingly opulent **Colonel Black Mansion** in Ellsworth and the elegant **Ruggles House** way Down East in Columbia Falls. In 1820 Maine finally became a state (the 23rd), but, as we note in our introduction to "The North Maine Woods," not without a price. The mother state (Massachusetts), her coffers at their usual low, stipulated an even division of all previously undeeded wilderness, and some 10.5 million acres were quickly sold off—vast, privately owned tracts that survive today as the unorganized townships.

An exception to this pattern is found in the lush St. John River valley in the very northeastern corner of the state. In a riverside meadow by Madawaska's **Tante Blanche Museum**, a large marble cross marks the spot on which several hundred displaced Acadians landed in 1787. Acadians trace their lineage to French settlers who came to Nova Scotia in the early 1600s and who, in 1755, were forcibly deported by an English governor. Today French remains the lingua franca on both sides of the river, currently the boundary between Maine and Canada. **Acadian Village**, a mini museum in Van Buren, only begins to tell the story. Check the **Maine Acadian Heritage Council** site (maineacadian.org) for an overview of historic sites and museums in the St. John valley.

This boundary was set only in 1842 when the Webster-Ashburton Treaty ended the bloodless Aroostook War. The US Government had ignored repeated pleas to help settle the boundary dispute, so the new, timber-rich state built its own northern forts (the **Fort Kent Blockhouse** survives) and raised a militia of more than 3,000. Aroostook County, created in 1840, attracted a number of new settlers who had discovered its good farmland and subsequently received land grants. In 1844 the state built massive **Fort Knox** at the mouth of the Penobscot River (see "Bucksport"), just in case. Never entirely completed, it's a spooky centerpiece for a state park, particularly popular at Halloween.

As we note in the introduction to "Brunswick and the Harpswells," it can be argued that the Civil War began and ended there. Unfortunately the state suffered heavy losses: Some 18,000 young soldiers from Maine died, as Civil War monuments along the **Civil War Trail** (mainecivilwartrail.org) attest. The end of the war, however, ushered in a boom decade. Outstanding displays in the **Vinalhaven Historical Society Museum** (see "The Fox Islands") and in the **Deer Isle Granite Museum** in Stonington (see "Deer Isle, Stonington") present the ways that Maine granite fed the demand for monumental public buildings throughout the country, and how both schooners and Down Easters (graceful square-rigged vessels) were in great demand (see the **Penobscot Marine Museum** in "Belfast, Searsport" and the **Maine Maritime Museum** in "Bath Area").

In the late 19th century many Maine industries boomed, tourism included. We describe Maine's tourism history in our introduction because it is so colorful, little recognized, and so much a part of what you see in Maine today.

Maine: The Pine Tree State from Prehistory to the Present by Richard Judd, Edwin Churchill, and Joel Eastman (University of Maine Press, 1995) is a good, readable history. For a shorter, entertaining, and reliable read, we recommend *The Lobster Coast: Rebels, Rusticators, and the Struggle for a Forgotten Frontier* by Colin Woodward (Penguin, 2005).

General Information

The **Maine Office of Tourism** maintains visitmaine.com and a 24-hour information line (1-888-624-6345) that connects with a live call center or with a fulfillment clerk who will send you the thick, helpful, four-season guide *Maine Invites You* (accompanied by a Maine highway map). Other useful state publications available on request at this writing include: *The Maine Art Museum Trail*, *Explore Maine by Bike*, *Maine Performs!* (a guide to performing arts), and the *Maine Birding Trail*. The *Guide to Inns and Bed & Breakfasts and Camps and Cottages*, a lodging guide, and *Maine Invites You* are published by the **Maine Tourism Association** (207-623-0363; maine tourism.com), a member-supported group that maintains well-stocked and -staffed welcome centers at its southern gateway at Kittery (207-439-1319) on I-95 northbound (also accessible from Rt. 1); in Yarmouth just off Rt. 1 and I-95 (207-846-0833); at the new West Gardiner Service Plaza (operated by the Maine Center for Craft/Maine Craft Association), I-95 Exit 102/103 and I-295 Exit 51; Hampden near Bangor on I-95 both northbound and southbound; Calais (207-454-2211); and Houlton (207-532-6346). There's also an information center near the New Hampshire line on Rt. 302 in Fryeburg (207-935-3639). In each chapter we describe the local sources under *Guidance*.

AIRPORTS AND AIRLINES **Portland International Jetport** (207-774-7301; portlandjetport .org). Portland is served by Delta (delta.com), United Airlines (united.com), American Airlines (AA.com), JetBlue (jetbluc.com), and Southwest Airlines (southwest.com). **Bangor International Airport** (207-947-0384; flybangor.com) offers flights to Florida via Allegiant Air (allegiantair.com); NYC and Detroit on Delta; American (aa.com) serves NYC, Philadelphia, and Washington, DC. **Hancock County Regional Airport** (bhairport.com) near Bar Harbor, **Augusta State Airport** (augustaairport .org), and **Knox County Regional Airport** (207-594-4131) in Owls Head near Rockland are all served by **Cape Air** (capeair.com). **Penobscot Island Air** (penobscotislandair.net), based at Owls Head, has regular flights to the islands of Vinalhaven, North Haven, and Matinicus. **Northern Maine Regional Airport** (flypresqueisle.com) is served by **Pen Air** (penair.com). **Manchester, NH**, and Boston's **Logan International Airport** are both popular gateways for Maine travelers; both are served by **Mermaid Transportation** (gomermaid .com) to Portland. **Concord Coach Lines** (see *Bus Service*) offers express service from Logan to Portland with continuing service to Augusta, Bangor, and coastal other destinations.

AIR SERVICES Also called flying services, these are useful links to wilderness camps and coastal islands. Aside from regularly scheduled service to several islands, **Penobscot Island Air** (see above) offers charter

ABENAKI

benaki, or Wabanaki, means "people of the dawn." Native Americans have lived in Maine and eastern Canada for many thousands of years, judging from shell heaps and artifacts found in areas ranging from coastal Damariscotta/Boothbay and Blue Hill to the Rangeley Lakes in western Maine. Ancient pictographs can be found on the Kennebec River and around Machias Bay. An excellent exhibit, *12,000 Years in Maine*, in the Maine State Museum (mainestatemuseum.org) in Augusta, depicts the distinct periods in this history and features the Red Paint People, named for the red pigments found sprinkled in their burial sites. They flourished between 5,000 and 3,800 years ago and are said to have fished from large, sturdy boats. The Abbe Museum (abbemuseum.org) in Bar Harbor, now a Smithsonian affiliate, is dedicated to showcasing the cultures of Maine's Wabanaki, the less than 7,000 members of the Penobscot, Passamaquoddy, Micmac, and Maliseet tribes who live in the state. The permanent collection of 50,000 objects ranges from 10,000-year-old artifacts to exquisite basketry and craftswork from several centuries. The timeline begins with the present and draws visitors back through 10,000 years and to its core, "The Circle of Four Directions." Early French missions at Mount Desert and Castine became battlegrounds between the French and English, and by the end of the 17th century thousands of Wabanaki had retreated either to Canada or to the Penobscot community of Old Town and to Norridgewock, where Father Sebastian Rasle insisted that the Indian lands "were given them of God, to them and their children forever, according to the Christian oracles." The mission was obliterated (it's now a roadside rest area), and by the end of the French and Indian Wars only four tribes remained. Of these the Micmacs and Maliseets made the unlucky choice of siding with the Crown and were subsequently forced to flee (but communities remain near the Aroostook County–Canadian border in Presque Isle and Littleton, respectively). That left only the Penobscots and the Passamaquoddys.

In 1794 the Penobscots technically deeded most of Maine to Massachusetts in exchange for the 140 small islands in the Penobscot River, and in 1818 Massachusetts agreed to pay them an assortment of trinkets for the land. In 1820, when Maine became a state, a trust fund was set aside but ended up in the general treasury. The state's three reservations (two belonging to the Passamaquoddys and one to the Penobscots) were termed "enclaves of disfranchised citizens bereft of any special status." Indians loomed large in Maine lore and greeted 19th-century tourists as fishing and hunting guides in the woods and as snowshoe and canoe makers and

flights to and from Boston or Portland airports to pretty much anywhere in Maine; its fleet includes floatplanes. Greenville, site of the September International Floatplane Fly-in, is home to **Currier's Flying Service** (207-695-2778) and **Jack's Air Service** (207-695-3020), which serve remote camps in the North Woods, as do Millinocket-based **Katahdin Air Service** (207-723-8378) and **West Branch Aviation** (207-723-4375). In Rangeley, **Acadian Seaplanes** (207-864-5307) offers a similar service for outlying camps in the Western Mountains.

AMTRAK Maine passenger service is not just back but a resounding success! Amtrak's **Downeaster** (amtrak.com) offers frequent roundtrips between Boston's North Station and Brunswick with stops in Wells, Old Orchard, Saco, Portland, and Freeport. More people every year are discovering the view of the shoreline you otherwise never see. Northbound the first Maine stop is **Wells** at a regional transportation center, served by taxis and a seasonal trolley to the beach. In Saco the station is just beyond the mighty falls (taxi service and shuttle bus). In **Old Orchard** the stop is a short walk from the beach and lodging. The **Portland** station doubles as a stop for Concord Coach Lines, and there's bus and taxi service to downtown; you can also rent a bike. In **Freeport** the stop is right at the outlets, while the **Brunswick** station is steps from lodging, dining, and shopping and an

guides, while Native American women sold their distinctive sweetgrass and ash-splint baskets and beadwork at the many coastal and inland summer hotels and boardinghouses.

In 1972 the Penobscots and Passamaquoddys sued to reclaim 1.5 million acres of land allegedly illegally appropriated by the state, and in 1980 they received an $80.6 million settlement, which they have since invested in a variety of enterprises. The Indian Island Reservation in Old Town is presently home to 610 of the tribe's 2,000 members, and the **Penobscot Nation Museum** (penobscotnation.org) there, while small, is open regularly and well worth a visit. The Passamaquoddy tribe today numbers about 2,500 members, roughly divided between the reservations at **Indian Township** on Schoodic Lake and at **Sipayik**, also known as **Pleasant Point** (wabanaki.com), near Eastport, site of the **Indian Ceremonial Days**, held annually in mid-August to celebrate Passamaquoddy culture and climaxing in dances in full regalia. Exhibits at the **Wabanaki Culture Center** (207-454-2521) in Calais currently focus on Passamaquoddy history and craftsmanship, including a 20-foot vintage-1872 birch-bark canoe, but plans call for the story of all four Wabanaki tribes to be told here. There is also a small **Passamaquoddy Cultural Heritage Center** in Indian Township, Princeton, north on Rt. 1.

The 1,000-member Aroostook Band of Micmacs is headquartered in Presque Isle; tribal offices for the 800-member Houlton Band of Maliseet Indians are in Littleton. The **Hudson Museum** at the University of Maine–Orono has a small display on local tribes. Members of all four tribes form the **Maine Indian Basketmakers Alliance** (maineindianbaskets.org), which makes and markets traditional ash-splint and sweetgrass baskets at special sales events, held in July in Bar Harbor and December at the University of Maine–Orono. **Nowetah's American Indian Museum** in New Portland exhibits the century craftsmanship (see "Sugarloaf and the Carrabassett Valley") and displays a large collection of authentic basketry.

Christina Tree

DISPLAY OF PASSAMAQUODDY BASKETS AT THE WABANAKI CULTURE CENTER

easy walk to Bowdoin College museums. Prices are reasonable; seniors and ages 15 and under are half price, and frequent packages lure Mainers to sports and entertainment events in Boston.

AREA CODE The area code throughout Maine is **207**.

BUS SERVICE **Concord Coach Lines** (1-800-639-3317; concordcoachlines .com) serves Portland, Augusta, Brunswick, Bath, Wiscasset, Damariscotta, Waldoboro, Rockland, Camden, Belfast, Searsport, Bangor, and the University of Maine at Orono (when school is in session). Its Boston/Portland/Bangor Express is the fastest service to

eastern Maine and we recommend it over **Greyhound Bus Lines** (1-800-231-2222), serving Augusta, Lewiston, Waterville, Portland, and Bangor. See exploremaine.org for details about public transit buses—the site offers options for daily service year-round from Bangor Airport (stopping at both bus terminals) to Calais, with stops in Machias and Perry, along with many flag-down stops (call ahead) in between. **Cyr Bus Line** (1-800-244-2335; johntcyr.com) offers daily bus service from Bangor to Caribou with stops in Sherman, Houlton, and Presque Isle.

FERRIES The Maine Department of Transportation maintains a brilliant website (exploremaine.org) with schedules for **Maine**

NORTH HAVEN FERRY

Christina Tree

State Ferry Service (1-800-491-4883) from Rockland to Vinalhaven, North Haven, and Matinicus, from Lincolnville to Islesboro, and from Bass Harbor to Swans Island and Frenchboro. They also list services to Monhegan Island, Isle au Haut, and the Cranberry Islands. Casco Bay islands are served by **Casco Bay Lines** (cascobaylines.com) from Portland. **Quoddy Loop Ferries** (quoddyloop.com) travel from Eastport and Campobello Island to the New Brunswick mainland via Deer Island, and from Black Harbor to Grand Manan. Check online for ferry service between Portland and Nova Scotia, which is supposed to be starting in 2016.

FIRE PERMITS Maine law dictates that no person shall kindle or use outdoor fires without a permit, except at authorized campsites or picnic grounds. Fire permits in the organized townships are obtained from the local town warden; in the unorganized townships, from the nearest forest ranger. Portable stoves fueled by propane gas, gasoline, or Sterno are exempt from the rule.

LITTER Littering in Maine is punishable by a $100 fine; this applies to dumping from boats as well as other vehicles. Most cans and bottles are redeemable.

HANDICAPPED ACCESS Within this book, handicapped-accessible lodging, restaurants, and attractions are marked with a wheelchair symbol (♿). **Maine Adaptive Sports & Recreation** (maineadaptive.org) offers an outstanding snow sports program, including cross-country and alpine skiing, snowshoeing, and snowboarding. Summer programs offer paddling, golf, and cycling.

INNS AND BED & BREAKFASTS For each edition we personally inspect hundreds of inns and B&Bs. Our choices reflect both what we have seen and the feedback we receive from others; they are not paid listings. The **Maine Innkeepers Association** maintains a website of its members at maineinns.com. Also check listings at visitmaine.com and mainetourism.com.

MAPS Free state maps are available from the **Maine Office of Tourism** (1-888-624-6345) and at the state visitors information centers, but we are sad to see the way these have deteriorated in recent years. The **AAA map** to Northern New England is a step up, and within this book we have done our best to detail obvious destinations. Sooner or later, however, serious Maine explorers have to invest in *DeLorme's Maine Atlas and Gazetteer* (delorme.com). **The Division of Parks and Lands** (maine.gov/doc/parks) offers a web page that finds any parks and public lands in the many regions of the state.

PUBLIC BROADCASTING **The Maine Public Broadcasting Network** (mpbn.net) offers statewide television and radio. **Maine Public Television** stations are **Channel 10** in Augusta and Presque Isle, **Channel 12** in Orono, **Channel 13** in Calais, and **Channel 26** in Biddeford. Local programming includes *Maine Watch*, highlighting important issues in Maine each week. **Maine's seven public radio stations** can be found on the dial at 90.1 in Portland, 90.9 in Bangor, 91.3 in Waterville, 90.5 in Camden, 89.7 in Calais, 106.1 in Presque Isle, and 106.5 in Fort Kent. *Maine Watch* and *Maine Things Considered* highlight state news.

POPULATION 1.33 million, according to the 2014 census. It has grown 4.2 percent since 2000, enough to hold on to its two congressional representatives.

TRAFFIC AND HIGHWAY TRAVEL TIPS Maine coastal travel has its sticky wickets. By far the worst is the weekend backup at the tolls at the entrance to the Maine Turnpike as well as those not far south in New Hampshire. The 109-mile toll highway (I-95) begins in Kittery. Exit numbers will throw you if your map predates 2004. Rather than sequential numbering, they represent the number of miles from the New Hampshire line. Tolls are a flat rate paid when getting on—and sometimes off—the turnpike. Get E-ZPass (ezpassmaineturnpike.com) and avoid peak travel times. Note that it takes no longer to reach a Downeast than a Midcoast destination, thanks to the way the highways run. The quickest way to Rockland or Camden from points south is I-295 to Brunswick and then coastal Rt. 1. Belfast and destinations east through the Blue Hill Peninsula, however, can be reached in roughly the same time by taking I-295 to I-95 at Augusta and Rt. 3 to coastal Rt. 1 at Belfast. You can reach Ellsworth (gateway to Mount Desert and points east) in equal time by traveling I-295 to I-95 to Bangor and then heading down Rt. 1A. For current information on road conditions and delays, dial 511 in Maine and 1-866-282-7578 from out of state, or go to 511maine.gov. For travel conditions and construction updates, phone 1-800-675-PIKE, or check maineturnpike.com.

SEAT BELTS Seat belts are the law in Maine, and **right turns on a red light** are permitted—unless otherwise stated—after a stop to check for oncoming traffic. **Headlights** should be turned on with windshield wipers.

WEDDINGS An estimated 9,700 couples were married in Maine in 2012, and judging from members of wedding parties whom we meet at B&B breakfast tables, a large percentage were from far-flung corners of the country. Check out *Real Maine Weddings* magazine (realmaineweddings.com). Several chambers of commerce, notably York, Kennebunkport, Boothbay, and Camden, are particularly helpful. Within the book we note properties that specialize in weddings with our ring symbol ⚭.

Arts

We have listed outstanding annual events within each chapter of this book; also see event listings on visitmaine.com and mainetourism.com. A community calendar is posted at mainepublicradio.org.

ART Maine's landscape has drawn major artists since the mid-19th century. The **Maine Arts Commission** (mainearts.com) offers a searchable database of artists, arts organizations, and events. Also see maineartmuseums.org for the state's leading art museums. Within each chapter we describe the best art destination. For more about art throughout the state, pick up a current copy of the *Maine Gallery & Studio Guide*, available at most galleries.

CRAFTS *Maine Guide to Crafts and Culture*, available free from the **Maine Crafts Association** (mainecrafts.org), is a geographic listing of studios, galleries, and museums throughout Maine. **United Maine Craftsmen,**

Inc. (207-621-2818; unitedmainecraftsmen .com), also sponsors six large shows each year. **Haystack Mountain School of Crafts** (haystack-mtn.org; see "Deer Isle, Stonington") is a summer school nationally respected in a variety of crafts, with three-week courses mid-June through mid-September. The surrounding area (Blue Hill to Stonington) contains the largest concentration of Maine craftspeople, many with open studios. For fiber studios, farms, and galleries listed at mainefiberarts.org, a printed or online tour map is also available. Also check out the **Center for Maine Craft** (207-588-0021) at the Gardiner rest area off I-95.

FILM Northeast Historic Film (1-800-639-1636; oldfilm.org) is based at "The Alamo," a vintage-1916 movie house in Bucksport. This admirable group has created a regional moving-image archive of films based on or made in New England that were shown in every small town during the first part of the 20th century. Request the catalog *Videos of Life in New England*. The **International Film & Television Workshops (207-236-8581)** in Rockport offer a variety of week-long courses in various aspects of film. The **Maine International Film Festival** is a 10-day event with more than 60 films shown in Waterville (miff.org). Portland hosts the **Maine Jewish Film Festival** (mjff.org) in mid-March. The **Camden International Film Festival** (camdenfilmfest.org) is now one of the largest. For an overview of festivals see the **Maine Film Office** website (filminmaine.com) and the **Maine Arts Commission** site (mainearts.maine.gov). There are still five functioning **drive-ins** in Maine: in Saco, Bridgton, Skowhegan, Westbrook, and Madawaska.

MUSIC Maine offers a wide variety of musical events, festivals, and live shows depending on your taste. **Bowdoin International Music Festival** (bowdoinfestival.org) in Brunswick is the state's most prestigious and varied chamber music series, and the **Kneisel Hall Chamber Music Festival** (kneisel.org) in Blue Hill is its oldest chamber music festival, also still outstanding. There is also, of course, the **Portland Symphony Orchestra** (portland symphony.org), which has a summertime pops series, and the **Bangor Symphony**

Orchestra (bangorsymphony.com). Music lovers should also take note of the **American Folk Festival** (americanfolkfestival.com) the last weekend in August in Bangor, the **Lincoln Arts Festival** (lincolnartsfestival.net) of classical and choral music held throughout the Boothbay Harbor region in summer months, and the **Bluegrass Festival at Thomas Point Beach** in August. Outstanding summer programs include the **Bowdoin International Festival** (bowdoinfestival.com); **Kneisel Hall** in Blue Hill (kneisel.org); **Monteux School of Conducting** in Hancock (monteuxschool .org); **New England Music Camp** in Oakland (nemusiccamp.com); and **Maine Jazz Camp** (mainejazzcamp.com) at the University of Maine–Farmington. **SummerKeys** (summer keys.com) in Lubec specializes in piano but welcomes students of all levels in a variety of instruments. See maineperforms.com for more information.

THEATER The **Ogunquit Playhouse** (ogunquitplayhouse.org) is among the oldest and most prestigious summer theaters in the country. Along the South Coast also check out the **Arundel Barn Playhouse** (arundel barnplayhouse.com) in Kennebunk and the **Hackmatack Playhouse** (hackmatack.org) in Berwick. In Portland note the **Portland Stage Company** (portlandstage.com); in Brunswick the **Maine State Music Theater at Bowdoin College** (msmt.org) is a big draw. Farther along the coast look for the **Camden Civic Theatre** (camdencivictheatre.com), based in the refurbished Camden Opera House; the **Belfast Maskers** (belfastmaskerstheater .com) in Belfast; the **Acadia Repertory Theatre** (acadiarep.com) in Somesville; and **Downriver Theatre Company** (downriver theatrecompany.com) in Machias. Inland you'll find the **Theater at Monmouth** (theater atmonmouth.org), **Lakewood Theater** (lake woodtheater.org) in Skowhegan, **Deertrees Theatre and Cultural Center** (deertreestheatre.com) in Harrison, **Celebration Barn Theater** (celebrationbarn .com) in South Paris, and **Carousel Music Theater** (carouselmusictheater.org) in Boothbay. **Penobscot Theatre Company** (penobscottheatre.org) in Bangor offers a variety of winter productions, as do the **Portland Players** (portlandplayers.org) and **Portland Stage Company** (portlandstage.com).

Year-round venues include the **Camden Civic Theatre** (camdencivictheater.com) in Camden, the **Waldo Theatre** (thewaldo.org) in Waldoboro, the **Public Theatre** (thepublictheatre.org) in Auburn, and **City Theater** (citytheater.org) in Biddeford. Most universities and colleges also offer performances throughout the school year. All are detailed in their respective chapters. Check out maineperforms.com for a full list of performance venues.

Food & Drink

Locally produced items include venison and beeswax as well as blueberries, Christmas wreaths, smoked seafood, teas, beer, wine, maple syrup, gin, vodka, and lobster stew, to name just a few. The Maine Department of Agriculture, Conservation and Forestry (getrealmaine.com) publishes several helpful guides. The website lists farmers' markets, orchards, farm stores, and much more.

AGRICULTURAL FAIRS The season opens in late June and runs through the first week of October, culminating with the large, colorful, immensely popular **Fryeburg Fair**. Among the best traditional fairs are the **Union Fair** (late August) and the **Blue Hill Fair** (Labor Day weekend). **The Common Ground Country Fair** (third weekend in September at the fairgrounds in Unity), sponsored by the Maine Organic Farmers and Gardeners Association (mofga.org), features organic Maine-grown food, farming techniques, dancing, and music and draws city folk and organic gardeners from all corners of the state. For details about fairs see the **Maine Department of Agriculture, Conservation and Forestry** website (getrealmaine .com). A vibrant tradition of harness racing at Maine fairs has been reinvigorated with a small percentage of revenues earned by Hollywood Casino in Bangor.

APPLES Fall brings plenty of pick-your-own opportunities across the state, and many orchards also sell apples and cider. For a map/guide to PYO orchards, see maineapples .org. Also check out Maine Apple Sunday throughout the state in mid-September and the Cornish Apple Festival in Cornish in late September.

BEER, WINE, AND SPIRITS Prohibition began in Maine, and before Bob and Kathe Bartlett could open Maine's first winery in 1982, they had to get the law changed. Just off Rt. 1 in Gouldsboro, **Bartlett Maine Estate Winery** (bartlettwinery.com) offers tastings of its prizewinning fruit wines utilizing Maine apples, blueberries, raspberries, and honey as well as regional pears and peaches, and has added **Spirits of Maine** to its name, with pear eau de vie and Calvados-style apple brandy among its labels. Currently the website mainewinetrail.com lists more than 20 visitor-friendly wineries that use hardy grapes as well as other fruit. **Cellardoor Vineyard** (mainewine.com) in Lincoln offers wine tastings in its state-of-the-art restored 18th-century barn at its vineyard in Lincoln and at "The Villa," Rt. 1 in Rockport. **Breakwater Vineyards** (breakwatervineyards.com) in Owls Head has planted some 3,000 vines; its tasting room commands a glorious view of Penobscot Bay. In this area also check out **Oyster River Winegrowers** (oysterriverwine .com) in Thomaston; in Union, **Sweetgrass Farm Winery and Distillery** (sweetgrass winery.com) uses fruit to craft gins and rum as well as fruit brandies and wine; **Savage Oakes** (savageoakes.com) in Union produces apple and grape wines. **Blacksmiths Winery** (blacksmithswinery.com) on Rt. 302 in South Casco produces both prizewinning grape and fruit wines. We also recommend **Maine Distilleries** (mainedistilleries.com), founded by brothers from an Aroostook farm who found a new use for their potatoes, winning national recognition for their Cold River Vodka and offering a tasting room in Freeport. Portland has had a surge in local, mostly Bayside, breweries and distilleries. **New England Distilling** (newenglanddistilling.com), one of the best, makes rum and gin and offers tastings. There is also **Twenty 2 Vodka** (twenty2vodka .com), **Maine Craft Distilling** (mainecraft distilling.com), and the newest big thing: **HoneyMaker mead** (mainemeadworks.com). For information on Maine's ever-evolving breweries and microbreweries and Maine's Beer Trail, check out mainebrewersguild.org. The **Maine Brewer's Festival** (learnyourbeer .com) in Portland is held the first weekend of November and often sells out. There is also a June Bangor's Beer Festival, a July Portland Brew Festival, and a September Maine Lakes

Brew Fest in Bridgton. Also check mainebeer tours.com.

BLUEBERRIES Maine grows 98 percent of US lowbush wild blueberries on an estimated 64,000 acres. Few growers allow U-pick, at least not until the commercial harvest is over. (One exception is **Staples Homestead Blueberries** in Stockton Springs.) Then the public can to go "stumping" for leftovers (except where posted)—but the berries might not be in the best shape. On the other hand, berrying along roads and hiking paths is a rite of summer. The **blueberry barrens**—thousands of blueberry-covered acres—spread across Cherryfield, Columbia, and Machias (site of the state's most colorful blueberry festival in August) in Washington County. For more about Maine's famous fruit, go to wildblue berries.com and wildblueberries.maine.edu. The Wild Blueberry Festival in Machias (machiasblueberry.com) in mid-August is one of the state's most colorful events; there are also blueberry festivals in Union and Rangeley.

CHEESE Maine's 31 cheesemakers claim to create more than 150 artisan cheeses, but with the exception of Seal Cove Farm in Lamoine (producing goat cheese since 1980), many are available only locally. Discover events like **Open Creamery Day** in early October at mainecheeseguild.org; other sites to check are pinelandfarms.org and cheese-me.com.

FARMS AND FARMERS' MARKETS The **Maine Department of Agriculture, Conser-** vation and Forestry's website (getrealmaine .com) is a terrific resource detailing farms, farmers' markets, agricultural events, and what's available season by season.

LOBSTERS Lobster is just another item on the menu elsewhere in the world, but in Maine it's an experience. It's no secret that Maine's clean, cold waters produce some of the world's tastiest lobster. This hardshelled crustacean has a long body and five sets of legs, including two large front claws, one large, flat, and heavy and the other smaller, thinner. They don't like light, hiding by day and emerging at night to eat mussels, sea urchins, and crabs. Most are more than five years old by the time they are caught, because Maine regulates the minimum (also maximum) size of what can be sold. The state also prohibits catching pregnant females, and imposes trap limits and license controls. In the 1880s most lobster was canned. Currently 70 percent of what's caught by Maine lobstermen is shipped live out of state. While elsewhere its appeal may be the fanciful ways it's prepared, in Maine it's the opposite. The shorter the time between a lobster's last crawl—not in a restaurant tank but in its home waters—and your plate, the better. The preferred cooking method: 10 to 15 minutes in boiling seawater for an average-sized (1- to 1½-pound) lobster. Selecting the lobster is a bit more complicated. Choices may include a "cull" (a lobster with one claw), a "chicken" (a female, usually 1 pound, and considered to have the most delicate meat), and "hardshell" or "softshell." Lobsters molt, usually shedding their shells in summer. The soft shell fills with seawater, which is replaced by new meat as the animal grows and the shell hardens. Which is better depends on whom you talk to. Many prefer "shedders" because the shells are easy to crack and the meat is sweet. These actually don't transport as well as the full and firmly meated "hard shells," so chances are you won't have a chance to sample one outside Maine. How to eat a lobster is a no-holds-barred experience best embarked upon (and always explained) at lobster pounds. See lobsterfrommaine.com for more, and check out the Lobster sidebars throughout this book for the best lobster pounds, shacks, and restaurants.

Nancy English

SOFTSHELLED LOBSTERS READY TO EAT

CHRIS AND JOHN DAVIS SERVE UP PEMAQUID OYSTERS

MAPLE SUGARING Maine produces roughly 450,000 gallons of syrup a year, and the **Maine Maple Producers Association** (mainemapleproducers.com) publishes a list of producers who welcome visitors on **Maine Maple Sunday** (also known as Sap Sunday), always the fourth Sunday in March.

OYSTERS AND CLAMS Maine, like the rest of New England, produces some of the best shellfish in the world. Feasting on raw oysters is a 2,000-year-old tradition in Maine, as evidenced by heaps of empty oyster shells ("middens") still to be seen in Damariscotta. By the mid-1800s native oyster beds had all but disappeared, but thanks to seeding methods these sweet and salty oysters are back and the Damariscotta River estuary remains their epicenter. Check out **Pemaquid Oyster Co.**, **Glidden Point Sea Farm**, **Mook Sea Farms**, **Muscongus Bay Aquaculture**, and **Norumbega Oyster, Inc.** For do-it-yourselfers, state law permits shellfish harvesting for personal use only, unless you have a commercial license. But rules vary with each town, so check with the town clerk (the source of licenses) before you dig, and make sure there's no red tide. Some towns do prohibit clamming, and in certain places there is a temporary stay on harvesting while the beds are being seeded.

PLOYE This traditional buckwheat Acadian pancake/flat bread, as delicate as a crêpe, is a specialty throughout the St. John Valley. The **Bouchard Family Farm** (1-800-239-3237) produces a line of French Canadian food products.

Museums

Seven of the state's museums have formed a partnership and created the **Maine Art Museum Trail** (maineartmuseums.org). The **Portland Museum of Art** (portlandmuseum.org) is known for its strong collection of works by impressionist and postimpressionist masters as well as Winslow Homer, whose recently restored studio in Prout's Neck is open (by reservation through the museum) for tours. **The Farnsworth Art Museum** with its **Center for the Wyeth Family in Maine** (farnsworthmuseum.org) in Rockland has a stellar collection of Maine art as well as frequent special exhibits. The seasonal **Ogunquit Museum of American Art** (ogunquitmuseum.org) is worth checking; the **Colby College Museum of Art** (colby.edu/museum) in Waterville has the largest exhibit area of any Maine museum, and exceptional quality as well. The **Bates College Museum of Art** (abacus.bates.edu/acad/museum) and **Bowdoin College Museum of Art** (bowdoin.edu/artmuseum) are described within their respective chapters. The **University of Maine Museum of Art** (umma.umaine.edu) in Bangor is another worth exploring.

Easily the most undervisited museum in the state, the outstanding **Maine State Museum** (mainestatemuseum.org) in Augusta has outstanding displays on the varied Maine landscape and historical exhibits ranging from traces of the area's earliest people to fishing, agriculture, lumbering, quarrying, and shipbuilding. It's a great place for families. The **Seashore Trolley Museum** (trolleymuseum.org) in Kennebunkport and the **Owls Head Transportation Museum** (obtm.org) near Rockland are family finds as well. Our favorites also include the **Peary-MacMillan Arctic Museum** at Bowdoin College in Brunswick, the **Wilson Museum** (wilsonmuseum.org) in Castine, and the **L. C. Bates Museum** (gwh.org) in Hinckley, a true "cabinet of curiosities" filled with stuffed animals and

Indian artifacts. The **Patten Lumbermen's Museum** (lumbermensmuseum.org) and the **Maine Forestry Museum** (rlrlm.org) in Rangeley are both glimpses of a recently vanished way of life in the North Maine Woods. The **Rangeley Outdoor Sporting Heritage Museum** (rangeleyoutdoormuseum.org) in Oquossoc focuses on the colorful history of fly-fishing in this area. The museum at the **Colonial Pemaquid Restoration** in Pemaquid, presenting archaeological finds from the adjacent early-17th-century settlement, is also unexpectedly fascinating. Also see the Abbe Museum under *Wabanaki*.

MAINE MARITIME MUSEUM (maine maritimemuseum.org) in Bath stands in a class by itself and should not be missed. The **Penobscot Marine Museum** (penobscot marinemuseum.org) in Searsport is smaller but still substantial, focusing on the merchant captains and their experiences in far corners of the world, featuring yearlong special exhibits. The **Marine Resources Aquarium** in Boothbay Harbor displays regional fish and sea creatures, many of them surprisingly colorful. The stars of the show are the sharks and skates in a large touch tank. The **Mount Desert Oceanarium** (theoceanarium.com) is a commercial attraction with several locations in the Bar Harbor area.

SHAKERS **Sabbathday Lake Shaker Village and Museum** (maineshakers.com/museum) in New Gloucester is the country's last functioning Shaker religious community. Visitors are welcome to walk the grounds, and can take seasonal tours of six of the 18 existing structures on 1,800 acres, visit the museum reception center and gift shop, and attend seasonal Sunday services in the meeting-house. Frequent workshops and special events are scheduled March through December. *Note:* With the exception of service dogs, no pets are allowed in the village, not even in a car.

Nature

APPALACHIAN TRAIL (appalachiantrail .org). The 267-mile Maine section of this 2,859-mile Georgia-to-Maine footpath enters the state in the Mahoosuc Range—accessible there from Grafton Notch State Park (the Mahoosuc Notch section is extremely difficult)—and continues north into the Rangeley and Sugarloaf areas, on up through The Forks in the Upper Kennebec Valley to Monson. East of Moosehead Lake it runs through Gulf Hagas and on around Nahmakanta Lake, through Abol Bridge to Baxter State Park, ending at the summit of 5,267-foot Mount Katahdin. Hikes along the trail are noted within specific chapters; lodging places catering to AT through-hikers include **Northern Outdoors** in The Forks, the **Sterling Inn** in Caratunk, **Lake Shore House** in Monson, **Little Lyford Pond Camps** (an AMC Wilderness Lodge; see below) near Gulf Hagas, and **Appalachian Trail Lodge** in Millinocket, which also serves hikers with food drops in the "Hundred Mile Wilderness" south of Katahdin. July, August, and September are the best months to hike this stretch. The **Maine Appalachian Trail Club** (matc.org) helps with maintenance and in other ways; it publishes a trail guide that can be ordered online.

BEACHES Given the rising summer temperature of the Atlantic Ocean—62 degrees in Portland and 63 degrees at Bar Harbor—swimming has become more enjoyable, but it still isn't the primary reason most folks come to the Maine coast. Still, Maine beaches (for instance at York, Wells, the Kennebunks, Portland, Popham, and Pemaquid) can be splendid walking, sunning, and kite-flying places. At **Ogunquit** and in **Reid State Park** in Georgetown, there are also warmer backwater areas in which small children can paddle. Other outstanding beaches include 7-mile-long **Old Orchard Beach** and, nearby, state-maintained **Crescent Beach** on Cape Elizabeth, **Scarborough Beach** in Scarborough, **Ferry Beach** in Saco, and **Sand Beach** in Acadia National Park. The state-maintained freshwater beaches are on **Lakes Damariscotta**, **St. George**, **Sebec**, **Rangeley**, **Sebago**, and **Moosehead**; also on **Pleasant Pond** in Richmond. All state beaches include changing facilities, restrooms, and showers; many have snack bars. The town of **Bridgton** has several fine little lakeside beaches, while **Lake George Regional Park** (between Skowhegan and Canaan) offers sandy beaches and facilities on two shores.

BIRDING Visit mainebirdingtrail.com to download the Maine Office of Tourism free map/guide to 80 birding locations in the state or to order the full *Maine Birding Trail* (Down East Books) guide, detailing 260 places to watch and hear birds across the state. Birding festivals begin in May with **Wings, Waves and Woods** in Deer Isle and Stonington and the **Down East Spring Birding Festival** (downeastbirdfest.org) in Cobscook Bay. The **Acadia Birding Festival** on Mount Desert Island and **Aroostook State Park Birding Festival**, between Houlton and Presque Isle, are both held in June. **Maine Audubon** (207-781-2330; maineaudubon.org), based at Gilsland Farm Audubon Center in Falmouth, maintains a number of birding sites and sponsors nature programs and field trips year-round, including naturalist-led van tours and boat cruises to see birds and other wildlife statewide. Adirondack-style lodges alongside Sunset Pond at 1,600 acre Borestone Mountain Audubon Sanctuary are available for group rental. **Laudholm Farm** in Wells, **Biddeford Pool**, **Scarborough Marsh**, **Merrymeeting Bay**, and **Mount Desert** are also popular birding sites. **Monhegan** is the island to visit in May and September. The **Moosehorn National Wildlife Refuge** (207-454-3521) in Washington County represents the northeastern terminus of the East Coast chain of wildlife refuges and is particularly rich in bird life.

Atlantic puffins are Maine's most popular bird to watch and they are smaller than you might expect. They lay just one egg a year and were almost extinct at the turn of the 20th century, when the only surviving birds nested on either Matinicus Rock or Machias Seal Island. Since 1973 Audubon has helped reintroduce nesting on Eastern Egg Rock in Muscongus Bay, 6 miles off Pemaquid Point, and since 1984 there has been a similar puffin-restoration project on Seal Island in outer Penobscot Bay, 6 miles from Matinicus Rock. The best time for viewing puffins is May through mid-August. The largest colony and the only place you are allowed to view the birds on land is **Machias Seal Island**, where visitors are permitted in limited numbers. Contact **Andrew Patterson** (boldcoast.com) in Cutler. With the help of binoculars (a must), you can also view the birds from the water via tours with **Cap'n Fish** (mainepuffin.com) from Boothbay Harbor, **Hardy Boat**

Cruises (hardyboat.com) from New Harbor, and the **Monhegan Boat Line** (monheganboat.com) from Port Clyde. The **Hog Island Audubon Camp** (maineaudubon.org) also offers guided boat cruises to Eastern Egg Rock. For those who can't make time to get out on the water, the **Project Puffin Visitor Center** (projectpuffin.org) in Rockland uses live-streaming mini cams and audio to provide a virtual visit with nesting puffins on Seal Island.

ISLANDS Most of Maine's 3,250 offshore islands are uninhabited. We describe those that offer overnight lodging—**Chebeague** and **Peaks Islands** in Casco Bay; **Monhegan**, **Vinalhaven**, **North Haven**, and **Islesboro** along the Midcoast; and in the Down East section **Isle au Haut**, **Swans Island** off Mount Desert Island, **Campobello** in New Brunswick (across the bridge from Lubec), and **Grand Manan** (also in Canada). In Casco Bay the ferry also serves **Cliff Island** (summer rentals are available); **Eagle Island**, former home of Admiral Peary, is served by daily excursion boats from Harpswell and South Freeport. For information on public and private islands on which low-impact visitors are welcome, contact the **Maine Island Trail Association** (207-596-6456; mita.org). MITA maintains 80 islands and charges $45 ($65 per family) for membership, which brings with it a detailed guidebook and the right to land on these islands. **The Island Institute** (207-594-9209; islandinstitute.org) serves as an umbrella organization for the island communities; with the $50 membership come its publications: *Island Journal* and *Working Waterfront*.

LAKES Maine boasts some 6,000 lakes and ponds, and every natural body of water of more than 10 acres is theoretically available to the public for "fishing and fowling." Access is, however, limited by the property owners. Because paper companies and other land management concerns permit public use (see *Camping*), there is ample opportunity to canoe or fish in solitary waters. **Powerboat owners** should check registration rules at www.maine.gov/ifw, also the source for obtaining a milfoil sticker as required by law for all motorized boats using Maine rivers, lakes, ponds, and streams. For more about the most popular resort lakes in the state, see the

Bridgton, Rangeley, Moosehead, and Belgrade Lakes chapters. **State parks on lakes** include **Aroostook** (camping, fishing, swimming; Rt. 1 south of Presque Isle), **Damariscotta Lake State Park** (swimming, picnicking; Rt. 32, Jefferson), **Lake St. George State Park** (swimming, picnicking, fishing; Rt. 3 in Liberty), **Lily Bay State Park** (swimming, camping, picnicking; 8 miles north of Greenville), **Peacock Beach State Park** (swimming, picnicking; Richmond), **Peaks-Kenny State Park** (swimming and camping on Sebec Lake near Dover-Foxcroft), **Rangeley Lake State Park** (swimming, camping; Rangeley), **Sebago Lake State Park** (swimming, picnicking, camping; near Bridgton), **Mount Blue State Park** (swimming, camping in Weld), and **Swan Lake State Park** (swimming, picnicking north of Belfast in Swanville).

MOOSE   The moose, Maine's state animal, has made a comeback from near extinction in the 1930s, but thanks to a deadly Winter Tick numbers are now substantially less than the 76,000 recorded just a few years ago. Moose are the largest animal found in the wilds of New England. They grow to be 10 feet tall and average 1,000 pounds. The largest member of the deer family, they have a large, protruding upper lip and a distinctive "bell" or "dewlap" dangling from their muzzle or throat.

"Bull" (male) moose have long been prized for their antlers, which grow to a span of up to 6 feet. They are shed in January and grow again. Female moose ("cows") do not grow antlers, and their heads are lighter in color than the bulls'. All moose, however, are darker in spring than summer, grayer in winter.

Front hooves are longer than the rear, as are the legs, the better to cope with deep snow and water. In summer they favor wetlands and can usually be found near ponds or watery bogs. They also like salt and so tend to create and frequent "wallows," wet areas handy to road salt (the attraction of paved roads).

Moose are vegetarians, daily consuming more than 50 pounds of leaves, grass, and other greenery when they can find it. In winter their diet consists largely of bark and twigs. Mating season runs from mid-September until late October. Calves are born in early spring and weigh in at 30 pounds. They grow quickly but keep close to their mothers for an entire year. At best moose live 12 years.

Your chances of spotting one are greatest in early morning or at dusk on a wooded pond or lake or along logging roads. If you are driving through moose country at night, go slowly, because moose typically freeze rather than retreat from oncoming headlights. The state records hundreds of often deadly collisions between moose and cars or trucks. The common road sign and bumper sticker reading BRAKE FOR MOOSE means just that. Be extremely wary at dusk, when vision is difficult and moose are active. For details about commercial moose-watching expeditions, check "Rangeley Lakes Region," "Moosehead Lake Area," and the "Katahdin Region."

PARKS AND NATURE PRESERVES   Within each chapter we describe these under *Green Space* or *To Do—Hiking*. The one not to miss is **Acadia National Park** (207-288-3338; nps.gov/acad), which occupies more than 40,000 acres offering hiking, ski touring, swimming, horseback riding, canoeing, and a variety of guided nature tours and programs, as well as a scenic 27-mile driving tour. See more on page 301.

ROCKHOUNDING   Maine is a famous source of pink and green **tourmaline**, especially plentiful in the Bethel area, site of the new **Maine Mineral and Gem Museum** (mainemineralmuseum.org) in Bethel. Thanks to the high price of gold, prospectors are back panning Maine streambeds. The **Maine Geological Survey** (207-287-2801) offers an introduction to Maine minerals and their sources.

SPORTING CAMPS   The Maine sporting camp—a gathering of log cabins around a log hunting lodge by a remote lake or stream—is a distinctly Maine phenomenon that began appearing in the 1860s. "Sports" (guests) were met by a guide at a train or steamer and paddled up lakes and rivers to a camp. With the advent of floatplanes (see *Air Services*), many of these camps became more accessible, and the proliferation of private logging roads has put most within reach of snowmobiles and sturdy vehicles. True sporting camps still cater primarily to anglers in spring and hunters in fall, but since summer is neither a hunting season nor a prime fishing season, they all host families who just want to be in the woods. True sporting camps still include a central lodge in which guests are served all three meals; boats and guide service are available. The **Maine Sporting Camp Association** (mainesportingcamps.com) maintains a list of more than 40 members. We describe those we have visited and recommend in our "Western Mountains and Lakes Region," "North Maine Woods," "Upper Kennebec Valley," and "Aroostook County" chapters.

SCENIC HIGHWAYS AND BYWAYS Books have been written about Maine's most scenic roads. Those officially recognized as **National Scenic Byways** include **the Old Canada Road**, 78 miles of Rt. 201 from Solon north to the Canadian border; the 52 glorious miles of Rt. 17 from Byron on up through **Rangeley Lakes**; and the 29 miles of Rt. 1 from Sullivan to **Schoodic**. The **All American Road** (the Loop Road in Acadia National Park) is a must. See exploremaine.org for descriptions of the 10 Maine Scenic Byways. Within each chapter we describe our own picks under *Excursions*.

WATERFALLS The following are all easily accessible to families with small children: **Snow Falls Gorge** off Rt. 26 in West Paris offers a beautiful cascade; **Small's Falls** on the Sandy River, off Rt. 4 between Rangeley and Phillips, has a picnic spot with a trail beside the falls; **Jewell Falls** is located in the Fore River Sanctuary in the heart of Portland; **Step Falls** is on Wight Brook in Newry off Rt. 26; and just up the road in Grafton Notch State Park is **Screw Auger Falls**, with its natural gorge. Another Screw Auger Falls is in Gulf Hagas, off the Appalachian Trail near the Katahdin Iron Works Rd., north of Brownville Junction. **Kezar Falls**, on the Kezar River, is best reached via Lovell Rd. from Rt. 35 at North Waterford. An extensive list of "scenic waterfalls" is detailed in the *Maine Atlas and Gazetteer* (DeLorme). Also check out 90-foot **Moxie Falls** in The Forks.

Outdoors

ATVS **Alliance Trail Vehicles of Maine** (atvmaine.org) offers information about the state's all-terrain vehicle clubs and riding opportunities. Registration information and more can be found at the Department of Inland Fisheries and Wildlife website, maine.

gov/ifw. The Department of Agriculture, Conservation and Forestry (maine.gov/dacf) has ATV trail maps too.

AMUSEMENT PARKS **Funtown/Splashtown USA** in Saco is Maine's biggest, with rides, water slides, and pools. **Aquaboggan** (pools and slides) is also on Rt. 1 in Saco. **Palace Playland** in Old Orchard Beach is a classic, with a carousel, Ferris wheel, rides, and a 60-foot water slide. **York's Wild Kingdom** at York Beach has a zoo and amusement area. **Seacoast Fun Park** in Windham and **Wild Acadia Fun Park** in Trenton have a water slide or tubing slide, mini golf, and rock climbing wall. Also see *Ziplines*.

BICYCLING The excellent Maine DOT site, exploremaine.org/bike, lists tours ranging from 20 to 100 miles. With the Office of Tourism, Maine DOT has published an *Explore Maine by Bike* guide to 33 loop tours, downloadable from its site. The **Bicycle Coalition of Maine** (bikemaine.org) serves as a conduit for information about both off- and on-road bicycling throughout the state and maintains a calendar of bicycling events, including the annual BikeMaine. Guided multiday tours are offered by **Summer Feet Cycling** (summerfeet.net) and **Discovery Bicycle Tours** (discoverybicycletours.com); a variety of tours are offered by **L.L. Bean** (llbean.com). Biking is popular on Swan's Island off Acadia and on islands in Casco Bay. Rt. 1 is heavily traveled and should be avoided. Dedicated recreation paths are appearing, notably in Portland, South Portland, and Brunswick/Bath, along the Kennebec between Augusta and Gardiner, and farther north between Solon and Bingham. Bicycling also makes sense in heavily touristed resort areas in which a car can be a nuisance; rentals are available in most coastal destinations. For good biking maps of various regions, **Map Adventures** (mapadventures .com) makes very readable small maps of bike routes, stocked at most bike shops and bookstores. **Mountain biking** is particularly popular on the carriage roads in **Acadia National Park**, along the 85-mile Sunrise Trail (sunrise trail.org) in Hancock and Washington Counties (also popular with ATVs), at **Sunday River Resort**, and at **Sugarloaf** and the neighboring **Maine Huts and Trails** system (maine huts.org).

BOAT EXCURSIONS You won't know what Maine is about until you stand off at sea to appreciate the beauty of the cliffs and island-dotted bays. For the greatest concentrations of boat excursions, see "Boothbay Harbor Region," "Rockland/Thomaston Area," and "Bar Harbor and Ellsworth." Also see *Coastal Cruises*; *Ferries in Maine* and *to Canada*; *Sailing*; and *Windjammers*.

CAMPING See "North Maine Woods" for details about camping within these vast fiefdoms, and also for camping in **Baxter State Park** (see "Katahdin Region") and along the **Allagash Wilderness Waterway** (see *Canoeing* in "Aroostook County"). For camping within **Acadia National Park**, see "Acadia National Park." For the same within the **White Mountain National Forest**, see "Bethel Area." For private campgrounds, the booklet *Maine Camping Guide*, published by the Maine Campground Owners Association (207-782-5874; campmaine.com), lists most privately operated camping and tenting areas. Reservations are advised for the state's 13 parks that offer camping (campwithme.com; also see *Parks, State*). We have attempted to describe the state parks in detail wherever they appear in this book (see Damariscotta, Camden, Cobscook Bay, Sebago, Rangeley, and Greenville). Note that state campsites can accommodate average-sized campers and trailers, but only Sebago and Camden Hills offer (up to 40-foot) trailer electric and water hookups. **Warren Island** (just off Islesboro) and **Swan Island** (just off Richmond) offer organized camping, and primitive camping is permitted on a number of islands through the **Maine Island Trail Association** (MITA; see *Islands*). Within this book we occasionally describe outstanding private campgrounds.

CAMPS AND LEARNING PROGRAMS FOR ADULTS **Outward Bound** (1-866-476-7651; outwardboundwilderness.org) offers a variety of adult-geared outdoor adventures in Maine as well as throughout the country. **L.L. Bean** (llbean.com) offers introductions to a variety of sports, with programs lasting from a couple of hours to multiday family adventures and **Outdoor Discovery Schools**. The **Hog Island Audubon Center** on Hog Island off Bremen offers programs sponsored by Audubon's

BAXTER STATE PARK   Courtesy of the Maine Office of Tourism

Project Puffin (see "Damariscotta/Newcastle"). The **AMC** (see *Appalachian Mountain Club*) also offers weeklong "Family Camp" programs at several Maine venues. Photographers should check out the **Maine Media Workshops** (theworkshops.com) in Rockport. Also see *Boatbuilding* (**WoodenBoat** offers much more than boatbuilding). **Road Scholar**, formerly Elderhostel (roadscholar.org), offers a variety of programs throughout Maine for everyone over age 50. Check out **Haystack Mountain School** under *Crafts* and arts workshops under *Artists, Art Programs, and Art Galleries*. Entries under *Music Schools* and *Sailing* also have workshop information. Potters should check out the **Watershed Center for Ceramic Arts** (watershedceramics.org) in Newcastle.

CAMPS, FOR CHILDREN More than 200 summer camps are listed in the exceptional booklet published annually by the **Maine Summer Camp Association** (1-800-536-7712; mainecamps.org). Also check out **Maine Camp Experience** (mainecampexperience .com).

CANOEING Developed by the Wabanaki who still proudly manufacture canoes in Old Town (see "Bangor Area"), the canoe remains popular on Maine rivers. The ultimate canoe trip in Maine (and on the entire East Coast) is the 7- to 10-day expedition up the **Allagash Wilderness Waterway**, a 92-mile ribbon of lakes, ponds, rivers, and streams in the heart of northern Maine's vast commercial forests. For further information, see *Camping*. Also see *To Do—Canoeing* in "Aroostook County." A map tracing Henry David Thoreau's three canoe/hiking journeys described in *The Maine Woods* has been produced by Maine Woods Forever (thoreauwabanakitrail.org). Also see *Books*.

DOGSLEDDING Racing is a long-established winter spectator sport in Maine, and both riding on and driving dogsleds is increasingly popular. Based in the Bethel area, two experienced outfitters offer multi-day expeditions. At **New England Dogsledding** (newenglanddogsledding.com) Steve Crone, a competitive racer based at the Tele-mark Inn, a rustic 1890s woodland lodge, offers multiple-day "Learn to Dogsled" packages, including treks into the Umbagog National Wildlife Refuge. So do Polly Mahoney and Kevin Slater at **Mahoosuc Guide Service** (207-824-2073; mahoosuc .com), who have been offering combination skiing and mushing trips for more than 20 years. They also offer four-day "Northern

Classic" trips from wilderness lodge to lodge near Moosehead Lake.

In the Moosehead Lake region also check out Stephen Medera's **Song in the Woods** (songinthewoods.com), based in Abbott, which offers a choice of trips. Don and Angel Hibbs have traveled more than 40,000 miles by dog team. In the Rangeley area check out **Rangeley Region Sled Dog Adventures** and **Morning-song Wilderness Tours**. The **Northeast Dogsled Championships** are held in Jackman in early March, followed closely by the **Can-Am Crown Sled Dog Races** in Fort Kent.

FISHING Check out the **Maine Department of Inland Fisheries and Wildlife** at maine .gov/ifw/fishing for basics such as licensing information and public boat-launch locations for freshwater fishing on Maine's lakes, ponds, rivers, and streams. **Registered Maine Guides** (maineguides.org) know where and how to fish, and offer frequent courses. One-day fishing licenses are available at general stores and from outfitters throughout the state; they come with a regulations book. The **Maine Department of Marine Resources** furnishes saltwater recreational fishing registry information, species information, and launch sites at maine.gov/dmr. The **Maine Association of Charterboat Captains** (mainecharter captains.org) is another great resource for saltwater fishing, and visitmaine.com has extensive fishing info. Also see the **Maine Sporting Camp Association** (mainesporting camps.com) and *Sporting Camps*; all these camps cater to fishermen.

GOLF The **Golf Maine Association** website (golfme.com) offers information and links to its member courses. Also check out the **Maine Golf Trail** (visitmaine.com) and the Maine State Golf Association (mesga.org). Within the book we list golf courses within each chapter. The major resorts catering to golfers are the **Samoset** in Rockport, the **Bethel Inn** and **Sunday River Resort** in Bethel, **Sebasco Harbor Resort** near Bath, the **Country Club Inn** in Rangeley, **Sugarloaf** in the Carrabassett Valley (where you should also inquire about **Moose Meadows**), and **Sunday River Golf Club** in Newry. The **Aroostook Valley Golf Club** (avcc.ca) near Fort Fairfield spans the Maine–New Brunswick border.

Courtesy of New England Dogsledding

YOU TOO CAN DOGSLED

HIKING Both the **Appalachian Mountain Club** (outdoors.org) and **Maine Huts and Trails** (mainehuts.org) maintain off-the-grid full-service lodges along 80-mile trail networks. Our personal favorite hikes are the Indian Trail up Mount Kineo at the midpoint in Moosehead Lake, along the cliffs on the island of Monhegan, and at West Quoddy Light, but the rite-of-passage hike for much of New England is up Mount Katahdin. While we list hikes within most chapters, we strongly suggest acquiring detailed trail guides. In addition to the *AMC Maine Mountain Guide* and the AMC map/guide to trails on Mount Desert, we recommend investing in *50 Hikes in Coastal and Inland Maine* by John Gibson and *50 Hikes in the Maine Mountains* by Cloe Chunn (both from Countryman Press), which offer clear, inviting treks up hills of every size throughout the state. The *Maine Atlas and Gazetteer* (DeLorme) also outlines a number of rewarding hikes. **Map Adventures** (map adventures.com) makes very readable small maps of bike routes. While hiking is generally associated with inland Maine and Acadia, in recent years tens of thousands of acres of dramatic shore property have been preserved, much of this traversed by coastal trails, which we have attempted to list chapter by chapter. The car-free island of **Monhegan** is beloved by hikers for its many dramatic trails. **Maine Trailfinder** (mainetrailfinder.com) is an amazing resource for hikers. Also see *Appalachian Trail* and *State Parks*. In recent years the Boston-based AMC, the country's oldest nonprofit outdoor recreation/conservation group, has acquired 66,500 acres in the North Woods (see "Moosehead Lake Area") along with three historic sporting camps, rechristening them "Wilderness Lodges." Over the past decade it has restored two of the camps (the third is set to reopen soon), linked by an 80-mile trail system geared to nonmotorized recreational use. With its reservation system and outreach to outdoors-minded folks throughout the Northeast, the nonprofit is raising the profile of this magnificent, under-visited woodlands corridor between Moosehead Lake and Baxter State Park. Both Little Lyford and Gorman Chairback Wilderness Lodges are within easy hiking distance of magnificent Gulf Hagas. The AMC has also long offered seasonal "family camp" programs at **Echo Lake** (amcecholakecamp.org)

on Mount Desert, and at **Cold River Camp** (amccoldrivercamp.org) in Evans Notch within the White Mountain National Forest.

HUNTING Hunters should obtain a summary of Maine hunting and trapping laws from the **Maine Department of Inland Fisheries and Wildlife** (mefishandwildlife.com). In 1897 the Maine legislature passed a bill requiring hunting guides to register with the state; the first to do so was Cornelia Thurza Crosby (better known as "Fly Rod" Crosby), whose syndicated column appeared in New York, Boston, and Chicago newspapers at the turn of the 20th century. Becoming a **Registered Maine Guide** entails passing tests in one of several categories—including hunting, fishing, whitewater rafting, canoeing, or sea kayaking—administered by the Maine Department of Inland Fisheries and Wildlife. There are currently several thousand, but just a few hundred are full-time professional guides. The website of the **Maine Professional Guides Association** (maineguides.org), can give you contact information, as can the **Maine Wilderness Guides Association** (mwgo.org). For more, check HUNTING at visit maine.com.

HORSEBACK RIDING **Northern Maine Riding Adventures** (mainetrailrides.com) is based in Dover-Foxcroft. In the Bethel area **Deepwood Farm** offers trail rides, summer camp, and sleigh rides; also near Bethel, **New England Riding and Driving** (newengland driving.com), based at Telemark Wilderness Lodge, offers "Learn to Carriage Drive" packages, including those for special-needs children. In the Moosehead Lake area **Rockies Golden Acres** (rockiesgoldenacres.webs.com) gives trail rides through the woods to Sawyer Pond with mountain views. Also check HORSEBACK RIDING at visitmaine.com.

HORSE RACING Harness racing, in a renaissance since gambling with slot machines has been allowed in Bangor—the earnings subsidize the "purses" or winnings at Maine's two harness racing tracks—can be found at **Scarborough Downs** April through November. The **Bangor Raceway** is open late May through late July. Both allow betting. Bangor offers slot machines and table games in a casino called **Hollywood Casino Hotel &**

Raceway. Many of the agricultural fairs also feature harness racing.

KAYAKING **Sea kayaking outfitters** that offer guided half-day and full-day trips, also overnight and multiday expeditions with camping on Maine islands, are too numerous to be listed here but are described within each relevant chapter. The leading outfitters are **Maine Island Kayak Company** (maineisland kayak.com) on Peaks Island off Portland; **Maine Sport Outfitters** (mainesport.com) in Rockport; **H2outfitters** (h2outfitters.com), based on Orrs Island, which offers an extensive array of trips both locally and around the world; **Old Quarry Ocean Adventures, Inc.** (oldquarry.com) in Deer Isle; **Tidal Transit** (207-633-7140) in Boothbay Harbor; **Midcoast Kayak** (midcoastkayak.com) in Damariscotta; and **Castine Kayak Adventures** (castine kayak.com). In Washington County, **Sunrise Canoe & Kayak Tours** (sunrisecanoeand kayak.com) offers rentals and tours in Machias Bay. **L.L. Bean** (llbean.com) offers instruction in kayaking at its **Outdoor Discovery Schools**, Rt. 1, Freeport. Inquire about their **Paddle Sport Weekend.** Also see maine paddlesports.org for a listing of members of the Maine Association of Sea Kayaking Guides and Instructors. Dorcas Miller's comprehensive *Kayaking the Maine Coast: A Paddler's Guide to Day Trips from Kittery to Cobscook* (Countryman Press) is an excellent resource for kayak owners and competent kayakers. Also see the **Maine Island Trail** under *Islands*. It's a great camping resource for sea kayakers.

Lake kayaking offers myriad options for paddlers. Kayaks, along with canoes, are available from most lakeside lodging places described in this book. Serious expeditions can be planned (see *Guide Services*) on adjoining lakes in the Grand Lake Stream and Rangeley regions as well as the North Woods. Jackman-based **Cry of the Loon Adventures** (cryoftheloon.net) offers guided camping on the classic 34-mile Moose River Bow Trip. Also see *Whitewater Rafting*; most of these outfitters also offer whitewater kayaking.

MAINE HUTS AND TRAILS Check maine huts.org for updates and details on this ambitious Kingfield-based, hut-to-hut trail system that is planned to eventually run from the Mahoosuc Mountains to Moosehead Lake. At present an 80-mile trail system, limited to nonmotorized use and groomed for cross-country skiing, connects the Carrabassett and Upper Kennebec Valleys. Along the way there are now four off-the-grid "huts"— Poplar Stream Falls, Stratton Brook, and Flagstaff Lake (all accessible from the Sugarloaf area), along with Grand Falls, 14.2 miles from West Forks. These comfortable lodges are fully staffed in-season, offering three meals in a main building, bunkhouses with private and semiprivate rooms, and a wood-fired sauna.

SAILING Windjammers and yacht charter brokers aside, there are a limited number of places that will rent small sailing craft, and fewer that will offer lessons to adults and children alike. **Linekin Bay Resort** (linekinbay resort.com) in Boothbay Harbor is billed as the only surviving full-service sailing resort on the East Coast. Qualified sailors can rent Rhodes 19-foot sailboats, and sailing lessons are offered for those of all abilities. The **Mansell Boat Rental Company** (mansellboat rentals.com), Southwest Harbor, rents sailboats by the day or longer. **Buck's Harbor Marine** (207-326-8839), South Brooksville, rents sail- and motorboats. Inquire about sailing lessons. Learn-to-sail programs are offered by **WoodenBoat School** (thewooden boatschool.com) in Brooklin, the **Camden Yacht Club** (camdenyachtclub.org), which offers a junior sailing program to non members, and **Bay Island Sailing School** (sailme.com) based in Rockland. **Old Quarry Ocean Adventures** (oldquarry.com) in Deer Isle rents a variety of sailboats and offers lessons. Other rentals and daysails are listed throughout the book. (Also see *Windjammers*.)

SKIING **Ski Maine Association** (207-773-SNOW; skimaine.com) provides information about alpine mountains and cross-country centers in Maine. **Sugarloaf** in the Carrabassett Valley and **Sunday River** in the Bethel area vie for the title of Maine's number one ski resort. Although now under the same Michigan-based ownership, the two are very different and complement each other well. Sugarloaf is a high, relatively remote mountain with New England's only lift-serviced snowfields on its summit and a classy, self-contained condo village at its base.

Sunday River, just an hour north of Portland, consists of eight adjoining (relatively low-altitude) mountains; snowmaking is a big point of pride, and facilities include a variety of reasonably priced and family-geared slope-side condo lodgings. **Saddleback Mountain** in Rangeley has an enthusiastic following and has recently been modernized and expanded. **Mount Abram** in the Bethel area is a true family area with a strong ski school and some fine runs. **Shawnee Peak** in Bridgton, in business since 1938, is a medium-sized, family-geared area that offers night as well as day skiing. The **Camden Snow Bowl** in Camden is small but satisfying.

Cross-country offerings are a widely varied lot. The **Sugarloaf Outdoor Center** is the state's largest. See separate entries in this section for the **Appalachian Mountain Club** (outdoors.org) and **Maine Huts and Trails** (mainehuts.org), each of which maintains 80 miles of groomed trails and offers guided and self-guided treks between fully staffed lodges. In **Bethel** there are three trail networks (Bethel Inn, Carter's Farm X-C Ski Center, and Bethel Nordic Ski Center). **Rangeley Lakes Trails Center** offers 55 groomed kilometers, and the town of **Millinocket** maintains extensive trail networks that enjoy dependable snow cover. In the Moosehead area the **Birches Resort** offers an extensive network and trailside yurts. **West Branch Pond Camps** (which connect with the AMC system and programs) also caters to skiers, as do **Chesuncook Lake House** and **Katahdin Lake Wilderness Camps**. All these options are detailed within their respective chapters. Also see the **Maine Winter Sports Center** facilities (mainewsc.org) in Aroostook County.

SNOWMOBILING See the **Department of Inland Fisheries and Wildlife** site (maine .gov/ifw) for information about registering a snowmobile in Maine. The **Maine Snowmobile Association** (MSA; mesnow.com) represents more than 290 clubs and maintains some 14,000 miles of an ever-expanding cross-state trail network. **Aroostook County**, given its reliable snow conditions, is an increasingly popular destination. See the **Upper Kennebec Valley** and **Jackman** as well as **Moosehead**, **Katahdin**, and **Rangeley Lakes** for details about outfitters who offer sled rentals, gear, and guided rides. **Northern**

SKIING AT SUGARLOAF

Outdoors in The Forks and **New England Outdoor Center** near Millinocket are two biggies (see *Whitewater Rafting*).

WHALE-WATCHING Each spring humpback, finback, and minke whales migrate to New England waters, where they remain until fall, cavorting, it sometimes seems, for the pleasure of excursion boats. One prime gathering spot is **Jefferies Ledge**, about 20 miles off Kennebunkport, and another is the **Bay of Fundy**. For listings of whale-watch cruises, see "The Kennebunks," "Portland Area," "Bar Harbor," and "Washington County." The East Quoddy (Campobello) and West Quoddy (Lubec) Lighthouses are also prime viewing spots. Whales are sighted more often than not on the ferry ride from Black Harbor, New Brunswick, to the island of Grand Manan, another hub for whale-watch cruises.

WHITEWATER RAFTING In Maine this phenomenon's beginnings coincided with the last log drive on the Kennebec River. Logs were still hurtling through Kennebec Gorge on that day in spring 1976 when fishing guide Wayne Hockmeyer and eight bear hunters from New Jersey plunged through it in a rubber raft. At the time Hockmeyer's rafting know-how stemmed solely from having seen *River of No Return*, in which Robert Mitchum steered Marilyn Monroe down the Salmon River.

Hockmeyer and his wife Suzie went on to found **Northern Outdoors**, still the foremost outfitters among those positioned around The Forks, near the confluence of the Kennebec and Dead Rivers and the rapids through nearby 12-mile-long Kennebec Gorge. Numbers on the rivers are now strictly limited and timed for the releases from the Harris Hydroelectric Station above the gorge. Several rafting companies—notably **Northern Outdoors** (northernoutdoors.com), **Crab Apple** (crabappleinc.com), and **Magic Falls Rafting Company** (magicfalls.com)—base facilities in and around The Forks.

The West Branch of the Penobscot represents the ultimate challenge in Maine rafting, best for experienced rafters. Here Matt Polstein's **New England Outdoor Center** (neoc.com) is the leading outfitter, with two bases, one just outside Baxter State Park and the second on Millinocket Lake with a mix of basic and upscale cabins. **Northern Outdoors** also offers base facilities here near Ripogenus Dam. Details are in our Upper Kennebec and Katahdin chapters.

WINDJAMMERS In 1936 artist Frank Swift outfitted a few former fishing and cargo schooners to carry passengers around the islands of Penobscot Bay. At the time these old vessels were moored in every harbor and cove, casualties of progress. Swift's fleet grew to include more than a dozen vessels. Competitors also prospered throughout the 1950s, but the entire windjammer fleet appeared doomed by rigorous Coast Guard licensing requirements in the 1960s. The 1970s and 1980s saw the rise of a new breed of windjammer captain. Most of those now sailing built or restored the vessel he or she commands or acquired it from the captain who did. Members of the current Maine windjammer fleet range from the *Stephen Taber* and the *Lewis R. French*, both originally launched in 1871, to the *Heritage*, launched in 1983.

Former *Taber* co-captain Ellen Barnes recalls her own discovery of windjammers: "No museums had gobbled up these vessels; no cities had purchased them to sit at piers as public relations gimmicks. These vessels were the real thing, plying their trade as they had in the past with one exception: The present-day cargo was people instead of pulpwood, bricks,

coal, limestone, and granite." Six are registered historic landmarks.

Choosing which vessel to sail on is the most difficult part of a windjammer cruise. Check the **Maine Windjammer Association** website (sailmainecoast.com) for details about its members.

ZIPLINES **Monkey Trunks** in Saco, **Monkey C Monkey Do** in Wiscasset, and **Take Flight Adventures** in Kittery add maneuvering with ropes to the seasonal mix of what coastal visitors can do. Inland, check out ziplines at **Sugarloaf** in summer months and at **Sunday River Resort** in both summer and winter seasons.

Sights to See

COVERED BRIDGES Of the 120 covered bridges that once spanned Maine rivers, just nine survive. The most famous, and certainly picturesque, is the **Artists' Covered Bridge** (1872) over the Sunday River in Newry, northwest of Bethel. The others are **Porter Bridge** (1876), over the Ossipee River, 0.5 mile south of Porter; **Babb's Bridge**, rebuilt after burning in 1973, over the Presumpscot River between Gorham and Windham; **Hemlock Bridge** (1857), 3 miles northwest of East Fryeburg; **Lovejoy Bridge** (1883), over the Ellis River in South Andover; **Bennett Bridge** (1901), over the Magalloway River, 1.5 miles south of the Wilson's Mills post office; **Robyville Bridge**

Bob Angell and the Maine Windjammer Association

PARADING WINDJAMMERS

(1876), Maine's only completely shingled covered bridge, in the town of Corinth; the **Watson Settlement Bridge** (1911), between Woodstock and Littleton; and **Low's Bridge**, carefully reconstructed in 1990 after a flood took the 1857 structure, across the Piscataquis River between Guilford and Sangerville.

FALL FOLIAGE Autumn days tend to be clear, and the changing leaves against the blue sea and lakes can be spectacular. Off-season prices sometimes prevail, in contrast with the rest of New England at this time of year. Check the Maine Department of Agriculture, Conservation and Forestry website (mainefoliage.com), for a map reporting leaf colors and places to visit. (The website is only actively updated Sept. 1–Oct. 15.)

FORTS Maine's 20 forts are actually a fascinating lot, monuments to the state's largely forgotten history. **Fort Knox** (see "Bucksport") is the state's grandest and offers a lively seasonal schedule of events. **Fort William Henry** at Pemaquid (see "Damariscotta/ Newcastle") is genuinely fascinating, while **Fort Edgecomb** off Rt. 1 in Edgecomb, just east of Wiscasset, is an easy hit. Also check

out **Fort George** in Castine, **Fort McClary** in Kittery, **Fort Popham** near Bath, **Fort Pownall** at Stockton Springs, **Fort O'Brien** in Machiasport, and, near the northern end of Rt. 1, our favorite: the **Fort Kent Blockhouse**. **Old Fort Western** in Augusta (oldfortwestern.org) is the oldest surviving wooden fort in New England.

LIGHTHOUSES More than 800 lighthouses still stand in the US and Maine has 66 of them, including the Machias Seal Island Light, maintained by the Canadian Coast Guard. But it's Maine that they symbolize. No longer simply photogenic icons, more than a dozen lighthouse stations now invite visitors to clamber up into their towers and explore their keeper's houses-turned museums, welcome centers, or lodging. As lighthouses have become automated, many have been adopted by "friends." The **American Lighthouse Foundation** (lighthousefoundation.org) serves as an umbrella organization for groups supporting nine Maine lights, and its site details open hours for those at the **Owls Head**, **Rockland Breakwater**, **Pemaquid Point**, **Wood Island** (off Biddeford Pool), and **Little River Lighthouse** off Cutler (lodging offered). At **Burnt**

Christina Tree

MONHEGAN LIGHTHOUSE

Island Light Station in Boothbay Harbor, guides dress as lighthouse keepers from the 1950s and show visitors how life was lived on an isolated island. Also in the Boothbay area, Cuckolds Lighthouse is now a luxurious bed & breakfast. See the Rockland chapter for details about these and **Goose Rocks Lighthouse** (beaconpreservation.org), a freestanding "spark-plug-style" light in the Fox Island Thorofare. Nearby, off Sprucehead, the Whitehead Light Station (whiteheadlightstation .org) welcomes visitors with seven guestrooms, summer workshops, and September rentals. Another popular island light is the vintage-1795 **Seguin Island Light Station** (seguinisland.org). Sited 2.5 miles off the mouth of Kennebec River, it's a 186-foot granite lighthouse on a 64-acre island. A far easier shot is the **Neddick (Nubble) Light,** just off Sohier Park in York, within camera range. True lighthouse buffs also make the pilgrimage to **Burnt Harbor Light** on Swan's Island and to **Matinicus Rock**, the setting for several children's books. **The Keeper's House** on Isle au Haut is another B&B. **Head Harbor Lighthouse** on the island of Campobello, accessible at low tide, is the ultimate adventure; it is also a prime whale-watching post. Descriptions of all these lights are detailed in their respective chapters. **Fort Point Light** at Stockton Springs and **Bass Harbor Head Light** at Bass Harbor are easily accessible by land. **Portland Head Light** on Cape Elizabeth, completed in 1790 and automated in 1990, is now a delightful museum featuring the history of lighthouses. Other lights that feature museums are the **Marshall Point Light** at Port Clyde, **Pemaquid Point** (the lighthouse itself is now open seasonally), **Monhegan Light** on Monhegan Island, **Grindle Point** on Islesboro, and **West Quoddy Head Light** in Lubec, now part of a state park with a stunning shore path. Rockland's Gateway Visitor Center is home to the **Maine Lighthouse Museum** (mainelighthousemuseum.com).

LOBSTERBOAT RACES The season's races represent one of the best spectator events along the Maine coast. Races begin mid-June in Boothbay Harbor, and the "World's Fastest Lobster Boat Races" are always held on Moosabec Reach between Jonesport and Beals Island on July 4. Other venues are Rockland, Stonington, Harpswell, Friendship, Winter Harbor, and Pemaquid. Participants accumulate points as they go along, and there's an awards ceremony and pig roast in late September.

Shopping

ANTIQUES A member directory listing hundreds of dealers is produced by the **Maine Antiques Dealers Association**. The association's active website lists members as well as auctions at maineantiques.org. The 60-plus-page *Maine Antique Dealer Directory* can be ordered online.

ANTIQUARIAN BOOKS Maine is well known among book buffs as a browsing mecca. **Maine Antiquarian Booksellers** posts a directory of 50 members at mainebooksellers.org.

BOOKSTORES Full-service, independent bookstores—those stores that stand ready to

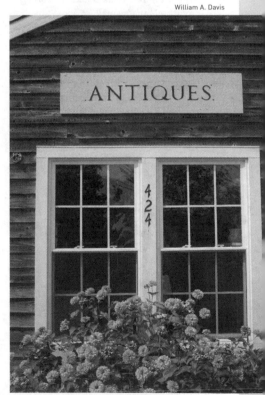

William A. Davis

ANTIQUES IN WINTER HARBOR

find the kind of book you are looking for, even if you don't know what it is—are becoming a rarity in urban centers, let alone seasonal coastal towns. Maine, however, still has its fair share. In Kennebunk Lower Village look for **Kennebooks**, in Portland for **Longfellow Books**, and in Brunswick for **Gulf of Maine Books** whose co-owner, poet Gary Lawless, is also founder of Blackberry Press, which has reissued many out-of-print Maine classics. In Bath there's **Bath Bookshop** and in Damariscotta there's the peerless **Maine Coast Book Shop** with its cyber café. **Book Stacks** in Bucksport also offers WiFi and coffee, while **Blue Hill Books** draws patrons from throughout East Penobscot Bay to its white-clapboard house up a side street. At the **Calais Bookshop**, Carole Heinlein presides over a an oasis of print, with antiquarian as well as new books, an impressive number of which she has read. Hats off, of course, to Bar Harbor–based **Sherman's Books and Stationery**, Maine's own distinctive chain with stores in Boothbay Harbor and Freeport. Finally, we have to mention **Dockside Books** in Stonington. It may be Maine's smallest bookstore, but it has the best view.

FACTORY OUTLETS We note individual outlet stores in their respective chapters throughout; we also describe the state's two major outlet clusters: in **Freeport** (freeport usa.com) and **Kittery** (thekitteryoutlets.com). **New Balance** also makes sneakers in Maine

Christina Tree

GARY LAWLESS OF GULF OF MAINE BOOKS SPECIALIZES IN MAINE AUTHORS

and maintains outlets in Norway and Skowhegan.

L.L. BEAN (llbean.com) was founded in 1912 by Leon Leonwood Bean. The company began as a one-room operation selling a single product, the Maine Hunting Shoe. Ninety out of the first 100 boots Bean sold that year fell apart. He refunded the purchasers' money, establishing a company tradition of guaranteed customer satisfaction still honored today in Freeport and in stores throughout the United States, Japan, and China. This Maine icon's 200,000-square-foot flagship store in Freeport is open 24 hours a day, 365 days a year. Outdoor clothing and equipment remain the company's mainstays, and they can now also be found in the Hunting and Fishing Store, the Bike, Boat & Ski Store, and the Home Store. **Outdoor Discovery Schools** and **Walk-On Adventures**, ranging from kayaking to fly-fishing, get customers into action year-round. See the Freeport chapter for details.

RENYS Billed as "A Maine Adventure," and "a part of the state's culture since 1949," Renys (renys.com) is a family-owned chain of 14 discount stores that, like hermit crabs, occupy spaces vacated by previous owners. The **Farmington** Renys fills a former music hall, the **Madison** space was an opera house, and in **Damariscotta** Renys Underground was a bowling alley. Several Renys fill former supermarkets, and in Bath, Gardiner, Dexter, Damariscotta, and Portland the shops effectively fill the void left by small-town clothing and department stores. Listing what Renys stocks is harder than saying what it doesn't. There are linens and shoes, name-brand clothing and toys, electronics, clamming and camping gear, stationery, Maine-made products, and always surprises. Renys has recently become less about odd lots (that niche is now filled by **Marden's**, Maine's other discount chain) and more about quality, service, and good value.

Further Reading

Anyone who seriously sets out to explore Maine should read the following mix of Maine classics and guidebooks: *The Maine Woods* by **Henry David Thoreau**, first published

RENYS

Maine has been home to the authors of many of our most beloved children's classics. **Robert McCloskey**, author of *Blueberries for Sal*, *Time of Wonder*, and *One Morning in Maine*, resided on an island off the Blue Hill Peninsula, also summer home to **E. B. White**, known for wonderful essay collections and his ever-popular children's novels *Charlotte's Web* and *Stuart Little*. Damariscotta-based **Barbara Cooney** wrote and illustrated some 200 books, among them *Miss Rumphius*, *Island Boy*, and *Hattie and the Wild Waves*.

Recent classics set in Maine include **Carolyn Chute**'s *The Beans of Egypt, Maine* (1985), *Letourneau's Used Auto Parts* (1988), *Merry Men* (1994), and *The School of Heart's Content Road* (2008); and **Cathie Pelletier**'s *The Funeral Makers* (1987) and *The Weight of Winter* (1991). *Maine Speaks*, an anthology of Maine literature published by the **Maine Writers and Publishers Alliance** (mainewriters.org), contains all the obvious poems and essays and many pleasant surprises. **Linda Greenlaw**'s *The Lobster Chronicles* (2002) describes the island of Isle au Haut. It's a good read with insights into life on all of Maine's surviving island communities. *The Lobster Coast* (Penguin, 2004) by **Colin Woodward** is a must read for anyone interested in "Rebels, Rusticators, and the Struggle for a Forgotten Frontier." *The Poacher's Son* (Macmillan) and five more locally set mysteries by former *Down East* editor **Paul Doiron** are all worth a read. Maine titles for all ages can be found at islandportpress.com.

posthumously in 1864, remains very readable and gives an excellent description of Maine's mountains. For those inspired to trace Thoreau's route there's *The Wildest Country: Exploring Thoreau's Maine* by **Parker Huber** (AMC Books), complete with maps and color photographs of local flora and fauna. Our favorite relatively recent Maine author is **Ruth Moore**, who writes about Maine islands in *The Weir*, *Spoonhandle*, and *Speak to the Wind* (originally published in the 1940s and reissued by Blackberry Books, Nobleboro). The 1940s classic *We Took to the Woods* by **Louise Dickinson Rich** is now published by Down East Books in Camden. **Sarah Orne Jewett**'s classic *The Country of the Pointed Firs and Other Stories* (W. W. Norton), first published in 1896, is set on the coast around Tenants Harbor and is still an excellent read. For an overview of Maine-related poetry and prose we highly recommend *The Maine Reader: The Down East Experience from 1614 to the Present* by **David R. Godine**.

Guides to exploring Maine include the indispensable *Maine Atlas and Gazetteer* (DeLorme) and, from Down East Books, *Islands in Time: A Natural and Cultural History of the Islands of the Gulf of Maine* by **Philip W. Conkling**. From AMC Books comes the serious hiker's *AMC Maine Mountain Guide*; also check out *50 Hikes in the Maine Mountains* by **Cloe Chunn** and *50 Hikes in Coastal and Inland Maine* by **John Gibson** (both Countryman Press).

SOUTHERN COAST

KITTERY, SOUTH BERWICK,
AND THE YORKS

OGUNQUIT AND WELLS

THE KENNEBUNKS

OLD ORCHARD BEACH, SACO,
AND BIDDEFORD

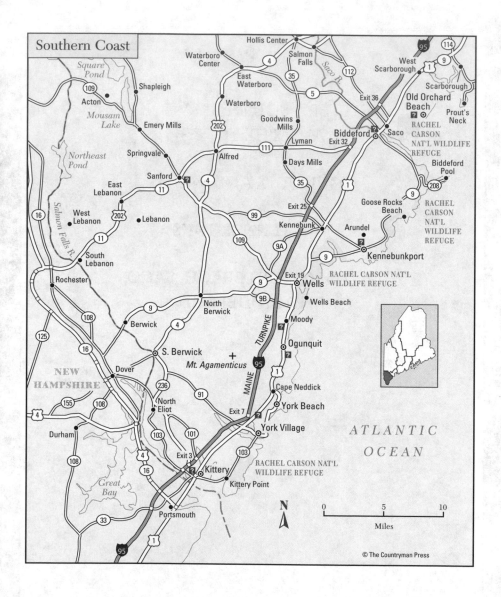

Southern Coast

SOUTHERN COAST

The smell of pine needles and salt air, the taste of lobster and saltwater taffy, the shock of cold green waves, and, most of all, the promise of endless beach—this is the Maine that draws upward of half the state's visitors, those who never get beyond its Southern Coast. The southern Maine coast makes up just 35 of the state's 4,500 coastal miles but contains 90 percent of its sand.

The early histories of these towns differ sharply, but all have been shaped since the Civil War by the summer tide of tourists. York Village and Kittery are recognized as the oldest communities in Maine; Wells dates to the 1640s, and Kennebunkport was a shipbuilding center by the 1790s. All were transformed in the second half of the 19th century, an era when most Americans—not just the rich—began to take summer vacations, each in his or her own way.

Maine's Southern Coast was one of the country's first beach resort areas, and it catered then—as it does today—to the full spectrum of vacationers, from blue-collar workers to millionaires. Before the Civil War, Old Orchard Beach rivaled Newport, Rhode Island, as the place to be seen; when the Grand Trunk Railroad to Montreal opened in 1854, it became the first American resort to attract a sizable number of Canadians.

The ebb and flow of tourist tides wash most dramatically over this stretch of Maine, cresting on summer weekends with an influx of day-trippers. Most of the big old summer hotels vanished by the 1950s, the era of the motor inns that now occupy their sites. Along Rt. 1 just a few of the 1930s-era motor courts survive, sandwiched between elaborate condo-style complexes with indoor pools and elevators. Inns and bed & breakfasts are once more an endangered species, thanks to web-based ways of finding short-term rentals and the demand for year-round homes and condo complexes. Luckily, the lay of the land—salt marsh, estuarine reserves, and other wetlands—largely limits development.

GUIDANCE **The Maine Beaches Association** (mainebeachesassociation.com) publishes a guide and maintains an umbrella website linking Southern Coast chambers.

The Maine Tourism Association's Kittery Information Center (207-439-1319; maine tourism.com) is open daily (except Christmas, Easter, and Thanksgiving), 8–6 in summer months (until 8 Fri.–Sat.), otherwise 9–5:30 (bathrooms open 24 hours daily). Maine's gatehouse in a real sense is on I-95 northbound in Kittery, with exhibits and rack cards from all Maine regions. The staffed information desk is good for local as well as statewide advice on lodging, dining, and attractions. There are also picnic tables under the pines.

KITTERY, SOUTH BERWICK, AND THE YORKS

T he moment you cross the Piscataqua River you know you are in Maine.
Kittery and York both have their share of deep coves and rocky ocean paths, and both towns claim to be Maine's oldest community. Technically Kittery wins, but York looks older . . . depending, of course, on which Kittery and which York you are talking about.

Kittery Point (Rt. 103), an 18th-century settlement overlooking Portsmouth Harbor, boasts Maine's oldest church and some of the state's finest mansions. The village of Kittery itself, however, has been shattered by so many highways and rotaries that it initially seems to exist only as a gateway, on the one hand for workers at the Portsmouth Naval Shipyard and on the other for patrons of the outlet malls strung along Rt. 1. (It's worth finding **Kittery Foreside**, the southernmost corner of town; some of the area's most interesting restaurants cluster here around **Wallingford Square**.)

In the late 19th century artists and literati gathered at Kittery Point. Novelist and *Atlantic Monthly* editor William Dean Howells, who summered here, became interested in preserving the area's colonial-era buildings. Novelist Sarah Orne Jewett, a contributor to *The Atlantic*, spearheaded restoration of the magnificent 18th-century Hamilton House in her hometown, nearby South Berwick. Her friend Sam Clemens (otherwise known as Mark Twain), who summered in York, was involved in an effort, led by local preservationist Elizabeth Perkins, to buy up that town's splendid old school, church, burial ground, and abundance of 1740s homes.

In 1896 Howells suggested turning York Village's "old gaol" into a museum. At the time you could count the country's historic house museums on your fingers. The Old Gaol today is one of eight buildings belonging to the **Museums of Old York**. Stop by the visitors center at the Remick Barn to learn about the town's multilayered history, including its origin as a Native American settlement called Agamenticus, one of many wiped out by a plague in 1616. It was settled by English colonists, but not until the mid-18th century did the present colonial village become a way-stop between Portsmouth and points east.

York is divided into so many distinct villages that Clemens once observed, "It is difficult to throw a brick . . . in any one direction without danger of disabling a postmaster." The town includes **York Village**, **York Harbor**, **York Beach**, and **Cape Neddick**—such different communities that they are sometimes referred to as "the Yorks."

York Harbor has been a low-key, high-priced retreat since the 1870s. The Stage Neck Inn is built on the site of the 19th-century, 300-room Marshall House, and several grand old summer "cottages" are part of the York Harbor Inn. York Harbor's mile-or-so-long shore path, first traced by fishermen, has been smoothed and embellished with the **Wiggly Bridge**, a graceful pedestrian suspension bridge across the river and through Steedman Woods.

Landscaping and public spaces were among the consuming interests of the 19th-century summer residents, who around the turn of the century also became interested in zoning. In *Trending into Maine* (1935) Kenneth Roberts noted York Harbor's "determination to be free of billboards, tourist camps, dance halls and other cheapening manifestations of the herd instinct and Vacationland civilization."

A York Harbor corporation was formed to impose its own taxes and keep out unwanted development. The corporation fiercely fought against the Libby Camps, a tent-and-trailer

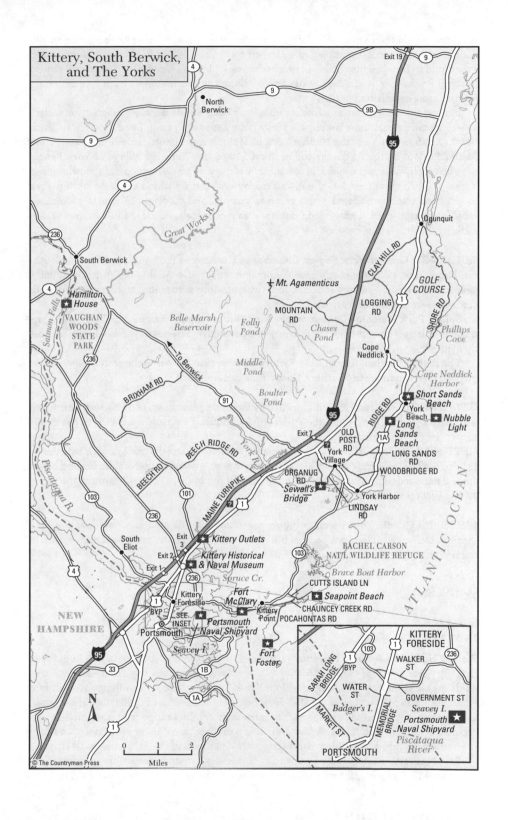

Kittery, South Berwick, and The Yorks

Exit 19
North Berwick
South Berwick
Ogunquit
Hamilton House
VAUGHAN WOODS STATE PARK
Mt. Agamenticus
GOLF COURSE
CLAY HILL RD
LOGGING RD
MOUNTAIN RD
SHORE RD
Phillips Cove
Great Works R.
Belle Marsh Reservoir
Folly Pond
Chases Pond
Cape Neddick
Cape Neddick Harbor
Middle Pond
Salmon Falls R.
To Berwick
BRIXHAM RD
Boulter Pond
Short Sands Beach
York Beach
Nubble Light
Long Sands Beach
LONG SANDS RD
WOODBRIDGE RD
BEECH RIDGE RD
York R.
Exit 7
OLD POST RD
York Village
RIDGE RD
Piscataqua R.
BEECH RD
ORGANUG RD
Sewall's Bridge
York Harbor
LINDSAY RD
RACHEL CARSON NAT'L WILDLIFE REFUGE
Brave Boat Harbor
South Eliot
Exit 3
Kittery Outlets
Kittery Historical & Naval Museum
CUTTS ISLAND LN
Seapoint Beach
CHAUNCEY CREEK RD
POCAHONTAS RD
Exit 2
Exit 1
Spruce Cr.
Fort McClary
Kittery Point
NEW HAMPSHIRE
Kittery Foreside
BYP
SEE INSET
Portsmouth Naval Shipyard
Portsmouth
Fort Foster
Seavey R.
Fort Foster
ATLANTIC OCEAN
MAINE TURNPIKE

KITTERY FORESIDE
SARAH LONG BRIDGE
BYP
WALKER ST
WATER ST
Badger's I.
MEMORIAL BRIDGE
GOVERNMENT ST
Seavey I.
Portsmouth Naval Shipyard
MARKET ST
PORTSMOUTH
Piscataqua River

N

0   1   2
Miles

© The Countryman Press

campground on the eastern edge of York Harbor. Roberts wrote that York Harbor was in danger of being almost completely swamped by "young ladies in shorts, young men in soiled undershirts, and fat ladies in knickerbockers." Libby's Oceanside Camp still sits on Roaring Rock Point, its trailers neatly angled along the shore. Across from it is matching Camp Eaton, established in 1923.

Beyond the campgrounds stretches mile-long **Long Sands Beach**, a magnet for surfers as well as swimmers. **Cape Neddick**, a rocky point separating Long Sands and Short Sands beaches, offers views of **"the Nubble,"** one of Maine's most photogenic lighthouses, from **Sohier Park** at its tip. At the far end of Short Sands, the Victorian village of **York Beach**, with its mostly seasonal shops and restaurants, old-style Fun-O-Rama games, bowling, and York's Wild Kingdom, evokes the 1890s "trolley era" during which a half-dozen big York Beach hotels accommodated 3,000 summer visitors, and 2,000 more guests patronized local boardinghouses. Today's lodgings are a mix of motels, condos, and cottages within walking distance of the beaches.

GUIDANCE **Greater York Region Chamber of Commerce** (207-363-4422; via the Southern Maine link, 1-800-639-2442; gatewaytomaine.org), 1 Stonewall Lane, York. Open daily, year-round. From I-95 Exit 7 (northbound) drive straight across Rt. 1 to this manned, well-stocked welcome center (restrooms).

Sohier Park Welcome Center, overlooking **Nubble Light**, York Beach. Open mid-Apr.–mid-May, daily 9–4; mid-May–Oct., daily 9–7. Operated by Friends of Nubble Light, primarily a gift shop with restrooms.

The Maine Tourism Association Kittery Information Center is the state's biggest and busiest. See *Guidance* in **Southern Coast** introduction.

GETTING THERE Use I-95 Exit 1 for **Kittery Foreside** (downtown) and **Kittery Point**; exit 3 for **Kittery Outlets**; exit 7 for the **Yorks** and **Ogunquit**. You really need a car to get here.

GETTING AROUND **York Trolley Company** (207-363-9600; yorktrolley.com). Late June–Labor Day, trolleys circle all day along the beaches and around the Nubble. Inquire about special narrated tours and service to the Kittery Outlet Malls. $4 one ride around the route, $2 one way, free 5 and under.

WHEN TO COME York Beach is highly seasonal, but this area can be appealing May through December. Thanks to the sizable year-round population, most restaurants remain open year-round. The Kittery outlets draw holiday shoppers.

✳ To See

IN KITTERY

Kittery Historical & Naval Museum (207-439-3080; kitterymuseum.com), 200 Rogers Rd. Ext. (Rt. 1, just north of the Rt. 236 rotary). Open June–Columbus Day, Wed.–Sun. 10–4. $5 adult, $3 children, $10 for a family of four. Look for the 129-foot-high flagpole, each foot commemorating a member of the USS *Thresher*, a submarine lost in 1963 during sea trials. Larger than it looks from the outside, the museum's exhibits range from ship models to a reconstructed garrison house. A film dramatizes the local area history—from a 1600s fishing settlement through a gilded resort area to the evolution of the Rt. 1 outlet mall strip.

Fort McClary, Rt. 103. A state park open seasonally (grounds accessible year-round). A hexagonal 1846 blockhouse on a granite base, it was the site of fortifications in 1715, 1776,

MUST SEE

Nubble Light, York Beach. From Rt. 1A (Long Beach Ave.), take Nubble Rd. out through the Nubble (a cottage-covered peninsula) to Sohier Park at the tip of the peninsula. The 1879 Cape Neddick Lighthouse Station is set on a small island of its own—but that's all the better for taking pictures from the park, which offers parking, restrooms, and a gift shop (also see *Guidance*).

Christina Tree

NUBBLE LIGHT

and 1808. Its picnic area is across the road, but the grounds of the fort itself, with a view of Portsmouth Harbor, are more inviting. This site was first fortified to protect Massachusetts' vessels from being taxed by the New Hampshire colony.

IN YORK HARBOR AND YORK BEACH

First Parish Church, York Village. A mid-18th-century meetinghouse with a fine cemetery full of old stones with death's heads and Old English spelling.

Sayward-Wheeler House (207-384-2454; historicnewengland.org), 79 Barrell Lane, York Harbor. Open June–Oct. 15, second and fourth Sat. of the month, 11–4; tours on the hour. $5, $4 seniors, $2.50 students. This circa-1718 house was built by a prominent resident who was locally respected despite his Tory leanings. It remained in the same family for 200 years and retains its Queen Anne and Chippendale furnishings, family portraits, and china brought back as booty from the expedition against the French at Louisburg in 1745.

IN PORTSMOUTH, NEW HAMPSHIRE

✪ ❧ **Strawbery Banke** (603-433-1100; strawberybanke.org), 14 Hancock St. Grounds open year-round, Tyco Visitors Center (with café) open May–Oct. and for special events off-season. $20 adults, $10 ages 5–17, $50 family. In Portsmouth's oldest neighborhood more than 40 buildings from the 17th and 18th centuries have been preserved, many restored

THE MUSEUMS OF OLD YORK

This nonprofit group maintains several historic properties in York, open Memorial Day weekend to mid-October, Tue.–Sat. 10–5, Sun. 1–5. Admission is $5 adults for one building, $12 for all; senior, child, and family rates. It's best to pay the umbrella price and spend several hours wandering through the 18th- and 19th-century buildings scattered throughout the village. Begin at the **Virginia Weare Parsons Education Center** and **Remick Gallery**, attached to the vintage-1754 **Jefferds Tavern**, corner of Lindsay Rd. and York St. (parking is on Lindsay Rd.). Exhibits change but are dependably outstanding; this is also a venue for special programs and hearth cooking demonstrations. If you have time to visit only one building, pick the **Old Gaol** with its dank and dismal cells and stories of luckless patrons, including women. Dating in part to 1719, this was the jail for the entire province of Maine until 1760. In the vintage-1742 **Emerson-Wilcox House** on York St. you'll find period rooms and changing exhibits. The **Elizabeth Perkins House**, Southside Rd. (at Sewall Bridge), is our favorite building, a 1730 house by the York River. It is filled with antiques gathered on world travels and decorative arts, and imbued with the spirit of Elizabeth Perkins, a real powerhouse behind the Colonial Revival movement in southern Maine. Nearby at 140 Lindsay Rd. are the 18th-century **John Hancock Warehouse and Wharf** and **George Marshall Store**, which was built in 1869 as a chandlery for the large schooners that once docked here; it's now a contemporary art gallery. The **Old School House** (1745) still retains graffiti carved into paneling by the students, and **Steedman Woods**, a nature reserve, offers views of the York River and Wiggly Bridge. Old York hosts programming year-round as well as a local historical research center in the headquarters, a former bank building at 207 York St. in the middle of York Village (207-363-1756; off-season 207-363-4974; oldyork.org).

EXCURSIONS

Kittery Point, Pepperrell Cove, and Gerrish Island. From Rt. 1, find your way to Rt. 103 and follow its twists and turns along the harbor until you come to the white **First Congregational Church** and a small green across from a striking, privately owned Georgian-style house. An old graveyard overlooking the harbor completes the scene. Park at the church (built in 1730, Maine's oldest), notice the parsonage (1729), and walk across the road to the old graveyard. The magnificent neighboring house was built in 1760 for the widow of **Sir William Pepperrell**, the French and Indian War hero who captured the fortress at Louisburg from the French. Knighted for his feat, Pepperrell went on to become the richest man in New England. For a splendid view of the harbor, continue along Rt. 103 to **Fort McClary**. Four large hotels once clustered in this corner of Kittery, but today it's one of the quietest spots along the Southern Coast. At the back of the parking lot across from the general store, a seemingly forgotten tomb is inscribed with a plaque commemorating **Colonel William Pepperrell**, born in Devonshire in 1646, died in Kittery in 1734. Just beyond you can still see the foundations of one of the former summer hotels. Turn right beyond Pepperrell Cove and follow Gerrish Island Lane to a T-intersection; then take Pocahontas Rd. (the name of another vanished hotel) to World War I-era **Fort Foster**, now a park. Also check out Chauncey Creek Lobster Pound and **Seapoint Beach**. Rt. 103 winds on by the mouth of the York River and into York Harbor.

South Berwick. A short ride north of the Rt. 1 outlets brings you to a bend in the Salmon Falls River that is anchored by a splendid 1780s Georgian mansion, restored through the efforts of Maine author Sarah Orne Jewett; a formal garden and riverside trails through the woods add to the unusual appeal of this place. From Kittery, take either Rt. 236 north from the I-95 Eliot exit or more rural Rt. 101 north from Rt. 1 at Exit 3 (turn right at its junction with Rt. 236). From York, take Rt. 91 north. Hamilton House and **Vaughan Woods State Park** are the first left after the junction of Rts. 236 and 91 (Brattle St.); follow signs. **Hamilton House** is open June–Oct. 15, Wed.–Sun. 11–4, with tours on the hour ($8 adults, $7 seniors, $4 children); grounds open every day dawn to dusk. The foursquare Georgian mansion, built in 1785 on a promontory above the Salmon Falls River, had fallen into disrepair by the time Jewett (1849–1909) was growing up in nearby South Berwick; she used it as the setting for her novel *The Tory Lover* and persuaded wealthy Boston friends to restore it in 1898. **Historic New England** (207-384-2454; historicnewengland.org) also maintains the **Sarah Orne Jewett House** farther up Rt. 236, at its junction with Rt. 4 (5 Portland St.), in the middle of the pleasant village of South Berwick. It's open June–Oct., Fri.–Sun. 11–5, with tours on the hour; $8, $7 seniors, $4 students. This is another fine 1774 Georgian house. Jewett, who is best known for her classic novel *The Country of the Pointed Firs*, grew up in the clapboard house next door, now the delightful town library. Here you learn that in the mid-19th century this picturesque village was home to extensive mills. The brick **Counting House Museum** (207-384-0000) by the Salmon Falls on Main St. (Rt. 4 at the bridge) is open June–Oct., weekends 11–4. It houses the Old Berwick Historical Society collection with exhibits on 17th- through 19th-century rural life in southern Maine.

to reflect life in three centuries for a variety of residents, from wealthy merchants and sea captains to working families and poor widows. This is a major museum, minutes across the bridge from Kittery.

FOR FAMILIES ✐ ♿ **York's Wild Kingdom** (207-363-4911; yorkswildkingdom.com), York Beach. In July and Aug. the zoo is open daily 10–6 and the amusement area noon–9:30; varying hours in shoulder seasons, so call ahead to check. This is an old-fashioned amusement area and zoo with monkeys, bears, ducks, swans, a white Bengal tiger, and a number of exotic animals. You'll also find mini golf, a butterfly kingdom, and both pony and elephant rides. $25 adults, $17.25 ages 4–10, and $5.21 ages 3 and under for zoo/ride admission; less for zoo or rides only.

✪ ✐ **Seacoast Science Center** (603-436-8043; seacoastsciencecenter.org, 570 Ocean Blvd. (Rt. 1A), Rye, NH. Open daily Mar.–Oct.; Sat.–Mon. Nov.–Feb. In nearby 135-acre Odiorne Point State Park, this is a handsome facility with kids-geared touch tanks and exhibits, tidal pool walks, many special events. Nominal admission.

Also See ROPES COURSE and SURF-ING under *TO DO*

✳ To Do

BICYCLING Mount Agamenticus (see *Green Space*) is webbed with trails beloved by mountain bikers. Also **Berger's Bike Shop** (207-363-4070) in York Village.

BOATING Isles of Shoals Steamship Co. (603-431-5500 or 1-800-441-4620; islesof shoals.com), Portsmouth, NH. Daily cruises in-season stop at **Star Island**, site of a vast old white summer hotel that's now a Unitarian conference center. Visitors are welcome to this barren but fascinating place, webbed with walking trails. The ride on the 90-foot replica of an old steamboat takes one hour each way.

Christina Tree

GUNDELOW CRUISES ARE OFFERED IN SEASON

Captain & Patty's Piscataqua River Tours (207-439-8976), Town Dock, Pepperrell Rd., Kittery Point. June–Oct. 15, frequent daily departures for a tour aboard the launch *Sir William Pepperrell*.

Gundalow Co. (603-433-9505; gundalow.org), 60 Marcy St., Portsmouth, NH. The gundalow was the traditional sailing barge of the Piscataqua and other local rivers; this replica offers several daily cruises in-season.

York Harbor Marine Service (207-363-3602; yorkharbormarine.com), 20 Harris Island Rd., York. Boston whalers and other runabouts can be rented to explore the river and nearby coast.

FISHING The website **gatewaytomaine.org** lists half a dozen deep-sea fishing boats operating from York Harbor and Kittery. **Surf casting** is popular along Long Sands and Short Sands Beaches and from Sohier Park in York. **Eldredge Bros. Fly Shop** (207-363-9269; eldredgeflyshop.com), 1480 Rt. 1, Cape Neddick, is a full-service outfitter offering guided freshwater and saltwater trips.

GOLF The Ledges Golf Club (207-351-3000; ledgesgolf.com), 1 Ledges Dr. (off Rt. 91), York. This is a destination course for much of southern Maine: 18 holes, carts, pro shop, favored by local residents.

Cape Neddick Country Club (207-361-2011; capeneddickgolf.com), Shore Rd., Cape Neddick. Designed in the early 1900s by Donald Ross, redesigned by Brian Silva in 1998, its 18 holes feature rolling fairways integrated with ledge outcroppings and wetlands.

The Links at Outlook (207-384-4653), Rt. 4, South Berwick. An 18-hole Scottish-style course and driving range.

ROPES COURSE Take Flight Adventures (207-439-8838; takeflightadv.com), 506 Blue Star Memorial Highway (Rt. 1 north from Exit 3), Kittery. Open seasonally. $42.50 adults, $27.50 ages 12 and under, $37.50 students. Reserve ahead and allow two hours for the guided climbing tour, plus an extra half hour for a training session, before you hit the high ropes. They also offer zipline tours of up to two hours through the neighboring woodland.

KAYAKING The tidal York River, stretches of the Piscataqua around and above Eliot, and the Salmon Falls River (accessible from Vaughan Woods State Park in South Berwick) are particularly appealing to kayakers. **Harbor Adventures** (207-363-8466; harboradventures .com), based in York Harbor, and **Excursions** (207-363-0181; excursionsinmaine.com), based at Dixon's Campground, 1740 Rt. 1, Cape Neddick, offer guided tours and rentals.

SWIMMING ✍ **Fort Foster**, posted from Rt. 103, Kittery, is shallow a long way out and also has low-tide tidal pools with crabs and snails. Great for small children.

Long Sands, Rt. 1A, York Beach, a 1.5 mile expanse of firm sand stretching from York Harbor to Cape Neddick, backed by Rt. 1A and summer cottages, is great for walking. Metered parking the length of the beach and a bathhouse midway. Lifeguards in high season. Popular with surfers, who have designated areas and hours. Accessed by the trolley (*Getting Around*).

Short Sands is still a substantial beach, wedged between Cape Neddick and York Beach Village, backed by Ellis Park, a green walkway with plenty of seating and changing rooms. Limited meter parking along Ocean Ave. (Rt. 1A) and in the public lot. Best to take the trolley (*Getting Around*).

York Harbor Beach is small and pebbly, but pleasant, with restrooms. Limited parking for nonresidents on Rt. 1A. This is also the entrance to York's Cliff Walk.

SHORT SANDS BEACH

LONG SANDS BEACH, YORK BEACH

SURFING Long Sands Beach is known for its long, steady rollers; in summer an area is staked off with orange markers for swimmers; surfers use either end of the beach. **Liquid Dreams Surf Shop** (207-351-2545; liquiddreamssurf.com), 171 Long Beach Ave., rents boards and offers lessons and camps for both surfing and stand-up paddle boarding.

✳ Green Space

PARKS **Fort Foster Park**, Kittery. Beyond Pepperrell Cove, look for Gerrish Island Lane and turn right at the T-intersection onto Pocahontas Rd., which leads, eventually, to this 92-acre town park. The World War I fortifica-

tions are ugly, but there is a choice of small beaches with different exposures (one very popular with sailboarders), extensive walking trails, and picnic facilities. Fee.

Mount Agamenticus (207-361-1102; agamenticus.org), York. Just 691 feet high but billed as the highest hill on the Atlantic seaboard between York and Florida. Views sweep down along the coast and back over hills that roll off to distant mountains. Once a ski area, now part of a 10,000-acre wooded preserve, its easiest access is from Mountain Rd. off Rt. 1 (turn at Flo's Hot Dogs). The summit is cluttered with satellite dishes and cell towers, but there are viewing platforms, especially popular for tracking hawks in spring and fall, and a new handicapped-accessible trail. Bring a picnic.

YORK HARBOR CLIFF PATH

Vaughan Woods State Park (207-384-5160), South Berwick. Seasonal. Take Old Fields Rd. off Brattle St. A 250-acre preserve on the banks of the Salmon Falls River; picnic facilities and 3 miles of nature trails. The first cows in Maine are said to have been landed here at Cow Cove in 1634.

Goodrich Park, York. A good picnic spot on the banks of the York River, accessible from Rt. 1 south; look for the entrance just before the bridge.

Hartley Mason Harbor Park, Rt. 1A, York Harbor, adjoining Harbor Beach. Created in 1998 when several classic York Harbor cottages were destroyed in accordance with the wills of their former owners, this is a great spot for a picnic.

WALKS Cliff Path and Fisherman's Walk, York Harbor. For more than a mile, you can pick your way along the town's most pleasant piece of shorefront. Begin at the Hancock Barn, walk east along Lindsay Rd. and left down Mill Dam Rd. to the shady Steedman Woods. Go across the **Wiggly Bridge** (a pedestrian suspension bridge), then continue across Rt. 103, past the Sayward House, along the harbor to York Harbor Beach. Continue east from the parking circle at York Harbor Beach until the path ends at a private property line. This portion is a bit rough, and walkers are advised to keep to the path. Returning the way you've come is no hardship.

✳ Lodging

Note: This area, especially York Beach, offers many summer rentals. The big local agency in York is **seasiderentals.com**.

INNS AND RESORTS *Note:* For details about the largest local resort, **The Cliff House** resort and spa, which sits on the Ogunquit–York line, see the "Ogunquit" chapter.

♂ ♿ (ᵖ) **York Harbor Inn** (207-363-5119 or 1-800-343-3869; yorkharborinn.com), York St., Rt. 1A, York Harbor. Open year-round. Over the past decade this full-service inn has expanded to 63 rooms in six buildings, including four former York Harbor mansions. The 22-room main inn offers some reasonably priced as well as luxurious units with ocean views, and a beamed common area said to be part of a 1637 house from the Isles of Shoals. Given the inn's two popular restaurants (see *Dining Out*), however, we suggest opting for the privacy of another building. **Harbor Hill** and **Harbor Cliffs B&B**, along with **Yorkshire House**, are all within steps of the original inn. Across Rt. 1A there's waterside Hartley Mason Park, with the beach and Cliff Walk at its base. Half a mile away two other mansions, 🐾 **Harbor Crest** and **Chapman Cottage**, adjoin

each other. Rooms in both are also luxurious, and each building has its own character and common space. Until recently a popular inn known for its dining, Chapman Cottage still offers a delightful **Tavern**. Check the website. $99-349.

✪ ♂ ♿ (ᵖ) **Dockside Guest Quarters** (207-363-2868 or 1-800-270-1977; docksidegq .com), 22 Harris Island Rd., York. Open late May.–late Oct. Sited on a peninsula in York Harbor, this is a gracious, family-run inn with views of fishing boats, sailing yachts, gulls, and the Boon Island Light. The Maine house forms the centerpiece of a 7-acre compound that includes four contemporary, multi-unit buildings. In all there are 25 guest rooms—including several with gas fireplaces and six apartment/suites with kitchenettes—all with private decks and water views. Breakfast is served buffet-style in the Maine House and guests have access to fishing equipment, bicycles, and boat rentals. River tours are also offered by innkeeper Eric Lusty. Two-night minimum stay during July and Aug. $180–340. Also see neighboring **Dockside Restaurant** (*Dining Out*).

♂ ♿ (ᵖ) **Stage Neck Inn** (207-363-3850 or 1-800-222-3238; stageneck.com), 8 Stage Neck Rd., York Harbor. Open year-round, this attractive 58-room resort is sited on its

VIEW FROM DOCKSIDE GUEST QUARTERS

own peninsula, beyond a small harbor beach. It offers water views, a formal dining room (see **Harbor Porches** in *Dining Out*), the less formal **Sandpiper Grille**, tennis courts, an outdoor pool, a small indoor pool and Jacuzzi, and a full-service spa. $286–470 per couple B&B in high season. Geared to groups off-season. Inquire about packages.

♂ (ᵖ) **The Union Bluff** (207-363-1333 or 1-800-833-0721; unionbluff.com), 8 Beach St., P.O. Box 1860, York Beach. Open year-round. First opened in 1868, repeatedly renovated. There's not much of a lobby, but the elevator accesses comfortable rooms with a view of the ocean and Short Sands Beach. All three meals are served, and there's a choice between the **Union Grill** and an informal pub. The 70 units are divided among the original hotel, a three-story motel-like annex with balconies, and the more recently added Meeting House, which also houses a function hall. $79–419.

B&BS (ᵖ) **Inn at Tanglewood Hall** (207-351-1075; tanglewoodhall.com), 611 York St., York Harbor. Open year-round. A shingled 1880s summer mansion set in woods and gardens. No water views, but handy to the most dramatic stretch of the Cliff Path.

There are six nicely decorated and air-conditioned guest rooms, all with queen bed and private bath, three with gas fireplace or porch. Owners Su and Andy Wetzel serve a full breakfast, included in $175–235 in high season, otherwise $115–175.

✪ **Morning Glory Inn** (207-363-2062; morninggloryinnmaine.com), 120 Seabury Rd., York. The core of this contemporary-looking

PORTSMOUTH HARBOR INN

B&B is a post-and-beam cottage built more than 200 years ago on the Isles of Shoals. Banked in flower gardens and down a rural road half a mile from the ocean, Margie and Doug Mindell offer three guest rooms, each with a patio or deck, bath, TV, DVD, and mini fridge. The original cottage is now a parlor and there's also a living/dining area, library, and guest coffee bar. $175–265 June–Sept., from $155 early spring and late fall, including full breakfast.

🦞 (ᵢₚ) **Bittersweet Bed & Breakfast** (207-351-3007; bittersweetbednbreakfast.com), 167 Cape Neddick Rd. Within walking distance of Short Sands Beach but handier to smaller Cape Neddick Beach, this is a 1910 farmhouse with seven guest rooms and pleasant common spaces, including a screened porch. Reasonable rates ($150 weekends in July and August, $125 weeknights, otherwise $95) only add to the appeal. Hosts Victor and Randy are knowledgeable about dining options.

Sea Rose Inn Bed & Breakfast (207-361-4159; searoseinnmaine.com), 2 Southside Road, York. Open May–Oct. Mike and Jean are veteran B&B hosts, and this newest venture is an 1850s house in a quiet spot just off Rt. 1. There are three inviting rooms, each with quality beds (one king, two queens) and bedding, and spiffy en-suite baths. There's a parlor and deck as well as a dining room. $175–195 includes full breakfast.

IN KITTERY AND THE BERWICKS

♻ (ᵢₚ) **The Portsmouth Harbor Inn and Spa** (207-439-4040; innatportsmouth.com), 6 Water St., Kittery Foreside. Open year-round. Lynn Bowditch welcomes guests to her 1871 redbrick inn just off the Kittery green, across from the Piscataqua River and within walking distance of the theaters, shops, and restaurants of downtown Portsmouth, NH (across the bridge). Common rooms are cheerful and spacious, and the five guest rooms are carefully, imaginatively furnished; all have private bath (some with claw-foot tub), air-conditioning, ceiling fan, and cable TV/VCR (there's an extensive video library). Add to all this a day spa in the Carriage House. $175–200 in-season includes a full breakfast. From $155 off-season.

OTHER LODGING View Point (207-361-3261; viewpointhotel.com), 229 Nubble Rd.,

York. Office open daily in summer, selected days off-season. A nicely designed oceanfront, condominium-style complex overlooking the Nubble Lighthouse. Units have a living room, kitchen, porch or patio, gas fireplace, phone, cable TV, CD stereo, VCR, and washer-dryer, and vary from one to three bedrooms. In summer from $320 (for a couple) with a two-night minimum; from $1,920 per week. From $169 off-season. Specials.

🖊 (ᵢₚ) **Cutty Sark Motel** (207-363-5131 or 1-800-543-5131), 58 Long Beach Ave., York Beach. Location! Family owned, this is the only lodging on the beach side of the road in York Beach. The 42 rooms are housed in multistory clapboard buildings wedged into a corner of the beach, above a private lawn overlooking the ocean. All units have picture windows with a water view. Lowest rates are for rooms without AC or phones. $170–265 in-season, from $119 off-season, includes a continental breakfast.

Christina Tree

PORTSMOUTH HARBOR INN

♦ ⛬ **The Anchorage Inn** (207-363-5112; anchorageinn.com), Rt. 1A, Long Beach Ave., York Beach. A total of 179 motel-style rooms, most with water views across from Long Sands Beach, a good choice for families. Facilities include indoor and outdoor pools; some rooms sleep four, some have TV, small fridge. $75–595.

♦ ⛬ **Sands by the Sea & the Sea Rose Suites** (207-363-2211; sandsbythesea.com), 15 Ocean Ave., York Beach. Open May–Oct. This 60-unit 1950s motel is family run. Spanking clean and recently renovated, with a pool (with waterfall) and Short Sands Beach across the road. $209–249 in high season, from $99 in spring and fall. Inquire about condo suites and cottages.

Star Island (603-430-6272; starisland .org), Isles of Shoals. Open mid-June–mid-Sept. New England's last vast, truly authentic old-fashioned coastal resort complex sits 10 miles offshore on Star Island, one of the nine Isles of Shoals. The Unitarian-Universalist and United Church of Christ has owned the vintage-1875, five-story Oceanic Hotel since 1916 and continues to operate it as a conference center, hosting some 40 weeklong and weekend programs each season. A total of 265 guests can find simple but comfortable lodging among the hotel buildings, several cottages, and "the motel" (private baths). Conference topics include photography, writing, painting, and many geared to nature and renewal.

✳ Where to Eat

DINING OUT

IN KITTERY

✪ **Anneke Jans** (207-439-0001; annekejans .net), 60 Wallingford Square. Open nightly from 5. This dramatically dark dining room creates the illusion of sitting in a theater. The drama unfolds in the well-lit kitchen, visible beyond a stainless-steel framed counter. The chefs perform well. The signature Bangs Island mussels with Great Hill blue cheese, bacon, shallots, and pommes frites ($21) beg for an encore. Entrées $18–35. Fully licensed with a wide selection of wines by the glass.

♦ **Robert's Maine Grill** (207-439-0300; robertsmainegrill.com), Rt. 1 north. Open year-round, 11:30–8 or 9. Same ownership as Bob's Clam Hut but an upscale version with an expanded menu, including a raw bar and ranging from lobster bruschetta to seafood paella. Family-geared, this is a local favorite. Chef Craig Spinney is a stickler for not just the freshest but also the best seafood (like scallops from Winter Harbor); ditto for produce. Kids menu. Entrées $18–36.

Anju Noodle Bar (207-703-4298), 7 Wallingford Square. Open except Mon., noon–9:30, 10 Thu.–Sat. A sleek, inviting space with an Asian menu that includes Asian-inspired small plates like a pork bun with kimchi mayo and rice cakes with duck confit as well as noodle dishes and a wide choice of wine and beer.

Tulsi (207-451-9511; tulsiindianrestaurant .com), 20 Walker St. Open for dinner Tue.–Sun., also Sun. buffet–2:30. Great northern Indian food. The shrimp balchow appetizer is fiery and aromatic. Try the Kashmiri lamb curry or tandoori salmon. Entrées $14–18. Cocktail options include a blue mango martini and ginger mojito.

IN YORK

♂ **Clay Hill Farm** (207-361-2272; clayhill farm.com), 220 Clay Hill Rd., Cape Neddick. Open year-round for dinner but generally closed Mon. and Tue. in winter. Call for off-season hours and reservations. A gracious old farmhouse set in landscaped gardens halfway up Mount Agamenticus, with valet parking and an elegant decor, the farm is geared to functions. You might begin with escargots in puff pastry, then dine on roasted half duckling or Maine-lobster-stuffed shrimp. Entrées $17–34.

♂ **The York Harbor Inn** (207-363-5119; yorkharborinn.com), Rt. 1A, York Harbor. Open year-round for dinner and Sunday brunch. Dine either in the pleasant dining rooms with water views or downstairs in the less formal **Ship's Cellar Pub** (open 11:30 AM–11 PM), evoking the paneled saloon of a luxurious sailing yacht. The menu is large, but fresh seafood is the specialty. Dinner entrées might include Yorkshire lobster supreme (lobster stuffed with a scallop-and-shrimp filling) and seafood ravioli, but there are also salads, sandwiches, and flat breads. Entrées $10–30.

The Tavern at Chapman Cottage (check for days, hours) offers a more intimate venue with light dining on the likes of spicy lamb pizza, duck confit quesadilla, and key lime pie.

✍ **Cape Neddick Inn Restaurant and Tavern** (207-351-1145; capeneddickinn.com), 1273 Rt. 1, Cape Neddick, York. Open for dinner from 4 PM year-round. Originally opened in 1926, burned to the ground in 1984, and rebuilt. Both the dining room and tavern have fieldstone fireplaces. A hands-down top pick among locals. Entrees $16–32. Children's menu.

✪ ✍ **Dockside Restaurant & Bar** (207-363-2722; dockside-restaurant.com), Harris Island Rd. off Rt. 103, York Harbor. Open for lunch and dinner late May–Oct., but check. Reservations suggested for dinner. Docking as well as parking. The view of yacht-filled York Harbor from Phil and Anne Lusty's glass-walled dining room, screened porch, and open patio is hard to beat. At lunch try the seared tuna salad or garlic shrimp spaghettini; at dinner the specialties are seafood, such as drunken lobster sauté with shrimp, and roast stuffed duckling. Entrées $19.50–33. Children's menu.

The York River Landing (207-351-8430; theyorkriverlanding.com), 150 Rt. 1. Open 11–9, Fri., Sat. until 10. A large (seating 300), nicely designed, shingled and open-timbered new seafood restaurant with windows maximizing its site on the York River. A large and eclectic selection of craft beers is a specialty, but there's plenty of choice when it comes to seafood and locally raised meat. Entrees $14–34.

Harbor Porches (207-363-3850; stageneck .com/harbor-porches), Stage Neck Rd., York Harbor. Open year-round for breakfast, lunch, dinner, and Sunday brunch. Glass-walled with unbeatable ocean views, this attractive dining room has shed its white tablecloths and offers a menu with light as well as serious entrées from $10 to $30.

Frankie & Johnny's Natural Foods (207-363-1909), 1594 Rt. 1, Cape Neddick. Open for dinner Thu.–Sun., closed Jan. No credit cards. BYOB. This colorful, funky place offers vegan and vegetarian dishes but also plenty of seafood and meat. It can hit the spot if you're in the mood for toasted peppercorn seared sushi-grade tuna or homemade "harvest" pasta. Daily specials. Entrées $16.75–27.75.

IN PORTSMOUTH, NH

Portsmouth, linked by three bridges to Kittery, is a destination dining town for much of this area. Herewith is a listing of our favorite dining spots there. For details please see *New Hampshire: An Explorers Guide*. The **Black Trumpet Bistro** (603-431-0887; 29 Ceres St.) with a French/Mediterranean menu is the standout. **Ristorante Massimo** (603-436-4000; 59 Penhollow St.) serves elegantly prepared Italian cuisine in a grotto-like setting. **Brazo** (603-431-0050; 75 Pleasant St.) is hip, upscale. **Cava** (603-319-1575; 10 Commercial Alley) is a sophisticated wine bar featuring a vertical garden and tapas. **Jumpin' Jay's Fish Café** (603-766-3474; 150 Congress St.) features a choice of 10 catches a day. **The Library** (603-431-5202; 401 State St.) is an atmospheric old reliable.

EATING OUT

IN KITTERY AND ALONG RT. 1 THROUGH YORK (SOUTH TO NORTH)

✪ **Beach Pea Baking Co.** (207-439-555), 59 State Rd. (Rt. 1 south), Kittery, south of the Exit 2 Kittery traffic circle. Open daily 7:30–6. The aromas alone are worth a stop. Known for artisan breads—from roasted garlic boules through country French and baguettes to focaccia and fabulous cakes—also sandwiches and salads to go or to eat in the small, cheerful dining room on the deck. Deservedly popular; parking can be a problem.

Wood Grill Pizza (207-439-9700), 68 Wallingford Square, Kittery. Open daily 11–9; Fri., Sat until 10. Terrific pizzas with options like "Nancy's White" (garlic spread, tomato slices, eggplant, and more) plus endless "make your own" toppings. Also salads, gluten-free options, nightly specials.

✪ **Loco Cocos Tacos** (207-438-9322; loco cocos.com), 36 Walker St. (Rt. 103), Kittery. Open daily 11–9. Cal-Mex fare, expanded from the original truck to a roomy restaurant with lounge, heated patio. A great spot for stoking after shopping, also a quick road-food hit from I-95. Tasty *enchiladas con mole*, chili, soups and salads, guacamole, cabbage slaw, four kinds of free salsa (try the green avocado sauce).

The Black Birch (207-703-2294; theblack birch.com), 2 Government St. Open Tue.–Thu. 3:30–10; Fri., Sat. until 11. Housed in a former post office building around the corner from Wallingford Square, this is a gastro bistro

LOBSTER

✪ **Chauncey Creek Lobster Pier** (207-439-1030; www.chaunceycreek.com), 16 Chauncey Creek Rd., Kittery Point. Open Mother's Day–Labor Day, daily 11–8; post Labor Day–Columbus Day, daily 11–7, closed Tue. Owned by the Spinney family since the 1950s, specializing in reasonably priced lobster dinners with steamers, served inside and out on a pier on a tidal river walled by pine trees. Also available: lobster rolls, chowders, baked beans, a chicken dinner, and a raw bar. On summer weekends expect a wait. BYOB.

✪ **Cape Neddick Lobster Pound and Harborside Restaurant** (207-363-5471; capeneddick .com), 60 Shore Rd. (Rt. 1A), Cape Neddick. Open Mar.–Nov. for lunch and dinner, but call for hours in shoulder seasons. In August come early or be prepared to wait. Sited by a tidal river, this attractive building with dining inside and on a deck is a local favorite. Besides lobster and clams, the menu offers a variety of choices. Entrées $8–35.

Fox's Lobster House (207-363-2643; foxslobster.com), 8 Sohier Park Rd., Nubble Point, York Beach. Open daily in-season 11:45–9. A tourist-geared and -priced place near the Nubble, with a water view and a seafood menu.

Foster's Café & Marketplace (207-363-3255; fostersclambake.com), 5 Axholme Rd., Rt. 1A, York Harbor. Open in-season with a full menu, from hot dogs to lobster dinners, live lobster to go, inside and outside seating—but this place is all about lobster bakes for groups, at their place or yours, anywhere in the world (including the White House).

Maine Lobster Outlet (207-363-9899; mainelobsteroutlet.com), 360 Rt. 1, York (just south of Rite Aid). Open Mon.–Thu. 8–6; Fri., Sat. 8–7. If you have a way to bring home cooked lobster, this is a great resource; primarily a wholesaler, the store sells more than just lobster at a good price.

Note: At this writing lobstermen rarely get more than $4–6 per pound in high season, but in this area restaurants routinely overcharge for lobster dinners. Beware.

with sleek, casual decor. The bar runs the length of the room; there's an open kitchen at the back, a common table in the middle, plus individual tables. Regional craft beers and a menu that changes frequently with plenty of small plates, larger plates like fish and chips and chicken picatta. $12–17.

✪ **Bob's Clam Hut** (207-439-4233; bobs clamhut.com), Rt. 1 south, next to the Kittery Trading Post, Kittery. Open daily year-round, 11–9. Here since 1956 and definitely the best fried clams on the strip—some say the entire coast. The menu includes all the usual fried (using "cholesterol-free oil") seafood plus burgers and sandwiches. Order at the takeout and look for seating either inside or at the picnic tables around back.

✍ ⟨𝜔⟩ **When Pigs Fly Wood-Fired Pizzeria** (207-438-7036), 460 Rt. 1, Kittery. Open 11:30–9 Sun.–Wed.; until 10 Thu.–Sat. Ron Siegel's nearby bakery now supplies retail outlets throughout the Northeast. This company store and 160-seat restaurant features pizza and dishes that beg for bread, like steamed mussels. Craft beers, full bar.

Stonewall Kitchen Café (207-351-2719), 2 Stonewall Lane, just off Rt. 1, beside the Chamber of Commerce, York. Open Mon.–Sat. 8–5, Sun. 9–4. Shorter hours off-season. At the Stonewall Kitchen flagship store (see *Selective Shopping*) you order from the espresso bar or deli and a server will find you in the café or (weather permitting) at an outside table. Breakfast breads and house granola for breakfast; daily soups, deli sandwiches (like BLT and avocado), and salads all afternoon.

Fishermen's Dock (207-351-8100; fishermensdock.com), 674 Rt.1, York. Open 11–9. This new place fills a gap: a fish market and moderately priced restaurant with fresh, tasty seafood at reasonable prices. We lunched on a generous mixed greens salad topped with perfectly grilled salmon.

🖋 **Wild Willy's Burgers** (207-363-9924), 765 Rt. 1, York. Daily (except Sun.) 11–7:30. This wildly popular family eatery features certified Angus ground chuck hand shaped daily into burgers, topped with more combinations than you thought possible.

✪ **Flo's Hot Dogs**, Rt. 1 North, Cape Neddick. Open seasonally 11–3; closed Wed. The steamed hot dogs are bargain-priced and have a loyal following. Flo has passed away, but her daughter-in-law Gail carries on. Go for the special relish and hold the mustard and ketchup.

IN YORK VILLAGE

🖋 **Fat Tomato Grill** (207-363-5333), 241 York St. Open Tue.–Sat. 11–8, Sun.–Mon. 11–4. Basic sandwiches, multiple kinds of burgers and dogs, fried green tomatoes, kids' menu, cheap, cheerful, and handy.

Rick's All Seasons Restaurant (207-363-5584), 240 York St. Open daily from 6 AM for breakfast until 2 PM weekdays, closing earlier on Sun. A reasonably priced local hangout; omelets, quiche, corned beef hash, and hot apple pie with cheese. Cash only.

IN YORK BEACH

✪ 🌿 🖋 **The Goldenrod** (207-363-2621; the goldenrod.com), Rt. 1A. Open Memorial Day–Columbus Day for breakfast, lunch, and dinner, 8 AM–9 PM. Still owned by the Talpey family, who first opened for business here in 1896. Lunch and dinner specials are served up at time-polished wooden tables in the big dining room with a fieldstone fireplace as well as at the old-style soda fountain. Their famous Goldenrod Kisses are made from saltwater taffy cooked and pulled in the windows. Usually 135 flavors of house-made ice creams. Salads and terrific club sandwiches and long-time favorites like cream-cheese-and-olive or –nuts.

Union Bluff Pub (207-363-1333), Union Bluff Hotel, 8 Beach St. Open year-round for lunch and dinner. A local favorite with a welcoming atmosphere and full sandwich and burger menu, pizzas, and dinner specials ranging from crab-stuffed haddock to filet mignon. Entrées $17.95–29.95. Full bar.

THE GOLDENROD, YORK BEACH

Christina Tree

🖋 **Lobster Cove** (207-351-1100), 756 York St. Open breakfast–dinner. Just west of Long Sands Beach with an upstairs deck and water views. The Talpey family, owners of The Goldenrod, have created this moderately priced eatery. No surprises, but a good dinner bet for broiled haddock or baked stuffed shrimp. Burgers all day plus a children's menu.

ELSEWHERE

Thistle Pig (207-704-0624; thistlepig.com), 279 Main St., South Berwick. Open Thu.–Mon. 11 AM–10 PM, Sun. 10 AM–10 PM. Not so out of the way (see Excursions) and a local favorite for locally sourced lunch and dinner, with signature pork dishes like fried pork shoulder with Buffalo sauce.

SNACKS, TREATS, AND TAKE-HOME
Dunne's Ice Cream (207-363-1277), 214 Nubble Rd., York Beach. Seasonal, noon–9. This tidy, spanking new ice cream takeout (with restrooms), owned by Fox's Lobster House, replaces Brown's, the area's former ice cream landmark.

Terra Cotta Pasta Company (207-475-3025), Rt. 1 north, below the Kittery traffic circle. Open Mon.–Sat. 9–7, Sun. 11–5. Pick up freshly made linguine and lasagna for supper or a full-bodied sandwich for a picnic at nearby Fort McClary.

✳ Entertainment

Ogunquit Playhouse (see *Entertainment* in "Ogunquit and Wells") is the nearest and most famous summer theater. Special children's presentations.

Hackmatack Playhouse (207-698-1807; hackmatack.org), in Berwick, presents summer-stock performances most evenings; Thu. matinees.

Seacoast Repertory Theatre (603-433-3372; seacoastrep.org), 125 Bow St., Portsmouth, NH. Professional theater productions.

The Dance Hall (207-703-2085), 7 Walker St., Kittery. A venue for frequent live dance and music performances. Check the website.

✳ Selective Shopping

ANTIQUES Half a dozen antiques dealers can be found along Rt. 1 between **Bell Farm Antiques** in York and **Columbary House Antiques** in Cape Neddick. Stop in one and pick up the leaflet guide. **York Antiques Gallery** (746 Rt. 1; open daily 10–5), showcases 65 quality dealers on four floors.

ART GALLERIES **York Art Association Gallery** (207-363-4049 or 207-363-2918), Rt. 1A, York Harbor. Annual July art show, films, and workshops.

George Marshall Store Gallery, 140 Lindsay Rd., York. Open mid-June–mid-Oct., Tue.–Sat. 10–5, Sun. 1–5. Housed in an 18th-century store maintained by the Museums of Old York. Exhibits feature regional contemporary art and fine crafts.

Kittery Art Association (207-451-9384; kitteryart.org), 8 Coleman Ave., Kittery Point. Open all year, Sat. noon–6, Sun. noon–5, also March–Nov. Thu. 2:30–5. Housed in a former firehouse marked from (and just off) Rt. 103, changing shows by member artists.

SPECIAL STORES **Kittery Trading Post** (207-439-2700; kitterytradingpost.com), 301 Rt. 1, Kittery. A local institution since 1926, this sprawling store completed a major expansion in 2004 and is always jammed with shoppers in search of quality sportswear, shoes, children's clothing, firearms, outdoor books, and fishing or camping gear. The summer-end sales are legendary and many items are often discounted, but this is not an outlet store.

IN YORK

Stonewall Kitchen (207-351-2712; stonewall kitchen.com), Stonewall Lane, Rt. 1, beside the Chamber of Commerce visitors center, York. Open 8–8 in high season, except 9–6 Sun.; check for off-season hours. What began as a display of offbeat vinegars at a local farmer's market is now a mega specialty food business. Owners Jonathan King and Jim Stott maintain that all their products—from roasted garlic and onion red pepper jelly to raspberry peach champagne jam—still represent homemade care. Sample them in the open-kitchen-style shop, pick up free recipes, and find kitchen supplies and more. There's also a café (see *Eating Out*) and a **cooking school** with a calendar of varied classes, some taught by celebrity chefs.

Rocky Mountain Quilts (207-363-6800 or 1-800-762-5940), 130 York St., York Village. Open by appointment. Betsey Telford restores quilts and sells antique quilts (more than 450 in stock, "from doll to king"), blocks, and fabrics from the late 1700s to the 1940s.

Woods to Goods (207-363-6001; woods togoods.com), 891 Rt. 1, York. Open daily 10–6; 10–5 off-season. Not all but many of the lamps, ship models, and other decorative items in this roadside shop are made by inmates of Maine prisons. The PRISON BLUES T-shirts and sweatshirts with the catchy line MADE ON THE INSIDE TO BE WORN ON THE OUTSIDE are produced by Oregon inmates.

IN KITTERY

OUTLET MALLS **Kittery Outlets** (1-888-548-8379; thekitteryoutlets.com). Open daily year-round, mid-Mar.–Dec., Mon.–Sat. 9–9, Sun. 10–6; shorter hours off-season. Take I-95 Exit 3. At this writing more than 120 discount stores within a 1.3-mile strip of Rt. 1 in Kittery represent a mix of clothing, household furnishings, gifts, and basics. All purport to offer savings of at least 20 percent on retail prices.

✪ **Sue's Seafood** (207-439-5608), 33 Old Post Rd. Sue Allen's classic seafood market is the place to pick up fish on your way home.

✳ Special Events

June–mid-October: **Gateway Farmers' Market** (gatewayfarmersmarket.org), behind the Greater York Region Chamber (see *Guidance*), Sat. 9–1 Jun.–Sept., also Thu. 9–1 in July, Aug. Many local products, crafts, produce, and food.

July: **Ellis Park Concerts** almost nightly at the gazebo at Short Sands Pavilion, York Beach. Schedule at gatewaytomaine.org. **Concerts at Hamilton House**, South Berwick (historicnewengland.org). **Sundays in the Garden Concert Series**, every Sunday in July, 5 PM at Hamilton House, South Berwick (southberwickmain.org); bring a picnic.

Late July/early August: **York Days Celebration**—flower show, church supper, concerts, square dances, parade, and sand castle contest.

August: **Summer House and Garden Tour,** York (oldyork.org), sponsored by the Museums of Old York.

Labor Day weekend: **Old York Antiques Show** (oldyork.org) fills Remick Barn, the Museums of Old York visitors center, York.

October: **Harvestfest** (the weekend after Columbus Day weekend) in York Beach (yorkharvestfest.com).

Saturday of Thanksgiving weekend: **Lighting of the Nubble, Sohier Park**, 5:45–7, with a shuttle bus from Ellis Park (207-363-1040). The famous lighthouse is illuminated in sparkling white lights for the Christmas season.

December: Christmas York **Festival of Lights Parade** (first weekend).

OGUNQUIT AND WELLS

O gunquit and Wells share many miles of uninterrupted sand, and the line between the two towns also blurs along Rt. 1, a stretch of restaurants and family-geared lodging places. Named for the English cathedral town, Wells was incorporated in 1653 and remains a year-round community of 10,000 with seasonal cottages, condo complexes, and campgrounds strung along the beach and Rt. 1—parallel strips separated by a mile-wide swatch of salt marsh.

Ogunquit was part of Wells until 1980 but seceded in spirit long before that, establishing itself as a summer resort in the 1880s and a magnet for artists in the 1890s through the 1940s. It remains a compact, walk-around resort village clustered between its magnificent beach and picturesque Perkins Cove; these two venues are connected by the mile-long Marginal Way, an exceptional shore path. The village offers a vintage movie house and the Ogunquit Playhouse, one of New England's most famous summer theaters.

With the 1980s came trolleys-on-wheels to ease traffic at Perkins Cove and the beach. With a year-round population of 1,100 and 3,000 rooms for rent, Ogunquit regularly draws 40,000 on summer and holiday weekends year-round. A reservation or summer weekends, or even on a weekday in August, is wise—but call the Ogunquit Chamber (listed below) if you are without one; they can usually help.

GUIDANCE **Ogunquit Chamber of Commerce** (207-646-2939; ogunquit.org), P.O. Box 2289, Rt. 1, Ogunquit (beside the Ogunquit Playhouse). Open year-round, Mon.–Fri. 10–4, Sat. 11–3; more hours on Fri., Sat., and Sun. in July and Aug. Staff are helpful, and this large visitors center (with restrooms) is well stocked with pamphlets, including *This Week in Ogunquit* with entertainment and more. The Ogunquit Chamber offers 90-minute walking tours in summer; call 207-967-2939 for schedule.

Wells Chamber of Commerce (207-646-2451; wellschamber.org), 136 Post Rd. (Rt. 1, northbound side) in Moody. Open year-round Mon.–Fri. 9–5; weekends in-season.

GETTING THERE *By car:* Coming north on I-95, take Exit 7 (York) and drive up Rt. 1 to the village of Ogunquit. Coming south on the Maine Turnpike/I-95, take turnpike Exit 19 (Wells).

By train: The **Downeaster** (1-800-USA-RAIL; amtrak.com), Amtrak's popular Boston–Portland service, makes five roundtrips daily, year-round. The Wells Transportation Center stop is at 696 Sanford Rd. (Rt. 109) near the Exit 19 tollbooth of the Maine Turnpike (I-95).

Coastal Taxi (207-229-0783; mainetaxicab.com). Friendly service available year-round.

GETTING AROUND Memorial Day–Columbus Day open-sided Ogunquit trolleys circle through the village of Ogunquit, Perkins Cove, and out Rt. 1 in Wells, stopping at the main entrance to Ogunquit Beach and at Footbridge Beach. Fare is nominal. Trolley stops are mapped, and maps are available from the chambers of commerce. They run weekends in June and daily from July 1 to Columbus Day.

PARKING Park and walk or take the trolley. In summer especially, the trolley is the easiest way to get around. There are at least seven public lots; call the chamber for rates. There is also free parking (one-hour limit) on Rt. 1 across from the Leavitt Theatre just north of

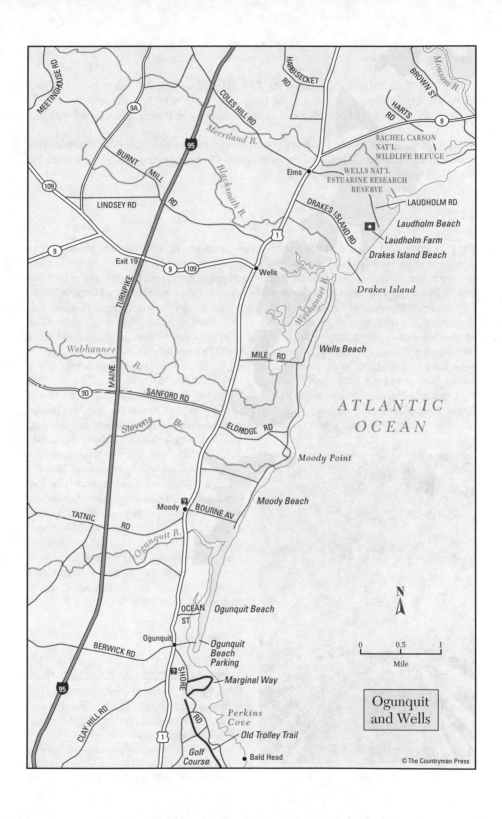

Ogunquit
and Wells

© The Countryman Press

Ogunquit Square or adjacent to Cumberland Farms. Parking at the main entrance to Ogunquit Beach is $10 to $25, depending on season and weather, per day.

PUBLIC RESTROOMS *In Ogunquit:* At Footbridge Beach, Main Beach, Perkins Cove, Jacob's Lot, the Dunaway Center, and the Ogunquit Chamber Welcome Center.
In Wells: At the jetty, Wells Harbor Pier, Wells Beach, and Drakes Island parking areas.

WHEN TO COME Ogunquit and Wells slow down in winter, but several restaurants stay open through the year. Visiting in September and October or June makes for a more leisurely experience with far less traffic.

✳ To See

Perkins Cove, Ogunquit. Maine's most painted fishing cove, with restaurants and shops now housed in weathered fish shacks. It is the departure point for the area's excursion and fishing boats, based beside the famous draw-footbridge. Parking is limited in summer, but public lots are nearby, and the trolley stops here regularly, or walk here via Marginal Way.

Ogunquit Museum of American Art (207-646-4909; ogunquitmuseum.org), Shore Rd., Ogunquit (0.4 mile west of Perkins Cove). Open May–Oct., Mon.–Sun. 10–5. $10 adults, $9 seniors and students, free under 12. Founded in 1952 and built superbly of local stone and wood, with enough glass to let in the beauty of the cove it faces, the museum displays selected paintings from its permanent collection, which includes the strong, bright oils of Henry Strater and other one-time locals such as Reginald Marsh.

Ogunquit Heritage Museum (207-646-0296; ogunquitheritagemuseum.org), 86 Obeds Lane, Ogunquit. Open June–Sept., Tue.–Sat. 1–5. Set inside the Captain James Winn House, an 18th-century Cape with a unique Federal staircase and original paneling and flooring, this museum exhibits artifacts of Ogunquit's artistic and fishing history. It also houses the Littlefield Genealogical Library.

                                                 ♿ ✹ **Historical Society of Wells and Ogunquit** (207-646-4775; historicalsocietyofwellsandogunquit.org), 936 Post Rd. (Rt. 1, opposite Wells Plaza). Open mid-May–mid-Oct., Wed.–Thu. 10–4. Housed in a historic meetinghouse still used for weddings, concerts, and numerous special events; also a genealogy library, old photos, memorabilia, ship models, and a gift shop.

Nancy English

THE DRAW-FOOTBRIDGE SPANNING PERKINS COVE

✳ To Do

APPLE, BLUEBERRY, AND VEGGIE PICKING Spiller Farm U-Pick (207-985-2575; spillerfarm.com), 85 Spiller Farm Lane, Wells. Pick apples (including Northern Spy), blueberries, strawberries, and more—like your own buttercup squash—and pay by the pound or piece. Hayride farm tours on fall weekends at this 130-acre 1894 farm. No credit cards. **Spillers' Farm Store** (207-985-3383), 1054 Branch Rd., Wells, does accept cards and is open year-round with farm products, Angus beef, pizza, and more.

BICYCLING **Wheels N Waves** (207-646-5774; wheelsnwaves.com), 365 Post Rd. (Rt. 1), Wells, and (207-641-2501), 161 Main St., Ogunquit. Rentals include mountain bikes, hybrids, and kids' bikes.

BOATING **Finestkind Cruises** (207-646-5227; finestkindcruises.com) offers scenic cruises and "lobstering trips." The **Bunny Clark** (207-646-2214; bunnyclark.com) offers deep-sea fishing trips from Perkins Cove.

GOLF **Merriland Farm** (207-646-0508; www.merrilandfarm.com), 545 Coles Hill Rd. (off Rt. 1), Wells. Nine-hole, par-three course on a working farm. Also a café (207-646-5040; merrilandfarmcafe.com).

MINI GOLF ♫ ♿ **Wells Beach Mini-Golf** (1-800-640-2267; wellsbeach.com), 1000 Post Rd. (Rt. 1), Wells. Open daily May 14–Oct. 14.
  ♫ **Wonder Mountain Fun Park** (207-646-9655; wondermountainfunpark.com), 270 Post Rd. (Rt. 1), Wells. Open Memorial Day–Labor Day. A human maze, two 18-hole courses—including Mountain Mania, complete with waterfalls—and an arcade with skee ball and video games.
  ♫ **Sea-Vu Mini Golf** (207-646-7732; sea-vucampground.com) is another Rt. 1 option in Wells. 18 holes.

SEA KAYAKING **World Within Sea Kayaking** (207-646-0455; worldwithin.com), Wells. Registered Maine Guide Andrew French offers kayak and paddleboard rentals from the Ogunquit River Inn and Suites on the Ogunquit–Wells line.

SURFING **Wheels N Waves** (207-646-5774; wheelsnwaves.com), 365 Post Rd. (Rt. 1), Wells, and (207-641-2501), 161 Main St., Ogunquit. Rentals include surfboards and wet suits. A two-hour lesson with equipment is $60; it's offered year-round, but in winter generally only those 13 and older can find equipment that fits. Summer surf camps. Anyone can get on the big paddleboards; speed paddleboards offer an incredible workout.

TENNIS Three public courts in Ogunquit. Inquire at **Dunaway Center** (207-361-9538). **Wells Recreation Area**, Rt. 9A, Wells, has four courts.

✳ Green Space

BEACHES Three-mile-long **Ogunquit Beach** offers surf, soft sand, and space for kite flying, as well as a sheltered strip along the mouth of the Ogunquit River for toddlers. It can be approached three ways: (1) The most popular way is from the foot of Beach St. There are boardwalk snacks, changing facilities, and toilets, and it is here that the beach forms a tongue between the ocean and the Ogunquit River; (2) The Footbridge Beach access (take Ocean St. off Rt. 1 north of the village) offers restrooms and is less crowded, $15 a day weekdays, $20 weekends for parking; and (3) Moody Beach parking lot, Wells. Be sure to park in the lot provided; $20 a day. Walk west onto Ogunquit Beach, not to Moody Beach, now private above the high-water mark.
  Wells Beach. Limited free parking right in the middle of the village of Wells Beach; also parking at the east end by the jetty. Wooden casino and boardwalk, clam shacks, clean

THE DEAD GRASS HAS BEEN BURNED OFF IN EARLY SPRING AT LAUDHOLM FARM

public toilets, a cluster of motels, concrete benches—a gathering point for older people who sit while enjoying the view of the wide, smooth beach.

Drakes Island, Wells. Take Drakes Island Rd. off Rt. 1. There are three small parking areas on this spit of land lined with private cottages.

NATURE PRESERVES AND PARKS **Wells Reserve at Laudholm** (207-646-1555; wells reserve.org), Laudholm Rd. (off Rt. 1, just south of its junction with Rt. 9; look for the blinking yellow light just south of the Maine Diner on Rt. 1), Wells. This 2,250-acre reserve on two estuaries, an area formed where ocean tides meet freshwater currents, is a National Estuarine Research Reserve with headquarters listed on the National Register of Historic Places. The reserve consists of two parts: the meadows, salt marshes, woodlands, and two barrier beaches at the mouth of the Little River; and Laudholm Farm, the former estate of railroad executive George C. Lord that began as a saltwater farm in the 1640s. Today it's a birder's mecca. A visitors center is open year-round (weekdays 10–4; also May–Oct., Sat. 10–4 and Sun. noon–4), with exhibits, restrooms, and parking. Seven miles of trails meander through fields, woods, and wetlands (bring a bathing suit if you want to swim at the beach). The Wells Reserve is open daily year-round (gates open daily 7 AM–sunset); entrance fee Memorial Day–Columbus Day is $3 adults, $1 ages 6–16; no dogs allowed. Guided trail walks and programs for adults and kids ages 6–9. The Laudholm Nature Crafts Festival is held the weekend after Labor Day. Punkinfiddle (punkinfiddle.org) in early fall is a celebration of National Estuaries Day with fiddle bands and artisan demonstrations like butter churning, apple pressing, and pumpkin rolling.

Rachel Carson National Wildlife Refuge, off Rt. 9 on the Wells–Kennebunk line. See the description in "The Kennebunks."

Dorothea Grant Common. Hidden away between Rt. 1 and the Dunaway Center, this quiet park surrounds the Ogunquit Heritage Museum at Winn House (see *To See*).

WALKS **Marginal Way.** In 1923 Josiah Chase gave Ogunquit this windy path along the ocean. A farmer from the town of York, just south of here, Chase had driven his cattle around rocky Israel's Head each summer to pasture on the marsh grass in Wells, just to the north. Over the years he bought land here and there until, eventually, he owned the whole promontory. He then sold off sea-view lots at a tidy profit and donated the actual ocean frontage to the town, thus

MARGINAL WAY IN OGUNQUIT

preserving his own right-of-way. There is very limited parking at the mini lighthouse on Israel's Head.

🚲 ♿ **Wells Harbor**. Here is a pleasant walk along a granite jetty and a good fishing spot. There is also a playground, and a gazebo where concerts are held.

Old Trolley Trail. An interesting nature walk and cross-country ski trail that begins on Pine Hill Rd. N., Ogunquit.

✳ Lodging

Note: Ogunquit's 2,500 "rooms" include many family-geared efficiencies, especially along Rt. 1. We do not attempt to critique them here, but all are listed on the Ogunquit Chamber of Commerce website (ogunquit.org) and in its Four Season Destination Resource Guide. All listings are in Ogunquit 03907, or have an Ogunquit mailing address, and are most convenient to Ogunquit, unless otherwise noted

RESORT 🚲 ♿ **The Cliff House** (207-361-1000; cliffhousemaine.com), Shore Rd., P.O. Box 2274. Open mid-Apr.–Nov. Opened in 1872 with a single building at the top of its spectacular location, the Cliff House now features a monumental spa facility and 32 large rooms that have gas fireplaces and, of course, ocean views. Guests ages 18 and older can use the "vanishing-edge" pool (set out on the terrace, it gives swimmers the illusion of a sea dip without the low temperature of Maine ocean water). The spa, open to the public as well as to guests, offers luxurious massages and facials.

Former innkeeper Kathryn Weare is the great-granddaughter of the woman who opened this 194-room hotel. This place rose from its own ashes after being run down during the temporary, exclusive use of the U.S. military, which employed it as a lookout for Nazi submarines in World War II. Although the decor in the main building rooms is undistinguished, furnishings are good quality. Every amenity you need is close at hand, from a dining room with that great view and good food (see *Dining Out*) to nearby golf courses, two indoor heated pools, and an exercise room. The most important feature, of course, is the sound of the waves hitting the rocks outside your bedroom.

High-season summer rates range $275–370 with no meals; $180–255 off-season.

RESORT MOTOR INNS Our usual format places inns before motels, but in the 1960s some of Ogunquit's leading resorts replaced their old hotel buildings with luxury "motor inns."

🚲 **The Sparhawk** (207-646-5562; the sparhawk.com), 85 Shore Rd., P.O. Box 936. Open mid-Apr.–late Oct. Fifty-two-unit oceanfront resort overlooks the confluence of the Ogunquit River and the Atlantic Ocean, as well as Ogunquit Beach (waves lap below the balconies). Twenty units in neighboring Ireland House (with balconies canted toward the water) are combination living room/bedroom suites. The Barbara Dean and Jacobs Houses, formerly village homes, add another 11 suites and four apartments, some with gas fireplace and Jacuzzi. Outdoor pool (heated mid-June–mid-Sept.), shuffleboard, croquet, tennis, and fitness center. One-week minimum stay July–mid-Aug.; $195–315 per night in high summer, $105–250 in spring and fall.

Parsons Post House Inn (207-646-7533; parsonsposthouse.com), 62 Shore Rd. Fourteen bright and comfortable rooms, all with private bath, were completely updated in 2015; the beds are extolled by visitors and the beach decor with blue-gray walls and

Nancy English

THE CLIFF HOUSE

white linens does more of the ocean's therapy, refreshing and rejuvenating visitors. Innkeepers Laura and John provide morning muffins and afternoon baked goods; the beach is a quarter of a mile for a day's sojourn. Rooms $125–249, Apr.–Nov.

INNS AND B&BS ♂ ⚐ **The Beachmere Inn** (207-646-2021 or 1-800-336-3983; beach mereinn.com), 62 Beachmere Place. Open year-round. Beachmere Inn consists of a rambling, updated mansion and a streamlined building that border a huge lawn overlooking Ogunquit Beach. The inn, owned by female members of the same family since 1937, has 39 rooms and 33 suites; Number 35 is a blue aerie set over Marginal Way and ocean waves. All rooms have kitchenette and cable TV, and most have a private balcony, deck, or terrace. A huge indoor hot tub, cedar sauna, massage rooms, exercise rooms, and children's play area are available to guests. High-season rates, $160–395, drop in the off-season after the last weekend in October to $65–195.

The Grand Hotel (207-646-1231 or 1-800-806-1231; thegrandhotel.com), 276 Shore Dr. Open Mar.–Nov. Twenty-eight suites in this hotel, originally a condominium complex. Each has two rooms, wet bar, fridge, cable TV, a king-sized bed, and a private deck or balcony; fireplace in top-floor rooms. There's an elevator, an interior atrium, an indoor pool, and an outdoor hot tub. $180–240 in high season, $95–210 right after Labor Day, from $70 off-season.

AERIAL VIEW OF BEACHMERE INN

The Trellis House (207-646-7909 or 1-800-681-7909; trellishouse.com), 10 Beachmere Place, P.O. Box 2229. Open May–Oct. This shingled, turn-of-the-20th-century summer cottage offers appealing common areas, including a wraparound screened porch. In 2015, Laurence Plotkin and Glen Porter handsomely redecorated eight guest rooms, all with full private bath, some with a water view. $169–299, two-night minimum, might include Trellis Benedict with crabcake. The inn is handy both to the village and to Perkins Cove via Marginal Way.

Marginal Way House and Motel (207-646-8801; marginalwayhouse.com), Wharf Lane, P.O. Box 697. Open late Apr.–Oct. Just a short walk from the beach and really in the middle of the village, this delightful complex is hidden down a waterside lane; its landscaped lawn has a water view. There are old-fashioned guest rooms—Number 8 has flowered wallpaper and a beach view—in the Main and Wharf Houses, each with private bath. Dockside houses six standard motel units, and there are seven (high-season weekly rental) apartments. Rates range from $55–279.

Rockmere Lodge (207-646-2985; rockmere.com), 150 Stearns Rd. Hospitality, devoted repeat guests, good books and art assembled in a shingle-style 1899 "cottage" with the sea spread at its feet. Innkeepers Andy and Bob have three beloved dogs, but no pets are allowed and no children under 12. That said, count on handsome, Victorian decor, books perhaps stocked in the bedside table, excellent breakfasts, and relaxing on the porch and in the bountiful garden. Rates range from $125–255.

Above Tide Inn (207-646-7454; above tideinn.com), 66 Beach St. Open May 15–Oct. 15. Right at the start of Marginal Way and steps from the bridge leading over to Ogunquit Beach, also steps from village shops and jutting right out into the water. Meghan and John Hubacz offer nine rooms, each with an outdoor sitting area, small fridge, TV, and shower or bath. All but one room have water views, and local artists painted the pictures hanging inside. Mid-July–Labor Day rates are $190–235; $100–140 off-season, continental breakfast included.

The Beauport Inn on Clay Hill (207-361-2400; beauportinn.com), 339 Clay Hill Rd.

THE RIVERSIDE MOTEL OVERLOOKING PERKINS COVE

Open year-round. A two-minute drive from town, this quiet stone manor set by a river has vintage-1835 English oak floor-to-ceiling paneling in its great room. Each room has a gas fireplace, cable TV, and DVD; there's also a two-room suite and a fully equipped apartment. A lap pool, steam room, and Jacuzzi are shared by guests. $150–275 (depending on the season) includes a full breakfast.

Beach Farm Inn (207-646-8493; beach farminn.com), 97 Eldridge Rd., Wells 04090. Open Apr.–Nov. This handsome restored farmhouse has been taking in guests since the 19th century, when it was a working salt-marsh farm. The tasteful early American decor is one of the charms, as is a swimming pool that beckons from the lawn. Eight attractive bedrooms, three with private bath—others can be rented with an unattached bath for private use—and two efficiency cottages. $109–159.

COTTAGES ✍ **Dunes on the Waterfront** (207-646-2612; dunesonthewaterfront.com), 518 Main St., P.O. Box 917. Open May–Oct. Owned by the Perkins family for more than 70 years, this is really a historic property, the best of the coast's surviving "cottage

colonies," as well as a great family find. The 36 units include 19 old-style white cottages with green trim, many with fireplace, scattered over well-kept grounds fronting on the Ogunquit River, with direct access to Ogunquit Beach by rowboat at high tide and on foot at low tide. All rooms have refrigerator and color TV. Minimum stay in July and Aug. in the larger cottages. $255–315 in-season, $170–195 off-season.

🐾 ✍ **Cottage in the Lane Motor Lodge** (207-646-7903; cottageinthelane.com), 84 Drakes Island Rd., Wells. There are 10 housekeeping cottages, all facing landscaped grounds under the pines (an artistic play structure and a pool form the centerpiece); salt marsh beyond. It's a 0.75-mile walk or bike ride to the beach. The quiet setting borders the Rachel Carson Wildlife Refuge and Laudholm Farm (see *Green Space*). A two-bedroom cottage runs $990 per week in-season, $560–750 off-season.

✍ **The Seagull Inn and Condominiums** (207-646-5164; seagullvacations.com), 1413 Post Rd. (Rt. 1), Wells. Two 3-story town houses (available year-round), 27 two-bedroom cottages, 1 one-bedroom cottage, all with a screened porch, fill what used to be an open field. Private driveway and gas grills; new cottages have ocean views. The seven remaining old cottages have been updated with bathrooms and kitchens. Two heated pools, one with hot tub, the other with a wading pool for children. Rentals by the week in summer (three-night minimum off-season), $800–1,500 for the housekeeping cottages; $2,800 a week for town houses.

MOTEL **Riverside Motel** (207-646-2741; riversidemotel.com), Shore Rd., P.O. Box 2244. Open mid-Apr.–Oct. Just across the draw-footbridge and overlooking Perkins Cove is this trim, friendly place with 42 units; also four rooms in the 1874 house. The property had been in the Staples family for more than 100 years before Geoff Scimone took over in 2009. All 4 acres are nonsmoking. All rooms have cable TV and full bath, most tiled, and all overlook the cove; fresh muffins, Congdon's Doughnuts, yogurt, and cereal served in the lobby 7:30–11 around the fireplace, with outdoor seating. $79–199, depending on season and location of room.

✳ Where to Eat

DINING OUT **Roost Café and Bistro** (207-646-9898; roostcafeandbistro.com), 262 Shore Rd., Ogunquit. Open Apr.–Dec. 1; May–Aug. open seven days a week; Sept.–Dec. open Wed.–Sun. Serving breakfast (available all day) starting at 8 AM, light fare at 3 PM at the bar, and dinner 5 PM–close. The menu is an eclectic mix, as the owners' priority is simply to "do food really well." Options range from Asian-inspired grilled swordfish with Korean BBQ and coconut scallion rice to a lobster pappardelle with house-made pasta. Reservations advised. Entrées $18–30.

✪ ♿ **Joshua's Restaurant** (207-646-3355; joshuas.biz), 1637 Post Rd. (Rt. 1), Wells. Open daily at 5 PM with the last seating at 9:15. The buzz about Joshua's just keeps getting better. The Mather family farm grows its own vegetables, and chef Joshua Mather puts them to spectacular use as sides for grilled rack of lamb, pork tenderloin with plum chutney, and haddock with caramelized onion crust. An elegant, refurbished farmhouse dining room and bar. Entrées $21–35.

The Velveteen Habit (207-216-9884; thevelveteenhabit.com) 37 Ogunquit Rd., Cape Neddick—but easily found from downtown Ogunquit. Located in the former Arrows Restaurant, this elegant spot sustains high-end dining with kitchen gardens, house-smoking, curing, and pickling; also sophisticated cocktails and fine wine. Two might feast on porterhouse steak, horseradish creamed kale and chimichurri; or a single lucky diner on haddock with smoked clams and roasted fennel. Entrées $17–33. Brats with cheddar grits ($14) on the bar menu make this just as good for a casual dinner. No dress code.

✪ **Angelina's Ristorante** (207-646-0445; angelinasogunquit.com), 655 Main St., Ogunquit. Open daily 4:30–10. Reservations recommended. Owner-chef David Giarusso Jr. might be tired, but he's scrupulously polite whenever you encounter him on a busy night at this deservedly popular Italian restaurant, and that's part of why people love it here. A garden terrace feels cool in the hot summer and the bustling rooms are always comfortable, but what's most important is on the plate, and it is wonderful. Good wine list. Entrées $16–31.

MC Perkins Cove (207-646-6263; mcperkinscove.com), Perkins Cove. Lunch and dinner daily in summer, closed some days of the week off-season. Wonderful water views and live Thu.-night entertainment. Owned by the inventive chefs of Arrows, this is a casual place for fresh raw oysters, grilled steak and fish, fried trout, and other seafood with splendid touches. Choose your own "evil carbos" and sauces. The even more casual bar menu is a deal. Entrées $19–37.

Five-O Shore Road (207-646-5001; five-o shoreroad.com), 50 Shore Rd., Ogunquit Village. Open for dinner in-season nightly, light fare served until 11 PM; Thu.–Sun. in winter. Brunch served Sun. 10–2. The beef tenderloin brochette we tried remains a high point of dining out, and the skilled preparation of everything else was memorable, too. Maine lobster with crab and corn caponata and dry-rubbed pork loin with roasted tomato polenta were on a summer menu. Good wine and cocktails. Entrées $23–39.

Gypsy Sweethearts (207-646-7021; gypsy sweethearts.com), 30 Shore Rd., Ogunquit.

LOBSTER

Note: Maine's southernmost beach resorts are the first place many visitors sample real "Maine Lobstah" the way it should be eaten: messily, with bib, butter, and a water view.

♪ **Barnacle Billy's, Etc.** (207-646-5575 or 1-800-866-5575; barnbilly.com), Perkins Cove. Open May–Oct. for lunch and dinner. What began as a no-frills lobster place (the one that's still next door) has expanded over 50 years to fill a luxurious dining space created for a more upscale waterside restaurant. Lobster and seafood dishes remain the specialty, and it's difficult to beat the view combined with comfort, which frequently includes the glow from two great stone fireplaces. Full bar; dinner entrées from $16.75, higher for a big boiled lobster. You can also order lobster at the counter and wait for your number, dine on the outdoor deck, or order burgers.

✪ ☞ ♪ ♿ **Lobster Shack** (207-646-2941), end of Perkins Cove. Open mid-Apr.–mid-Oct., 11–8 in-season. A family-owned, old-style, serious lobster-eating place since the 1940s (when it was known as Maxwell and Perkins). The tables are wide slabs of shellacked pine with plenty of room for lobster by the pound, steamer clams, good chowder, house coleslaw; also reasonably priced burgers, apple pie à la mode, wine, beer.

♪ **Ogunquit Lobster Pound** (207-646-2516), Rt. 1 (north of Ogunquit Village). Open Apr.–Dec. Summer hours are 4–9, fall hours (starting in Sept.) are 4:30–9. Expanded gradually over the years, this log landmark retains its 1930s atmosphere and is still all about selecting your lobster and watching it (if you so choose) get steamed in the huge outdoor pots. "Steamers" (steamed clams) are the other specialty. The large menu, however, now includes angelhair pasta, fried foods, and sirloin steaks. Beer and wine are available. Entrées $4–30 and up for lobster.

☞ ♪ **Fisherman's Catch** (207-646-8780; fishermanscatchwells.com), 134 Harbor Rd., Wells Harbor. Open May–Columbus Day, daily 11:30–9 in summer, closing earlier off-season. Set in a salt marsh, with rustic tables; a traditional seafood place with unbeatable prices. Good chowder and really good lobster stew, homemade crabcakes, lobster dinners, children's menu, beer on tap, all provided by a family that takes good care of you. Try the bread pudding with whiskey sauce. Entrées $6.99–22.99 plus.

Open Apr.–Oct. for dinner Tue.–Sun. from 5:30; weekends off-season. Meals with a Caribbean twist are served in a charming old house that is the dependable neighborhood dinner spot for demanding locals. Chef-owner Judie Clayton's green secret pumpkinseed sauce is a tangy delight on the rack of lamb. Poblano rellenos and pan-seared sea scallops with pineapple and roasted sweet potato. Many wines available by the glass. Entrées $19–32.

The Front Porch Restaurant (207-646-4005; frontporchrestaurant.net), 9 Shore Rd., Ogunquit. Closed Tue.; otherwise open 5–close except Sat. (noon–close). A popular nightspot boasts a fine fish taco with cilantro slaw, good macaroni and cheese, and burgers. Count on a crowd on summer weekends, with entertainment upstairs in the piano bar (see *Entertainment*). The menu is served in all

three spaces except during shows. Steaks, flat breads, and grilled fish, too. Entrées $10–29. Reservations not accepted.

Jonathan's Restaurant (207-646-4777; jonathansrestaurant.com), 92 Bourne Lane, Ogunquit. Open year-round. There are two entirely distinct parts to this big place. The downstairs restaurant consists of a series of nicely decorated rooms (one with a 600-gallon tropical aquarium). The mainstream fare is well made, including grilled steak, scampi Provençal, and caramelized salmon fillet. Entrées $21.95–33.95. For more about what happens upstairs, see *Entertainment*.

Varano's Restaurant (207-641-8550; varanos.com), 60 Mile Rd., Wells. Open daily at 4:30. A family-owned Italian restaurant that combines a welcoming professional staff with good food. Prosciutto and melon might be

A GARDEN AT THE ENTRANCE TO CAFFÉ PREGO

a summer appetizer, and whole-wheat vegetarian pasta keeps up the good work. Grilled lamb, house pork sausage, and lobster with black fettuccine. Entrées $14.95–31.95. Reservations not accepted.

EATING OUT **Amore Breakfast and Café Amore** (207-646-6661; amorebreakfast.com), 309 Shore Rd., Ogunquit. Open early spring–mid-Dec., in-season 7 AM–1 PM daily, closed Wed. and Thu. in the fall, extended hours in the café and evening hours in summer. Relaxed and pleasant, this restaurant makes exuberant omelets and a lobster eggs Benedict as pretty as an ocean sunrise. Also panini and sandwiches including a lobster roll, and a place to park. Breakfast $4–14; lunch $6–12.

Caffé Prego (207-646-7734; cafeprego .com), 44 Shore Rd., Ogunquit. Open daily. Pizza, well-made pasta and panini, Italian pastries and desserts, cappuccino and espresso all vie for your appreciation. In any case, you can finish with house gelato in compelling flavors like kiwi and chocolate. Entrées $8.75–21.75.

Oarweed Oceanside Restaurant (207-646-4022; oarweed.com), Perkins Cove. Open end of Apr.–Oct., daily at 11 AM for lunch and dinner. This seaside restaurant has outdoor seating in warm weather, but inside or out you can feast your eyes on the water—and on your plate, where you might choose a good crab roll, lobster roll, crabcakes, steamed lobster, roast chicken, or the perfectly done steamers, an essential ingredient in the shore dinner. Entrées $3.50–34.

Jake's Seafood (207-646-6771; jakes seafoodrestaurant.com), 127 Post Rd. (Rt. 1), Moody. Open daily 5 AM–9 PM Apr.–Oct., breakfast and lunch Nov.–Mar. Very popular, this spot specializes in good American cooking, fresh seafood, and ice cream.

Congdon's Donuts Family Restaurant (207-646-4219; congdons.com), 1090 Post Rd. (Rt. 1), Wells. Open 6–3 daily in summer (closed Wed.), fewer days in winter. Fresh muffins, breads, pastries, doughnuts, and a full menu for breakfast and lunch. The doughnuts are fried in lard; this place is one of the very few left that does so, and it makes a great doughnut.

Mike's Clam Shack (207-646-5999; mikes clamshack.com), 1150 Post Rd. (Rt. 1), Wells. Open daily in-season 11:30–closing. An enormous place with enormous crowds and a reputation for good fried clams. Sandwiches, burgers, pasta, and fried seafood. $5.50–24.95.

⌀ **Billy's Chowder House** (207-646-7558; billyschowderhouse.com), Mile Rd., Wells. Open daily 11:30–close mid-Jan.–early Dec. Overlooking Wells Harbor and a salt marsh, a family favorite with famous chowder and a selection of fried seafood, steamed shellfish, broiled scallops, and, of course, boiled lobster. There's also plenty of meat on the menu, including a hot dog and fries. Entrées $14–32.95.

Maine Diner (207-656-4441; mainediner .com), 2265 Post Rd. (Rt. 1), Wells, near the junction of Rts. 1 and 9. Open year-round; Sun.–Thu. 7 AM–8:30 PM, Fri. and Sat. 7 AM–9 PM. This packed place can boast about its seafood chowder, made with shrimp, scallops, lobster, and clams in a milky broth. Avoid the chicken potpie. Entrées $3.50–30.95.

⌀ **Village Food Market and Cafe** (207-646-2122; villagefoodmarket.com), 230 Main St., Ogunquit. This landmark grocery store has changed with the times, adding daily baked goods, soups, salads, a deli—and a new brick-oven pizzeria called Cornerstone. Call before 11 for a picnic order to avoid the line.

SNACKS **Bread & Roses Bakery** (207-646-4227; breadandrosesbakery.com), 28 Main St., Ogunquit. Over the years Mary Breen's pleasant bakery has expanded into an attractive café serving muffins and coffee, irresistible

72 | SOUTHERN COAST

VILLAGE FOOD MARKET

cinnamon butter puffs, and other delectable pastries. Lunch on panini, big salads, and fresh thick-crust pizza.

Scoop Deck (207-646-5150; facebook .com/thescoopdeck), Eldridge Rd. (just off Rt. 1), Wells. Open Memorial Day–Columbus Day. Mocha chip and Dinosaur Crunch (blue vanilla) are among the more than 55 flavors; the ice cream is from Thibodeau Farms in Saco. Fall flavors include pumpkin pie and apple crisp. Also yogurt, brownies, and hot dogs.

Borealis Breads (207-641-8800), Rt. 1, Wells. Open daily. Great bread and sandwiches—don't overlook the fabulous breadsticks—and the brownies and other treats are excellent. More than 100,000 pounds of whole-wheat flour for the breads is milled from wheat grown in Aroostook County.

✳ Entertainment

THEATERS **Hackmatack Playhouse** (207-698-1807; hackmatack.org), 538 School St. (Rt. 9), Berwick, stages live performances mid-June–Labor Day.

Arundel Barn Playhouse (207-985-5552; arundelbarnplayhouse.com), 53 Old Post Rd., Arundel. Mid-June–Labor Day. Box office opens in May for preseason. Professional musical theater in a restored 1800s barn.

Leavitt Fine Arts Theatre (207-646-3123; leavitttheatre.com), 259 Main St., Ogunquit Village. An old-time theater with new screen and sound; showing first-run films since 1923 and live entertainment, including comedians.

Ogunquit Playhouse (207-646-5511; ogunquitplayhouse.org), Rt. 1 (just south of Ogunquit Village). Open May–Oct. Billing itself as "America's Foremost Summer Theater," this grand old summer-stock theater opened for its first season in 1933 and is now owned by the Ogunquit Playhouse Foundation. It continues to feature top stars in productions staged Tue.–Fri. at 8 PM, Sat. at 8:30 PM; matinees are offered several days of the week.

OTHERS **Jonathan's Ogunquit** (207-646-4777; jonathansrestaurant.com), 92 Bournes Lane, Ogunquit. Year-round, national performers. You can check the current schedule on the website.

Ogunquit Performing Arts (207-646-6170) sponsors the Chamber Music Festival in June and the Capriccio annual summer arts festival; also film, music, social dances, and theater year-round.

The Front Porch Restaurant (207-646-4005; frontporchrestaurant.net), 9 Shore Rd., Ogunquit. Performances and piano and the chance to join in the show tunes; special events with live entertainment.

Hope Hobbs Gazebo at Wells Harbor Park is the site of Sat.-night concerts in summer.

✳ Selective Shopping

ANTIQUES SHOPS Rt. 1 from York through Wells and the Kennebunks is studded with antiques shops, among them is **MacDougall-Gionet** (207-646-3531; macdougall-gionet .com), open Tue.–Sun. 10–5, a particularly rich trove of formal and country furniture in a barn; 60 dealers are represented. **R. Jorgensen Antiques** (207-646-9444; rjorgensen .com) has nine rooms filled with antique furniture, including fine formal pieces from a number of countries. Open Mon.–Sat. 10–5, Sun. noon–5.

ART GALLERIES In addition to the Ogunquit Museum of Art there is the **Barn Gallery**, home of the Ogunquit Art Association (207-646-8400; barngallery.org, ogunquitart association.com), Shore Rd. and Bourne Lane,

BARN GALLERY

Ogunquit. Open late May–early Oct., Mon.–Sat. 11–5 and Sun. 1–5. The Barn Gallery showcases work by members; also stages frequent workshops, lectures, Wed.-night films about artists, Tue.-night workshops working with a model, and concerts. Another is the **Van Ward Gallery** (207-646-0554; vanwardgallery.com), 49 Shore Rd., Ogunquit.

BOOKS Boston book lovers drive to Wells to browse in the cluster of exceptional bookstores along Rt. 1, including **Annie's Book Stop** (207-646-3821; anniesbookstopwells .com), 676 Post Rd., Wells. Hours change with the season. Mysteries, new releases, old favorites both used and new. **Douglas N. Harding Rare Books** (207-646-8785; hardingsbooks.com), 2152 Post Rd., open year-round, is huge and excellent with some 200,000 titles, including rare finds, maps, and prints. **The Arringtons** (207-646-4124), 1908 Post Rd. (Rt. 1), specializes in military subjects as well as vintage paperbacks and postcards.

SPECIAL SHOPS **Perkins Cove**, the cluster of former fish shacks by Ogunquit's famous draw-footbridge, harbors more than a dozen shops and galleries.

Crickets Corner Toys and Kites (207-646-2261; cricketscornertoys.com), 41 Shore Rd., Ogunquit. Beach toys, games, stuffed animals, and a huge variety of kites.

Harbor Candy Shop (207-646-8078; harborcandy.com), 26 Main St., Ogunquit. Open year-round Thu.–Sun. 9 AM–9 PM, Fri.–Sat. 9 AM–10 PM. Open since 1956, this family-owned store makes turtles with Belgian chocolate and handmade caramel (made from cream and sugar and no preservatives); they are their most popular item.

Pine Tree Farm Market and Café (207-646-7545; facebook.com/PineTreeFarm MarketCafe), 411 Post Rd., Wells. A fine place to find a good sandwich, breakfast, or wine, cheese, pickles, and more, like flowers and pumpkins in fall.

✳ Special Events

April: Big **Patriots Day celebration** at Ogunquit Beach.

June: **Ogunquit Chamber Music Festival** (first week). **Laudholm Farm Day** (midmonth). **Wells Week** (end of the month)—a weeklong celebration centering on Harbor Park Day, with boat launchings, a chicken BBQ, a sand-sculpture contest, and a crafts fair. **Métis of Maine Annual Powwow**—dance, rituals and crafts made by people of Native American ancestry, Wells.

July: **Fireworks** on July 4, sand-castle building, family fun day, and three-day **Harbor Fest** in Wells.

September: **Open Homes Day**, sponsored by the Wells Historical Society. **Nature Crafts Festival** (second weekend) at Laudholm Farm. **Capriccio**, a celebration of the performing arts, and **Kite Day** in Ogunquit. **Punkinfiddle** (punkinfiddle.org), a celebration of National Estuaries Day.

October: **Ogunquit Fest**, with tours and costume parade, and October Fest.

December: **Christmas parade** in Wells. **Christmas by the Sea** (second weekend) in Ogunquit.

THE KENNEBUNKS

The Kennebunks began as a fishing stage near Cape Porpoise as early as 1602, but the community was repeatedly destroyed by Native American raids. In 1719 the present "port" was incorporated as Arundel, a name that stuck through its lucrative shipbuilding and seafaring years until 1821, when it became Kennebunkport. Later, when the novel *Arundel*, by Kenneth Roberts (born in Kennebunk), had run through 32 printings, residents gave the old name to North Kennebunkport.

That the Kennebunks prospered as a shipbuilding center is obvious from the quantity and quality of its sea captains' and shipbuilders' mansions, the presence of its brick custom-house (now the library), and the beauty of its churches.

In his 1891 guidebook *The Pine-Tree Coast*, Samuel Adams Drake noted that "since the beginning of the century more than eight hundred vessels have been sent out from the shipyards of this river." He recalled: "When I first knew this place, both banks of the river were lined with shipyards . . . all alive with the labor of hundreds of workmen." But by the 1890s, Drake noted, shipbuilding was "moribund" and Kennebunkport had become "a well-established watering-place."

In 1872 this entire spectacular 5-mile stretch of coast—from Lords Point at the western end of Kennebunk Beach all the way to Cape Porpoise on the east—was acquired by one developer, the Sea Shore Company. Over the next couple of decades no fewer than 30 grand hotels and dozens of summer mansions evolved to accommodate the summer visitors that train service brought. The Kennebunks then shared the 1940s-to-1960s decline suffered by Maine coastal resorts, losing all but a scattering of old hotels.

According to the locals, the Kennebunks developed an almost countercultural feel in the 1960s and '70s. Then the tourist tide again turned, and over the past few decades the area has grown increasingly upscale: Inns have been rehabbed and dozens of B&Bs and inns have opened. Dock Square's world-class shopping district now rivals those in Palm Beach and other swanky spots, but a walk through the historic streets of Kennebunkport is free and quite idyllic. And a meal at one of the lobster shacks is as rustic, delicious, and affordable as any on the Maine coast.

Nancy English

You can bed down a few steps from Dock Square's lively shops and restaurants or out at Goose Rocks, where the only sound is the lapping of waves on endless sand. Most B&Bs are, however, the former sea captains' homes grouped within a few stately streets of each other, many within walking distance of both Dock Square and the open ocean.

GUIDANCE **Kennebunk/Kennebunkport Chamber of Commerce** (207-967-0857 or 1-800-982-4421; visitthekennebunks.com), main office, 16 Water St., Kennebunk; kiosk,

ON THE BRIDGE BETWEEN KENNEBUNK AND KENNEBUNKPORT

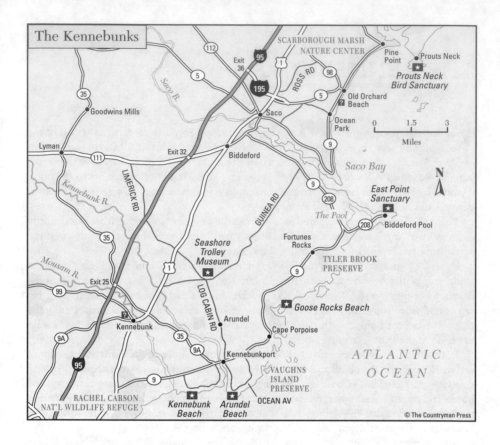

The Kennebunks

1 Chase Hill Rd., Kennebunk. Open Mon.–Fri. year-round, plus Sat. and Sun. late May–late Oct. Staff are unusually helpful, and the chamber publishes an excellent free guide.

GETTING THERE *By air:* **Portland International Jetport** is served by various airlines and taxi services.

By car: Drive up I-95 to Exit 25 and take Rt. 35 into Kennebunk, on to Kennebunkport and the Kennebunk beaches. Coming up Rt. 1, take Rt. 9 east from Wells.

By train: See *Amtrak* in "What's Where." The Downeaster service from Boston's North Station takes about two hours. Starting in 2017, Amtrak makes a seasonal stop at 12 Depot St., Kennebunk; until then, transportation is available from Wells.

GETTING AROUND Kennebunk is a busy commercial center straddling the strip of Rt. 1 between the Mousam and Kennebunk Rivers. A 10-minute ride down Summer St. (Rt. 35) brings you to Kennebunkport. Then there are the Kennebunk beaches, Cape Porpoise, Goose Rocks Beach, Cape Arundel, and Kennebunk Lower Village. Luckily, free detailed maps are readily available.

Intown Trolley (207-967-3686; intowntrolley.com), Kennebunkport, offers narrated sight-seeing tours; $16 adults, $6 ages 3–17, free for those 2 and under. The tickets are good for the day, so you can also use them to shuttle between Dock Square and the Kennebunk beaches.

PARKING A municipal fee parking lot is hidden behind the commercial block in Dock Square. You can find free parking at 30 North St., a short walk to Dock Square, and another fee lot near the bridge in Lower Village. Good luck!

WHEN TO COME One nice side effect of the Kennebunk tourist trade: This is the least seasonal resort town on the Southern Coast. Most inns and shops stay open through Christmas Prelude in early December, and many never close. Visit in fall, when crowds thin out.

✳ To See

MUSEUMS **The Brick Store Museum and Archives** (207-985-4802; brickstoremuseum .org), 117 Main St., Kennebunk. Open year-round, Tue.–Fri. 10–4:30, Sat. 10–1. Admission $7.50 adults, $6 seniors; $3 children 6-16. This block of early-19th-century commercial buildings, including William Lord's **Brick Store** (1825), hosts a permanent exhibit documenting the region from the days of Native Americans, the arduous settlement years, and the subsequent colonial era through the period of shipbuilding glory. Changing exhibits focus on a wide variety of subjects.

✎ **Seashore Trolley Museum** (207-967-2800; trolleymuseum.org), 195 Log Cabin Rd., about 3 miles from Kennebunkport. Open daily, rain or shine, Memorial Day–Columbus Day, weekends in May and through Oct.; $10 adults, $7.50 ages 6–16, $8 seniors over 60, children under 6 free. This nonprofit museum preserves the history of the trolley era, displaying more than 250 vehicles from all over the world. The impressive collection began in 1939, when the last open-sided Biddeford–Old Orchard Beach trolley was retired. Five million passengers traveled this line in 1907. A 3-mile trolley excursion takes visitors through woods and fields. An 8,000-hour effort restored an electric locomotive that sometimes operates and is always on display; the vehicle is on the National Historic Register and is the subject of an exhibit about public transportation in the early 20th century.

Kennebunkport Historical Society (207-967-2751; kennebunkporthistoricalsociety .com) has three facilities. **The Pasco Center**, 125 North St., free, is open year-round (the Benson Blacksmith Shop and Clark Shipwrights Office hours vary), **The Town House School**, 135 North St., is used for research ($10 an hour) and open year-round for

THE CONDUCTOR DESCRIBES THE "BOWLING ALLEY" STREETCAR FROM NEW HAVEN, CONNECTICUT, DURING THE TROLLEY RIDE AT SEASHORE TROLLEY MUSEUM

Nancy English

abbreviated hours. Free on-site parking at both. The society also maintains **"White Columns,"** aka the Nott House, 8 Maine St. (no parking), a Greek Revival mansion with Doric columns, original wallpaper, carpets, and furnishings. Kirsten Camp, executive administrator, provides a fabulous 30-minute tour of the Nott House from 10 AM to 3 PM on the hour in summer, $10; the First Families Museum, also in White Columns, is devoted to President George H. W. Bush.

HISTORIC SITES **Wedding Cake House**, Summer St. (Rt. 35), Kennebunk. This privately owned 1826 house is laced up and down with ornate white gingerbread. Legend has it that a local sea captain had to

EXCURSIONS

Take a scenic drive along Ocean Avenue, starting in Kennebunkport, which follows the **Kennebunk River** for a mile to Cape Arundel and the open ocean, then winds past many magnificent summer homes. Stop along **Parson's Way**, located off Ocean Ave. on the right just after the Colony Hotel, and enjoy the park benches that take advantage of the magnificent view of the mouth of the Kennebunk River and **Gooch's Beach**. Continue north and east to **Walker's Point**, former president George H. W. Bush's summer estate (it fills a private 11-acre peninsula). Built by his grandfather in 1903, its position is uncannily ideal for use as a president's summer home, moated by water on three sides yet clearly visible from pullouts along the avenue. Continue along the ocean (you don't have to worry about driving too slowly, because everyone else is, too). Follow the road to **Cape Porpoise**, site of the area's original 1600s settlement. The cove is still a base for lobster and commercial fishing boats, and the village is a good place to lunch or dine. Continue along Rt. 9 to **Clock Farm Corner** (you'll know it when you see it) and turn right onto Dyke Rd. to **Goose Rocks Beach**; park and walk. Return to Rt. 9 and cross it, continuing via Goose Rocks Rd. to the Seashore Trolley Museum and then Log Cabin Rd. to Kennebunkport.

Nancy English

THESE VISITORS TO GOOSE ROCKS BEACH LAST SAW ONE ANOTHER 26 YEARS EARLIER—ALSO AT GOOSE ROCKS BEACH

rush off to sea before a proper wedding cake could be baked, but he more than made up for it later.

South Congregational Church, Temple St., Kennebunkport. Just off Dock Square, built in 1824 with a Christopher Wren–style cupola and belfry; Doric columns added in 1912.

Louis T. Graves Memorial Library (207-967-2778), 18 Maine St., Kennebunkport. Built in 1813 as a bank, which went bust, it later served as a customhouse. It was subsequently donated to the library association by artist Abbott Graves, whose pictures alone make it worth a visit. You can still see the bank vault and the sign from the custom collector's office. At the Perkins House next door, the book saleroom is full of bargains and open during the library's hours.

First Parish Unitarian Universalist Church, Main St., Kennebunk. Built between 1772 and 1773, with an Asher Benjamin–style steeple added between 1803 and 1804 along with a Paul Revere bell. In 1838 the interior was divided into two levels, with the church proper elevated to the second floor. Popular legend holds that the pulpit was carved from a single log found floating in the Caribbean Sea and towed back to Maine.

✳ To Do

BICYCLING **Aquaholics** (207-967-8650; aquaholicsurf.com), 166 Port Rd., Kennebunk, and **Coastal Maine Kayak** (207-967-6065; coastalmainekayak.com), 8 Western Ave., Kennebunk, rent bikes. **Kennebunkport Bicycle Co.** (207-251-3135), 34 Arundel Rd. (off North St.), Kennebunkport, rents a variety of bikes. Open seasonally. The Kennebunks lend themselves well to exploration by bike, a far more satisfying way to go in summer than by car.

BOATING **The *Rugosa*** (207-468-4095; rugosacharters.com), at The Nonantum Resort, Ocean Ave., Kennebunkport. Several daily trips to Goat Island Lighthouse, where you can visit the tower, at high tide only. Lobstering demonstrations with traps pulled, and a cocktail cruise in the evening.
    The Landing School of Boat Building and Design (207-985-7976; landingschool.edu), 286 River Rd., Arundel, offers a Sept.–June program in building and designing sailing craft. Visitors welcome if you call ahead.

CARRIAGE RIDES **Rockin' Horse Stables** (207-967-4288; rockinhorsemaine.com), 245 Arundel Rd., Kennebunkport. Tour Kennebunkport's historic district (25 minutes) in a spiffy white vis-à-vis carriage with burgundy-colored velvet seats and antique lanterns. Sleigh rides all winter and wagon and carriage rides at Christmas Prelude (see *Special Events*).

FISHING **Stone Coast Anglers, Inc.** (207-985-6005; stonecoastanglers.com), Kennebunk. Captain Paul J. Rioux specializes in chartered boat trips along the coast for up to three guests as well as guided wading trips for saltwater and game fish.

GOLF **Cape Arundel Golf Club** (207-967-3494; capearundelgolfclub.com), 19 River Rd., Kennebunkport, 18 holes. The local links former president George H. W. Bush frequented are open to the public daily. Three-day advance tee time reservations accepted. **Webhannet Golf Club** (207-967-2061; webhannetgolfclub.com), 26 Golf Club Dr., off Sea Rd., Kennebunk Beach, 18 holes. Open to the public but semiprivate, with limited tee times especially in July and Aug. **Dutch Elm Golf Course** (207-282-9850; dutchelmgolf.com), Arundel, 18 holes; cart and club rentals, lessons, pro shop, snack bar, putting greens. ✐ **Hillcrest Golf** (207-967-4661), Rt. 9, Kennebunk. Open daily 8 AM–dark; balls and clubs furnished.

KAYAKING **Harbor Adventures** (207-363-8466; harboradventures.com), Kennebunkport. Guided sea kayak tours for individuals and groups. **Coastal Maine Kayak** (207-967-6065; coastalmainekayak.com), 8 Western Ave., Kennebunk (next to Federal Jack's), offers kayak tours, rentals, a sea kayak guide course, a women's retreat, and kayak rolling sessions. The trip to Cape Porpoise Lighthouse is good for beginners and old hands.

SAILING **Schooner *Eleanor*** (207-967-8809; gwi.net/schoonersails). Two-hour sailing trips aboard a traditional, gaff-rigged, 55-foot schooner set sail from the docks at the Arundel Wharf Restaurant.
    The Pineapple Ketch (207-468-7262; pineappleketch.com), 95 Ocean Ave., Kennebunkport. Daily two-hour tours and private charters at 11, 2, and sunset, mid-May–Oct., on

this 38-foot ketch with red sails and a black hull. $40 per person. Book tours in-season at 207-967-4050.

SURFING **Aquaholics** (207-967-8650; aquaholicsurf.com), 166 Port Rd., Kennebunk, is the place for a surf lesson, whether you are 3 or 73. Weeklong surf camps run right into winter, and with a wetsuit on, the cold is nothing compared with the fun. Stand-up paddle clinics and tours, surf shop, and a full line of rentals.

WHALE-WATCHING AND OCEAN TOURS This is a popular departure point for whale-watching on Jefferies Ledge, about 20 miles offshore. If you have any tendency toward seasickness, be sure to choose a calm day or take anti-nausea medication. Chances are you'll see more than a dozen whales. Frequently sighted species include finbacks, minkes, rights, and humpbacks. **First Chance** (207-967-5507 or 1-800-767-2628; firstchance whalewatch.com), 4 Western Ave. in the Lower Village (at the bridge), also offers a scenic lobster cruise.

✳ Winter Activities

CROSS-COUNTRY SKIING **Harris Farm** (207-499-2678; harrisfarm.com), 252 Buzzell Rd., Dayton. A 500-acre dairy farm with more than 20 miles of trails. Equipment rentals available, including snowshoes and ice skates. Located 1.5 miles from the Rt. 5 and Rt. 35 intersection.

SLEIGH RIDES **Rockin' Horse Stables** (207-967-4288), 245 Arundel Rd., Kennebunkport, offers 30- to 40-minute sleigh rides on a 100-acre farm.

✳ Green Space

BEACHES The Kennebunks discourage day-trippers by requiring a permit to park at major beaches. Day, week, and seasonal passes must be secured from the chamber of commerce, town hall, police department, or local lodging places. You can also park in one of the town lots and walk, bike, or take a trolley to the beach.

Goose Rocks Beach, a few miles north of Kennebunkport Village on Rt. 9, is the area's most beautiful beach: a magnificent, wide, smooth stretch of silver-white sand backed by high dunes. Children here seem to mimic their less frenetic 19th-century counterparts, doing wonderfully old-fashioned things like flying kites, playing paddleball, and making sand castles.

Kennebunk and **Gooch's Beaches** in Kennebunk are both long, wide strips of firm sand backed by Beach Ave., divided by Oak's Neck. Beyond Gooch's Beach, take Great Hill Rd. along the water to **Strawberry Island**, a great place to walk and examine tidal pools. Please don't picnic. Keep going and you come to **Mother's Beach**, small and very sandy.

Arundel Beach, near the Colony Hotel at the mouth of the Kennebunk River, offers nice rocks for climbing and good beachcombing for shell and beach-glass enthusiasts.

NATURE PRESERVES ✐ ♿ **Rachel Carson National Wildlife Refuge** (207-646-9226; fws .gov/northeast/rachelcarson). Headquarters for this almost 50-mile, 5,000-acre preserve is just south of the Kennebunkport line at 321 Port Rd. (Rt. 9) in Wells. The refuge is divided among 10 sites along Maine's Southern Coast. Pick up a leaflet guide to the mile-long, wheelchair-accessible nature trail here. Kayakers can enter the refuge traveling up the rivers, but no put-ins or takeouts allowed to avoid disturbing the wildlife. (Also see Laud-holm Farm in "Ogunquit and Wells.")

Kennebunkport Conservation Trust (207-967-3465; kporttrust.org), P.O. Box 7004, Cape Porpoise, maintains a number of properties. These include the **Tyler Brook Preserve** near Goose Rocks, the 148-acre **Emmons Preserve** along the Batson River (access from unpaved Gravelly Rd. off Beachwood Rd.), the nearly 1,000-acre **Kennebunkport Town Forest**, and the **Vaughns Island Preserve**, which offers nature trails on a wooded island separated from the mainland by two tidal creeks. Cellar holes of historic houses are accessible by foot from 1½ hours before to 1½ hours after low tide. The trust also maintains historic **Goat Island Lighthouse**.

The Nature Conservancy (207-729-5181) owns 135 acres of the **Kennebunk Plains Preserve** and assists in the management of 650 state-owned acres in West Kennebunk (take Rt. 99 toward Sanford), with nearly 4 miles of shoreline on the Mousam River in Kennebunk.

WALKS **Henry Parsons Park**, Ocean Ave., is a path along the rocks leading to Spouting Rock and Blowing Cave, both sights to see at midtide. A great way to view the beautiful homes along Ocean Ave.

St. Anthony Monastery and Shrine (207-967-2011), Kennebunk. Some 44 acres of peaceful riverside fields and forests on Beach Ave., now maintained by Lithuanian Franciscans as a shrine and retreat. Visitors are welcome; gift shop. (See the Franciscan Guest House in *Other Lodging*.)

HIKING **The Eastern Trail** (easterntrail.org). Download the trail guide from the website and find the parking area for this off-road and on-road trail that will someday connect with the Florida Keys; in Kennebunk, it's at the elementary school.

✳ Lodging

All listings are in Kennebunkport 04046 unless otherwise noted.

INNS AND B&BS *Top dollar:* **Captain Lord Mansion** (207-967-3141 or 1-800-522-3141; captainlord.com), P.O. Box 800, at the corner of Pleasant and Green Sts. Open year-round. This three-story Federal home, built in 1812, is topped with a widow's walk from which guests can contemplate the town and sea. All 16 rooms have a gas fireplace and private bath; large high beds are equipped with steps to climb into them. The decor here is possibly the most elaborate in the state, and the Merchant Captain's Suite may have the most elaborate bathroom, including its gas fireplace. $289–550 per room in high season, $149–399 off-season, breakfast and tea included. Spa services include massage for couples and facials.

White Barn Inn (207-967-2321; whitebarninn.com), 37 Beach Ave., P.O. Box 560C, Kennebunk 04043. Open year-round. The "barn" is an elegant dining room (see *Dining Out*) where guests have breakfast and can dine. Built in the 1860s as a farmhouse, later enlarged as the Forest Hills House, this complex lies midway between Dock Square and Kennebunk Beach. Courteous staff wear black, a sleek hotel version of the brown-robed Franciscan friars nearby (see the Franciscan Guest House in *Other Lodging*). Choose an antiques-furnished room in the farmhouse; a suite in the Carriage House with four-poster king bed, fireplace, and marble bath; a cottage suite with specially crafted furnishings, a double-sided fireplace, Jacuzzi, and steam shower. $320–860 per couple for rooms includes breakfast, tea, and use of touring bikes. The yacht *True Blue* can be rented by the day and meals arranged on board. Three waterfront cottages are also for rent. A 5.35 percent housekeeping fee is added.

Hidden Pond (207-967-9055; hiddenpondmaine.com), 354 Goose Rocks Rd. Two-bedroom cottages and "bungalows" offer a private vacation home feeling in a wooded landscape. Modern and stylish, Hidden Pond caters to the wealthy, with every possible amenity, including a "WC," yoga, a spa, a shop with good cheese and wine, and a personal chef on order to make dinner in your bungalow. A shuttle takes you to a sister property at Goose Rocks Beach, to the beach itself, and to downtown Kennebunkport and fine dining. $399–549. See *Dining Out* for Earth, the lodging's restaurant.

Moderately expensive: ♂ 🍴 **Nonantum Resort** (1-888-205-1555; nonantumresort.com), 95 Ocean Ave., Kennebunkport. Open mid-April to mid-Dec. A sprawling, comfortable, nicely cared-for inn on the Kennebunk River, with boat excursions from the dock, Nonantum can be counted on for kids' activities, a pool, good breakfasts, well-trained staff, and comfortable rooms, many with river views. It's an easy walk to the shops and other restaurants, too, and hosts events like Ballroom Dance Weekend and a Halloween Bash. It's owned by Mainers. $209–309, with reduced rates off-season.

Cape Arundel Inn (207-967-2125; cape arundelinn.com), 208 Ocean Ave., P.O. Box 530A. Open mid-Feb.–New Year's Eve. The most dramatic location in town, facing the open ocean with just the estate of former president George H. W. Bush interrupting the view. Rich Malconian bought this inn in 2011. Seven rooms in the main house and six in an addition as well as a carriage house make up the accommodations; those in the addition all have picture windows and a deck facing the water, parking in back, and TV. The carriage house water-view suite (up a flight of stairs) has a deck and sitting area. Interesting art hangs in the living room, some of it by Jack

THE SUNROOM AT THE CAPTAIN JEFFERDS INN, WHERE A CUP OF COFFEE OR TEA IS ALWAYS AVAILABLE

Nahil, the inn's previous owner. The dining room, which is open to the public for dinner (see *Dining Out*), is deservedly well loved. $320–425 in-season, from $135 off-season, includes a continental breakfast.

🐾 ♂ **The Captain Jefferds Inn** (207-967-2311 or 1-800-839-6844; captainjefferdsinn.com), 5 Pearl St., Box 691. Erik and Sarah Lindblom are your hosts at this handsome Federal-era mansion with 16 rooms; nine have a gas fireplace, and all have air-conditioning, feather beds, and down comforters. Baxter, in the carriage house, is decorated in a "Maine camp" style—except for the two-person whirlpool with a round stone surround. First-floor Chatham has a four-poster and two wingback chairs by the fireplace. The spacious common rooms include a sunporch where tea and coffee are always available. $149–379, depending on season.

♂ **Maine Stay Inn and Cottages** (207-967-2117 or 1-800-950-2117; mainestayinn.com), 34 Maine St., Box 1800A. Open year-round. The inn offers six guest rooms in the main house and 11 suites in five cottages nestled in nicely landscaped grounds. The house was built in 1860 by Melville Walker and given to his wife as a Christmas present five years later. The cottages are simple on the outside but handsomely outfitted inside with efficiency kitchens, deep whirlpool tubs, and some with gas fireplaces. A breakfast, perhaps baked eggs with cheddar and Parmesan, and afternoon tea are offered by friendly owners Judi and Walter Hauer, who bought the inn in 2008. $229–379 in-season, $129–279 off-season.

Tides Beach Club (207-967-3757; tidesbeachclubmaine.com), 254 Kings Hwy., Goose Rocks Beach. Open late May–Oct. Twenty-one renovated rooms, some overlooking Goose Rocks Beach, are painted in pastels and outfitted with comfortable beds and high-tech amenities. Fans of the previous owners' Tides-Inn-By-the-Sea will be in for a shock because the Victoriana has vanished, traded in for cool colors and modern graphic prints. Fans of contemporary style will be thrilled. The beach across the narrow road remains its eternal self, a wide sweep of white sand banded by a ribbon of dunes. Rates $399–829 in-season.

♂ ♂ **Seaside Inn** (207-967-4461; kennebunkbeach.com), 80 Beach Ave., Kennebunk 04043. Open year-round. A modern

22-room inn set on a quiet stretch of one of Maine's best public beaches, it is the only one in the area directly on the ocean. This property has been in the Gooch-Severance family for nine generations, beginning in the 1640s when King Charles II conveyed the land to John Gooch, who ferried folks across the river. All of that seems to make this the oldest inn in the country—and the history is detailed on the website. The cheery breakfast room is an 1850 former boathouse for the 19th-century inn that stood here until the 1950s. Inn rooms feature two queen beds, air-conditioning, cable TV, phone, mini fridge, and balcony or patio. Three-day minimum in oceanfront rooms in high season. $105–259 per night, including extended continental breakfast and access to a local fitness center.

Bufflehead Cove Inn (207-967-3879; buffleheadcove.com), Box 499, off Rt. 35. Open May–Nov. This hidden gem, sequestered on 6 acres at the end of a dirt road and overlooking an 8-foot-deep tidal cove, sits a mile from the village of Kennebunkport. Harriet Gott, a native of nearby Cape Porpoise, her husband Jim, and their son Erin offer four good-looking guest rooms, a suite, and a separate deluxe cottage. River View cottage lies off by itself with a deck, kitchen, wood-burning fireplace, and whirlpool tub. The inn's living room has a hearth and deep window seats. $155–395 includes a full breakfast on the white porch if the weather is fine, and afternoon wine and cheese.

✦ ♿ **Kennebunkport Inn** (207-967-2621 or 1-800-248-2621; kennebunkportinn.com), 1 Dock Square, P.O. Box 111. Open year-round. Owners Debbie Lennon and Tom Nill have redecorated the 50 rooms; Number 303 is a "mansion room" with canopy four-poster, gas fireplace, and bathtub. The inn has four sections—the main house (originally an 1890s mansion), a 1980s Federal-style addition, a 1930s river house with smaller rooms, and the Wharfside, with 14 rooms including three family suites. In summer a small, enticing pool on the terrace offers respite from the Dock Square hubbub, and guests can dine in **One Dock** year-round. The cocktail lounge with a huge old bar offers evening piano music. High-season rates $205–349 per room, less off-season.

The Captain Fairfield Inn (207-967-4454 or 1-800-322-1928; captainfairfield.com), P.O.

Box 3089, corner of Pleasant and Green Sts. Open year-round. Owners Rob and Leigh Blood bought the inn in 2004, adding a wine list and small plates to serve guests afternoon or evening. Homemade cookies, included, are served in the afternoon, and the three-course breakfast features local ingredients. The lawn with two "fire tables" stretches back across the width of the block. Notable among the nine handsome rooms, the Library features a private porch and garden and double whirlpool; Sweet Liberty has a tiled rainfall shower; and the Breakwater Room is contemporary. $259–409 in high season, $159–300 in low.

Lower priced: ✦ ♣ ✦ ♿ **The Edgewater Inn** (207-967-3315; edgewaterinnmaine .com), 126 Ocean Ave., P.O. Box 2578. Open Apr.–Dec. A friendly little hotel with a casual atmosphere, owned and run by Peter Ciriello and Caroline Neish, The Edgewater Inn has 12 small but pleasant rooms and Coveside Cottage for rent; some also have a refrigerator and a fireplace. Portland Head, with oak furniture, shares a deck on the inlet on the inn's west side, where herons and other waterbirds find their own breakfast. In-season $259–309 for a double, cottage higher, includes a fantastic full breakfast and afternoon refreshments.

Chetwynd House Inn (207-967-2235; chetwyndhouse.com), 4 Chestnut St., P.O. Box 130. Open year-round. In 1972 Susan Chetwynd opened Chetwynd, Kennebunkport's first B&B. Now owned by Robert Knowles, her son, it remains a gracious 1840s home near Dock Square. The four antiques-furnished guest rooms have private bath, TV, refrigerator, and air-conditioning; a top-floor junior suite has skylights and a river view. Generous breakfasts—with eggs cooked to order and a quarter melon with peaches, blueberries, and bananas or other fruit—are served family-style at the dining room table. $269–299 in-season.

Harbor Inn (207-967-2074; harborinn kennebunkport.com), 90 Ocean Ave., P.O. Box 538A. Open year-round. Kathy and Barry Jones, longtime area residents, fill this fine old house with flowers and their warm friendliness. The five rooms and two-room suite (all with private bath) feature a mix of family antiques, paintings, and prints, and the long front porch is lined with wicker. It's a short walk to the ocean, a longer but pleasant walk to Dock Square. $155–225 for rooms in-season,

$125 off-season. Woodbine Cottage in-season is $225 a night or $1,500 weekly.

The Waldo Emerson Inn (207-985-4250 or 1-877-521-8776; waldoemersoninn.com), 108 Summer St. (Rt. 35), Kennebunk 04043. This special house was built in 1784 by a shipbuilder who inherited the land and original 1753 cottage (the present kitchen) from Waldo Emerson, the great-uncle of the famous poet and essayist. The building was later a stop on the Underground Railroad. The inn has four cozy guest rooms with private bath and air-conditioning, each with a wood-burning fireplace. A quilt store is on the property, and the Wedding Cake House is next door. $165–185 high season per couple includes a full gourmet breakfast and afternoon tea in one of the two handsome 18th-century parlors (one with a large-screen TV). Complimentary beach parking and bikes.

OTHER LODGING **The Franciscan Guest House** (207-967-4865; franciscanguesthouse.com), 26 Beach Ave., Kennebunk 04043. Open mid-Mar.–mid-Dec. With private bath, air-conditioning, and television, the 65 rooms here have the feeling of Maine the way it used to be. This 1908 estate on the Kennebunk River was converted to a guest house in the 1960s; the friars live in the Tudor great house. The 44-acre garden is open to the public year-round during daylight hours (no pets), and walking the riverside trails might take half an hour, past formal gardens and the Stations of the Cross, Our Lady of Lourdes, and other shrines and fountains. Maps of the trees and shrubs planted under Frederick Law Olmsted's design, and of the shrines, are available. $69–199; less off-season, with breakfast often made by the Lithuanian cook—a cross between a European and an American breakfast that might include homemade farmer's cheese, raisin bread, carrot bread, and potato bread. A moderately priced buffet dinner is served most nights in the height of summer.

🐾 🐱 ✒ ♿ **Yachtsman Lodge and Marina** (207-967-2511; yachtsmanlodge.com), Ocean Ave., P.O. Box 560C. Open May–early Dec. This 30-room inn is great for the cruising crowd, who can sail right up the Kennebunk River to the lodge and take advantage of its 59-slip marina. The Yachtsman features rooms decorated to resemble the inside of a yacht, with private riverside patios. $179–399 includes continental breakfast in the marble-tiled breakfast room or under the pergola. Children and pets are OK, and wheelchair access is easy. Bicycles and canoes are available for guests.

❋ Where to Eat

DINING OUT ✪ **Ocean** (207-967-2125; capearundelinn.com), Ocean Ave., Kennebunkport. Open daily mid-Feb.–Dec. for dinner, closed Mon. off-season. This dining room, matching its great location facing the ocean, presents skilled cooking and fine service. Chef Pierre Gignac once ran his own restaurant, 98 Province, in Ogunquit, which was excellent, and continues his fine work in Ocean with an emphasis on classic French cuisine. Duck Magret a l'orange cannot, perhaps, be improved on; monkfish gigot comes with tomato beignets. $31–37.

✪ ♿ **Pier 77** (207-967-8500; pier77 restaurant.com), Pier Rd., Cape Porpoise. Open daily for lunch and dinner June–Sept.; Wed.–Sun., St. Patrick's Day–May and Columbus Day–Dec.; The Ramp is open 11:30–9 Wed.–Sun. Well-made dinners upstairs and lunches downstairs in the **Ramp**, a bar filled with sports memorabilia, deserve the big following they've earned. Duck cassoulet, chicken and dumplings, and seafood stew were on a fall menu, and pulled pork sandwiches or fried clams—perhaps dug by the man you spotted on the

Nancy English

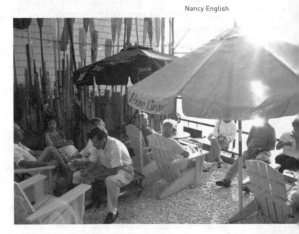

THE RAMP AT PIER 77

flats as you came inside—might be for lunch. Entrées $17–30.

White Barn Inn (207-967-2321; whitebarn inn.com), 37 Beach Ave., Kennebunkport. Open for dinner year-round Mon.–Sat. (except Jan.), daily in summer. Reservations required with credit card; $25 per-person fee charged if canceled less than 24 hours in advance. This award-winning restaurant is set in two restored 19th-century barns with a three-story glassed rear wall, exposed beams, and extravagant seasonal floral displays. Original art, hotel silver, and fine linens are accessories to extraordinary meals. The four-course prix fixe menu changes frequently, but count on lobster among the entrées and foie gras to start. $109 prix fixe plus tax, beverage, and gratuity. The bistro menu offers à la carte dishes.

On the Marsh Bistro (207-967-2299; onthemarsh.com), Rt. 9, Kennebunk Lower Village. Open daily for dinner May–Oct.; closed Mon. and Tue. off-season. Continental dining with style overlooking a lovely salt marsh. Executive chef Jeff Savage takes pride in his high-quality ingredients. Grilled bison New York strip sirloin with chive popovers and seared scallops with lobster risotto were on a fall menu, when the bar menu listed house creton (a French Canadian pork spread) and a meatball sub. The wines are wonderful, with hundreds to choose from. Entrées $21–37.

Tides Beach Club (207-967-3757; tides beachclubmaine.com), Goose Rocks Beach, 6 miles northeast of Dock Square. Open late May–Oct. 1 for lunch. Under new ownership and with completely new decor, Tides Beach Club serves signature cocktails alongside its raw oysters; you might also try steamed mussels with tomato, citrus, and saffron. Of course you can also get a lobster, or a steak, or a steak with lobster. Entrées $19–42.

Salt & Honey (207-204-0195; thesaltand honey.com), 24 Ocean Ave., Kennebunkport. Jackson Yordeon started serving lobster omelets, huevos rancheros, and braised short rib hash for breakfast, a steak sandwich for lunch, and IPA-beer-battered chicken apps and fish-and-chips for dinner in 2015. The large portions are popular and the good drinks too. Entrées $15–24.

  ♿ **Bandaloop** (207-967-4994; bandaloop .biz), 2 Dock Square. Open daily for dinner in summer, less often in winter. Entrées and

sauces can be paired as you like, but the menu always offers several entrées and specials. Seared scallops with pistachio-cilantro pesto might appeal more than the fantastic mac-and-cheese (half portion is still large); a rack of lamb with buttermilk sweet potato mash hit the spot one fall. Desserts like dark chocolate torte or fruit crisp deserve to be enjoyed. Entrées $17–31.

Earth (207-967-6550; earthathiddenpond .com), 354 Goose Rocks Rd. Open to the public for dinner only. Local ingredients, of course. Herb-infused cocktails are served in this space mixing rustic earthiness and high style. Outdoor dining in good weather, and outdoor bonfires to keep you there after sunset. Duck breast with lily buds, swordfish with bacon and corn, a burger, and snacks of house pickle "relishes" appeared on one menu. Entrées $18–38.

50 Local (207-985-0850; localkennebunk .com), 50 Main St., Kennebunk. For anyone hungry for something grown nearby, this is the place; anyone else who simply likes to dine well will be equally satisfied. Try mussels, Taunton Bay oysters, and lobster spring rolls to start; steak frites, fish stew, and vegan noodle bowl are some entrée possibilities. Entrées $14–29.

  ♿ **Academe at the Kennebunk Inn** (207-985-3351; thekennebunkinn.com), 45 Main St., Kennebunk. Open Wed.–Sat. for dinner; daily for the more informal tavern menu, lunch on weekdays. Chef-owners Brian O'Hea and Shanna Horner O'Hea make high-quality meals at a moderate price. Braised beef short rib with garlic and Parmesan tater tots, or the famous lobster potpie were on a fall menu. Entrées $11–35.

  ♿ **Stripers Waterside Restaurant** (207-967-3625; stripersrestaurant.com), 131–133 Ocean Ave., Kennebunkport. Open in-season daily for lunch and dinner. This upscale seafood place has a long, thin aquarium harboring little blue fish that match pale blue slipcovered chairs. But the real view is out the window where the river flows by. Pork porterhouse with onion jam and yellowfin tuna with grilled squash and poached lobster were on one menu. Entrées $20–34.

One Dock Prime (1-800-248-2621; kennebunkportinn.com), One Dock Square, Kennebunkport. Steaks are a specialty, but you will likely also find swordfish, pork chops, and sea scallops. Entrées $21–38.

LOBSTER

✪ ✿ ♿ **Nunan's Lobster Hut** (207-967-4362), Rt. 9, Cape Porpoise. Open for dinner weekends in May and then daily June–mid-Oct. A long telescope of a building full of old benches, with buoys hanging from the rafters, Nunan's has been feeding lobster lovers since 1953, when Bertha Nunan started working here. Her two sons and their wives are in charge, with decades of experience to guide them. The place can fill up by 5:15; people outside get a number and wait for a table. A 1½-pound lobster comes with melted butter, potato chips, a roll, and pickles. Grilled cheese and a hamburger supply other tastes, and pie, brownies, and cheesecake are on the dessert list. Beer and wine. No credit cards.

✿ **Mabel's Lobster Claw** (207-967-2562), Ocean Ave., Kennebunkport. Open Apr.–early Nov., daily for lunch and dinner. An informal favorite with locals, including former President Bush. Reservations recommended for dinner. Specialties include stuffed lobster Savannah, lobster stew, and shore dinner (clam chowder, lobster, and steamed clams). The lunch special is a lobster roll in a buttery, grilled hot-dog roll, and the mussels marinara is great anytime. Entrées $13–30.

✿ ♿ **The Clam Shack** (207-967-3321 or 207-967-2560), Kennebunkport (at the bridge). Clams, lobsters, and fresh fish. A year-round seafood market and Mother's Day–Columbus Day takeout stand that's worth the wait. Other seafood markets include **Cape Porpoise Lobster Co.** (207-967-4268) in Cape Porpoise, where the locals get their fish and steamed lobster to go, and **Port Lobster** (207-967-2081), 122 Ocean Ave., Kennebunkport, which offers live or cooked lobsters packed to travel or ship, and lobster, shrimp, and crab rolls to go (several obvious waterside picnic spots are within walking distance). Other local businesses get their picked lobster here; it won't be fresher anywhere else.

Nancy English

THE CLAM SHACK

EATING OUT Old Vines (207-967-2310; old vineswinebar.com), 173 Port Rd., Kennebunk. Open Wed.–Mon. from 5. A popular wine bar that opened in 2009, Old Vines serves snacks and small plates with its glasses of wine from featured vineyards. More than 20 are sold by the glass; try the Noemus Rioja from Spain or Château Bousquette, a sparkling rosé from France. Small plates of spiced almonds, cheeses, and cured meats might be the start of a delicious meal centered on a soppressata panini or quiche of the day. $6–21.

🐾 🍴 **The Wayfarer** (207-967-8961; wayfarercapeporpoise.com), 1 Pier Rd., Cape Porpoise. Open Tue.–Sat. for breakfast, lunch until 2; Sun. breakfast–noon. Closed Mon. New England cuisine with a twist—mac and cheese, arugula salad, lobster fettuccine, and meat loaf vie for attention. BYOB.

🐾 🍴 **Alisson's** (207-967-4841; alissons .com), 5 Dock Square, Kennebunkport. Open at 11 for lunch and 5 for dinner. Casual dining in this busy, family-run spot features standards with occasional outstanding twists, like the Dee Dee Burger with blue cheese. Count on reliably good casual food. Entrées $8–22.

🐾 🍴 ♿ **Federal Jack's Restaurant & Brewpub** (207-967-4322; federaljacks.com), 8 Western Ave., Kennebunk Lower Village. Open from 11:30 for lunch and dinner, offering a variety of handcrafted ales. This is the original Shipyard Ale brewery with parking right in the thick of things. The spacious and sunny restaurant is upstairs, with a seasonal terrace dining on the river. Try the Blue Fin stout with Captain Jack's Feast—chowder, lobster, and mussels. Live acoustic music on weekends. The pub fare is the best way to go.

Cape Porpoise Kitchen (207-967-1150; capeporpoisekitchen.com), 1 Mills Rd., Cape Porpoise. Open year-round. Take-out and catering are the focus, and this is the right place to go for a fabulous BLT or many other delicious sandwiches, salads, and baked goods for a picnic on the beach. Wine, beer, cheese, and gifts, with a small seating area if the weather is bad. No restroom.

ICE CREAM **Rococo Artisan Ice Cream** (207-251-6866; rococoicecream.com), 6 Spring St., Kennebunkport. Open May–Oct. Based on Argentinian ideas about gelato and dairy, Rococo Ice Cream puts the flavors up front and never stops inventing them. Blue Fin Stout, Blueberry Chipotle, and Goat Cheese with Honey and Fig give you an idea—but the proof is in the eating.

✳ Entertainment

🍴 **Arundel Barn Playhouse** (207-985-5552; arundelbarnplayhouse.com), 53 Old Post Rd. (just off Rt. 1), Arundel. Opened in 1998 in a revamped 1800s barn, this is a thoroughly professional, classic summer theater with performances June–Labor Day: Tue.–Sat., some Sundays; matinees Wednesdays and some Fridays. Tickets $28–39.

🍴 **Hackmatack Playhouse** (207-698-1807; hackmatack.org), 538 Rt. 9, Beaver Dam, Berwick. Local actors, rave reviews.

🍴 **River Tree Center for the Arts** (207-967-9120; rivertreearts.org), 35 Western Ave., Kennebunk. Encompassing the Chappell School of Music and the Irvine Gallery and School of Art, this multifaceted organization stages local concerts, productions, and happenings, as well as workshops in the visual and performing arts for all ages.

Also see **Federal Jack's** under *Eating Out* and *Entertainment* in "Ogunquit and Wells."

✳ Selective Shopping

ANTIQUES SHOPS The Kennebunks are known as an antiques center, with half a dozen shops, most on Rt. 1, representing a number of dealers. One on Rt. 9 that's sure to offer endless interest is **Antiques on Nine** (207-967-0626), 81 Western Ave., Kennebunk, overflowing with things strange and wonderful.

ART GALLERIES You'll find some 50 galleries, many seasonal; **Mast Cove Galleries** (207-967-3453) on Maine St., Kennebunkport, is touted as the largest gallery in Maine, with more than 100 artists represented. Pick up a free copy of the annual *Guide to Fine Art, Studios, and Galleries*, published by the Art Guild of the Kennebunks (207-324-4912) and available at the chamber of commerce and most galleries.

FARMS 🍴 **Harris Farm** (207-499-2678; harrisfarm.com), Buzzell Rd., Dayton. July–Oct. Fresh milk, eggs, produce, and maple syrup are sold. Pick-your-own pumpkins on the last Sunday in Sept. and the first two Sundays in Oct., with hayrides offered to the pumpkin patch. A half-hour ride through beautiful, wooded forest and farms, this farm is 1 mile down Buzzell Rd. from Rt. 35.

Blackrock Farm (207-967-5783; black rockfarm.net), 293 Goose Rocks Rd.,

Kennebunkport. A beautifully planted perennial garden and nursery with unusual plants and trees, as well as a pick-your-own raspberry patch. Bring a picnic and feast your eyes on the stone walls, grape arbor, and sculpture.

SPAS **The Breakwater Inn & Spa** (207-967-5333; thebreakwaterinn.com), 127 Ocean Ave., P.O. Box 560C, Kennebunkport. Full-service spa with massage, facials, body wraps, steam room, and fitness center. All facilities are open to the public.

Cottage Breeze Day Spa & Boutique (207-967-2259; cottagebreeze.com), 31 Western Ave., Kennebunk. Full-service spa. With any luck Judy will be your massage therapist, and what fine therapy it will be. Utterly comfortable treatment rooms and an array of body products.

SPECIAL SHOPS **Farm + Table** (207-604-8029; farmtablekennebunkport.com), 8 Langsford Road. A quick right turn at Cape Porpoise Kitchen brings you to a gorgeous red barn, elegantly outfitted with the home goods that furnish the serene refuge you plan on living in very soon.

KBC Coffee & Drygoods (207-967-1261; federaljacks.com), 8 Western Ave., Kennebunkport. Hidden beneath Federal Jack's, this is a source of Kennebunk Brewing Company ales (bottled or in a returnable "Growler") and brew gear as well as souvenir clothing and gifts; also good for cappuccino and homemade fudge.

Hearth and Soul (207-985-7466; hearthandsoulme.com), 35 Main St., Kennebunk. Open Tue.–Sat. "Primarily Primitives" is the motto at this quirky, charming place. Braided rugs, furniture, a folk art wall mural, and bricks of milk paint.

Daytrip Society (207-967-4440; daytripsociety.com), 4 Dock Square, Kennebunkport. Essentials and fripperies in good taste, from Pendleton blankets and good Thermoses to old books and new cards. Around the corner, ✐ **Daytrip Jr.** (207-967-8345; daytripjr.com), 9 Ocean Ave., sells fine toys and games, some perfect for a long drive.

✳ Special Events

Many of the events below are listed with the Kennebunk/Kennebunkport Chamber of Commerce (207-967-0857 or 1-800-982-4421; visitthekennebunks.com), P.O. Box 740, Kennebunkport 04043.

February: **Winter Carnival Weekend** with hay- and sleigh rides in Kennebunk. Weekend **"February Is for Lovers"** events (207-967-0857).

May: **May Day Festival** on Main Street, Kennebunk.

Summer: **Farmers' Market** (kennebunkfarmersmarket.org) during the growing season.

June: **The Kennebunkport Festival**, with food, wine, and works of art.

July: Old-fashioned **July 4** picnic, fireworks, and band concert.

August: **Riverfest** (first Saturday).

September: **Harvest Fest**—parades, music, and good food.

October: **Presidential Road Race** (presidentialroadrace.com).

November: **Holiday Auction. Holiday Presents Weekend**.

December: **Christmas Prelude** (first full and second weekends)—Dock Square is decked out for Yuletide and there are champagne receptions, church suppers, concerts, carols, holiday fairs, and house tours.

OLD ORCHARD BEACH, SACO, AND BIDDEFORD

Old Orchard's name stems from an apple orchard, one of the first in Maine, planted in 1657 by pioneer settler Thomas Rogers. It was also one the first Maine towns to prosper by catering to tourists.

In 1837 a canny local farmer, Ebenezer C. Staples, recognized the region's summer playground potential. Initially taking in boarders on his farm for $1.50 a week, he later opened the first hotel, the still-operating Old Orchard Beach Inn. Staples's instincts proved right: The new railroads soon brought a wave of tourists from both the United States and Canada to frolic on Old Orchard's superb 7-mile-long white-sand beach. Thanks to the Grand Trunk Railroad, Old Orchard became the closest ocean beach resort to Montreal. The area, which has a large Franco-American population, is still a popular destination for French Canadian visitors, especially when the exchange rate is in their favor.

When the first pier at Old Orchard Beach was built in 1898, it stood 20 feet above and 1,800 feet out over the water and was constructed entirely of steel. The pavilions housed animals, a casino, and a restaurant. In the decades that followed, the original pier was rebuilt many times after being damaged by fire and storms, until a wider and shorter wooden pier was built in 1980.

Nancy English

THE PIER AT OLD ORCHARD BEACH

An amusement area appeared in 1902 and grew after World War I. The 1920s brought big-name bands such as those led by Guy Lombardo and Duke Ellington to the Pier Casino, and thousands danced under a revolving crystal ball.

Fire, hard economic times, and the decline of the railroad and steamboat industries all took their toll on Old Orchard Beach over the years, but then a major revitalization plan widened sidewalks, added benches and streetlights, and passed and enforced ordinances that prevent "cruising." For families, it can't be beat, with the beach, amusement park rides, mini golf just down the road, and reasonable lodging rates.

The area is also well known for the camp meetings that began in the mid-1800s, first by Methodists, then by Baptists and the Salvation Army. These meetings continue throughout the summer in the Ocean Park community today.

Biddeford and Saco, separated by the Saco River, are often called "the twin cities."

Although it also includes the stately old seaside resort village of Biddeford Pool, the city of Biddeford is essentially a classic mill town with a strong French Canadian heritage and mammoth 19th-century brick textile mills that have largely stood idle since the 1950s. Those buildings along the Saco River, long victims of desuetude, have been revitalized—at first slowly, but rapidly in recent years—by housing, businesses, and restaurants. Run of the Mill, a brew pub with good food and a terrific terrace, was one of the first on the Saco side; in Biddeford, Lincoln Mill Hotel, led by Tim Harrington, who owns much of the Kennebunks' upscale lodgings, is scheduled to open in 2017. North Dam Mill now holds nearly 120 businesses that include Portland Pie and an auction house as well as light manufacturing such as HyperLite Moutain Gear and a clothier named Suger. Saco Island Mills feature a year-round farmers'/artisans' market, as well as public services like lawyers and Social Security administration. Saco is home to Maine's first green train station, where Amtrak stops five times daily on its way to and from Boston year-round.

GUIDANCE **Old Orchard Beach Chamber of Commerce** (207-934-2500; to get a free vacation planner by mail, 1-800-365-9386; oldorchardbeachmaine.com), P.O. Box 600 (1st St.), Old Orchard Beach 04064, maintains a year-round walk-in information center (open 8:30–4:30 weekdays, also Sat. and Sun., June–Aug.) and offers help with reservations.

Biddeford+Saco Chamber of Commerce & Industry (207-282-1567; biddefordsaco chamber.org), 28 Water St., Suite 1, Biddeford 04005, stocks many local brochures at its Welcome Center. Hours are 8–4:30 weekdays year-round and 8–noon on weekends June 15–Sept. 15; helpful, friendly staff.

GETTING THERE *By air:* **Portland International Jetport** is 13 miles north, and rental cars are available at the airport. You can also fly your own plane into **Sanford Airport**.

By hired car: **Maine Limousine Service** (207-883-0222 or 1-800-646-0068; mainelimo .com), P.O. Box 1478, Scarborough 04070, can also pick you up and bring you to the region.

By car: Exits 32, 36, and 42 off the Maine Turnpike (I-95) take you easily to Rt. 9 and the center of Old Orchard Beach and Main St. in Biddeford and Saco. You can also find the towns from Rt. 1.

By train: **The Downeaster** (1-800-USA-RAIL; amtrak.com), Amtrak's train service between Boston and Freeport, makes five stops a day year-round at Saco and seasonally, May–Oct., at Old Orchard Beach.

GETTING AROUND From many accommodations in Old Orchard Beach, you are close enough to walk to the pier, the town's center of activity. **Shuttle Bus**, the local transportation service, connects the downtowns of Biddeford, Saco, Portland, and Old Orchard Beach. Call 207-282-5408 or go to shuttlebus-zoom.com for schedules.

MUST SEE

Saco Museum (207-283-3861; sacomuseum.org), 371 Main St., Saco. Open year-round Tue., Wed., Thu. noon–4; Fri. noon–8; Sat. 10–4; Sun. noon–4 June–Dec. 15. $5 adults, $3 seniors, $2 students, under 6 free (free to all 4–8 Fri.). Larger than it looks from the outside and very well maintained and organized. An exhibit about art and industry fills the first floor, and one room presenting a factory girl bedchamber is furnished with the artifacts of a millworker—including a racy novel. A dress-up trunk allows visitors to try on mid-1800s fashion. Original paintings include 13 portraits by deaf painter John Brewster Jr.—whose subjects seem tenacious and inured to suffering—as well as furniture, tools, and natural history specimens. Lectures and special exhibits. The institute's **Dyer Library** next door has an outstanding Maine history collection.

PARKING There are a number of privately owned lots in the center of Old Orchard Beach and one municipal lot. Most charge $5–15 for any length of time—10 minutes or all day. There are meters on the street if you don't mind circling a few times to catch an available one, but at 15 minutes for a quarter, you're better off in lots if you plan to stay long.

WHEN TO COME Biddeford is especially worth visiting during La Kermesse, the colorful four-day Franco-American festival in late June. This festival—which features a colorful parade (some marching bands wear snowshoes), concerts, dances, fireworks, and public suppers with traditional stick-to-the-ribs French Canadian food—is one of the largest ethnic events in New England. Old Orchard Beach quiets way down after Columbus Day, but there are still many places to stay and four year-round restaurants for off-season visitors. The pier closes after Columbus Day weekend.

✳ Villages

Ocean Park is a historic community founded in 1881 by Free Will Baptists and well known for its outstanding religious, educational, and cultural programs. The Ocean Park Association (207-934-9068; oceanpark.org) sponsors lectures, concerts, movies, and other events throughout the summer in the cluster of old buildings known as Temple Square. Within the community you'll also find a recreation hall, shuffleboard and tennis courts, and an old-fashioned ice cream parlor. The entire community is a state game preserve, and you can find great walking trails through cathedral pines.

Pine Point. This quiet and less crowded end of the beach offers a selection of gift shops, restaurants, and lobster pounds.

Camp Ellis. At the end of a peninsula where the Saco River blends with the ocean. Residents fight a constant battle with beach erosion, and some of the homes are ever

Nancy English

FISHING THE CAMP ELLIS BREAKWATER

closer to the shore. Fishing trips, whale-watching, a long breakwater great for walking, interesting shops, and a couple of restaurants.

Biddeford Pool. A small yachting port with lots of low-key charm where well-to-do families have been summering in the same big old shingled houses for generations. You'll find a few shops, a lobster pound, and a small restaurant, but not much else. Although politically part of blue-collar Biddeford, "the pool" is socially closer to fashionable nearby Kennebunkport.

✳ To Do

APPLE PICKING ✄ **Snell Family Farm** (207-929-6166; snellfamilyfarm.com), 1000 River Rd. (Rt. 112), Buxton. Pick-your-own apples in Sept. and Oct., when the farm stand moves from its summer spot across the street over toward the farmhouse, and the greenhouse is jammed with pumpkins ready for carving. In summer and fall the farm stand is stuffed with the best produce imaginable.

FOR FAMILIES The Rt. 1 strip in Saco and nearby Old Orchard Beach makes up Maine's biggest concentration of "family attractions." Kids go wild. Parents fear they may go broke.

✄ **Funtown/Splashtown USA** (207-284-5139; funtownsplashtownusa.com), Rt. 1, Saco. Open daily (depending on the weather) mid-June–Labor Day, weekends in spring and fall. Water activities and a large amusement park. In addition to the 100-foot wooden roller coaster Excalibur, the park has bumper cars, New England's largest log flume, plenty of carnival rides, a hydrofighter, kiddie rides, and antique cars. Purchase discount tickets at the Biddeford+Saco Chamber Welcome Center.

✄ **Aquaboggan Water Park** (207-282-3112; aquaboggan.com), Rt. 1, Saco. Open mid-June–Labor Day. Several water slides, including a high-thrills slide with a choice of mats or tubes, Aquasaucer, swimming pool, bumper boats, mini golf, arcade, shuffleboard, toddler area, and wave pool.

✄ **Monkey Trunks** (603-452-8812; monkeytrunks.com), 1 Cascade Rd., Saco. A high-ropes-and-ziplines park that opened in the summer of 2011, Monkey Trunks was an immediate hit. A giant swing, a 50-foot leap, and more for $39–49, depending on height.

✄ **Pirate's Cove Adventure Golf** (207-934-5086; piratescove.net), 70 1st St., Old Orchard Beach. Two 18-hole up-and-down mini golf courses, waterfalls, ponds.

✄ **Palace Playland** (207-934-2001; palaceplayland.com), 1 Old Orchard St., Old Orchard Beach. Open daily June–Labor Day; arcade open through Columbus Day on weekends. For more than 60 years fun seekers have been wheeled, lifted, shaken, spun, and bumped in Palace Playland rides. There's a carousel (though it no longer contains the original 1906 horses), a Ferris wheel, a 60-foot-high (Maine's largest) water slide, and a roller coaster. You can pay by the ride or buy an all-day pass.

GOLF Dunegrass (207-934-4513; dunegrass.com), 200 Wild Dunes Way, Old Orchard Beach, 18 holes. **Biddeford-Saco Country Club** (207-282-5883), 101 Old Orchard Rd., Saco, 18 holes. **Deep Brook Golf Course** (207-282-3500; deepbrookgolfcourse.com), 36 New County Rd. (Rt. 5), Saco, nine holes. **Cascade Golf Center** (207-282-3524), 955 Portland Rd., Saco, driving range.

MUSEUMS Biddeford Mills Museum: (207-229-6387; biddefordmillsmuseum.org), 2 Main St., Suite 17-301G, Biddeford. Former mill workers lead reservation-only tours in the mill works and an underground canal. Daily tours run mid-June–mid-October from 10–noon. $10 donation.

EXCURSIONS

From Saco there's a loop that heads up Rt. 112, past the Way-Way General Store. On the right a few miles out is the Saco Heath Preserve, worth a stop to explore. From there, continue on Rt. 112 until it intersects with Rt. 202. Turn left and stay on 202 until you see the intersection with Rt. 5. Turn left again and follow Rt. 5 along the river, back to the center of Saco.

Harmon Historical Museum (207-934-9319; harmonmuseum.org), 4 Portland Ave., Old Orchard Beach, is open June–Sept., Tue.–Fri. 11–4, Sat. 9–noon; winter hours by appointment. Home of the Old Orchard Beach Historical Society, the building is full of exhibits from the town's past. Each year, in addition to the regular school, fire, and aviation exhibits, there is a special exhibit. Pick up the timeline of the area's history and the walking map of historic sites.

TENNIS The **Ocean Park Association** (207-934-9068; oceanpark.org) maintains public tennis courts, open to the public for a fee in summer.

✳ Green Space

BEACHES Obviously, **Old Orchard Beach** is the big draw in this area, with 7 miles of sand and plenty of space for sunbathing, swimming, volleyball, and other recreation.

Ferry Beach State Park is marked from Rt. 9 between Old Orchard Beach and Camp Ellis in Saco. The 100-plus-acre preserve includes 70 yards of sand, a boardwalk through the dunes, bike paths, nature trails, a picnic area with grills, lifeguards, changing rooms, and pit toilets. Even in the middle of summer it isn't terribly crowded here. $6 per nonresident, $1 ages 5–11, free under 5 or over 65 with identification. Off-season the Iron Ranger (a green pole with a green can beside the booth) collects reduced fees on the honor system.

Bay View Beach, at the end of Bay View Rd. near Ferry Beach, is 200 yards of mostly sandy beach; lifeguards, $2 per hour parking.

Camp Ellis Beach, Rt. 9, Saco. Some 2,000 feet of beach backed by cottages; also a long fishing pier and breakwater. The commercial parking lots fill quickly on sunny days.

Pine Point, off Rt. 9, Scarborough, has a small and uncrowded beach near the fisherman's co-op. The larger beach area, closer to Old Orchard, with snack bar, changing room, and bathrooms, charges fees in summer for parking in the adjacent lot.

HIKING Saco Bay Trails (sacobaytrails.org), P.O. Box 720, Saco 04072, publishes a trail guide for Saco, Biddeford, and Old Orchard Beach. Copies are sold for $10 in local shops and at the Biddeford+Saco Chamber of Commerce.

Saco Heath Preserve (nature.org), Rt. 112 (2 miles from I-95 Exit 36), Saco. This small Nature Conservancy preserve shouldn't be overlooked. The sign is hard to spot; look for it on the right a few miles out of Saco. A quiet, peaceful stroll through a peat bog on a mile-long wooden boardwalk and woodland trail through the 1,223-acre preserve brings visitors close to heathland plants like Labrador tea and sheep laurel. Atlantic white cedar nurtures rare-in-Maine Hessel's hairstreak butterflies.

East Point Sanctuary, off Rt. 9 (east of Goose Rocks Beach) in Biddeford Pool. A 30-acre Maine Audubon wildlife sanctuary well known to birders, who flock here during migrating seasons. Beautiful any time of year. From Rt. 9 turn right just beyond Goose Rocks Beach onto Fortune Rocks Beach Rd. to Lester B. Orcutt Blvd.; turn right, drive almost to the end, and look for a chain-link fence and AUDUBON sign. The trail continues along the golf course and sea.

LIGHTHOUSE TOUR **Wood Island Lighthouse** (207-286-3229; woodislandlighthouse .org), Biddeford Pool. Tours are offered by the Friends of Wood Island Lighthouse, departing from Vines Landing in Biddeford Pool; by phone reservation only. The tours last 1½ hours and are offered July and Aug.; donations of $10 encouraged. The 42-foot stone tower, attached keeper's house, and stone oil house can be entered on this 35-acre island where seabirds nest and others rest on their migrations. A half-mile boardwalk takes visitors from the boat landing to the lighthouse.

✳ Winter Sports

CROSS-COUNTRY SKIING ⚡ **Harris Farm Cross-Country Ski Center** (207-499-2678; harrisfarm.com), 280 Buzzell Rd., Dayton. Open daily 9 AM–dusk when there's snow. This 500-acre dairy and tree farm offers 40 kilometers of groomed trails, from easy to difficult, over hills, by ponds and streams, and through the woods. Rentals include snowshoes.

✳ Lodging

INNS AND B&BS **The Atlantic Birches Inn** (207-934-5295 or 1-888-934-5295; atlantic birches.com), 20 Portland Ave., Old Orchard Beach 04064. A Victorian, shingle-style home built in the area's heyday. Five guest rooms in the main house are named for former grand hotels; they're cheerful, with a mix of old and new furnishings. The in-ground pool is perfect on a hot day. $131–192 in high season includes continental breakfast with fresh muffins, fruit salad, and whole-grain bread.

⚡ **Old Orchard Beach Inn** (207-934-5834 or 1-877-700-6624; oldorchardbeachinn.com), 6 Portland Ave., Old Orchard Beach 04064. Ebenezer Staples's original hostelry, part of this inn dates from the 1730s, and the building is on the National Register of Historic Places as Maine's oldest continuously operated inn. All 18 rooms, one a two-bedroom suite, have air-conditioning, cable TV, and private bath. $125–450 high season, $89–225 off-season, with a continental breakfast that includes homemade muffins and breads.

The Nautilus by the Sea (1-800-981-7018; thenautilusatoceanpark.com), 2 Colby Ave., Ocean Park 04063. This 12-room B&B, built in 1890 as a private home, is smack up against the beach. Many rooms have beach or ocean views, with the most dramatic vista from the fourth-floor "penthouse suite," where at night you can watch the beam of Wood Island Light play across the water. Owners Jim and Charlotte Katz run this updated inn. $135-225 in-season, $105-190 off-season, with full breakfast.

OTHER LODGING **Aquarius Motel** (207-934-2626; aquariusmotel.com), 1 Brown St., Old Orchard Beach 04064. A small, family-owned and -operated 14-unit motel that's exceptionally clean and right on the beach. The patio is a great place to relax after a day of sightseeing. $159 for a double with kitchenette in-season. Family-sized units also available. Many special rates in early spring and late fall.

Ocean Walk Hotel (207-934-1716 or 1-800-992-3779; oceanwalkhotel.com), 197 E. Grand Ave., Old Orchard Beach 04064. Forty-four well-kept rooms, from studios to oceanfront suites. The top-floor rooms in one building have very high ceilings, giving them a light, airy, spacious feel. Indoor pool. $175–300 in-season, $75–200 off-season.

♿ **Sea View Motel** (207-934-4180 or 1-800-541-8439; seaviewgetaway.com), 65 W. Grand Ave., Old Orchard Beach 04064. Forty-nine rooms, some with ocean views. Pretty landscaping, with an outdoor pool and a beautiful fountain in front. The simple rooms, some with kitchenette, are modern, bright, and well maintained. $98–290 in-season, $57–125 off-season.

SEA VIEW MOTEL

* **The Gull Motel, Inn & Cottages** (207-934-4321; gullmotel.com), 89 W. Grand Ave., Old Orchard Beach 04064. An attractive motel with an outdoor pool, immaculate and family oriented. The inn is right on the beach, with a great porch. Cottages also available by the week. Inn rates $80–150 per night; motel rates $75–160; cottages $1,250 per week.

* & **Billowhouse** (207-934-2333 or 1-888-767-7776; billowhouse.com), 2 Temple Ave., Ocean Park 04063. This 1881 Victorian seaside guest house is Mary Kerrigan's retirement project, completely renovated yet with old-fashioned charm. There are three ground-level efficiency apartments and six kitchenette units in the adjoining motel. The four B&B units include a large three-room suite with private deck, in-room Jacuzzi, and full kitchen; a two-room suite with private deck and outside hot tub; two oceanfront rooms with private bath share a deck overlooking the ocean. $135–250 in-season, less for extended stays, breakfast included for B&B guests only; $95–155 off-season.

CAMPGROUNDS Camping is a budget-minded family's best bet in this area. There are at least a dozen campgrounds here (more than 4,000 sites in the area), many geared to families and offering games, recreational activities, and trolley service to the beach in-season.

Following are a few recommendations; check with the chamber for a full listing.

Silver Springs Campground and Cottages (207-283-3880; silverspringsmaine .com), 705 Portland Rd. (Rt. 1), Saco 04072. May–mid-Oct. Thirteen cottages and 130 sites (with full RV hookups) keep Mary Ann and Bryce Ingraham busy. "Most people who come, come back," Mary Ann said. The framework for the cottages is still from the 1930s, but inside and out they are new, with interiors finished with V-match pine boards and all new appliances. Two swimming pools and a rec hall. Camping sites $42–48, cottages $80–175 in-season. Discounts off-season.

* & **Bayley's Camping Resort** (207-883-6043; bayleys-camping.com), 52 Ross Rd., Scarborough 04074. Just down the road from Pine Point are paddleboats, a swimming pool, Jacuzzi, fishing, game room, special programs for children and adults—and a shuttle to take you to Pine Point Beach and Old Orchard's downtown. More than 400 sites and 50 rental trailers. $47–86 depending on hookups.

❂ * & **Powder Horn** (207-934-4733; maine campgrounds.com), P.O. Box 366, Old Orchard Beach 04064. A 450-site campground with plenty of recreation options—playgrounds, shuffleboard, horseshoes, volleyball, rec hall and game room, activities program, mini golf, and trolley service to the beach in-season. $50–65 per night in-season, $40–50 off-season. **Hidden Pines** is a sister campground next door with basic to premium sites.

✳ Where to Eat

DINING OUT & **Joseph's by the Sea** (207-934-5044; josephsbythesea.com), 55 W. Grand Ave., Old Orchard Beach. Open Apr.–Dec., hours vary. Dinners are still as polished and well made. Wonderful grilled steaks, seared scallops, and the popular Pasta Maison—Maine shrimp, scallops, salmon, and mussels on angel-hair pasta with real cream. For once the cream is light, enhancing and not overwhelming the seafood. Entrées $18–29.

Custom Deluxe (207-494-7110; facebook .com/CustomDeluxeMaine), 140 Main St., Biddeford. Open Tue.–Fri. 11–2 and 5-9:30, Sat. 5–9:30. Thomas Malz and Megan McVey opened this ambitious place in 2015; the French dishes fit right in with the mill town

RUN OF THE MILL

history. Moules Normandie—mussels cooked with cider and served with shoestring fries—and brisket with Montreal spice were on the first menu. Entrées $11–15.

Run of the Mill (207-571-9648; therunof themill.net), 100 Main St., Saco. This micro-brewery set on Saco Island in the Saco River has a fabulous outdoor deck in good weather and finely crafted ales and good food year-round. The hand-cut fries are memorable, and of course what could be better with "Basement Bitter"? Shepherd's pie and bangers and smash keep the UK close at hand. Entrées $9–20.

♪ **The Landmark** (207-934-0156; landmarkfinedining.com), 28 E. Grand Ave., Old Orchard Beach. Open at 5 for dinner Apr.–Dec.; daily June–Columbus Day; call for hours off-season. Fine dining in a 1910 Victorian house and on an outdoor terrace in fine weather. Menu specialties include a creamy lobster stew, garlicky pasta with mussels, lacquered duck, and barbecued ribs, all quite good. Entrées $18–27. Early-bird specials.

Bufflehead's (207-284-6000; buffleheads restaurant.com), 122 Hills Beach Rd., Bidd-eford. Open year-round, daily for lunch and dinner in summer; call for hours off-season. Offering indoor and outdoor seating with a terrific ocean view, this great family place makes quality food. Try the fried sole with Creole meunière sauce, or baked scallops. Entrées $11–28.

EATING OUT Los Tapatios Mexican Restaurant (207-602-6284), 11 Adams St., Bid-deford. Big plates of Mexican mainstays; the mole comes recommended, and the margari-tas are just as generously made. Friendly ser-vice and a dedication to pleasing you makes your visit feel delightful. Modest prices.

Huot's Restaurant (207-282-1642; huots seafoodrestaurant.com), Camp Ellis Beach, Saco. Open mid-Apr.–mid-Sept., Tue.–Sun. 11–9. The third generation of the Huot family is carrying on the tradition of good, fresh sea-food at this clean, simple spot in Camp Ellis, begun in 1935. Entrées $7–25.

Traditions (207-282-6661), 162 Main St., Saco. A cozy little restaurant specializing in pasta and traditional Italian meat and seafood dishes. Open for lunch and dinner. Entrées $8–16.

New Moon (207-282-2241; thenewmoon restaurant.com), 17 Pepperell Square. Cozy restaurant in Pepperell Square. Breakfast on the Irish Benedict with red flannel hash, and

LOBSTER

Lobster Claw (207-282-0040), 4 Ocean Park Rd. (Rt. 5), Saco. Lobsters cooked outside in giant kettles, stews and chowders, cozy dining room, and takeout available. Twin lobster specials, also steamers, fried seafood. Lobster packed to travel.

Goldthwaite's (207-284-5000; poollobster.com), 3 Lester B. Orcutt Blvd., Biddeford Pool, is good for a lobster roll or something else at the counter; enjoy your food at a picnic table in back near the water.

GOLDTHWAITE'S AT BIDDEFORD POOL

Nancy English

try baked stuffed lobster for dinner. Open 7:30 AM–2 PM daily, 5–9 Thu.–Sat.

Palace Diner (207-284-0015; palace dinerme.com), 18 Franklin St., Biddeford, was lionized by *Bon Appétit* magazine in 2014—the brown butter banana bread, Palais Royale burger, challah French toast, and excellent fries are all worth the national press they are getting. Open 8–2 daily.

Cole Road Café (207-283-4103; coleroad cafe.com), 1 Cole Rd., Biddeford. Open for breakfast and lunch Tue.–Sat. 7 AM–1 PM; breakfast only on Sun. starting at 8. Deservedly popular, this colorful, friendly place makes all the breakfast standards; specials might include blueberry-stuffed French toast with cream cheese. Joyce Rose has run Cole Road Café for 20 years. Breakfast $3–10.

Hanabi (207-284-5454; facebook.com/Saco .Hanabi), 15 Pepperell Square, Saco. Fine sushi and Korean entrées.

TAKE-OUT Near Old Orchard Beach's pier and on the main drag are an abundance of take-out stands and informal restaurants serving pizza, burgers, hot dogs, fried seafood, fried dough, pier fries, ice cream, and more. Our favorites are **Bill's** for pizza and **Lisa's** for pier fries.

Rapid Ray's (207-282-1847), 179 Main St., Saco. Open daily until around midnight. A local icon since 1953. Quick and friendly service from people who seem to know everyone who walks through the door. Burgers, hot dogs, lobster rolls, and the like at great prices.

✳ Entertainment

City Theater (207-282-0849; citytheater.org), Main St., Biddeford. This 500-seat, 1890s theater offers a series of live performances.

    Saco Drive-In (207-284-1016), Rt. 1, Saco. Double features in spring and summer.

✳ Selective Shopping

Cascade Flea Market, 885 Portland Rd. (Rt. 1), Saco. One of Maine's largest outdoor flea markets, open daily in summer.

    Stone Soup Artisans (207-283-4715; stonesoupartisans.com), 228 Main St., Saco. Quality crafts from more than 50 Maine artisans. Pottery and jewelry, all made in Maine.

    Saco Island Farmers' Market this year-round farmers'/artisans' market features organic meat and vegetables, handmade products, and live entertainment. Wed.–Sat. 7–noon, May–Oct.

✳ Special Events

January: **Annual Lobster Dip**—hundreds of participants dip into the chilly Atlantic to benefit Special Olympics of Maine in Old Orchard Beach.

    Late June: **La Kermesse**, Biddeford—parade, public suppers, dancing, and entertainment highlighting Franco-American culture and traditions. **Saco Sidewalk Arts Festival**, Saco.

    Early July: **Greek Heritage Festival**, St. Demetrius on Bradley St. in Saco.

    July 4th: **Community Parade** and art show in Ocean Park Square.

    Late July: The **Lobster Bowl Shriners Football Game** in Biddeford.

    June–Labor Day: **Fireworks** at the Old Orchard Beach square Thu. at 9:45 PM.

    August: **Ocean Park Festival of Lights** and **Salvation Army camp meetings** under the pavilion in Ocean Park. **Beach Olympics**—three days of competitions, music, displays, and presentations to benefit the Special Olympics of Maine. Annual **5K Race and Kids' Fun Run**, scholarship fund-raiser.

    September: **Annual Car Show**—with a car lineup and parade, Old Orchard Beach.

    October: **Saco HarvestFest**.

    December: **Celebrate the Season by the Sea**—a tree-lighting ceremony with horse-drawn hay-wagon rides, refreshments, a holiday bazaar, caroling, and a bonfire on the beach, in Old Orchard.

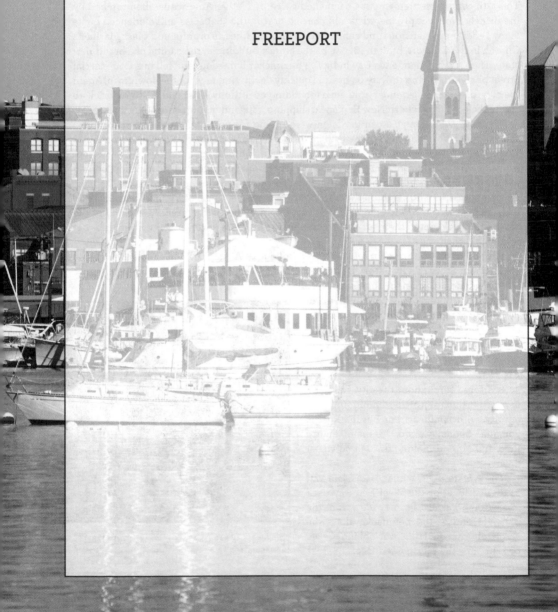

CASCO BAY

PORTLAND AREA

FREEPORT

PORTLAND AREA

L ively, walkable, and sophisticated, Maine's largest city is also a working port. Greater Portland accounts for one-quarter of Maine's total population, but Portland's most populated area is a 3½-mile-long peninsula facing Casco Bay. Visitors head down Congress Street to the Old Port, more than five square brick and stone blocks built during the city's peak shipping era and now laced with restaurants, cafés, shops, and galleries.

Portland's motto, "Resurgam" ("I shall rise again"), could not be more appropriate. The 17th-century settlement was decimated twice by Native Americans, then torched by the British. Finally it prospered as a lumbering port in the 1820s—as still evidenced by its many Federal-era mansions and commercial buildings, like the granite-and-glass Mariner's Church in the Old Port, built in 1820 to be the largest building in the capital of a brand-new state. Then, on Independence Day in 1866, a firecracker flamed up and fell in a Commercial Street boatyard, setting the city on fire and quickly destroying most of the downtown. Again the city rose like the legendary phoenix, rebuilding beautifully, this time in sturdy brick, to create the core of northern New England's shipping, rail, and manufacturing businesses.

These very buildings, a century later, were "going for peanuts," in the words of a real estate agent who began buying them up in the late 1960s, when Portland's handsome Grand Trunk Station was demolished. At that time, artists and craftspeople were renting shopfronts down by the harbor for $50 per month. They formed the Old Port Association, hoping to entice people to stroll through that no-man's-land. During its first winter, the Old Port Association strung lights through upper floors to convey a sense of security and shoveled their own streets, a service the city had ceased to provide to that area. At the end of the season they celebrated their survival by holding the first Old Port Festival, a street fair that is still held each June.

Higher up on Congress Street, the Maine College of Art (MECA) has replaced Porteus Department Store in a five-story Beaux Arts building and maintains the street-level Institute of Contemporary Art. With a student body of more than 420 and a far larger continuing-education program, MECA has had a visual impact up and down Congress Street, which is now called the Arts District.

Scattered throughout the city are members of Portland's growing immigrant community, with families from Bosnia, Russia, Somalia, Sudan, Congo, Vietnam, Puerto Rico, and Mexico, making this Maine's most diverse city.

The Western Promenade was laid out as an overlook for the West End way back in 1836; the Eastern Promenade was at the opposite end of the peninsula, along the verge of Munjoy Hill, overlooking Casco Bay. In 1879 the city gained Deering Oaks

Nancy English

TWO HORSES IN HARNESS TAKE A BREAK AT THE STANLEY THOMAS PULLEN FOUNTAIN

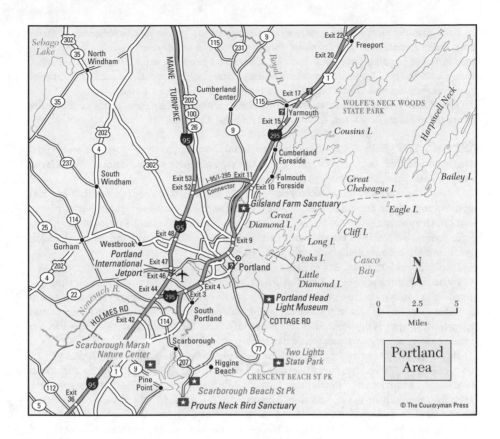

Park and was blessed by the design of city civil engineer William Goodwin. In 1917, with turn-of-the-century plans by Frederick Law Olmsted, a dream of James Phinney Baxter, a mayor of Portland, came true when Baxter Boulevard along Back Cove was opened to pedestrians.

Commercial Street is a departure point for the fleet of Casco Bay Lines ferries that regularly transport people, mail, and supplies to nearby Peaks Island and to the Diamond Islands, Chebeague, and Cliff Island, more than an hour's ride. The waterfront is, moreover, the departure point for deep-sea fishing, harbor cruises, whale-watching, and daysailing.

Beyond South Portland lies Cape Elizabeth, home of the vintage-1791 Portland Head Light and its museum. Nearby Scarborough to the south and both Falmouth and Yarmouth, just north of the city, also offer secluded seaside reserves for walking, boating, and birding.

GUIDANCE **Greater Portland Convention and Visitors Bureau** (207-772-5800; visit portland.com) publishes *Visit Portland Maine*, listing restaurants, sights, museums, and accommodations, including cottages. **Visitors information centers** are at 14 Ocean Gateway Pier (east of the end of Commercial St.), Portland 04101, open year-round. July–Columbus Day the schedule is Mon.–Fri. 9–5, Sat.–Sun. 9–4. Another center is at the **Portland International Jetport** (207-775-5809), open daily 10 AM–midnight.

Portland's Downtown District (207-772-6828; portlandmaine.com), 549 Congress St., Portland 04101, offers information about performances, festivals, and special events. They publish a guide to services, attractions, dining, and lodging.

For current entertainment, weather, and dining ratings, go to pressherald.com, the *Portland Press Herald* site. The *Portland Forecaster* (theforecaster.net)—a free weekly available in street vending boxes and at coffeehouses and shops—carries listings for galleries, music, and events. A website, portlandfoodmap.com, holds the most complete listing of Portland restaurants and is the best source for food-related events in the city.

The Maine Tourism Association (207-846-0833; mainetourism.com) staffs a major state information center on Rt. 1 in Yarmouth, just off I-295 Exit 17.

GETTING THERE *By air:* **Portland International Jetport** (207-774-7301; portlandjetport .org) is served by major carriers, and car rentals at the airport include National, Avis, Hertz, Budget, Enterprise, and Alamo.

By bus: **Concord Coach Lines** (207-828-1151 or 1-800-639-3317; concordcoachlines.com) stops en route from Boston to Bangor and coastal points at a modern station just off I-295 Exit 5A. **Greyhound** (1-800-231-2222; greyhound.com) offers frequent service among Portland, Boston, and Maine's coastal and inland points, using the Greyhound terminal, which unfortunately is dingy and offers little parking.

By car: From I-95, take I-295 to Exit 4 (Portland Waterfront).

By train: Amtrak service (1-800-USA-RAIL; amtrak.com). The **Downeaster** now runs five times daily between Boston's renovated North Station and Portland's clean rail–bus station on outer Congress St.; the trip takes about 2½ hours and then heads north to Freeport and Brunswick. Stops in Old Orchard Beach (seasonal), Saco/Biddeford, and Wells give another option to Portland visitors who would like to skip driving.

By ferry: Ferry service from **Nova Star Cruises** (novastarcruises.com) linking Portland, Maine, to Yarmouth, Nova Scotia, has a schedule of daily trips leaving Yarmouth at 9:30 AM and arriving in Portland at 6:30 PM, returning from Portland at 8 PM to arrive back in Yarmouth at 8 AM. Additional boats may be running at a future date, with a planned schedule in place from May 1 to the end of October. Check the web for the most up-to-date service. The 528-foot *Nova Star* has 163 cabins, a casino, a theater, and restaurants with a capacity of 1,215 passengers, along with room for 336 cars and 38 trucks.

GETTING AROUND **The Metro** (207-774-0351; gpmetrobus.net) city buses connect airport and city, and offer convenient routes around the city. $1.50 one-way, $5 day pass, or $13.50 for a 10-ride ticket; 75 cents for those over 65 or with disabilities; $1 for high school students.

PARKING Portland meters are 50 cents per half hour, but the $15 parking ticket after the meter expires makes parking expensive. Use one of the city's many parking garages. The **Fore Street Garage** (439 Fore St.) puts you at one end of the Old Port, and the **Custom House Square Garage** (25 Pearl St.) at the other. Beware private Unified Parking Partners-run lots: They boot cars that overstay their prepaid ticket.

✳ To See

MUSEUMS All listings are in Portland unless otherwise noted.

Maine Historical Society (207-774-1822; mainehistory.org), 485 Congress St. Maine Historical Society's offices are here, as are **Wadsworth-Longfellow House**, the **MHS Museum** and **MHS Research Library**, as well as the **Maine Memory Network** (mainememory.net). The Wadsworth-Longfellow House offers a 45-minute guided tour of the house. Built in 1785 by the grandfather of Henry Wadsworth Longfellow, this was the first brick dwelling in

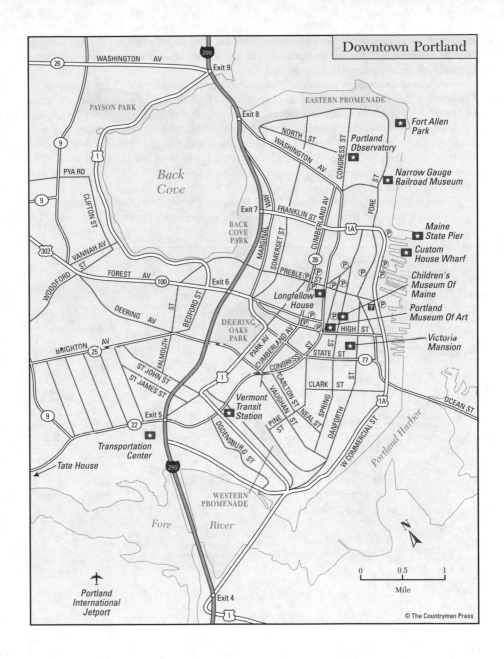

Downtown Portland

© The Countryman Press

town. Peleg Wadsworth was a Revolutionary War hero, and the entire clan of Wadsworths and Longfellows was prominent in the city for nearly two centuries. A small garden is hidden behind the house; another is a couple of blocks down Congress beside the granite First Parish Church (No. 425), marking the site on which Maine's constitution was drafted in 1819.

✐ ♿ **The Museum at Portland Head Light** (207-799-2661; portlandheadlight.com), 1000 Shore Rd. in Fort Williams Park, Cape Elizabeth. Memorial Day–Oct., open daily 10–4; Columbus Day–mid-Dec. and mid-Apr.–Memorial Day, open weekends 10–4. $2 adults,

$1 ages 6–18. This is the oldest lighthouse in Maine, first illuminated in 1791 per order of George Washington. It is now automated, and the former keeper's house has been transformed into an exceptional lighthouse museum.

Institute of Contemporary Art/MECA (207-879-5742; meca.edu/ica), 522 Congress St. Changing exhibits frequently worth checking; free. The ICA is a street-level gallery at the Maine College of Art (MECA), with more than 420 full-time students.

⚓ **The International Cryptozoology Museum** (207-518-9496; cryptozoologymuseum .com), 11 Avon St., Portland. $7 admission ages 13 or older, $5 ages 12 and under, "infants-in-arms" free. Meet the "Feejee Mermaid," a haunting movie prop, and the 8-foot-tall Crookston Bigfoot. This collection of mysterious creatures is the lifework of Loren Coleman and includes a life-sized colossus squid, 14 feet long.

⚓ **Maine Narrow Gauge Railroad Co. & Museum** (207-828-0814; mainenarrowgauge .org), 58 Fore St. Open May–Oct., daily 10–4, trains 10 to 3 on the hour, and seasonally for

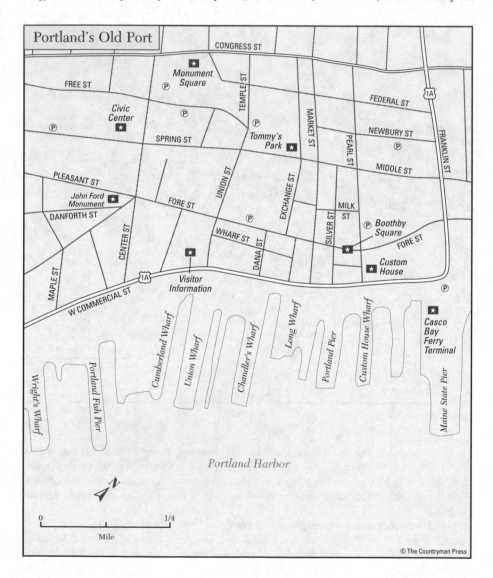

MUST SEE

🖊 ♿ **Portland Museum of Art** (207-775-6148; for a weekly schedule of events and information, 207-773-ARTS; portlandmuseum .org), 7 Congress Square. Open Tue., Wed., Thu., Sat., and Sun. 10–5, Fri. 10–9; Memorial Day–Columbus Day also open Mon. 10–5; closed New Year's Day, Thanksgiving, and Christmas. $12 adults, $10 students and seniors (with ID), and $6 ages 13–17; under 13 free. Free admission Fri. 5–9 PM. Maine's largest art museum is a striking building designed by I. M. Pei's firm. Featured American artists include Winslow Homer, Edward Hopper, Rockwell Kent, Louise Nevelson, Andrew and N. C. Wyeth, John Singer Sargent, and Marguerite Zorach; the museum also has interesting European works by Renoir, Degas, Prendergast, Matisse, and Picasso. Neighboring McLellan House, the lovely Federal-period home of the museum's original collection, along with the Sweat Memorial Galleries, showcases an impressive collection of 19th-century American paintings and decorative arts.

THE WATERFRONT SIDE OF THE WINSLOW HOMER STUDIO

The Portland Museum of Art bought the Winslow Homer Studio in 2006 from the artist's great-grandnephew, who had enjoyed the building as a summer house and used to leave it unlocked for art lovers to visit. That informality is no more, but with a knowledgeable docent in charge, your visit will linger in memory as a glimpse of an irascible genius. The building was restored to look much the way it did when Winslow Homer lived and painted here during summers from 1884, when the studio, a former carriage house, was embellished with a second-floor porch by local architect John Calvin Stevens, until 1910 when Homer died at 74 from natural causes at the studio.

Visits require tickets and reservations ($55 for nonmembers, $30 for members; $25 for students with valid ID; two tours Thu.–Sun. are offered in fall and spring, Fri. and Mon. in the summer, lasting 2½ hours). An upscale bus takes groups of no more than 10 to the studio from the museum.

Nancy English

PORTLAND MUSEUM OF ART DOCENT CAROL PATTERSON LEADING A TOUR AT CANNON ROCK, NEAR THE WINSLOW HOMER STUDIO

special events. A 1.5-mile roundtrip excursion along Casco Bay is offered regularly May–Oct. Leading up to Christmas, you can take the Polar Express; excursion fares are $10 roundtrip adults, $9 seniors, $6 ages 3–12. The museum sells the tickets. From the 1870s to the 1940s, five narrow-gauge lines carrying visitors linked rural Maine communities.

♂ & **Children's Museum and Theatre of Maine** (207-828-1234; kitetails.com), 142 Free St. Open Memorial Day–Labor Day, Mon.–Sat. 10–5, Sun. noon–5; otherwise, closed Mon. but open 9–11 for members; $10 per person (under 18 months free). Next door to the Portland Museum of Art, this fun museum features three levels of interactive, hands-on exhibits designed to help the young and old learn together. Permanent exhibits include "Have a Ball," in which kids make ramps and set balls in motion, a car repair shop and lobster boat, an ATM, a science center, a toddler area, and a black-box room that's a walk-in camera obscura.

♂ & **Portland Fire Museum** (207-772-2040; portlandfiremuseum.com), 157 Spring St. (near the corner of State). Open through the year during First Friday Art Walk, the first Friday of each month, at 6; call for more hours. The only remaining firehouse in Portland with horse stalls, this wonderful old brick structure was built in 1837 and originally housed a girls' grammar school. The artifacts (including a 1938 pumper truck) chronicle the city's contentious relationship with fire, from the city's destruction by fire at the hands of the British in 1775 to the Great Fire of 1866.

Portland Science Center (207-812-3850; portlandsciencecenter.com), 68 Commercial St., Maine Wharf. $19.50 adults, $15.50 children. Opened in 2015 with a highly publicized and controversial exhibit of plasticized human bodies, the Portland Science Center promises to be a memorable stop in anyone's day. "Body Worlds" is an exhibit that has toured the world, revealing the inner structure of healthy and unhealthy human bodies to the eye. Exhibits provide "edutainment," with subject matter mythic and compelling.

HISTORIC SITES All listings are in Portland unless otherwise noted.

♂ **Victoria Mansion**, the Morse-Libby House (207-772-4841; victoriamansion.org), 109 Danforth St. (at the corner of Park St.). Open for tours May–Oct., daily 10–3:45 (closed major holidays), Sun. 1–4:45; $15 adults, $13.50 seniors and AAA members, $5 children 6–17, under 6 free. Christmas hours and rates: day after Thanksgiving–first week of Jan., open daily; $15 adults (no senior discount), $5 students. Ruggles Sylvester Morse, a Maine native who made his fortune as a New Orleans hotelier, built this elaborately gilded, frescoed, carved, and many-mirrored mansion in 1858 as a summer home after relocating south just before the Civil War. The Italianate brownstone palazzo features a three-story grand hall with stained-glass windows, a stunning skylight, and a flying staircase with 377 balusters hand carved in black walnut. It was rescued from destruction and opened to the public in 1941.

Tate House Museum (207-774-6177; tatehouse.org), 1267 Westbrook St. Follow Congress St. (Rt. 22) west across the Fore River and turn left on Westbrook St. Open June–Oct., Wed.–Sat. 10–4, Sun. 1–4. $12 adults, $10 seniors, $5 ages 6–12, under 6 free. George Tate, mast agent for the Royal Navy, built this Georgian house in 1755 to reflect his important position. Both the interior and exterior are unusual, distinguished by clerestory windows, a gambrel roof, wood paneling, and elegant furniture.

Neal Dow Memorial (207-773-7773), 714 Congress St. Open year-round, tours given by appointment. Donation requested. Currently the headquarters of the Maine Women's Christian Temperance Union, this handsome Greek Revival mansion was built in 1829 by Neal Dow, the man responsible for an 1851 law that made Maine the first state to prohibit alcohol. He also championed women's rights and abolition.

GUIDED TOURS ✪ **Greater Portland Landmarks Center for Architecture and Preservation**, Safford House (207-774-5561; portlandlandmarks.org), 93 High St., Portland 04101.

THE ICONIC PORTLAND HEAD LIGHT IS IN FORT WILLIAMS PARK, CAPE ELIZABETH

Greater Portland Landmarks fills an 1858 bow-fronted Italianate building, designed by architect Charles Alexander, which was saved from destruction by this nonprofit organization in the 1970s after a block of historic homes was demolished to widen Spring Street. Landmarks has led walking tours of Portland's historic neighborhoods, including Friday 11 AM tours of Portland's "Golden Age" in 2015. Also note the organization's excellent books and its series of walking guides, available at the observatory, the center, or online. Landmarks runs the **Portland Observatory** at 138 Congress St., high on top of Munjoy Hill. It's open late May to mid-Oct., 10–5; $10 adults, $8 seniors, $5 ages 6–16. Climb the 103 steps to the top of Captain Lemuel Moody's masterpiece and watch the ships entering Casco Bay.

⚓ **Portland Discovery Land and Sea Tours** (207-774-0808; portlanddiscovery.com), 170 Commercial St., Portland. Mid-May–Oct. One trip is a narrated, 105-minute trolley tour that begins on Commercial St. in the Old Port and includes Portland Head Light. Another is the sunset lighthouse cruise. $24 adults, $17 children. Boat tours take in lighthouses.

Downeast Duck Tours (207-774-3825; downeastducktours.com), departing from Commercial St., by Casco Variety. The Duck Tour, about an hour long, takes you around Portland and into Casco Bay after the amphibious vehicle rolls into the harbor. Narrated tours run mid-May–mid-Oct., daily, with five a day before Labor Day and fewer in fall. $27 adults, $25 seniors, $20 ages 6–12, free ages 3 and under.

✳ To Do

BICYCLING **Map Adventures** (207-879-4777; mapadventures.com) makes very readable small maps of bike routes. **Portland Trails** (207-775-2411; trails.org) prints a *Map and Trail Guide*. The Maine Department of Transportation publishes a spiral-bound book with bike routes in Maine; separate tours are published in smaller books. These maps are stocked at **Back Bay Bicycle** (207-773-6906; backbaybicycle.com; 333 Forest Ave., Portland) and **Cycle Mania** (207-774-2933; cyclemania1.com; 59 Federal St., Portland), which sponsor weekly group rides. Cycle Mania and **Gorham Bike and Ski** (207-773-1700; gorhambike.com; 693

EXCURSIONS

No one seems quite sure how many islands there are in Casco Bay. Printed descriptions range from 136 to 222. Seventeenth-century explorer John Smith dubbed them the Calendar Islands, saying there was one for every day of the year. Regular year-round ferry service runs to six of the islands, five of which invite exploration.

PEAKS ISLAND Just 3 miles from Portland and a 20-minute ferry ride, Peaks is the most accessible island. Ferry service runs regularly both in summer and off-season because many of the island's approximately 1,000 year-round residents commute to the mainland for work and school. In summer the population swells to between 5,000 and 6,000, and day-trippers are common. The 5-mile shore road around the island is great for walking or bicycling. Rent a pair of wheels at **Brad's ReCycled Bike Shop** (207-766-5631), 115 Island Ave.; when Brad isn't there, you fill out a form, place payment in the box, and return the bikes when you're through. The **Fifth Maine Regiment Museum** (207-766-3330; fifthmainemuseum.org), Seashore Ave., is a striking building erected in 1888 to house Maine's largest collection of Civil War memorabilia (local history exhibits are on the second floor). **Maine Island Kayak Co.** (207-766-2373 or 1-800-796-2373; maineislandkayak.com) offers excellent, superbly guided half-day to multiday trips in Casco Bay along the Maine coast with renowned kayaking instruction. **The Cockeyed Gull** (207-766-2800), 78 Island Ave., serves the best dinner on the island, including Korean specialties, and has a deck perched over the bay. The **Inn on Peaks Island** (207-766-5100; innonpeaks.com), 33 Island Ave., has big, airy rooms and is open year-round with its own lunch and dinner restaurant, **The Pub**. All rooms include TV/DVD, phone, ceiling fan, fireplace, whirlpool tub, and balcony, $135–300 for a double. **DownFront** (207-766-5500), 50 Island Ave., at the top of the hill from the boat, sells great ice cream, candy, clothing, souvenirs, and the "cookie colossus."

CHEBEAGUE ISLAND is the largest in Casco Bay: 4.5 miles long and 2 miles wide. Its population of 350 swells to eight times that in summer. A bike is the best way to explore. **Mack Passano** (207-846-7829), 168 South Rd., is known as the Bike Man of Chebeague and was written up in *Down East* magazine. He offers more than 100 secondhand bikes for free. **The Chebeague Island Inn** (207-846-5155; chebeagueislandinn.com), the island's dowager lodging and an elegant place for a summer

Congress St., Portland) are the city bike shops that rent bicycles. They recommend you make a reservation, and they also stock DOT bike trail booklets and Portland Trails maps.

Eastern Trail (207-284-9260; easterntrail.org) is an ambitious trail system that will someday connect Casco Bay to Kittery (and Maine to Florida) with a 68.8-mile off-road greenway. Parts of the route now stretch through Scarborough Marsh, with its flocks of birds and summer scenery, up through South Portland where it is also called the **Greenbelt Trail**.

Mountain Division Trail (mountaindivisiontrail.org), Standish. Running from Standish through Gorham to Windham, the Mountain Division Trail is packed gravel with some paved sections. Four intersections take you across roads, but the 5-mile-plus trail is off-road. Horses travel on it, too.

BOATING **Chebeague Transportation Company** (207-846-3700; chebeaguetrans.com) runs the ferry that travels between Cousins Island and Chebeague. Call for directions and parking details.

Casco Bay Lines (207-774-7871; cascobaylines.com), Casco Bay Ferry Terminal, 56 Commercial St. at the foot of Franklin Arterial, Portland. Founded in 1845, this business was said to be the oldest continuously operating ferry company in the country when it went

meal, is open May–mid-Oct., with 21 rooms available at $150–370. **The Niblic** (207-846-1015) is a little store next to the boatyard where visitors can buy local crafts and snacks and drinks, as well as a good lunch. You can pick up takeout at **Doughty's Island Market** (207-846-9997). To relax and enjoy the scenery, head to **Chandler's Cove**, a white-sand beach, or the beach near **Coleman's Cove**. Golfers will want to try the **Chebeague Island Golf Club** (207-846-9478; chebeague.org), a beautiful nine-hole course founded in 1920, where nonmembers can play anytime except Mon. or Thu. morning. The **Chebeague Island Historical Society** has restored the old District No. 9 Schoolhouse, open all day in summer with a visitors center and museum. Call 207-846-5237 for details. **Casco Bay Lines** ferries dock at the southern end of the island, and **Chebeague Transportation Company** (207-846-3700; chebeaguetrans.com) runs the ferry that travels between Cousins Island and Chebeague. Call for directions and parking details.

LONG ISLAND Three miles long and approximately a mile wide, Long Island, like the others, has a thriving summer population, and rental cottages can make you a part of it. **Coveside of Long Island** (207-766-0092), 285 Beach Ave., is run by Emily Jacobs, who serves a terrific breakfast. The B&B is within walking distance of Long Island's prettiest beach, **Singing Sands**.

GREAT DIAMOND ISLAND A pleasant half-hour ferry ride from downtown, this 2-mile-long island is the site of Fort McKinley, built sturdily of brick in the 1890s, now restored as **Diamond Cove** (diamondcove.com), a resort-style development featuring 121 town houses. The **Inn at Diamond Cove** (207-775-7090; innatdiamondcove.com) is a luxury lodging that opened in 2015 following a $12 million renovation of the soldiers' barracks in Fort McKinley Park (and a fire that gutted the first renovation when it was almost done). The inn has its own dedicated transportation from the dock in Portland. $309–$569. **Diamond's Edge** (207-766-5850; diamondsedge.com) takes good care of meals; a casually elegant restaurant open late May–Oct., dinner only except mid-June–Labor Day, when lunch is also served. A popular place for weddings.

CLIFF ISLAND is a full 1½-hour ride down the bay. It is the most rustic of the islands, with 8 miles of dirt roads, no overnight accommodations, a peaceful feel, and sandy beaches.

bankrupt in 1980. The present, quasi-municipal Casco Bay Island Transit District now carries 870,000 passengers and 26,000 vehicles out to the bay's beautiful islands every year.

✿ *Lucky Catch* **Lobstering** (207-761-0941; luckycatch.com), 170 Commercial St., Portland. Instead of just eating them, why not land one of those tasty crustaceans yourself? Early May–late Oct., Captain Tom takes tourists and locals out to haul traps on the *Lucky Catch* five times daily Mon.–Sat., with side trips to Portland Head Light and White Head Passage. Each 80- to 90-minute cruise costs $30 per adult, $28 for seniors and ages 13–18, $20 ages 2–12; children under 2 free.

✪ *Odyssey* **Whale Watch** (207-775-0727; odysseywhalewatch.com), Long Wharf, Portland. Whale-watches daily at 10 AM June–Oct. on the *Odyssey*, a 93-passenger boat. $49 adults, $39 children 12 and under.

BOWLING **Bayside Bowl** (207-791-2695; baysidebowl.com), 58 Alder St., provides excellent food and drink in a hipster setting, and the bowling is a lot of fun. Live music on weekend nights.

BREWERIES, WINERIES, AND DISTILLERIES Portland is famous for its microbreweries, and many give tours, either on a regular basis or by appointment. **The Maine Brew Bus**

(207-200-9111; themainebrewbus.com), 111 Commercial St., Portland, takes care of the driving and scheduling for $50 to $75 or so, depending on the tour chosen. For information, contact individual breweries. Three fine breweries that share the same industrial neighborhood start with long-established **Allagash Brewing** (207-878-5385 or 1-800-330-5385; allagash.com), 50 Industrial Way, with world renowned Curieux, limited editions like Nancy, made with sour cherries, and classic Allagash White. Make a reservation online for a tasting. **Bissell Brothers** (207-808-8258; bissellbrothers.com), 1 Industrial Way, touts Substance as its "slightly dank" flagship ale, and a brew schedule at the website lists what is ready in their tap room. **Foundation** (207-370-8187; foundationbrew.com), 1 Industrial Way, #5, has several unique offerings. Epiphany, Eddy, Wanderlust, and Burnside are some possible brews to sip as you wander the brewery and ask staff questions on a self-directed tour. **Oxbow** (207-315-5962; oxbowbeer.com), 49 Washington Ave., makes Farmhouse Ale and Space Cowboy, both Belgian-style ales brewed in Newcastle

Nancy English

THE BARREL ROOM AT ALLAGASH

and easy to taste in the Portland Tasting Room. Other microbreweries include **D. L. Geary Brewing** (207-878-BEER; gearybrewing.com), 38 Evergreen Dr.; **Gritty McDuff's Brew Pub** (207-772-2739; grittys.com), 396 Fore St.; **Peak Organic Brewing Company** (207-586-5586; peakbrewing.com), 110 Marginal Way; **Liquid Riot Bottling Company** (207-221-8889; liquidriot.com), 250 Commercial St; and the largest of all, **Shipyard Brewing** (207-761-0807; shipyard.com), 86 Newbury St. In East Bayside, the funky, post-industrial part of town hugging I-295, **Rising Tide Brewing Company** (207-370-2337; risingtidebrewing.com), 103 Fox St., has tours Fri. and Sat. and a tasting room to sample Spinnaker, a wheat beer made in summer, or Ursa Minor, "dark as squid ink and moody as the sea." **Bunker Brewing Co.** (207-450-5014), 122 Anderson St., makes Mockingbird, if you are in luck. **Urban Farm Fermentory** (207-773-8331; urbanfarmfermentory.com), 200 Anderson St., Bay 4, makes hard cider, kombucha, and mead, each sold by the 32-ounce growler, with tastings on weekend evenings. **Sweetgrass Winery and Distillery** (207-761-8446; sweetgrasswinery.com), 324 Fore St., offered a tasting of four wines or spirits for $5 in 2015, with a nice glass for a souvenir. The Apple Brandy is sublime and we are all awaiting the barrel-aged bourbon with respectful impatience (release date 2018). Lamb, bitters, vanilla extract, and blankets also for sale from the Union, Maine, farm. **Cellardoor at the Point** (mainewine.com) is planned to open in 2016 on Thompson's Point, Portland's new music, circus, and brewery hotspot. The wines are made with grapes grown in Lincolnville, less than two hours up the coast. **New England Distilling** (207-878-9759; newenglanddistilling.com), 26 Evergreen Dr., Portland, is distilling Ingenium gin and Eight Bells rum. **Maine Craft Distilling** (207-798-2528; mainecraftdistilling.com), 101 Fox St., makes Chesuncook gin, Ration rum, and Queequeg spiced rum.

SAILING CLASS IN CASCO BAY

FOR FAMILIES ✒ **Southworth Planetarium** (207-780-4249; usm.maine.edu/planet), University of Southern Maine, 96 Falmouth St., Portland. Astronomy shows throughout the year.

GOLF **Sable Oaks Golf Club** (18 holes, 207-775-6257), South Portland, is considered among the most challenging and best courses in Maine; **Riverside North** (18 holes, 207-797-3524) and **Riverside South** (nine holes, 207-797-5588), in Portland; **Val Halla** (18 holes, 207-829-2225), in Cumberland; and **Twin Falls** (nine holes, 207-854-5397) in Westbrook.

    Willowdale Golf Club (207-883-9351; willowdalegolf.com), off Rt. 1, Scarborough, has 18 holes. **Nonesuch River Golf Club** (207-883-0007; nonesuchgolf.com), off Rt. 114, Scarborough, also has 18 holes.

RACING **Scarborough Downs** (207-883-4331; scarboroughdowns.com), off I-95 Exit 6 in Scarborough. From Apr.–Dec. Scarborough Downs, the largest facility of its kind in New England, has live harness racing with betting windows; year-round thoroughbred and harness racing is available via simulcast with off-track betting.

    Beech Ridge Motor Speedway (207-885-5800; beechridge.com), Holmes Rd., Scarborough. Summer stock-car racing Thu.–Sat., May–Oct.

SAILING *Bagheera* (207-766-2500 or 1-87-SCHOONER; portlandschooner.com), Maine State Pier, Portland. Built in 1924 of long-leaf yellow pine, oak, and mahogany, this vintage Alden sailed all over the world before making Casco Bay her home port in 2002. She can carry as many as 48 passengers. Four cruises daily, Memorial Day–Labor Day, three daily until Columbus Day. $42 for adults, $21 for children. *Wendameen*, a schooner built in 1912, is available for private charters and overnight cruises.

    The *Frances* (207-749-9169; mainesailingadventures.net) offers cruises daily Memorial Day–Columbus Day, along with many theme cruises like yoga, wine, and music.

SEA KAYAKING ✒ **Maine Island Kayak Co.** (207-766-2373 or 1-800-796-2373; maineislandkayak.com), 70 Luther St., Peaks Island. Late May–Oct. Exceptional guides, state-of-the-art equipment, and a commitment to the leave-no-trace philosophy are crucial in heavily trafficked Casco Bay. This company offers instruction in kayaking and trips throughout the summer. **Portland Paddle** (207-730-9730; portlandpaddle.net), East End Beach, Portland. Guided kayak tours and kayak and paddleboard rentals.

✳ Green Space

BEACHES ✎ ⓹ **Crescent Beach State Park** (207-799-5871), 66 Two Lights Rd., Cape Elizabeth; 8 miles from Portland on Rt. 77. A mile of sand complete with changing facilities, a playground, picnic tables, and a snack bar. Good for young children because it's protected from heavy surf.

✎ ⓹ **Wolfe's Neck Woods State Park** (207-865-4465; off-season, 207-865-6080), 426 Wolfe's Neck Rd. (take Bow St., across from L.L. Bean), Freeport. Open Apr.–Oct. Day-use fee. A 233-acre park with shoreline hiking along Casco Bay, the Harraseeket River, and salt marshes, as well as excellent birding, with ospreys the local stars.

Kettle Cove is just down the road from Crescent Beach—follow the road behind the (excellent) ice cream shop on Rt. 77. Free, but parking is limited. This spot is good for bird-watching during migration seasons.

Higgins Beach, farther down Rt. 77 in Scarborough, is an extensive strand within walking distance of lodging—but there is no parking on the street. Private lots charge a fee. The swell can kick up quite a bit here, so beware the undertow. Surfers are always here when the waves are high.

Scarborough Beach State Park (scarboroughbeachstatepark.com), 414 Black Point Rd. (Rt. 207), 3 miles south of Rt. 1 on Prouts Neck. Open Memorial Day–Sept. ($5 admission), also for walking year-round. A 243-acre park with a superb beach, but only a 65-foot stretch is technically public. Get there early because parking is minimal and open-ocean lovers like this one best.

PARKS ✎ **Deering Oaks**, Portland's 51-acre city park, designed by city civil engineer William Goodwin, has a pond, ducks and, rarely, a beaver and a moose, a fountain, a playground, a fine grove of oak trees, a shrub rose garden, and a refurbished urban "ravine" complete with a wading pool and spray jets for summertime frolicking. A farmers' market is held here Sat. morning May–Nov., and fabulous winter lights designed by Pandora LaCasse.

Two Lights State Park, 66 Two Lights Rd., Cape Elizabeth, is open year-round. No swimming, but 40 acres of shore with stunning water views for picnicking and fishing.

Also see **Fort Williams Park** in *Excursions* and **Fort Allen Park** under Eastern Promenade in *Walks*.

NATURE PRESERVES ✎ **Gilsland Farm Audubon Center** (207-781-2330; maine audubon.org), 20 Gilsland Farm Rd., Falmouth (3 miles east of Portland). Open Mon.–Sat. 9–5; Sun. noon–5 in warm weather, 2–5 in cold weather. Maine Audubon's headquarters are located at this 65-acre wildlife sanctuary, along with trails, rolling fields, river frontage, and salt marsh. The education center features exhibits throughout

DEERING OAKS WADING POOL IS A PERFECT REFUGE ON A HOT DAY.

Nancy English

FREEDOM TRAIL MARKER

the year and a wildlife discovery room for children.

Scarborough Marsh Audubon Center (207-883-5100), Pine Point Rd. (Rt. 9), Scarborough. Open daily mid-June–Labor Day, 9:30–5:30. The largest salt marsh (3,000 acres) in Maine, this is a great place for quiet canoe and kayak exploration. This Maine Audubon center offers canoe and kayak rentals, exhibits, a Maine Audubon Nature Store, and guided walking and canoe and kayak tours throughout the summer.

Fore River Sanctuary, (207-775-2411; trails.org). Located near Maine Turnpike Exit 8, off Brighton Ave., Portland, and managed by Portland Trails. This 85-acre preserve is hidden behind a suburban neighborhood where explorers might not think to look. The 2.5 miles of hiking trails offer access to Portland's only waterfall, **Jewell Falls**.

Prouts Neck Cliff Walk and Wildlife Sanctuary. Winslow Homer painted many of his seascapes in a small studio here (now owned by Portland Museum of Art). This exclusive community on Prouts Neck is not far from the Black Point Inn. Winslow Homer Road marks the start of the Cliff Path (unmarked), a beautiful stroll along the rocks, around Eastern Point, and back almost to the inn. You can also walk through the sanctuary between Winslow Homer Road (just east of St. James Episcopal Church) and Library Lane, donated by Winslow's brother Charles.

WALKS **Portland Trails** (207-775-2411; trails.org), 305 Commercial St., Portland, an organization committed to developing hiking and walking trails in the city, sells a map describing several city parks and more than 50 miles of trails as well as bus routes to take you there. The website has a page with links to every trail in Portland on an expandable map.

✐ **The Eastern Promenade.** Follow Congress St. east to the Portland Observatory atop Munjoy Hill and then continue the extra block to the Eastern Promenade, a park-lined street high on this same bluff with sweeping views of Casco Bay. Follow it around, back toward the harbor, to 68-acre **Fort Allen Park**, which dates to 1814, set on a blustery point above the bay. Down along the bay itself the paved **Eastern Promenade Trail** runs along the base of Munjoy Hill, good for biking and walking. The railroad museum's excursion train runs alongside it.

🐾 ♿ **The Western Promenade** is Portland's most architecturally interesting residential neighborhood. Pick up a copy of the Portland Landmarks leaflet *Guide to the Western Promenade* from the seasonal visitors bureau at Ocean Gateway.

🐾 ✐ ♿ **Baxter Boulevard.** A 3.5-mile path around the tidal flats of Back Cove connects with the Eastern Promenade Trail. It's a popular spot for dog walking, jogging, and biking. Park across from the Hannaford Bros. store.

Eastern Cemetery, Congress St. and Washington Ave. (near the Portland Observatory on Munjoy Hill). The oldest cemetery in Portland, it is listed by the National Trust for Historic Preservation. Its 6 acres hold more than 4,000 headstones dating from the mid-17th century to the early 19th; some are embellished with angels and death's heads. **Spirits Alive**

(spiritsalive.org) runs guided tours here ($10 adults, $5 children under 12) in summer and a Halloween Walk Among the Shadows tour.

Portland Freedom Trail (207-591-9980; portlandfreedomtrail.org). A granite-and-bronze marker at the Eastern Cemetery on Congress St. was the first of a series of 13 markers at places in the city where abolitionists lived, preached, and harbored escaping slaves on the Underground Railroad. The website offers a Freedom Trail Map for a self-guided walking tour. The Abyssinian Church on Newbury St. was Maine's first black church when it was built in 1829 and is undergoing restoration. A pro-slavery riot erupted after a sermon criticizing slavery in 1842 at First Parish Church at the head of Temple St.

Clark's Pond Trail, maintained by the South Portland Land Trust (southportland landtrust.org). Home Depot in South Portland is located at the trailhead of this plunge into the woods, a 1.1-mile trail located near the Maine Mall with a secret waterfall and turkeys and deer.

Cape Elizabeth Land Trust (207-767-6054; capelandtrust.org), 330 Ocean House Rd., Cape Elizabeth. The Cape Elizabeth Land Trust has preserved 650 acres of the town's land and developed many miles of trails on those acres and via rights-of-way that connect the scattered parcels.

✳ Lodging

HOTELS There are more than 2,000 hotel and motel rooms in and around Portland.

IN THE OLD PORT 04101

✐ ♿ **Portland Regency** (207-774-4200 or 1-800-727-3436; theregency.com), 20 Milk St. Stay in one of 95 rooms (including suites) housed in a century-old armory. Rooms come with reproduction beds (a king or two doubles), white down comforters, cable TV, and air-conditioning; some suites feature a whirlpool tub. Downstairs gym and day spa with luxurious locker rooms, each with private sauna; also coed sauna and steam room, and 10-person, tiled whirlpool with a waterfall. $139–329.

The Press Hotel (207-808-8800; thepress hotel.com), 119 Exchange St. A wall of manual typewriters recalls the building's origin as a newspaper office, but the reporters hammering typewriter keys never saw anything like the luxurious bedrooms and baths upstairs. This hotel is part of Marriott's Autograph Collection, a set of unique lodgings worldwide. Its **Union** is a fine dining restaurant (see below) that makes sure the burgers are topnotch. $199–600.

🐾 ✐ ♿ **Portland Harbor Hotel** (207-775-9090 or 1-888-798-9090; theportlandharbor hotel.com), 468 Fore St. Amenities include cable TV and radio, marble bath,

European-style glass shower, granite counters; Jacuzzi suites feature an oval spa tub and separate sitting area with sofa bed. Fitness center. **Eve's at the Garden** serves fine dinners. $129–399, depending on view and season. Pets are allowed on the first and second floors for a $25 fee per day.

🐾 ♿ **Residence Inn Portland Downtown/ Waterfront** (207-761-1660; marriott.com), 145 Fore St. Comfortable rooms, many overlooking the harbor. There are 137 studios, 34 one-bedroom suites, and 8 two-bedroom suites. All have full kitchen and sleeping area with king bed; a hot breakfast buffet is included. Guest laundry room. Onetime fee for pets. $169–349.

Nancy English

THE PRESS HOTEL LOBBY

Hampton Inn Downtown Portland (207-775-1454; hamptoninn.com), 209 Fore St. New in 2011, this hotel was built on the site of the old Jordan's Meats factory, famous for its red hot dogs. Now the good-sized rooms, some with harbor views, are proving restful. Other perks include the free breakfast and Sebago Brewing Company on the first floor. $129–449 depending on season.

IN MIDTOWN PORTLAND

♂ ♿ **Holiday Inn by the Bay** (207-775-2311 or 1-800-HOLIDAY; innbythebay.com), 88 Spring St. 04101. Portlanders love to hate this ugly, 11-story, downtown highrise, especially since it took over a beautiful neighborhood. But the harbor and skyline views are great from the inside. Amenities include an indoor pool, small fitness center, cable TV with in-room movies, free parking, laundry facility, and a restaurant and lounge. Two suites and 239 rooms range from $180 to $240 in high season.

The Westin Portland Harborview (207-775-5411; starwoodhotels.com), 157 High St. This hotel resurrects the glory of the original Eastland Hotel it took over. Gutted and completely modernized, the hotel stands across from the Portland Museum of Art. Its 289 rooms feature upscale modern furnishings. The Top of the East never looked this good; go to the top of the building for a panoramic view of the city and a drink.

BEYOND PORTLAND

✪ ♂ ♿ **Black Point Inn** (207-883-2500 or 1-800-258-0003; blackpointinn.com), 510 Black Point Rd., Prouts Neck 04074. Open May–Nov. 1. This vintage-1878 summer hotel now has just 25 rooms. The oldest elevator in the state of Maine is still hand operated by a polite staff member. Guests use the Prouts Neck Country Club's 18-hole golf course and 14 tennis courts, as well as kayaks, boats, and bikes. Two sandy beaches, an outdoor heated pool. Rates $410-695 for double MAP (Modified American Plan) per night plus 18 percent guest service charge (covers all gratuities). Live jazz on the porch Tue. nights.

♂ ❀ ♂ ♿ **Inn by the Sea** (207-799-3134; innbythesea.com), 40 Bowery Beach Rd., Cape Elizabeth 04107. Open year-round. A 15-minute drive from downtown Portland, this shingled beachside complex maintains a high reputation. The 61 accommodations include traditional guest rooms with gas-burning fireplace and mini fridge, two-bedroom cottages with kitchen, and suites with a bedroom and living area, mini fridge, and microwave. **Sea Glass,** the inn's popular restaurant, serves all three meals. $200–2,000 depending on season and accommodation, plus 5 percent hotel fee.

♂ **Higgins Beach Inn** (207-883-6684; higginsbeachinn.com), 34 Ocean Ave., Scarborough 04074 (7 miles south of Portland). Open mid-May–mid-Oct. A well-cared-for 1890s three-story wooden summer hotel near sandy, gorgeous Higgins Beach. The dining room, **Garofalo's,** features seafood and pasta dishes from owner Diane's Sicilian family recipes (entrées $16–27). Upstairs the 22 guest rooms are archetypal summer hotel rooms— simple, clean, and airy—13 with private bath. $200 double with private bath, $90 with shared bath, with a minimum two-night stay in summer.

The Breakers Inn (207-883-4820; thebreakersinn.com) 2 Bay View Ave., Higgins Beach, Scarborough. One of co-author Chris Tree's favorite inns in Maine, this B&B in a 1900 private home draws praise from its guests who delight in its location. Fifteen guest rooms, some pine-paneled and some overlooking the sea, hold antiques and classic summer cottage decor, and the nights are filled with the sound of crashing waves. $150–215 depending on season; no credit cards.

INNS AND B&BS Pomegranate Inn (207-772-1006 or 1-800-356-0408; pomegranateinn.com), 49 Neal St., Portland 04102. In eight amazing rooms, bold, hand-painted walls by Portland artist Heidi Gerquest create an energetic atmosphere; five have a gas fireplace. Count on a fantastic breakfast from innkeeper Dana Moos, author of *The Art of Breakfast,* like egg roulade with leeks, Parmesan, and lobster. $229–329 per room in-season, $189–299 off-season, of course including breakfast.

Morrill Mansion Bed & Breakfast (207-774-6900; morrillmansion.com), 249 Vaughan St., Portland 04102. Seven bedrooms are named for local neighborhoods and old families in this elegant B&B, next to Maine Medical Center and on the edge of the West End, an easy walk to midtown. The building was completely done over by owner David Parker, and all rooms have queen beds, private bath, and cable TV/DVD. $99–239 includes a breakfast buffet with an egg custard, French toast, warm fruit crisp and yogurt, and more. Afternoon treats, perhaps whoopie pies, are served in the second-floor guest living room.

The Mercury (207-775-0224 or 1-800-600-1557; mercuryinn.com), 273 State St., Portland 04101. This small Victorian on the hill below Portland's main street, Congress, is the favorite stop for visitors who like a quiet place with all the basic comforts. Six rooms have been furnished by owners Tim Karu and Jacob Krueger with bright, clean, modern furnishings; all show the owners' concern for the environment. $110–175.

Inn on Carleton Bed & Breakfast (207-775-1910; innoncarleton.com), 46 Carleton St., Portland 04102. A beautiful building in the hands of a hospitality professional. Buddy Marcum has revitalized this town house in Portland's West End, updating the beds and the rooms with modern furniture and embellishing the classic structure to make it a fine addition to Portland's small inns. Marcum is a flight attendant; when he's working part time, his well-trained staff cater to his guests. $120–225.

West End Inn (207-772-1377 or 1-800-338-1377; westendbb.com), 146 Pine St., Portland 04102. This 1871 brick town house combines natural elegance with colorful decor. The most popular of the six rooms is Cliff Island, with 12-foot ceilings, private deck, and white and blue accents. All have private bath, cable TV, ceiling fan, and air-conditioning. $119–229 includes full breakfast.

Inn at Park Spring (207-774-1059 or 1-800-437-8511; innatparkspring.com), 135 Spring St., Portland 04101. At one of the most convenient locations in town, Nancy and John Gonsalves offer six well-appointed guest rooms with private bath and sitting area. The handsome Museum Room is painted yellow and furnished with two wing chairs and a four-poster queen bed. Breakfast is served in the formal dining room with floor-to-ceiling windows; a French toast croissant stuffed with marmalade and cream cheese could be on the menu. $125–225.

The Chadwick Bed & Breakfast (207-774-5141 or 1-800-774-2137; thechadwick.com), 140 Chadwick St., Portland 04102. Under the management of innkeeper E. Scot Fuller. Four rooms on the second floor have cushy beds, flat-screen TV and DVD, and private bath (but two are across the hall). A full breakfast completes the experience. The back garden and a big sitting room with capacious chairs and couches are ideal for relaxation. $100–250.

🦐 🐾 ✑ ♿ **Inn at St. John** (207-773-6481 or 1-800-636-9127; innatstjohn.com), 939 Congress St., Portland 04102. A 39-room hotel built in 1897 to accommodate railroad passengers arriving at Union Station (unfortunately long gone), this place is convenient for guests arriving by Greyhound and Vermont Transit, though it's a hike to downtown. Attractive rooms are well managed by innkeeper Paul Hood. $59–295, depending on season, includes continental breakfast.

✳ Where to Eat

DINING OUT

IN PORTLAND

✪ **Back Bay Grill** (207-772-8833; backbaygrill .com), 65 Portland St. It's always a good night for dinner at Back Bay Grill, where a lot of history hasn't made the dining room stiff, perhaps because the mural on the wall always provides such a good example of bon temps—and you can be assured of fine service and excellent wine. Scottish salmon with chanterelles in-season or braised pork chops with

BACK BAY GRILL

fava beans might be on the always appealing menu. Entrées $25–36.

Piccolo (207-747-5307; piccolomaine.com), 111 Middle St. Damian Sansonetti, from New York's Bar Boulud, and his wife and business partner, Ilma Jeil Lopez, a pastry chef with her own New York credentials from Le Bernadin, prepare exquisite Italian-inspired meals tailored to the best provisions of each season.

Fore Street (207-775-2717; forestreet.biz), 288 Fore St. Open for dinner nightly. Reservations a must in summer, but there are open tables at 5:30 when the dining room opens. Sam Hayward oversees meals full with his signature integrity. Great roast pork, turned on a spit in the open kitchen, or fish roasted in a wood-fired oven, or roast quail, or just a few chicken livers quickly sautéed, and the best steamed mussels with garlic almond butter. The local vegetable side dishes are not to be missed, nor are desserts like peach tarte tatin. Entrées $18–35.

Hugo's (207-774-8538; hugos.net), 88 Middle St. An original, adventurous menu of small plates creates an evening packed with revelations. Combinations of flavors and quirky juxtapositions, perhaps porchetta with toothwort or sweet onion agnolotti, leave diners in a reverie. Plates $22, five courses for $90.

✪ **Miyake** (207-871-9170; miyake restaurants.com), 468 Fore St. Open for lunch and dinner Mon.–Sat. In-season a variety of wild salmon allows a taste of the Pacific's best. Uni, cracked fresh from the urchin shell, and ankimo are exceptional, and the miso soup is of the highest quality. Omakase nigiri, $70, presents 10 pieces of the freshest fish possible.

♿ **five fifty-five** (207-761-0555; five fifty-five.com), 555 Congress St. Chef-owner Steve Corry makes even hamburgers an unusual pleasure. But try black pepper ice cream or other flavors the evening menu offers for real adventure. A fall menu offered paper-wrapped flounder, served with couscous and black olive tangerine butter; a steak might come with crispy potatoes. Entrées $15 (from the bar menu)–35. Reservations advised.

Emilitsa (207-221-0245; emilitsa.com), 547 Congress St. The starter freebie, a yellow lentil puree with toasted pita, alerts you to an

FORE STREET'S WOOD-BURNING OVEN BEING RESTOCKED

emphasis on vibrant flavors. Spanakopita was never so fresh, moussaka as light lamb chops and chicken livers as savory. Ask for the right Greek wines and discover how perfectly they pair. Entrées $25–36.

✪ **Caiola's** (207-772-1110; caiolas.com), 58 Pine St. A short walk into the West End, this professional kitchen is run by Abby Harmon, whose sure touch makes scallops perfect and grilled swordfish even better. The burger is a moist marvel, and the steak, pork chop, house cannelloni, and more are, too. Manager Lisa Vaccaro makes the atmosphere welcoming. Entrées $22–27.

Scales (207-761-0380; forestreet.biz), 72 Fore St. Owned by Dana Street of Street & Co. and Sam Hayward of Fore Street, this new place on the waterfront is a reprise of a smaller seafood restaurant that did fried fish perfectly and sold the city's best fried oysters. Crab bisque, JFK Lobster Stew, herring or mackerel "toasts," and a paper cone filled with a variety of fried fish are on the menu.

Paciarino (207-774-3500; paciarino .com), 470 Fore St. Fabiana de Savino and Enrico Barbiero make fresh pasta daily to be lunched on with fresh tomato sauce or with pesto, or enjoyed at dinner in somewhat larger portions. The light, deft touch with fine olive oil (the gold-foil-wrapped bottle is an elixir, friends assert) and other fine imported products also for sale make a meal here utterly refreshing and *saporito*—which is "tasty" in Italian. Entrées $16–18.

Central Provisions (207-805-1085; central -provisions.com), 414 Fore St., burst into the foodie scene with culinary fireworks that haven't let up. Small plates, each crafted to make memories, like caramelized sheep's cheese, suckling pig, or orrechiete with garlic scapes, will lure you back for more. Entrées $14–24, but since you will order multiple plates, expensive.

Isa Bistro (207- 808-8533; isaportlandme .com), 79 Portland St. Closed Tuesday. Lamb merguez sliders glimmer on the menu; the tagliatelle Bolognese is perfect, and so is the braised rabbit. Three meatballs and a dish of sautéed Brussels sprouts is a perfect supper. Entrées $16–22.

Outliers Eatery (207-747-4166; outlier seatery.com), 231 York St. Cool urban style reigns in this glimmering room, while lobster gnocchi and duck confit hash (a brunch dish) make the meals extremely satisfying. Entrées $15–29.

Vinland (207-653-8617; vinland.me), 593 Congress St. Open since the fall of 2013, David Levi features snacks of reindeer lichen, beet chips with strained yogurt, cucumber and chive, and something called Angel Egg, his spin on a deviled egg, at this Maine-sourced restaurant on Congress Square, near the art museum; main courses are determined by the season.

&. **Local 188** (207-761-7909; local188.com), 685 Congress St. Open Tue.–Sat. for dinner, and Sunday brunch. A tapas bar and dinner restaurant with a great lounge and bar. The Spanish bias is evident, as is local produce and a stray influence from Turkey or elsewhere. Spanish wines are a specialty. Try the gazpacho, the garlic shrimp, grilled chorizo, or paella. Entrées $18 and up; tapas $4–14.

Ribollita (207-774-2972; ribollitamaine .com), 41 Middle St. Open for dinner Mon.– Sat. The classics are the draw at this welcoming place, with handmade pasta in butternut squash ravioli one example, and the creamiest flan in town. Entrées $12.50–20.

The East Ender (207-879-7669; eastender portland.com), 47 Middle St. A cider-brined local pork chop and a plate of baby back ribs argued for a return visit to this friendly, comfortable place with an affection for good meat

and Wed.-night half-off wine by the bottle. Entrées $16–22.

&. **Street & Company** (207-775-0887; streetandcompany.net), 33 Wharf St. Open for dinner daily at 5:30. Reservations recommended. The noisy, packed dining rooms here, and a comfortable bar with upholstered seats, are filled with lovers of the wonderful fish, inventive specials, and comfortable standards like lobster diavolo for two, mussels Provençal, and scallops in Pernod and cream. The raw bar serves up the best oysters in town. Entrées $18–32.

Liquid Riot Bottling Company (207-221-8889; liquidriot.com), 250 Commercial St. Open daily 11:30–1 AM. A microbrewery that experiments with fermentation both in the glass and on the plate. Pub food in a fantastically cool space.

Union (207-808-8700; thepresshotel.com), 390 Congress St. The glossy restaurant in The Press Hotel opened in 2015 to praise for scallops with crisp pork belly and roasted cod with clams, confit lamb shoulder and white anchovy tempura. Entrées $19–30.

✪ **Sonny's** (207-772-7774; sonnysportland .com), 83 Exchange St. Open daily. Sonny's bar area in an elegantly renovated old bank is perfect for an inventive cocktail, and its tables and booths are a fine place to enjoy South and Central American and Southwestern flavors. Dishes might include beef brisket enchiladas or a roasted poblano cheeseburger. Entrées $14–24.

Ebb & Flow (207-780-0227; ebbandflowme .com), 100 Commercial St. Using its big beautiful space to show off seafood made with Mediterranean inspiration, Ebb & Flow has gotten better and better; roasted sardines and grilled octopus, braised lamb shank and pork chops with prosciutto and fig, ending with a cheesecake worth indulging in and galakto-boureko, Greek custard pie. $24–34.

Boda (207-347-7557; bodamaine.com), 671 Congress St. Closed Mon. "Very Thai" means fragrances and flavors turned up a notch from the typical Thai restaurant; it also means exceptional dishes anyone can love. Romelo salad with betel leaves, a range of skewered meats and vegetables, and entrées like pork hock with star anise. Entrées $12–14.

Zapoteca (207-772-8242; zapoteca restaurant.com), 505 Fore St. Eat at the lively bar or in the dining room and enjoy ceviche with crab and Maine shrimp; enchiladas stuffed with the same under green chili sauce; or a local rib eye with lime, oregano, and cilantro salsa.

The Corner Room (207-879-4747; thecornerroomkitchenandbar.com), 110 Exchange St. Harding Lee Smith runs four "Rooms." This one features fresh pasta in all shapes and sizes with lamb ragu, mushrooms, and cream, or all'Amatriciana can be counted on for lunch or dinner. Pizza and a long antipasto list of cheeses and cured meats. $15 and up.

The Grill Room (207-774-2333; thegrill roomandbar.com), 84 Exchange St. Harding Lee Smith takes care of grilled steaks with The Grill Room, where you can also order wood-oven pizza and, depending on the season, grilled swordfish, skewered scallops with rosemary and mushroom risotto, and a grilled rib eye with béarnaise and frites. The bar is a good place to meet a friend. Entrées $12–37.

Boone's Fish House and Oyster Room (207-774-5725; boonesfishhouse.com), 86 Commercial St. Fried and fresh seafood, raw oysters, a more inventive menu—local lamb flat bread and Asian-inspired dishes—upstairs where the open deck is a summer destination.

ON MUNJOY HILL

& **The Front Room** (207-773-3366; thefront roomrestaurant.com), 73 Congress St. Open daily for all three meals. Bustling and hectic on weekends, you can find meat loaf, roast pork chops, grilled flatiron steak, and mushroom ragu with polenta. Easy to understand why it's full, but the noise can overwhelm. Entrées $15–21.

& **Blue Spoon** (207-773-1116; bluespoon me.com), 89 Congress St. Open for lunch and dinner Tue.–Sat., brunch on Sat. This small restaurant at the top of Munjoy Hill cooks up straightforward dishes with skill and keeps them reasonably priced. Local stuff in-season, but the juicy burger and large bowls of mussels with lemon and garlic are mainstays. Entrées $15–20.

Lolita Vinoteca + Asador (207-775-5652; lolita-portland.com), 90 Congress St. Guy and Stella Hernandez bring years of refining small plates into bursts of fine flavor to Lolita,

with its lamb kefte with figs and market fish accented with aioli. Open for lunch Sat.–Sun., dinner daily. Medium plates $14, large $24.

OUTSIDE PORTLAND

Gather (207-847-3250; gathermaine.com), 189 Main St., Yarmouth. Open Tue.–Sat. for dinner, Sun. brunch 9:30–1:30. The kitchen works on the stage of an old Masonic Hall, making Neapolitan-style pizza with house-made sausage, or local pork with milk and cheese polenta; the fried Brussels sprouts are excellent. Entrées $13–22.

& **The Point Restaurant at The Black Point Inn** (207-883-2500 or 1-800-258-0003; blackpointinn.com), 510 Black Point Rd., Prouts Neck. Open May–Jan. 1, reservation required in the formal restaurant. Fine casual entrées in the **Chart Room**, no reservations accepted, range $16–31; Sun. brunch. The cocktails on the porch overlooking the coastline are always fine. Entrées $24–34.

& **Saltwater Grille** (207-799-5400; saltwatergrille.com), 231 Front St., South Portland. Open daily for lunch and dinner, with fabulous views across the bay to Portland. Entrées include marinated hanger steak with mashed potatoes, baby back ribs, and roast salmon—all in enormous portions. Entrées $19–30.

The Purple House (brescaandthehoney bee.com), 378 Walnut Hill Rd., North Yarmouth. Krista Kern Desjarlais bought this small building in North Yarmouth in 2015 for her wood-fired bakery, with once-a-month dinners by reservation only. Montreal-style bagels, boiled in water with a little honey and undergoing a slow rise, are a specialty. Cuban coffee and her other signature, fantastic ice cream.

EATING OUT

IN AND AROUND THE OLD PORT

✪ **Petite Jacqueline** (207-553-7044; bistropj .com), 190 State St. French bistro fare priced right. Quiche, roast chicken, perhaps choucroute garnie on Friday for the plat du jour, and always tarte tatin. Entrées $13–26.

Bao Bao Dumpling House (207-772-8400; baobao-maine.com), 133 Spring St. Cara Stadler's Portland branch serves Vietnamese iced coffee. The boiled peanuts are a fantastic starter; the dumpling menu includes soup dumplings and other "wrapped treasures."

Eventide Oyster Co. (207-774-8538; eventideoysterco.com), 86 Middle St. Count on fresh oysters and the best choices of wine to go with them. Crab salads, grilled squid, chowders, fried oyster sides, and dinner of grilled beef brisket are all keenly tailored to taste delicious. The atmosphere is boisterous, not to mention loud. Excellent cocktails.

The Honey Paw (207-774-8538; thehoney paw.com) 78 Middle St. Closed Tue. Part of a little triumvirate in this one block of Middle Street, The Honey Paw serves eclectic noodles like ramen and ravioli with exalted flavors. Count on good wine. $14–36.

✎ **El Rayo** (207-780-8226; elrayotaqueria. com), 101 York St. (and 245 Rt. 1, Scarborough). Tacos, of course, like *al pastor*, filled with braised pork with grilled pineapple salsa, and great sides and beginners like ceviche, fried plantains, and fundido—baked cheese with chorizo. Big burritos, daily specials; finish with *dulces suenos*, mocha milk with tequila and Kahlúa. Excellent margaritas.

Vignola Cinque Terre (207-772-1330; vignolamaine.com), 10 Dana St. Open daily for dinner, Sat. for lunch and Sun. for brunch. Vignola Cinque Terre focuses on pizza, cured meats, and straightforward entrées like grilled skirt steak, pork loin, and a cassoulet with cotechino. Entrées $12–28.

Duckfat (207-774-8080; duckfat.com), 43 Middle St. Open daily 11 AM–dinner. Sister restaurant to Hugo's (see *Dining Out*), with the soul of a gourmand on a budget. Incredible fries rise from a mix of duck fat and vegetable oil. Panini are crisp cases of vegetable ratatouille or bacon, goat cheese, and tomatoes. Rich milk shakes, tender beignets, sweet dessert sandwiches of brioche and jam. Salads and iced coffee for a light lunch. Panini $6–13.50.

Sur Lie (207-956-7350; sur-lie.com), 11 Free St. Tapas and wine, wine and tapas—try the hanger steak and Lanzos Tempranillo or the fried oysters and Contadi Castaldi "Rose" with its bubbles. Cheese plates, charcuterie, and dessert, all carefully arranged on various little plates, or perhaps a piece of slate, with perfect little garnishes. $8–14.

Pai Men Miyake (207-541-9204; miyake restaurants.com), 188 State St. Deep bowls of miso broth with pork belly and noodles might be the main attraction, but the pork buns and crab and scallop hamayaki with eel sauce will have you licking your chops. The sake list is elaborate and worth your while. $9–14.

✎ **Flatbread Pizza** (207-772-8777; flat breadcompany.com), 72 Commercial St. Open daily 11:30 AM–dinner. One of a small chain of pizza joints (nine others include one in Paia Maui, Hawaii). Flatbread bakes its pies in a clay, wood-fired oven shaped like a low igloo—right in the middle of the restaurant. Kids are always sitting on a stone, mesmerized by the fire. Our favorite pizza features house maple-fennel sausage, sun-dried tomatoes, onions, mushrooms, mozzarella, and Parmesan. Outside deck overlooks the ferry terminal.

Schulte & Herr (207-773-1997), 349 Cumberland Ave. Open Tue.–Sun. 8–3. Fresh German food, from crisp potato pancakes with house lox, to tangy cucumber salad and spaetzle with Emmentaler, to a poppy-seed cake with vanilla sauce that was authenticated by our critical German companion.

Salvage BBQ (207-553-2100; salvagebbq .com), 919 Congress St. A big space dedicated to slow-smoked meat. Brisket, ribs, and chicken can be devoured with sides of slaw, collard greens, and smoked corn in-season. Peach pie and pecan pie for dessert.

Taco Escobarr (207-541-9097; taco escobarr.com), 548 Congress St. Closed Sun. A quick, cheap meal of three crisp, puffy, or soft tacos wrapped around braised chicken or carne asada is a welcome thing. The hot salsa is guaranteed to raise your temperature.

Tiqa (207-808-8840; tiqa.net), 327 Commercial St. Tiqa serves Middle Eastern- and Mediterranean-inspired dishes like kibbeh nayyeh from Lebanon, kabobs and kefta, and Maine lobster paella. A big terrace for outside dining or an aperitif; wines from the Middle East as well as elsewhere. Entrées $18–35.

Slab (207-245-3088; slabportland.com), 25 Preble St. Thick, soft, irresistible Sicilian slab pizza devised by baking fanatic Stephen Lanzalotta. Even when the sauce is skimpy and the dough undercooked, the slab addicts come back hoping for better and more, always more. You can get a salad, or chickpea hummus, or meatloaf or caponata, and fantastic Italian pastry. Thursday night concerts at the outside picnic tables; excellent assortment of local beers.

PORTLAND'S BEST COCKTAILS

Every self-respecting bar has a cocktail list with some ambition, and gems are scattered around Portland, like Boda's "The Fuge's Dilemma" made with a bourbon infused with 11 tigers—bitter and medicinal—or the perfect Old Fashioned at Eventide. But we depend on **Hunt & Alpine Club** (207-747-4754; huntandalpineclub.com), 75 Market St., for repeated brilliance from the diabolic cocktail shaker of John Myers—like the Modern, with scotch, sloe gin, lemon, and bitters; or their perfect version of the classic Penicillin, with scotch, ginger, honey, and lemon. The Scandinavian menu includes smoked trout deviled eggs and chewy brown bread and butter to go with the oysters. At **The Bearded Lady's Jewel Box,** (207-747-5384; the beardedladysjewelbox.com), 644 Congress St. (and probably no sign on the door), where you are one of the jewels, Nan'l Meiklejohn devises the cocktail list. If a TransEurope Express with scotch, Punt e Mes vermouth, yellow chartreuse, Campari, bitters, and a green chartreuse rinse isn't your go-to choice there will be something even stranger and just as delicious on the cocktail menu. The food is not the point: It's best to eat before you get there.

HUNT AND ALPINE CLUB

Nancy English

✪ **Empire Chinese Kitchen** (207-747-5063; portlandempire.com), 575 Congress St. A good Chinese restaurant that opened in the summer of 2013, Empire Chinese Kitchen serves dumplings, garlic string beans, dim sum, Peking duck buns, and lobster longevity noodles. Up to $19.

Benkay (207-773-5555; sushiman.com), 2 India St. A sushi bar with Western- and Japanese-style tables, one in the shape of a dory.

Sapporo Restaurant (207-772-1233; sappororestaurant.com), 230 Commercial St. Open for lunch and dinner daily. Portland's oldest sushi place has kept its high standards. You can count on Sapporo for a great dinner.

Jewel of India (207-828-2001; thejewelof india.com), 45 Western Ave., South Portland. Owned by the same family that made its reputation in Biddeford, this branch serves the same aromatic dishes.

AROUND PORTLAND

Bonobo (207-347-8267; bonobopizza.com), 46 Pine St. Open for lunch Wed.–Fri. 11:30–2:30,

Sat. noon–4; dinner Sun.–Thu. 4–10, Fri.–Sat. 4–11. A wood-fired oven bakes pizza with a thin crust made with wet dough; many organic ingredients are used. Sausage and onion is one popular pie. The house pizza, Bonobo, holds mushrooms, prosciutto, spinach, cream, fontina, and thyme. Pizza $12.50–16.50.

Oh No Café (207-774-0773; ohnocafe.com), 87 Bracket St. Home of the best breakfast sandwiches in Portland and a smoked salmon on bialy that will feed your soul. Beer and wine to purchase for take-out only.

✪ **Otto and Enzo** (207-773-7099; ottoportland.com), 576 Congress St. Exceptional pizza by the slice ($3.50) or pie. This is the spot to satisfy an appetite for thin-crust, remarkable pizza, perhaps with mashed potato and bacon, grilled eggplant and tomato, or classic pepperoni. Sister restaurant **Otto** (207-358-7870), 225 Congress St., is just as convivial; same terrific pizza.

🍴 🍷 ♿ **Becky's Diner** (207-773-7070; beckys.com), 390 Commercial St. Open daily 4 AM–9 PM, this is a genuine local favorite, known for soups and pies. Breakfast on fruit salad, a granola-and-yogurt bowl, and delicious grilled, homemade corn and blueberry muffins. Also reasonably priced lunch and dinner specials, and good chowder.

🍴 🍷 **Artemisia Café** (207-761-0135), 61 Pleasant St. (just behind and to the east of Holiday Inn by the Bay). Lunch Mon.–Fri., brunch Sat. and Sun., dinner Thu.–Sat. Salads, wraps, and sandwiches, from salade Niçoise to the Tuscan grill with portobello mushrooms, pesto, and goat cheese. A friendly spot for a quiet and good brunch or dinner.

Blue Rooster Food Co. (207-747-4157; blueroosterfoodcompany.com), 5 Dana St. Open 11 AM–2 AM. A sandwich shop with a few stools and benches around its small perimeter. Blue Rooster serves bacon-wrapped hot dogs with cheese sauce and crispy onions, along with a pastrami Cuban and the Godfather—mortadella, salami, Swiss, and provolone. Check out the twist on poutine made with tater tots.

Portland Patisserie (207-553-2555; portlandpatisserie.com), 46 Market St. Excellent croissants and pain au chocolat, crêpes savory and sweet, salads (including Niçoise), quiche, pâté de campagne on baguette, wine, beer, coffee, macarons and other desserts.

BEYOND PORTLAND

✪ **158 Pickett Street Café** (207-799-8998), 158 Benjamin Pickett St., South Portland. Breakfast and lunch Tue.–Sun. They make the bagels so exactly right: chewy, slightly sour, utterly delicious, and golden brown. A variety of original soups in winter, local salads in summer, and sandwiches like ham and Brie with roasted grapes on baguette, Anestes Fotiades's favorite (and see portlandfoodmap.com, his work of art).

Enio's Eatery (207-799-0207), 347 Cottage Rd., South Portland. A well-respected couple who have worked in many kitchens and local establishments over the years offer a fine wine list and calamari, lamb, halibut, and excellent desserts.

🍷 **The Lobster Shack at Two Lights** (207-799-1677; lobstershacktwolights.com), 225 Two Lights Rd., Cape Elizabeth (off Rt. 77 at the tip of the cape, near Two Lights State Park). Open Apr.–late Oct., 11–8. Dine inside or out at this local landmark built in the 1920s, set below the lighthouse and next to the foghorn, where Herb and Martha Porch sell amazing quantities of lobster, chowder, fried Maine shrimp, scallops, clams, and lobster and crabmeat rolls. BYOB.

Elsmere BBQ and Wood Grill (207-619-1948; elsmerebbq.com), 448 Cottage Rd., South Portland. A former gas station with reclaimed wood and concrete rehab, Elsmere serves Texas BBQ slow-cooked on a custom-built smoker and local craft beer.

Nancy English

KEN'S PLACE

🍴 ✂ **The Good Table** (207-799-4663; the goodtable.net), 526 Ocean House Rd. (Rt. 77), Cape Elizabeth. Open Tue.–Sun. for breakfast, lunch, and dinner 8 AM–9 PM in summer, from 11 AM in winter, with 3 PM Sun. closing year-round. Beloved by its loyal regulars, the restaurant serves home-style standards, but the specials board is where the best meals can be found.

Ken's Place (207-883-6611), 207 Pine Point Rd., Scarborough. Open daily for lunch and dinner Apr.–Oct. You can depend on David Wilcox to make sure things are running smoothly here, and that the kitchen is scrupulous about changing the oil and serving the freshest seafood. Great fried clams.

COFFEE Coffee by Design (207-772-5533; coffeebydesign.com), 620 Congress St. and 67 India St., is a friendly local chain in a cheerful spot with plenty of tables and its own roasted beans in the coffee and espresso. **Arabica** (207-899-1833; arabicacoffeeportland.com), 2 Free St. We like this place's high ceilings and its cinnamon toast. The coffee is the best in town. **Crema** (207-210-6473), 9 Commercial St.—also owned by the owners of Arabica—makes perfect espresso with their own perfectly roasted beans. Of course, people who flock to **Bard Coffee** (207-899-4788; bardcoffee.com), 185 Middle St., would say their own favorite spot, with its expert espresso, is even better. **The Speckled Ax** (207-660-3333), 567 Congress St., provides a traditional glass of seltzer with a wood-oven-roasted espresso, which beat out Bard in one newly returned-from-Italy Mainer's opinion.

DOUGHNUTS The Holy Donut (207-874-7774; theholydonut.com), 194 Park Ave. and 7 Exchange St., Portland, makes Maine potato doughnuts with unique flavors like chocolate sea salt and Allen's coffee brandy. The potato is mashed and added to the dough, which helps create the moist consistency of the doughnuts.

BAGELS Union Co. Bagels (207-747-4400; unionbagel.com), 147 Cumberland Ave. With organic flour, these are hand-rolled, boiled, and baked über authentic NYC bagels.

PASTRY AND PIES Standard Baking Co. (207-773-2112; standardbakingco.com), 75 Commercial St. (below Fore Street restaurant). Artisanal French and Italian breads are exceptional, and so are the rolls, baguettes, brioches, and pain au chocolat. **Ten Ten Pié** (207-956-7330) 171 Cumberland Ave., Portland. "Unlike any other bakery in Maine," one customer crows, and what else could be true when the offerings range from bento boxes of cold ramen salad with marinated egg and savory pies to lingonberry pinwheels and macarons. **Scratch Baking** (207-799-0668; scratchbakingco.com), 416 Preble St., South Portland. The best bagels for those of us who like slow-rise, crisp crust often sell out on weekends; sandwiches on the other breads baked here; extraordinary cookies, cakes, pies. **Little Bigs** (207-747-4233; littlebigs maine.com), 340 Main St., South Portland; supplies Mainers with its own version of a cronut—along with Nutella- and banana-filled doughnuts, and savory pies like a breakfast calzone or potato-crusted egg pies. **Two Fat Cats** (207-347-5144; twofatcatsbakery.com), 47 India St., Portland. Cupcakes, terrific blueberry pie, red velvet cake, and many other delectables.

ICE CREAM AND GELATO Beal's Ice Cream (207-828-1335; bealsicecream.com), 12 Moulton St., is in the middle of the Old Port (and has four other locations), making 17 percent butterfat premium ice cream. **Mount Desert Island Ice Cream** (207-210-3432; mdiic.com), 51 Exchange St., just up the street, makes its own terrific ice creams, some spiked with hot chili—but who can resist the salted caramel? **Gorgeous Gelato** (207-699-4309; gorgeousgelato.com), 434 Fore St., calls itself the only authentic gelato in Portland and uses cream and whole milk in its brilliantly flavored confections. Mariagrazia Zanardi and her husband, Donato Giovine, from Milan, make gelato with "70 percent less fat" than premium ice cream. **Gelato Fiasco** (207-699-4314; gelatofiasco.com), 425 Fore St., moved in across the street in late 2011. Time to take a stroll and compare them all.

✳ Entertainment

All listings are in Portland unless otherwise noted.

Cross Insurance Arena (207-775-3458; crossarenaportland.com), 1 Civic Center

Square. An arena with 6,733 seats, the center hosts year-round concerts, ice-skating spectaculars, Portland Pirates hockey games, and more.

Thompson's Point (thompsonspoint maine.com) at Thompson's Point, a small peninsula that juts out into the Fore River, is the new site of a **Circus Conservatory**, a winery that hosts open-air concerts in the summertime, with an orchard of Trees of Forty Fruits that can be harvested for months, once mature.

MUSIC **Portland Symphony Orchestra** (207-773-6128; portlandsymphony.com), Merrill Auditorium, 20 Myrtle St. (just off Congress St. behind City Hall). The winter series runs Sept.–May; in summertime, outdoor pops concerts at different locations along the shores of Casco Bay.

PORTopera (207-879-7678; portopera.org), Merrill Auditorium. This critically acclaimed company puts on an opera in mid-summer.

Portland Ovations (207-773-3150; portland ovations.org). A series of orchestra, jazz, and musical theater performances staged in fall and winter at Merrill Auditorium.

Port City Music Hall (207-899-4990; portcitymusichall.com), 504 Congress St. Contemporary, popular music.

PROFESSIONAL SPORTS The **Portland Sea Dogs** (1-800-936-3647; portlandseadogs.com), a Double-A baseball team and Boston Red Sox affiliate, play in Hadlock Stadium on Park Ave. (next to the Expo). The **Maine Red Claws** (207-210-6655; nba.com/dleague/maine), an NBA Development League affiliated with the Boston Celtics, had their first season in 2009–10, playing in the Portland Expo Building on Park Ave.

THEATER **Portland Stage** (207-774-0465; portlandstage.com) is based in the city's old Odd Fellows Hall (25A Forest Ave.), now an elegant, intimate, 290-seat theater. This Equity group stages a variety of shows Oct.–Apr.

Portland Players (207-799-7337), Thaxter Theater, 420 Cottage Rd., South Portland. An excellent community theater; the Players put on productions Sept.–June.

Lyric Music Theater (207-799-1421), Cedric Thomas Playhouse, 176 Sawyer St., South Portland. Four musicals each winter.

ANGELA ADAMS'S STORE   Nancy English

St. Lawrence Arts Center (207-775-5568; stlawrencearts.org), 76 Congress St. An umbrella performance space for musicians, filmmakers, dance companies, and other artists. **The Good Theater** (207-885-5883), a resident theater company, performs four stage productions and one musical each season. The schedule changes constantly, so call to see what's doing.

✳ Selective Shopping

All listings are in Portland unless otherwise noted.

Angela Adams (207-774-3523; angela adams.com), 131 Middle St. This store sells the swirling, colorful carpets and handbags designed by Angela Adams: Pricey rugs are coveted nationwide. Sales held at the end of each retail season.

Ferdinand (207-761-2151; ferdinandhome store.com), 243 Congress St. Just steps from Angela Adams, Ferdinand is stuffed with low chic—T-shirts with charming animals and inexpensive pins, earrings, and jewelry, all infused with owner Diane Toepfer's eccentric aesthetic.

Sea Bags (207-780-0744; seabags.com), 24 Custom House Wharf, sells fashionable, eco-friendly tote bags made in Portland, from recycled sails.

ANTIQUES Allen and Walker (207-772-8787), 684 Congress St. A mix of 1960s modern and older antiques, with some Japanese pottery.

ART GALLERIES Art Walks are held the first Friday of every month, when galleries citywide hold open houses.

Greenhut Galleries (207-772-2693 or 1-888-772-2693; greenhutgalleries.com), 146 Middle St. Peggy Golden Greenhut represents many of Maine's top artists and sculptors.

June Fitzpatrick Gallery (207-772-1961; fitzpatrickgallery.com), 522 Congress St. Well established and showcasing contemporary and fine art.

Susan Maasch Fine Art (207-478-4087; susanmaaschfineart.com), 4 City Center. Established and new artists.

BOOKSTORES Longfellow Books (207-772-4045; longfellowbooks.com), 1 Monument Way, is Portland's literary hot spot, stocking a full range of titles and hosting frequent readings by local and national authors. **Sherman's Maine Coast Book Shops** (207-773-4100; shermans.com), 49 Exchange St., opened this fifth Maine location in 2015 with book signings and toys.

Antiquarian-book lovers should check out **Carlson-Turner Books** (207-773-4200; carlsonturnerbooks.com), 241 Congress St. **Yes Books** (207-775-3233), 589 Congress

HARBOR FISH OYSTERS

Nancy English

St., founded by Pat Murphy, is considered by some to be the best used-book store in Maine.

FOOD Micucci Grocery (207-775-1854; micuccigrocery.com), 45 India St. Order prosciutto and Parmigiana at the counter, shop for wine, olive oil, and maybe an Italian pastry while you wait.

Maine's Pantry (207-228-2028; mainespantry.com), 111 Commercial St. Many of the best food products made in Maine can be found here—like Stanchfield Farms' high-quality jams and jellies, and Captain Mowett Blue Flame hot sauce.

Len Libby's Candies (207-883-4897; lenlibby.com), 419 Rt. 1, Scarborough. The candies made here are good, but the real draw is the enormous moose named Lenny—made with 1,700 pounds of milk chocolate, the only life-sized chocolate moose in the world, put together in 1997.

Browne Trading Market (207-775-7560; brownetrading.com), 260 Commercial St. Open Mon.–Sat. 10–6. Formerly a fish wholesaler serving upscale restaurants throughout the United States, now selling its own smoked salmon, trout, shrimp, scallops, mussels, fresh seafood, and caviar, along with a wide assortment of cheeses and wine.

Harbor Fish Market (207-775-0251 or 1-800-370-1790; harborfish.com), 9 Custom House Wharf. Open Mon.–Sat. 8:30–5:30. The epicenter of fish, lobster, crabs, oysters, clams, eels, and squid, to name a few, which you can ship anywhere you like.

Nancy English

LONGFELLOW BOOKS

SPECIAL SHOPS **Portmanteau** (207-774-7276; portmanteauonline.com), 11 Free St. Nancy Lawrence began by stitching canvas bags but has long since established a reputation for the distinctive tapestry handbags, totes, backpacks, luggage, and cloaks fabricated in her store.

Leroux Kitchen (207-553-7665; leroux kitchen.com), 161 Commercial St. Everything you could possibly need to make a gourmet meal, from marble mortars and pestles to Henckels knives, Viking cookware to wines and prepared foods.

Vena's Fizz House (207-747-4901; venas fizzhouse.com), 345 Fore St., Portland. This emporium of bar gadgets, glassware, and specialty drink ingredients deserves a visit when nonalcoholic drinks are served, whenever it's open; on Wed.–Sat. after 4 (and all day Sunday), you can order alcoholic craft cocktails to sample the stuff you might want to bring home from the biggest collection of bitters you are likely to encounter. A short food menu offers lobster BLT, nuts, pickles.

Cabela's (cabelas.com), Haigis Pkwy., Scarborough 04070. Located at I-95 Exit 42. Cabela's, a nationwide outdoor retail chain, opened this new 130,000-square-foot showroom in spring 2008.

❋ Special Events

Mid-March: **Maine Jewish Film Festival** (mjff.org).

June: **Old Port Festival** (second Sunday)—a celebration that began in the 1970s with the revival of the Old Port; includes a parade, various performances, street vendors, and special sales.

July: **July 4th Portland Stars and Stripes Extravaganza**. The Portland Symphony and a guest perform on the Eastern Promenade before the fireworks.

Mid-July: **Yarmouth Clam Festival**—arts and crafts, plenty of clams, performances, more. **Maine Brewer's Festival Summer Session** (mainebreweersguild.org), now at Thompson's Point. More than 50 Maine microbreweries show off their beers.

August: **Cumberland Crafts Fair**, Cumberland Fairgrounds. **Sidewalk Art Festival**, Congress St.

September: **Cumberland County Fair**, Cumberland.

October: **Harvest on the Harbor**, Portland.

Post-Thanksgiving–Christmas: **Victorian Holiday Portland**—with tree lighting, the arrival of Father Christmas, costumed carolers, and special events through Christmas.

FREEPORT

Think of Freeport, and you'll likely think of shopping. This is one coastal town that welcomes visitors every day of the year, even on Christmas morning, when the famous L.L. Bean store is open for business. A 24-hour, 365-day-a-year superstore, L.L. Bean has been a landmark since the famous boot was developed back in 1912. But it was with the influx of seconds and factory stores in the early 1980s that the reputation of Freeport as a shopping mecca took hold.

The retail facades, however, belie a rich and varied history dating back more than 200 years. The first known residents of the area were several tribes of the Wabanaki. Attempts by colonists to settle in the area resulted in a series of wars throughout the 1600s and early 1700s. By 1715 epidemics of European diseases and the settlers' persistence ended the Native American hold on the area, and a peace treaty with the Penobscots was signed in 1725.

Originally a part of North Yarmouth, Freeport was granted a charter, separating it from the town in 1789. A longtime legend (somewhat controversial, because there is no documented evidence of the occurrence) holds that in 1820 the papers separating Maine from Massachusetts were signed in the historical Jameson Tavern.

During the War of 1812, shipbuilding became an important industry, with one famous boat inspiring Whittier's poem, "The Dead Ship of Harpswell." In the 1880s shoe factories sprouted up in Freeport, adding another industry to its economy.

When an electric trolley was built to connect Portland and Yarmouth with Brunswick and Lewiston, it passed through Freeport. Many trolley companies built parks to encourage ridership; likewise, a developer built the Casco Castle Hotel to draw tourists to South Freeport. The hotel burned down, but a stone tower remains (on private property) and can be best viewed from Winslow Memorial Park or from the harbor.

Despite the proliferation of shops, the village has retained the appearance of older days—even McDonald's has been confined to a gracious old house, with no golden arches in sight. The Freeport Historical Society operates a research library and museum in a historic house in the midst of the retail sector.

GUIDANCE **FreeportUSA** (207-865-1212 or 1-800-865-1994; freeportusa.com), P.O. Box 452, Freeport 04032, operates a visitors center in a relocated historic hose tower on Depot St. Brochures, information, and restrooms can be found here.

The Maine Tourism Association's welcome center in Kittery stocks some Freeport brochures, and there is another state information center on Rt. 1 just south of Freeport, in Yarmouth, at Exit 17 off I-95.

GETTING THERE Excellent bus service on **Concord Coach Lines** (see *Getting There* in "Portland Area") runs from Boston to Brunswick. The Amtrak **Downeaster** (1-800-USA-RAIL; amtrak.com) offers service through to Brunswick with stops in Freeport, with five round-trips daily.

✳ Villages

South Freeport has been a fishing center from its beginning, when it was known as Strout's Port. Between 1825 and 1830 up to 12,000 barrels of mackerel were packed and shipped

DOWNTOWN FREEPORT

from here each year. Later the area specialty became lobster packing. Offering a very different feel from the chaotic shopping frenzy of downtown Freeport, the harbor features great seafood. From here you can take a cruise to explore Eagle and Seguin Islands in summer.

Porter's Landing. Once the center of commercial activity, this now quiet residential neighborhood nestles amid rolling hills, woods, and streams. The village is part of the Harraseeket Historic District on the National Register of Historic Places.

�֎ To See and Do

🔍 🎯 ✎ ♿ **Desert of Maine** (207-865-6962; desertofmaine.com), 95 Desert Rd., Freeport. Open daily, early May–mid-Oct., 9–5. Admission runs $10.50 adults, $7.75 ages 13–16, $6.75 ages 4–12. Narrated tram tours and self-guided walks through 40 acres of sand that was once the Tuttle Farm. Heavily farmed, then extensively logged to feed the railroad, the topsoil eventually gave way to the glacial sand deposit beneath it, which spread . . . and spread until entire trees sank below the surface. Children love it, especially the gem hunt, when you sluice for gems from a bag of "tailings" guaranteed to contain small or large gemstones or fossils (from $6 to $8.50). Camping available (see *Lodging*).

BOATING **Atlantic Seal Cruises** (207-865-6112; atlanticsealcruises.com), Town Wharf, South Freeport. Memorial Day–mid-Oct. Captain Thomas Ring runs daily narrated trips (if the eight-person minimum is met) into Casco Bay, including three-hour cruises to Eagle Island, the former summer home of Admiral Robert E. Peary, the first person to reach the North Pole; six-hour cruises from South Freeport to Seguin Island Lighthouse to see—and climb inside—the fascinating first-order Fresnel lens, and a visit to the museum run by the Friends of the Seguin Lighthouse Caretakers (with 50-foot humpback whale and porpoise sightings on the trip to the island).

BREWERY The excellent **Maine Beer Company** (207-221-5711; mainebeercompany.com), 525 Rt. 1, has a tasting room for a special introduction to their beer, with a view of the brewery through wide glass windows.

CANOEING The **Harraseeket River** in Freeport is particularly nice for canoeing. Start at Mast Landing, the northeastern end of the waterway; there are also launching sites at Winslow Memorial Park on Staples Point Rd. and at South Freeport Harbor.

GOLF **Freeport Country Club** (207-865-0711; harrisgolfonline.com), 2 Old County Rd., Freeport. Nine holes, golf clinics, driving range, pro shop, and snack bar.

MUSEUM ✎ **Harrington House** (207-865-3170; freeporthistoricalsociety.org), 45 Main St., Freeport. Hours vary depending on season; check the website under VISIT US. Donations appreciated. Built of local brick and granite, this 1830 house and its garden are maintained by the Freeport Historical Society as a museum, research library, and archive.

MUST SEE

L.L. BEAN (1-877-755-2326; llbean.com), 95 Main St. Open 24 hours a day, 365 days a year, as are the three other stores listed below (but not the outlet). With a kids' department, a camping department, a pond stocked with brown or brook trout, and a trail "rock" to test new hiking boots, the building resembles a fancy shopping mall more than it does a single store. Back in 1912 Leon Leonwood Bean developed his boot, or Maine Hunting Shoe, a unique combination of rubber bottom and leather top. "You cannot expect success hunting deer or moose if your feet are not properly dressed," Bean wrote in his very first catalog. Ninety out of the first 100 boots he built literally fell apart at the seams, so Bean refunded the purchasers' money and began a company tradition of guaranteed customer satisfaction, including all-night hours for the outdoorsmen who passed through in the wee hours. Bean himself died in 1967.

Nancy English

L.L. BEAN BIKE, BOAT & SKI STORE

L.L. Bean Hunting and Fishing Store (1-877-755-2326, llbean.com), 95 Main St. All the fishing equipment is here, along with archery gear and hunting rifles. Bean also sells used guns, and will buy guns in good condition. Fish and game mounts are hung around the store, giving the place a hunting lodge atmosphere.

L.L. Bean Bike, Boat & Ski Store (1-877-755-2326, llbean.com), 95 Main St. When the weather warms up, the bike and boat displays bloom; when it's getting colder it's time for all the ski equipment, snowshoes, toboggans, and sleds to take a bigger share of the space.

L.L. Bean Home Store (1-877-755-2326, llbean.com), 12 Nathan Nye St., Freeport. Opened in the summer of 2009, the Home Store stocks attractive, inexpensive quilts based on vintage designs, good-quality flannel and cotton sheets, towels, hooked-wool pillows, and furniture like a wicker side table.

SPECIAL LEARNING PROGRAMS L.L. Bean Outdoor Discovery Schools (1-888-552-3261; llbean.com/adventure), Rt. 1, Freeport. You can get your toes wet—literally, if you're kayaking—with L.L. Bean's Discovery Series. For a fee, participants can take a shuttle bus from the downtown store to enjoy 1½ hours of (Memorial Day–Columbus Day) fly casting, kayaking, archery, and clay shooting—and, when the snow permits, until March, cross-country skiing and snowshoeing.

The L.L. Bean Outdoor Discovery Schools also offer half-day or longer tours and classes that cover the basics—like "Introduction to Stand-Up Paddleboarding." A two-night Casco Bay Island Kayak Camping Trip includes lobster dinner.

✳ Green Space

✐ **Winslow Memorial Park** (207-865-4198; freeportmaine.com), Staples Point Rd., South Freeport. Open Memorial Day–Sept. A 90-acre municipal park with a sandy beach and large grassy picnicking area; also boating and 100-site oceanside campground ($20–27 per night for nonresidents). Facilities include restrooms with showers. $2 nonresident admission fee.

✐ **Mast Landing Audubon Sanctuary** (207-781-2330; maineaudubon.org), Upper Mast Landing Rd. (take Bow St. south), Freeport. Maintained by Maine Audubon, this 140-acre sanctuary offers trails through apple orchards, woods, meadows, and along a millstream. Several paths radiate from a 1-mile loop trail. You might even get lucky and see mink, deer, or porcupines.

🐾 ✐ **Bradbury Mountain State Park** (207-688-4712; bradburymountain.com), Rt. 9, 528 Hallowell Rd., Pownal (6 miles from Freeport: from I-95, take Exit 20 and follow signs). Open year-round. $4.50 nonresidents ages 12 and older, $1 ages 5–11, under 5 free. The summit, accessible by an easy (even for young children) 0.5-mile hike, yields a splendid view of Casco Bay and New Hampshire's White Mountains. Facilities in the 800-acre park include a small playground, a softball field, hiking trails, toilets, and a 35-site overnight camping area.

✐ **Pettengill Farm** (207-865-3170; freeporthistoricalsociety.org), Pettengill Rd., Freeport. Managed by the Freeport Historical Society (which conducts periodic guided tours), the grounds are open anytime. A saltwater farm with 140 acres of open fields and woodland that overlooks the Harraseeket Estuary, with a totally unmodernized vintage-1810 saltbox house.

✐ ♿ **Wolfe's Neck Woods State Park** (207-865-4465), 425 Wolfe's Neck Rd. (take Bow St., across from L.L. Bean), Freeport. Open Apr.–Nov. A 233-acre park with shoreline hiking along Casco Bay, the Harraseeket River, and salt marshes, with excellent birding. Ospreys nest here, and an eagle is nearby. Guided nature walks and scattered picnic tables and grills. Day-use fee for nonresident adults.

✳ Lodging

All listings are in Freeport 04032 unless otherwise noted.

INNS AND B&BS 🐾 ✐ ♿ **Harraseeket Inn** (207-865-9377 or 1-800-342-6423; harraseeketinn.com), 162 Main St. The Gray family—Nancy, her son Chip, and daughter Penelope (all former Maine Guides)—have a passion for Maine expressed through meticulous and warm innkeeping. Two blocks north of L.L. Bean, their inn began as a five-room B&B in the 1800 Federal house next door. Many of the rooms feature antiques and reproductions, canopy bed, and Jacuzzi; 20 have a fireplace. The inn has formal dining rooms (see *Dining Out*) and the casual and popular Broad Arrow Tavern (see *Eating Out*). Glassed-in pool overlooking the gardens. Rates in-season are $190–325, full buffet breakfast and afternoon tea included.

Hilton Garden Inn Freeport (207-865-1433; hiltongardeninn.com), 5 Park St. Reliable and with all the best amenities, this Hilton Garden Inn has 99 rooms, indoor pool, hot tub, exercise room, restaurant, and bar. A gas fireplace burns in the lounge, where you can enjoy a drink. The inn is a five-minute walk to the shops.

🐾 ✐ **White Cedar Inn** (207-865-9099 or 1-800-853-1269; whitecedarinn.com), 178 Main St. Open year-round. This restored Victorian is the former home of Arctic explorer Donald B. MacMillan, who traveled nearly to the North Pole with Admiral Peary—until frostbite set in. Seven bedrooms come with private bath, down comforters, and air-conditioning; some have a fireplace. Owners Rock Nadeau and Monica Kissane, who are constantly updating the inn's rooms, serve a full breakfast at small tables in the sunroom. Doubles $135–225.

Brewster House (207-865-4121; brewster house.com), 180 Main St. The bright, warm colors of the tasteful and well-appointed rooms and immaculate bathrooms at Brewster House will put any traveler at ease. Scott and Mary Gile bought this established business in 2013. As low as $169 for the rooms and $279 for a two-bedroom suite, including breakfast that might be blueberry-stuffed French toast.

The James Place Inn (207-865-4486 or 1-800-964-9086; jamesplaceinn.com), 11 Holbrook St. Victoria and Robin Baron have furnished their pretty B&B with charm, luxury, and beautiful furnishings. Single guests enjoy a stay in the Rose Room, with a stunning spool bed and a single whirlpool bath. All seven rooms have air-conditioning and cable TV; one features a kitchenette. Full breakfast at the café tables on the deck or in the pretty glassed-in breakfast room. $149–199.

☗ **Applewood Inn** (207-865-9705; applewoodusa.com), 10 Holbrook St. Jay and Jennifer Yilmaz have five rooms in well-kept, modern buildings for nightly rentals, one with a full kitchen. Local artists are the creators of much of the engaging decor. Breakfast included in the $165–300 in-season rates; longer-term rentals available. The family also operates several AJ Dogs stands and an ice cream stand on Freeport's busy Main Street.

✪ ☗ ✔ ♿ **Royalsborough Inn at the Bagley House** (207-353-6372 or 1-800-765-1772; royalsboroughinn.com), 1290 Royalsborough Rd., Durham 04222. A 10-minute drive from downtown Freeport in a serene country setting, this is the oldest house in town, built as a public house in 1772. The town's first worship services were held here, and this was the site of the first schoolhouse. Marianne and Jim Roberts have furnished eight rooms with antiques and down and alpaca comforters. $140–180 double in-season includes full breakfast and afternoon refreshments.

MOTELS **The Village Inn** (207-865-3236; reservations only, 1-800-998-3649; freeport villageinn.com), 186 Main St., has rates starting at $75 and is within easy walking distance of all the shops. The very basic decor is perfectly clean, and the owners since 1986, Lewis and Jackie Corliss, are down-home Mainers who can tell you the history of their transformed town or help you get your disabled car fixed, as they did for us.

On Rt. 1 south of Freeport near the Yarmouth town line are a number of modern motels. Among these is the ☗ **Best Western Freeport Inn** (207-865-3106 or 1-800-99-VALUE; freeportinn.com), 31 Rt. 1. Set on 25 acres of lawns and nature trails, this place offers an upscale motel ambience at reasonable prices. Outdoor swimming pool and playground. Pets are allowed in 22 of the 80 rooms. Doubles are $125–214. The Freeport Café serves breakfast all day (seasonal hours).

CAMPGROUNDS ☗ ✔ ♿ **Cedar Haven Campground** (207-865-6254; reservations only, 1-800-454-3403; cedarhavenfamily campground.com), 39 Baker Rd. Open May–Oct. Fifty-eight mostly wooded sites, each with fireplace and picnic table. Water and electricity hookups, five with sewer and cable TV as well. Ten tent sites. Store with wood, ice, and groceries; mini golf, playground, and pond for swimming. Two miles from Rt. 1 and downtown Freeport. $31–50 per night.

☗ ✔ ♿ **Desert Dunes of Maine Campground** (207-865-6962; desertofmaine.com), 95 Desert Rd. Located next to a kitschy attraction with a natural glacial sand deposit (see *To See and Do*), this campground offers 50 wooded and open sites with hookups, hot showers, laundry, convenience store, propane, fire rings, picnic tables, horseshoe pits, nature trails, and swimming pool. Campsites are $30–39 per night.

✳ Where to Eat

All listings are in Freeport unless otherwise noted.

DINING OUT ♿ **Harraseeket Inn Maine Dining Room** (207-865-9377 or 1-800-342-6423), 162 Main St. Open year-round for dinner and Sun. brunch 11:30–2. Continental cuisine and elegant service in three formal dining rooms. The chefs use fresh, in-season, and often organic ingredients from local gardeners and farmers. Entrées $24–38. The

Harraseeket is also known for its Sunday brunch, which can feature caviar, oysters on the half shell, lobster, and a crêpe station.

✪ **Azure Café** (207-865-1237; azurecafe .com), 123 Main St. Alfresco dining in good weather allows careful surveillance of the shoppers, but warm, handsome rooms and a bar inside make sure you can enjoy the good food year-round. The focus is on Italy, with ravioli stuffed with butternut squash and ricotta, or grilled filet mignon skewers glazed with roasted garlic balsamic. Maine seafood risotto marries the best of both coastlines. Steamed lobster is sold for the best price in town, guaranteed. The classic pasta dishes are worth exploring. Entrées $13–32.

Mediterranean Grill (207-865-1688; mediterraneangrill.biz), 10 School St. Open daily in summer for lunch and dinner, closing earlier off-season. A Turkish dinner awaits you here: everything from falafel and stuffed eggplant to kebabs, moussaka, and lamb shanks. Choose from Turkish wines as well as the usual from California, and baklava to end. Entrées $16–23.

EATING OUT 🍷 ♿ **The Broad Arrow Tavern** (207-865-9377), Harraseeket Inn, 162 Main St. Open 11:30–10:30, with drinks until midnight. A ground-floor dining room overlooking the terrace, this place is packed with fans of the delicious food, unstuffy pub atmosphere, and collection of stuffed animals on the wall (moose, fish, deer). The open kitchen has a wood-fired oven and grill, and serves up

everything from pizzas, sandwiches, and grilled steak to a Caesar salad.

Tuscan Brick Oven Bistro (207-869-7200; tuscanbrickovenbistro.com), 140 Main St., has a wood-fired oven fennel sausage and burrata pizza, a daily risotto, and classic Italian entrées from gnocchi to spicy zuppa di pesce. Entrées $11–34.

Petrillo's (207-865-6055; petrillosfreeport .com), 5 Depot St., is where all the locals go for a good burger; a brunch pizza with eggs, spinach and prosciutto; or a fine plate of seafood linguine. Entrées $8–21.

✪ **Jacqueline's Tea Room** (207-865-2123; jacquelinestearoom.com), 201 Main St. Open 10:30–3 Tue.–Sat. Make a reservation for tea with all the trimmings; four courses and unlimited tea, with tea sandwiches of smoked salmon or cucumber, delicate, crumbling scones with clotted cream and lemon curd, and cakes, tarts, and English toffee. Tea is chosen from a list of 100-plus teas (also available to purchase) and served in 2-cup teapots during a leisurely two hours.

Conundrum (207-865-0303; conundrum winebistro.com), 117 Rt. 1, South Freeport. This bistro, set right under the Big Indian, serves good burgers and other casual meals in an intimate, red room along with varieties of pâté and cheese (also sold in the neighboring shop, Old World Gourmet; see *Snacks*), which you can order as entrées. The wine selection is amazing, and you can enjoy a taste before deciding on a glass, or half glass, to drink. Entrées $10–27.

🍷 ♿ **Gritty McDuff's** (207-865-4321), 187 Lower Main St. The only brewpub in Freeport, this branch of the popular Portland pub offers outdoor dining, lobster, seafood, pizza, and pub food. Great ales brewed right here, and a tasty lamb burger with feta, too.

✪ 🍷 **Harraseeket Lunch & Lobster Co.** (207-865-4888), foot of Main St., South Freeport (turn off Rt. 1 at the giant wooden Indian, then turn right at a stop sign a few miles down). Open May–Columbus Day. At this traditional lobster shack in the middle of the Harraseeket boatyard, order lobsters and clams on one side, fried food on the other, and eat at picnic tables (of which there are never enough at peak hours) overlooking a boat-filled harbor. Lobsters are fresh from the pound's boats; homemade desserts. There is

AZURE CAFÉ

Nancy English

STEAMERS AND A POUND-AND-A-HALF LOBSTER AT
HARRASEEKET LUNCH & LOBSTER

also a small inside dining room. Be aware that it is a busy place; you may have to wait to eat.

SNACKS AND TAKEOUT Old World Gourmet (207 865 4477), Rt. 1 (next to the Big Indian). Imported cheese, pâté, prepared food, and wine are ready to fill picnic baskets or take over dinner duty.

Royal River Natural Foods (207-865-0046; rrnf.com), 443 Rt. 1. A great place to buy vegetarian snacks for the road, such as organic fruits and local vegetables, freshly made soups, pasta and green salads, sandwiches, and muffins, which you can eat in the café, too.

✳ Selective Shopping

OUTLETS 🛍 As noted in the chapter's introduction, Freeport's 74-plus downtown factory outlets, with more on the edges of town, constitute what may have become Maine's mightiest tourist magnet. *Boston Globe* writer Nathan Cobb called it "a shoppers' theme park spread out at the foot of L.L. Bean, the high church of country chic."

A $45 million open-air commercial center, Freeport Village Station, opened in 2009 on more than 3 acres of L.L. Bean–owned land in the middle of town; it holds factory outlets for Calvin Klein, Talbots, Nike, Coach, Izod, PacSun, Van Heusen, Brooks Brothers, and the L.L. Bean Outlet itself.

L.L. Bean Outlet Store, 1 Freeport Village Station. Seconds, samples, and irregular merchandise of all kinds. You never know what you'll find, but it's always worth a look. Unlike the main store, the outlet is open only during the hours for Freeport Village Station: Mon.–Sat. 9–9, Sun. 10–6.

Thomas Moser Cabinetmakers (207-865-4519 or 1-800-708-9041; thosmoser.com), 149 Main St. Open Mon.–Sat. 10–6, Sun. 11–5. Fine furniture inspired by Shaker, Arts and Crafts, Japanese, Danish, and art deco designs. This family business has been a Freeport institution for more than 35 years.

&. **Cuddledown of Maine Factory Store** (207-865-1713 or 1-888-235-3696; cuddledown .com), 554 Rt. 1. Comforters, pillows, gift items, all filled with goose down. The annual sale in mid-July is worth the trip.

Brahms Mount (207-869-4025; brahms mount.com), 115 Main St. The specialty here is beautiful fabrics—linen and cotton blankets and throws, scarves, pillows, and towels. Sold throughout the country at exclusive stores, they are on display here in all their sumptuous glory.

SPECIAL SHOPS
All listings are in Freeport unless otherwise noted.

Brown Goldsmiths (207-865-4126; brown goldsmiths.com), 11 Mechanic St. Open Mon.–Sat. Original designs in rings, earrings, and bracelets.

Maine Distilleries (207-865-4828; maine distilleries.com), 437 Rt. 1, south of Rt. 295 Exit 20. Using Maine potatoes grown on his farm in Fryeburg, Donnie Thibodeau and his brother, neurosurgeon Lee Thibodeau, teamed up with a professional brewer and former Olympic ski coach Bob Harkins to open Maine's first vodka distillery in 2005.

🖉 **DeLorme's Map Store** (207-865-4171), Rt. 1 (south of downtown Freeport). A large bank of computers invites visitors to try mapping software. Many people come just to see Eartha, the world's largest rotating and revolving globe, which spins quietly in a glassed-in lobby.

Edgecomb Potters/Hand in Hand Gallery (207-865-1705 or 1-800-343-5529; edgecombpotters.com), 8 School St. Fine contemporary American crafts, including colorful porcelain made in Maine, jewelry, blown glass, and iron.

✪ ✏ ♿ **Mangy Moose** (207-865-6414 or 1-800-606-6517; themangymoose.com), 112 Main St. Moose, moose, and more moose. Susan Culkins has put together a fun store filled with clothing, books, art, and mounts— meaning stuffed moose, mountain lion, bobcat, caribou, and bear heads. A beautiful rustic quilt with machine-embroidered pine-cones was reasonably priced, but the moose antler chandelier rang up at $6,000.

Sherman's Maine Coast Book Shops (207-869-9000; shermans.com), 128 Main St. A branch of the Maine bookseller (also in Bar Harbor, Camden, Boothbay Harbor, and Port-land), featuring Maine books and gifts, cards, and toys.

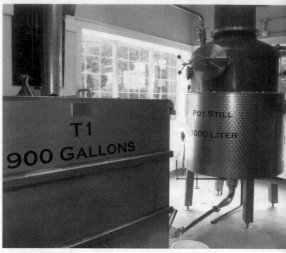

COLD RIVER VODKA   Nancy English

✳ Special Events

Mid-February: **L.L. Bean Kids Winter Fun Week; Winter Festivities and Flavors of Freeport** (freeportusa.com).

Early June: **L.L. Bean Paddlesport Weekend.**

Summer: Frequent musical and comedy performances in the **L.L. Bean Discovery Park.**

Fall: **Pettengill Farm Days**—living history demonstrations, horse-drawn wagon rides, inside/outside house tours, children's days, fresh-pressed cider. **Fall in the Village Art and Music Festival.**

December: **Sparkle Weekend** (first full weekend)—caroling, horse-drawn wagons, Santa arriving in a Maine yacht, and **Tuba Concert.**

MIDCOAST AND THE ISLANDS

BRUNSWICK AND THE HARPSWELLS

BATH AREA

WISCASSET AREA

BOOTHBAY HARBOR REGION

DAMARISCOTTA/NEWCASTLE/
WALDOBORO AND PEMAQUID AREA

ROCKLAND/THOMASTON AREA

MIDCOAST ISLANDS

Monhegan; The Fox Islands: Vinalhaven and
North Haven; Matinicus

CAMDEN/ROCKPORT AREA

Isleboro

BELFAST, SEARSPORT, AND
STOCKTON SPRINGS

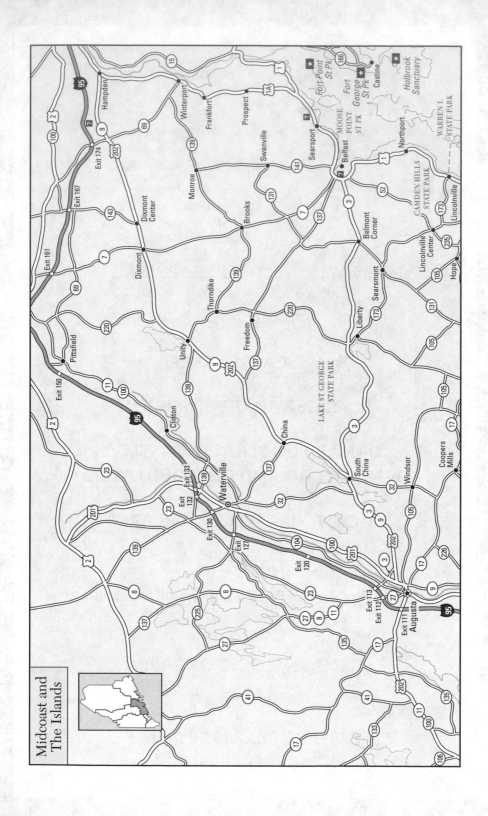

Midcoast and
The Islands

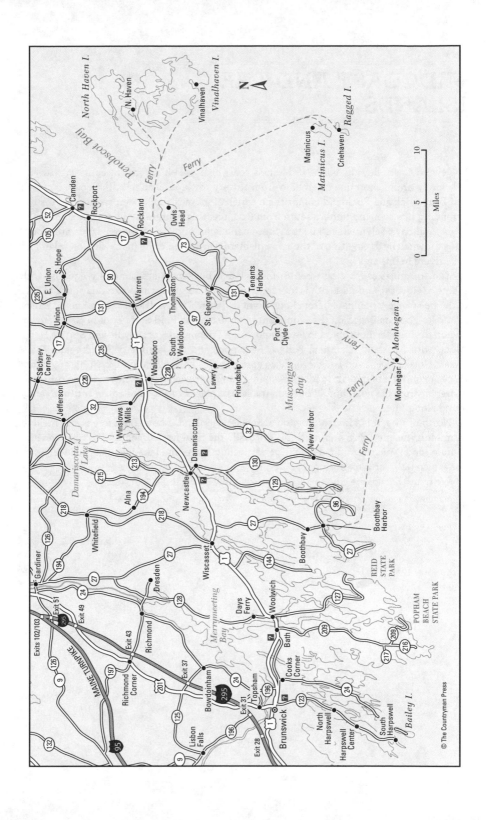

MIDCOAST AND THE ISLANDS

Beyond Casco Bay the shape of Maine's coast changes—it shreds. In contrast with the sandy arc of shoreline stretching from Kittery to Cape Elizabeth, the coast between Brunswick and Rockland comprises a series of more than a dozen ragged peninsulas extending like so many fingers south from Rt. 1, creating countless big and small harbors, coves, and bays. Scientists tell us that these peninsulas and the offshore islands are mountains drowned by the melting of the same glaciers that sculpted the many shallow lakes and tidal rivers in this area.

The 100 miles of Rt. 1 between Brunswick and Bucksport are generally equated with Maine's Midcoast, and its depth is greater than the name suggests. It extends south of Rt. 1 to the tips of every peninsula, from Potts Point in South Harpswell and Land's End on Bailey Island; to Popham Beach on the Phippsburg Peninsula and Reid State Park in Georgetown; and on through the Boothbays to Pemaquid Point, Friendship, Port Clyde, and Spruce Head. Along with Rockland, Camden, Belfast, Searsport, and the islands of Monhegan, Vinalhaven, North Haven, and Islesboro, these communities have all catered to summer visitors since steamboats began off-loading them in the mid-19th century. Each peninsula differs in character from the next, but all offer their share of places to stay and eat in settings rarely found along Rt. 1.

North of Rt. 1, this Midcoast region also extends inland. Above Bath five rivers meld to form Merrymeeting Bay, and north of Newcastle the tidal Damariscotta River widens into 13-mile-long Damariscotta Lake. This gently rolling, river- and lake-laced backcountry harbor is also well worth exploring.

We hope that no one who reads this book simply sticks to Rt. 1.

BRUNSWICK AND THE HARPSWELLS

Brunswick is Maine's premier college town, home to **Bowdoin College** with its venerable campus and museums. It's also essentially car-free, with train and bus service from Boston and Portland to a station that's steps from lodging, dining, shops, and galleries.

The Civil War began and ended in Brunswick, or so say local historians. A case can be made. Harriet Beecher Stowe was attending a service in Brunswick's **First Parish Church** when she is said to have had a vision of the death of Uncle Tom and hurried home to begin penning the book that has been credited with starting the war. Joshua Chamberlain, a long-time parishioner in this same church, was the Union general chosen for the honor of receiving the surrender of the Confederate infantry at Appomattox.

Brunswick began as an Indian village named Pejepscot, at the base of the Androscoggin River's Great Falls. In 1688 this became a Massachusetts outpost named Fort Andross, on a site subsequently occupied by a series of mills. Its (roughly) 16,000 residents are a mix of Franco-Americans whose great-grandparents were recruited to work in mills, Bowdoin-related families and retirees, and professionals who commute to work in Portland or Augusta (Brunswick is halfway between).

Brunswick's Maine Street is the state's widest, laid out in 1717 with a grassy "mall"—a long strip of greenery, the scene of concerts and farmers' markets. Set a just a bit above and beyond downtown, the handsome Bowdoin campus is visitor friendly. It's the July and August venue for the **Bowdoin International Music Festival**, and for the **Maine State Music Theatre**. Both the **Bowdoin College Museum of Art** and the **Peary-MacMillan Arctic Museum** are must-sees.

South of Brunswick one peninsula and several bridge-linked islands stretch seaward, defining the eastern rim of Casco Bay. Collectively they form the town of Harpswell—better known as **"the Harpswells"** because it includes so many coves, points, and islands (notably Orrs and Bailey)—which claims more shoreline than any other town in Maine. Widely known for their seafood restaurants, these are Maine's most convenient peninsulas, yet seem much farther Down East.

GUIDANCE ☀ (ᵗᵖ) **Brunswick Visitor Center** (207-721-0999; brunswickdowntown.org), 16 Station Ave, just off upper Maine St. (look for the railroad tracks). Open daily year-round, 10-6:30 in summer. From Rt. 1 take Pleasant St. (see intro) and turn right at the "?". It's a place not only to pick up local info, but also to board **Amtrak's Downeaster** or a **Concord Coach** to Portland or Boston.

Harpswell Business Association (harpswellmaine.org) publishes a useful guide map pinpointing lodging and the many restaurants, boat excursions, and galleries on the peninsulas south of Brunswick. Check out the website.

GETTING THERE *By bus:* **Concord Coach** (concordcoachlines.com) offers 2½-hour service from Boston's Logan International Airport and South Station.

By car: The I-295 (formerly I-95) exit for Brunswick and coastal points north is Exit 28 to Rt. 1. Continue straight ahead up Pleasant St., which forms a T with Maine St. Southbound on I-295 take Exit 31A.

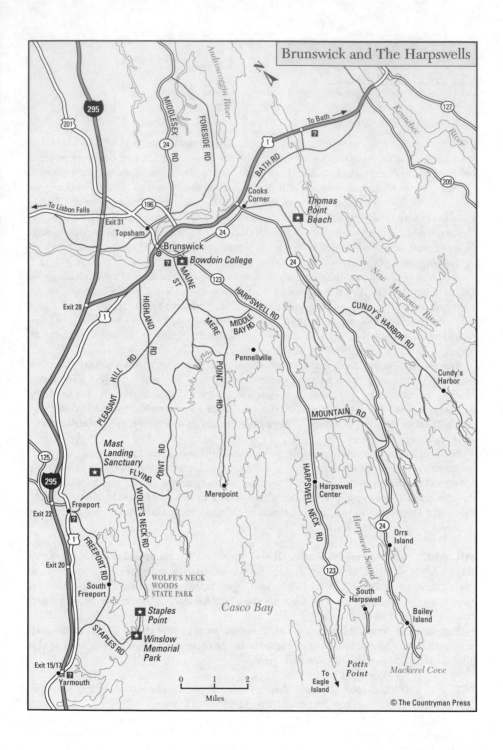

Brunswick and The Harpswells

© The Countryman Press

MUST SEE

Bowdoin College (207-725-3100; bowdoin.edu), Brunswick. Tours begin at the admissions office. Visitors may park in lots off Bath Rd., College St., and Sills Dr.

Maine was part of Massachusetts when the college was founded in 1794, and the school is named for a Massachusetts governor. Nathaniel Hawthorne and Henry Wadsworth Longfellow were classmates here in 1825. The college has been coed since 1971; roughly 50 percent of its 1,700 students are female. Bowdoin ranks high among the nation's liberal arts colleges both in status and in cost (though financial aid is substantial).

Bowdoin College Museum of Art (207-725-3275; bowdoin.edu/artmuseum), Park Row. Open year-round, Tue.–Sat. 10–5, Thu. until 8:30, Sun. 2–5. Closed Mon. and holidays. Free. The entrance to this 1894 copper-domed building designed by McKim, Mead & White is through a discreet glass pavilion facing the street. Thirteen galleries house changing exhibits, and a rotunda with murals by Abbott Thayer, Kenyon Cox, and John LaFarge is hung with early pieces from the museum's extensive collection. Check the website for current exhibits, which frequently feature contemporary artists.

Peary-MacMillan Arctic Museum (207-725-3416; bowdoin.edu/arctic-museum) Hubbard Hall, open year-round, Tue.–Sat. 10–5, Sun. 2–5. Closed Mon. A colorful, well-displayed collection of clothing, trophy walruses and seals, polar bears and caribou, and other mementos showcases expeditions to the North Pole by both Robert Peary and Donald Baxter MacMillan (class of 1898), who assisted Peary on his 1909 expedition and went on to dedicate his life to exploring Arctic waters and terrain until 1954. Displays include an interactive touch screen, photo blowups, and artifacts to tell the story, also changing exhibits about the Arctic. See the Admiral Peary & Eagle Island sidebar.

Courtesy of Bowdoin College

BOWDOIN COLLEGE MUSEUM OF ART

By train: **Amtrak's Downeaster** (1-800-USA-RAIL; amtrak.com) offers regular daily service from Boston to Brunswick via Portland, Freeport, and other points between.

By air and limo: **Mid-Coast Limo** (1-800-937-2424; midcoastlimo.com) makes runs by reservation from Portland International Jetport. **Mermaid Transportation** (1-800-696-2463; gomermaid.com) picks up at Boston and Manchester airports as well.

PUBLIC RESTROOMS **Brunswick Visitor Center**, 16 Station Ave. See *Guidance.*

JOSHUA LAWRENCE CHAMBERLAIN

Joshua Lawrence Chamberlain (1828–1914) was Maine's greatest Civil War hero, a college professor who became one of the most remarkable soldiers in American history. Thanks to the Ken Burns PBS series, *The Civil War*, and to the film *Gettysburg*, Joshua Chamberlain has been rediscovered. This scholar-soldier also presided as president of Bowdoin College after serving four terms as governor of Maine.

The Pejepscot Historical Society (pejepscothistorical.org) maintains Chamberlain's old home at 226 Maine St., across from the Bowdoin campus, open late May–mid-Oct., Tue.–Sat. 10–4, Sun.1–4. Guided tours are on the hour; the last begins at 3. $8.50 adults, $4 children. It's a fascinating house, with many original furnishing as well as Chamberlain's uniforms, medals, saddle sword, bullet-dented boots, and the ornate chair he used as governor and college president. Here you learn that the Bowdoin graduate was teaching rhetoric and languages (he was fluent in eight) at his alma mater when the war began.

Of all his military achievements, Chamberlain is best remembered for his valor and leadership on the second day of the Battle of Gettysburg, July 2, 1863. A lieutenant colonel commanding an inexperienced and understrength regiment, the 20th Maine Volunteer Infantry, he defended Little Round Top, a key position on the extreme left of the Union line. Repeatedly attacked by a much larger Confederate force, he refused to retreat; when there was no more ammunition and most of his men were dead or wounded, he ordered an unorthodox bayonet charge that routed the Southern troops.

Had the Confederates taken Little Round Top they could have outflanked the Union army and won the battle—and with it, possibly, the war. He ended the war as a major general and was chosen by General Ulysses S. Grant to accept the surrender of the Confederate Army of Northern Virginia at Appomattox. As the Confederate regiments marched into the Union camp to lay down their arms, Chamberlain had his troops salute them, a gesture of respect that infuriated some Northerners but helped reconcile many Southerners to their defeat.

Late in life Chamberlain wrote *The Passing of the Armies*, an account of the final campaign of the Union's Army of the Potomac. Filled with vivid descriptive passages, the book is still in print.

JOSHUA LAWRENCE CHAMBERLAIN

WHEN TO COME Brunswick is lively year-round, but the museums and several good restaurants are closed Mondays.

✳ To See

The Harpswells, including Orrs and Bailey Islands: Given its great seafood restaurants and scenic coves, we try to spend the night along the way. From Main Street, follow Rt.

123 south past Bowdoin College 9 miles to the picturesque village of **Harpswell Center**. The white-clapboard Elijah Kellogg Church faces the matching Harpswell Town Meeting House, built in 1757. The church is named for a former minister who was a prominent 19th-century children's book author. Continue south through West Harpswell to **Potts Point**, where multicolored 19th-century summer cottages cluster on the rocks like a flock of exotic birds that have wandered in among the gulls.

Retrace your way up Rt. 123, and 2 miles north of the church turn right onto Mountain Rd., leading to busier Rt. 24 on Great (also known as Sebascodegan) Island. Drive south along **Orrs Island** across the only remaining **Cribstone Bridge** in the world, a National Historic Civil Engineering Landmark. (Its granite blocks are laid in honeycomb fashion—without cement—to allow tidal flows.) This bridge brings you to **Bailey Island**, with its restaurants, lodging places, picturesque **Mackerel Cove**, and rocky **Land's End**, with a statue honoring all Maine fishermen. To find the **Giant Stairs** (see *Walks*), turn off Rt. 24 at Washington Ave. and park at the Episcopal chapel. Otherwise continue on Rt. 24 and take Cundy's Harbor Rd. 4.3 miles to another picturesque fishing harbor with good places to eat.

Pejepscot Historical Society Museums (207-729-6606; pejepscothistorical.org). Founded in 1888 and named for an ancient Indian settlement, this is one of Maine's oldest historical societies. It maintains three downtown Brunswick museums: the **Joshua L. Chamberlain Museum** (see sidebar); The **Pejepscot Museum & Research Center**, 159 Park Row, open summer, Tue.–Fri. 10–4; winter, Wed.–Fri (free admission), a massive, cupola'd mansion that displays changing exhibits on Brunswick, Topsham, and Harpswell history; and the adjoining **Skolfield-Whittier House** (open late May–mid-Oct. for tours Wed.–Sat. 10 and 4), a high Victorian mansion filled with the photos and paintings of three generations.

The First Parish Church United Church of Christ (207-729-7331; firstparish.net), Maine St. at Bath Rd., Brunswick. Open July–mid-Aug. for Tue. noon organ concerts and tours, and year-round for Sun. services. Designed in the 1840s by Richard Upjohn, architect of New York City's Trinity Church. It's open-beamed, with deeply colored stained-glass windows and a vintage 1883 tracker organ. The large sanctuary window was donated by Joshua Chamberlain, one of the first people to be married here.

✲ To Do

BICYCLING The **Androscoggin River Bicycle Path**, a 2.6-mile, paved bicycle/pedestrian trail, begins at Lower Water St. in Brunswick and runs along the river to Grover Lane in Cooks Corner. It connects with Topsham along the way via a bicycle lane on the Merrymeeting Bridge.

BOATING **Casco Bay Lines** (207-774-7871) offers a daily seasonal excursion from Cook's Lobster House on Bailey Island. It takes an hour and 45 minutes to circle around Eagle Island and through this northern end of Casco Bay.

Check **harpsellmaine.org** for an extensive list of fishing and sailing in Casco Bay.

Atlantic Seal Cruises (207-865-6112) picks up at Cook's Lobster. We can recommend Capt. Thomas Ring's Eagle Island and Casco tours. See description in Freeport section.

Sail Casco Tours (277-833-731; sailcasco.com). Capt. Ian Marshall's charter sails aboard his 38-foot *Island Packet*, based in Harpswell, and is a local favorite.

Sea Escape Charters (207-833-5531; seaescapecottages.com) offers Bailey Island–based fishing charters for mackerel and stripers in Casco Bay, also scenic cruises aboard the 35-foot ketch *Tevake* and 70-foot schooner *Alert*.

GOLF **Brunswick Golf Club** (207-725-8224), River Rd., Brunswick. Incorporated in 1888, an 18-hole course known for its beauty and challenging nature. Snack bar, lounge, and cart rentals. **Mere Creek Golf Club** (207-721-9995) is a nine-hole course at Brunswick Landing (former Brunswick Naval Station) and is open to the public.

SEA KAYAKING ☸ **H2outfitters** (207-833-5257; h2outfitters.com). Based just north of the Cribstone Bridge on Orrs Island, this is one of Maine's oldest kayaking outfitters. No rentals. Lessons for all abilities, from beginners to instructor certification; guided day trips and overnight excursions, also a variety of international kayaking vacations.

    Seaspray Kayaking (207-443-3646; seaspraykayaking.com), 320 State Rd., West Bath. Sited on the New Meadows River, Seaspray offers rentals and guided tours and trips.

SWIMMING ✤ **White's Beach** (207-729-0415), Durham Rd., Brunswick. Open mid-May–mid-Oct. A pond in a former gravel pit (water no deeper than 9 feet). Facilities include a small slide for children. Sandy beach, lifeguards, picnic tables, grills, and a snack bar. Inquire about campsites.

    ✤ **Thomas Point Beach** (207-725-6009), off Thomas Point Rd., marked from Rt. 24, Cooks Corner. Open Memorial Day–Labor Day, 9 AM–sunset. Admission fee. The beach is part of an 85-acre private preserve on tidal water overlooking the New Meadows River and Thomas Bay. It includes groves for picnicking (hundreds of picnic tables plus a main lodge snack bar, playground, and arcade), tent and RV sites. It's the scene of the **Maine Highland Games** in August and **Bluegrass Festival**, Labor Day weekend.

    ✤ **Coffin Pond** (207-725-6656), River Rd., Brunswick. Open mid-June–Labor Day 10–7. Admission fee. A strip of sandy beach surrounding a circular, spring-fed pond. Facilities include a 55-foot-long water slide, a playground, and changing rooms.

WALKS **Giant Stairs**, Bailey Island. Turn off Rt. 24 at Washington Ave., park at the Episcopal church, and walk down to Ocean St.; follow the path along the water and follow the small sign to the well-named "stairs."

    Brunswick-Topsham Riverwalk. A 1.25-mile walking loop links the Frank J. Wood ("Green") Bridge to the "swinging" footbridge across the Androscoggin River, built in 1892 by the firm that built the Brooklyn Bridge.

    Brunswick-Topsham Land Trust (207-729-7694; btlt.org), 108 Maine St., Brunswick. The land trust has preserved more than 700 acres in the area. Pick up a map and guides to the nature loops at **Skolfield Nature Preserve,** Rt. 123, Brunswick (4 miles or so south of town), the **Bradley Pond Farm Preserve** in Topsham, a 2.5-mile trail system in a 162-acre preserve; and **Crystal Spring Farm Trail**, a 2.5-mile trail on the 160-acre farm on Pleasant Hill Rd. in Brunswick.

    Town of Harpswell Walking Trails. By far the most famous of these leads to the **Giant Stairs** (see above), but there are half a dozen more options. Stop by the town offices on Mountain Rd. (between Rts. 24 and 123) and pick up pick a copy of the *Harpswell Guide* to local trails, landings, and other spots worth finding.

    Swan Island (207-547-5322; mefishwildlife.com). At the head of Merrymeeting Bay, the island is 4 miles long and less than a mile wide, a haven for wood ducks, mergansers, bald eagles, wild turkeys, and more. It was the site of an Indian village in 1614, when Captain John Smith stopped by. It's open by self-access year-round; limited transport and tours are offered seasonally by reservation. No pets allowed. Managed by the Maine Department of Inland Fisheries and Wildlife, which requires reservations for overnight camping. The landing is in Richmond Village.

ADMIRAL PEARY AND EAGLE ISLAND

In the 1890s the North Pole was the equivalent of the moon in the 1960s. The race was on among nations to be the first to reach it. On April 6, 1909, Robert E. Peary (1856–1920) was the man who claimed that honor for America. Peary was a naval engineer who had sailed south to help survey a possible Nicaraguan canal route in the 1880s, but eventually became obsessed with the Far North. On his own time and financing, he began leading Greenland-based expeditions in 1886. Working with native Inuit and their dog teams, Peary pushed steadily north in subsequent expeditions. He designed the *Roosevelt*, a steam and sail vessel with a shallow draft, to navigate among icebergs, and on its second voyage it is said to have sailed to

ADMIRAL ROBERT E. PEARY GREETS THE CROWDS IN NOVA SCOTIA ON HIS RETURN FROM THE NORTH POLE.

within 150 miles of the North Pole. The remaining distance was covered on sled and foot during the following spring. Dismissing their support team, Peary, along with his African American assistant Matthew Henson and four Inuit, finally reached the geographic pole, taking measurements and photographs to document the feat. Controversy continues to dog the accuracy of their final position, but this saga entranced the world.

It was on Eagle Island that Josephine Peary finally received the news of her husband's triumph. Peary had bought the 17-acre Casco Bay island soon after graduating from Bowdoin because its rocky headland resembles the prow of a ship. The shingled summer home he built there is positioned atop that bluff, facing northeast. Peary designed the three-sided living room hearth, made from island stones and Arctic quartz crystals, and stuffed many of the birds on the mantel. The player piano is one octave short because it had to fit aboard the *Roosevelt*.

The **Eagle Island State Historic Site** (207-624-6080; pearyeagleisland.org) is open mid-June–Labor Day, 10–sunset. The house offers a rare glimpse into era as well as life. A nature path circles the island (trails open July 15, after bird-nesting season), and there are also picnic sites and a small beach. See *Boating* for transport from Bailry Island; **Marie L. Cruises** (207-833-5343) also offers regular trips from Dolphin Marina in South Harpswell. There are guest buoys and a dock.

Also see the **Peary-MacMillan Arctic Museum** (Must See).

Christina Tree

EAGLE ISLAND STATE HISTORICAL SITE

✳ Lodging

IN AND AROUND BRUNSWICK

✪ ☗ ((ɐ)) **Middle Bay Farm Bed & Breakfast** (207-373-1375 or 1-800-299-4914; middlebay farm.com), 287 Pennellville Rd., Brunswick 04011. Open year-round, this handsome clapboard farmhouse dates to the 1830s and overlooks a tidal cove. Sited at the end of a country road, it's minutes from downtown Brunswick and also from seafood restaurants in the Harpswells. In the early 1900s it was a summer boardinghouse (Helen Keller is said to have stayed here). Phyllis Truesdell is a warm and skilled hostess who makes guests feel invited. There's a living room with a baby grand, a gracious dining room, and a big country kitchen. The four spacious guest rooms are decorated with many bright and tasteful touches; our current favorite is the Star Room, with its stenciled floor and writing desk. All have private full bath, water view, sitting area, and cable TV/VCR hidden in an armoire. There's also a porch from which to survey lawn, sky, and water. The neighboring Sail Loft Cottage houses two rustic suites, each with a living area, cooking facility, and two small bedrooms. The 5 landscaped acres are on a rise above Middle Bay tidal cove; kayaks and canoes are available. $170–190 in-season, $150–175 off-season, includes a full breakfast.

✪ ☗ ✎ ♿ ((ɐ)) **Brunswick Inn** (207-729-4914 or 1-800-299-4914; thebrunswickinn .com), 165 Park Row, Brunswick 04011. This 1840s Greek Revival home with long windows and a pillared porch offers the charm of a gracious country inn, but within easy walking distance of both the Bowdoin campus and downtown restaurants. It's buffered from traffic by the town's wide green mall. Innkeeper Eileen Hornor has hung common spaces and guest rooms with well-chosen art by local artists (most of it for sale), added a flowery patio, and decorated the double parlors invitingly. On cool days wood fires glow in the parlors, the breakfast room, and the Great Room at the rear of the house, a space with comfortable seating and a full-service bar (open to the public Tue.–Sat. evenings). The 15 guest rooms are divided among the original house, a contemporary carriage house with its own

BRUNSWICK INN

Gary Pennington

common space, and a self-contained "Garden Cottage" in which pets are welcome. Each room is equipped with phone, desk, and clock-radio; TV on request. $150–260 includes a full breakfast.

✎ ♿ ((ɐ)) **The Brunswick Hotel & Tavern** (207-837-6565; thebrunswickhotelandtavern .com), 4 Noble St., Brunswick 04011. Handy to the Bowdoin campus and the Brunswick Station, this is a three-floor, 48-room, four-suite facility obviously geared to Bowdoin parents, alums, and hopefuls. Rooms are comfortably, sleekly furnished, most with two queens. Decor is notably masculine, featuring earth colors and pictures of polar bears (the college mascot). The **Tavern** serves all meals. Rooms run $159–300 EP, but check for packages.

✎ ♿ ((ɐ)) **The Daniel** (207-373-1824 or 1-877-373-2374; thedanielhotel.com), 10 Water St., Brunswick. This is a contemporary inn with elevator-accessed guest rooms and suites. With its recent change in name and ownership, it is getting good reviews, as is its **Coast Bar + Bistro**, open for lunch and dinner. Handy to the Androscoggin River Recreation Path (a great place to walk and jog), it's minutes by car from downtown but not an easy walk. $159-379, including continental breakfast with fresh baking.

((ɐ)) ☗ **Black Lantern Bed & Breakfast** (207-725-4165 or 1-888-306-4165; blacklantern bandb.com), 57 Elm St., Topsham 04086. Open year-round. Longtime local B&B owners Tom and Judy Connelie offer comfortable rooms, a view of the Androscoggin River, direct access to the bike path (also good for jogging) along its banks, as well as a dock with good access for kayakers. Just across the river from downtown Brunswick, this hospitable old house has three cheerful guest rooms, all with private bath, two with river views, and the third with a gas fireplace. $110–125, $95–100 off-season, includes a full breakfast.

IN HARPSWELL

✪ 🐾 (ᵞᵖ) **Harpswell Inn** (207-833-5509 or 1-800-843-5509; harpswellinn.com), 108 Lookout Point Rd., Harpswell 04079. Open year-round. Innkeepers Richard and Anne Moseley have deep ties to Harpswell and delight in sharing local secrets and history. Their gracious three-story white-clapboard B&B was built as the cookhouse for an adjacent boatyard and subsequently became the Lookout Point House, one of no less than 52 summer hotels and boardinghouses to be found in Harpswell during the steamboating era. The eight guest rooms vary widely and come with and without hearth, deck, and water views; the three suites have kitchens, decks, and more (check the website). The large living room has a massive stone fireplace, ample seating, and plenty to read. Lawns slope to the shore with plenty of comfortable spots from which to view the resident blue heron and Middle Bay. In high season $145–190 for rooms, $239–259 for suites (less off-season), with a very full breakfast, including Anne's blueberry cake if you're lucky. Off-season discounts. Richard, a professional chef, caters for groups of 50 inside and 150 with an outdoor tent. Pets are

THE HARPSWELL INN

Christina Tree

accepted in four cottages, available for weekly rental.

🦞 🐾 ✐ (ᵞᵖ) **The Driftwood Inn** (207-833-5461; thedriftwoodinnmaine.com), 81 Washington Ave., Bailey Island 04003. Open late May–mid-Oct.; the dining room (which is open to the public) is open June–Labor Day. Sited on a rocky point within earshot of a foghorn and walking distance of the Giant Stairs Driftwood is classically "Maine rustic," meaning naturally air-conditioned, shared baths (some are now private), and heated by fireplaces. Innkeeper David Conrad's family has owned Driftwood for more than 60 years, and this 1905 complex is one of the last of its breed along Maine's coast. Breakfast and a full-course dinner are open to the public The cottages contain a total of 16 doubles (some have queens) and eight singles (nine with half-bath); there are also six housekeeping cottages. We recommend Rooms 6 and 7 in Driftwood, pine-walled with a firm queen bed, a half-bath, and windows on the water. Prices vary with the view and bath facilities. There is a small saltwater swimming pool set in the rocks. $80–145 per couple (no minimum stay). Housekeeping cottages, available by the week, are $705–770. No credit cards. Pets in the cottages ($25 fee).

Log Cabin, An Island Inn (207-833-5546; logcabin-maine.com), Rt. 24, Bailey Island 04003. Open Apr.–Oct. Built decades ago as a lavish log summer home with a huge hearth (a moose head, of course, hangs above), it offers nine rooms—four with kitchen, two with

Christina Tree

DRIFTWOOD INN

hot tub, all with private bath, fridge, coffee machine, and waterside deck—and access to the heated swimming pool. Breakfast is included for high-season rates from $189-339. Dinner is still served to guests only.

✪ ☗ **The Captain's Watch B&B** (207-725-0979; captainswatchbandb.com), 926 Cundy's Harbor Rd. and Pinkham Point Rd., Harpswell 04079. Open most of the year. Donna Dillman offers four spacious guest rooms with water views in a former Civil War–era inn with an octagonal cupola, set on a 250-foot-high bluff. Upstairs rooms are handsome, furnished with antiques (two share access to the cupola); a first-floor barnboard-sided room with a king bed and picture window is equally attractive. Full breakfasts are served in the paneled dining room or, weather permitting, on the deck. Walk down to the picturesque working harbor. $150–185 includes breakfast.

✐ ♿ **Bailey Island Motel** (207-833-2886; baileyislandmotel.com), Rt. 24, Bailey Island 04003. Open mid-May–mid-Oct. Located just over the Cribstone Bridge. A real find, an attractive two-story gray-shingled building on the water's edge, offering water views and landscaped lawns with rocks and a dock to walk out on. Kudos to owner Chip Black. The 11 rooms are fresh, clean, and comfortable, with cross-ventilation from windows. Cable TV. No smoking. Coffee and muffins are included in $105–140. Guests are welcome to tie their boat up to the dock or a mooring or push off in their kayaks. Walk next door to lunch or dinner at Morse's Cribstone Grill or across the way to Cook's Lobster House.

Check **harpswell.org** for cottage rentals on Orrs and Bailey Islands.

✳ Where to Eat

DINING OUT

IN BRUNSWICK

Note: This is a college town, and the quality of the food is higher than prices imply.

✪ **Henry & Marty** (207-721-9141; henryandmarty.com), 61 Maine St. Open for dinner Tue.–Sun. Reservations recommended. Filling two warmly colored and decorated store-fronts with a welcoming ambience, whether you come for a glass of wine and thin-crust pizza or for paella Valencia. This is a long-established favorite with a full bar that's an oasis for single diners ($14–28).

✪ **Trattoria Athena** (207-721-0700), 25 Mill St (parallel to and accessible from Rt. 1 North). Open for dinner Wed.–Sat., family-style. Lunch Tue.–Sat. in summer. Seating just 30 (reservations are a must), this is as genuine as a trattoria can be in Maine, chef-owned and locally sourced as much as possible with from-scratch pastas. The Italian and Greek menu may include stuffed grape leaves and carpaccio as well as mussels of the day. Entrées might include saltimbocca alla Romana and braised lamb ($23-26).

Tao Restaurant (207-727-9002; tao-yuan .me), 22 Pleasant St. Open for dinner Tue.–Sat. Cordon Bleu–trained chef-owner Cara Stadler brings experience in top Shanghai and European restaurants to a menu inspired by seasonal, local produce. Dine on a spicy greens salad followed by barley miso glazed eggplant or tea-smoked lamb. Entrées $11.80–13.80, but plates are small, meant to be shared; ordering three or four per person is recommended. A three-course pre-theater dinner menu is $48.

✪ ☖ **The Great Impasta** (207-729-5858 thegreatimpasta.net), 42 Maine St. Open daily (except Sun.) for lunch and dinner. A great stop even if you're simply traveling up or down Rt. 1, but arrive early to get a booth (plaques honor booth regulars). Specialties include pasta dishes like seafood lasagna and *Frutti di Mare* risotto (native scallops and Gulf shrimp sautéed with white wine, over creamy cheese risotto). Wine and beer served. Entrées $14–26.

EATING OUT

IN BRUNSWICK

✪ ☖ ✐ **Frontier Café & Cinema Gallery** (207-725-5222; explorefrontier.com), 14 Maine St. (Fort Andross). Open Tue.–Thu. 9–9, Fri., Sat. 11–10, Sun. 11-9. A theater, gallery, café, and pub is a winning combination. Long windows along two walls overlook the Androscoggin River, its dam, and frequently ospreys, sometimes eagles and peregrine falcons. There are coffees and teas, draft beers, and a full bar. The widely ranging menu might include fish-and-chips, Thai green curry, steak, rice-battered fried fish tacos as well as "marketplates" representing different parts of the world. Owner Michael "Gil" Gilroy, who

LOBSTER

Note: The peninsulas stretching south from Brunswick into Casco Bay have been a destination for lobster lovers since steamboatin' days.

✪ ✎ **Dolphin Marina & Restaurant** (207-833-6000; dolphinmarinaandrestaurant.com), 515 Basin Point Rd., South Harpswell (marked from Rt. 123, also accessible by water). Open 11:30–8 Apr.–Nov., daily in summer; Thu.–Sun. in shoulder months. The prime seafood destination-dining spot in the Harpswells, this snazzy restaurant sits at the very tip of Basin Point, walled in windows with sweeping views of Casco Bay. The fish chowder and lobster bisque are a specialty of the Saxton family, who opened their marina coffee shop in 1966. It grew so popular that lines eventually snaked around the building, and several years ago they built this larger, beautifully designed restaurant. The current menu has expanded, too, but the draw is still the daily hauled and handpicked lobster and crab and broiled seafood that have been luring patrons from Brunswick (45 minutes) and beyond for decades. All dinners continue to include a blueberry muffin, and no one passes on dessert. Nightly specials. Fully licensed.

✪ **Morse's Cribstone Grill** (207-833-7775), Rt. 24 at the Cribstone Bridge, Bailey Island. Open seasonally for lunch and dinner. Cathy and Sheldon Morse are local lobster dealers and their restaurant is a local favorite—glass-walled and right on the water. How can you beat fresh lobster meat cooked and picked in-house, mixed with just the right amount of mayonnaise, and served in a buttered and grilled roll—while watching cormorants and gulls on an island just offshore? Nothing fancy here, just steamers, lobster, broiled and fried scallops, haddock, chowders, stews, and fresh greens topped with chicken, haddock, sea scallops, or lobster. Wine and beer.

LOBSTER DEALER SHELDON MORSE BESIDE MORSE'S CRIBSTONE GRILL

Christina Tree

✎ **Cook's Lobster & Ale House** (207-833-2818; cookslobster.com), Bailey Island. Open year-round, 11:30–10. In 2015 the area's most famous lobster house changed hands for only the second time since 1955, and changes are afoot. More deck seating, a larger pub specializing in local brews, and more of a focus on groups are promised. What won't change is the seafood menu and site surrounded on three sides by water. Chances are it will still be a good idea in July and August. Try to get here before noon, when the Casco Bay liner arrives with its load of day-trippers.

✎ **Holbrook's Lobster Wharf** (207-729-9050), Cundy's Harbor. Open Memorial Day–mid-June on weekends, then daily until Labor Day, 11–8. A nicely sited lobster landmark with a harbor view. Tables are topped with umbrellas and banked in flowers, and lobster is available right off the boat in all the usual ways. BYOB.

✎ **Erica's Seafood** (207-833-7354; ericasseafood.com), Basin Point, South Harpswell. Mother's Day weekend–Columbus Day, 11–7. Just before Dolphin Marina (see above), this shop and takeout place with picnic tables offers lobster (hauled off the wharf here) with a view; also chowders, seafood rolls, and the basics, homemade whoopie pies.

Libby's Market (207-729-7277), 42 Jordan Ave., Brunswick. This small variety store is worth finding for the town's best lobster and crab rolls. The owner's lobsterman husband hauls daily, so the meat hasn't sat in a fridge. It's just the right temperature and mix, served in a choice of sizes and toasted buns. There are picnic tables, but better to take it to enjoy with a view.

traveled the world for his previous work, has used largely salvaged and recycled materials to turn this raw factory space into his vision of a cultural crossroads. Check the website for current events; also see *Entertainment*. Parking is okay in the big lot up front; also look for the rear entrance lot just before the bridge.

✪ **Scarlet Begonias** (207-721-0403), 16 Station Ave. Open Mon.–Sat., lunch–dinner. The first and still one of the most popular Brunswick bistros, now in Brunswick Station. Doug and Colleen Lavallee, and now their son, are still in the kitchen serving up some great sandwiches, chunky, fresh-herbed pastas, salads, also fabulous pizzas. A savory bean and ham soup with half of a grilled sandwich hit the spot on a rainy day. Wine and beer.

✪ **El Camino** (207-725-8228), 15 Cushing St. Open for dinner Tue.–Sat. An unpromising exterior disguises a hip, funky interior, the setting for highly inventive Mexican food, with a dedication to using chemical-free seafood and meats as well as organic—local wherever possible—produce. The chips are warm, the selection of beers large, and the margaritas famous. Vegans as well as vegetarians have options.

Enoteca Athena (207-721-0100; enoteca athena.com), 97 Maine St. Open Tue.–Sun. from 3. An attractive wine bar featuring Greek and Italian labels and a light Mediterranean menu that can hit the spot.

✪ **Lemongrass Vietnamese Restaurant** (207-725-9008; lemongrassme.com), 212 Maine St. Open Tue.–Sun. 11–9. A bright, inviting space with local art is the setting for fresh, delicious, authentic Vietnamese cuisine. The specialties are pho (noodle soups) and goi salads with a tangy sauce and choice of tofu, fish, or meat toppings.

✎ **Sea Dog Brewing** (207-725-0162; seadogbrewing.com), Great Mill Island, 1 Main St., Topsham. Open Mon.–Sat. 11–1 AM Sun. 11:30–1 AM. Music Thu.–Sat. Housed in a picturesque (former) paper mill, vintage 1868. A big, friendly brewpub with seasonal outdoor dining overlooking the churning Androscoggin. This is a good bet for families. Specialties include fried scallops, grilled or teriyaki sirloin, potato-crusted haddock, and cioppino (seafood stew). There is a wide choice of house beers and ales.

Bangkok Garden Restaurant (207-725-9708), 14 Maine St., Fort Andross. Open daily except Sun. for lunch and dinner. This attractive restaurant is the local pick for classic Thai curries and seafood dishes.

✪ ✎ **Wild Oats Bakery and Café** (207-725-6287), Tontine Mall, 149 Maine St. Open Mon.–Sat. 7–5, Sun. 8–5. Set back from Maine St. with tables on the terrace and inside. A town meeting place serving coffees and teas, from-scratch pastries and breads, healthy build-your-own sandwiches, and salads. For those too impatient to stand in line, there are freshly made salads in the cooler. Outside seating, too, weather permitting.

Fat Boy Drive-In (207-729-9431), 111 Bath Rd. Open for lunch and dinner, late Mar.–mid-Oct. This is no 1950s reconstruct, just a real carhop-staffed drive-in that's survived because the frappés, hot dogs, and burgers are so good and reasonably priced.

Miss Brunswick Diner (207-729-5948), 101 Pleasant St. (Rt. 1 northbound). Open daily 5 AM–9 PM. A convenient road-food stop, a remake of a diner that originally stood in Norway (Maine) but has now been here several decades; the neon lights, booths, and jukebox are all new, but the food is what it claims to be: "home cooking at a down-home good price."

Gelato Fiasco (207-607-4002), 74 Maine St. Open daily 11–11. Owners Josh and Bruno make a couple dozen flavors of their irresistible ice cream from scratch daily.

IN THE HARPSWELLS

The Driftwood Inn (207-833-5461; see *Lodging*). Open seasonally; non-guests must reserve by 4:40. The pine-walled, many-windowed dining room in this rustic resort sits almost atop the water; dinner is served promptly at 6 when the bell rings. The menu offers a wide choice of local seafood as well as rib eye. Salad and rolls included in $18–21; BYOB. There's also a child's and breakfast menu.

Block & Tackle (207-725-5690), 842 Cundy's Harbor Rd. (off Rt. 24), Harpswell. Open seasonally 11–8, breakfast from 7 AM on weekends. A family-run and -geared restaurant. Try shrimpster stew, real house-made clam cakes, or the fried mushrooms.

BIGS—Bailey Island General Store (207-833-2400). The local gathering spot with an open grill, popular for breakfast and pizza. Also good for screen repair and bait.

✳ Entertainment

MUSIC **Bowdoin International Music Festival** (207-373-1400; bowdoinfestival.org), Brunswick. Famed in classical music circles since 1964, this late June–early Aug. festival brings together talented young performers and internationally acclaimed musicians for a series of both classical and contemporary works. Most concerts are staged in state-of-the-art Studzinski Recital Hall on the Bowdoin campus. Additional concerts are staged throughout the local community.

Music on the Mall (207-729-4439). July–Aug., concerts at 6 PM Wed. on Brunswick's grassy downtown mall and in the **Harpswell Bandstand by the Sea,** Thu. in June and Aug., and Sun. at 2 PM in Sept.

Also see First Parish Church under *To See.*

THEATER ⚓ **Maine State Music Theatre** (207-725-8769; msmt.org), Bowdoin College, Brunswick. June–late Aug., matinees and evening performances. Special children's shows. Air-conditioned Pickard Theater is housed in Memorial Hall, an 1873 memorial to the Bowdoin students who fought and died in the Civil War—ordered built, of course, by Joshua Chamberlain. This highly professional Equity company strives for a mix of classics and new scripts and frequently gets rave reviews.

FILM **Evening Star Cinema** (207-729-6796 or 1-888-304-5486; eveningstarcinema.com),

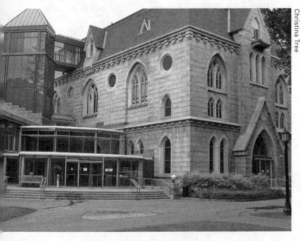

Christina Tree

PICKARD THEATER AT BOWDOIN COLLEGE

Tontine Mall, 149 Maine St., Brunswick. First runs but also alternative film: foreign, art, and documentary.

Frontier Café & Cinema Gallery (207-725-5222; explorefrontier.com), 14 Main St., Fort Andross. Check the website for frequent films and lectures in the 75-seat cinema (seats are recycled from the Biddeford Theater, converted into swivel/rocking chairs and coffee tables). Visual storytelling, and special events, too (also see *Eating Out*).

✳ Selective Shopping

ART

IN BRUNSWICK AND TOPSHAM

Second Friday Art Walks (207-798-6985; artwalkmaine.org/brunswick), May–Sept., are major events, with open houses at many studios as well as galleries and art venues.

Bayview Gallery (207-729-5500), 58 Maine St., features traditional Maine landscapes. **Icon Contemporary Art** (207-725-8157), 19 Mason St., just off the Rt. 1 end of Main St., is open year-round, Wed. 1–5, Sat. 1–4. A serious contemporary gallery with changing exhibits of sculpture, original drawings, and paintings.

Spindleworks (207-725-8820; spindleworks.org), 7 Lincoln St., an artists' cooperative for people with disabilities that produces some striking handwoven fiber clothing and hangings, quilts, accessories, paintings, prints, T-shirts, rag rugs, and more.

IN THE HARPSWELLS

The Gallery at Widgeon Cove (207-833-6081; widgeoncove.com). Open most of the year, but call before coming. This waterside gallery features Georgann Kuhl's landscapes, striking works composed of thousands of individual pieces of her handmade papers, and the gold and silver jewelry and sculptures of Condon Kuhl; it's worth a detour. **Ash Cove Pottery** (207-833-6004), farther down the road, displays a variety of hand-thrown and -glazed functional stoneware by Susan Horowitz and Gail Kass. On Rt. 24 (north of Mountain Rd.) the former Gunpoint Church now serves as a gallery for **Sebascodegan Artists** (named for the island on which it stands), a cooperative with 20 members. It's open July 4–Labor Day, Mon.–Sat. 10–5.

FARMERS' MARKET Brunswick May–Nov., Tue. and Fri. 8–2 on "the Mall"—the park-like green strip on upper Maine St. Local produce and products.

SPECIAL STORES

IN BRUNSWICK

✪ **Gulf of Maine Books** (207-729-5083), 134 Maine St. A laid-back, full-service bookstore with a wide-ranging inventory, particularly rich in Maine titles, poetry, also great cards. The owners (they have been called "curators") are photographer Beth Leonard and Gary Lawless, founder of Blackberry Press (note the full line here), which has reissued out-of-print Maine classics. Lawless is a poet with an international following.

    Cabot Mill Antiques (207-725-2855; cabotiques.com), 14 Maine St. (at Rt. 1), Fort Andross. Open daily 10–5. A vast, 160-dealer space with quality antiques; flea markets on summer weekends.

    Wyler's & Local (207-729-1321), 148/150 Maine St., is a great mix of quality pottery, glassware, jewelry, and clothing. It now also includes "Local," good for gourmet items and a deli, making it a great picnic source.

    Wilbur's of Maine Confections (207-729-4462; wilburs.com), 143 Maine St. Open daily. We dare you to pass up a "Double Decadence" (a dark chocolate truffle with hazelnuts). The chocolate is handmade in Freeport, and there's a large inventory of other candies.

IN HARPSWELL

Black Sheep Wine Shop (207-725-9284; blacksheepwine.com), 105 Mountain Rd., Harpswell. With more than 600 different labels, a range of prices (at least 90 under $12 a bottle), friendly service, and frequent tastings, dinners, and classes, this has become a destination for wine lovers. Also a selection of Maine-crafted beers.

    Island Candy Company (207-833-6639) 1795 Harpswell Islands Rd. (Rt. 24), Orrs

BRUNSWICK FARMERS' MARKET ON THE MALL   Christina Tree

Island. Open 11–8 in summer; fewer days and hours off-season. Closed in snow season. Melinda Harris Richter makes everything from lollipops to truffles.

✳ Special Events

Check the Thu. edition of Brunswick's *Times Record* for current happenings.

    June–Aug: See *Entertainment* for details about the **Bowdoin International Music Festival** and **Maine State Music Theatre.**

    ✎ *July–August:* **Music on the Mall in Brunswick** concerts are Wed. evenings.

    July: **Bailey Island Fishing Tournament** (to register, phone Cook's Lobster House at 207-833-2818). **Harpswell lobster boat races.**

    August: **Topsham Fair** (first week)—a traditional agricultural fair complete with ox pulls, crafts and food competitions, a carnival, and livestock; held at Topsham Fairgrounds, Rt. 24, Topsham. **Maine Highland Games** (third Saturday), Thomas Point Beach, a daylong celebration of Scottish heritage with piping, country dancing, sheepdog demonstrations, and Highland fling competitions. **Brunswick Outdoor Arts Festival.**

    September: **Annual Thomas Point Bluegrass Festival** (Labor Day weekend; thomaspointbeach.com) is huge. Also see brunswickdowntown.org for a **Taste of Brunswick.**

BATH AREA

Over the years some 5,000 vessels have been built in Bath. Think about it: In contrast to most communities—which retain what they build—here an entire city's worth of imposing structures have sailed away. Perhaps that's why, with a population of fewer than 9,000, Bath is a city rather than a town. The granite city hall, with its rounded, pillared facade and cupola—with a Paul Revere bell and a three-masted schooner for a weather vane—seems meant for a far larger city.

American shipbuilding began downriver from Bath in 1607 when the 30-ton pinnace *Virginia* was launched by Popham Colony settlers. The tradition continues with naval vessels regularly constructed at the Bath Iron Works (BIW).

With around 5,700 workers, BIW currently employs fewer people than worked in Bath's shipyards in the 1850s. At its entrance a sign proclaims: **THROUGH THESE GATES PASS THE WORLD'S BEST SHIPBUILDERS.** This is no idle boast, and many current employees have inherited their skills from a long line of forebears.

Obviously, this is the place for a museum about ships and shipbuilding, and the **Maine Maritime Museum** has one of the country's foremost collections of ship models, journals, logs, photographs, and other seafaring memorabilia. It includes a 19th-century working shipyard and offers tours of BIW as well as river and coastal cruises.

Both BIW and the Maine Maritime Museum are sited on a 4-mile-long reach of the Kennebec River where the banks slope at precisely the right gradient for laying keels. Offshore, the channel is 35 to 150 feet deep; the open Atlantic is 18 miles downriver.

Bath's 19th-century prominence as "City of Ships" is reflected in the blend of Greek Revival, Italianate, and Georgian Revival styles in the brick storefronts along Front Street and in the imposing wooden churches and mansions in similar styles along Washington, High, and Middle Streets. Front Street offers a healthy mix of shops and restaurants, and the riverfront itself has once more become a focal point.

Today BIW, with its 400-foot-high towers at the end of Bath's Front Street, still dominates the city's economy, but Bath now styles itself "Maine's Cool Little City." Its downtown hums with newfound energy, a visitor-friendly mix of culture and commerce. Take the plunge from Rt. 1 down the steep northbound exit ramp just before the soaring Sagadahoc Bridge. Pick up walking and parking maps at the visitors center in the former rail station

Christina Tree

BATH'S FRONT STREET

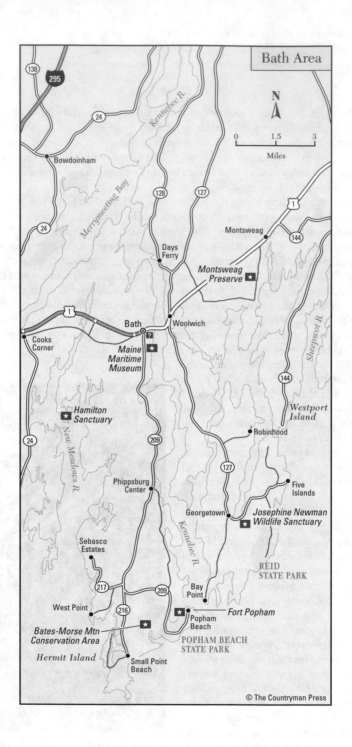

Bath Area

N

0   1.5   3
Miles

138 295

24

Bowdoinham

128 127

Kennebec R.

Merrymeeting Bay

24

Montsweag

1

144

Days Ferry

Montsweag Preserve ★

Bath

Woolwich

Cooks Corner

Maine Maritime Museum ★

1

Sheepscot R.

144

Westport Island

Hamilton Sanctuary ★

New Meadows R.

Robinhood

24

209

127

Phippsburg Center

Five Islands

Georgetown

Josephine Newman Wildlife Sanctuary ★

Kennebec R.

Sebasco Estates

REID STATE PARK

217

209

Bay Point

West Point

216

Fort Popham

Popham Beach ★

Bates-Morse Mtn Conservation Area ★

POPHAM BEACH STATE PARK

Hermit Island

Small Point Beach

© The Countryman Press

and explore shops and restaurants along Front Street, then settle into an Adirondack chair in Waterfront Park.

Save a day or two to explore the peninsulas south of Bath. **Phippsburg Peninsula**'s perimeter is notched with coves filled with fishing boats, and **Popham Beach** near its southern tip is a grand expanse of sand. **Reid State Park** on **Georgetown Island**, just across the Kennebec River, is the Midcoast's other major sandy strand. North of Bath, Merrymeeting Bay is a major flyway, well known to birders.

GUIDANCE The **Visitors Center** (207-443-1513; visitbath.com) in the rehabbed Bath Railroad Station, 15 Commercial St. (from Rt. 1 take Historic Downtown Bath exits). Open May–Oct., daily in high season, otherwise Mon.–Fri. with a manned info desk, restrooms, and brochures; pick up the Bath map/guide.

BATH'S CITY HALL

Christina Tree

GETTING THERE *By car:* Rt. 1 barrels by the city, with views only from high on the Sagadahoc Bridge, too late if you're heading north. Take the downtown exit just south of the bridge. From points south take I-95 to I-295 to either Exit 28 (Brunswick) or Exit 31 (Topsham) and the connector (Rt. 196) to Rt. 1. We prefer Exit 28 (it's less confusing), but if it's a peak traffic time try your luck with 31.

By bus: **Concord Coach** (1-800-639-3317; concordcoachlines.com), en route to and from Boston, stops in Bath at Coastal Plaza off Rt. 1.

By air and limo: **Mid-Coast Limo** (1-800-937-2424; midcoastlimo.com) makes runs by reservation from Portland International Jetport.

GETTING AROUND **Bath Trolley** operates a loop throughout the city, daily July–Labor Day, weekends in the shoulder seasons.

PUBLIC RESTROOMS Bath Railroad Station **Visitors Center** (see *Guidance*) and **Waterfront Park**.

WHEN TO COME Bath itself remains lively year-round, but the Popham and Georgetown areas are June–Columbus Day destinations.

✳ To See

Bath Historic District. In the 18th and 19th centuries Bath's successful families built impressive mansions. **Sagadahoc Preservation, Inc.** (207-443-2174; sagadahocpreservation .org. Check the website for the excellent *Self-Guided Walking and Driving Tours* page and events or find them at the Old Winter Street Church, 880 Washington St.

MUST SEE

MAINE MARITIME MUSEUM (207-443-1316; www.mainemaritime museum.org), 243 Washington St., Bath (watch for the turnoff from Rt. 1). Open daily year-round 9:30–5 except Thanksgiving, Christmas, and New Year's Day. $15 adults, $13.50 seniors, and $10 ages 6–16. Docking and mooring available. Sited just south of Bath Iron Works on the banks of the Kennebec River, this extensive complex—10 riverside acres—includes the brick-and-glass **Maritime History Building** and the **Percy & Small Shipyard**, the country's only sur-

viving wooden shipbuilding yard (its turn-of-the-20th-century belts for driving machinery have been restored). Museum exhibits focus on the era beginning after the Civil War, when 80 percent of this country's full-rigged ships were built in Maine, almost half of those in Bath.

The pride of Bath, you learn, were the Down Easters, a compromise between the clipper ship and the old-style freighter that plied the globe from the 1870s through the 1890s, and the big multimasted schooners designed to ferry coal and local exports like ice, granite, and lime. A fine example of the latter, the six-masted *Wyoming* was the largest wooden sailing vessel ever built. A full-scale steel sculpture suggests its mammoth size and height.

BATH-BUILT DOWN EASTERS PLIED THE GLOBE

The museum's permanent collection of artwork, artifacts, and documents totals more than 21,500 pieces, and there is an extensive research library. Permanent exhibits include *Distant Lands of Palm and Spice*, a fascinating, occasionally horrifying glimpse of where and why Maine ships sailed—including the 18th-century West Indies sugar and slave trade and the imperialis-

THE SIZE OF A SIX-MASTER SHIP BUILT HERE IS SUGGESTED BY THIS SCULPTURE

Patten Free Library (207-442-5141), 33 Summer St., Bath. Open Tue.–Fri. Set in landscaped grounds is one of the most inviting libraries we know. Artwork includes a half model of the six-masted *Wyoming* and the colorful mural of exotic creatures by Dahlov Ipcar in the children's room. Note the *Spirit of the Sea* sculpture by William Zorach in the adjoining park.

Maine's First Ship (207-443-4242; mfship .org). Open July–Labor Day daily except Sun.; otherwise look for the OPEN flag on a long wooden "Historic Freight Shed" at the head of Commercial St. You can watch the ongoing reconstruction of the pinnace *Virginia,* built in 1607 at the mouth of the Kennebec by members of the Popham Colony—who climbed aboard and sailed back to England in 1609.

tic exploration around Cape Horn, the Pacific, and Asia in the 19th and early 20th centuries. You hear the wind whistling in the rigging and follow the individual stories of multiple captains.

Beyond the Maritime History Building, exhibits are housed in half a dozen buildings, widely scattered on the museum grounds. One of our favorites, *Lobstering and the Maine Coast*, includes a collection of lobstering boats and interactive activities for kids. The Donnell House, the late-Victorian home of a prominent Bath family, is open seasonally.

THE MAINE MARITIME MUSEUM'S EXHIBITS INCLUDE A KID-FRIENDLY PILOTHOUSE, MARINE PAINTINGS, AND FIGUREHEADS

Exhibits aside, this museum involves visitors in the significance of its surroundings. A seasonal trolley tour highlighting the history of the neighboring General Dynamics' Bath Iron Works is not to be missed. You can also choose from half a dozen regularly offered seasonal cruises (see *To Do*) with historic narrations down the Kennebec and around into Sheepscot Bay. There's plenty for children, too, from a hands-on pilothouse and elaborate pirate-boat climbing structure to summer camps. Check the website for frequent lectures, workshops, concerts, and special events.

✳ To Do

BIRDING Hamilton Sanctuary, West Bath. A Maine Audubon Sanctuary (maineaudubon .org) sited on a peninsula in the New Meadows River, offering a 1.5-mile trail system and great bird-watching: common eiders, snowy egrets in the cove, and shorebirds in the mudflats at low tide. In spring there are bobolinks, red-winged blackbirds, meadowlarks, and several species of warblers. Take the New Meadows exit off Rt. 1 in West Bath; turn left on New Meadows Rd., follow it 4 miles to the sanctuary.

Thorne Head Preserve, Bath. Follow High St. 2 miles north to the end and you will find easy, wooded paths in this 96-acre Kennebec Estuary Land Trust's preserve with views of the Kennebec River, rich in common warblers and vireos. The trust publishes a widely available guide to all nine of its preserves; see kennebecestuary.org.

Also see *Green Space*.

BOATING Maine Maritime Museum (mainemaritimemuseum.org; see *Must See*) offers an extensive choice of regularly scheduled one- to three-hour narrated tours down the Kennebec River and to Merrymeeting Bay.

River Run Tours (207-442-7028; riverruntours.com), based in Woolwich. Captain Ed Rice offers charter tours for up to 15 people throughout this area.

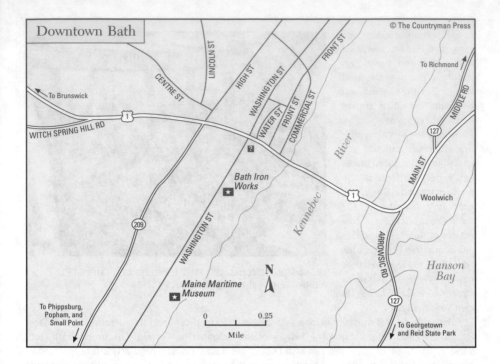

Seguin Island Light Station (seguinisland.org). Sited 2.5 miles off the mouth of Kennebec River, this 186-foot granite lighthouse stands on a bluff on a 64-acre island. It was commissioned by George Washington in 1795; the current tower and keeper's house are vintage 1859 and maintained by **Friends of Seguin Light Station** (72 Front St., Bath; 207-443-4808). Buildings are open Memorial Day–Columbus Day, Tue.–Fri., weather permitting. The island has no dock. Visitors off-load into a dinghy, and the uphill hike is steep. What you see is a keeper's house and museum and the view from tower. Plan to bring a picnic and stay a few hours, exploring hiking paths. Check the website for charter runs from Bath and Boothbay Harbor. The shortest, most frequent service is the **Seguin Island Ferry** (207-841-7977) from Popham Beach.

CANOEING AND KAYAKING This area's many coves and quiet stretches of smaller tidal rivers lend themselves to kayaking, and outfitters have multiplied in recent years. **Seaspray Kayaking** (207-443-3646; seaspraykayaking.com), with bases at Sebasco Harbor and 320 State Rd., on the New Meadows River, offers rentals and tours.

FISHING Surf fishing is popular at Popham Beach. Nearly 20 boats offer fishing on the river. See **visitbath.com** for a list of fishing charters.

GOLF **Bath Country Club** (207-442-8411; thebathgolfclub.com), Whiskeag Rd., Bath, has 18 holes and a pro shop; lessons available. **Sebasco Harbor Resort Golf Club** (207-389-9060) is a recently renovated, waterside nine-hole course open to the public. Reservations advised. Also see the Brunswick chapter.

EXCURSIONS

The Phippsburg Peninsula. From the Maine Maritime Museum drive south on Rt. 209, down the narrow peninsula that's the town of Phippsburg. Pause at the first causeway you cross. This is Winnegance Creek, an ancient shortcut between Casco Bay and the Kennebec River; note the **Winnegance General Store** (*Eating Out*). Continue south on Rt. 209 until you come to **Bisson's Center Store** on your right. Turn left on Parker Head Rd. into the tiny hamlet of Phippsburg Center. This is one of those magical places, far larger in memory than in fact—perhaps because it was once larger in fact, too, as you can see in the **Phippsburg Historical Society** (open July–Sept., Mon.–Sat. 2–4). A **giant linden tree** was planted in 1774 between the white-clapboard Congregational church (1802) and its small cemetery. Note the year of the striking Georgian mansion next door (now **The 1774 Inn**). Also look for the stumps of piers on the river shore beyond, remnants of a major shipyard. Continue along the peninsula's east shore on Parker Head Rd., past a former millpond where ice was once harvested. At the junction with Rt. 209, turn left and note the entrance to **Popham Beach State Park** with its 3 miles of sand. Rt. 209 ends shortly beyond at Fort Popham, a granite Civil War-era fort (with picnic benches) at the mouth of the Kennebec River, 15 miles below Bath. It's a favorite spot for fishermen and a destination for eating seafood by the water at **Spinney's Restaurant** and **Percy's General Store** (see *Eating Out*). This is also a departure point for excursions to **Sequin Island Light**. A pedestrian wooded road leads to World War I and II fortifications that constitute **Fort Baldwin Memorial Park**; a six-story tower yields views up the Kennebec and out to sea.

Along the shore at **Popham Beach**, note the pilings, in this case from vanished steamboat wharves. Around the turn of the 20th century, two big hotels served the passengers who transferred here from Boston to Kennebec River steamers, or who simply stayed a spell to enjoy the town's spectacular beach.

Returning back up Rt. 209, consider two detours. The first is a left on Rt. 216, which runs south to Small Point with limited beach access and camping on **Hermit Island** at its end. Note access to the **Morse Mountain** preserve (great walk, great beach) near the start.

A few curves north on Rt. 209, turn left on Sebasco Rd. (Rt. 217) to find **Sebasco Estates** and **Anna's Water Edge**, the reason many drive out this way from Bath.

Arrowsic and Georgetown Islands. Just east of the Sagadahoc Bridge (at the Dairy Queen that's been there forever), turn south on Rt. 127. Cross a shorter bridge and you are on Arrowsic Island.

Christina Tree

POPHAM BEACH VILLAGE

Note Robinhood Rd., which leads to two of the area's top restaurants (see *Dining Out*). Farther down Rt. 127, in Georgetown Center, look for **Georgetown Pottery**. South of **Georgetown Country Store** (good for sandwiches), turn right to find the **Georgetown Historical Society and Cultural Center** (207-371-9200; georgetownhistoricalsociety .org) at 20 Bay Point Rd.; check the website for a schedule of lectures and events. Continue on Rt. 127 to **Reid State Park**, the big draw (see *Swimming*). The road ends at the **Five Islands Lobster Co.** (see *Eating Out*).

SWIMMING 🐾 If you're traveling with a dog, it's important to know that they're allowed only in picnic areas, not on the beaches.

✍ **Popham Beach State Park** (for current parking and tide updates, 207-389-9125), Rt. 209, Phippsburg; 14 miles south of Bath. One of the best state park swimming and walking beaches in Maine: 3 miles of sand at the mouth of the Kennebec River, a small part of the park's 519 acres. Facilities include bathhouses, showers, and picnic areas with grills. Also a sandbar, tidal pools, and smooth rocks. It can be windy; extra layers are recommended. Day-use fees are charged mid-Apr.–Oct.: $6 adults ($4 Maine residents), $2 seniors, $1 ages 5–11, under 5 free.

✍ **Reid State Park** (207-371-2303), Rt. 127, Georgetown (14 miles south of Bath and Rt. 1). Open daily year-round. A 766-acre preserve with rock ledges, woodlands, and salt marshes as well as sand beaches. Good for year-round walking and birding. The bathhouse and snack bar overlook 2 miles of sand in three distinct beaches that seldom become overcrowded, although the limited parking area does fill by noon on summer weekends. You can choose surf or slightly warmer sheltered backwater. Little River, around the corner from Half-Mile Beach, is a tidal estuary that warms on sunny days, good for children. Entrance fee $6.50 adults ($4.50 Maine residents), $2 over age 65, $1 ages 5-11).

✍ **Charles Pond**, Rt. 127, Georgetown (about 0.5 mile past the turnoff for Reid State Park; 15 miles down the peninsula from Rt. 1). The best all-around swimming hole in the area, this long and narrow pond has clear water and is surrounded by tall pines.

✍ **Sewall Pond**, Arrowsic. This large pond is visible from Rt. 127, but the beach is on the far side. Heading south, turn left on Old Post Rd.; the parking area is a mile or so on your left. It's another 0.25 mile to the pond.

✍ **Pleasant Pond** (207-582-2813), **Peacock Beach State Park**, off Rt. 201, north of Richmond. Open Memorial Day–Labor Day. A sand-and-gravel beach with lifeguards on duty. Water depth drops off gradually to about 10 feet in a 30-by-50-foot swimming area removed from boating and enclosed by colored buoys. Picnic tables and BBQ grills.

SPECIAL LEARNING PROGRAMS **Shelter Institute** (207-442-7938; shelterinstitute .com), 873 Rt. 1, Woolwich. A year-round resource center for those who want to build or retrofit their own energy-efficient home; a wide variety of classes.

Halcyon Yarn (see *Special Shops*) offers classes in fiber arts, including weaving, knitting, felting, spinning, crocheting, and rug hooking.

Rock Gardens Inn (see *Lodging*) offers widely respected, weeklong art workshops.

✳ Green Space

✍ **Fort Baldwin Memorial Park**, Phippsburg. The short, narrow road around a one-lane corner to Point Sebago leads to the site of the **Popham Colony**. An interpretive panel details the extent of the 1607–08 settlement here. Climb the six-story tower (steep stairs, but the railing is sturdy) for a view up the Kennebec and, downriver, out to sea. There are also remnants of fortifications from World Wars I and II.

✍ **Fort Popham Historic Site** (207-389-1335), Hunniwell's Point at Popham Beach. Open Memorial Day–Sept. Picnic sites are scattered around the ruins of this 1861 granite fort, built to guard the Kennebec during the Civil War. Beach and ocean fishing access.

Josephine Newman Wildlife Sanctuary, Georgetown. Bounded on two sides by salt marsh, these 119 acres maintained by Maine Audubon provide good birding along 2.5 miles of walking trails. Look for the sign on Rt. 127, 9.1 miles south of Rt. 1.

Bates-Morse Mountain Conservation Area consists of some 600 acres extending from the Sprague to the Morse River and out to Seawall Beach. A 2-mile hike over a hill accesses an unspoiled beach. Pack a picnic, a towel, and some water—but no dogs and please, no radios. Seawall Beach is an important nesting area for piping plovers and least terns. Look for the small sign on the left to Morse Mountain Rd. soon after Rt. 216 veers off from Rt. 209. Parking is limited; don't park on the road or you will get a ticket.

Montsweag Preserve, Montsweag Rd., Woolwich. A 1.5-mile trail takes visitors through woods, fields, and a salt marsh, and along the water. This 45-acre preserve is owned by The Nature Conservancy. From Rt. 1, take a right onto Montsweag Rd. 6.5 miles from Bath, then 1.3 miles and a left into the preserve.

Note: The **Phippsburg Land Trust** protects a constantly evolving number of preserves and offers guided walks throughout summer and fall. See phippsburglandtrust.org.

Also see *Swimming* and *Birding*.

✳ Lodging

RESORTS ♂ ☀ ♪ ♿ ((ᵠ)) **Sebasco Harbor Resort** (207-389-1161 or 1-800-225-3819; sebasco.com), 29 Kenyon Rd., Sebasco Estates. Open May–Oct. This 550-acre, 133-room, family-geared waterside resort dates back to 1930, featuring a nine-hole golf course, tennis courts, a large swimming pool, kayaking, and full children's and adult programs. Scenic excursions, lobster cookouts, and live entertainment are also offered. The newest additions are Harbor Village Suites and the Fairwinds Spa Suites ($219-499), handy to the full-service **Fairwinds Spa**. Lodging is otherwise divided among the main lodge, a lighthouse-shaped annex ($199-399), and 22 widely scattered and differing cottages ($249-559, based on two people). Add $48 per person MAP (breakfast and dinner); children 12 and under eat free from the children's menu. Weddings and family reunions are specialties. Informal dining is at **The Ledges**, more formal at **The Pilot House**. A spa menu is also available. Golf is $30 for nine holes (walking). Pets are accepted in some cottages ($25 per night).

✪ ♪ **Rock Gardens Inn** (207-389-1339; rockgardensinn.com), Sebasco Estates. Open late June–mid-Sept. A hidden gem, sited on its own narrow peninsula between a cove and bay, within the Sebasco Harbor Resort grounds. Accommodating just 60 guests, it offers access to all of Sebasco's facilities as well as to its own pool and dock with kayaks. Rock Gardens dates back to 1911, and Ona Barnet has preserved the old-style atmosphere of the dining room with its painted tables and the library with its well-thumbed books. Traditions include a weekly lobster bake and cocktail party. The 10 cottages (accommodating three to eight) and three inn rooms are tastefully furnished and constantly updated. Request a water view. Aug. is family-geared. In June, July, and Sept. a series of Sebasco Art Workshops features some well-known teachers. In high season $130–200 per person MAP plus 15 percent for service, less in June and Sept.; children's rates. A four-course dinner (BYOB) as well as breakfast is included; five-night minimum in July and Aug., but check for cancellations.

B&BS

IN BATH

✪ ☘ ☀ ♪ ♿ ((ᵠ)) **The Inn at Bath** (207-443-4294 or 1-800-423-0964; innatbath.com), 969 Washington St. Open year-round. Elizabeth

Christina Tree

COVESIDE BED AND BREAKFAST

GREY HAVENS

Knowlton is the hospitable keeper of this restored 1840s Greek Revival home in the city's historic district. There are twin living rooms with marble fireplaces and eight luxurious guest rooms with private bath, including a two-bedroom suite. Four rooms have a wood-buring fireplace and all have air-conditioning, cable, DVDs, and are thoughtfully furnished but differ in decor. $170–200, from $150 off-season, with a breakfast that includes homemade granola, fresh fruit, and always a hot entrée, perhaps quiche. $25 per additional guest. Children (over 5) and dogs are welcome for a $10 fee.

((y)) **The Kennebec Inn** (207-443-5324; kennebecinn.com), 696 High St. South of Rt. 1 but an easy walk to downtown shops and restaurants, this is a graceful 1850 captain's mansion backing on landscaped lawns with an in-ground pool. There's an elegant parlor with working hearth and four guest rooms divided between the house and (attached) carriage house—all with private baths and thoughtfully, traditionally furnished. $159–205 includes a full breakfast served at the dining room table. Innkeepers Ken and Rachel Parlin invite guests to cook their own lobsters on the grill outside.

((y)) **Benjamin F. Packard House** (207-443-6004 or 1-888-361-6004; benjaminpackard .com), 45 Pearl St. This striking Italianate house was built solidly to house a local shipbuilder in 1790 and remained in the same family until 1985. Amy and Mark Hranicky are enthusiastic hosts. They have created an extensive, brick-floored garden as an alternative to the more formal gathering room with its working hearth. The four guest rooms include two that work well as a family suite. $140–180 in-season, from $100 off-season, includes a choice of a full breakfast.

((y)) **Pryor House** (207-443-1146 or 1-866-977-7969; pryorhouse.com), 360 Front St. Don and Gwenda Pryor offer three crisp, attractive guest rooms with air-conditioning and private bath in this late-Federal-style home. The Tall Chimney Room features a small deck and big Jacuzzi. Common space is inviting. Breakfast, which may be tomato basil quiche, banana crêpes, or blueberry French toast, is included ($145–165). Guest pets are possible but carefully screened.

& ((y)) **Hampton Inn** (207-386-1310; bathbrunswickarea.hamptoninn.com), 140 Commercial St. This four-story, 94-room inn is right downtown. Elevator-accessed rooms come with a king or two queens; facilities include a lap pool and Jacuzzi as well as a fitness center and laundry room. $129–250, breakfast included.

ON THE PHIPPSBURG PENINSULA SOUTH OF BATH

♂ **The 1774 Inn at Phippsburg** (207-389-1774; 1774inn.com), 44 Parker Head Rd., Phippsburg. Open May–Oct. This imposing cupola-topped, foursquare mansion was built by the Kennebec River in 1774 and served as home to Maine's first U.S. congressman. It has been beautifully restored by Brits Jacqueline Hogg and John Atkinson. Guests can choose from four splendid Federal-style guest rooms furnished with antiques, three smaller but thoughtfully decorated rooms in an ell, and the open-timbered but luxurious "Woodshed" with its own porch and steps out into the garden. Grounds slope to the river. The paneling is original throughout, and rooms are furnished with an eye to elegance and comfort. $180–260 includes a full breakfast served by the hearth in the original kitchen.

♂ ❀ **EdgeWater Farm** (207-389-1322 or 1-877-389-1322; ewfbb.com), 71 Small Point Rd., Phippsburg 04562. Year-round. This circa-1800 farmhouse, set in 4 acres of gardens and fruit trees, offers six guest rooms with private bath, kitchen privileges, and access to a large dining/living room. It's well suited to small-group gatherings. There's also an apartment that sleeps seven to 13, and an indoor pool. $140–225.

ON THE GEORGETOWN PENINSULA

❂ ❀ ((•)) **Coveside Bed and Breakfast** (207-371-2807 or 1-800-232-5490; covesidebandb.com), Georgetown (Five Islands). Open Memorial Day–mid-Oct. Tucked into a corner of a quiet, lobster-filled cove is a rare retreat created by Carolyn and Tom Church. The seven guest rooms are divided between a century-old farmhouse and a matching shingled cottage with its own common space and screened porch. All of the many-windowed rooms face the water; those in the cottage have French doors opening onto decks. Some have a gas fireplace and/or a Jacuzzi, but really any room here is special. All have high, angled, or cathedral ceilings with fans, and there's a sense of uncluttered spaciousness and real comfort. Weather permitting, the multicourse breakfast is served on the brick terrace from which the lawn slopes away beneath high trees to the shorefront. Carolyn and Tom are consummate hosts who go way beyond the norm in helping guests with local dining and sightseeing. Beach passes, a canoe, and bikes are free to guests, and there's exercise equipment in a rec room with TV. $150–235.

♂ **The Mooring** (207-371-2790; the mooringb-b.com), 132 Seguinland Rd., Georgetown. Open May–Oct. Paul and Penny Barabe, the great-granddaughter of Walter Reid, donor of the land for his namesake state park, share their home as a B&B. The five guest rooms all have private bath; there are gracious common spaces, and a wicker-furnished porch overlooks the lawns and water. Weddings for up to 125 are a specialty. $150–210 includes a full breakfast.

♂ **Grey Havens Inn** (207-371-2616 or 1-855-473-9428; greyhavens.com), 96 Seguinland Rd. Open early May–Oct. The donor of the land for neighboring Reid State Park also built this turreted, gray-shingled summer hotel, opened in 1904. A huge parlor window—said to be the first picture window in Maine—as well as most of the 13 guest rooms and the long veranda command views of Sheepscot Bay. Rooms and baths have been renovated; the spacious old parlor with its tongue-and-groove paneling has been whitened and lightened with bright, contemporary furnishings. The restaurant, **"Blue,"** is open to the public for dinner (see *Dining Out*). Rooms are $215–395.

1774 INN AT PHIPPSBURG

Christina Tree

mid-June–mid-Oct., $175–350 in shoulder weeks. Weekends tend to be booked for weddings.

OTHER LODGING 🦆 🚣 **Hermit Island Campground** (207-443-2101; hermitisland .com), 6 Hermit Island Rd., Phippsburg 04562; winter mailing address: 42 Front St., Bath 04530. This 255-acre almost-island at Small Point offers 275 nicely scattered campsites, 51 on the water. Only tents, small to medium pop-ups, and small pickup campers are permitted. Owned since 1953 by the Sewall family, Hermit Island also has a central lodge with a recreation room and snack bar where kids can meet. Beyond the camping area are acres of private beach and hiking trails through unspoiled woods and meadows. From $37 per night. Repeat customers mail in their summer reservations for a week or longer on Jan. 1, but shorter stays can be booked, beginning in March, by phone. No pets.

✴ Where to Eat

DINING OUT Also see "Brunswick and the Harpswells."

IN BATH

✪ **Solo Bistro** (207-443-3373; solobistro.com), 128 Front St. Open Mon.–Sat. from 5 nightly for dinner (reserve), also Sat., Sun. 10:30–2 for brunch. The best restaurant in Bath. Pia Neilson's decor is Scandinavian, simple, and sleek, and the chef's way with locally sourced ingredients is inspired. The menu changes monthly, but there's always a wide choice, from a bistro burger and enticing vegan dish to a choice of fish and meat. Live jazz Fri. Entrees: $18–30 and nightly prix fixe for $25, Wed. for $18.

✪ **Kennebec Tavern and Marina** (207-442-9636; kennebectavern.com), 119 Commercial St. Open lunch–dinner until 9 weekdays, 10 Fri. and Sat. A spacious, casual oasis with booths and tables overlooking the Kennebec River, and a seasonal waterside deck. The usual choice of seafood, chicken, and steak. Easy access from Rt. 1. Entrées $12–36. It fits under both *Dining* and *Eating Out*.

🚣 **Beale Street Barbeque and Grill** (207-442-9514; mainebbq.com), 215 Water St. Open for lunch and dinner. No reservations. The feel, with deep booths and soft lighting, is that of a neighborhood restaurant, but the food is authentic Tennessee: pulled pork and ribs, smoked hot sausage and chicken and sausage jambalaya, also plenty of fresh seafood. From $11 for a pulled pork bulkie to $30 for a BBQ sampler. Also fits under both *Dining and Eating*.

ON THE GEORGETOWN PENINSULA

"Blue" at Grey Havens Inn (207-371-2616), Seguinland Rd. (marked from Reid State Park). Open seasonally, Tue.–Sun. 5–9 in high season, Wed.–Sun. in shoulder months. White-clothed tables are well spaced in this large, classic, tongue-and-groove-paneled dining room with views out across Sheepscot Bay. The restaurant offers traditional fine dining. Nightly blackboard specials. Entrées $20–32, but you can also dine on mussels and a salad or on tasty burgers.

The Osprey & Tavern at Riggs Cove (207-371-2530; robinhoodmarinecenter.com), 340 Robinhood Rd. (just off Rt. 127, near Reid State Park). Open mid-June through Aug.,

Christina Tree

THE OSPREY RESTAURANT AT ROBINHOOD MARITIME CENTER

11–11. Reserve. This yachtsmen's haven with water views is squirreled away in the Robinhood Marine Center. Inside and outside seating with water views. New owners in 2015 garnered rave reviews for the seafood menu; also microbrews and light fare.

EATING OUT

IN BATH

🍸 ♿ **Mae's Cafe** (207-442-8577; maescafeand bakery.com), 160 Center St. (corner of High). Open 8–3, serving until 2. Breakfast omelets and specials like lobster Benedict are available all day, and the lunch menu has a loyal following. Try a crab melt or a flat-bread pizza with sautéed lobster, onion, spinach, and mozzarella. The bakery case is filled with delectable cakes—most patrons walk away with at least a cookie. Fully licensed.

Byrnes Irish Pub (207-443-6776; byrnes irishpub.com), 38 Centre St. Open 11 on, from 10 on Sundays. Single-malt whiskeys and selection of Maine and imported beers are the draw, but this is also a good place to eat. Frequent live music.

✪ **Starlight Café** (207-443-3005), 15 Lambard St. Open weekdays 7–2; also Sat. June–Christmas. This bright, funky eatery and bakery is a real find. Large, luscious sandwiches. Create your own by picking bread, meat, cheese, veggies, and daily specials. Limited indoor seating, but it's a short walk to a bench by the Kennebec River.

✪ **The Cabin** (207-443-6224), 552 Washington St., across from the Bath Iron Works. The exterior is a bit shabby, but inside it's a great local spot boasting "the only real pizza in Maine." Booths, patio seating in warm weather, pitchers of beer, terrific pizza. The menu includes pasta and subs. Best in the evening, after the BIW closes for the day.

🍸 **J. R. Maxwell &Co.** (207-443-2014), 122 Front St. Open year-round for lunch and dinner daily. Bath's shopping street place to eat. Lunch on crabcakes and blueberry pie or dependably good burgers. Dinner choices are vast, plus nightly specials. $9–25.

Winnegance General Store (207-443-3300), 38 High St., Bath. Open Mon.–Wed. 6–6, Thu.–Sat. 6 AM–8 PM, Sun. 6–4. South of town on Rt. 209, just before the Winnegance River. Recently restored and wildly popular. Local chefs Shawn Shutt and Holly Snowden

WINNEGANCE GENERAL STORE & CAFE   Christina Tree

get raves for breakfasts like scallop, shrimp, and lobster with cheddar omelets and lunch staples like crabmeat tacos served on a bed of mixed greens (we could only eat one of the two). Wine and beer. Limited seating inside, outside picnic tables. Also check out **Schutty's** (207-798-9167), 410 State Rd., West Bath. The couple's seasonal, wildly popular food truck widely known for fresh seafood with flair. Open seasonally Mon.–Sat. 11–8, Sun. 11–4.

🍸 **Best Thai II** (207-443-8655; bestthai maine.com), 23 Elm St. Open Tue.–Sun. for lunch and dinner, closed Mon. Our favorites are the volcano noodle soup and mango fried rice; plenty here to please. Beer and wine.

ON THE PHIPPSBURG PENINSULA

✪ 🍴 🍸 **Anna's Water's Edge** (207-389-1803), Black's Landing Rd., Phippsburg. Open Memorial Day–Labor Day, 11:30–8:30. Reservations accepted. Well marked from Rt. 209. Sited on a commercial fishing wharf 16 miles south of Bath, but worth the drive on a summer evening, it's a great place for a full shore dinner, with a full menu ranging from sandwiches to surf and turf. Standout chowder and crabcakes. Nightly specials. Liquor served.

✪ 🍸 **Spinney's Restaurant** (207-389-1122), 987 Popham Rd (end of Rt. 209). Open daily 8 AM–9 PM, June–Oct.; call for hours in May and Oct. Our kind of beach restaurant with tables on the glassed-in porch and water views, also on a sand-side deck. Glen and Diane Theal specialize in fresh fish and seafood, fried, steamed, and broiled; good lobster and crabmeat rolls. Fully licensed.

Percy's General Store (207-389-2010), Popham Beach. Seasonal. Locals head for the back room with its water-view booths, good for breakfast on through lobster rolls, fried clams, and lobster dinner specials.

North Creek Farm (207-389-1341; north creekfarm.org), 24 Sebasco Rd., Phippsburg. Open year-round 9–6:30. Suzy Verrier's nursery and extensive perennial gardens are also the setting for a great little eatery with limited inside seating and picnic benches. The tables by the woodstove are inviting off-season, as are the freshly made soups. Homemade pies are another draw. The store sells her organically grown produce, eggs, cut flowers, wine and beers, cheese, gardening implements, and gifts.

ON THE GEORGETOWN PENINSULA

✪ ⚓ **Five Islands Lobster Co.** (207-371-2990; fiveislandslobster.com), Georgetown. Fourteen miles south of Rt. 1 at the end of Rt. 127 on Five Islands wharf. Open seasonally, 11:30–8. It's hard to beat the view from this end-of-the-road commercial lobster wharf. A genuine, old-style lobster pound, it's all

outdoors and all about steamed lobsters and clams with corn and potatoes, lobster rolls, fried clams, and fried seafood. Onion rings are also a specialty. BYOB.

Five Islands Farm (207-371-9383; five islandsfarm.com), Rt. 127, Five Islands. Open mid-May–Dec., Wed.–Mon. 10:30–6. Heidi Klingelhofer's small, shingled emporium overflows with flowers and is a seasonal trove of Maine cheeses, wines, local produce, and specialty foods. Cheese is Heidi's passion, and she carries one of the largest selections of Maine artisan cheeses available.

Also see *Dining Out*.

✳ Entertainment

✪ ⚓ **Chocolate Church Arts Center** (207-442-8455; chocolatechurcharts.org), 804 Washington St., Bath. Gallery and box office open Tue.–Thu. Call ahead. The church is an 1847 Stick Gothic beauty with a soaring, graceful interior and amazing acoustics, converted to a 375-seat theater. Sept.–June presentations include plays, concerts, and a wide variety of

Christina Tree

VIEW FROM FIVE ISLANDS LOBSTER

guest artists, many of them big names. The website also lists summer events.

Gazebo Series band concerts. July and Aug., Tue. and Fri., 7 PM, Library Park, Bath.

Music on the Dock (visitbath.com). July–Aug., "Saturdays at Six," concerts at Waterfront Park.

See **Solo Bistro**, **Byrnes Irish Pub**, and the **Kennebec Tavern** for live music.

✳ Selective Shopping

ART **Third Friday Art Walks & Trolley Tour** (visitbath.org) involving some two dozen venues, more than half of them galleries and studios. Live music, performance too.

☼ **Georgetown Pottery** (georgetown pottery.com), 813 Rt. 1 (207-443-8722) in Woolwich (12 miles north of Bath) and on Rt. 127 in Georgetown (207-371-2801), 9 miles south of Rt. 1. Both showrooms are open daily. Jeff Peters has been handcrafting his distinctive style of pottery since 1972. The extensive selection includes dishes, mugs, and other practical pieces in a variety of hand-painted and deeply colored designs, from casseroles to ikebana "Zen pots." The new Rt. 1 facility includes the adjoining Portage Co. store featuring Maine-crafted furnishings and more. We still prefer the original Georgetown store in which you can watch potters at work.

Saltbox Pottery (207-443-5586; saltbox pottery.com), 4 Shaw Rd., Woolwich. Open May–Dec., Mon.–Sat. 10–5:30. Traditional-style stoneware, wheel-thrown and functional. We couldn't resist a butter dish.

☼ **Markings Gallery** (207-443-1499; markingsgallery.com), 50 Front St., Bath. Open 10–5 in-season; call ahead off-season. This gallery, owned by local artists and craftspeople, is exceptional not only for the quality of what it shows but also for its careful blend of clay, glass, jewelry, woodworking, mixed media, and more. There's plenty here, but the shop isn't cluttered.

Centre St. Arts Gallery (207-442-0300; centrestartsgalleryllc.com), 11 Centre St., is a cooperative gallery showing the work of 20 local artists as well as juried shows; also offers classes and workshops.

Old Post Office Gallery (207-371-2015; leapetersonart.net), 833 Five Islands Rd. (Rt.

Christina Tree

MARKINGS GALLERY IN BATH INCLUDES HANDCRAFTED CLOTHING

127), Georgetown. Open late May–mid-Sept., Fri.–Mon. Owned by several artists and displaying work by a select number. Great local landscape cards by Lea Peterson.

BOOKSTORES **Mustard Seed Bookstore** (207-389-4084; themustardseedbookstore. com), 74 Front St., Mon.–Sat. 9:30–6; Thu. until 8 (frequent readings). Tea as well as books are taken seriously here; plenty of comfortable seating.

Open Door Books (207-443-8689; open doorbooks.us), 178 Front St., Bath. John Ring has a great selection of used, rare, and out-of-print books.

CLOTHING STORES Anchored by **Renys** (#46), one in a chain of exceptional small Maine department stores, **Front Street** has evolved into an exceptional mix of shops. Check out **Bohemian Rose** at #106 (casual to formal) and Contemporary Clothing Cooperative (#110). Don't miss the back room at **Markings Gallery** (#50) with tempting one-of-a-kind hats, bags, scarves, and more.

FARMERS' MARKET **Bath Farmers Market** (bathfarmersmarket.com) is held Sat. mornings; check the website for precise times and venue. In winter the market is held in the Freight Shed on Commercial St.

FLEA MARKET **Montsweag Flea Market** (207-443-2809), Rt. 1, Woolwich. Open Wed.

and Fri.–Sun., 6:30–3. A field filled with tables weighted down by every imaginable collectible and curiosity. Wed. is Antique Day; on weekends look for collectibles, crafts, and good junk. Come early.

SPECIAL SHOPS **Halcyon Yarn** (207-442-7909 or 1-800-341-0282; halcyonyarn.com), 12 School St., Bath. Warehouse open Mon.–Sat. 10–4, Wed. until 8. A destination and mecca for knitters, spinners, and rug hookers with yarns distributed worldwide. Inquire about workshops.

Bath's Front Street is lined with mid-19th-century redbrick buildings. Clothing aside (see above), **Renys** (#46) is a trove of genuine bargains. In a quick visit we unearthed turtlenecks, kitchen mitts, stationery, nail files, and a set of pillowcases for a total of $21.50. This is one of the best stores in this standout Maine chain (renys.com). **Springer's Jewelers** (#76) is a vintage emporium with mosaic floors, chandeliers, and ornate glass sales cases. **Now You're Cooking** (#49) is a major kitchen supply store with a wide following

and cooking classes. **Lisa-Marie's Made in Maine** (#170) fills three storefronts with work by more than 100 artisans, and **Island Treasure Toys** (#182) caters to kids of all ages. Also see **Markings Gallery** and **Mustard Seed Bookstore** above.

✱ Special Events

Details for most events are at visitbath.com.

Three days surrounding the Fourth of July: **Bath Heritage Days**—a grand celebration with an old-time parade of antique cars, marching bands, clowns, guided tours of the historic district, crafts sales, art shows, musical entertainment in two parks, food, bed races, bucket relays, and fireworks over the Kennebec.

Saturday of Columbus Day weekend: **Autumn Fest**. Scarecrow-making, open houses.

December: **Old-Fashioned Christmas** (all month), with competitions and special events.

WISCASSET AREA

Sea captains' mansions and mid-19th-century commercial buildings line Rt. 1 in this historic village, and on summer weekends motorists have time to study them as they inch along. When the bridge across the Sheepscot River was rebuilt and widened, it was supposed to ease the traffic snarl, but Wiscasset is the only village through which cars heading up and down the Midcoast on Rt. 1 must all file slowly, stopping at pedestrian crossings.

It's an obvious stop. The places to eat are varied and good, antiques stores abound, and the historic buildings are worth visiting.

Still the shire town of Lincoln County, Wiscasset is half as populous as it was in its shipping heyday which, judging from the town's clapboard mansions, began after the Revolution and ended around the time of the Civil War. Lincoln County Courthouse, built in 1824 on the town common, is the oldest functioning courthouse in New England.

From Wiscasset, Rt. 27 runs northwest to Dresden Mills, and from there it's just a few miles to the haunting Pownalborough Court House. Rt. 218 veers northeast, paralleling the Sheepscot River through backcountry to Alna, home of the Wiscasset, Waterville & Farmington Railway and Head Tide Village. Rt. 144 heads south down the spine of the quiet Westport Island.

GUIDANCE **Wiscasset Area Chamber of Commerce** (207-882-9600; wiscassetchamber .com) publishes a walking guide and maintains a useful website.

GETTING THERE *By bus:* **Concord Coach** (1-800-639-3317; concordcoachlines.com).

By car: Note the shortcut around traffic northbound: Turn right on Lee St., continue to Fore St. and Water St., and either park or continue north (right) on Rt. 1.

By air and limo: **Mid-Coast Limo** (1-800-937-2424; midcoastlimo.com) makes runs by reservation from Portland International Jetport.

PUBLIC RESTROOMS are in the Waterfront Park, corner of Water and Fore Sts.

✳ To See

IN WISCASSET VILLAGE

Nickels-Sortwell House (207-882-7191; historicnewengland.org), 121 Main St. (Rt. 1). Open June 1–Oct. 15, Fri.–Sun. Tours every half hour, 11–4. Admission $8, $7 seniors, $4 students. This classic Federal-era mansion in the middle of town was built by a shipowner and trader. After he lost his fortune the house became a hotel, and in 1895 a Cambridge, Massachusetts, mayor purchased it; it's now maintained by Historic New England with furnishings from varied periods.

Castle Tucker (207-882-7169; historicnewengland.org), 2 Lee St. Same nonprofit owner as the Nickels-Sortwell House, same season, tour hours, and admission price, but open Wed.–Sun. Castle Tucker was built in 1807 by Judge Silas Lee, who overextended his resources to present his wife with this romantic mansion. Highlights include a freestanding elliptical staircase, Victorian furnishings, and original wallpapers.

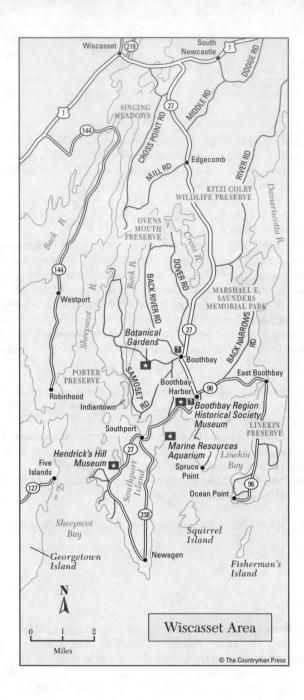

Wiscasset Area

© The Countryman Press

Old Lincoln County Jail and Museum (207-882-6817; lincolncountyhistory.org), 133 Federal St. Open June–Sept., Sat., Sun. noon–4. $5 adults, free 16 and under. The museum consists of a chilling 1811 jail (in use until 1930) with damp, thick, granite walls (some bearing interesting 19th-century graffiti), window bars, and heavy metal doors. The jailer's house (in use until 1953) displays tools and changing exhibits.

IN DRESDEN

⚓ **Pownalborough Court House** (207-882-6817; lincolncountryhistory.org), 28 Court House Rd., off Rt. 128. Open June–Sept., Sat., Sun. noon–4; in July, Aug. also open Tue.-Fri. 10–4. $5 adults; free under 15. Worth the drive. Maine's only surviving pre–Revolutionary War courthouse, this striking three-story building, which includes living quarters upstairs for the judge, gives a sense of this countryside along the Kennebec in 1761, when it was built to serve as an outpost tavern as well as a courtroom. The courthouse is on the second floor, and the third floor is a museum of rural life. Bring a picnic (there are tables). Take Rt. 27 north for 8 miles to Dresden Mills, then Rt. 127 south for 3.7 miles to Rt. 197 and on to Rt. 128, where you head north for 1.3 miles.

IN EDGECOMB

⚓ **Fort Edgecomb State Memorial** (207-882-7777), 66 Old Fort Rd.; the turnoff from Rt. 1 is just across the Sheepscot River. The fort is open Memorial Day–Labor Day, daily 9–6. Nominal donation. This 27-foot, two-story octagonal blockhouse, built in 1808, overlooks a narrow passage of the Sheepscot River. For the same reasons that it was an ideal site for a fort, it is today an ideal picnic site, and tables are provided.

FOR FAMILIES ✪ ⚓ **Wiscasset, Waterville, and Farmington Railway Museum** (207-882-4193; wwfry.org), 97 Cross Rd., Sheepscot Station, Alna (just off Rt. 218, 4.5 miles north of Wiscasset). The museum is open 9–5 on Sat. year-round, Also Sun. in summer. Check the website for trains, which run most weekends, six times a day in summer, less off-season. Volunteers preserve the history of this 2-foot narrow-gauge railroad. The museum's pride is Engine No. 9, an 1891 two-footer locomotive, billed as the oldest in the United States. Volunteers have built replicas of the engine house and shop, original station, and freight shed, which now houses the gift shop and museum. It's a 37-minute roundtrip run on 2.6 miles of track. Trains are usually pulled by a diesel locomotive, but on special occasions a vintage-1904 steam engine is used. Rides are $7 per adult, $6 seniors, $4 ages 4–12.

⚓ **Monkey C Monkey Do** (207-882-6861; monkeycmonkeydo.com), 698 Bath Rd. (corner of Rt. 1 and Rt. 144), Wiscasset. Open daily mid-June–Labor Day, weekends Memorial Day Weekend–Columbus Day. Full course: $25 ages 4–13, $35 older students, $40 adults. From $15 for a sampling; $99 for a family pass. Three ziplines and a great swing with 30 obstacles to navigate at heights of 12–40 feet. Reservations recommended.

✳ Green Space

The **Back River Trail at Eaton Farm** (chewonki.org/about/nature_trails.asp). This is a 4.5-mile coastal trail. From Rt. 1 turn right onto Old Ferry Rd in Wiscasset (at Norm's Used Cars). Take the third right onto Ready Point Rd., which is 0.5 mile past Chewonki Neck Rd. Follow Ready Point Rd. until you see a well-marked sign on the right for Eaton Farm Trail. There is ample parking there and a kiosk for hikers.

Christina Tree

AT THE WISCASSET, WATERVILLE, AND FARMINGTON RAILWAY MUSEUM

EXCURSIONS

Take a scenic drive across Rt. 218 to picturesque Sheepscot Village. The 32-acre Bass Falls Preserve, maintained by the **Sheepscot Valley Conservation Association** (207-586-5616), is 1.2 miles east of Rt. 218; from the parking lot a mile-long trail leads down to the river. Back on Rt. 218 continue north past the **Alna Meeting House** to Head Tide Village, another quiet cluster of old homes around the **Old Head Tide Church** (1858). Note the swimming hole beneath the milldam. The **Alna Store** on Rt. 218 just south of **Head Tide** is a great source of sandwiches and hot specials.

Sunken Garden, Main St., Wiscasset. Down a few steps, easy to miss, but a wonderful little garden surrounded by a stone wall. Planted by the Sortwell family in the foundation of an old inn, the property was donated to the town in 1959.

Sherman Lake Rest Area, Rt. 1 between Edgecomb and Newcastle. Pick up the fixings in Wiscasset and picnic at this scenic rest area. Since the dam broke, this "lake" is now a tidal river. It's still a lovely spot, though, complete with restrooms.

Morris Farm (207-882-4080; morrisfarm.org) 156 Gardiner Rd. (Rt. 27), Wiscasset. A 60-acre organic working farm, with trails open to the public during daylight hours; phone to check on current programming: day camps and farm tours and store.

❋ Lodging

INNS AND B&BS **Squire Tarbox Inn** (207-882-7693 or 1-800-818-0626), 1181 Main Rd. (Rt. 144; turn off Rt. 1 south of Wiscasset), Westport 04578. Open mid-Apr.–Dec. "A good country inn must be tasted," maintains Swiss chef Mario De Pietro, and food is indeed what draws most patrons to this handsome Federal-style farmhouse. Boards and timbers in the low-ceilinged dining room date to 1763, while the parlor and four largest guest rooms, all with working fireplace, are in the "new" (1825) section of house. The remaining seven, more rustic guest rooms are in the converted 1820s Carriage Barn, off a sitting room with a gas fireplace, books, and games. De Pietro and his wife, Roni, perpetuate the inn's reputation for hospitality as well as food, encouraging guests to follow walking paths on their 13 acres, row on the saltwater pond, or explore Westport Island on a mountain bike. $139–199 per couple; off-season $119–179 per couple, including breakfast with freshly baked crois-sants, homemade muesli, and a hot dish pre-pared with fresh-laid eggs from the house hens. Also see *Dining Out*.

✪ 🐾 🖉 ((ɣ)) **Snow Squall Inn** (207-882-6892 or 1-800-775-7245; snowsquallinn.com), 5 Bradford Rd., Wiscasset 04578. Open more or less year-round. Melanie Harris, a trained yoga instructor and massage therapist, and Paul Harris, a professional chef, who met in Bermuda, offer spaciously comfortable accommodations in this 1850s house (named for a clipper ship) with ample common space, gardens, and lounges with hearths and TV. The four guest rooms in the main house have a private bath, king or queen bed, phone, and air-conditioning. Each of the three suites in the Carriage House has two bedrooms (1½ baths) and a private entrance, good for families. $117–170 for rooms, from $160-181 per couple for suites, less off-season. A full breakfast is included. Inquire about massage and yoga.

🦞 ((ɣ)) **Marston House** (207-882-6010 or 1-800-852-4137; marstonhouse.com), Main St., P.O. Box 517, Wiscasset 04578. Open May–Oct. The front of the house is Paul and Sharon Mrozinski's antiques shop, specializ-ing in 18th- and early-19th-century textiles and painted furnishings. In the Carriage House behind—well away from the Rt. 1 traffic noise—are two exceptional guest rooms, each with private entrance, working fireplace, and private bath. Breakfast is served in the flow-ery gardens or in your room. $150 per couple, $125 per night for two nights or more.

OTHER 🦞 **Wiscasset Motor Lodge** (207-882-7137; wiscassetmotorlodge.com), 596 Bath Rd. (Rt. 1), Wiscasset 04578. Open Apr.–Nov.

Attractive, clean, comfortable motel with either a queen or two queen beds and air-conditioning. On Rt. 1; some rooms are quieter than others. $79–108 in high season, from $65 in shoulder seasons.

Chewonki Campground (207-882-7426; chewonkicampground.com), 235 Chewonki Neck Rd., Wiscasset 04578. Sited on 50 waterside acres. The website lets you check out actual, unusually spacious sites for RVs and tents. For tentative tenters a couple are already rigged, ready to rent. Amenities include saltwater pools, a tennis court, a camp store, a rec hall, lawn games, and kayak rentals. Not far enough off Rt. 1 or the local airport to eliminate all traffic noise. Sites are $48–78 in-season, less in shoulders.

✳ Where to Eat

DINING OUT **Squire Tarbox Inn** (207-882-7693; squiretarboxinn.com), 1181 Main Rd. (Rt. 144; turn off Rt. 1 south of Wiscasset), Westport (see *Lodging*). Open daily (except Mon.) Memorial Day–Oct.; Thu.–Sat. in Apr., May, Nov., and Dec. Reserve. Dinner is served 6–8:30 PM in an 18th-century former summer kitchen with a large colonial fireplace and ceiling timbers that were once part of a ship. In warm-weather months there's an attractive screened and canopied deck. Swiss chef-owner Mario De Pietro now shares the kitchen with his Swiss-trained daughter Lara. Ingredients are increasingly farm-to-table in classic dishes like rosemary-roasted rack of lamb or sautéed sliced veal with Swiss-style rösti potatoes. Much of the fruit and veggies come from the inn's extensive organic farm. Entrées $23.50–30. A 15 percent gratuity is added.

Little Village Bistro (207-687-8232), 65 Gardiner Rd. (Rt. 27) open Tue.–Sat. 4–9. Reserve! Tony Bickford, a top Boothbay Harbor chef, has opened his own little restaurant and it's a winner. Just about everything is locally sourced and made from scratch. The reasonably priced menu includes comfort food like slow braised Bolognese and vegetarian dishes like pea and goat cheese tortellini with wild mushrooms (both $14), as well as crab-stuffed haddock and crispy seared duck breast (both $20) and rack of lamb ($26).

✪ ♿ **Le Garage** (207-882-5409; legarage restaurant.com), 15 Water St., Wiscasset.

Open 11 AM–dinner, from 8:30 Sun (brunch). A former 1920s garage with a glassed-in porch overlooking the Sheepscot River (request a table on the porch). Frequently less crowded for lunch (seafood crêpes are the specialty) than restaurants on the main drag. Owned by Lee Rust's family; chefs change but specialties remain seafood chowders, stews, Newburgs, and creamed finnan haddie. Entrées $21–26.50, also a pub menu.

EATING OUT ✪ *Sarah's* (207-882-7504; sarahscafe.com), Main and Water Sts., Wiscasset. Open daily year-round, 11–8, with an outdoor deck for summer dining. The extensive menu includes good pizza (try the Greek pizza with extra garlic), salads, sandwiches in pita pockets or baked in dough, vegetarian dishes, Mexican fare, and lobster more than 15 different ways. Well known for their soup and bread bar.

Montsweag Roadhouse (207-443-6563; montsweagroadhouse.com), 942 Rt. 1, Woolwich, nearer to Wiscasset than Bath. Open 11–1 AM. Serving food until 9, until 10 Fri. and Sat. This distinctive red building is an old apple storage barn, a restaurant since the 1930s but now with a pleasantly split personality. Come on a weeknight and it's a quiet, spacious family-geared place with booths and a large, reasonably priced menu and full bar. On Fri. and Sat. this place hops with live bands.

Treats (207-882-6192), 80 Main St., Wiscasset. Open Mon.–Sat. 8–6, Sun. 10–4. A food store known for baked goods plus terrific soups and sandwiches, with an eat-in table. The town's picnic source.

✳ Selective Shopping

ANTIQUES SHOPS Antiques are everywhere in Wiscasset. On and just off Water Street, in or attached to attractive old homes, more than 20 shops by our last count. Pick up a map (available in most shops) and browse the day away; many specialize in nautical pieces and country primitives. **Wiscasset Village Antiques** (207-882-4029; avalon antiquemarket.com), Rt. 1, 2 miles south of Wiscasset Village. Open daily 9–7 in-season. More than 100 dealers. See the Bath chapter for details about the Montsweag Flea Market,

LOBSTER

Red's Eats (207-882-6128), Rt. 1 and Water St., just before the bridge, Wiscasset. Open Apr.–Sept. until 2 AM on Fri. and Sat., until 11 weeknights, and noon–6 on Sun. The lines can be an hour long and the seating is at picnic benches, but the lobster rolls—packing an entire lobster into one small hot-dog roll—continue to get rave reviews. Whether or not this is "Maine's #1 Lobster Roll" is a matter of taste. The lobster is cold, fresh from the fridge, served with a choice of drawn butter or mayo. Fried clams are the other specialty but there are also crabcakes, hot dogs, fried zucchini, and more. It's been operated by members of the Gagnon family since 1977.

Christina Tree

RED'S EATS

Sprague's Lobster (207-882-1236), 22 Main St., Wiscasset. Open seasonally, 11–7. No lines, no legend, but a great view from picnic tables on a pier beside the river. This is the other great place for lobster any way; also really good clam fritters.

The Sea Basket (207-882-6581), 303 Bath Rd. (Rt. 1), Wiscasset. Open Wed.–Sun. 11–8. A long-established road stop known for fresh seafood; a lot of it is fried, but with an eye to keeping it heart healthy. Known for lobster stew, lobster rolls, and sea scallops.

south of Wiscasset on Rt. 1, open seasonally on Wed. and weekends.

ART GALLERIES Wiscasset Bay Gallery (207-882-7682; wiscassetbaygallery.com), 67 Main St., Wiscasset. Changing exhibits in spacious exhibit rooms. Specializes in 19th- and 20th-century Maine and New England marine and landscape paintings.

Maine Art Gallery (207-882-7511; maine artgallery.org), 15 Warren St. Open June–Nov., Tue.–Sat. 10–4, Sun. 11–4. Housed in a vintage-1807 brick schoolhouse, a nonprofit gallery since 1954. Frequently changing exhibits. Worth finding.

OTHER Sheepscot River Pottery (207-882-9410; sheepscot.com), 34 Rt. 1, Edgecomb, just north of Wiscasset; home base for one of Maine's major potteries.

Old Salt Books and Gifts (207-882-4700), 49 Water St., Wiscasset. Maine products, gifts, cards, young adult books, more. The newest occupant of the Old General Store.

Big Al's Supervalues (201-882-6423; bigalssupervalues.com), south of Wiscasset Village on Rt.1. An odd-lots trove of everything you don't need and a few things you might. Toys, gadgets, Maine souvenirs, party supplies, etc. Free coffee.

BOOTHBAY HARBOR REGION

The water surrounding the village of Boothbay Harbor is more than just a view. You must cross it—via a footbridge—to get from one side of town to the other, and you can explore it on a wide choice of excursion and charter boats and in sea kayaks. It is obvious from the very lay of this old fishing village that its people have always gotten around on foot or in boats. Though parking has increased in recent years, cars still feel like an intrusion. In the peninsula's other villages—Boothbay, Southport, and East Boothbay—roads are walled by pines, permitting only occasional glimpses of water.

Boats are what all four of the Boothbays have traditionally been about. Boats are built, repaired, and sold here, and sailing and fishing vessels fill the harbors. Excursions range from an hour-long sail around the outer harbor to a 90-minute crossing (each way) to Monhegan Island. Fishermen can pursue giant tuna, stripers, and blues, and nature lovers can cruise out to see seals, whales, and puffins.

In the middle of summer Boothbay Harbor itself is chockablock full of tourists licking ice cream cones, chewing freshly made taffy and fudge, browsing in shops, looking into art galleries, listening to band concerts on the library lawn, and, of course, eating lobster. You get the feeling it's been like this every summer since the 1870s.

Boothbay Harbor is just a dozen miles south of Rt. 1 via Rt. 27, which runs down the middle of the peninsula. The coastline is, however, a different story, measuring 100 miles

Christina Tree

BOOTHBAY HARBOR

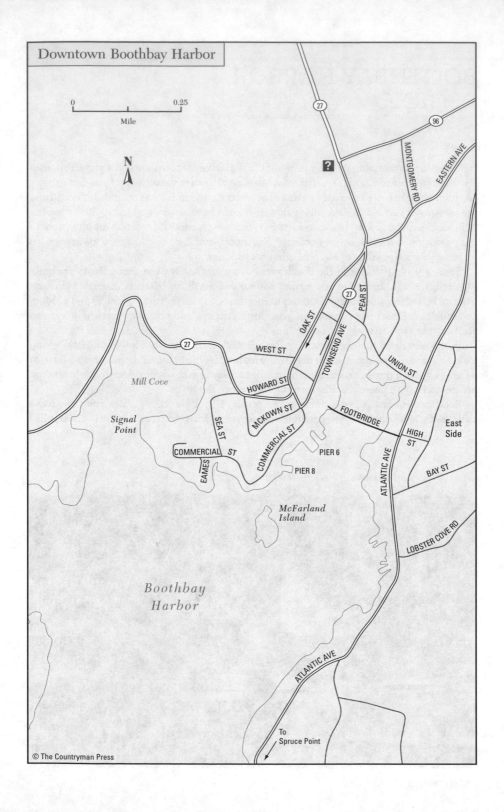

Downtown Boothbay Harbor

0   0.25
Mile

N

as it wanders down the Sheepscot, around Southport Island and up into Boothbay Harbor, out around Spruce Head, around Linekin Bay, out Ocean Point, and back up along the Damariscotta River.

Thanks to the fervor of developers from the 1870s on, this entire coastline is distinguished by the quantity of its summer cottages, many of which can be rented by the week for less than you might think. Still, thanks to the Boothbay Region Land Trust, there are now over 30 miles of accessible waterside preserves, with trails meandering through hundreds of acres of spruce and pine, down to smooth rocks and tidal pools. It was this landscape that inspired Rachel Carson, who first summered on the peninsula in 1946 and built a cottage on the Sheepscot River in 1953, to write much of *The Edge of the Sea* (1955) and then *Silent Spring* (1962), the book that changed global thinking about human beings' relation to basic laws of nature.

GUIDANCE **Boothbay Harbor Region Chamber of Commerce** (207-633-2353; boothbay harbor.com), 192 Townsend Ave. (Rt. 27), southbound, just before the light but north of Hannaford Supermarket at the junction with Rt. 96. Open weekdays 8–5 year-round, also weekends 10–4 June–Columbus Day. Pick up the chamber's annual *Visitor & Resource Guide* and (indispensable) map detailing local parking lots. The chamber also keeps cottage listings and tracks availability for cottages weekly and for lodgings daily.

Boothbay Information Center (207-633-4743; boothbay.org/bcc), Rt. 27, Boothbay, after the fire station. Open daily 9–9 (until 6 on Sun.) late June–Columbus Day, also Fri.–Sun. Memorial Day–late June. A friendly walk-in center that does its best to help people without reservations find places to stay. It keeps an illustrated scrapbook of options, also a cottage rental list.

GETTING THERE *By car:* Take I-295 from Portland, getting off at Exit 28 (Brunswick) or Exit 31 (Topsham). Follow signs to Rt. 1 north through Bath and Wiscasset, turning onto Rt. 27 into Boothbay and Boothbay Harbor.

GETTING AROUND **The Rocktide Trolley** (on wheels) runs every 30 minutes daily, 10–5, mid-June–Labor Day. From the east side of town, starting at the Rocktide Inn, to Brown's Wharf Inn, across to the heart of the Boothbay Harbor Region, up onto 27 north, stopping at the Meadow Mall, the Flagship Inn, and the Boothbay Region YMCA.

PARKING Finding a spot in the center of Boothbay Harbor can mean circling the block a couple of times. Still, we had little trouble on an August weekend, armed with a local map showing parking lots (see *Guidance*). Boothbay Harbor offers free street parking and a dozen public parking lots.

PUBLIC RESTROOMS In Boothbay Harbor restrooms are open Memorial Day–Columbus Day by the small park at the Town Landing; also during office hours at the town hall, Howard Street. Locations are marked on the chamber of commerce map.

WHEN TO COME Some lodgings and restaurants stay open year-round, but those bright warm days on the water can't be beat.

✳ To See

✪ ✎ **The By-Way**. Don't miss Boothbay Harbor's old-fashioned harborside boardwalk area. Walk from the By-Way down to the footbridge across the harbor.

FOR FAMILIES ✪ ✎ **Maine State Aquarium** (207-633-9559), McKown Point Rd., West Boothbay Harbor. Open Memorial Day weekend–Sept. daily 10–5; in Sept., Wed.–Sun. $7 adults, $5 seniors, $3 ages 3–12. At this octagonal waterside aquarium, kids and adults alike can view tanks filled with sea creatures found in Maine waters such as striped bass, cod, alewives, and a 14-pound lobster. Dip your hands into the touch tank and view "chained sharks," skates, and alewives (larger than we'd thought). Presentations several times a day in summer, but get there early to ensure a good view.

✎ ♿ **Boothbay Railway Village** (207-633-4727; railwayvillage.org), Rt. 27 (about 3 miles north of Boothbay Harbor). Open daily 9:30–5, June–mid-Oct.; special rides for Halloween and Thanksgiving, plus a Polar Express in early Dec. Regular admission $10 adults, $5 ages 2–18. A 2-foot narrow-gauge railway with a coal-fed steam engine wends its way through a miniature village made up of several restored buildings, including vintage railroad stations, the Boothbay Town Hall (1847), and the Spruce Point chapel (1923). Displays include a general store, a doll museum, and a 1920s-era home with an authentic 1929 GE refrigerator and period furniture. More than 55 antique autos (1907–49) are also on display. Many special events, including a weekend antique auto meet (more than 150 cars) in late July.

✎ **Dolphin Mini Golf & Shell Museum** (207-633-4828), 510 Wiscasset Rd. (Rt. 27), Boothbay. Open daily May–mid-Sept. The museum, housed in a covered bridge, boasts one of the world's largest private collections of seashells, including lobster claws and sand dollars (free). The 18 holes of mini golf include lakes stocked with fish and a covered bridge. All this plus Round Top ice cream.

LIGHTHOUSES ✪ ✎ **Burnt Island Lighthouse Program** (maine.gov/dmr/burntisland). This 1821 lighthouse, a mile out from the inner harbor, remains an active light station owned by the Maine Department of Marine Resources. Visitors are greeted by docents in 1950s dress portraying the island's last lighthouse keeper and his family, guiding them around their '50s furnished home and up into the light. See *Boating/Balmy Days Cruises* for frequent excursions in July/Aug.

Hendrick's Head Light, Southport Island. Built in 1829, privately owned but can be viewed from Hendrick's Beach. The story goes that a keeper here found a floating bundle after a shipwreck. He adopted the baby inside, the wreck's only survivor.

The Inn at the Cuckolds Lighthouse (innatcuckoldslighthouse.org). Just half a mile off the outer tip of Southport Island, this vintage-1892 station is now a luxurious, two-suite bed & breakfast. Check the website for visuals and for a schedule of weekly tours and periodic events. Also See *Lodging.*

Ram Island Light is a distinctive landmark off Ocean Point. Built in 1883, it's now automated and the island itself is maintained by a nonprofit trust.

MUSEUMS ✎ **Boothbay Region Historical Society Museum** (207-633-0820; boothbay historical.org), 72 Oak St., Boothbay Harbor. Open year-round, Thu.–Sat. 10–2. Free. Seven rooms are filled with vintage lobster traps, Native American artifacts, ship's bells, a Fresnel lens from Ram Island, and genealogical resources. The gift shop stocks books, maps, coins, photos, and more.

✎ **Hendricks Hill Museum** (207-633-1102; hendrickshill.org), 419 Hendricks Hill Rd., Rt. 27, Southport Island. Open July and Aug., Tue., Thu., and Sat. 11–3. The house looks much as it did in 1810, with a period kitchen including a beehive oven, pictures of Southport's grand hotels, as well as other village memorabilia, wooden boats, and farm implements. Farther down the road stop by **Southport Memorial Library**, which has an impressive monarch butterfly collection.

MUST SEE

Coastal Maine Botanical Gardens (207-633-4333; mainegardens.org), 132 Botanical Garden Dr., off Barter's Island Rd., Boothbay. Gardens and buildings open Apr. 15–Oct. 31 daily 9–5, until 6 in July/Aug. $16 adults, $14 seniors 65 and over, $8 ages 3–17, under 3 free. These magnificent 270 shorefront acres contain more than 80,000 plants from more than 1,300 species, 350 of them native. This property was slated for development in the 1970s when a small group of local residents dedicated themselves to this project, some mortgaging their homes.

Come early to get a parking spot in summer! Plan to spend at least three hours, quite possibly a day. Begin with the website, which offers monthly updates of what's in bloom as well as events and a mapped lay of the land. From the visitors center, with its gift shop and the **Gardens Kitchen Café** (open 11–4), paths radiate out to themed gardens. The **Children's Garden** begins with spouting whales and a maze lawn, and includes a lupine meadow, Mr. McGregor's garden, a story barn, tree house, a shallow pond, and more. The **Garden of the Five Senses** adds the scent of grosso lavender and other aromatic plants, the texture of lamb's ears and creeping thyme, the noise of flowing water and frogs and wooden boards underfoot, and the taste of herbs like Russian tarragon to the beauty you can drink in with your eyes. A downward-sloping path brings you to the **Meditation Garden**, centered on a magnificent stone basin. From here the path can connect with the **Shoreland Trail**, along which you can find the **Fairy House Village** and **The Landing**, where you can rent **kayaks** to paddle along the Back River or board the electric-powered tour boat **_Beagle_** for a one-hour cruise out into the Sheepscot River (sheepscotrivercruises.com). Wooded trails loop back to the **Giles Rhododendron Garden**, set off by a waterfall. Free shuttles ease the way from multiple parking lots, and guided cart tours are available by reservation. Pets are allowed only in the parking area; there is a dog walk and water spigot. Count on the café for meals made with produce picked just outside the door in summer.

THE AGC COLORING COTTAGE LURES SMALL VISITORS

Coastal Maine Botanical Gardens

✳ To Do

BIKE RENTALS Tidal Transit Co. (207-633-7140; kayakboothbay.com), by the footbridge, Boothbay Harbor, rents bikes in-season.

BOATING ✐ **Balmy Days Cruises** (207-633-2284; balmydayscruises.com), Pier 8, Boothbay Harbor, offers cruises to Monhegan Island every morning early June–early Oct. and weekends in shoulder seasons. The crossing takes 90 minutes each way, and you have close to four hours on the island. Bring a picnic and hit the trail. Here are also harbor tours, party fishing, and tours to **Burnt Island Lighthouse** (see *Also See*).

   ✐ **Cap'n Fish Boat Cruises** (207-633-3244; mainewhales.com), Pier 1 (red ticket booth), Boothbay Harbor. Mid-May–mid-Oct. Daily cruises include whale-watching, lighthouses, trap hauling, and more.

   Sheepscot River Cruises (207-633-6598), The Landing at **Coastal Maine Botanical Gardens** (see Must See). Electric boat *Beagle* offers hourly cruises.

   West Harbor Recreation (207-370-0678), West Boothbay, offers both power and sailboats.

SAILING Boothbay Harbor Yacht Club (207-633-5750), 156 Western Ave., West Boothbay Harbor 04575. Moorings available for sailing/cruising to visitors. Launch service 8–2, heads, showers, laundry, dining room/lounge access. Closed Mon. Free WiFi wireless Internet access at mooring, ice available, plus other amenities.

   Daysails are offered by **Schooner** *Lazy Jack* (207-633-3444; sailschoonerlazyjack.com), ☙ **Schooner** *East Wind* (207-633-6598; schoonereastwind.com), **Friendship Sloops** *Sarah Mead* (207-380-5460) and *Bay Lady* (207-633-2284; balmydayscruises.com).

Christina Tree

BOOTHBAY OFFERS PLENTY OF WAYS TO GET OUT ON THE WATER

HENDRICKS HEAD BEACH

✪ **Linekin Bay Resort** (207-633-2494; linekinbayresort.com), 92 Wall Point Rd., Boothbay Harbor. Overnight moorings (all chain), onshore facilities. Qualified sailors can rent 19-foot Rhodes sailboats, and sailing lessons are offered for all abilities.

SPORTFISHING See boothbayharbor.com for details about the following: **Breakaway Sportfishing** (207-350-5118), **Redhook Charters** (207-633-3807), **Sweet Action Charters** (207-318-4898), and **Charger Charters** (207-380-4556). **Oak Street Provisions** (207-633-1290), 43 Oak St., Boothbay Harbor, rents tackle and bait, sells fishing licenses.

GOLF **Boothbay Harbor Country Club** (207-633-6085; boothbayharborcc.com), Country Club Dr. (off Rt. 27), Boothbay. Open Apr.–Nov. Eighteen holes, expansive new clubhouse and restaurant; open to the public through short-term memberships and member inns; carts and clubs for rent.

RECREATIONAL FACILITY ✍ **Boothbay Region YMCA** (207-633-2855; brymca.com), Townsend Ave., Rt. 27 (on your left as you come down the stretch that leads to town). An exceptional facility open to nonmembers (user fee charged) with two new swimming pools and other programs for children. Tennis, racquetball, gymnastics, aerobics, soccer, swimming in a heated six-lane indoor pool, saunas, exercise and weight-lifting rooms, and a fieldhouse with a three-lane track.

SEA KAYAKING ✍ **Tidal Transit Company** (see *Bike Rentals*) offers guided tours as well as hourly, half-day, and full-day rentals (basic instruction included); their rentals are also available at the landing at the Maine Coastal Botanical Garden.

SWIMMING Beaches are all private, but visitors are permitted in a number of spots:
    Hendricks Head Beach. Follow Rt. 27 toward Southport, across the Townsend Gut Bridge to a circle (white church on your left, monument in the center, general store on your right); turn right and follow Beach Rd. to the beach; roadside parking and calm, shallow water.
    🐾 **Grimes Cove** has a little pebble beach with rocks to climb at the very tip of Ocean Point, East Boothbay. Follow Rt. 96 to the end.
    🐾 **Barrett Park**, Lobster Cove (turn off Atlantic Ave. at the Catholic church, east side of Boothbay Harbor), is a town park with restrooms and two rocky Linekin Bay beaches.

🐾 **Knickerkane Park**, Barter's Island Rd., Boothbay. Paths lead from the parking lot to a small island with picnic tables and swimming. The road in is a bit rough, but that seems to keep crowds away from this small beach with a dock.

TENNIS Public tennis courts are located across Rt. 27 from the YMCA, which also has indoor courts.

WALKS Ocean Point, at the tip of the East Boothbay peninsula, offers beautiful views of the ocean and several windswept islands, but parking can be tricky. Leave your car in the lot operated by the Linekin Preserve or other designated parking area and walk, though be mindful of NO TRESPASSING signs. Explore the rocky beach and its tidal pools. On a clear day you can see both Ram Island and the Cuckolds lighthouses.

Also see *Green Space*.

✳ Green Space

Boothbay Region Land Trust (207-633-4818; bbrlt.org), 137 Townsend Ave., Boothbay Harbor. Open Mon.–Fri. 9:30–4:30. The trails are open year-round and free, donations appreciated. Download maps from the website or pick up a copy of the spiral-bound, illustrated *Take a Hike,* published by the land trust—a guide to 22 preserves with a total of more than 30 miles of trails. The 1,700 acres of land under the trust's protection include several islands. In the **Porter Preserve** (23 wooded acres, including a beach) on Barters Island, an osprey peered at us from its nest atop a marker along a ledge just offshore, and another ledge was so thick with seals that they seemed like some kind of brown growth—until a dog barked and the entire ledge seemed to heave and rise, then flop and splash off in different directions.

✳ Lodging

The chamber of commerce lists more than 100 lodging places in its regional guide and keeps a list of vacation rentals. See *Guidance*.

RESORTS ♂ 🐾 ♂ **Spruce Point Inn Resort & Spa** (207-633-4152 or 1-800-553-0289; sprucepointinn.com), 88 Grandview Ave., Boothbay Harbor. Open mid-May–mid-Oct. Boothbay Harbor's premier full-service resort is sited on 57 acres at the tip of a peninsula jutting into Boothbay Harbor. Roughly 100 rooms are divided between the handsome 1940s inn and "lodges," self-contained town houses and cottages scattered over landscaped grounds. There are no less than 22 types of rooms, varying widely in size and decor. Public rooms in the inn include an attractive library and two restaurants; elegantly casual **Bogie's** and oceanfront **88** for fine dining. We loved swimming in the cold saltwater pool and warming back up again in the hot tub, both on the edge of the bay. Amenities also include a heated freshwater pool, clay tennis courts, lawn games, a fitness center, a full-service spa, and a private pier. Guests can also take advantage of kayaks, bicycles, and sails on the Friendship Sloop *Sarah Mead*. Organized children's programs are offered in July and Aug. EP high-season rates for rooms in the inn are $225–625, cottages $295–1,500, cottage rooms $195–390, modern lodge rooms $340–595, and town houses $745–845. A resort fee is added.

♂ ♂ ♿ **Newagen Seaside Inn** (207-633-5242 or 1-800-654-5242; newagenseasideinn.com), 60 Colony Rd. (Rt. 27), Southport Island, Cape Newagen. Open mid-May–mid-Oct. When the original resort opened in the 1920s, owner Joshua Brooks—founder of the Eastern States Exposition—had both electricity and Rt. 27 extended to this southern tip of Southport Island to serve it. In 1943 the original inn burned in a fire said to be set

Christina Tree

PORCH AT LINEKIN BAY RESORT

as a signal to German U-boats. Brooks then had the present large, admittedly plain-faced facility built, painted, and open within three months. Rachel Carson frequented the inn and its splendid grounds; her ashes were scattered here. Even if you don't stay here, be sure to find your way to the property's pine-shaded shore. Rooms and suites in the main inn have all been recently renovated, another junior suite added in the Little Inn annex, and a gorgeous new ocean-view cottage added. There's also a new pool and a brand-new restaurant, open for both lunch and dinner (see *Dining Out*). Amenities include tennis courts, bicycles, lawn games, rowboats, and the Pine Room, which houses two funky 1940s-era candlepin bowling lanes, pool table, and table tennis. Weddings fill the place on weekends but midweeks are quiet and good value. Rooms $165–255 and suites $235–305, depending on room and season. Cottages, $295–455. Rates include full breakfast.

✍ & **Ocean Point Inn** (207-633-4200 or 1-800-552-5554; oceanpointinn.com), 191 Shore Rd., P.O. Box 409, East Boothbay. Open Memorial Day–Columbus Day. This 110-year-old resort has a great location, longtime owners, and an enthusiastic following. All rooms have private bath, air-conditioning, cable TV, mini refrigerator, and phone; most have water views, and some have a fireplace. Guests relax in the heated pool with a hot tub or the Adirondack chairs overlooking the ocean. There's an oceanfront dining room (see *Dining Out*). $99–299 in-season, continental breakfast included; full buffet breakfast is extra.

Ocean Gate Resort (207-633-3321 or 1-800-221-5924; oceangateinn.com), Southport 04576. Several multistory buildings with water views are ranged along the shore, and attractive cottages come with and without views on this 45-acre wooded property. A breakfast buffet and use of canoes and kayaks is included in the rates: $104–299. Facilities include a heated pool, miniature golf, fishing pond, tennis, and more.

✪ ✍ ❀ ✍ (⟨•⟩) **Linekin Bay Resort** (207-633-2494; linekinbayresort.com), 92 Wall Point Rd., Boothbay Harbor. Open Memorial Day–Columbus Day weekends. Styled as the last all-inclusive sailing resort on the East Coast, Linekin Bay has been owned by the same family since 1909. It's been evolving ever since, which explains its range of lodging—35 rooms in five different lodges (family groups can rent an entire lodge), along with 30 cottages (one or two rooms). High-season rates—$150–190 per adult, less for children (free under 3)—include the use of a fleet of Rhodes 19s, and lessons are offered. Three meals, served family-style in the open-timbered central lodge, are also included along with Kids Camp and the use of canoes, kayaks, rowboats, standup paddleboats, and tennis and fishing gear. Facilities include a heated bayside saltwater pool and tennis court, a TV room (nightly movies), an old-fashioned game/library area, a bar and deck, as well as kids' rec room and play areas. Weddings for up to 150 in shoulder months.

INNS AND B&BS ✪ ✍ & (⟨•⟩) **Topside** (207-633-5404 or 1-888-633-5404; topsideinn.com), 60 McKown St., Boothbay Harbor. Open May–Oct. This spacious captain's house sits atop McKown Hill with sweeping water views from its windows and the Adirondack chairs on its long, sloping lawn. Some 20 rooms are divided between the light-filled and unfussily elegant main house and two "guest houses," two-story former motel units that Mark and Buzz have transformed so completely that "Leeward," especially, is a tempting choice over the house. Common space includes a book-stocked living room as well as a guest pantry (fridge, coffee, and snacks) and multiwindowed dining room.

TOPSIDE INN

Breakfast, which includes house granola, fruit, and freshly baked breads, perhaps deviled eggs with salmon or shrimp creole with grits and a fried egg, is included in $179-239. Downtown Boothbay Harbor is a quick, short walk downhill (the uphill return seems steeper).

✪ ((ᵞ)) **Five Gables Inn** (207-633-4551 or 1-800-451-5048; fivegablesinn.com), 107 Murray Hill Rd. (off Rt. 96). East Boothbay. Open Memorial Day weekend–mid-Oct. Steve and Susan Plansteiner are the owners of this special inn. Fifteen of the 16 rooms offer views of Linekin Bay; most have queen-sized beds (many with handmade quilts), and five have a working fireplace. The smaller third-floor gable rooms offer some of the best water views. There's a living room/dining area with a wraparound porch, spacious enough for guests to find their own corner, also space around the hearth that invites conversation. Breakfast and afternoon tea is included in $145–260 double.

Blue Heron Seaside Inn (207-633-7020; blueheronseasideinn.com), 65 Townsend Ave., Boothbay Harbor. Boothbay natives Laura and Phil Chapman have restored this elegant harbor-side home as a B&B with six rooms outfitted with refrigerator/freezer, private bath, air-conditioning, and cable TV, with access to decks overlooking the harbor. Guests can use the inn's kayaks. $195–285 in-season includes a full breakfast, perhaps

Vickery French toast with baked apples. Then walk out the door and you are right in the village.

Welch House Inn (207-633-3431; welchhouse.com), 56 McKown St., Boothbay Harbor. Harbor views from this hilltop roost but also easy access to shops and restaurants, longtime hospitable hosts Susan and Michel, attractive guest and common rooms plus common decks add up to a great experience. The nine antiques-furnished rooms in the main house are available year-round and five more (less formal) in the Sail Loft are seasonal. $160-250 in high season (from $150 off-season) includes a locally sourced full breakfast, maybe pumpkin pancakes or crabmeat quiche.

MOTELS Boothbay Harbor has number of large, inviting motels, many on the harbor.

♿ **Flagship Inn & Suites** (207-633-5094; boothbaylodging.com), 200 Townsend Ave. (Rt. 27), Boothbay Harbor. Open year-round. This completely renovated, affordable motel offers 82 rooms and family suites. Amenities include a swimming pool, hot tub, and cable TV. $74–149, depending on the season. On-site restaurant.

🐾 **Mid-Town Motel** (207-633-2751; midtownmaine.com), 96 McKown St., Boothbay Harbor. Open May–Oct. Billed as "a true 1950s classic," this is a pleasant, spanking-clean motel with either a queen or a double and twin in each room and an easy walk to downtown shops and the waterfront. $95 July–Labor Day, from $69 off-season.

The Inn at the Cuckolds Lighthouse (1-855-212-5252; innatcuckoldslighthouse.com). Sited half a mile off the outer tip of Southport Island, this vintage-1892 station is now a luxurious, two-suite B&B open late May–late Sept. $1,350 per night Mon.–Thu., $1,600 Fri–Sun. Two-night minimum. Check the website for open house days on which public tours are offered.

COTTAGES The following are variations on old-style cottage colonies, still a good option, especially with children and/or pets.

🐾 ((ᵞ)) **Harborfields on the Shore** (207-633-5082; harborfields.com), 24 McKown Point Rd., West Boothbay Harbor 04575. A friendly, quiet family resort on a 10-acre harborfront

VIEW FROM THE WELCH HOUSE INN

property. Cozy cottages feature woodstoves, full kitchens, and great views of the harbor. Floats for boating, swimming, and fishing are available, as are moorings and a small tidal beach. Pets welcome. From $999 per week in high season.

Thompson Cottages (207-633-5304; thompsoncottages.com), 7 Thompson's Hill Rd., Southport 04576. Three 1-bedroom cottages and one 3-bedroom cottage come fully equipped, located on Townsend Gut. Alice and Dick Thompson have been hosting guests here since 1968. From $735 per week.

Note: Contact the chambers of commerce for lists of rental cottages. The Boothbays offer one of the coast's largest concentrations of vacation rentals.

CAMPING ❀ ✍ ♿ **Gray Homestead Campground** (207-633-4612; graysoceancamping .com), 21 Homestead Rd., Southport Island 04576. Open mid-May–Columbus Day. You can't beat the location—301 acres on the east coast of Southport Island. Forty-two sites for tents and RVs. Stephen Gray's family has been here since 1800. $37–52 per night for RVs; from $11 for tent sites.

✳ Where to Eat

DINING OUT ✪ ✍ **Ports of Italy** (207-633-1011; portsofitaly.com), 47 Commercial St., Boothbay Harbor. Open for dinner daily from 4:30, Apr.–mid-Oct. This is a long-standing local favorite. Sante Calandri carries on the tradition of genuine northern Italian cuisine. The pasta is homemade, the upstairs dining room is attractive, and there's a seasonal porch as well as free parking. Specials aside, the menu rarely changes. We can never pass up the tagliolini alle vongole, angel hair tossed with clams, white wine, and olive oil—unless it's for saltimbocca di vitello, veal scaloppini with fresh sage and prosciutto in a white wine sauce. Entrées $18–32.

The Thistle Inn (207-633-3541; thistleinn .com), 55 Oak St., Boothbay Harbor. Open year-round for dinner. Reservations recommended. No water views, but attractive dining rooms and seasonal deck. The focus is on local seafood and produce, a place to feast on Glidden Point oysters, pan-seared scallops, or yellow fin tuna. Entrées $25-32. Pub menu also available.

✒ ✳ **Newagen Seaside Inn** (207-633-5242), 60 Newagen Colony, Southport. Open seasonally for lunch; usually closed Sat. night. Given its location at the tip of Southport Island, this is also a good place to come for lunch, maybe flat bread with foraged mushrooms, caramelized onion, bacon, and Parmesan cream sauce. The dinner menu is dictated by available local ingredients. Walk off your meal by the water. Entrées $17–36.

The Rocktide Inn (297-633-4455; rocktideinn.com), 35 Atlantic Ave., Boothbay Harbor. Open daily for breakfast and dinner; drinks 4–11 in high season. Closed Columbus Day–mid-June. Come by boat or car for dinner (jackets required in the formal dining room, not in the casual dining room) or a Rocktide martini in the **On the Rocks Lounge**. The view of the sunset is magnificent, and locals rate the dinners highly. Entrées $12–30.

✒ **Ocean Point Inn Restaurant** (207-633-4200 or 1-800-552-5554), East Boothbay. Open mid-June–Columbus Day weekend. Reservations suggested. Three informal dining rooms with ocean views. Choices usually include seafood, duck, rib eye, and Delmonico steak. Entrées $18–29.

EATING OUT ✪ **The Boathouse Bistro & Tapas Bar** (207-633-0400; theboathousebistro .com), 12 By-Way, Boothbay Harbor. Open mid-March–Christmas for lunch and dinner. We love this place! Three different atmospheres—all casual—on each of the three floors, and the view improves as you climb (the top deck is open). Lunch on hot tapas like a lobster crêpe and dine on Italian seafood stew. On our last visit a lobster, mango, and avocado salad and white wine filled the bill ($25.92 total).

✪ **Oliver's** (207-633-8888), 36 Cozy Harbor Rd., Southport. Open May–Sept., Wed.–Sun. 11:30–8; Sun. brunch at 10. A nicely designed, casual restaurant on a hidden cove, accessible by land and water. It replaces and incorporates pieces of a much-loved local 1940s store. Eat at a shaded picnic table on the pier, in the zany, screened interior, and ideally—if you can nail a table—upstairs on the second-floor porch. The menu covers the basics and includes pleasant surprises. The blackened fish taco also comes with salsa and creamy avocado coleslaw. Beer and wine are served.

McSeagull's (207-633-5900; mcseagulls online.com), 14 Wharf St., Boothbay Harbor. Open daily 11:30–closing. Wharfside dining so popular it can get packed in high season. It's a local gathering place off-season because it's good. The book-sized menu ranges from pizzas to grilled as well as fried seafood platters. Try the northern white beans stewed in lobster stock, served with poached lobster.

✒ **Lobsterman's Wharf** (207-633-3443), Rt. 96, East Boothbay (adjacent to a boatyard). Open mid-May–Columbus Day, serving 11:30–9, until 10 on weekends. The large menu includes all the usual seafood, lobster stew, and crabcakes, as well as spinach salad and pastas. Entrées $7–30.

✪ **Baker's Way** (207-633-1119), 89 Townsend Ave., Boothbay Harbor. Open 6 AM–9 PM daily. Just the place for fried apple dumpling, you think, and then you smell lemongrass cooking and wonder where you are. There are two worlds here: a full bakery, very popular with locals, and a restaurant that serves traditional Vietnamese foods. Available 11 AM–closing, appetizers include steamed buns with ground pork, onion, garlic, peas, eggs, and scallions, and fresh spring rolls. Try the stir-fried squid—or chicken or shrimp—and dine in the back garden. BYOB.

Waves Restaurant (207-315-6021), 43 Commercial St., Boothbay Harbor. Open daily 7–11, 12–3, and 4–10. Still the same wooden booths that regulars loved all those years when this was Ebb Tide, but the food has a creative spark under new owners Jie and Ian Ronan. Try the fried haddock sliders at lunch and crabby haddock at dinner. Beer and wine are also served.

The **Blue Moon Café** (207-633-2220; blue moonboothbayharbor.com), 54 Commercial St., Boothbay Harbor. Open for breakfast and lunch daily, 7:30–2:30; Sun. brunch 7:30–noon. This little café with a seaside deck makes perfect crabcakes, and the side salad is filled with fresh greens. We needed a hot, fish-studded chowder in a hurry and got it, served in a china bowl, on the waterside deck.

Bet's Fish Fry, Boothbay Center common. Open seasonally Tue.–Sat. 11–2, 5–7. "Free beer tomorrow." This takeout is a great place to grab a scrumptious fried haddock sandwich. One is more than enough for two.

LOBSTER

🦞 🐾 ✂ ♿ **The Lobster Dock** (207-633-7120; thelobsterdock.com), 49 Atlantic Ave., Boothbay Harbor, at the east end of the footbridge. Open 11:29–8:01 (later on Fri. and Sat.) Memorial Day weekend–early Oct. This is our in-town place for a lobster roll, either hot with drawn butter or cold with a dab of mayo. Also lobster and shore dinners, steamed clams, mussels, steaks, and prime rib.

✂ ♿ **Robinson's Wharf** (207-633-3830; robinsons-wharf.com), Rt. 27, Southport Island (just across Townsend Gut from West Boothbay Harbor). Open daily year-round, 11:30–9. There's plenty of room inside, but on a sunny day sit on the dock at one of the picnic tables and watch the boats unload their catch. Lobsters and lobster rolls, fried shrimp, clams, scallops, fish chowder, lobster stew, and homemade desserts.

✂ **Cabbage Island Clambakes** (207-633-7200; cabbageislandclambakes.com). Late June–early Sept., the boat departs Pier 6 at Fisherman's Wharf daily, carrying passengers to 6-acre Cabbage Island in Linekin Bay. This is a traditional clambake with lobsters, clams, corn, and potatoes steamed in seaweed then served on picnic tables. In bad weather a circa-1900 lodge seats up to 100 people by a huge fireplace. About $62 per person plus tax, including boat ride.

Christina Tree

THE LOBSTER DOCK

GENERAL STORES **The East Boothbay General Store** (207-633-7800), 255 Ocean Point Rd., East Boothbay. Open mid-May–mid-Oct. Tucked into a bend of Rt. 96, this is a popular stop to grab an apple Brie bacon wrap for breakfast, or a sandwich from the deli, to eat in or to bring down to Ocean Point. Wine, beer, a variety of cheeses, and soft serve.

Southport General Store (207-633-6666), 443 Hendrick's Hill Rd., Southport. Pick up deli sandwiches or pizza and head for the shore.

Trevett Country Store (207-633-1140), 381 Barters Island Rd., Boothbay. Open daily 7 AM–8 PM, a mile up the road beyond the botanical gardens. Several knowledgeable friends had recommended this as the area's best lobster roll, but we were disappointed. The setting is great: Tables on the deck overlook the Barter's Island bridge.

SNACKS ✎ **Down East Ice Cream Factory** (207-633-3016), the By-Way, Boothbay Harbor. Homemade hard ice cream and frozen yogurt, and a make-your-own sundae bar; all sorts of toppings, including real hot fudge. Open 10:30–10:30 in the height of summer; hours vary off-season.

✎ **Daffy Taffy and Fudge Factory** (207-633-5178), the By-Way, Boothbay Harbor. Open 10–10 in the height of the season, fewer hours off-season. No credit cards. Watch taffy being pulled, designed, and wrapped—then chew! The fudge is made with fresh cream and butter.

Oak Street Provisions (207-633-1290; oakstreetprovisions.com), 43 Oak St., Boothbay Harbor, offers fresh seafood, meats, beer, wine, and specialty foods.

✳ Entertainment

The Opera House at Boothbay Harbor (207-633-5159; boothbayoperahouse.com), 86 Townsend Ave., Boothbay Harbor. This vintage-1894 theater is a nonprofit performance center, staging roughly 100 events annually. Check the website for current concerts, lectures, community events, and more.

Carousel Music Theater (207-633-5297; carouselmusictheater.org), 196 Townsend Ave. (Rt. 27), Boothbay. July 4–Columbus Day, 7:30 PM. Patrons are asked to come at 6:30 and have a drink, order supper, and then sit back with dessert and coffee to watch a musical revue.

Lincoln Arts Festival (207-633-3913; lincolnartsfestival.org). Concerts throughout the summer in varied locations.

Thursday evening band concerts on the library lawn, Boothbay Harbor.

✳ Selective Shopping

ART GALLERIES **First Friday Art Tours** (artwalkmaine.org/boothbay). June–Oct. On the first Fri. of each month more than a dozen local studios hold open houses.

Gleason Fine Art (207-633-6849; gleason fineart.com), 31 Townsend Ave., Boothbay Harbor. Tue.–Sat. 10–5. Museum-quality paintings by the likes of Fairfield Porter, James

Fitzgerald, and Scott Kelley, and more of the best contemporary artists in Maine.

Boothbay Region Art Foundation (207-633-2703; boothbayartists.org), 1 Townsend Ave., Boothbay Harbor. Open May–late Oct., Mon.-Sat. 10–5, Sun. noon–5. Six juried shows are held each season in this long-established gallery with two floors full of varied art.

ARTISANS **Abacus Gallery** (207-633-2166; abacusgallery.com), 12 McKown St., Boothbay Harbor. We love this shop, which since its 1971 opening has spawned sister stores in four Maine towns. Check out the jewelry, whimsical wooden sculptures, hand-painted furniture, and unusual gifts.

Boothbay Harbor Artisans (207-633-1152; mainecraftcoop.org/boothbay), 4 Boothbay House Hill Rd., Boothbay Harbor. A cooperative crafts market featuring quilts, soap, stained glass, pottery, maple syrup, jewelry, and more.

A Silver Lining (207-633-4103; asilver lining.com), 17 Townsend Ave., Boothbay Harbor. Working metalsmiths. Original, exceptional sculpture and jewelry in brass, sterling, and gold.

Edgecomb Potters (207-882-9493 or 1-800-343-5529; edgecombpotters.com), Rt. 27, Edgecomb. Open year-round. One of Maine's largest, most famous pottery stores (with branches in Portland and Freeport). A two-tiered gallery filled with deeply colored pots, vases, and table settings, lamps, bowls, cookware, and jewelry. There's also a sculpture garden and a small seconds corner.

Macdonald Stained Glass, Ltd. (207-633-4815; macdonaldglass.com), 7 Wall Point Road, Boothbay Harbor. Housed in a converted vintage garage (call for directions), this studio-gallery is a source of stained glass in many shapes. Visitors welcome.

SPECIAL SHOPS **Sherman's Maine Coast Book Shops** (1-800-371-8128; shermans.com), 5 Commercial St., Boothbay Harbor. This two-story emporium is the flagship for Maine's oldest, largest bookstore chain. Plenty of stationary, souvenirs, and much more

The Palabra Shop (207-633-4225; palabra-shop.com), 53 Commercial St., Boothbay Harbor. Open in summer, Sun.–Thu. 9–6, opening later on weekends. Owned by the same family

SHERMAN'S MAINE COAST BOOK SHOPS

for more than 50 years, a warren of 10 rooms offering everything from kitschy souvenirs to handcrafts and jewelry to a few antiques.

✳ Special Events

April: **Fishermen's Festival**—contests for fishermen and lobstermen, cabaret ball, crowning of the Shrimp Princess, tall-tale contest, boat parade, and blessing of the fleet.

June: **Windjammer Days**—parade of windjammers into the harbor, fireworks, band concert, parade of floats and bands up Main St., visiting U.S. Navy and Coast Guard vessels, live music on the waterfront, food, children's activities, and two crafts shows.

July: **Antique Auto Days**, Boothbay Railway Village, Rt. 27. **Boothbay Region Fish and Game Saltwater Fishing Tournament**, Boothbay Harbor (207-633-3788). **YMCA Southport Regatta** entails a variety of ways of circling Southport Island.

Early September: Boothbay Region Harbor Fest (boothbayharborfest.com).

Mid-September: **Clawdown**—participating restaurants compete with "lobster bites." Reserve ahead (207-633-2553); this is always a sellout.

October: **Fall Foliage Festival**—foliage cruises, crafts sales, live entertainment, steam train rides.

November: **Early-bird sale**. Stores open early to tempt shoppers. Stroll the streets in your pajamas as part of the pajama parade and then watch the fast-paced fun of the bed races.

Early December: **Harbor Lights Festival**. Mr. and Mrs. Claus arrive by boat; parade, crafts, holiday shopping.

DAMARISCOTTA/ NEWCASTLE/WALDOBORO AND PEMAQUID AREA

Damariscotta is a small region of large, quiet lakes, long tidal rivers, and almost 100 miles of meandering coastline, all within easy striking distance of Rt. 1. It encompasses the Pemaquid Peninsula communities of Bristol, Pemaquid, New Harbor, and Round Pond, as well as Lake Damariscotta and the twin villages of Damariscotta and Newcastle at its foot, and nearby Waldoboro.

Damariscotta's musical name is an Algonquian word loosely translated as "plenty of alewives," and in spring spawning alewives can indeed be seen climbing more than 40 feet up through a series of pools linking Great Salt Bay to the fresh water in Damariscotta Lake.

Fourteen miles stem-to-stern, Damariscotta Lake seems longer, changing character as it wanders north through three towns, its largely wooded shoreline patched with rolling farmland. Great Bay, the north basin, is wide and deep, good for catching smallmouth bass and trout, while South Arm is skinny and shallow, great for swimming.

The area's first residents also found an abundance of oysters here, judging from the shells they heaped over the course of 2,400 years on opposite banks of the river just below Salt Bay. Of late, the local oyster industry is once again thriving.

Native Americans also had a name for the peninsula jutting 10 miles seaward from this spot: Pemaquid, meaning "long finger." Its protected harbors loomed large on 16th- and 17th-century maps, the nearest mainland havens for Monhegan and a busy fishing center for European fishermen. It was from these fishermen that the Pemaquid Native American Samoset learned the English with which he welcomed the Pilgrims at Plymouth in 1621. It was also from these fishermen that Plimoth Plantation, the following winter, secured supplies enough to see it through to spring.

The site of Maine's "Lost City" is a mini peninsula bordered by the Pemaquid River and Johns Bay. A round stone tower at its entrance re-creates part of a fort built here in 1692. In recent decades more than 100,000 artifacts have been unearthed in the adjacent meadow, many of them now on display in a small state-run museum.

Pemaquid Light, marking the far tip of this peninsula, is pictured on Maine's quarter because it looks just like a lighthouse should. It stands atop dramatic but clamber-friendly rocks composed of varied seams of granite schist and softer volcanic rock, ridged in ways that invite climbing, and pocked with tidal pools that demand stopping.

Christina Tree

DAMARISCOTTA WATERFRONT

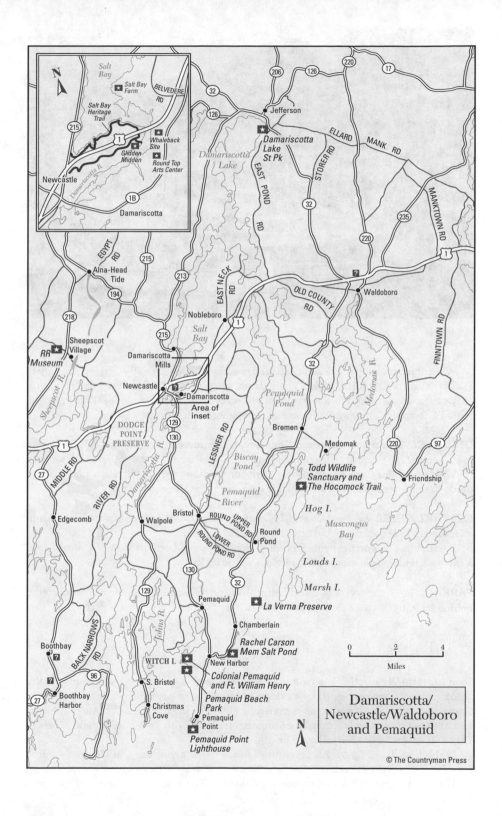

Damariscotta/
Newcastle/Waldoboro
and Pemaquid

© The Countryman Press

NEW HARBOR

While there is plenty to see and to do (and to eat) in this area, it's all scattered just widely enough to disperse tourist traffic. The villages are small. Downtown Damariscotta, with easy off/on access to Rt. 1, is a few waterside streets built of mellow old local brick; it's the region's compact shopping, dining, and entertainment hub.

GUIDANCE **Damariscotta Region Chamber of Commerce** (207-563-8340; damariscotta region.com). The chamber office is open year-round weekdays 9–5 at 67 Main St., Newcastle.

Waldoboro Business Association (waldoborobusiness.org) publishes a handy map/guide to this low-profile but lively town at the head of the Medomak River.

GETTING THERE *By bus:* **Concord Coach** (concordcoachlines.com) stops in Damariscotta and Waldoboro en route from Portland to Bangor.

By car: Most inns on the peninsula will pick up guests in Damariscotta, but you do need a car—or a boat—to get around. The obvious way is up Rt. 1.

PARKING in Damariscotta is much better than it first looks. Large lots are sequestered behind buildings on both sides of Main Street.

✳ Villages

Damariscotta/Newcastle. The twin villages of Newcastle (pop. 1,752) and Damariscotta (2,218 residents) are connected by a bridge and form the commercial center of the region. Damariscotta's Main Street is the commercial hub here, lined with 1840s brick buildings and filled with shops and restaurants. Damariscotta Mills, with its fish ladder and access to Lake Damariscotta, is a few miles up Rt. 215.

Waldoboro (pop. 1,337). An inscription in the cemetery of the Old German Church (see *Historic Churches*) relates the deceptive way in which landholder General Samuel Waldo lured the town's first German settlers here. The church and much of the town overlook the tidal Medomak (pronounced with the emphasis on *med*) River. Bypassed by Rt. 1, this village includes some noteworthy art galleries and the **Waldo Theatre** (see *Entertainment*). The **Waldoborough Historical Society Museum** (waldoborohistory.us), 1664 Main St., is on Rt. 220, just south of Rt. 1.

Round Pond, Bristol. The name evokes the shape of the village's harbor, said to have been a pirate base. This was once a major shipbuilding, and later on a quarrying, center. It remains a working fishing harbor with competing places to eat lobster and a famous Independence Day parade.

New Harbor, Bristol. A photogenic working harbor. Take South Side Rd. to Back Cove and walk out on the wooden pedestrian bridge for a great view. Note the memorial to Samoset, who is said to have sold land here, creating the first deed executed in New England. The village itself is far bigger than it looks at first.

Pemaquid Beach, Bristol. Just off the beaten track to Pemaquid Point Lighthouse, this is a tranquil seasonal community with a public beach (see *Swimming*), a reconstructed 17th-century fort, and a museum displaying artifacts from its early-17th-century settlement (see *Must See*).

South Bristol. Chances are you will have time to enjoy the view at "The Gut," the narrow channel spanned by a busy swing bridge. Rt. 129 continues south to Christmas Cove, a long-established summer colony.

Jefferson, the village at the head of Damariscotta Lake, also at the junction of Rts. 126, 32, and 206. Old farmhouses, a general store, and summer homes along the river now form the core of the village, and **Damariscotta Lake State Park**, with its sandy beach, is on the fringe. Be sure to drive west a couple of miles on Rt. 213 to **Bunker Hill**, with its old church commanding a superb panorama down the lake.

✳ To See

Alewives Fish Ladder, Rt. 215 in **Damariscotta Mills** at the intersection of Austin Rd. Look for parking just south of the bridge; a walkway beyond the bridge leads into the site. Originally built in 1807 and recently rebuilt, this is a stone-lined series of stepped pools and raceways. For roughly a month beginning in early May, alewives—also known as river herring—climb the 50 feet from Salt Bay up to Damariscotta Bay while gulls, cormorants, ospreys, and eagles circle. On an early June morning the swarming fish were so thick you could smell them.

Thompson Ice House, Rt. 129 in South Bristol. Open July and Aug., Wed., Fri., Sat. 1–4. A 150-year-old commercial icehouse displays traditional tools for cutting ice from an adjacent pond and a video on how ice continues to be harvested here. Small blocks of this ice costs $1 in the outside cooler. On the Sunday closest to July 4 an ice cream social here features hand-churned ice cream made with the ice.

Christina Tree

ALEWIVES FISH LADDER

⚓ **Old Rock Schoolhouse**, Bristol (halfway between Bristol Mills and Round Pond; follow signs from Rt. 130 to Rt. 132). Dank and haunting, this 1835–99 rural stone schoolhouse once was one of 20 one-room schoolhouses scattered through town. Open in summer, Wed. and Sun. 1–3; costumed volunteers offer to teach all comers.

MUST SEE

✪ ✐ **PEMAQUID POINT LIGHTHOUSE** (lighthousefoundation.org), Rt. 130 (at the end), Pemaquid Point. The tower is open Memorial Day–Columbus Day 10:30–5, but closed on rainy days. Pemaquid Point is owned by the town, which charges a per-person entry fee during summer. The lighthouse, built in 1824 and automated in 1934, is a beauty. It's just a 39-step climb to the top of the tower, but the light looms high above the rocks below and the real place to appreciate it is gained by climbing down, not up. The rocks offer a wonderfully varied example of geologic upheaval, with tilted strata and igneous intrusions. The tidal pools are exceptional, but take care not to get too close to the dangerous waves. The rocks stretch for half a mile to Kresge Point. **The Fishermen's Museum** (207-677-2494) in the former lighthouse keeper's home (May–late Oct., daily 9–5) displays photographs, ship models, and other artifacts related to the Maine fishing industry and lighthouses. Donations requested. The complex also includes the Pemaquid Art Gallery, picnic tables, and public toilets.

✪ ✐ **Colonial Pemaquid State Historic Site** (207-677-2423; friendsofcolonialpemaquid.org), Pemaquid Beach. Marked from Rt. 130, this 8-acre complex is open Memorial Day–Labor Day, 9–6; nominal fee. This small peninsula at the mouth of the Pemaquid River offers a glimpse into many layerings of history, beginning with a circa-1610 seasonal English fishing station that evolved into a year-round fur-trading outpost circa 1630–50. The foundations of homes, a customhouse, and a tavern are now on view and a period house has been reconstructed. The 17th-century tools and pottery, Spanish oil jars, and wampum found in these cellar holes are displayed in the museum.

Fort William Henry, the crenellated stone tower reconstructing the 1692 fort, displays exhibits on the early explorations of Maine and on the French and Indian Wars. It also enshrines the "Rock of Pemaquid," suggesting that settlers alighted on it long before the Pilgrims stepped onto that rock in Plymouth. The neighboring square clapboard Fort House contains a library, a restored parlor, changing exhibits, and a gift store. Picnic tables command water views. For a schedule of frequent summer lectures, tours, and reenactments, check the website.

FORT WILLIAM HENRY

Christina Tree

Chapman-Hall House, 270 Main St., Damariscotta. Open June–early Oct., weekends noon–4, volunteer-dependent. Built in 1754, this is the oldest homestead in the region. The house has been restored with its original kitchen and an herb garden. $5 admission.

HISTORIC CHURCHES This particular part of the Maine coast possesses an unusual number of fine old meetinghouses and churches, all of which are open to the public.

Old German Church (207-832-5100), Rt. 32, Waldoboro. Open daily during July and Aug., 1–4. Built in 1772 with square-benched pews and a wineglass pulpit; note the inscription in the cemetery: "This town was settled in 1748 by Germans who immigrated to this place with the promise and expectation of finding a prosperous city, instead of which they found nothing but wilderness." Bostonian Samuel Waldo—owner of a large tract of land in this area—had not been straight with the 40 German families he brought to settle it. This was the first Lutheran church in Maine and is the setting of one of Andrew Wyeth's most famous Helga paintings.

St. Patrick's Catholic Church (207-563-6038), Academy Rd., Newcastle (Rt. 215 north of Damariscotta Mills). Open year-round daily, to sunset. This is the oldest surviving Catholic church (1808) in New England. It's an unusual building: brick construction, very narrow, and graced with a Paul Revere bell. The pews and stained glass date to 1896 and there's an old graveyard out back. It's used for daily Mass, but a spacious, new addition with a clerestory roof and glass-walled sanctuary is now used on Sunday.

St. Andrew's Episcopal Church (207-563-3533), Glidden St., Newcastle. A charming half-timbered building on the bank of the Damariscotta River. Set among gardens and trees, it was the first commission in this country for Henry Vaughan, the English architect who went on to design the National Cathedral in Washington, DC.

Old Walpole Meeting House, Meeting House Rd., off Rt. 129, South Bristol. Open Sun. during July and Aug. for 3 PM services. A 1772 shingled meetinghouse with box pews and a pulpit with a sounding board.

Harrington Meeting House, 278 Harrington Rd., Pemaquid. Open during July and Aug., Mon., Wed., Fri., 2–4:30. Donations accepted. The 1775 building with its original box pews has been restored and serves as a museum of Old Bristol. A nondenominational service is held here once a year, usually on the third Sun. in Aug.

OTHER 🎧 **Skidompha Library** (207-563-5513; skidompha.org), 184 Main St., Damariscotta. Open Tue.–Sat. from 9 AM; until 7 PM Thu. and 1 PM on Sat., otherwise until 5 PM. This stunning library forms the heart of town, the scene of many programs geared to visitors as well as regulars. There are also frequent authors' nights and classic films.

Fawcett's Antique Toy & Art Museum (207-832-7398), 3506 Rt. 1., Waldoboro. Memorial Day–Columbus Day, open Thu.–Mon. 10–4, then weekends noon–4 until weekend before Christmas. $5 admission. Comic book and antique toy lovers alert: This is a major collection of original cartoon art, billed as the finest Lone Ranger collection in the world, also antique Disneyana, space toys, and the like. Antique toys bought and sold.

✳ To Do

BIRDING 🐦 **Audubon Camp, Hog Island** (hogisland.audubon.org). The center, 0.25 mile offshore at the head of Muscongus Bay, is a venue for nature and ornithology programs, including seasonal sessions sponsored by Audubon's Project Puffin, which reintroduced Atlantic puffins to nearby islands. Five miles of spruce trails, wildflower and herb gardens, and mudflats surround rustic bungalows. The dining room is in a restored 19th-century

EXCURSIONS

Damariscotta Lake. From Newcastle, Rt. 215 winds along past the Alewife Fish Ladder in Damariscotta Mills. Continue by St. Patrick's Church through farm country on Rt. 213 when 215 jogs west (note the scenic pullout across from the Bunker Hill Church, with a view down the lake) to Jefferson. Lunch at **Damariscotta Lake Farm** or pick up a sandwich at the **Jefferson General Store** and take it to **Damariscotta Lake State Park** (see *Swimming*). In the middle of Jefferson you'll find the dockside (below a twin file of cottages) **Damariscotta Lake Watershed Association** (dlwa.org), a source of local maps, books, and a summer sailing program for kids.

Sheepscot Village and Alna Head Tide. From Rt. 215 beyond St. Patrick's Church (see above) turn left at "Cowshit Corner" (there's a sign) onto W. Hamlet Rd. and then right on Old Country Rd. through rolling, open country to the picturesque village of Head Tide. (You can also reach this point directly from Rt. 1 on Sheepscot Rd. in Newcastle.) This is a cluster of old buildings around the river and its reversing falls. Cross the river and turn north on Rt. 218 to the **Alna Store** (207-586-5515), good for hot specials as well as sandwiches, local meat, and eggs. Continue on to **Head Tide**, another scenic village with a beautiful church and overlook at a small dam. Cut back to the store and turn down Dock Rd. (it's on the corner) and then right (south) on Rt. 194, which becomes Rt. 215. This is a lovely loop, one of the best in the area for bicycling.

Pemaquid Peninsula. Follow Rt. 129 south from Damariscotta, across the South Bristol Bridge to Christmas Cove. Backtrack and cross the peninsula via **Harrington Meeting House** Rd. to **Colonial Pemaquid** and **Pemaquid Beach** (glorious at sunset). Turn south on Rt. 130 to **Pemaquid Point Lighthouse** and return via Rt. 32 and **Round Pond**; take Biscay Rd. back to Damariscotta or continue on Rt. 32 into Waldoboro.

COWSHIT CORNER

Christina Tree

farmhouse. For puffin-watching and birding cruises, see Hardy Boat Cruises (below). Also see *Green Space*.

BOATING ⚓ **Hardy Boat Cruises** (Stacie and Captain Al Crocetti: 207-677-2026 or 1-800-278-3346; hardyboat.com), Shaw's Wharf, New Harbor, May–Oct. The 60-foot Maine-built *Hardy III* offers daily (twice daily in high season) 50-minute-long runs to **Monhegan Island** (for a detailed description, see "Midcoast Islands"). Pick a calm day. It doesn't matter if it's foggy, but the passage is no fun if it's rough. Another cruise circles **Eastern Egg Rock**, one of only five Maine islands on which puffins breed, with narration by an Audubon naturalist. There are also seal-watching, a lighthouse (Pemaquid Light), and harbor cruises. Nominal fee for parking roughly 0.25 mile back up the road.

♿ **Damariscotta River Cruises** (1-888-635-4309; damariscottarivercruises.com), Schooner Landing, Main St., Damariscotta. Check the website for daytime and evening (drinks and live music) cruises aboard the former navy launch *Teciani*, "The River Tripper."

Lake Pemaquid Camping (lakepemaquid.com), Egypt Rd., Damariscotta, rents canoes, kayaks, and paddle- and motorboats.

FISHING Damariscotta Lake is a source of bass, landlocked salmon, and trout. See Mill Pond Inn under *Bed & Breakfasts.*

GOLF **Wawenock Country Club** (207-563-3938), Rt. 129 (7 miles south of Damariscotta), Walpole. Open May–Nov. A nine-hole course with 18 tee boxes and a full-service clubhouse.

HIKING **Monhegan Island,** easily accessible from New Harbor (see *Boating*), is webbed with coastal shore and cliff trails beloved by hikers and birders. A day trip gives you a sampling, but it's best to spend the night for a full exploration.

KAYAKING **Midcoast Kayak** (207-563-5732; midcoastkayak.com), 47 Main St., Damariscotta, offers a variety of guided paddles in and around Muscongus Bay, also rentals. **Maine Kayak** (1-866-624-6352; mainekayak.com) offers guided trips, rentals, and packages from a variety of bases, including New Harbor. Both outfitters are geared to coastal paddling, but we have used a rental to explore **Damariscotta Lake**. There's boat access off Rt. 213 and spruce-topped islands to paddle to. You can also launch at the Jefferson General Store near Damariscotta State Park and paddle up Davis Stream.

SWIMMING ✪ **Pemaquid Beach Park** (207-677-2754), Rt. 130, Pemaquid. A town-owned area open Memorial Day–Labor Day, 9 5. Nominal admission, 12 years and older. A quarter mile of fine, white sand. Bathhouse, restrooms, refreshment stand, and picnic tables. This is also a great place to walk and watch the sunset in the evening.

ও **Damariscotta Lake State Park** (207-549-7600), Rt. 32, Jefferson, 9 miles north of Rt. 1. A sandy beach with changing facilities, picnic tables, and grills at the northern end of the lake. There's a new pavilion for group events and plenty of tree shade. $4 per Maine resident, $6 per out-of-stater; $2 out-of-state seniors.

Ice House Park, Damariscotta Mills. A sign reads NO FOUL LANGUAGE AND NO ALCOHOLIC BEVERAGES, but nothing prohibits kids from jumping off the bridge. Just up from the fish ladder, this is a neighborhood place, good for getting wet when you need to.

On Pemaquid Peninsula the big freshwater swimming holes are at **Biscay Pond** (from Rt. 1, take Biscay Rd. 3 miles) and **Bristol Mills Swimming Dam** on Rt. 130, 5 miles south of Damariscotta.

✳ Green Space

NATURE PRESERVES **Damariscotta River Association** (207-563-1393; draclt.org), 110 Belvedere Rd., 0.25 mile north of Rt. 1 in Damariscotta. Open year-round. DRA headquarters at Salt Pond Farm offers hay fields, salt- and freshwater marshes, and woods laced with walking/skiing paths. This is also the site of seasonal Friday farmers' markets, a summer concert series, special programs, and tours. DRA properties total more than 1,200 acres in over a dozen easily accessible places, including Great Salt Bay Preserve Heritage Trail, which loops around Glidden Point and leads to the **Glidden Midden,** 30 feet deep and said to date back 2,400 years. **Dodge Point Preserve** is a 506-acre property on Newcastle's River Rd. (2.6 miles south of Rt. 1), which includes a sand beach as well as a freshwater pond, a beaver bog, and trails.

ℐ **Rachel Carson Memorial Salt Pond**, Rt. 32, north of New Harbor. The pond is on the opposite side of the road from the parking lot. There's a beautiful view of the open ocean from here, and at low tide the tidal pools are filled with tiny sea creatures. Look for blue mussels, hermit crabs, starfish, and green sea urchins. Here Rachel Carson researched part of her book *The Edge of the Sea*. Inland from the pond, the preserve includes fields and forest.

✂ **Todd Wildlife Sanctuary and the Hocomock Trail**, Bremen (take Keene Neck Rd. off Rt. 32). A visitors center (207-529-5148) is open June–Aug., daily 1–4. The nature trail leads down to the beach. This is a great family picnic spot, accessible with short legs.

Hidden Valley Nature Center (hvnc.org), 131 Egypt Rd., Jefferson (0.5 mile south from Rt. 215). Nearly 1,000 acres of diverse land, 25 miles of trails to Little Dyer Pond, good for cross-country skiing and snowshoeing. Three cabins and several campsites, ongoing programs.

❋ Lodging

INNS AND B&BS ☀ ♿ **Bradley Inn** (207-677-2105 or 1-800-942-5560; bradleyinn.com), 3063 Pemaquid Point, New Harbor. Open Apr.–Dec. Warren and Beth Busteed are energetic innkeepers who have established a culinary reputation for this turn-of-the-20th-century inn (see *Dining Out*), the area's only inn serving dinner. The 14 guest rooms and two suites are divided among the main house, the Carriage House, and a cottage, all nicely furnished and each with private bath. Clunker bicycles are free, and the inn is less than a mile from Pemaquid Lighthouse and Kresge Point. Amenities include a spa with sauna and treatment rooms. High-season rooms are $225–475 (for a Carriage House suite); off-season from $160; $50 pet fee; special birding and spa weekends.

IN NEWCASTLE/DAMARISCOTTA

✪ 🐾 (⬤) ✂ **Mill Pond Inn** (207-563-8014; millpondinn.com), Rt. 215, Damariscotta Mills. Open year-round. Enter the red door of this much-expanded 1780 gray-clapboard house and you immediately feel at home. Sherry and Bobby Whear have been welcoming guests since 1986, and many have returned time after time. The five individually decorated and shaped rooms (check the website) include three 2-bedroom suites, one with its own entrance. $150–160 per couple ($20 for a second room) includes breakfast, maybe a crabmeat omelet with veggies from the garden. Less off-season. The alewives begin running in May and by mid-June you can take a dip off the dock or ask Bobby for a ride in his antique

motorboat. A Registered Maine Guide, Realtor, bartender, and co-host of *Wuzzup?*—a weekly series on Lincoln County TV (lctv .org)—Bobby enjoys tuning guests into local secrets. No credit cards.

☀ (⬤) **Newcastle Inn** (207-563-5685 or 1-877-376-6111; newcastleinn.com), 60 River Rd., Newcastle 04553. Open year-round. Julie Bolthuis offers 14 tasteful and comfortable rooms, all with private bath, some with water views, several with four-poster beds, eight with gas fireplace, and two with Jacuzzi. An inviting little bar with French doors opens onto a wide deck with water views—the breakfast venue, weather permitting. The grounds overlook the Damariscotta River. $145–295, includes a three-course breakfast. Per diem charge for dogs.

Alewives & Ales (207-563-1561; alewivesandales.com), P.O. Box 809, 22 High St., Damariscotta. This Federal-style mid-19th-century house on a quiet street south of town is a B&B with three guest rooms. Host Mimi McConnell tells us that the name honors Damariscotta's spring alewife migration, and brewing "ale" is her husband's Ray's hobby. A very full breakfast, served at the dining room table, is included in rates of $150–200; less off-season.

(⬤) **Oak Gables** (207-563-1476 or 1-800-335-7748; oakgablesbb.com), 36 Pleasant St., Damariscotta. Open year-round. The setting is 9 acres on the Damariscotta River with a heated swimming pool and boathouse (with a Ping-Pong table). Martha Scudder's gracious house has four second-floor guest rooms, shared bath ($120–185 with breakfast), and a river-view efficiency suite on the ground floor ($185 in-season), also available by the week. Inquire about weekly rentals for the riverside three-bedroom cottage and a two-person studio. Well-behaved children welcome.

ON THE PEMAQUID PENINSULA SOUTH OF DAMARISCOTTA

✪ 🐾 ✎ ♿ ((ᵗ)) **Gosnold Arms** (207-677-3727; winter, 561-575-9549; gosnold.com), 146 Rt. 32, New Harbor 04554. Open mid-May–mid-Oct. Sited at the entrance to a working harbor steps from Shaw's Wharf, this friendly inn has been owned by the Phinney family for more than three decades. It rambles on along the water, with rockers on the porch and ample rainy-day space. There are 10 simple but comfortable guest rooms upstairs (all private bath, eight with water views) and 20 cottage units, six with deck or sunporch, smack-dab on this working harbor. The Hillside units at the back of the property are good for families. Breakfast on the enclosed porch is served buffet-style, the better to catch the boat to Monhegan (island bound guests are permitted to park here). Inn rooms $118–152, cottages $138–216. Rates include breakfast; 15 percent less in June and Sept.

✪ ((ᵗ)) **The Inn at Round Pond** (207-809-7386; theinnatroundpond.com), 1442 Rt. 32, Round Pond. The mansard-roofed third floor was added to this 1830s home a century or so ago when it became the Harbor View Hotel. Sue and Bill Morton have created a delightful B&B with soothing colors, comfortable antiques, and original art. There are four delightful suites and a Garden Cottage hideaway for all guests to share, fitted with books, puzzles, and wicker. A full breakfast is included in $175–185, less off-season.

♂ ((ᵗ)) **The Hotel Pemaquid** (207-677-2312; hotelpemaquid.com), 3098 Bristol Rd., New Harbor 04554. Open mid-May–mid-Oct. A vintage-1888 summer hotel a short walk from Pemaquid Point but without water views. There's a Victorian-style lobby and living room with armchairs and a big stone hearth. The 30 rooms are divided among the main house and new annexes. Most rooms have private bath (four rooms in the inn itself share two baths). Coffee is set out at 7. From $108 off-season (private bath) to $291 in Aug. for a Carriage House suite sleeping four, with a living room, kitchen, and deck.

IN WALDOBORO 04572

✪ 🐾 ((ᵗ)) **Blue Skye Farm** (207-832-0300; blueskyefarm.com), 1708 Friendship Rd. (Rt. 220). Open year-round. This is an exquisite house, dating back to 1775 but with an elegant Federal facade. It retains all its original woodwork and working fireplaces in two of the six guest rooms as well as in common rooms; the stenciling in the front hall is thought to be by Moses Eaton. Stenciling aside, walls are all painted white and small-paned windows are thinly veiled in European-style lace café curtains. Peter and Jan Davidson spent a year restoring the house, which dates from 1775 and is set in 100 acres of marsh, meadows, and woods. Original detailing includes Indian shutters and a scalloped cupboard as well as paneling and mantels. Rooms are tastefully, comfortably furnished in antiques, and tempting, well-thumbed books line walls between the guest rooms. A full breakfast is served, and guests have access to the kitchen as well as outdoor grills for other meals. The entire house can rented and candlelit lobster dinners arranged. $149–165, less off-season.

COTTAGES 🐾 ✎ Check with the Damariscotta area chamber and **Newcastle Square Vacation Rentals** (207-563-6500; mainecoast cottages.com).

🐾 ✎ **The Thompson House and Cottages** (207-677-2317; thompsoncottages.net), New Harbor. Open May–Nov. Merle and Karen Thompson are the third generation of a family that's been offering hospitality since they began taking guests in 1920. There are still two sparkling-clean rooms in the 1874 house ($80), but the big attractions are the housekeeping cottages (maximum of five people), many with ocean views and facing New Harbor or Back Cove, all with fireplace (wood supplied). $1,150–1,850 per week in-season.

🐾 **Ye Olde Forte Cabins** (207-677-2261; yeoldefortecabins.com), 18 Old Fort Rd., Pemaquid Beach. Nostalgia buffs take note: Eight classic 1922 cabins stepped roof-to-roof along a wide central lawn sloping to a private beach on John's Bay. There's a cookhouse equipped with everything you need to make meals, along with immaculate men's and women's shower houses. From $115 per day

($575 per week) in high season for a cabin with private bath and double bed to $216 per day ($820 per week) for oceanfront cabins with private shower sleeping four. Guests bring kayaks, canoes, and fishing rods. Moorings available.

✎ ☀ ✐ **Moody's Motel** (207-832-5362; moodysdiner.com), Waldoboro. Open May 15–Oct.15. Moody's Diner is a Rt. 1 icon; less well known is the vintage motor court squirreled away behind the eatery in a quiet hilltop meadow. P. B. and Bertha Moody built the first cabins in 1927. Still in the family, there are 18 spanking-clean cottages, each with a screened porch, bath with shower, cable TV, and heat; five have kitchens. The grounds include lawn games and swings. $67 for a one-bedroom unit with twins; $77 for a two-bedroom, sleeping four; $87 for kitchenette units. Pet fee.

CAMPING ✐ ♿ **Lake Pemaquid Camping** (207-563-5202), Damariscotta. Off Biscay Rd. More than 200 tent and RV sites, also cabin and cottage rentals on 7-mile Lake Pemaquid. Facilities include tennis, a pool, 18-hole mini golf, game room, laundry facilities, sauna, Jacuzzi, snack bar, store, and a marina with boat rentals.

✳ Where to Eat

Note: Wherever you eat in this area, sampling **Damariscotta oysters** is a must, as the river once yielded firm, distinctively sweet and salty oysters served in the world's best restaurants. By the mid-1800s native oyster beds had about disappeared due to overharvesting, but have recently been reseeded thanks to the University of Maine's Darling Marine Center. The leading local producers are **Pemaquid Oyster Co.** (pemaquidoysters.com) and **Glidden Point Sea Farm** (oysterfarm.com), which has a retail shop at 707 River Rd., Edgecomb.

DINING OUT

IN DAMARISCOTTA/NEWCASTLE

✪ ✎ ✐ **Damariscotta River Grill** (207-563-2992; damariscottarivergrill.com), 155 Main St. Open for lunch, dinner, Sunday brunch. A brick-walled, two-floor, middle-of-Main-Street gem. Head upstairs to a seat by the window or at the copper bar (note the stellar collection of hockey pucks). Begin either meal with an order of oysters on the half shell, served with the house horseradish. Rick Hirsch and Jean Kerrigan have long been committed to turning local ingredients

MILL POND INN

LOBSTER

Muscongus Bay is a particularly prime lobster source, and genuine lobster pounds are plentiful around the harbors of the Pemaquid Peninsula.

Harbor View Restaurant at the Pemaquid Fisherman's Co-Op (207-677-2642; pemaquid lobstercoop.com/PRestaurant.html),32 Co-Op Rd. off Pemaquid Harbor Rd., Pemaquid Harbor. Open Memorial Day–Columbus Day, 11–8. Maine's oldest continuously run fishermen's cooperative supplies the lobster and this is the place to feast on it—along with steamed clams and mussels, and shrimp. Indoor and outdoor tables with a great view across Johns Bay to Colonial Pemaquid.

Broad Cove Marine (207-529-5186; broadcovemarine.com), 371 Momak Rd. (look for the BCMS sign on Rt. 32), Bremen. Open daily in-season 10–7. You can't get closer to a working harbor. Lobster and clams, live and cooked, oysters on the half shell, and lobster and clam rolls as fresh as they come. Dockside deck on the Medomak River.

Shaw's Wharf (207-677-2200), Rt. 32, New Harbor. Open early May–mid-Oct., daily for lunch and supper. This is a popular, long-established lobster pound on one of Maine's most picturesque harbors. It's also the departure point for the Hardy Boat Cruises and can get busy. Pick your lobster out of the pool below and feed on it upstairs at picnic tables, either inside or out. Chowders and stews, a wide choice of sandwiches, dinner salads, sides, and seafood dinners are also on the menu—but there's no corn. Excellent fish chowder. Fully licensed.

On the dock at Round Pond, two competing lobster shacks are both open daily for lunch through dinner in-season:

Muscongus Bay Lobster Company (207-529-5528). Sheltered picnic tables on the deck. Sample the area's oysters on the half shell, as well as the freshest crabmeat, lobsters, corn, and fixings.

Round Pond Lobster (207-529-5725). Really no-frills, but locals swear by it. BYOB.

BROAD COVE MARINE, BREMEN

Christina Tree

into memorable dishes like lobster cakes on sweet corn sauce. It's a big menu with dishes of all sizes to share. Children's menu. Award-winning wine list. Entrées $17.81–23.98. Check out the new Prep Kitchen selling food and wine on the ground floor (entrance from the parking lot).

✐ **King Eider's Pub** (207-563-6008; kingeiderspub.com), 2 Elm St. Open year-round 10:30 AM–11 PM. The downstairs pub is a good foggy-evening spot for light grub and a boutique brew. Crabcakes as well as oysters are the specialty in the pleasant upstairs restaurant. The dinner menu is large, ranging from burgers to char-grilled steaks. Entrées $20–27.99.

✐ **Newcastle Publick House** (207-563-3434; newcastlepublickhouse.com), 52 Main St., Newcastle. Open daily 11–11, midnight Fri., Sat. Housed in a landmark brick building at the junction of Rts. 1 and 125, this is an informal family-friendly pub with a focus on local ingredients. Here you can feast on the town's famed oysters, then dine on shepherd's pie or wild mushroom fettuccine or a veggie burger. Draft beer selections. Entrées $14–23, also pub menu and pizzas.

Savory Maine (207-563-2111; savorymaine dining.com), 11 Water St. Open daily year-round. Almost downtown but hidden away down by the river, this vintage-1825 school-house-turned-church-turned-restaurant with a deck is a delightful spot. Owner Grace Goldberg is dedicated to using wild, organic, and local ingredients. Lunch on a DLT (dulse, lettuce, and tomato) and dine on scallops Florentine or the gnocchi of the day with seasonal veggies. Wine and beer. Most dinner entrées $15.95–24.95.

ON THE PEMAQUID PENINSULA

Bradley Inn (207-677-2105; bradleyinn.com), Pemaquid Point Rd., New Harbor. Call to check, but generally open Thu.–Tue. in-season; Thu.–Sun., Nov.–Mar. Fine dining is what these two attractive dining rooms are about. The rooms are decorated in nautical antiques and soothing colors; tables are well spaced and candlelit. The locally sourced à la carte menu might include wild salmon with crab-fried brown rice, kale chips, and a soy ginger glaze. Entrées $25–37. The inviting

bar features house cocktails and grilled flat breads.

✐ **The Anchor** (207-529-2600; theanchor restaurant.com). In 2015, the Anchor Inn acquired a new name, kitchen, and rehabbed interior after 66 years. Andrea and Dan Reny are the new hands-on proprietors. (Dan has run neighboring Muscungus Bay Lobster for a decade.) The bar area has been expanded, but this is still a tiered dining room overlooking the harbor, and it's still wise to request a table on the waterside tier. The menu is simpler, focused on local seafood. At lunch we ordered a crab and avocado wrap and our request to wrap it in lettuce was graciously granted. Dinner entrées include steak and duck, but go for the lobster and shrimp ravioli. $18-29 dinner entrées and a reasonably priced bar menu that includes lobster "popcorn" and Medomak River softshell clams as well as local oysters.

EATING OUT

IN DAMARISCOTTA

Schooner Landing (207-563-7447; schooner landingmaine.com), Schooner Wharf, Main St. Open May–Sept. daily for lunch and dinner, just weekends in Apr. and Oct.; the pub remains open for live music on weekends through winter. Harborside on the Damariscotta River, informal and draft brews. Eat inside or out. Pemaquid oysters are the feature, fresh on the half shell, baked, stewed, or fried. Plenty of lobster and other seafood, sandwiches, burgers, and beers. Check out free oyster Fridays, music, and other events.

Weatherbird Café (207-563-8993), 72 Courtyard St. If you are browsing the shops and want a quick but delicious lunch, this bakery and market serves up deli sandwiches on fresh-baked breads and panini.

✿ ❀ **Larson's Lunch Box** (207-563-57550), 430 Upper Main St. (Business Rt. 1). May–late Oct., daily except Wed. 11–4. Beloved by locals, this roadside stand is known for its fresh and generous crab and lobster rolls. Billy and Barbara Ganem have installed a serious restaurant kitchen and also pride themselves on from-scratch clam chowder, sweet potato fries, and cookies. Burgers, too. Picnic tables.

✐ **Best Thai** (209-563-1440), 74 Main St. Open Tue.–Sat. for lunch and Tues.–Sun. for

MOODY'S DINER

dinner. The decor and presentation convey the message that this is the best Thai food around.

S. Fernald's Country Store (207-563-8484), 50 Main St. Owner Sumner Richards presides over the soda fountain and limited seating and takes pride in the '50s feel of this local gathering place.

ON OR JUST OFF RT. 1

✪ ⊕ ❤ ♿ **Moody's Diner** (207-832-7785; moodysdiner.com), Rt. 1, Waldoboro. Open daily 6 AM–9:30 PM. A clean and warm, classic 1927 diner run by several generations of the Moody family along with other employees who have been here so long they've become part of the family. Renovated and expanded, it retains all the old atmosphere and specialties, including killer pies and family-style food— corned beef hash, meat loaf, and stews—at digestible prices. You can buy T-shirts and other Moody's paraphernalia, but you can also still get chicken or turkey potpie and a great crabmeat roll. Prices haven't soared with fame.

❤ **Bullwinkle's Family Steakhouse** (207-832-6272), Rt. 1, Waldoboro. Locally loved and a good bet for road food. Steaks are the specialty, along with baby back ribs, seafood baskets, and subs.

✪ ❤ **The Narrows Tavern** (207-832-2210), 15 Friendship St., Waldoboro. Open 11:30 AM–1 AM, dinner until 9. Check the tavern's Facebook site for frequent music. A welcoming village pub with picnic-style tables at which patrons mix; the TV is unobtrusive, and the brick walls are hung with local art. Standout

fish chowder as well as salads, pastas with fresh veggies and fish, and burgers with sweet potato fries. Great pies. Selection of wine by the glass as well as brews.

Rising Tide Co-op (207-563-5556; risingtide.coop), 323 Main St., Damariscotta. A long-established local food co-op with a first-rate deli and café.

ON THE PEMAQUID PENINSULA: RT. 130

❤ **Cupboard Café** (207-677-3911), 137 Huddle Rd., New Harbor. Open Apr.–Dec., Tue.–Sat. 8–3, Sun. 8–noon. A family-run log eatery specializing in from-scratch baking (try the cinnamon buns) within striking distance of Pemaquid Light and the beach. Luncheon options include blackboard specials as well as salads, burgers, and sandwiches. Chicken pie is a signature dish.

The Contented Sole (207-677-3000) at Colonial Pemaquid. Open seasonally for lunch and dinner, this large wharf-side restaurant managed by the Bradley Inn is hidden down by the water, away from the tourist flow. Full menu from pizza and fish tacos to lobster scampi and steak. Fully licensed.

ON THE PEMAQUID PENINSULA: ALONG RT. 129 TO CHRISTMAS COVE

Harborside Café (207-644-8751), South Bristol. Open year-round for breakfast, lunch, supper. Just north of the drawbridge at "the Gut," this is a general store that's recently been slicked up by new owners with a coffee bar. It still offers local favorites, including pizza, omelets all day, sandwiches, fried seafood, chowder, and fresh fruit pies.

Island Grocery (207-644-8552; islandgrocery.net), 12 West Side Rd., South Bristol. Open mid-June–Labor Day. Just off Rt. 129, serving the seasonal community. Beth Fisher has created a bright combination store-café with fresh-baked muffins, scones, and yummy frozen custard.

Coveside Restaurant & Marina (207-644-8282; covesiderestaurant.com), Christmas Cove, South Bristol. Open seasonally, 11–9. Geared to customers arriving by yacht (call for moorings) and to the neighboring summer colony, not worth driving all the way to Christmas Cove—but a great amenity if you get there. Check to make sure they are open.

ELSEWHERE

🍴 **Morse's Kraut House** (207-832-5569; morsessauerkraut.com), 3856 Washington Rd. (8 miles north of Rt. 1 on Rt. 220), Waldoboro. Open year-round, daily except Wed., 9–4, deli until 6, from 8 Sat., Sun. Since 1918 sauerkraut has been made from fresh cabbage and sold on the premises, which now include a store and a restaurant featuring build-your-own sauerkraut dishes. Maine natives James Gammon and Cody LeMontagne are carrying on the tradition, also offering a selection of European deli meats, cheeses, delicacies, and pastries.

Borealis Breads Bakery and Sandwich Shop (207-832-0655), 1614-1702 Rt. 1, Waldoboro. Open Mon.–Fri. 8:30–5:30, Sat. and Sun. 9–4. Maine's most popular bread, made from all-natural ingredients, including local grains, and baked here on a stone hearth; more than a dozen kinds. Take-out soups, sandwiches, and more.

ICE CREAM ✪ 🍴 **Round Top Ice Cream** (207-563-5307), 526 Main St. (Business Rt. 1), Damariscotta. Open early Apr.–Columbus Day, 11:30–9, until 8 off-season. You'll find delicious Round Top Ice Cream, made with 15 percent butterfat, offered at restaurants

throughout the region, but this is the original shop just up the road from the farm where it all began in 1924. The ice cream comes in 60 flavors, including fresh blueberry.

✳ Entertainment

Lincoln Theater (207-563-3424; lcct.org), entrance off Main St., Damariscotta. The biggest hall east of Boston in 1875, later boasting the largest motion-picture screen in the state. A second-floor theater has been restored (with elevator access) by the Lincoln County Community Theater, which stages its own productions here. Also first-run films and special programs.

🍴 **Colonial Pemaquid State Historic Site** (207-677-2423; friendsofcolonialpemaquid .org) is a venue for frequent reenactments, lectures, and other special events (see *Historic Sites*).

✳ Selective Shopping

ANTIQUES **Robert Foster** (207-563-8110; fosterauctions.com) holds frequent auctions at his gallery, 811 Rt. 1, Newcastle. **The Art of Antiquing** (207-529-5300), 4 Back Shore Road, Round Pond (just of Rt. 32) is open seasonally, Wed.–Sun. 10–5, specializing in fine domestic and European antiques.

ART

IN DAMARISCOTTA UNLESS OTHERWISE NOTED

Twin Villages Art Walk, June–Dec., third Fri. 4–7. Twenty venues.

River Gallery (207-563-6330), Main St. Open in-season Mon.–Sat. 10–3; features 19th- and early-20th-century landscapes.

Damariscotta Pottery (207-563-8843), Elm St. Extension (around back of the Weatherbird). Open year-round except Sun. Majolica ware, decorated in bright floral designs. You won't see this advertised. It doesn't have to be. Watch it being shaped and painted.

The Stable Gallery (207-563-1991; stablegallerymaine.com), 26 Water St. Open daily mid-May–mid-Oct. A cooperative showing

Bill Davis

MORSE'S IS DESTINATION DINING AND SHOPPING.

PHILIPPE GUILLERM GALLERY, WALDOBORO

works of member artists and a variety of craftspeople.

Gifts at 136 (207-563-1011), 136 Maine St. An exceptional selection of sculpture, pottery, jewelry, artwork, artisan chocolates, too.

Watershed Center for Ceramic Arts (207-882-6705; watershedceramics.org), 19 Rick Hill Rd., Newcastle. An old brickworks serves as a studio in which artists use the local clay to create work. Inquire about two-week workshops, studio tours, and Salad Days.

Sheepscot River Pottery (207-882-9410), 115 Main St. The big shop is on Rt. 1 in Edgecomb, but this gift shop features the distinctive hand-painted dinnerware, plates, lamps, and more.

IN WALDOBORO

Philippe Guillerm Gallery (207-701-9085; guillermsculptures.com), 882 Main St., Waldoboro Village. Open Apr.–Nov., Tue.–Fri. 10–4. Paris-born and -bred Philippe Guillerm has devoted the past 25 years to sailing—collecting exotic and local woods and sculpting them into amazing shapes, from whimsical violins to human forms. The gallery in a former bank building is also—beyond the teller's window—his working studio. Also changing art exhibits.

Tidemark Gallery (207-832-5109; tidemarkgallery.com), 929 Main St.,

Waldoboro Village. Open Wed.–Sat. 10–5. A quality contemporary gallery with frequently changing shows and varied media.

IN NEW HARBOR AND PEMAQUID POINT

Pemaquid Craft Co-op (207-677-2077), 2565 Bristol Rd. (Rt. 130), New Harbor. Open May–Oct., daily 10–6, then Fri.–Sun. until Dec. 24. Fifteen rooms filled with work by 50 Maine crafters.

North Country Wind Bells (207-677-2224; mainebuoybells.com), 544 Rt. 32, Chamberlain. Open daily June–Labor Day, weekdays off-season. North of New Harbor on the pretty coastal road to Round Pond. Buoy wind bells, wilderness bells, and lighthouse bells are made and sold, along with garden and home accessories.

SPECIAL SHOPS

IN DAMARISCOTTA

✪ 🐾 ✎ **Renys** (207-563-3177; renys.com), Main St. First opened in Damariscotta in 1949, family-owned Renys has since become a small-town Maine institution, with 14 stores from Wells to Ellsworth as well as many inland. Corporate headquarters are south of town. Main Street hosts two stores: The original sells quality clothing, while Renys Underground offers everything from tea to TVs, bedding, china, and toys; a wide assortment of canned and boxed foodstuffs at amazing savings; a wide assortment of shoes, sandals, and boots; beach equipment; and all manner of staples and things you didn't realize you needed. The antithesis of Walmart, Renys has been the subject of two Maine musicals. The biggest sales of the year here begin at 6 AM on the first Saturday of November.

✪ ✎ **Sherman's Maine Coast Book Shops** (207-563-3207), 158 Main St. With its name change in 2016, this becomes the sixth store in Maine's largest bookstore chain. According to owner Jeff Curtis, the quality of this beloved, formerly independent bookstore will remain, along with the internet cafe.

Weatherbird on Main (207-563-1177), 132 Main St. An exceptional women's clothing store, expanded from the corner it previously occupied at Weatherbird's Courtyard Street store (see *Eating Out*).

ELSEWHERE

⚓ **Granite Hall Store** (207-529-5864), Rt. 32, Round Pond. Open daily May–Dec. 10–8:30. This distinctive, mansard-roofed building was constructed as a dance hall in 1873 at the center of a busy little port. Check out the movie screen and piano upstairs, relics of its silent-movie days. Sarah Herndon has preserved this sense of the past but filled it with reasons to explore, from the penny candy up front to Scottish scarves, Irish hats, and Maine-made woolens, books, and cards, plus an ice cream take-out window.

Alewives Fabrics (207-563-5002), Rt. 215, Damariscotta Mills. Open daily, year-round. Two miles north of Rt. 1, this is an excellent fabric store. The selection is outstanding, including Marimekko, batik, and Asian. Also quilting supplies. We stopped because we were looking for and found pillow forms.

FARMERS' MARKET **The Damariscotta Farmers Market** (damariscottafarmers market.org) is held mid-May–Oct., Fri. 9–noon at Round Top Farm, 526 Main St. (Business Rt. 1); also Mon. late June–late Sept. at **Rising Tide Co-op** (see *Eating Out*).

✴ Special Events

Note: See damariscotta.com for details.

February: Annual **ice harvest** at the Thompson Ice House, South Bristol. Sunday of Presidents Weekend.

May–early June: Alewives climb the fish ladder in Damariscotta Mills to spawn in Damariscotta Lake, and an **Alewives Festival** featuring smoked and grilled alewives is held the Sunday of Memorial Day weekend (*To See*).

July: Annual July 4 **fireworks** in Damariscotta and Wiscasset and a famously unorthodox **parade** in Round Pond. **Great Salt Bay Music Festival** at Damariscotta River Association.

Early August: **Olde Bristol Days**, Old Fort Grounds, Pemaquid Beach—parade, fish fry, chicken BBQ, bands, bagpipers, pancake breakfast, boat race, much more.

September: **Pemaquid Oyster Festival** at Schooner Landing, Damariscotta.

October: **Annual Pumpkinfest & Regatta** (first weekend) has become one of the biggest events of the year; it includes a parade of river-worthy pumpkins.

November: **Early Bird Sale at Renys** (first Sat.) and at stores throughout town. Free coffee, doughnuts, and bargains. From 6 AM.

December: **Coastal Christmas Fest**.

ROCKLAND/ THOMASTON AREA

Long billed as the "Lobster Capital of the World," Rockland is now better known as home of the Farnsworth Museum, with its exceptional collection of Maine-based paintings, and for the galleries, shops, attractions, and restaurants lining its mile-long, floridly brick Main Street. Departure point for ferries to the islands of Vinalhaven, North Haven, and Matinicus, it is also home port for the majority of Maine's windjammers, as well as for several daysailers and excursion boats.

In the past couple of decades this city of nearly 7,300 has been transformed almost completely. Never a "tourist town" like Camden or Boothbay, Rockland is fiercely proud of its working waterfront. Its sardine-packing and fish-processing plants are, however, gone, and the huge harbor, protected by a nearly mile-long granite—and walkable—breakwater, is now sparkling clean and equipped to accommodate pleasure boats. Old waterside industrial sheds have disappeared, replaced by offices and restaurants. The harborside walking trail lengthens with every edition of this book. A former newspaper plant is now the chamber of commerce visitors center and the Maine Lighthouse Museum.

Still, Rockland prides itself on its grit. The city's industrial base still includes FMC Bio-Polymer (processing carrageenan from seaweed) and homegrown Fisher Snowplow. The harbor, Maine's second largest after Portland, remains home to a sizable fishing and lobstering fleet along with tugs and U.S. Coast Guard and commercial vessels.

Initially known for its shipbuilding, the city became synonymous in the late 19th century with the limestone it quarried, burned, and shipped off to be made into plaster. When wallboard replaced plaster, Rockland quickly switched to catching and processing fish. In the 1990s, with fishing on the decline, city entrepreneurs once more looked to widen their base. Initially MBNA, the national credit card company, seemed a gift from the gods, tidying the southern rim of the harbor into an office "campus" and building a public boardwalk along its rim. In 2005, however, the firm sold out and disappeared.

Truly amazing is the way Rockland's resurgence has continued to be powered by the economic engines of fine art, food, and cultural attractions. The vacated office space was filled, and restaurants moved in to take advantage of waterfront views.

A century ago summer people heading for Bar Harbor, as well as the islands, took the train as far as Rockland, switching here to steamboats. Today a similar summer crowd rides the bus to the ferry terminal or flies into Knox County Regional Airport on Owls Head, just south of town, transferring to rental cars, air taxis, or windjammers to charter boats as well as ferries.

Southwest of Rockland, two peninsulas separate Muscongus Bay from Penobscot Bay. One is the fat arm of land on which the villages of Friendship and Cushing doze. Nearer is the skinnier St. George Peninsula with Port Clyde at its tip, departure point for the year-round passenger ferry service to Monhegan Island.

GUIDANCE **Penobscot Bay Regional Chamber of Commerce** (207-596-0376 or 1-800-562-2529; mainedreamvacation.com), 1 Park Dr., Rockland. Open daily Memorial Day–Labor Day, Mon.–Fri. 9–5 and Sat. 10–4; then weekdays and 10–2 Sat. through the Columbus Day weekend. The chamber's visitors centers (the second is in Camden at 2 Public Landing)

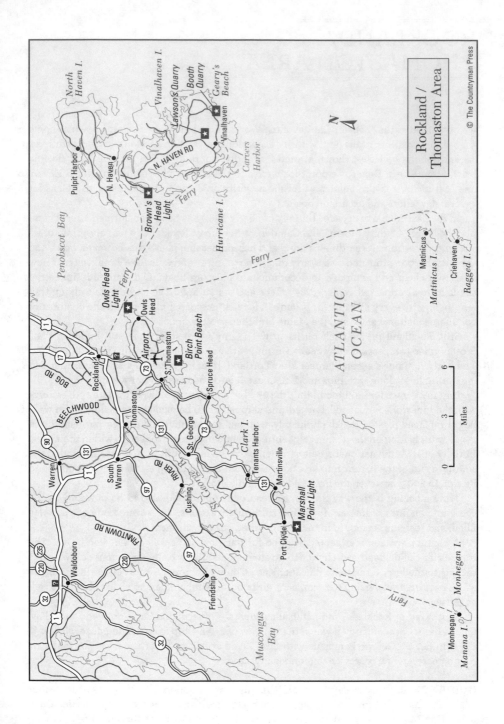

Rockland /
Thomaston Area

© The Countryman Press

PORT CLYDE

serve the Rockland area, which includes Owls Head, Thomaston, the peninsula villages, and the islands.

GETTING THERE *By air:* **Knox County Regional Airport** (207-594-4131) at Owls Head, just south of Rockland. Frequent daily service is via **Cape Air** (1-866-227-3247; capeair.com) to Boston's Logan Airport, with baggage connections to major carriers. **Penobscot Island Air** (penobscotislandair.net) offers both scheduled and charter service to Vinalhaven, North Haven, and Matinicus. Rental cars are available at the airport. Also see *By taxi* under *Getting Around*; all offer service to Portland International Jetport (see "Portland Area"). **Mid-Coast Limo** (1-800-937-2424; midcoastlimo.com) also serves Boston's Logan Airport.

   By bus: **Concord Coach** (1-800-639-3317; concordcoachlines.com) stops in Rockland at the Maine State Ferry Terminal.

   By boat: For moorings contact the harbormaster (office, 207-594-0312; dock, 207-594-0314).

GETTING AROUND *By taxi:* **Schooner Bay Limo & Taxi** (207-594-5000), **Hit the Road Driver Service** (207-230-0095; cell, 207-691-0295), and **Joe's Taxi** (207-975-3560) will get you there.

   By ferry: Frequent service from the **Maine State Ferry Service Terminal** (207-596-2022 or 1-800-491-4883) to Vinalhaven, North Haven, and, less frequently, to Matinicus (see "Midcoast Islands"). **Monhegan Boat Line** (207-372-8848) serves Monhegan from Port Clyde.

   Note: Rockland can be accessed and thoroughly enjoyed without a car.

PARKING Try to park in a free, all-day municipal lot off Tillson Ave. Note that street parking is limited to two hours and strictly enforced.

WHEN TO COME Rockland stages a series of festivals that draw weekend crowds from mid-July through September. The biggest is the Maine Lobster Festival, first weekend in August. The Farnsworth Museum, major galleries, restaurants, and lodging all remain open year-round.

✳ Villages and Islands

Friendship (pop. 1,200). Best known as the birthplace of the classic Friendship sloop, first built by local lobstermen to haul their traps (originals and reproductions of this sturdy vessel hold races here every summer), Friendship remains a quiet fishing village. The **Friendship Museum** (207-832-4852), housed in a former brick schoolhouse at the junction of Rt. 220 and Martin Point Rd., is open late June–Labor Day, Mon.-Sat. 1–4 and Sun. 2–4, also weekends March–Columbus Day. Displays feature Friendship sloops.

St. George is a town composed of several distinct villages along Rt. 131 on the St. George Peninsula, a 15-mile-long land finger between the tidal St. George River and the Atlantic. The most visible of these is **Tenants Harbor**, a fishing village with a terrific sculpture of St. George and the Dragon in front of the town office. There's a good little library and, beyond, rock cliffs, tidal pools, old cemeteries, and the kind of countryside described by Sarah Orne Jewett in *The Country of the Pointed Firs*. Jewett lived just a few bends down Rt. 131 in Martinville while she wrote the book.

Port Clyde marks the end of Rt. 131 and the tip of the peninsula. The departure point for the year-round ferries to Monhegan, it's tranquil and picturesque—with the exception of ferry departures and arrivals, when it's chaotic. The Ocean House Hotel is a great place to spend the night before boarding the ferry. Linda Bean (as in L.L. Bean) owns the working wharf (207-372-6543). She also owns the Dip Net restaurant, the Port Clyde General Store, and the neighboring Seaside Inn and gallery. This is a great spot for kayaking (see *To Do*), and Marshall Point Light (see *To See*) is around the bend.

Thomaston (pop. 2,800). Passing through Thomaston on Rt. 1 you notice the handsome brick downtown and line of handsome captains' homes, evidence of early-19th-century wealth from shipbuilding. In the 1840 census, three of the nation's seven millionaires lived in town. To dramatize its history Thomaston has installed 25 plaques along Main, Knox, and Water Sts., each with a photo taken at that spot a century ago with text in both English and French. Leaflet guides to this **Museum in the Streets** are available at the library. The **Thomaston Historical Society** (207-354-2314; thomastonhistoricalsociety.com) at the foot of Knox St. is open June–Aug., Tue.-Thu. 2–4. The state prison has moved to Warren but left behind its popular Maine State Prison Showroom (see *Selective Shopping*). Montpelier, home of the General Knox Museum (see *To See*), is just north of town at the junctions of Rts. 1 and 131.

Union (pop. 2,350) is 15 miles west of Rockland via Rt. 17, a little less if you follow Rt. 131 north along the St. George River. It's sited between Round Pond and Seven Tree Pond and surrounded by gentle hills and farm country. The **Union Fair** in August has been held since 1892. This place is also a good spot to swim, eat, and explore the **Matthews Museum of Maine Heritage** (matthewsmuseum.org) at the fairgrounds, open Wed.-Sat. in July and Aug., noon–4.

Islands. An overnight or longer stay on an island is far preferable to a day trip. From Rockland you can take a Maine State (car) Ferry to **Vinalhaven** and **North Haven**. Together these form the Fox Islands, divided by a narrow passage. Vinalhaven is Maine's largest offshore island, with its largest year-round population and lobstering fleet. A number of shopping, eating, and lodging options cluster around Carver's Harbor, a 10-minute walk from the ferry. North Haven offers fewer and more seasonal places to eat, shop, and stay, but a more open landscape. **Matinicus**, also accessible from Rockland, is the most remote of Maine's island communities, and quietly beautiful. Tiny **Monhegan**, accessible from Port Clyde, offers the most dramatic cliff scenery and the most hospitable welcome to visitors.

MUST SEE

✪ ♿ **Farnsworth Art Museum and Wyeth Center** (207-596-6457; farnsworthmuseum.org), 16 Museum St., Rockland. Open year-round. Memorial Day weekend–Oct. 31, daily 10–5, also Wed. and First Fridays 5–8 (free); Nov.–Dec. 31, closed Mon.; Jan.–Memorial Day weekend, Wed.–Sun. 10–5. Admission to the museum and Farnsworth Homestead (see below) is $12 adults, $10 senior citizens and students over 17; no charge under 17; free for all Wed. 5–8. Add $5 to include a visit to the Olson House (see below). This exceptional art museum was established by Lucy Farnsworth, who amazed everyone when, on her death at age 97 in 1935, she left $1.3 million to preserve her house and build a library and art gallery to honor the memory of her father. From the beginning the collection included paintings of Maine by Winslow Homer, George Bellows, and a (then) little-known local summer resident, Andrew Wyeth.

Since the early 1990s the Farnsworth has more than doubled its space and now occupies 3 acres in the middle of downtown Rockland. The collection numbers over 14,000 objects housed in five buildings with 28 galleries. The museum remains Maine-focused. A permanent exhibit traces the evolution of Maine landscape paintings with Hudson River School artists like Thomas Cole and 19th-century marine artist Fitz Henry Lane; American impressionists Frank Benson, Willard Metcalf, Childe Hassam, and Maurice Prendergast; early-20th-century greats like Rockwell Kent and Charles Woodbury; and such "modernists" as John Marin and Marsden Hartley. Rockland-raised painter and sculptor Louise Nevelson is also well represented. In recent years contemporary art holdings have been significantly expanded to include works by Alex Katz, Neil Welliver, Janet Fish, Bernard Langlais, and Robert Indiana, along with such photographers as Elliot Porter and Rockland native Kosti Ruohomaa.

Gardens connect the main museum with the Wyeth Center, a two-story exhibit space in a former church, displaying works by N. C. Wyeth (1882–1945) and Jamie Wyeth (born 1946). Exhibits vary. Andrew Wyeth's paintings are shown in the main museum.

Farnsworth Homestead (207-596-6457), 21 Elm St., Rockland. Open late May–mid-Oct., Tue.–Sun. 11–5. Tours on the hour. Free with museum admission. Built in 1850 for successful businessman William A. Farnsworth and his growing family, this was the nearly lifelong home of his daughter and museum founder Lucy Copeland Farnsworth. The Greek Revival–style Farnsworth Homestead has a richly decorated Victorian interior, with original furniture, carpets, wallpaper, paintings and prints, gas lighting fixtures, and many of the family's original belongings.

Courtesy of Farnsworth Art Museum

TURKEY POND BY ANDREW WYETH, 1944

✻ To See

The Olson House (207-596-6457), Hawthorn Point Rd., Cushing. Open Memorial Day–Columbus Day, daily 11–4. $10 adults, $8 seniors and students over 17. Administered by the Farnsworth Art Museum, this house served as a backdrop for many works by Andrew Wyeth, including *Christina's World*. It's been intentionally left unrestored except for interpretive materials. On Pleasant Point, accessed by quiet back roads, this saltwater farm makes a good bicycle destination. Built in the late 1700s, it was remodeled in 1872 but remained in the same family, ultimately passing to Alvara and Christina (1892–1968) Olson. Owned by the Farnsworth since 1991, it evokes the familiar painting.

MUSEUMS AND HISTORIC HOMES ✐
General Henry Knox Museum (Montpelier) (207-354-8062; knoxmuseum.org), 30 High St., Thomaston. Guided tours Memorial Day–Columbus Day, Thu.–Fri. 10–4; more days open on website. Admission $10 adults, $8 seniors, $4 ages 5–14 (family: $18). A 1926 re-creation of the grand mansion built (on another spot) in 1794 by General Henry Knox (1750–1806), the portly 5-foot-6-inch, 300-pound Boston bookseller who became

EVERYTHING AT THE OWLS HEAD TRANSPORTATION MUSEUM WORKS

a Revolutionary War hero, then our first secretary of war. He married a granddaughter of Samuel Waldo, the Boston developer who owned all of this area and for whom the county is named.

✐ **Owls Head Transportation Museum** (207-594-4418; owlshead.org), 117 Museum St., Owls Head. Off Rt. 73, 2 miles south of Rockland, adjacent to the Knox County Regional Airport. Open daily year-round (except Christmas, Thanksgiving, and New Year's Day) 10–5. Check the website for frequent special-event days. On non-event-days admission is $10 adults, $8 seniors, free under 18. One of the country's outstanding collections of antique planes and automobiles. In the exhibition hall you can take a 100-year journey through the evolution of transportation, from horse-drawn carriages to World War I fighter planes; from a 16-cylinder Cadillac to a Rolls-Royce; from the Red Baron's Fokker triplane to a vintage 1923 popcorn wagon from Old Orchard Beach.

CAPTAIN JIM SHARPE AT HIS SAIL, POWER & STEAM MUSEUM

William A. Davis

✐ **Project Puffin Visitor Center** (207-596-5566; projectpuffin.org), 311 Main St., Rockland. Open daily June–Oct. 10–5 (until 7 Wed in July and Aug.), then weekends until Dec.; call for off-season hours. Free. Live-streaming mini cams and audio provide a virtual visit with nesting puffins. A joint project of National Audubon and Maine Audubon, this is a must-stop, with exhibits cleverly designed for children, like the "burrow" into which they can crawl and observe puffins feeding their chicks in a similar burrow.

Sail, Power & Steam Museum (207-701-7627; sailpowersteammuseum.org), 75 Mechanic St., Sharps Point South. Open May–Nov.; check the web or call for hours. $5 adults, $3 ages 7–16. Free over

65. Nineteenth-century sail and steam vessels are the focus of this evolving museum, sited in the historic, still-working Snow Family Shipyard. It's the brainchild of Captain Jim Sharp, who helped restore Maine windjammer *Stephen Taber* and Arctic explorer Donald MacMillan's schooner *Bowdoin* (now owned by the Maine Maritime Academy). The growing collection includes half models, marine paintings and prints, and a vintage-1674 brass navigational instrument owned by Nathaniel Bowditch.

⚓ **The Coastal Children's Museum** (207-975-2530; coastalchildrensmuseum.org), 75 Mechanic St. at Sharps Point South. $5 admission, under 2 free. Wed.–Sat. 10–4, Sun. 1–4. More than 16 hands-on, interactive displays include a touch tank, a full-sized sailboat, and a lobster trap you can crawl through.

✳ To Do

BICYCLING **Side Country Sports** (207-701-5100; sidecountrysports.com), 41 Main St., Rockland. Rent bikes year-round (and skis and snowboards) for one, five, or seven days.

Georges River Bikeways is the name of a free map/guide that traces routes along the river and in its watershed area from Thomaston north into Liberty. Check with the Georges River Land Trust (207-594-5166), 328 Main St., Rockland.

BOATING Check with the chamber of commerce for a complete list of current excursions. Also see the Maine State Ferry Service under *Getting Around*. The ferry rides to both North Haven and Vinalhaven are reasonably priced and a good way to get out on the water. Both islands make good day trips, but Monhegan is far more walkable. See the Midcoast Islands chapter for details about all three islands.

Monhegan Boat Line (207-372-8848; monheganboat.com) in Port Clyde offers frequent 50-minute service to the island using its two boats, the *Elizabeth Ann* (built in 1995 for this run, with both open top and lower enclosed decks) and the smaller *Laura B* (built in 1943 for World War II duty). The same boats are also used for seasonal "Puffin/Nature" cruises to Eastern Egg Rock and to view the area's lighthouses.

Captain Jack Lobster Boat Adventure (207-542-6852; captainjacklobstertours.com), 130 Thomaston St., Rockland. Memorial Day–Columbus Day. Lobster-boat tours that may include an onboard lobster dinner.

Daysails and longer: **Summertime Cruises** (1-800-562-8290; schoonersummertime.com), 115 South St., Rockland. Captain Bill Brown offers three- and six-day cruises on a 53-foot pinky schooner for up to six passengers throughout the summer, plus day sails in spring and autumn.

A Morning in Maine (207-691-7245; amorninginmaine.com), Rockland Middle Pier. A classic coastal ketch with an overall length of 55 feet, captained by marine biologist Bob Pratt, offers sails ranging from a few hours to overnights for up to 21 people.

Johanson Boatworks (207-596-7060 or 1-877-456-4267), 11 Farwell Dr., Rockland, offers sailboat charters. **Bay Sailing** (207-831-8425; bay-sailing.com), the Pier at the Pearl, Rockland, offers yacht charters, boat rentals, and an ASA sailing school.

SEA KAYAKING **Breakwater Kayak** (207-596-6895; breakwaterkayak.com), behind Landings Restaurant (see *Eating Out*) on Commercial St., Rockland. Two-hour to multiday guided kayaking tours.

Port Clyde Kayaks (207-372-8100; portclydekayaks.com), Port Clyde. Based at an outfitting shop near the Port Clyde wharf. Guided tours take you across Port Clyde Harbor to Marshall Point Light and among the nearby Georges Islands.

FISHING, HUNTING, AND CANOEING **Saltwater Fishing & Guide Service** (207-542-8915), **Cramer Guide Services** (207-233-3979), and **Ten Mile Guide Service** (207-542-8777).

Maine Outdoors (207-785-4496; maineoutdoors.biz), 69 Beote Rd., Union, offers fishing and other paddling adventures.

GOLF **Rockland Golf Club** (207-594-9322; rocklandgolf.com), 606 Old County Rd., Rockland. Open Apr.–Oct. This 18-hole public course gets high marks from pros; complete with a modern clubhouse serving meals from 7 AM.

✳ Green Space

BEACHES ✐ **Johnson Memorial Park**, Chickawaukee Lake, Rt. 17, 2 miles north of downtown Rockland. Restrooms, picnic area, a sand beach, and warm water add up to the area's best swimming, good for small children.

✐ **Birch Point Beach State Park**, also known as Lucia Beach, off Ash Point Rd. in Owls Head. Sandy, with smooth boulders for sunning, wooded walking trails, and picnic benches. Marked from Rt. 73 (Dublin Rd. to Ballyhac Rd.).

Drift Inn Beach in Port Clyde, down Drift Inn Rd. by the Harpoon Restaurant, just off Rt. 131; a small beach in a great spot.

WALKING/PICNICKING **Rockland waterfront**. The area's most spectacular stretch of the **Rockland Harbor Trail** begins on the Samoset Hotel property just over the Rockport line and runs 1.7 miles out along the Rockland Breakwater to the lighthouse.

Harbor Park at the public landing marks the beginning of the trail south along the water past Sandy Beach Park (picnic benches) to Mechanic St. and on to Snow Marine Park. Along the way you'll find benches, flowers, and a gazebo.

Owls Head Light State Park. This classic lighthouse is set into a beautiful point with walks and views on both the bay and harbor sides, picnic tables. See *Lighthouses* for directions.

Waldo Tyler Wildlife Sanctuary, Buttermilk Lane (off Rt. 73), South Thomaston, is a birding spot on the Weskeag River.

The Georges River Land Trust (207-594-5166), 8 N. Main St., Rockland, publishes a map/guide to the Georges Highland Path, a foot trail through the hills of the Georges River watershed. Maps are available at the chamber of commerce.

Christina Tree

OWLS HEAD LIGHT

✳ Lodging

INNS AND B&BS

IN ROCKLAND 04841

((ᵞ)) **Berry Manor Inn** (207-596-7696 or 1-800-774-5692; berrymanorinn.com), 81 Talbot Ave., P.O. Box 1117. This expansive 19th-century shingle-style mansion is a sumptuous retreat. The 12 guest rooms, divided among the second and third floors of the mansion and the second floor of the carriage house, all have queen- or king-sized bed, flat-screen TV, phone, air-conditioning, and luxurious bath; almost all have a gas fireplace. A two-room, two-bath suite in the carriage house has a separate living room. $125–305 for rooms, $420 for the suite mid-June–mid-Oct., less off-season, including a multicourse breakfast and a guest pantry stocked with goodies that include homemade pies.

((ᵞ)) **LimeRock Inn** (207-594-2257 or 1-800-546-3762; limerockinn.com), 96 Limerock St. P. J. Walter and Frank Isganitis are the innkeepers of this 1890s Queen Anne–style mansion on a quiet residential street with a wraparound front porch and two living rooms to relax in. The eight guest rooms, all with private bath, are opulently furnished with antiques. The turret room is over the top, but our favorite is the airy Island Cottage room at the back of the house, opening on the garden. Amenities include a 24-hour guest pantry and computer. $169–249 ($129–169 off-season) includes a full breakfast.

✪ ❁ ⅃ ((ᵞ)) **Granite Inn** (207-594-9036 or 1-800-386-9036; oldgraniteinn.com), 546 Main St. An 1840s mansion built of local granite, set in a flower garden across from the Maine State Ferry Terminal (also the Concord Coach stop). Ideal if you come without a car and are bound for an island, but innkeepers Edwin and Joan Hantz have added plenty of other reasons to stay here. Joan is a graphic artist with an eye for blending contemporary furnishings and antiques. There are eight guest rooms, including two suites. Two front second-floor bedrooms—the largest—overlook the water and ferry terminal. The two-room suites (the second bedrooms have twin beds) represent good value for families or couples who don't mind

sharing a bath. $95–215 per night includes a breakfast featuring fresh fruit, from-scratch baked goods, bacon or sausage, and a hot entrée, maybe lemon crêpes with wild blueberry compote.

✪ ⅃ ((ᵞ)) **The Captain Lindsey House** (207-596-7950 or 1-800-523-2145; lindseyhouse.com), 5 Lindsey St. This was built in 1837 as one of Rockland's first inns, and the feel is that of a small, boutique hotel. With richly paneled public rooms and nine spacious guest rooms (one handicapped accessible), it's both a gem and the most convenient lodging to the Farnsworth Museum and Main Street shops. Run by schooner captains Ken and Ellen Barnes, who also restored and operated the windjammer *Stephen Taber* for more than 25 years, each guest room is different, but all have air-conditioning, TV, and private bath. $131–228 includes a full buffet breakfast, served in the garden, weather permitting.

❁ ☙ **Ripples Inn at the Harbor** (207-594-2771 or 1-800-375-5771; ripplesinnattheharbor.com), 16 Pleasant St. Open year-round. Sandi Dillon provides rooms that are not overly fussy but nicely decorated with an eye to comfort. There are four rooms and a family suite (accommodating four) with a whirlpool tub and private entrance. In addition to the usual common spaces, "The UN-common Room" has a microwave, fridge, and TV. $100–240 (for a two-bedroom suite) with full breakfast.

ON SPRUCE HEAD AND ON THE ST. GEORGE PENINSULA

❁ ((ᵞ)) **Craignair Inn** (207-594-7644 or 1-800-320-9997; craignair.com), Clark Island Rd., Spruce Head 04859. Main building open year-round. Michael and Joann O'Shea offer 20 guest rooms that are divided between the main house (Room 12 is a corner room with a queen and three windows with water views) and the Vestry, a former chapel set in gardens in the rear with water views from the second floor. The dining room overlooks the water and is open to the public for dinner (see *Dining Out*). Walk across the causeway to the Clark Island shoreline and a granite quarry that's good swimming. In high season from $90 for a room with shared bath to $200 for a private room with water view, $80–140

off-season, including a full breakfast. $20
extra for a pet.

🐾 🛜 **East Wind Inn** (207-372-6366
or 1-800-241-8439; eastwindinn.com), 21
Mechanic St., P.O. Box 149, Tenants Harbor
04860. Open May–Oct. This tall, distinctive,
19th-century building, an inn since the 1920s,
when patrons arrived by steamboat, offers
expansive waterside grounds and superlative
views from the veranda and sunny dining
room, as well as from six updated suites and
two bedrooms, all with private bath, and 10
rooms in the Meeting House annex. In 2012
Randy Deutsch took over from longtime
innkeeper Tim Watts and has sustained
the inn's traditional ambience while adding
updated comforts. From $172 in high season;
$148–200 off-season, including a full break-
fast. See the inn's restaurant and Quarry
Tavern in *Eating Out*.

🐾 🛜 **Weskeag Inn** (207-596-6676 or 1-800-
596-5576), Rt. 73, P.O. Box 213, South Thomaston 04858. Open year-round. Handy to the
Owls Head Transportation Museum and to
Knox County Regional Airport (pickups provided, perhaps in one of Gray Smith's antique
cars). A handsome and hospitable 1830s home
overlooking the Weskeag estuary in the tiny
village of South Thomaston. The lawn (available for weddings) sweeps to the river's edge.
Six attractive guest rooms have private bath;
two share or are rented as a suite. Our pick
would be the third-floor rooms with dormers
and water views. $135–150 in-season, $100–112
off-season, including breakfast.

🐾 🛜 **Ocean House Hotel** (207-372-6691
or 1-800-269-6691; oceanhousehotel.com),
P.O. Box 66, Port Clyde 04855. Open May–
Oct. This friendly old village inn is the logical
place to spend the night before or after taking
the neighboring ferry to Monhegan. Built to
board local mariners in the 1820s, it's earned
a loyal following under longtime ownership
by the Murdock family. Second- and third-
floor rooms include one apartment. This is a
good place for a single traveler, thanks to the
single rates and the ease of meeting fellow
guests, but families are welcome. Rooms from
$110, $125–145 with private bath, less solo, full
breakfast included. No credit cards.

Mill Pond House Bed & Breakfast (207-
372-6209; millpondhouse.com), 453 Port
Clyde Rd., Tenants Harbor 04860. Leslie Kor-
pinen's rambling 1860s farmhouse is a homey,

EAST WIND INN, TENANTS HARBOR   *Christina Tree*

attractive B&B with three second-floor guest
rooms, from $70 single (shared bath) to $105
double (private bath), morning muffins and
fruit included.

MOTELS ♿ 🛜 **Trade Winds Motor Inn** (207-
596-6661 or 1-800-834-3139; tradewinds
maine.com), 2 Park Dr., Rockland 04841. Open
year-round. This locally owned 120-unit motel
is composed of several wings, obviously
added over the decades. Units vary from
"non-view" basics (from $74 off-season) to
balcony rooms ($134–154) and "deluxe suites"
($214–234 in high season). Amenities include
a health club, pool, and restaurant.

✳ Where to Eat

DINING OUT

IN ROCKLAND

✪ **Primo** (207-596-0770; primorestaurant
.com), 2 S. Main St. (Rt. 73). Open May–Jan.,
daily in summer, otherwise Wed.–Mon.
5:30–9:30; call first. Reservations are a must.
This very special restaurant, rated among the
best in Maine, grows much of what it serves.
"Primo" was chef and co-owner Melissa
Kelly's grandfather, a butcher. Kelly follows
tradition by raising her own pork and making
several kinds of sausages as well as preparing
cuts of meats and overseeing the gardens,
greenhouses, and beehives on the 4-acre,

intensely cultivated property. With two James Beard Foundation Best Chef: Northeast Awards, the second for Primo, she knows how to make your dinner, from mushroom pizza ($18) to sautéed pork scaloppine with prosciutto in sage-mushroom Madeira. The house cannoli are crisp, rich, and excellent. Delectable pastas are $32–34, entrées $33–45. The menu, along with a pizza and small plates, is also available upstairs, a lively space with a long copper bar and $1-per-oyster nights.

Suzuki's Sushi Bar (207-596-7447; suzukisushi.com), 419 Main St. Open Tue.–Sat. for dinner. Where better to sample the full variety of the ocean's yield than a sophisticated Japanese restaurant? Keiko Suzuki's extensive menu includes raw nigiri dishes and spicy sushi rolls, entrées such as shrimp with shiitake, and many delectable salads and vegetarian dishes. Entrées $10–30.

In Good Company (207-593-9110; ingoodcompanymaine.com), 415 Main St. Open from 4:30 except Mon. No reservations. A wine bar in a living-room-like setting, serving salads, cheeses, nibbles, and light meals such as cedar-planked salmon and cold sliced beef tenderloin. $5–20.

✪ 🐾 **Café Miranda** (207-594-2034; cafemiranda.com), 15 Oak St. Open year-round 5–9:30. Reserve for dinner. In 1993 Kerry Altiero was the first chef in Rockland to offer the hip kind of dining for which the city has since become known. His small restaurant has, however, neither expanded (unless you

count seasonal café tables) nor moved from its side street. Single diners sit up at the counter watching an amazing variety of food emerge from the brick oven, with more than 40 entrées on the menu, including a kale dish roasted with mushrooms, garlic, and feta, followed by mussels roasted with curry. Entrées $19–28.

✪ **Rustica** (207-594-0015; rusticamaine.com), 315 Main St. Open Mon.–Sat. 11–3 and 5–10, Sun. 11–8; Tue.–Sat. off-season. No reservations. High quality at reasonable prices, a pleasant atmosphere, and decent wine are a winning combination for this "cucina Italiana." Chef-owner John Stowe serves up hearty soups, wild mushroom pasta, and three-cheese lasagna (house-made pasta layered with portobello, crimini, and shiitake mushrooms, Swiss chard, and three cheeses, served on a bed of marinara). Entrées from $12 for pizzas; $17–21 for pasta and entrées such as veal Marsala and pan-roasted cod.

Comida (207-593-8473; comidarestaurant.com), 421 Main St. Spanish cuisine brings chorizo into action with mussels in one dish, parsnip soup in another. Roasted chicken with mole and seared cod with sofrito are some of the Platos Grandes. $19–26.

Salt Water Farm (207-236-0554; saltwaterfarm.com), 24 Central St. In the Union Hall Building's spacious first floor, Salt Water Farm is both a restaurant and a cooking school, sourcing supplies from the local water and farms. Celery root and little neck clam chowder, a crab melt, baked beans, and lemon meringue pie were on one menu, which changes often. $13–22.

Archer's on the Pier (207-594-2435; archersonthepier.com), 58 Ocean St. Open Mon.–Sat. 11–10, and for jazz brunch on Sun. Chef-owner Lynn Archer, the dynamo powering the Brass Compass Café, runs Archer's at a prime site overlooking both the harbor and bay (formerly the Boathouse). Plenty of seafood: $31 in 2013 for twin lobster dinner; $27 for duck confit with butternut risotto. Lunch includes the lobsters along with slow-roasted beef and gravy on toast.

ELSEWHERE

✪ **The Slipway** (207-542-1829; theslipwaymaine.com), 24 Public Landing, Thomaston. Open May–Oct., lunch and dinner except

KERRY ALTIERO USES HIS WOOD-FIRED OVEN IN CREATIVE WAYS AT CAFÉ MIRANDA

Tue. Scott Yakovenko enjoys an enthusiastic following at this waterside venue (formerly the Harborside). We recommend the fried oysters, crisp and still juicy, grilled scallops and grilled swordfish with pesto, topped off with perfect blueberry pie, a dessert staple made by Scott's mother. The chef's specialty remains a seafood-studded bouillabaisse. The dining room is good looking, but best views are from the porch and seasonal deck and wharf. Entrées $18.50–24.

Thomaston Café and Bakery (207-354-8589; thomastoncafe.com), 154 Main St., Thomaston. Open year-round Mon.–Sat. 7:30–2, Sun. brunch 8:30–2. Dinner Fri. and Sat. 5:30–8. Chef-owners Herbert and Eleanor Peters have won many awards and acquired a strong following. Lunch on fresh-made soups, great sandwiches, fish cakes with home fries, salads. The dinner menu might include lobster ravioli with brandied lobster cream sauce. Entrées $17–25.

The East Wind Inn's **Wan-e-set Restaurant** and **Quarry Tavern** (207-372-6366 or 1-800-241-8439; eastwindinn.com), 21 Mechanic St., Tenants Harbor. Open May–Oct., tavern open year-round except for time off in January: call first. Local specialties prepared with creativity.

Craignair Inn & Restaurant (207-594-7644), Clark Island Rd., off Rt. 73, Spruce Head. Open May–Oct. for dinner; Fri., Sat. in spring and fall. Walk the shore before dining by a water-view window. Signature dishes include Craignair crabcakes served with risotto with Dijon rémoulade and fresh vegetables ($18), seared scallops and black Japonica rice ($23), and crispy pan-seared duck breast with cranberry orange reduction. Wines are limited but reasonably priced.

EATING OUT

IN ROCKLAND

Atlantic Baking Co. (207-596-0505), 351 Main St. Open Mon.–Sat. 1–6, Sun. 8–4; Tue.–Sat. in winter. Sited across from the Farnsworth Museum, this busy place seduces passersby with the aroma of fresh-baked bread. There's a blackboard sandwich menu and plenty of help-yourself salads and such in deli cases. Yummy soups and breads. The plastic and Styrofoam do seem at odds with the from-scratch, PC ethos of the place.

Home Kitchen Café (207-596-2449; homekitchencafe.com), 650 Main St. Fresh and vibrant ingredients, attentive and skillful cooking turn out invigorating breakfast omelets—bacon, roasted red pepper, and Cooper cheese, for instance—and a good haddock sandwich. Many items to choose from, and both breakfast and lunch are served all day.

✪ **The Brass Compass Café** (207-596-5960), 305 Main St. Open Mon.–Sat. 5–3, Sun. 6–3. Lynn Archer's friendly eatery is a find. Seafood stews, sandwiches, and salads, generous portions, good value. Yummy onion rings and fries. The house special is a lobster club, with one and a quarter lobsters, bacon, lettuce, and tomato on Lynn's toasted, fresh-made white bread.

✪ **Rock City Café** (207-594-4123), 316 Main St., open 7–7, until 9 Thu.–Sat. Rock City Coffee—chai and teas, too—along with bagels, scones, and pastries baked on premises. The soups and wraps are exceptional, and sandwiches come on Borealis sourdough. We feasted on a summer-veggie grilled panini loaded with roasted eggplant, squash, red onion, and tomatoes. Local beer and wine. In sleek new quarters, still the town meeting and gathering place. Live music, weekends.

Sunfire Mexican Grill (207-594-6196), 488 Main St. Open for lunch Tue.–Sat. 11–3, for dinner Wed. and Sat. 5–8. This is exceptional Mexican fare, all the basics but with very fresh veggies (try the mango avocado salad) and just the right taste. Beer, wine.

✦ **Rockland Café** (207-596-7556; rocklandcafe.com), 441 Main St. Open daily 5:30 AM–

Christina Tree

ROCK CITY CAFÉ IS ROCKLAND'S GATHERING SPOT

LOBSTER

McLoons Lobster Shack (207-593-1382; mcloonslobster.com), 315 Island Rd., South Thomaston. Open 11–7 Memorial Day to Columbus Day. Corn chowder and lobster stew along with the lobster just off the boats you watch pull in and unload.

Miller's Lobster Co. (207-594-7406; millerslobster.com), 83 Eagle Quarry Rd., Spruce Head. Open 11–7 Late June to early Sept. Lobsters (of course), steamers, a view of the sea, and fresh blueberry pie.

9 PM. This is a reliable family eatery, good for fish-and-chips, soups, salad, clam rolls, and daily specials. Warning: The crabcakes are more like crab pancakes. Look for the green-and-white-striped awning.

The Brown Bag (207-596-6372), 606 Main St. (north of downtown). Open Mon.–Sat. 6:30 AM–4 PM. This expanded storefront restaurant is a local favorite, with an extensive breakfast and sandwich menu, soups, chowders, and daily specials. Make your selection at the counter and carry it to your table when it's ready.

✔ *Trackside Station* (207-594-7500; tracksideme.com), 4 Union St. Open daily for lunch and dinner. Ironically this is just off the beaten track and as a result it's either briefly mobbed or relatively empty. The vintage railroad station makes an attractive dining space. It's decorated with blowup photos from Rockland's past. We lunched happily on a fresh crabmeat cheese melt.

✔ *Wasses Wagon*, 2 N. Main St. A local institution for hot dogs.

✳ Entertainment

The Strand Theatre (207-594-0070; rocklandstrand.com), 345 Main St., Rockland. Vintage 1923, a beautifully restored classic downtown 350-seat theater offering films, concerts, and live performances including a summer Wed.-evening series of Bay Chamber Concerts, also streamed performances ranging from the Metropolitan Opera to the Super Bowl.

The Farnsworth Art Museum (207-596-6457; farnsworthmuseum.org) in Rockland stages a year-round series of Sunday films and other weekly cultural events.

✳ Selective Shopping

ART AND CRAFTS GALLERIES

IN ROCKLAND

Arts in Rockland (AIR; artsinrockland.com) publishes a widely available downtown map of the two dozen galleries hosting **First Friday Receptions** (5–8) during the seasonal **Art Walks**. Galleries include the oldest (since 1982) and prestigious **Caldbeck Gallery** (caldbeck.com), at 12 Elm St.; goldsmith Thomas O'Donovan's **Harbor Square Gallery** (harborsquaregallery.com), filling three floors of a former bank building (374 Main St.) with art but also featuring fine jewelry. The **Dowling Walsh Gallery** (dowlingwalsh.com) is another highlight. Others to check: **Art Space Gallery** (207-594-8784; artspacemaine.com), 342 Main St. Also check out **Playing with Fire! Glassworks and Gallery** (playingwithfireglassworks.com), 497 Main St.

Archipelago Fine Arts (thearchipelago.net) at the Island Institute (386 Main St.) represents roughly 300 artists and craftspeople on "hinged" as well as real islands. Changing exhibits. The **Island Institute** (207-594-9209; islandinstitute.org) is a nonprofit organization focusing on the human dimension of Maine's 15 surviving year-round island communities (a century ago there were 300). The monthly *Working Waterfront* newspaper, as well as the glossy *Island Journal*, focus on shared concerns ranging from fisheries to schools to mapping.

The Museum Store at the Farnsworth Art Museum (207-596-5789; shop.farnsworthmuseum.org) is itself a standout trove of quality gifts including jewelry, books, and toys as well as art books, cards, and prints.

SPECIAL SHOPS

ALONG MAIN ST. IN ROCKLAND

Hello Hello Books (207-593-7780; hellohello books.com), No. 316. In the rear of the Rock City Café but with its own side-street entrance. Open daily except Tue. Lacy Simons offers a wide but obviously selective stock of used and new books. The **Black Parrot** (207-594-0138; No. 328) specializes in its colorful fleece-lined reversible garments but carries a mix of clothing, toys, cards, and more. **The Grasshopper Shop** (207-596-6156; No. 400) is a major link in a small Maine chain featuring clothing and a widely eclectic and colorful inventory. **Fiore Artisan Olive Oils and Vinegars** (207-596-0276; No. 503) is all about extra-virgin unfiltered olive oils and aged balsamic vinegars from the world over; sample them in the tasting room.

SOUTH FROM THE JUNCTION OF RTS. 1 AND 73, WHICH BEGINS AT THE SOUTHERN END OF MAIN ST., ROCKLAND

Rock City Coffee Roasters (207-594-5688; rockcitycoffee.com), 252 Main St. Roasted on the spot, the source of this widely distributed brew.

✪ **Trillium Soaps** (207-593-9019; trillium soaps.com), 216 S. Main St. A find for all of us with dry skin. Using organic olive oil, Peter and Nancy Digirolamo make small batches on the spot in some two dozen varieties, like rosemary-lime, clove, and bay rum. Also moisturizing bath soap including palm and coconut. Reasonably priced.

✪ **Jess's Market** (207-593-5068; jess market.com), 118 S. Main St. This is definitely the place in Rockland to buy lobster and a wide variety of very fresh fish, clams, mussels, oysters, and crab. Also the best takeout crab rolls.

Breakwater Vineyards (207-594-1721; breakwatervineyards.com), 35 Ash Point Dr., Owls Head (turn off Rt. 73 onto North Shore Dr.). Open Memorial Day–Columbus Day weekends, Wed.–Sun. noon–5. This 32-acre estate, with expansive views across the harbor and bay to the Camden Hills, has some 3,000 vines of hardy vinifera grapes. Bill and Jean Johnson presently offer oaked and unoaked Chardonnays, a dry Riesling, a Pinot Noir, and a blueberry wine.

Art of the Sea Galleries (207-594-9396; artofthesea.com), 5 Spruce Head Rd. (Rt. 73), displays nearly 100 museum-quality, full-rigged ship models; also half models and hundreds of nautical paintings and prints.

ALONG RT. 131 TO PORT CLYDE

Check out **St. George Pottery** (4.5 miles south of Rt. 1), George Pearlman's combination studio and contemporary ceramics gallery. **Noble Clay** (529 Port Clyde Rd.) in Tenants Harbor, open year-round, displays Trish and Steve Barnes's white-and-blue-glazed porcelain pottery with whimsical and botanical designs. **Mars Hall Gallery** (marshallgallery .net), 621 Port Clyde Rd., Tenants Harbor, is well worth a stop. **Ocean House Gallery** (207-372-6930; oceanhousegallery.com), end of Port Clyde Rd., is a seasonal gallery in the inn. **The Store Upstairs** over the Port Clyde General Store is worth a look: kitchenware and gadgets, oilcloth, children's books and toys, gifts.

IN THOMASTON

Maine State Prison Showroom (207-354-9237), 358 Main St. (Rt. 1), Thomaston, at the south end of town. Open daily 9–5. A variety of wooden furniture—coffee tables, stools, lamps, and trays—and small souvenirs, all carved by inmates. Prices are reasonable, and profits go to the craftsmen.

Oyster River Winegrowers (207-354-7177; oysterriverwinegrowers.com). The Tasting Room, 12 Oyster River Rd. (Rt. 131 north), Thomaston, is open May–Halloween, usually noon–6. Brian Smith is an experienced vintner who is just beginning to harvest his own vines. In the meantime he's souring Merlot grapes from the Finger Lakes and Petite Syrah from California.

IN UNION

Savage Oaks Vineyard & Winery (207-785-2828; savageoaks.com), 174 Barrett Hill Rd. (north of the junction of Rts. 17 and 131). Tasting room open Mother's Day–Oct., then weekends until Christmas, 11–5. Elmer (Buddy) and Holly Savage have been growing grapes on their 95-acre farm for a decade. A variety of red and white wines are available for sampling, along with three blueberry wines made from their 15 acres of wild blueberries.

Sweetgrass Farm Winery & Distillery (207-785-3024; sweetgrasswinery.com), 347 Carroll Rd., marked from Rt. 17 west of Union village. Tasting room open daily Mother's Day through Dec., 11–5. Keith and Constance Bodine produce fruit wines and highly respected spirits using Maine-grown apples, cranberries, blueberries, and rhubarb. Best sellers and prize winners are many: We love Back River gin and the apple brandy. The property also includes the **Carroll Farm Trail**, part of the Medomak Valley Land Trust; visitors are welcome to hike, snowshoe, and ski.

✳ Special Events

June: **Summer Solstice Night**, a Main Street Rockland street fair.

July: **Thomaston Fourth of July** festivities include a big parade, footraces, live entertainment, a crafts fair, BBQ, and fireworks. The **North Atlantic Blues Festival** (midmonth), Harbor Park, Rockland (northatlanticbluesfestival.com) is huge. **Maine Windjammer Parade of Sail** (midmonth), Rockland Harbor. **Friendship Sloop Days** (last weekend) includes a regatta and festivities in Rockland and a parade, BBQ, and children's activities in Friendship.

August: **Maine Lobster Festival** (first weekend, plus the preceding Wed. and Thu.), Harbor Park, Rockland (mainelobsterfestival .com). This is probably the world's biggest lobster feed, prepared in the world's largest lobster boiler. Patrons queue up on the public landing to heap their plates with lobsters, clams, corn, and all the fixings. King Neptune and the Maine Sea Goddess reign over the event, which includes a parade down Main Street, concerts, an art exhibit, and more. **Maine Boats, Homes & Harbor Show** (midmonth), Harbor Park, Rockland. **Union Fair and State of Maine Wild Blueberry Festival** (third week; unionfair.org)—a real agricultural fair with tractor- and ox-pulling contests, livestock and food shows, a midway, and the crowning of the Blueberry Queen.

November–December: **Rockland Festival of Lights** begins on Thanksgiving—parade, Santa's Village, sleigh rides.

MIDCOAST ISLANDS

Monhegan; The Fox Islands: Vinalhaven and North Haven; Matinicus

Monhegan

This island is endless and wonderful in its variety. It's possessed of enough beauty to supply a continent.
—Artist George Bellows, on first seeing Monhegan

Eleven miles at sea and barely a mile square, Monhegan is a microcosm of Maine landscapes, from 160-foot sheer headlands to pine woods, from wildflower-filled inland meadows to the smooth, low rocks along Lobster Cove. "Backed like a whale" is the way one mariner in 1590 described the island's shape: headlands sloping down to the small off-island of Manana, a blip on Monhegan's silhouette.

Monhegan is known for the quality and quantity of its artists and the grit of its lobstermen, who fish October through June. The island's first recorded artist arrived in 1858, and by the 1870s a hotel and several boardinghouses were filled with summer guests, many of them artists. In 1903 Robert Henri, a founder of New York's Ashcan School and a well-known art teacher, discovered Monhegan and soon introduced it to his students, among them George Bellows and Rockwell Kent. The island remains a genuine art colony. Jamie Wyeth owns a house built by Rockwell Kent, and Rockwell Kent passed his studio on to James Fitzgerald. More than 20 artists regularly open their studios to visitors.

The island continues to draw artists in good part because its beauty not only survives but also remains accessible. Prospect Hill, the only attempted development, foundered around 1900. It was Theodore Edison, son of the inventor, who amassed property enough to erase its traces and keep the island's cedar-shingled cottages (which still number around 130) bunched along the sheltered harbor, the rest preserved as common space and laced with footpaths.

In 1954 Edison helped organize Monhegan Associates, a nonprofit corporation dedicated to preserving the "natural, wild beauty" of the island. Ironically, this was one of the country's few communities to shun electricity until relatively recently. A number of homes and one inn still use kerosene lamps. Vehicles are limited to a few trucks for those with businesses and golf carts for those with medical needs. Visitors come to walk, to paint, to bird, and to relax.

Captain John Smith is said to have discovered the island in 1614, a quadricentennial celebrated in 2014. Native American

THE FITZGERALD STUDIO IS OPEN TO VISITORS

THE VILLAGE ON MONHEGAN

artifacts on display in the Monhegan Museum may date back as far as 8,000 years. The island's present settlement has been continuous since 1790; it's been a "plantation" since 1839. The year round population of less than 50 swells in summer to a little more than 600, not counting roughly 100 seasonal employees, 300 overnight guests, and up to 300 day-trippers. At this writing the number of working lobstermen is down to eight, and there are three children in the white-clapboard school.

Monhegan has three inns, a B&B, several nightly rental units, and a limited number of weekly rental cottages. Fog and a frequently rough passage insulate it to some degree, but on summer days a high tide of day-trippers from Boothbay Harbor and New Harbor, as well as Port Clyde, washes over this small, fragile island. More worrisome still are skyrocketing real estate prices. Monhegan Island Sustainable Community Association (MISCA) is now dedicated to ensuring affordable housing for year-round residents.

GUIDANCE *A Visitor's Guide to Monhegan Island, Maine*, a free 10-page leaflet, comes with every boat ticket to the island in the hope that visitors will read about the dangers and rules as well as the obvious beauty of the cliff-side trails on the island's backside. The *Monhegan Associates Trail Map*, also available on the boats, is well worth $1 (see *Hiking*), and the free Studio Locations sheet (see the chapter intro) is also handy if you want to meet resident artists. Also check **monheganwelcome.com**, **monhegan.com**, and **monhegan associates.org**.

GETTING THERE **Monhegan Boat Line** (207-372-8848; monheganboat.com) operates both the sleek *Elizabeth Ann* and the beloved old *Laura B* from Port Clyde; reservations a must. Service is three times daily in-season, less frequent in spring and fall, and only Mon., Wed., and Fri. in winter. It's a 50- or 70-minute trip, depending on which boat you catch. Mid-May–Columbus Day weekend **Hardy Boat Cruises** (1-800-278-3346; hardyboat.com) offers a 50-minute run from New Harbor with two daily roundtrips early June–Sept. **The Ocean House** in Port Clyde and the **Gosnold Arms** in New Harbor are within walking distance of these two services, taking the sting out of making morning boats. The *Balmy Days II* (1-800-298-2284; balmydayscruises.com) also offers seasonal roundtrips from Boothbay.

EQUIPMENT AND RULES Come properly shod for the precipitous paths. Hikers should wear long pants and socks against poison ivy; bring sweaters and windbreakers. Wading or swimming anywhere but Swim Beach (on the harbor) can be lethal. During one of our visits a young man was washed away by a rogue wave. Kayaking is also dangerous. Flashlights are a must for overnight visitors. Hiking boots and rain gear are also good ideas. Public phones are few; cell phone reception has improved, thanks to an tower that now dwarfs the lighthouse. Smoking is prohibited beyond the village. So is camping. Do not bring bicycles. Dogs must be leashed at all times. And *please* don't pick the flowers.

PUBLIC RESTROOMS The two public pay toilets are on a lane behind the Monhegan House.

GETTING AROUND Several trucks meet each boat as it arrives and provide baggage service. Otherwise visitors have no access to motorized transport.

WHEN TO COME The spring migration season brings birds and birders. June can be rainy and foggy—but also glorious and always flowery, with wild strawberries to be found along hiking paths. July and August are prime time, but September is best for hiking; birds and birders return.

✳ To See

Monhegan Island Light, built of granite in 1850 and automated in 1959, caps a hill that's well worth climbing for the view alone. The **Monhegan Historical & Cultural Museum** (207-596-7003; monheganmuseum.org) is a real gem. In July and Aug. it's open daily 11:30–3:30; in late June and all Sept. it's 1:30–3:30. $5 per adult. A spellbinding display of island art, including prints by George Bellows and Rockwell Kent, and annual special exhibits in the neighboring gallery. Flora, fauna, some geology, lobstering, and island history are interpreted through artifacts, including documents dating back to the 16th century. The neighboring **Art Gallery** houses annually changing exhibits.

The **Kent-Fitzgerald-Hubert House**, Horn's Hill. Open seasonally, Tue. and Sat. 1–3. Built by Rockwell Kent, it later served as a home and studio for James Fitzgerald (1899–1971), one of the most distinctive and prominent artists for whom Monhegan has been a home and inspiration.

Monhegan Memorial Library (207-596-0549), 1 Main St. Open May–Oct. A welcoming shingled cottage walled with books. There's a large children's section, and visitors can borrow books. Note special events.

✳ To Do

ART WALKS **Open studios**. In contrast to the once-a-month art walks popular in many communities, on Monhegan more than 20 resident artists welcome visitors to their studios on most summer days. Pick up the ubiquitous map/guide and schedule, or look for shingles hung outside houses, listing the hours they're open. Don Stone is the current dean of Monhegan painters, and his studio on the way to Burnt Head is open by chance or appointment. Stop by the **Lupine Gallery** (see *Selective Shopping*) to spot work by resident artists you may fancy. Everywhere you see artists at work and soon your own fingers may begin itching. Check out weeklong **Monhegan Island Workshops** (calebstoneart.com) in June and Sept. Don't miss the great paintings in the island's museums (see *To See*).

BIRDING Positioned in the middle of the Atlantic flyway, Monhegan is one of the best birding places on the East Coast. Your local Audubon Society may have a trip going in May or mid- through late Sept.

HIKING Pick up a current Monhegan Associates Trail Map before setting out on the island's network. Day-trippers are advised to take the **Burnt Head Trail** (No. 4) and loop back to the village via the **Whitehead Trail** (No. 7), descending by the lighthouse, or vice versa. This way you get a sense of the high bluffs and the unusual rocks in Gull Cove. Beyond this well-trod loop, trails are marked with few guideposts. It's easy to get turned around in **Cathedral Woods** (justly famed and known for its "fairy houses"), which, along with **Pulpit Rock**, should be reserved for an unhurried day. The path along the southern outer tip of the island, from Burnt Head to Christmas Cove, is ledgy and unsuitable for children and shaky hikers. The relatively flat trail from the village to **Lobster Cove** at the southern tip of the island is a favorite and has recently been improved. It can, however, be the muddiest and slipperiest of all after rains. Be sure to bring a flashlight if you are setting out toward evening, just in case you get lost—the fate of our brother-in-law, who wandered around all through the night.

✳ Lodging

ALL LISTINGS ARE ON MONHEGAN ISLAND 04852

Note: Lodging is limited but remarkably varied.

INNS ✪ **Island Inn** (207-596-0371; islandinn monhegan.com). Open Memorial Day–Columbus Day weekend. This shingled, cupola-topped, gabled, classic 1907 summer hotel with a long, rocker-lined veranda is steps from the ferry dock and overlooks the boat-filled harbor and Manana Island. The public rooms are a winning mix of old-fashioned and chic, with a comfortable living room and book-stocked side porches. The nicely decorated dining room has the harbor view (see *Dining Out*). The 28 rooms and four suites are divided between the main inn and Pierce Cottage (with remodeled suites) behind it. Eight rooms still share baths. In high season (July–Labor Day), from $170 per couple (shared bath, meadow view) to $420 for the top suite. Otherwise $130–295, depending on room and week. $10 charge for one-night stays. Children under 5 are free. All rates include a full breakfast, served buffet-style, usually featuring lobster scramble.

⌀ **Monhegan House** (207-594-7983; monheganhouse.com), P.O. Box 345. Open Memorial Day–early Oct. Holden and Susan Nelson have revived Monhegan's oldest continuously operating summer hotel, adding two suites with bath and a deck. This is the island's oldest inn and set in the middle of the village. The 28 rooms are on four floors. No closets, and most baths and showers (plentiful and immaculate) are in a wing off the middle of the second floor. For couples and families we recommend the third floor; for singles the bargain-priced fourth-floor rooms have the best views (coveted by artists). The downstairs lobby is hung with art, warmed by a gas fireplace, and equipped with books and games. Children are welcome and free under age 3. A full breakfast is included in the rates ($99–189 in high season, $193–224 for suites; $88–149 in low). Head in for breakfast before 8 AM, because it's open to the public and very popular. Dinner is also excellent (see *Dining Out*).

✪ 🍴 🐾 ⌀ ((ŷ)) **The Trailing Yew** (207-596-6194; trailingyew.com). Open mid-May–mid-Oct. This quirky institution has a loyal following among artists and writers (ourselves included). New England's last genuine 19th-century-style "summer boardinghouse," it's the place for the many solo travelers drawn to Monhegan. Now owned by the Chioffi family and friends, the inn's 33 rooms are more comfortable but still lit with kerosene lamps, divided among the main house and adjacent annexes and cottages on the grounds and The Mooring Chain (good only for groups) up the road. With the exception

Christina Tree

THE TRAILING YEW

of The Cabin, baths are shared and have electricity (guests are asked to charge electronic devices in the office). In shoulder seasons it's advisable to bring a sleeping bag. Dining is at 6:30; guests gather beforehand in Adirondack chairs on the porch and lawn, again around shared tables, and the conversation is usually lively (BYOB). Dinner is open to the public: $32 for four courses, tax and gratuity included. $140 per person solo, $240 double includes breakfast and dinner; sliding scale for ages 2–12. $10 pet fee. No credit cards.

B&BS ✪ 🐾 Shining Sails (207-596-0041; shiningsails.com), P.O. Box 346. Open year-round. Lobsterman John Murdock and his wife, Winnie, offer two rooms and five exceptional apartments in their welcoming village home overlooking the water. All five waterview units have a deck, the better to savor the sunset and stars. All rooms are tastefully decorated, featuring original island art. On foggy days a woodstove warms the living room, where an ample continental breakfast is served daily, May–Columbus Day. The Murdocks are helpful hosts and this place is so justly popular; it's advisable to book far in advance for July and Aug., but there are always some openings. $150–220 per night with breakfast, $110–165 off-season. Four apartments are also for rent at the Inn at Fish & Maine.

GUESTHOUSES AND DAILY RENTALS
Hitchcock House (207-594-8137; hitchcock house.com), Horn's Hill. Hidden away on Horn's Hill with a delightful garden and a large, sheltered deck, which serves as common space for guests. In the house itself Barbara Hitchcock offers two appealing housekeeping units, both with decks with views down across the meadows to the village and water. There are also two upstairs guest rooms, each with a small fridge and a hot pot, sharing one bath; a "cabin" in the garden has a full kitchen, living room, and bath. July–Labor Day weekend efficiencies are $125 per night, $815 per week; rooms are $90 per night, $555 per week, less off-season.

Tribler Cottage (207-594-2445; tribler cottage.com). Open mid-May–mid-Oct. On the edge of the meadow, at the base of Lighthouse Hill, this remains in the same family that has been welcoming visitors since the 1920s. Richard Farrell offers two housekeeping apartments. Hillside apartment has a sundeck and living room with fireplace; both apartments have a gas heater. $140–160 per couple per night based on three-night stay; $945–1,085 weekly.

WEEKLY RENTALS Cooking facilities come in handy here: You can buy lobster, good fresh and smoked fish, and a limited line of vegetables (bring meat and staples). **Shining Sails Cottage Rental** (207-596-0041; shiningsails.com) manages more than two dozen rental cottages, available by the week. **Brackett Rentals** (207-594-9151; brackettrentals.com) offers upward of 20 units. Also check with Maryann Body (207-596-0175). It's wise to get in your bid in early for the summer.

✳ Where to Eat

Note: Restaurants are BYOB, but wine is readily available in island stores.

DINING OUT The Island Inn (207-596-0371). Open to the public Memorial Day–Columbus Day for breakfast and dinner, also for lunch July 4–Labor Day. This classic, turn-of-the-20th-century dining room has contemporary decor and water views. The breakfast frequently features lobster casserole. Reserve a table overlooking the water for dinner. We can vouch for pan-seared scallops on a bed of mixed greens and tangy Maine crabcakes with the house herb and chive aioli. Entrées $19–34.

Monhegan House Open nightly late June–Labor Day, then weekends. The attractive, many-windowed dining room at the back of the inn overlooks the village and meadow. Breakfasts feature house-made breads and omelets. The dinner menu changes nightly and always includes a vegetarian option; it might offer a house-made onion and lavender sausage, haddock en papillote, honey-brined chicken, or cumin-scented scallops. Entrées $22–27.

EATING OUT ✪ The **Fish House Market**, Fish Beach. Open daily. The seasonal source of the freshest of seafood for anyone with cooking facilities. Better yet, anyone can enjoy Damariscotta oysters, steamed clams, the island's best crab and lobster rolls, and daily specials to eat at picnic tables on Fish Beach with the island's best view of the sun setting behind Manana Island (BYOB).

The Barnacle. Sited beside the ferry wharf and owned by the Island Inn, the Barnacle offers limited seating on the deck and inside. Sandwiches, soups, and pastries; also espresso and prepared sandwiches. Wine and beer sold.

The Novelty, behind Monhegan House. Pizza, soups and sandwiches, quiche, salads, and hot wraps. Freshly made cookies are great hiking fuel as you set off up Horn's Hill. Hand-dipped ice cream and frozen yogurt hit the spot on the way down. Wine, beer, splits of champagne. Outside shaded seating.

Black Duck Emporium. Open Memorial Day–Columbus Day in the former general store. Sited at the center of the village, next to the post office, this is the current island gathering place, good for snacks and pastry as well as coffee, tea, etc.

✳ Entertainment

Check the Rope Shed or monhegan.com for frequent evening concerts, jams, art lectures, and poetry readings in venues such as the schoolhouse, church, and library.

✳ Selective Shopping

The Lupine Gallery (207-594-8131; lupinegallerymonhegan.com), 48 Main St. Open early May–Columbus Day, 11–4:30. Bill Boynton and Jackie Bogel offer original works by 100 artists who paint regularly on the island. This is a very special gallery, showcasing the work of many professional artists within walking distance. Sited just uphill from the ferry dock, it's a good place to judge which studios you want to visit. Great cards, prints, and art books, also artists' supplies and framing.

Black Duck Emporium. Open Memorial Day–Columbus Day. This longtime island gift store has expanded to fill the former general store, offering cappuccino and pastries as well as imaginative T-shirts, books, kitchenware, pottery, and jewelry.

Winterworks. Open more or less daily Memorial Day–Columbus Day, by the ferry dock. A former fish house is now the island co-op, filled with work produced by the island's craftspeople: good quality knitted goods, jewelry, and Christmas decorations.

Monhegan Brewing Co. (monheganbrewing.com). Open May to Oct., with small-batch handcrafted beers, two IPAs and a Lobster Cove APA, with two sodas, perhaps—ginger beer and root beer are also sold.

Nancy English

FISH BEACH

The Fox Islands: Vinalhaven and North Haven

The Fox Islands Thorofare, a rowable stretch of yacht-filled water, separates Vinalhaven and North Haven, two islands of more than a dozen out in Penobscot Bay. The two differ deeply, even geologically. It's said that they were once oceans apart. Frequent Maine State Ferry service links both islands to Rockland but no ferry stops at both.

Maine's largest off-shore island, Vinalhaven is the size of Manhattan but home to less than 1,200 residents (Maine's largest year-round island community) plus an equal number of widely scattered summer people. Life eddies around the village of Carver's Harbor at the island's southern end. Vinalhaven was once a world-known source of granite, and two former quarries are now swimming holes. There are also wildflower-filled moors, wooded coastal paths, and sheltered paddling places.

There is, however, no yacht club or golf course, and yachtsmen will be hard-put to find a guest mooring among the fishing boats in Carver's Harbor, home to one of the world's largest lobstering fleets. In recent years three 1.5-megawatt wind turbines have been installed on the north side of Vinalhaven, capable of generating all the electricity needed for both islands.

North Haven is half as big, with just 355 year-round residents, some 1,500 in summer. Founded well over a century ago by Boston yachtsmen, its summer colony includes some of the country's wealthiest and most influential families. The former general store by the ferry dock is now Waterman's Community Center, with a 140-seat state-of-the-art theater, the venue for summer lectures, concerts, and plays.

The village of North Haven offers gift shops and galleries, seasonal restaurants, and gracious year-round lodging and dining. Beyond the village a 10-mile loop beckons bicyclists through rolling, open fields, spotted with buttercups and idyllic farmhouses, most of them summer homes. Sheltered Pulpit Harbor is a favorite mooring for windjammers and yachtsmen. There's also a public golf club and a private yacht club, the North Haven Casino, home to the island's distinctive dinghies.

GUIDANCE Town offices on **North Haven** (207-867-4433) and **Vinalhaven** (207-863-4471) field most questions. The Vinalhaven Chamber site is vinalhaven.org. On-island, pick up a free copy of *The Wind*, the island's newsletter. For North Haven check northhavenmaine.org.

GETTING THERE **Maine State Ferry Service** (in Rockland: 207-596-5400). The islands are serviced by different ferries; from Rockland it's a 75-minute ride. Day-trippers never have a problem walking on; the bike fee is nominal. Each ferry takes a set number of cars, and only a handful of these spaces can be reserved; otherwise, cars are taken in order of their position in line. For the morning boats, it's wise to be in line the night before. It doesn't make sense to bring a car unless you plan to stay awhile.

Note: **Concord Coach Lines** (concordcoachlines.com) stops daily at the Rockland Ferry Terminal.

Penobscot Island Air (207-596-7500; penobscotislandair.net) will fly you in from Portland or Boston as well as Rockland to either Vinalhaven or North Haven.

GETTING AROUND *By boat:* Shuttle service between North Haven and Vinalhaven is possible through **J. O. Brown & Sons Boatyard** (207-867-4621) in North Haven. Try calling from the phone on the boat landing on the Vinalhaven side of the Thorofare. On Vinalhaven the **Tidewater Motel** rents cars. Also see *Bicycling*.

Note: Day-trippers to North Haven will find shopping and food within steps of the ferry dock, but on Vinalhaven it's 0.4 mile from the ferry to the village and another mile or so to the quarries and Lanes Island Nature Preserve. A bike comes in handy.

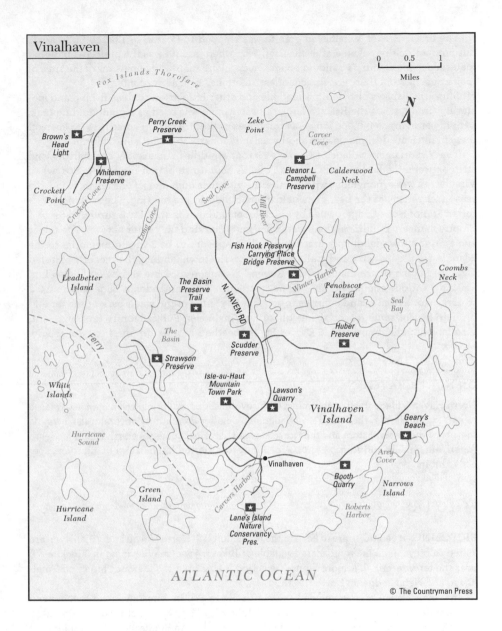

Vinalhaven

0   0.5   1
Miles

Fox Islands Thorofare

Brown's Head Light

Perry Creek Preserve

Zeke Point

Carver Cove

Whitemore Preserve

Crockett Point

Crockett Cove

Seal Cove

Mill River

Eleanor L. Campbell Preserve

Calderwood Neck

Long Cove

Fish Hook Preserve, Carrying Place Bridge Preserve

Coombs Neck

Leadbetter Island

The Basin Preserve Trail

N. HAVEN RD.

Winter Harbor

Penobscot Island

Seal Bay

Ferry

The Basin

Scudder Preserve

Huber Preserve

White Islands

Strawson Preserve

Isle-au-Haut Mountain Town Park

Lawson's Quarry

Vinalhaven Island

Geary's Beach

Hurricane Sound

Green Island

Vinalhaven

Booth Quarry

Arey Cove

Narrows Island

Carters Harbor

Roberts Harbor

Hurricane Island

Lane's Island Nature Conservancy Pres.

ATLANTIC OCEAN

© The Countryman Press

WHEN TO COME Only June–Aug. can you count on all visitor-geared facilities being open on both these islands. September, however, is beautiful.

✳ To See

The Vinalhaven Historical Society Museum (207-863-4410; vinalhavenhistoricalsociety .org), 41 High St. Open daily 11–4, mid-June–mid-Sept. Within walking distance of the ferry, worth the uphill climb. An outstanding community museum housed in the former church, built in 1838 in Rockland and floated over on a barge in 1878. It has also served as a theater and skating rink. Displays feature the island's granite industry.

The first order for Vinalhaven granite was shipped to Boston in 1826 to build a jail, but production skyrocketed after the Civil War, when granite was the preferred building material for the country's building boom. On an island map, 40 red pins mark the sites of major quarries, but there are also countless "motions," or backyard pits.

Museum displays also depict island life and other industries, such as fishing and lobstering (in the 1880s the Basin, a large saltwater inlet, was used as a giant holding tank, penning as many as 150,000 lobsters until prices peaked). Knitting horse nets (to keep off flies) in intricate designs was yet another island industry that's now an art form.

The Victorian-era village of Carver's Harbor straddles a causeway and narrow land strip between the harbor and Carver's Pond. A boomtown dating from the 1880s, when Vinalhaven was synonymous with granite, the village is built almost entirely of wood, the reason why many of the best of its golden-era buildings are missing. The strikingly Victorian Star of Hope Lodge, owned by artist Robert Indiana, is one of two surviving Second Empire mansard buildings (there were once four) marking the center of town. The 6-foot eagle on the town landing is limestone. Still, it appears to be a fitting memorial to the island's granite industry and craftsmen. Also on the town landing, the recently restored Old Fire Engine House displays "Old Ruben," a vintage-1888 fire truck. You'll also find amazing antique equipment and public restrooms. A Galamander, a huge wagon used to carry stone from island quarries to schooners, stands in the small park at the far end of Main St. For some reason the neighboring Vinalhaven Public Library (207-863-4401; vinalhavenpubliclibrary.org), 6 Carver St., is sheathed in pink granite from Jonesboro, Maine.

ON NORTH HAVEN

North Haven Village itself is charming, with several shops, galleries, and a choice of places to eat. Pulpit Harbor, the island's second, much smaller community several miles away, is the site of the general store and the North Haven Historical Society's North Island Museum (open Sun. in July and Aug., 2–4:30). A general store, period kitchen and living room, special exhibits.

✳ To Do

BICYCLING If you take care to keep to the roadside, both North Haven and Vinalhaven are suited to bicycling. Bike rentals are available at Bikesenjava (see *Bicycling* in "Rockland") near the ferry terminal. A more limited selection is available at Tidewater Motel on Vinalhaven and Nebo Lodge on North Haven.

In North Haven we recommend the North Shore Rd. In Vinalhaven we recommend the Granite Island Rd. out along the Basin or following Main St. the other direction out to Geary's Beach (see *Green Space*). The North Haven Rd. is an 8-mile slog up the middle of Vinalhaven, but the rewards are great: Browns Head Light, the Perry Creek Preserve, and views of North Haven.

GOLF **North Haven Golf Club** (207-867-2054), open June–Sept. A waterside course, nine holes.

SEA KAYAKING **Tidewater Motel** in Carver's Harbor, Vinalhaven, rents kayaks and will transport you to put-ins like the Basin, a long tidal inlet that's great for spotting seals.

SWIMMING On Vinalhaven, ✪ **Lawson's Quarry**. From the middle of Carver's Harbor, turn (uphill) at the Bank Building and continue up and up High St., past the historical society, and then turn right on North Haven Rd. for 0.5 mile. For Booth Quarry begin at the east (uphill) end of Main St., 1.5 miles past the Union Church (E. Main St.).

✳ Green Space

ON VINALHAVEN

The **Vinalhaven Land Trust** (207-863-2543; vinalhavenlandtrust.org) maintains 17 preserves mapped on its website and in handouts available at 12 Skoog Park near the ferry dock. Our favorites include: Lane's Island Preserve, a 15-minute walk from town, 40 acres of fields, marsh, moor, and beach with trails along the beach and up into the meadows facing open ocean; Grimes Park, beside the ferry terminal, a 2-acre point of rocky land with two small beaches; and Geary's Beach—explore the trails, lunch at the picnic tables, and enjoy a view of Isle au Haut and Matinicus.

Christina Tree

SWIMMING AT LAWSON'S QUARRY

Christina Tree

LANE'S ISLAND PRESERVE

✳ Lodging

ON VINALHAVEN 04863

♻ 🏠 ✂ 📶 **Tidewater Motel and Gathering Place** (207-863-4618; tidewatermotel.com), 15 Main St., Carver's Harbor. Open except Jan.–Feb. "I don't want to leave this room," we wrote about Room 16, an aerie with a deck overlooking a harbor full of lobster boats, all turned into the wind like gulls. Phil and Elaine Crossman's waterside motel spans a tidal stream connecting the harbor with Carver's Pond. The water swooshing under rooms once powered a gristmill, granite-polishing mill, and blacksmith shop. The 19 units come in varied sizes and shapes, including suites and efficiencies, one fit for reunions or a small conference. Rooms have harbor-side decks and all have a microwave, coffeemaker, small fridge, full bath, and small TV. The Crossmans also loan bikes and rent kayaks, meet the ferry, and help guests around the island. All the town's eating options are within steps.

Elaine Crossman is a noted artist, and Phil is the island chronicler. His genuinely funny book of essays, *Away Happens*, captures island life. $185–210 for rooms, from $100 off-season. $8 for each additional person over two; kids 10 and under are free, and families with more than one older kid are only charged for one; morning coffee, juice, and muffins are included. Inquire about Millstream Cottage.

🏠 **Libby House** (207-863-4696; libby house1869.com), Water St. Open June–Sept. This proud home was built in 1869 by T. E. Libby, namesake of an island ferry (he was responsible for bringing the Maine State Ferry Service to Vinalhaven). It's on the edge of the village, on the way to Lane's Island Preserve. Guests share the long sunporch with its rocking chairs and upright piano, as well as a living room with a fireplace and access to the dining room and kitchen fridge. The four guest rooms (private baths) are furnished with comfortable antiques. There's also a downstairs two-bedroom apartment with a full kitchen. Longtime host Philip Roberts asks guests to remove their shoes on entering.

Christina Tree

VIEW FROM THE TIDEWATER MOTEL

$110–140 for rooms, $160 for the apartment. Pets accepted Sept.–June.

ON NORTH HAVEN 04853

✪ ❀ ✎ ♿ (ᵖ) **Nebo Lodge** (207-867-2007; nebolodge.com), 11 Mullins Lane, P.O. Box 358. Open May–Oct. Built handsomely in 1912 as an inn but privatized in 1956, reopened in 2006 by a dedicated local group of women who included now U.S. Representative Chellie Pingree and her daughter Hannah. Their goal was to preserve it both as a place for residents to dine together and as an island entrée for visitors. The inn building offers eight crisp guest rooms, four with shared bath, many with tufted wool rugs, throw pillows, and linens by nationally known designer and island native Angela Adams. Two third-floor rooms are the brightest and most attractive, both with private bath. The sitting room is delightful, with a rosy Angela Adams rug. There's a strong commitment here to all things green and local. The dining room with its working fireplace is justly busy (see *Dining Out*). Your cell phone may not work, but there is wireless Internet. All rooms have a small fridge. Bikes are available, and the innkeeper can arrange a boat trip. High season (July–Columbus Day) $150–$275. There is a wheelchair-accessible garden unit with kitchenette in a neighboring house. Rates include a continental breakfast. Pets are accepted on a case-by-case basis; cleaning fee. Check the website for frequent special events.

COTTAGE RENTALS Davidson Realty (207-863-2200; maineislandliving.com) specializes in summer rentals. High-season weekly vacation rentals range from $700 for a village house to $4,000 for a summer mansion overlooking the Fox Islands Thorofare. Also check vinalhaven.org.

✳ Where to Eat

ON VINALHAVEN

Salt (207-863-4444), 64 Min St. Open Thu.–Sun. for dinner, Sun. brunch, Fri.–Sat. off-season. A limited menu focused on local

NEBO LODGE, NORTH HAVEN

seafood and Maine-raised meat, house-made specialties from pâté to pastries.

The Haven (207-863-4969), 49 Main St. Open June–Jan. Tory Pratt is the island's favorite caterer and the back, harbor-side dining room (reservations recommended) offers superb seafood dishes, also pasta and steak. Entrées $17–25.

✎ **The Harbor Gawker** (207-863-9365), Main St., middle of the village. Open mid-Apr.–mid-Nov., Mon.–Sat. 11–8. Lobster rolls, crabmeat rolls, and baskets of just about anything. Owned by the Morton family since 1975, this is a great, casual spot with views of the millrace and Carver's Pond. Order at the counter: from-scratch soups and chowders, seafood baskets, and blueberry pies, along with ice cream and a dairy bar. It's a big menu, from hot dogs through salads and wraps to quesadillas and lobster dinners.

Surfside (207-863-2767), Harbor Wharf, W. Main St. Donna Webster opens at 4 AM for the lobstermen and is open for lunch and dinner, but check. A great harbor-side breakfast spot with tables on the deck and specials like a crabmeat or lobster omelet, or a tomato herb cheese omelet with fish cakes.

Greet's Eats (207-863-2057), West Main St. near the ferry dock. Greta McCarthy's food truck gets raves for lobster rolls and burgers.

ON NORTH HAVEN

Nebo Lodge (207-867-2007; nebolodge.com), 11 Mullins Lane, North Haven Village. Open

July and Aug., Mon.–Sat.; Fri. and Sat. in May, June, and Sept.–mid-Oct. Reserve. This is a very special inn (see *Lodging*) right in the village with a menu that changes nightly. Chef Amanda Hallowell is committed to using as much locally grown produce as possible. A "first taste" might be fried green tomatoes with chive dressing or the house-made pickle plate with locally produced chèvre and rye bread. On a June evening we dined on roast organic duck, raised at Turner Farm, with rhubarb crème brûlée and cardamom-ginger ice cream. The à la carte menu ranges from $8 for an appetizer to $38 for Lobster Bohemienne and includes "light suppers" like hand-ground burger and house-made pizza. The full bar offers classic cocktails as well as island originals like the "Oystertini." Free transport across the Thorofare is offered to patrons coming from Vinalhaven. Inquire about roundtrip "dinner cruises" from Rockland Harbor.

Cooper's Landing (207-867-2060). Open July and Aug. for lunch and dinner; check in June and Sept. Mickey Campbell runs this handy little restaurant, which offers seating inside and out at the summer heart of the village. Burgers, veggie options, lobster and crab rolls, fish cakes, chowder and salads, wine and beer. The low-cal chocolate shake, made from unsweetened chocolate and hemp milk, comes highly recommended.

❋ Entertainment

Waterman's Community Center (207-867-2100; watermans.org), North Haven Village. This exceptional center right at the ferry dock includes a theater, the venue for frequent productions, concerts, and presentations. Check the calendar for contra dance, workshops, and children's activities. Open daily year-round 7–4 for coffee, tea, muffins, sodas, and bagels in an airy, nonprofit community center with couches, tables, board games, and newspapers.

Smith Hokanson Memorial Hall at Vinalhaven High School (207-863-4800) in Carver's Harbor is the stage for lectures, theater, and a variety of community activities.

❋ Selective Shopping

IN CARVER'S HARBOR ON VINALHAVEN

❧ **The Paper Store** (207-863-4826) is the nerve center of the island, the place everyone drops by at least once a day. This is also the place to check for current happenings like plays and concerts, and to get a chart of the island.

New Era Gallery (207-863-9351; neweragallery.com), Main St. Open Memorial Day–Dec. Painter and printmaker Elaine Austin Crossman's gallery shows work by some of Maine's most prominent painters, sculptors, photographers, and fiber artists. Note the widely celebrated three-dimensional traditional knotted netting sculptures by Stephanie Crossman; also check out the sculpture garden and special exhibits.

❧ **Go Fish** (207-863-4193), Main St. Open seasonally, Tue.–Sat. 10–4:30. A great kids-geared shop with books, healthy toys, games, penny candy, original island T-shirts, and much more.

Five Elements Gallery & Studio (207-863-2262), 50 Main St. Original jewelry in dichroic glass, worth a look.

Second Hand Prose, Main St. Open Mon.–Sat. 9–4:30. Run by Friends of the Library and featuring secondhand books. Good selection of Maine and maritime titles.

IN NORTH HAVEN VILLAGE

North Haven Gift Shop and Gallery (207-867-4444). Open Memorial Day–mid-Sept. (but closed Sun.), 9:30–5. Since 1954 June Hopkins (mother of Eric) has run this shop with rooms that meander on and on, filled with pottery, books, accessories, jewelry, and much more, including bags by the island's famous young designer, Angela Adams. Gallery exhibits change frequently. Hopkins keeps running accounts for summer families and knows the names of members of as many as six generations of a family when they walk in.

Hopkins Wharf Gallery (207-867-4647). Open July and Aug. 10–5; by appointment in spring and fall. Owned by David Hopkins (brother of Eric) and David Wilson, this is a contemporary gallery featuring work by island-related artists. It's also a source for works by longtime North Haven summer resident Frank Benson.

✳ Special Events

Year-round: **North Haven Arts Enrichment Presentations** include exceptional plays, concerts, and lectures performed in Waterman's Community Center in North Haven Village at the ferry landing. For details, phone 207-867-2100; watermans.org.

Summer season: **Concerts**, primarily classical, chamber, and jazz, are staged on both islands, sponsored by Fox Islands Concerts.

July 4: **Parade** in Vinalhaven.

July–August: **Saturday Farmers' Market** at the ball field, North Haven Village, features crafts as well as produce. **Saturday Flea Market**, 10 AM in the field next to the Galamander, Carver's Harbor, Vinalhaven. **Union Church Baked Bean Supper** (every other Thu. in

FOURTH OF JULY PARADE, VINALHAVEN

Christina Tree

summer), Vinalhaven. Check vinalhaven landtrust.org for the schedule of frequent morning walks and evening talks.

For details about other regular occurrences on both islands, consult *The Wind*, a weekly newsletter published on Vinalhaven.

Matinicus

Home to some 30 hardy souls in winter, most of whom make their living lobstering, Matinicus's population grows to about 200 in summer. Maine's outermost island, it lies 23 miles at sea beyond the outer edge of Penobscot Bay. Quiet and unspoiled, it's a haven for birds, with some 650 species identified. Walking trails thread the meadows and shore, and there are two sand beaches—one at each end of the 750-acre island. Matinicus Rock is offshore, a protected nesting site for puffins, a lure for birders in June and July. Matinicus and neighboring Ragged Island (better known as Criehaven, the name of its seasonal village) are the setting for Elizabeth Ogilvie's trilogy: *High Tide at Noon, Storm Tide,* and *Ebb Tide.*

GETTING THERE The flying time via **Penobscot Island Air** (207-596-7500) from Owls Head is 15 minutes, but flights may be canceled because of weather—and the fog can hang in there for days. That's when you contact matinicusexcursions.com; it's an hour's ride. Inquire about puffin-watching trips. The **Maine State Ferry** (207-596-2022) takes 2¼ hours to ply between Matinicus and Rockland, four times a month May–Oct., and once a month the rest of the year. At this time there is no overnight lodging, but check for rentals.

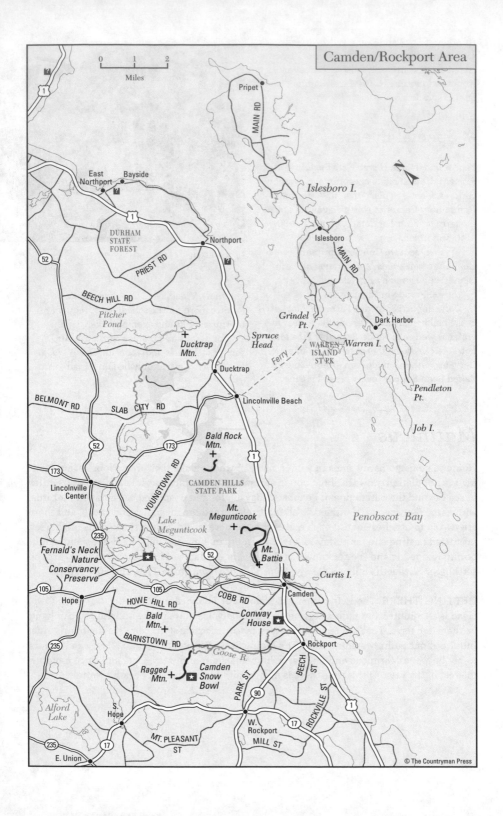

0 1 2
Miles

Pripet

MAIN RD

East
Northport   Bayside

Islesboro I.

Northport

DURHAM
STATE
FOREST

PRIEST RD

Islesboro

MAIN RD

BEECH HILL RD

*Pitcher
Pond*

*Ducktrap
Mtn.*

*Spruce
Head*

*Grindel
Pt.*

Dark Harbor

BELMONT RD   SLAB CITY RD

Ducktrap

Ferry

WARREN
ISLAND
ST PK

Warren I.

*Pendleton
Pt.*

Lincolnville Beach

*Bald Rock
Mtn.*

Job I.

YOUNGTOWN RD

173

CAMDEN HILLS
STATE PARK

Lincolnville
Center

*Mt.
Megunticook*

Penobscot Bay

235

*Lake
Megunticook*

*Mt.
Battie*

Fernald's Neck
Nature
Conservancy
Preserve

Curtis I.

Hope

HOWE HILL RD

COBB RD

Camden

Conway
House

*Bald
Mtn.*

BARNSTOWN RD

Goose R.

Rockport

235

*Ragged
Mtn.*

Camden
Snow
Bowl

PARK ST

BEECH ST

ROCKVILLE ST

*Alford
Lake*

S.
Hope

90

W.
Rockport

17

MT. PLEASANT
ST

MILL ST

E. Union

© The Countryman Press

Smack on Rt. 1, Camden is the most popular way station between Kennebunkport or Boothbay Harbor and Bar Harbor. Seemingly half its 19th-century captains' homes are now B&Bs. Shops and restaurants line a photogenic harbor filled with private sailing and motor yachts. It's also a poor man's yacht haven—open year-round—with a thriving fishing industry. The ski area would make a good winter vacation destination as well as a summer tour.

Here, in 1936, artist Frank Swift refitted a few former fishing and cargo schooners to carry passengers around the islands in Penobscot Bay. He called the boats windjammers. Half a dozen members of Maine's current windjammer fleet are still based here (the rest are in neighboring ports), and several schooners offer daysails. You can also get out on the water in an excursion boat or a sea kayak.

From the water you can see two aspects of Camden not apparent from land. The first is the size and extent of the Camden Hills. The second is the size and number of the palatial old waterside "cottages" along Beauchamp Point, the rocky promontory separating Camden from Rockport. Here, as in Bar Harbor, summer residents were wise and powerful enough to preserve the local mountains, seeding the creation of the present 6,500-acre Camden Hills State Park, one of Maine's more spectacular places to hike.

Camden's first resort era coincided with those colorful decades during which steam and sail overlapped. As a stop on the Boston–Bangor steamboat line, Camden acquired a couple of big (now vanished) hotels. In 1900, when Bean's boatyard launched the world's first six-masted schooner, onlookers crowded the ornate neighboring steamboat wharf to watch.

In contrast with Boothbay and Bar Harbor, Camden has always been a year-round town and never overdependent on tourism. Camden's early business was, of course, building and sailing ships. By the mid-1800s half a dozen mills lined the series of falls on the Megunticook River, just a block or two from the waterfront. The vast wooden Knox Woolen Company—the "Harrington Mill" portrayed in the movie *Peyton Place*—made the felts used by Maine's paper mills to absorb water from paper stock. It operated until 1988, and now holds a hodgepodge of restaurants, businesses, and homes.

Culturally enriched by its sophisticated populace—workaday residents, retired diplo-

Nancy English

LUGGAGE AWAITS DEPARTURE TIME ON THE WHARF IN CAMDEN HARBOR

mats, military and intelligence officers, and summer people alike—Camden (along with Rock-port) offers a bonanza of music, art, and theatrical productions, all of surprising quality. There are also world-renowned programs in filmmaking, computer science, woodworking, and photography.

Ironically, only a small fraction of the thousands of tourists who stream through Camden every summer takes the time to discover the extent of its beauty. The tourist tide eddies around the harborside restaurants, shops, and galleries and continues to flow on up Rt. 1 toward Bar Harbor. Even in August you are likely to find yourself alone atop Mount Battie (accessible by car as well as on foot) or Mount Megunticook (highest point in the Camden Hills), or in the open-sided Vesper Hill Children's Chapel, with its flowers and sea view. Few visitors see, let alone swim in, Megunticook Lake or set foot on the nearby island of Islesboro.

A decade or two ago you could count on your fingers the number of places to stay here, but Camden has since become synonymous with B&Bs. A total of some 1,000 rooms can now be found in hotels, motels, inns, and cottages as well as the B&Bs between Camden and neighboring Lincolnville and Rockport.

GUIDANCE **Penobscot Bay Regional Chamber of Commerce** (207-596-0376 or 1-800-562-2529; mainedreamvacation.com), 2 Public Landing (and also at its home base, 1 Park Dr., Rockland). Open daily Memorial Day–Labor Day, Mon.–Fri. 9–5 and Sat. 10–4; then weekdays and 10–2 Sat. through the Columbus Day weekend. The chamber's visitors centers serve the Rockland and Camden area, which includes Owls Head, Thomaston, the peninsula villages, and the islands.

GETTING THERE *By air:* **Knox County Regional Airport**, at Owls Head, about 10 miles from Camden, offers daily flights to and from Boston. **Bangor International Airport** and **Portland International Jetport** offer connections to all parts of the country.

Nancy English

CAMDEN HARBOR

By bus: **Concord Coach Lines** (1-800-639-3317; concordcoachlines.com) stops on Rt. 1 at the Maritime Farms, just south of Camden, en route from Bangor to Portland and Boston and vice versa.

By limo: **Mid-Coast Limo** (207-236-2424 or 1-800-937-2424; midcoastlimo.com) makes runs from Portland International Jetport by reservation. **Schooner Bay Limo** (207-594-5000; schoonerbaytaxi.com) goes to Portland and elsewhere.

By car: Our preferred route, to bypass Rt. 1 traffic, is to take I-295 to Gardiner, then follow signs to Rt. 226. When this road ends, take a right onto Rt. 17, which winds through pretty countryside to Rt. 90, and then intersects with Rt. 1 leading into Camden.

PARKING is a problem in July and August. In-town parking has a stringently enforced two-hour limit (just 15 minutes in a few spots, so be sure to read the signs). There is parking just a two- to five-minute walk away; the chamber recommends parking on Chestnut St., Union St., Mechanic St., and Washington St. The chamber has a map that highlights all-day parking areas.

WHEN TO COME Camden and Rockport are open year-round with a thriving fishing industry; the ski area makes this area a good winter destination as well as a summer tour. But for sailing and swimming, summer is the time to come, and fall foliage contrasts beautifully with the blue water.

✲ Villages

Rockport's harbor is as picturesque as Camden's, and the small village is set high above it. Its quiet, subdued charm provides a nice respite from the hustle of Rt. 1. Steps (you have to look closely for them) lead down to Marine Park, a departure point in 1816 for 300 casks of lime shipped to Washington, DC, to help construct the Capitol. In the small park you'll see the restored remains of a triple kiln, a saddleback steam locomotive, and a granite sculpture of André the Seal, the legendary performer who drew crowds every summer in the early and mid-1980s. The village (part of Camden until 1891) includes the restored Rockport Opera House, site of Bay Chamber Concerts, the Maine Media Workshops program, and restaurants and shops.

Lincolnville's landmarks—the Lobster Pound Restaurant, Maine State Ferry to Islesboro, and the Whale's Tooth Pub, formerly a customhouse with a big fireplace—serve as centerpieces for proliferating shops, restaurants, and B&Bs. The beach offers a nice swimming spot on hot days.

✲ To See

LIGHTHOUSE Curtis Island Light. A public park, the island is nevertheless accessible only by boat, and the lighthouse is not open to the public. The best views are from sightseeing cruises out of Camden Harbor, but if you walk down to where Bayview St. connects with Beacon, there's a good lookout.

MUSEUMS ✐ ♿ **Old Conway Homestead and Cramer Museum** (207-236-2257; conway house.org), Conway Rd. (off Rt. 1 at the Camden–Rockport town line). Open July and Aug., Wed.–Sat. 1–4; admission charged. Open June and Sept. by appointment. Administered by the Camden-Rockport Historical Society, this restored early-18th-century farmhouse features antiques from several periods. The barn holds collections of carriages, sleighs, and

EXCURSIONS

Drive or, better yet, bicycle around **Beauchamp Point**. Begin on Chestnut St. in Camden and follow this peaceful road by the lily pond and on by the herd of **belted Galloway cows** (black on both ends and white in the middle). Take Calderwood Lane through the woods and by the **Vesper Hill Children's Chapel**, built on the site of a former hotel and banked with flowers, a great spot to get married or simply to sit. Continue along Beauchamp Ave. to Rockport Village to lunch or picnic by the harbor, and return via Union St. to Camden.

early farm tools; don't miss the Victorian privy, blacksmith shop, and 1820 maple sugar house, where sugaring demonstrations are held each spring. **The Cramer Museum** displays local memorabilia and changing exhibits.

Schoolhouse Museum (207-789-5445), Rt. 173, Lincolnville Beach. Open Mon., Wed., and Fri. 1–4, June–Oct., other times by appointment. Admission is free. A small museum detailing the history of Lincolnville, with exhibits that change often and include stereoptics and tintypes, early settlers' tools, and Native American artifacts. The museum also publishes *Ducktrap: Chronicles of a Maine Village*, an excellent book on local history, and *Staying Put in Lincolnville, Maine*, both by local author Diane O'Brien.

OTHER SITES **Cellardoor Vineyard** (207-763-4478; mainewine.com), 367 Youngtown Rd., Lincolnville, 11–6 daily, May–Oct., and **Cellardoor Winery at the Villa** (207-236-2654), aka The Yellow House, Rt. 1 (at Rt. 90), Rockport; noon–5 daily in winter, 11–6 Apr.–Oct. Vines in this 7-acre Lincolnville vineyard were completely removed in 2008 and 2009. Some were dead and others didn't produce the best wines, according to Bettina Doulton, who purchased the business in 2007. New grape varietals planted, better suited to the climate, include Seyval Blanc, Frontenac Gris, and Marquette. To supplement the crop, the business buys grapes from the West Coast to make, for instance, its excellent Viognier.

✳ To Do

BICYCLING ☙ **Camden Hills State Park**, Rt. 1, Camden, has a 10-mile (roundtrip) ride through the woods on a snowmobile trail. Bikes are not allowed on hiking trails. The **Camden Snow Bowl** also offers a number of rides through woods and swamps, as well as riding on ski trails. It's a hearty ride, but the views from the top are terrific.

☙ **Georges River Bikeways**. The Georges River Land Trust (207-594-5166) puts out a pamphlet highlighting several good biking routes, with many scenic spots within the Georges River watershed.

Maine Sport Outfitters (207-236-7120 or 1-800-722-0826; mainesport.com), Rt. 1, Rockport, rents Raleigh hybrids as well as bike trailers and car racks for a day or extended periods. Rentals include helmets, locks, water bottles, and cable. **Map Adventures** (1-800-891-1534; mapadventures.com) makes a very readable small map of bike routes and trails in the Camden Hills, stocked here.

BOATING See also Windjammers.

Yacht charters are offered spring to autumn along the Maine coast. Most charters run for a week, although sometimes it's possible to charter a boat just for a long weekend, with or without crew. For more information, contact **Johanson Boatworks** (207-596-7060 or 1-877-4-JOHANS), which rents everything from J-40 sloops to Ericson 38s. **Rockport**

Charters (207-691-1066; rockportcharters.com) offers, with advance notice, 20-passenger, three-hour wildlife charters to see puffins, eagles, ospreys, and more. Leaving from both Camden and Rockland, as well as Rockport, Captain Robert Iserbyt also provides transportation for workers out to North Haven.

It would be a shame to be in Camden and not spend some time on the water. The two-hour sailing excursions are a wonderful way to get a taste of what the harbor has to offer if your time is limited. Remember to bring a jacket, because the air can get chilly once you're offshore, even on a sunny day. Wander down the wooden boardwalk and check the offerings, which include:

& **Schooner Appledore II** (207-236-8353; appledore2.com), an 86-foot schooner (the largest of the daysailing fleet), has sailed around the world and now offers several trips daily, including sunset cruises. Licensed bar.

Schooner Surprise (207-236-4687; camdenmainesailing.com), a traditional, historic, 57-foot schooner, offers entertaining, informative two-hour sails. Captain Jack and wife Barbara Moore spent seven years cruising between Maine and the Caribbean, educating their four children on board in the process.

Schooner Olad (207-236-2323; maineschooners.com), a 57-foot schooner, offers two-hour sails and charters.

Schooner Heron (207-236-8605 or 1-800-599-8605; woodenboatco.com), runs lobster lunch, midafternoon, and evening sails (BYOB, with hors d'oeuvres served) out of Rockport for a maximum of 36 passengers. With typically eight to 20 passengers on the regular sails, this 65-foot schooner, built in 2003 in Camden by its owners, is available for private trips.

& **Betselma** (207-236-4446), a motor launch, provides one-hour coastal and two-hour island trips (owner Les Bex was a longtime windjammer captain) out of the harbor and down the coast.

& **Lively Lady Too** (207-236-6672 or 418-839-7933; livelyladytoo.com), a traditional lobster boat, takes passengers on two-hour ecotours that can include watching lobster traps being hauled and swinging in close to an island for bird-watching. A monitor shows video of the ocean floor.

Schooner Lazy Jack II (207-230-0602). Two-hour sails and private charters from Camden Harbor with Captain Sean O'Connor.

& **Maine State Ferry** from Lincolnville Beach to Islesboro (207-734-6935). At $10 roundtrip per passenger, $27.50 per vehicle, and $8.50 per bicycle, this is the bargain of the local boating scene. An extra $12 each way secures your reservation. (See Getting There under "Islesboro.")

BOWLING **Oakland Park Bowling Lanes** (207-594-7525), 714 Commercial St., Rockport. Susan and Joe Plaskas have updated this old-fashioned bowling alley with refinished lanes, air-conditioning, and tile flooring, retaining the 1950s decor. Video games and air hockey too.

GOLF **Goose River Golf Club** (207-236-8488; gooseriver.com), Simonton Rd., Rockport. Nine holes, but you can play through twice using different starting tees. Cart rentals; clubhouse. Tee times recommended any time of the week; you can request up to a week in advance.

& **Golfers Crossing Miniature Golf** (207-230-0090). Water hazards and obstacles complete this mini golf experience on Rt. 1 in Rockport.

Samoset Resort Golf Course (clubhouse, 207-594-1431), Rockport, has an 18-hole, par-70 course with seven oceanside holes and ocean views from 14 holes. A renovation includes a redesigned 18th hole featuring a stone seawall, a remodeled 185-yard, par-three 5th hole, and renovations to hole 4. The clubhouse has a pro shop, locker rooms, and the **Clubhouse Grille**. Carts are available.

HIKING **Bald Rock Mountain**. This 1,100-foot mountain in Lincolnville once had a ski area at the top. Great views of Penobscot Bay and the Camden Hills. You'll find the trailhead 1.25 miles down a dirt road from the gate on Ski Lodge Rd. (off Youngtown Rd.). The climb is about 0.5 mile long and moderate. Ask about overnight camping at the Camden Hills State Park headquarters on Rt. 1 in Camden.

Georges Highland Path is a 40-mile trail network created and maintained by the Georges River Land Trust (207-594-5166; grlt.org). Trails wind through the Oyster River Bog, a magnificent semi-wilderness area with a 7.2-mile trail that links the Thomaston Town Forest with the Ragged Mountain section. A map put out by the trust details distances and hiking times and shows where the trailheads are.

Coastal Mountain Hiking (207-236-7731), Camden, offers guided hikes and packed lunches.

See also **Beech Hill** and **Camden Hills State Park** in *Green Space*.

SEA KAYAKING **Ducktrap Sea Kayak Tours** (207-236-8608; ducktrapkayak.com), Lincolnville Beach, offers two-hour and half-day guided tours in Penobscot Bay. Most patrons are first-time kayakers. Group and family tours, rentals, and lessons.

Maine Sport Outfitters (207-236-8797 or 1-800-722-0826; mainesport.com), on Rt. 1 just south of Rockport, offers courses in kayaking, guided excursions around Camden Harbor and out into Penobscot Bay, and island-based workshops. They also rent kayaks and canoes (also see *Special Learning Programs*).

SPECIAL LEARNING PROGRAMS *🏄* **Camden Yacht Club Sailing Program** (207-236-4575; off-season, 207-236-7033), Bayview St., Camden, provides sailing classes for children and adults, boat owners and non-boat owners, during late June, July, and Aug.

📷 **Maine Media Workshops College** (207-236-8581; mainemedia.edu), 70 Camden St., Rockport. This nationally respected year-round school for photography, cinematography, television production, and related fields offers a choice of 200 programs that vary in length from one week to three months for every skill level. The faculty includes established, recognized professionals from across the country; the students come from around the world. Housing is provided for most of the students, and the school helps arrange accommodations for others. Also a gallery with changing exhibitions, open to the public.

The Center for Maine Contemporary Art (207-236-2875; cmcanow.org; see *Entertainment* and *Selective Shopping*), 11 Lime St., and reopening in 2016 at 21 Winter St., Rockland (formerly Maine Coast Artists). Exhibits and professional development for artists, including workshops.

Maine Sport Outfitters (207-236-8797; mainesport.com), Rockport. This Rt. 1 complex is worth a stop whether you're up for adventure sports or not. The place has evolved from a fly-fishing and canvas shop into a multitiered store that's a home base for a wide variety of local kayaking tours and multiday kayaking workshops geared to all levels of ability, based at facilities on Gay Island.

Center for Furniture Craftsmanship (207-594-5611; woodschool.com), 25 Mill St., Rockport. June–Oct. Hands-on one- and two-week workshops for novice, intermediate, and advanced woodworkers and cabinetmakers. Twelve-week intensive courses are also offered three times a year. A nine-month comprehensive course runs from Sept. to June.

SWIMMING *🏊* Saltwater swimming from Camden's **Laite Memorial Park and Beach**, Upper Bayview St.; at **Lincolnville Beach**, Rt. 1 north of Camden; and in Rockport at **Walker Park**, across the road from Marine Park. Freshwater swimming at **Megunticook Lake**, Lincolnville (**Barret Cove Memorial Park and Beach**; turn left off Rt. 52 northwest of Camden), where you'll also find picnic grounds and a parking area; **Shirttail Beach**, Camden (Rt. 105); and at the **Willis Hodson Park** on the Megunticook River, Camden (Molyneaux Rd.). At the **Penobscot Bay YMCA** (207-236-3375), Union St., visitors can pay a day-use fee that entitles them to swim in the Olympic-sized pool (check hours for family swimming, lap swimming, and other programs); use the weight rooms, rock climbing gym and sauna; and play basketball in the gym.

TENNIS There are two public tennis courts at the **Camden Snow Bowl** on Hosmer Pond Rd. (first come, first served). In addition, **Samoset Resort** (207-593-1545), Rockport, has outdoor courts, as does the **Rockport Recreation Park** (207-236-9648).

WALKING **The Camden-Rockport Historical Society** (207-236-2257) has prepared a brochure (available at the chamber of commerce and the Cramer Museum) with a 2.5-mile walk past historic buildings. The brochure includes historical details and a sketch map. An expanded bicycle or car tour encompassing two towns is also included.

WINDJAMMERS ⚓ Windjammer cruises are offered late May–mid-Oct. Nine traditional tall ships sail from Camden, Rockport, and Rockland on three- to six-day cruises throughout Penobscot Bay. For brochures and sailing schedules, contact the **Maine Windjammer Association** (1-800-807-WIND; sailmainecoast.com).

Angelique (1-800-282-9989; sailangelique.com), Camden, is a 95-foot ketch that was built expressly for the windjammer trade in 1980. Patterned after 19th-century English fishing vessels, she offers 15 passenger cabins, a pleasant deck-level salon with piano, belowdecks showers, and rowboats for exploring the coast.

Lewis R. French (1-800-469-4635; schoonerfrench.com), Camden, was launched on the Damariscotta River in 1871 and is the oldest documented vessel in America's windjammer fleet. Before becoming a passenger vessel, the French carried cargo such as lumber, firewood, bricks, granite, lime—even Christmas trees—along the coast. She had three major rebuilds, the most recent in 1976 when she was brought into passenger service. Sixty-five feet long, the *French* accommodates 21 passengers in 13 private cabins with freshwater sinks and portholes that open. Hot, freshwater shower on board. Captain Garth Wells enjoys getting his guests actively involved in the experience of sailing an authentic 19th-century schooner.

Mary Day (1-800-992-2218; schoonermaryday.com), Camden, was the first schooner built specifically for carrying passengers. At 90 feet, she's among the swiftest; Captains Barry King and Jen Martin have extensive sailing experience. Features include a fireplace and parlor organ and hot, freshwater showers on the deck. The *Mary Day* accommodates up to 28 passengers, and meals include a New England boiled dinner, baked goods made in the galley's woodstove, and a lobster bake on every cruise.

Grace Bailey, Mercantile, **and** *Mistress* (207-236-2938 or 1-800-736-7981; mainewind jammercruises.com), Maine Windjammer Cruises, Camden. For years known as the *Mattie, Grace Bailey* took back her original name following a thorough restoration in 1990. Built in 1882 in New York, the 81-foot *Grace Bailey* once carried cargo along the Atlantic coast and to the West Indies. She has belowdecks showers. *Mercantile* was built in Maine in 1916 as a shallow-draft coasting schooner; 78 feet long, she has been in the windjammer trade since its beginning in 1942. There are belowdecks showers. *Mistress*, the smallest of the fleet at 46 feet, carries just six passengers. A topsail schooner built in 1960 along the lines of the old coasting schooners, she is also available for private charter. All three cabins have private heads, but there is no shower on board.

WINDJAMMER *GRACE BAILEY*

✳ Winter Sports

CROSS-COUNTRY SKIING **Camden Hills State Park** (207-236-3109) marks and maintains some trails for cross-country skiing, and there's a ski hut on Mount Battie (see *Green Space*).

Tanglewood 4-H Camp (207-789-5868 or 1-877-944-2267), 1 Tanglewood Rd., off Rt. 1 near Lincolnville Beach. Ungroomed, scenic cross-country trails that wend through woodlands and along streams. Maps with a description of trails are at the kiosk at the trailhead on the loop of the road.

DOWNHILL SKIING ✍ **Camden Snow Bowl** (207-236-3438; camdensnowbowl.com), Hosmer Pond Rd., Camden. With an 850-foot vertical drop, 11 trails for beginners through experts, a new chairlift and a new conveyor lift following a $6.5 million investment, Camden Snow Bowl has a base lodge, rental and repair shop, ski school, and cafeteria, plus the Jack Williams Toboggan Chute. In early February the Snow Bowl hosts the annual U.S. National Toboggan Championship Races at the toboggan chute with outlandishly costumed teams making mad runs down the chute at 40-plus miles an hour, bottoming out on the ice-covered Hosmer Pond. $39 full-day adult weekend pass, $29 students.

✳ Green Space

✍ ♿ **Camden Hills State Park** (207-236-3109; off-season, 207-236-0849), 280 Belfast Rd., Rt. 1, Camden. $4.50 nonresident adults, $3 Mainers, $1 ages 5–11; free under 5 and over 65 for residents, $1.50 nonresidents 65 and older. In addition to Mount Battie, this 6,500-acre park includes Mount Megunticook, one of the highest points on the Atlantic seaboard, and a shoreside picnic site. You can drive to the top of Mount Battie on the road that starts at the park entrance, just north of town. At the entrance pick up a Camden Hills State Park brochure, which outlines 19 trails with distance and difficulty level. In winter many of the trails convert to cross-country ski runs, given snow. There are 106 campsites available May 15–Oct. 14.

Warren Island State Park, also administered by Camden Hills State Park, is just a stone's throw off the island of Islesboro. The park features picnic tables, trails, and tent sites. Accessibility is the problem: You can arrange to have a private boat carry you over from the mainland, rent your own boat in Camden, or paddle out in a sea kayak. Because of this, the island boasts a peace and quiet often hard to find on the mainland in high season.

MERRYSPRING NATURE CENTER

Nancy English

Marine Park, off Russell Ave. (just after you cross the bridge), Rockport. A nicely landscaped waterside area with sheltered picnic tables. Restored lime kilns and a locomotive remind visitors of the era when the town's chief industry was processing and exporting lime. During a stroll you're likely to see several painters capturing the picturesque harbor on canvas.

Merryspring Nature Center (207-236-2239; merryspring.org), Camden. Open to the public year-round during daylight hours. A 66-acre private preserve with walking trails; herb, daylily, demonstration, and rose gardens; raised beds; and an arboretum. The Goose River borders the preserve, accessible via Conway Rd. from Rt. 1 in Camden. Birders frequent the gardens on the lookout for barred owls and warblers. If you're lucky you'll see white-tailed deer, ermine, porcupine, raccoon, rabbit, and even moose. Weekly talks in summer. Free to members, $5 for nonmembers.

Fernald's Neck Preserve (207-236-7091; coastalmountains.org). Owned by the Coastal Mountains Land Trust, located at the end of Fernald Neck Rd. off Rt. 52, past Youngtown Rd., Lincolnville and Camden. Open dawn until 7:30 PM, no pets allowed. The preserve's 326 acres cover most of a wooded peninsula that juts into Lake Megunticook. Signs showing walking trails are at the trailhead kiosk and trail intersections. Trails lead to stunning water views. Trails can be boggy: Wear boots or old shoes.

CAMDEN AMPHITHEATRE

Nancy English

Camden Harbor Park and Amphitheatre (207-236-3440), Atlantic Ave., Camden. The amphitheater, designed by Fletcher Steele in 1929, has been nominated as a National Historic Landmark; it's a magical setting for summertime concerts or weddings, and a good place to sit, think, or read anytime. Across the street Harbor Park covers a manicured slope down to the water, with the Megunticook River waterfall in its midst. Picnic on one of the benches overlooking Camden Harbor.

The Beech Hill Preserve (207-236-7091; coastalmountains.org), Beech Hill Rd., Rockport. The Coastal Mountains Land Trust cares for 295 acres on this hilltop preserve, bare of trees and the perfect place to drink in the intricate coastline of Midcoast Maine. More than 100 species of birds stop here at some point in the year, feasting on the organic blueberries that attract people, too—although access is limited to the annual free picking days. The berries are harvested and sold to support the preserve. A sod-roofed stone house at the top of the hill called Beech Nut is on the National Register of Historic Places. A trail map is available by download, or with a call to the land trust.

Curtis Island, in the outer harbor. A small island with a lighthouse that marks the entrance to Camden, this is a public picnic spot and a popular sea kayaking destination.

✱ Lodging

ALL LISTINGS ARE IN CAMDEN
04843 UNLESS OTHERWISE NOTED

Camden Accommodations (207-236-6090 or 1-800-344-4830; camdenac.com), 43 Elm St., is a vacation rental agency with more than 85 private properties in the Camden area.

Camden Bed & Breakfast Association (camdeninns.com), Camden. The brochure lists 13 members with descriptions of each and contact information.

RESORT ✒ ♿ **Samoset Resort** (207-594-2511 or 1-800-341-1650; samoset.com), 220 Warrenton St., Rockport 04856. Open year-round. The original Samoset lodge burned down in 1972; a renovation in 2011 brought this resort closest yet to its luxurious beginnings. Set on 230 oceanfront acres, the Samoset holds 178 rooms and suites, many with ocean views, balcony, or patio, all with private bath, TV, and air-conditioning; and four cottages, including the two-bedroom Flume Cottage perched on a rocky outcropping above the water. The Samoset has a world-class 18-hole golf course and golf pro shop, outdoor tennis courts, fitness center, spa, sauna, and indoor and heated, handicapped-accessible outdoor pools. Samoset takes wonderful care of families with young children with a children's program. The dining room, La Bella Vita (see *Dining Out*), and the adjacent Enoteca (see *Eating Out*) have floor-to-ceiling windows overlooking the water. Rooms $249–479, off-season $129–329.

INNS ♿ **Inn at Ocean's Edge** (207-236-0945; innatoceansedge.com), P.O. Box 258, Lincolnville 04849. Look for the entrance off Rt. 1 a couple of miles north of the Camden line. Open May–Oct. This modern hotel features a main inn with three common areas and 18 guest rooms; the Hilltop building with 12 rooms, each with a balcony, sits up the hill. Almost every room features a water view, and all have a Jacuzzi, gas fireplace, TV, VCR, stereo. The Spa building holds two luxury suites. Steps lead down to a private shingle beach. Breakfast might include Grand Marnier French toast. An elegant heated pool, spa with treatment rooms, sauna, and whirlpool are available to guests. $205–495 includes breakfast. Children 14 and up welcome.

Camden Harbour Inn (207-236-4200 or 1-800-236-4266; camdenharbourinn.com), 83 Bayview St. This luxury inn names its rooms for former Dutch ports and colonies, and each room's decor takes flight from the places evoked—like Java, with an orange-red headboard and green-gold pillows. Views of the harbor, some fireplaces, thick feather beds, TV/DVD, CD player, and much more. You can arrange a lobster picnic on the beach, too. Natalie's is the site of breakfast (included in rates of $225–1,090) and fine dining (see *Dining Out*).

✒ ♿ **Whitehall** (207-236-3391; whitehall maine.com), 52 High St. (Rt. 1). Open mid-May–Oct. This old inn has been spruced up by new corporate owners Lark Hotels, though the vintage-1904 Steinway looks much the way it did on the summer evening in 1912 when a young local woman, Edna St. Vincent Millay, read her poem "Renascence" to assembled guests. One of the guests, swept away by Millay's verse, paid for her Vassar education. Thirty-six guest rooms in the main inn and several two-bedroom suites have private bath, air-conditioning, and flat-screen TV; all come with an iPad for the visit stocked with local information. See *Dining Out* for The Pig and Poet restaurant. Rooms $159–509.

Hartstone Inn (207-236-4259 or 1-800-788-4823; hartstoneinn.com), 41 Elm St. Open year-round. Mary Jo and Michael Salmon

THE LOBBY OF WHITEHALL

and their innkeepers are in charge of three properties: the first building on Rt. 1, the Hideaway House, and the Manor House. Some of the 11 guest rooms and 12 suites (all with private bath) offer a fireplace and canopy bed. Dinner is served in the main inn (see *Dining Out*). In high season $125–285 double with full breakfast and afternoon tea and cookies; low season $105–185. Spa services offered. Guests can take a group cooking class between Nov. and May.

Cedarholm Garden Bay Inn (207-236-3886; cedarholm.com), Rt. 1, Lincolnville Beach 04849. The pleasures of privacy and setting make a stay extraordinary. Down a road set in the midst of the landscaped grounds are the four cottages, Osprey, Puffin, Tern, and Loon, each with fireplace, Jacuzzi, queen (or king) bed, wet bar with microwave oven, small fridge, and a fabulous view of the ocean from a private deck. Two upper cottages, closer to Rt. 1, have a private bath, wet bar, and mini fridge. Continental breakfast includes muffins baked with berries grown here, in-season. All guests have access to a shared deck right on the beach. Upper units begin at $175 per night; luxury cottages, $300–495 per night.

B&BS ✪ ♪ **The Hawthorn Inn** (207-236-8842; camdenhawthorn.com), 9 High St. (Rt. 1). Open year-round. Owners Ted and Lisa Weiss offer 10 guest rooms at this Victorian mansion. The inn is a short walk from Camden Village and its harbor. The luxury rooms in the Carriage House have a double Jacuzzi,

TV/DVD, fireplace, and private deck or patio. Breakfast could include blueberry walnut pancakes. A landscaped garden spreads out beyond the two-tiered deck and terrace, where breakfast is served in fine weather. Children are welcome; some rooms accommodate more than two people. $175–295 in high season.

The Camden Maine Stay (207-236-9636; camdenmainestay.com), 22 High St. (Rt. 1). Open year-round. Innkeepers Claudio and Roberta Latanza welcome guests to this 1802 Greek Revival house, one of the best known in Camden's High Street Historic District. Stay in one of four standard rooms and four suites with names like the Common Ground Room, which has a cathedral ceiling and private deck over the garden. The 2-acre property is embellished with impeccable gardens. Breakfast in the formal dining room or on the sunporch. Afternoon tea included. $155–270 double room rate, in-season; $120–260 off.

Norumbega (207-236-4646 or 1-877-363-4646; norumbegainn.com), 63 High St. (Rt. 1). Open year-round. With one of the most imposing facades of any B&B anywhere, this turreted stone "castle" has long been a landmark just north of Camden, and new

LIBRARY SUITE AT NORUMBEGA

DINING ROOM AT NORUMBEGA

with CD player. The Quarterdeck Room with skylights has its own entrance, fireplace, TV/DVD, library, sofa, Jacuzzi whirlpool tub, and separate shower. Ironed linens and feather beds make for blissful sleep. Breakfast, perhaps orange yogurt pancakes and sausage, is a choice of several dishes from a menu. $125–280 high season, $99–199 low.

A Little Dream (207-236-8742; littledream .com), 60 High St. (Rt. 1). Open year-round except March. Raised up on a hill over busy Rt. 1, this place feels wonderfully secluded, with seven guest rooms including a carriage house suite called the Isle Watch. Overlooking the harbor and Curtis Island, it has a gas fireplace, king canopy bed, soaking tub, and covered porch complete with porch swing. If you stay here or in Treetops July 4, you can view three separate fireworks displays from your rooms. $159–295 double includes breakfast, perhaps lemon ricotta pancakes. Foreign guests are always welcome: Innkeeper JoAnna Ball speaks Italian, German, and French. Her husband, Bill Fontana, is a sculptor.

🐾 ✈ **Inns at Blackberry Common** (207-236-6060 or 1-800-388-6000; blackberryinn .com), 82 Elm St. Open year-round. Cyndi and Jim Ostrowski's two buildings hold some of the prettiest interiors in town. Settees covered in silk damask, ornate Oriental rugs, and decorative swords set the style. Stay in the Bette Davis room, where the movie star slept after the cast party for *Peyton Place*, with a queen brass bed and antique lighting fixture. In-house dinners offered Nov.–June on Sat. nights. $129–249 in-season, $149–189 off, including a full breakfast served in the dining room or in the courtyard.

The Inn at Sunrise Point (207-236-7716 or 1-800-435-6278; sunrisepoint.com), Sunrise Point Rd., P.O. Box 1344. Open May–Oct. Set on a 4-acre waterfront estate just over the town line in Lincolnville, this small, luxurious B&B is now run by Daina Hill. Five cottages named for Maine painters and writers—among them Winslow Homer and Richard Russo—have an incredible view, fireplace, private deck, and Jacuzzi. The Wyeth Loft Suite offers king bed, gas fireplace, small deck, and TV/DVD; an attached bedroom can be rented. Count on fine linens on all the sumptuous beds. Three rooms and the loft are $300–445,

owners Phil Crispo, a CIA-trained chef, and Sue Walser have sunk their resources and energy into an extensive renovation to keep it that way. Inside you'll find an ornate staircase with fireplace and love seat on the landing, a formal parlor, and a dining room with a blue-tiled fireplace. Nine guest rooms and two suites named for European castles come with king or queen bed, private bath, antiques, and TV. Doubles $209–629, including full breakfast. The inn serves dinner to its guests and has a liquor license.

The Blue Harbor House (207-236-3196 or 1-800-248-3196; blueharborhouse.com), 67 Elm St. Open year-round. This friendly 11-room inn serves cocktails and hors d'oeuvres to guests (by reservation, starting at $10 per person); breakfast, included in the rates, is served on the spacious sunporch and might include quiche Florentine for a main course. Fresh Scottish shortbread was baking for the afternoon snack on our visit. Rooms are pleasantly decorated with handmade quilts; all have private bath, telephone, air-conditioning, and TV/VCR. The Captain's Quarters has a kitchenette. Doubles $95–205.

The Camden Windward House (207-236-9656 or 1-877-492-9656; windwardhouse .com), 6 High St. (Rt. 1). Open year-round. Kristen and Jesse Bifulco have added a cozy wine bar upstairs with a second-floor deck overlooking Mount Battie; they have been entertaining guests since 2005. The five guest rooms and three suites all have private bath, air-conditioning, cable TV, and clock-radio

cottages $330–595, full breakfast, perhaps poached eggs with asparagus and chive oil, included.

The Belmont (207-236-8053 or 1-800-238-8053; thebelmontinn.com), 6 Belmont St. Open mid-May–Oct. This inn, with a peaceful location a few blocks off Rt. 1, has been undergoing a renewal under the ownership of Anita Zeno. An 1890s Edwardian house with a wraparound veranda with a blue ceiling, the Belmont has six guest rooms with private bath and several with a gas fireplace. Full breakfast, afternoon tea always available. $199–289 per night in-season.

The Victorian by the Sea (207-236-3785 or 1-800-382-9817; victorianbythesea.com), Lincolnville Beach 04849. Open year-round. Jeanne and Rob Short own this 1889 shingle-style Victorian "cottage" overlooking the water, away from Rt. 1. Seven guest rooms each have a queen bed, private bath, and fireplace. The Victorian Suite, with a turret room, chaise lounge, and fireplace, overlooks Penobscot Bay. The $165–250 in-season rate includes full breakfast with, perhaps, blueberry buttermilk scones.

OTHER LODGING 🐚 🐾 *High Tide Inn* (207-236-3724 or 1-800-778-7068; hightideinn .com), Rt. 1. Open May–late Oct. Set far enough back from Rt. 1 to preclude traffic noise, this no-frills, easygoing complex appeals to singles and couples (who tend to choose one of the five rooms in the inn) and families (who often opt for a cottage, two-bedroom deck house, or motel unit, five with connecting sleeping rooms). Most of the very clean 31 rooms have breathtaking views—especially for the price. The complex fills 7 quiet acres of landscaped grounds that slope to the water and more than 250 feet of private ocean beach. Continental breakfast with just-baked popovers and muffins. Pets allowed in only four of the cottages. $89–195.

🐾 🐚 ♿ **Lord Camden Inn** (207-236-4325 or 1-800-336-4325; lordcamdeninn.com), 24 Main St. Open year-round. This inn is named for the British nobleman who championed the American cause in the House of Lords during the Revolutionary War. Occupying a restored 1893 brick Masonic hall, the 36 rooms offer cable TV, private bath, telephone, air-conditioning, and elevator. Most rooms

have two double beds and private balcony overlooking the town and harbor or the hills beyond. June–Nov., rates include a full breakfast with a make-your-own waffle stand; continental breakfast off-season. $99–289.

CAMPING 🐚 🏕 ♿ **Megunticook Campground by the Sea** (207-594-2428; megunticook campgrounds.com), 620 Commercial St., Rockport 04856. Open May 15–early or mid-Oct. Wooded, oceanfront campground with 100 sites and 10 rustic camping cabins. Facilities include a store, recreation hall, fishing, heated pool, and oceanfront picnic area and gardens for Sat.-night lobster bakes. $35–45 in-season. **Camden Hills RV Resort** (207-236-2498), 30 Applewood Rd. in Rockport, is a sister park.

✳ Where to Eat

DINING OUT ✪ **Francine Bistro** (207-230-0083; francinebistro.com), 55 Chestnut St., Camden. Open Tue.–Sat. 5:30–10; reservations recommended. Small, intimate, and sometimes noisy. Chef-owner Brian Hill has been earning high praise since 2003. Chewy, moist bread with a marvelous crust is one mark of excellence. The dry-aged steak has an astonishingly good flavor, as does the venison, and the seared line-caught Chatham cod is both moist and crisp. Count on Hill to seek out the best ingredients in Maine. Excellent wine list. Entrées $24–30.

Long Grain (207-236-9001), 31 Elm St. Reservations recommended. Customers extoll the crab fried rice, coconut soup with chicken or tofu, and the Thai beef salad, Nua Nam Tok, aromatic with lime; house noodles in organic farmers greens are simply fantastic. $9.20–15.

Natalie's (207-236-7008; camdenharbour inn.com), at the Camden Harbour Inn, 82 Bayview St., Camden. Open daily for dinner 5:30–9 and employing the coast's best seafood and farm products to make French-inspired meals—perhaps seared duck breast with turnip purée and black mission figs or halibut with crushed cauliflower and royal trumpet mushrooms. Fine wine list. Three-course prix fixe dinner $68; bar menu $18–35.

Fresh (207-236-7005; freshcamden.com), 1 Bay View Landing. For once, the server's recommendation of the crabcakes was founded in reality—they are excellent. Good wine, lobster risotto, fish-and-chips, burgers; sidewalk seating is delightful in good weather. $18–28.

✪ 🐾 ♿ **Chez Michel** (207-789-5600), Lincolnville Beach (across from the beach). Open Apr.–mid-Nov., dinner Tue.–Sun., lunch and dinner on Sun. This restaurant serves French food and has been winning repeat loyal customers since 1989. The mussels marinière with garlic, onion, and white wine is a great appetizer, and even better for dinner (with salad, potato, and French bread). New England-style fisherman's chowder with haddock, Maine shrimp, clams, and scallops, and steak au poivre are always good. Raspberry pie in-season inspires requests with reservations. Entrées run $17–24.

Pig + Poet (207-236-3391; whitehall maine.com), 52 High St. Chef Sam Talbot, a good-looking TV "personality," collaborated on a menu that includes grilled clams with nori butter and porchetta with egg and Poet hot sauce—in honor of Edna St. Vincent Millay, who in life and in her poetry burned the candle at both ends. A Sazerac or a Hemingway daiquiri could sustain the tradition. $15–32.

Hartstone Inn (207-236-4259 or 1-800-788-4823; hartstoneinn.com), 41 Elm St., Camden. Open year-round. The menu for the five-course, prix fixe dinner ($55) changes nightly—with only one available each night. Menus are on the website, so you can choose what you prefer, perhaps finding seared duck breast with sweet potatoes or grilled swordfish with pesto.

40 Paper (207-230-0111; 40Paper.com), 40 Washington St., has won praise for many of its more than 40 cocktails; carbonara made with bucatini and whatever local vegetables are in season may be starring on an ever-changing menu with an Italian focus.

EATING OUT

IN CAMDEN

The Drouthy Bear (207-542-7741; drouthy bear.com), 50 Elm St. A Scottish pub with Scotch eggs and kedgeree, bangers and mash, and ploughman's platter. Mushy peas on the side and a long list of good ale—for the drouthy among us, otherwise known as thirsty.

🐾 ♿ **Peter Ott's** (207-236-4032), 16 Bayview St. Open year-round for casual dinner, with a large menu that features grilled sirloin steak and salmon with maple chipotle glaze. Entrées are served with the salad bar unless you choose something lighter. $17–31.

🐾 ♿ **Camden Deli** (207-236-8343; camdendeli.com), 37 Main St. Open 7 AM–10 PM daily. Breakfast and more than 40 sandwich choices combining all the regular deli meats and cheeses as well as some less expected choices, like a pressed Cubano or a Monte Cristo, for lunch. The back dining room overlooks the waterfall in downtown Camden, and another dining room upstairs, with a deck open in summer, does, too.

🐾 ♿ **Camden Bagel Café** (207-236-2661), 25 Mechanic St. Open Mon.–Sat. 6:30 AM–2 PM, Sun. 7:30–2. Bagels with substance are baked here, some in whole wheat. The plain interior makes a good refuge as you enjoy a bagel with cream cheese or with an egg and bacon for breakfast. Soups and chili when things cool down.

🐾 ♿ **Cappy's Chowder House** (207-236-2254; cappyschowder.com), 1 Main St. Open year-round—for more than 30 years. Lunch and dinner daily in summer; closing some days in winter. Croissant sandwiches, burgers, and full meals for lunch; seafood entrées, pasta, and meat dishes for dinner.

🐾 ♿ **The Waterfront Restaurant** (207-236-3747; waterfrontcamden.com), Bayview St. Open for lunch and dinner; you can watch the activity in the harbor. Popular and with a well-trained staff, this place fills up fast and

Nancy English

PETER OTT'S WATERSIDE DINING

VIEW FROM THE BACK DECK OF CAMDEN DELI

doesn't take reservations. Dinners include a shore dinner (clam chowder, corn on the cob, steamers, mussels, and a lobster) and steaks. $18–24.

IN ROCKPORT

Shepherd's Pie (207-236-8500; shepherds pierockport.com), 18 Central St. A gastropub devised by Francine Bistro chef-owner Brian Hill that serves excellent food. Chefs Mark Senders and Patrick Duffy are in charge of the shepherd's pie made with lamb shanks braised with Madeira, served with buttermilk potato purée; a duck, smoked peanut butter, and hot pepper jelly sandwich was driving people wild recently. Seasonal tarte tatin. Entrées $13–22.

Sweet Sensations and 3 Dogs Café (207-230-0955; mainesweets.com; 3dogscafe.com), 309 Commercial St. (Rt. 1). Open daily and early in summer; shorter hours in winter. The café and bakery offer dinosaur cookies,

meringues, and much, much more. Lunch is soup, salad, and sandwiches—perhaps the Vinalhaven, a BLT with applewood-smoked bacon on organic whole wheat bread. Lunch $7–14.

Enoteca (207-593-1529), at Samoset Resort. Open daily for breakfast, dinner, and Sunday brunch, year-round. Brick oven–fired pizza and an Italian American menu, with a large fireplace indoors and an outdoor firepit on the terrace (open until mid-Sept.) and floor-to-ceiling windows overlooking the water.

TAKEOUT **The Market Basket** (207-236-4371), Rts. 1 and 90, Rockport. Open Mon.–Fri. 7–6:30, Sat. 8–6:30, Sun. 9–4. This specialty food store offers a wide variety of creative salads, French bread, soups, entrées, sandwich specials for takeout, more than 500 wines from around the world, and more than 75 varieties of cheese. Baked goods like double chocolate mini cakes are another reason to visit.

🦞 **Scott's Place** (207-236-8751), Elm St. (Renys parking lot), Camden. Open 10:30–4, Mon.–Sat. Since 1974 this tiny building in the parking lot of a small shopping center has served thousands of toasted crabmeat and lobster rolls, chicken sandwiches, burgers, veggie burgers, hot dogs, and chips. Prices are among the best around, and it's open year-round.

✳ Entertainment

Bay Chamber Concerts (207-236-2823; baychamberconcerts.org), 58 Bay View St., Suite 1, Camden 04843. This renowned organization has presented outstanding concerts since 1961. In July and August they sponsor Thu.-evening chamber music concerts in the Rockport Opera House with its gilded interior, and Wed.-evening concerts at the beautifully restored Strand in Rockland. The series celebrated its 50th year in 2010. Winter-season selections include classical and jazz music concerts and dance performances.

Camden Civic Theatre (207-236-2281; camdencivictheatre.com), Main St., Camden. A variety of theatrical performances are presented in the restored Camden Opera House, a second-floor theater with plum seats and

LOBSTER

⌗ ♿ **Lobster Pound Restaurant** (207-789-5550), Rt. 1, Lincolnville Beach. Open every day for lunch and dinner from the first Sun. in May to mid-Oct. This is a mecca for lobster lovers—some people plan their trips around a meal here. Features lobster, boiled or baked, also clams, other fresh seafood, roast turkey, ham, steaks, and chicken. A family-style restaurant that seats 246 inside and has an outside patio near a sandy beach. Takeout and picnic tables offered across the beach.

Graffam Brothers Seafood (207-236-8391), 211 Union St., Rockport. Open late spring to sometime in Oct. Across the street from the fish store are picnic tables where you can enjoy lobsters, clams, and more. This takeout-only spot serves hand-cut French fries, lobster rolls made with freshly picked lobster, and lobster dinners, with hot dogs, chicken fingers, and salads for alternatives.

---

cream-and-gold walls. Tickets are reasonably priced.

⌗ ♿ **The Center for Maine Contemporary Art** (207-236-2875; cmcanow.org), 11 Lime St., and reopening in 2016 at 21 Winter St., Rockland. Open year-round, Tue.–Sat. 10–5; also open Sun. 1–5. $5 admission for nonmembers; members, children under 18, and Rockport residents free. Promoting contemporary Maine art and artists since 1952 through exhibitions and education. The gallery sponsors more than 20 shows each season, an art auction, a crafts show, gallery talks, a shop, and an evening lecture series.

Everyman Repertory Theatre (207-236-0173; everymanrep.org), Rockport. Noel Coward's *Blythe Spirit* was performed in June 2012 at this nonprofit, professional theater dedicated to fine acting, inspired playwrights, and reasonable ticket prices.

✳ Selective Shopping

Avena Botanicals (207-594-0694; avena botanicals.com), 219 Mill St., Rockport. Open in summer Mon.–Fri. 9–5, off-season Mon.–Thu. 9–5, Fri. 9–1. Walk in the botanical garden in growing season, when you can drink in the scents serenaded by the chorus of crickets and honeybees. At the apothecary you can purchase creams, salves, teas, and tinctures, during the same hours, year-round. Check the website for the summer schedule of free herb walks with Deb Soule, the herbalist founder.

ART GALLERIES **Bay View Gallery** (207-236-4534; bayviewgallery.com), 33 Bayview St., Camden. One of the largest galleries in the Midcoast area. Original paintings and sculptures by contemporary artists working in Maine. Custom framing.

A Small Wonder Gallery (207-236-6005; smallwondergallery.com), 1 Public Landing (across from the chamber of commerce), Camden. A small gallery with well-chosen, limited-edition graphics, watercolors, hand-painted tiles and more.

ARTISANS **Windsor Chairmakers** (207-789-5188; windsorchair.com), Rt. 1, Lincolnville Beach. Filling two floors of an old farmhouse are Windsor chairs and tables, highboys, and four-poster beds, all offered in a selection of finishes. A gallery in a wing of the connected farmhouse shows a line of Shaker-style furniture. Visitors can tour the workshop to see furniture being made.

Maine Artisans (207-789-5376), Rt. 1, Lincolnville Beach. Open daily May–Oct., this charming store sells work by weavers, potters, and sock makers, among others.

The Foundry (207-236-3200; remsen.com), 531 Park St., West Rockport (next to the Baptist church). Richard Remsen makes 20-inch-long fishing lures out of handblown glass that are outfitted with metal hardware.

Michael Good Gallery (1-800-422-9623; michaelgood.com), 325 Commercial St. (Rt. 1), Rockport. Original and extraordinary pottery, jewelry, sculpture, and accessories.

BOOKSTORES ♿ **Down East** (207-594-9544), Rt. 1, Rockport. The headquarters for Down East Enterprises (publishers of *Down East, Fly Rod & Reel,* and *Shooting Sportsman* magazines, as well as a line of New England books) is located in a handsome old mansion that includes a bookshop, open 8–5 Mon.–Fri. year-round.

✎ **The Owl and Turtle Bookshop** (207-236-7335), 33 Bayview St. One of Maine's best bookstores. Maine authors and Maine history, children's books, and signings by such exemplary local authors as Tess Gerritsen. The café serves its own blend of local coffee and is the perfect place to rejuvenate yourself after an afternoon in town.

Sherman's Maine Coast Book Shops (207-236-2223 or 1-800-803-5949; shermans.com), 14 Main St., Camden. Another in the fine chain of Sherman's bookstores on the Maine coast, Camden's branch has expanded in its new, sun-filled location and is packed with books, toys, puzzles, cards, and gifts.

SPECIAL SHOPS

ALL SHOPS ARE IN CAMDEN AND OPEN YEAR-ROUND UNLESS OTHERWISE NOTED

✎ **The Smiling Cow** (207-236-3351; smilingcow.com), 41 Main St. Seasonal. Three generations ago a mother and five children converted this stable into a classic gift shop, one with unusual warmth; members of the fifth generation are now employed inside. We like the Maine-themed items like fragrant, locally made soaps.

The Cashmere Goat (207-236-7236; thecashmeregoatknit.com), 20 Bayview St. Drop-in classes will get you started on the project the soft, irresistible cashmere will inspire you to undertake. Alpaca fiber, wool, and cotton, too.

✎ **Heavenly Threads** (207-236-3203), 57 Elm St. (Rt. 1). Open Mon.–Fri. 10–4, Sat. 10–1, closed Mon. off-season. Wealthy summer folks and locals both donate to this extremely clean shop full of surprising finds, maybe Calvin Klein for under $5. Proceeds benefit Coastal Hospice, Rockland Soup Kitchen, and more.

Glendarragh Lavender (207-236-8151; mainelavender.com), 22 Main St. Just standing inside this store is calming; the lavender grows on a 26-acre farm near town and is sold here in many forms, ready to soothe, salve, and sustain you.

Ducktrap Bay Trading Company (1-800-560-9568; ducktrapbay.com), 20 Main St. Many of these pieces—decoys, wildlife and marine art, scrimshaw, and paintings—have earned awards for their creators.

Danica Candleworks (207-236-3060), 569 West St. (Rt. 90), West Rockport. In a building with a Scandinavian-inspired exterior especially pretty when it snows, you'll find a candle factory and a shop that sells high-quality hand-dipped and scented candles and accessories.

❋ Special Events

February: **U.S. National Toboggan Championships**—teams from all over the country compete in two-, three-, and four-person races, often in costume (Camden Snow Bowl); **Winterfest**; and **Camden Conference**.

March: **Maine Maple Sugar Sunday**.

Mid- to late July: **Annual Open House and Garden Day**, sponsored by the Camden Garden Club. Very popular tour of homes and gardens in Camden and Rockport held every year for five decades. **Summer HarborArts**, a juried arts and crafts show (third Saturday and Sunday), Camden Harbor Park. **The Annual Hope Jazz Festival**, Hope.

August: **Merryspring's Annual Kitchen Tour**—see uniquely designed kitchens in Camden, Rockport, and Lincolnville, plus demonstrations and tastings. **Union Fair** and **Blueberry Festival** (late month), Union Fairgrounds (see "Rockland/Thomaston Area").

Labor Day weekend: **Camden Windjammer Festival**, Camden Harbor. A celebration of the windjammer industry featuring a parade of boats, music, nautical history, fireworks, and the Schooner Bum Talent Contest.

October: **Fall HarborArts**, a juried arts and crafts show, Camden Harbor Park—75 artisans displaying work for sale. **VinFest**, Cellardoor Winery, Lincolnville. **Lincolnville Fall Festival**, Lincolnville. **PopTech**, Camden.

December: **Christmas by the Sea** (first weekend)—tree lighting, Santa's arrival, caroling, holiday house tour, refreshments in shops. Rockport Garden Club **Holly Berry Fair**.

Islesboro

A 14-mile-long, string-bean-shaped island just 3 miles off Lincolnville Beach (a 20-minute ferry ride), Islesboro is a private kind of place, best visited with a car or a bicycle.

There are three distinct communities on the island. The town of Islesboro with the necessary services (town office, post office, health center, and fire department) sits in the center between Dark Harbor and Pripet. Dark Harbor (described by Sidney Sheldon in his best seller *Master of the Game* as the "jealously guarded colony of the super-rich") has long been a summer resort village, where huge "cottages" peek from behind the trees along the road to Pendleton Point. Pripet is a thriving year-round neighborhood of boatbuilders and fishermen.

GETTING THERE Take the car-carrying **Maine State Ferry** (207-789-5611 or 207-734-6935); $10 round-trip per passenger, $27.50 per vehicle, and $8.50 for a bicycle, with reservations from the mainland or island available for a fee. The ferry lands mid-island at Grindle Point. The crossing is a 3-mile, 20-minute ride, the schedule depending on the season. If you go for a day trip only, pay close attention to when the last ferry leaves the island to avoid being stranded. At the landing you'll find a clean ferry terminal with public restrooms. When you board the Maine State Ferry, ask for a map and schedule. The detailed and informative island map shows a full view of the island as well as business locations, a ferry schedule, a brief description of the island, and a historical society events calendar.

GUIDANCE The **Islesboro town office** (207-734-2253), 150 Main Rd., is a great source of information, with friendly service both on the phone and in person.

WHEN TO COME Only in summer will visitors be able to visit a bookstore, one café, and a historical society museum with a gallery.

✵ To See and Do

The old lighthouse on **Grindle Point** (built in 1850, now automated) and keeper's cottage now house the seasonal **Sailors' Memorial Museum** (207-734-2253), open July–Labor Day, 9:30–4:30, closed Wed. and Sun. Look for summer musical and theatrical performances at the **Free Will Baptist Church**. Check out the **Up Island Church**, a fine old structure with beautiful wall stencils and fascinating old headstones in the adjacent graveyard.

The layout of the island makes at least a bicycle necessary to get a real feel for the place. But the roads are narrow and have no shoulder. Bicyclists should use great caution. Even so, after both driving and biking the island, we prefer biking. In Dark Harbor you'll see huge "cottages" and impressive architecture. In summer you'll also find the **Dark Harbor Shop** (207-734-8878), with souvenirs, gifts, ice cream, and a deli. "We haven't changed in 40 years—change comes slowly to Islesboro," said owner Bill Warren, laughing. Open daily the Fri. of Memorial Day weekend to Labor Day. A picnic area and town beach at Pendleton Point have spectacular views. The trip down the other side of the island will take you past the **Islesboro Historical Society** (207-734-6733) in the former high school, a beautiful stone building which houses an annual arts and crafts show.

BELFAST, SEARSPORT, AND STOCKTON SPRINGS

Belfast's long, Victorian brick Main Street slopes steadily downward, away from Rt. 1, toward the confluence of the tidal Passagassawakeag River and Belfast Bay and the site of the largest boatyard downeast.

With just 7,100 residents and a small-town feel, Belfast is a city and the seat of Waldo County. Magnificent Greek Revival and Federal homes, proof of early prominence, line High and Church Streets. Lower blocks suggest a checkered commercial history that included a sarsaparilla company, a rum distillery, and a city-owned railroad. Now it's a bustling, hip small town with exceptional food and drink.

High above downtown Belfast, Rt. 1 crosses the Passagassawakeag River into East Belfast, threading a string of shops, restaurants, and a mix of 1940s motor courts and motor inns with water views.

In Searsport Rt. 1 becomes, suddenly and briefly, a mid-19th-century brick-and-granite downtown. Visit the Penobscot Marine Museum to learn that more than 3,000 different vessels have been built in and around Penobscot Bay since 1770. Searsport alone launched eight brigs and six schooners in one year (1845), and for many years boasted more sea captains than any other town its size, explaining the dozens of 19th-century mansions lining Rt. 1.

If you have the time, take the scenic route to this region from Augusta, poking through the communities of Unity, Thorndike, and Brooks, detouring to Liberty then down to Belfast. Rt. 1 continues to shadow the shore as it narrows into what seems more like a broad river.

GUIDANCE **The Belfast Area Chamber of Commerce** (207-338-5900; belfastmaine.org), P.O. Box 58, Belfast 04915, maintains an information center at 14 Main St. near the waterfront; open daily June–mid-Oct., 10–6; mid Oct.–May, Mon.–Fri. 9–2.

GETTING THERE *By car:* The most direct route to this region from points south and west is via I-95, exiting in Augusta and taking Rt. 3 to Belfast. Exit 113 on I-95 accesses a connector to Rt. 3, offering motorists bound for the Midcoast a way around Augusta. If you're coming up Rt. 1, take the first turnoff for downtown Belfast.

By bus: **Concord Coach Lines** (1-800-639-3317; concordcoachlines.com) stops in both Searsport and Belfast.

PUBLIC RESTROOMS At the public landing at the bottom of Main Street, open May–mid-Oct.

Nancy English

BUSKING ON THE MAIN STREET IN BELFAST

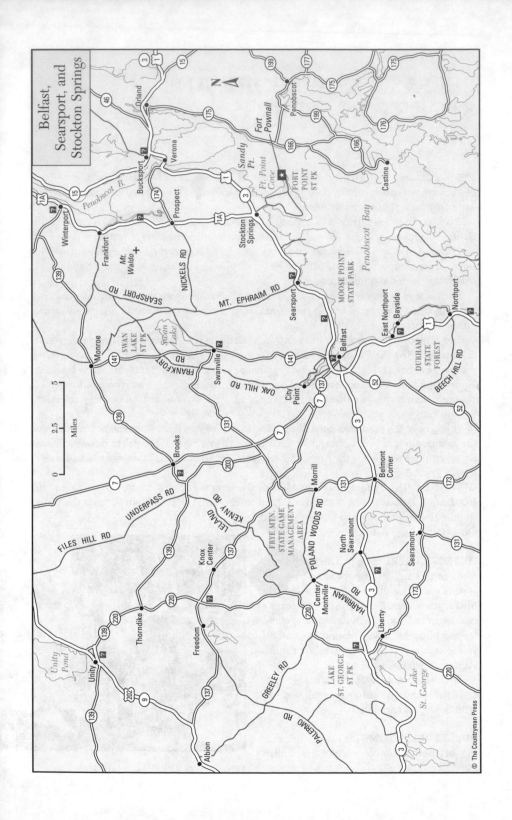

Belfast, Searsport, and Stockton Springs

© The Countryman Press

WHEN TO COME The town chugs along through winter, with most inns and restaurants open throughout the year; still, the summer season gives the ocean a friendlier look and fills the farm stands. Come to Belfast anytime to enjoy the downtown.

�֍ Villages

Brooks. In the center of this quiet county, surrounded by hills, this town has the most scenic golf course around.

Liberty, straddling Rt. 3, is home to Lake St. George State Park and to the extraordinary **Liberty Tool Company** (207-589-4771; jonesport-wood.com), Main St. Open June–mid-Oct., daily, fewer days off-season, closed Jan. and Feb. and reopening in Mar. with a big sale on the first Saturday. Antique and used tools and every other thing that you can imagine—clocks, lanterns, books, postcards. Tools for sale can be looked at Sat. morning, or call 1-888-405-2007. The octagonal Liberty post office, located across the street from Liberty Graphics, dates to 1867 and houses the Liberty Historical Soci-

WOODWORKING AND CARPENTRY TOOLS OVERFLOW THE SHELVES AT LIBERTY TOOL COMPANY

ety (207-589-4393), open weekend afternoons in July and Aug. **Liberty Graphics** (207-589-4035; libertygraphicstshirts.com), Main St., open daily in summer, fewer days off-season, sells T-shirts, including organic cotton versions, printed with water-based designs from nature and designs by Frank Lloyd Wright.

Northport. A low-key community with pleasure boats in the harbor and golf clubs, as well as a mid-19th-century former Methodist campground with hundreds of gingerbread cottages on the bay.

Unity. Home to a rural college, a raceway, and the fairgrounds for the popular late-Sept. Common Ground Fair.

Stockton Springs. Rt. 1 now bypasses this former shipbuilding town. Follow East St. down to Fort Point.

✖ To See

MUSEUMS **Davistown Museum** (207-589-4900; davistownmuseum.org), 58 Main St., Liberty. Skip Brack, meticulous owner of Liberty Tool Company, has sorted out the finest antique tools of his collection to create this museum above Liberty Graphics. Its specialty is a collection of signed shipbuilders' edge tools. Contemporary Maine artists, 108 in total, exhibit their work in this space, and a permanent collection is also on display, most in the top floors. As the website states, the art and artifact combination at Davistown Museum "is unique among Maine's museums and galleries." Native American artifacts. Children can make a sculpture out of odds and ends gathered from the tool store. Suggested donation $3.

MUST SEE

Penobscot Marine Museum (207-548-2529; penobscot marinemuseum.org), Rt. 1, Searsport. Open May–mid-Oct., Mon.–Sat. 10–5 and Sun. noon–5. $12 adults; children 7–15 are $8. Family rate $30. (The library is open Mon.–Fri. 9–1.) The 13 buildings include eight on the National Register of Historic Places. The museum shop is at the entrance to the complex on Rt. 1. More than 50 small craft, one of the largest collections in New England, are on display, including peapods, dories, canoes, and lobster boats. A meticulously restored ship captain's home re-creates prosperous Maine coast life in the 19th century, while a commercial fishing exhibit in Searsport's original town hall shows the working side of the maritime community. Other artifacts show the changing faces of Maine, from the Wabanaki natives to the shipbuilders of the 1800s. The galleries in the **Captain Jeremiah Merithew House** hold a world-class collection of paintings by father, son, and grandson marine artists Thomas Buttersworth (Sr. and Jr.) and James Buttersworth, whose depictions of ships in storm and calm are luminous and exciting. The museum displays scrimshaw-carved whales' teeth, ship models, and artifacts of the China trade. Tours include scheduled visits to the adjacent First Congregational Church to view glorious stained-glass windows and a 100-year-old organ with over 1,000 pipes. Three children's activity areas include a "marine science lab," a ship's capstan, and a large-scale model of a square-rigger's mast and sails that kids can manipulate. Other exhibits focus on the working-class people who made their living in the granite, lime, ice, lumber, and tourism industries.

Belfast Historical Society and Museum (207-338-9229; belfastmuseum.org), 10 Market St., Belfast. Open mid-June–mid-Oct.; in summer Tue.–Sat. 11–4, from Labor Day Fri.–Sat. 11–4; by appointment year-round. A ship model of the *Charlotte W. White* has been restored for display. A self-guided "Museum-in-the-Streets" walking tour is installed downtown.

Safe Harbor Church, Rt. 1, Searsport. Phone 207-548-6663 or pick up the key across the street and check out the fabulous stained-glass windows in this church, built in 1815. It's now maintained as a meditation space and holds regular services.

Bryant Wood Stove Museum (207-568-3665; bryantstove.com), 27 Stovepipe Alley (junction of Rts. 220 and 139), Thorndike. Open year-round, Mon.–Sat. 8–4:30. What began as a stove shop has evolved into a fascinating museum. The front room is crammed with restored woodstoves (for sale). Walk through these to the doll circus, with its array of mechanical, musical dolls from Barbie to Disney characters and everything in between. The back room houses a collection of player pianos, nickelodeons, and vintage automobiles. Worth the drive.

✷ To Do

BERRY PICKING **Staples Homestead Blueberries** (207-567-3393 or 207-567-3703), 302 Old County Rd., Stockton Springs. Turn at the ball field on Rts. 1/3, then drive 3 miles to the T at County Rd.; turn right. Open 8–5 daily while its certified organic berries are in-season (Aug.). Friendly owners Basil and Mary Staples will instruct you in the mysteries of blueberry raking, then let you go to it, or you can pick by hand.

BEER **Liberty Craft Brewing** (207-322-7663; libertycraftbrewing.com), 7 Coon Mountain Lane, Liberty. Queen Bee Honey Lager, imperial porter, and golden pilsner are a few of the ales on tap at this destination brewery with a pub food menu.

BOATING Community rowing is a summer tradition: Sign up and enjoy the free sport at the town dock. **Downeast Windjammer Cruises** (207-546-2927; downeastwindjammer

.com), Thompson Wharf, Belfast. The *Patience* cruises Penobscot Bay daily June–Sept., offering a choice of itineraries.

Miss Nina (207-505-1618; sailingmissnina.com), Belfast Harbor. June–Oct. 1, sail this 61-foot wooden ketch with Captain Dan and Amy Miller for half- and full-day charters; six-passenger maximum.

Schooner Timberwind (207-619-0654), Thompson's Wharf, Belfast. Day sails and sunset cruises. Built in Portland in 1931 as a pilot schooner, this pretty 96-foot vessel was converted to a passenger vessel in 1969; it moved to Belfast from Rockland in 2015.

Belfast Bay Company Lobster Boat Trips (207-323-1443; belfastbaycompany.com). Take the *Clara K* from Belfast to visit Castine or Holbrook Island Sanctuary. $45–75.

COOKING CLASSES (207-505-5231; belfastbreezeinn.com) 192 Northport Ave. Sandi Knapp, of the **Belfast Breeze Inn**, offers cooking classes in the summer along with music performances and a dinner show.

GOLF **Country View Golf Club** (207-722-3161) in Brooks is the most scenic in the area: nine holes, par 36, cart and club rentals, lessons, clubhouse. **Northport Golf Club** (207-338-2270), Northport. A fully irrigated nine-hole course, pro shop, snack bar, driving range, and rentals.

KAYAKING **Water Walker Sea Kayaks** (207-338-6424; touringkayaks.com), Belfast. Ray Wirth, a Registered Maine Guide and ACA-certified open-water instructor, offers tours ranging from several hours in Belfast Harbor or around Sears Island to full-day trips to other islands to overnight trips.

SWIMMING **Lake St. George State Park** (207-589-4255), Rt. 3, Liberty. Open May 15–Oct. 15. A great way station for travelers going to or from Down East. A deep, clear lake with a small beach, lifeguard, bathhouse, 38 campsites, and a boat launch. **Swan Lake State Park**, Rt. 141, Swanville (north of town; follow signs), has a beach with picnicking facilities. **Belfast City Park**, Rt. 1, Belfast (south of town), holds a swimming pool, tennis courts, picnicking facilities, and a gravel beach. **Sandy Point Beach** is off Rt. 1 north of Stockton Springs (it's posted HERSEY RETREAT; turn toward the water directly across from the Rocky Ridge Motel).

TRAINS **Belfast and Moosehead Lake Railway** (brookspreservation.org), Upper Bridge Station, High St., Belfast. Train rides leave the station twice a day on weekends in summer, taking passengers over 7 miles of track and bridges along the harbor and river.

WINE **Winterport Winery** (207-223-4500; winterportwinery.com), 279 S. Main St., Winterport. Open May–Dec., Tue.–Sat. 11–5; Mar.–Apr., Fri.–Sat. 11–5; closed Jan.–Feb. Taste the wine and ales from Penobscot Bay Brewery. A line of ice cream made with Half Moon Stout is worth sampling.

✳ Green Space

Also see Lake St. George State Park and Belfast City Park under *Swimming*.

Moose Point State Park, Rt. 1, south of Searsport. Open May 30–Oct. 15. A good spot for picnicking; cookout facilities are in an evergreen grove and an open field overlooking Penobscot Bay. Also check out **Mosman Park** in downtown Searsport with its playground and picnic benches by tidal pools and the public landing.

EXCURSIONS

Rt. 3, past Lake St. George and Sheepscot Pond, through the China Lakes region, is the most direct path between Belfast and Augusta, but take time to detour down Rt. 173 to **Liberty** to see the octagonal post office and the **Liberty Tool Company** and **Davistown Museum** (see *Museums*). For a leisurely tour of the villages between Belfast and Augusta, head north from East Belfast on Rt. 141 to Monroe. Ask for directions to **Stone Soup Farm** to see their gardens, then check out **Monroe Falls**, just off Rt. 139, and maybe have a picnic. Head out on Rt. 139, through Brooks, and then on toward Thorndike, where you'll want to stop at the **Bryant Museum**. Follow Rt. 139 into Kennebec County to Fairfield to meet up with I-95, or detour yet again onto Rt. 202, which will bring you through the China Lakes region to Augusta.

Fort Pownall and Fort Point State Park, Stockton Springs (marked from Rt. 1; follow the 3.5-mile access road). The 1759 fort built to defend the British claim to Maine (the Penobscot River was the actual boundary between the English and French territories) was burned twice to prevent its being taken; only earthworks remain. The adjacent park, on the tip of a peninsula jutting into Penobscot Bay, is a fine fishing and picnic spot.

Sears Island. After decades of debate about the future of this island (it was slated to be a container port, nuclear power plant site, LNG port, and more), it's open to the public. There are 940 acres and about 5 miles of shorefront to explore, just as migratory birds do. Good for walking, biking, kayaking, and fishing; visit the sand beaches to view the Camden Hills. It's connected to the mainland by a causeway. Off Rt. 1, take Sears Island Rd.

Carleton Pond Waterfowl Production Area, Troy. Part of the Maine Wildlife Refuge System. One thousand acres are accessible by canoe or kayak. Unstaffed. Contact the Maine Coastal Islands Wildlife Refuge Rockport office (207-236-6970), P.O. Box 495, Rockport 04856, for information and for regulations on duck and geese hunting.

✳ Lodging

RESORTS ✳ **Point Lookout** (207-789-2000 or 1-800-515-3611; visitpointlookout.com), 67 Atlantic Hwy., Northport (on the Lincolnville line). Open year-round. The 106 luxurious one-, two-, and three-bedroom cabins at Point Lookout, a gorgeous setting, started their existence as a corporate retreat built by MBNA in the mid-1990s. In 2008 these pine-paneled cabins were transformed into a resort. Each one holds a cable TV/DVD, a propane fireplace, and a screened porch, and more than half have cooking facilities; a small number have ocean views. **Copper Pine Café** takes care of breakfast and lunch, perhaps a panini with fresh mozzarella and tomatoes. Fitness center with massage and Zumba and yoga classes offered, plus bowling, racquetball, virtual golf, an artificial turf soccer field, a baseball field, and hiking trails. $271–350 in high season.

INNS AND B&BS

IN BELFAST 04915

The Belfast Bay Inn (207-338-5600; belfast bayinn.com), 72 Main St. Ed and Judy Hemmingsen, former owners of the Bluenose Inn in Bar Harbor, have transformed a brick building on Main Street into a boutique hotel that pulls out all the stops. The eight luxury rooms are filled with gorgeous upholstered furniture and plush beds, art, refrigerators, cable TV/DVD; some have views of the harbor, fireplace, dining area, and/or a balcony. Breakfast in a garden courtyard. Spa services. $198–378.

The Alden House (207-338-2151 or 1-877-337-8151; thealdenhouse.com), 63 Church St. This gracious 1840 Greek Revival mansion holds Italian marble mantels and sinks and a circular staircase inside its substantial walls. Larry Marshal and Rosemarie Cyr are the innkeepers overseeing the six guest rooms—five with private bath—a charming open porch, and comfortable furnishings. $129–179 includes a full breakfast served at separate tables.

The Jeweled Turret Inn (207-338-2304 or 1-800-696-2304; jeweledturret.com), 40 Pearl St. Open year-round. A handsome 1890s gabled and turreted house that's ornate inside and out, with a fireplace in the den said to be made of stones from every state in the Union at that time. This now lovely house suffered neglect before Carl and Cathy Heffentrager began transforming it in 1986, reviving its original glory by restoring the wood stairs and decking of the stone-edged verandas, where guests love to lounge in rockers and a swing. $130–169.

IN SEARSPORT 04974

Captain A. V. Nickels Inn (207-548-1104; captainnickelsinn.com), 127 E. Main St. (Rt. 1). Open June–Dec. Brenda and Michael Liston bought this inn in 2011 and gave it a complete renovation, upgrading the eight bedrooms and suites (all with private bath) with European antiques, flat-screen TV, and more. Each room is named for a port of call. Paris, with a four-poster bed, wine-red walls, and white moldings, is our top choice. Twin parlors, a library, and a porch are fine places for relaxation. Overnight guests receive a three-course breakfast and wine and cheese in the afternoon. $165–255. Two resident terriers.

COTTAGES 🐾 **Bayside Village**, built in the 1800s, has about 50 cottages on Penobscot Bay in Northport rented by the week by Bayside Cottage Rentals (207-338-5355; bayside cottagerentals.com). Margaret Lacoste's agency is open spring, summer, and fall, renting the cottages out for between $550 and $1,595 a week May–mid-Oct. Originally a Methodist campground, the cottages are ornately trimmed with Victorian gingerbread, some with stone fireplace. The village offers a main common, a swim float and dock on the pebble beach, sailing lessons, and a little yacht club with children's activities in summer.

MOTELS 🐾 🐾 **Ocean's Edge Fireside Suites** (207-338-2090 or 1-800-303-5098), 159 Searsport Ave. (Rt. 1), Belfast 04915. The location of this three-story facility is terrific. All 83 units (with two queen beds, king beds, or suites) have a balcony overlooking the bay; amenities include a full-service restaurant, guest laundry, indoor "mineral" pool (no chlorine) with sauna and hot tub, and lobby computer. $89–329 in summer includes continental breakfast. Try the two-night specials in winter midweek—the pool is heated to 86 degrees.

✳ Where to Eat

DINING OUT **The Lost Kitchen** (207-382-3333) 22 Mill St., Freedom. Open Wed.–Sat. Sixteen miles west of Belfast and worth the drive, The Lost Kitchen wows its visitors with a short, excellent menu. A neighboring farm's chickens are roasted with a magic that leaves the skin crisp and the meat moist; the chef, Erin French, knows exactly what she is doing. The mill building that houses this restaurant received equally painstaking attention during its renovation. Plum croustades or spring-dug parsnip cake—dessert will correspond to the season. Entrées $26–42.

Meanwhile in Belfast (207-218-1288; meanwhile-in-belfast.com), 2 Cross St. With owners from Salerno on Italy's Amalfi Coast, you can count on the best wood-fired oven pizzas with thin, crisp dough, fantastic fresh mozzarella, flavorful olive oil—all the reasons Italian pizza is justifiably renowned. Travelers are seeking this pizza out; locals are devotees. $10–20.

Nancy English

BAKING THE PIZZA AT MEANWHILE IN BELFAST REQUIRES CONSTANT ATTENTION

The Gothic (207-338-4684; matthew
kenneycuisine.com/hospitality/the-gothic),
108 Main St. Brunch and dinner, vegetarian
and vegan only. Belfast National Bank is
long gone, but its ambitious architecture still
graces this restaurant. Matthew Kenney, who
has traveled the world, brought back some
new ideas about cooking; local vegetarians
are grateful. Almond gazpacho, sweet potato
fritters, and poppy seed spaetzle are just some
of the delicious offerings.

Delvino's Grill & Pasta House (207-338-
4565; delvinos.com), 52 Main St., Belfast.
Open daily. The Italian classics are made well
at Delvino's, where you can also dine on a
blue cheese burger, fresh fish, or rib eye. Local
buffalo and Maine beef are usually offered.
Or try the mushroom sacchetti—pasta stuffed
with portobello and porcini mushrooms and
cheeses, topped with peppered cream sauce.
House desserts change daily. Entrées $8–22.

The Captain's Table and **Port of Call
Restaurant & Tapas Lounge** (207-548-1104;
captainnickelsinn.com), 127 E. Main St. (Rt.
1), Searsport. Open June–Dec. Reservations
recommended; no table is turned over at
this restaurant dedicated to relaxed, fine
dining. Three- and four-course meals from a
changing menu might include seared duck
in a cherry reduction. $49 for four courses.
Entrées from The Captain's Table (or from the
bar—perhaps steak or vodka lobster, $16–26)
can be enjoyed in Port of Call.

DOWNING OYSTERS AT THREE TIDES IN BELFAST

EATING OUT **Chase's Daily** (207-338-0555),
96 Main St., Belfast. Breakfast and lunch Tue.–
Sat., dinner Fri. from 5:30, Sun. brunch 8–1.
This high-ceilinged restaurant features enticing produce from the owners' Chase Farm in
Freedom, sold in the back. The freshness of
the ingredients and the great cooking combine to make the vegetarian fare wonderful.
Thin-crusted Margherita pizza with fresh
tomatoes and pools of melted mozzarella is
great in late summer, as are soft corn tacos
stuffed with black beans, spicy pepitas, feta,
crema, shredded cabbage, and lime. Freshly
baked bread and treats like sunken chocolate
cake for dessert. Meals $7–19.

✪ **Three Tides** (207-338-1707; 3tides
.com), 2 Pinchy Lane, Belfast. Open Tue.–Sat.
from 3 PM, Sun. 1–8, later opening in winter.
A fun spot with a serpentine concrete bar
and an outdoor deck over the river, where
you can drink special cocktails and eat piz-
zettes ($8.50), salads, and quesadillas. The
oysters, mussels, steamers, and lobsters are
very fresh; the lobsters are from their own
lobster pound. The **Marshall Wharf Brewing
Company** next door makes the exceptional
microbrews; Cant Dog Imperial IPA is a "hops
monster," exhilarating and bitter. An open-air
terrace downstairs serves oysters raw and
roasted, drinks, and French fries.

✐ ♿ **The Ocean's Edge Restaurant** (207-
338-2090), 159 Searsport Ave., Belfast. Open
daily 4–9, closed Sun. off-season. Not just

CHERRY TARTS AT CHASE'S DAILY, BELFAST

LOBSTER

✪ **Young's Lobster Pound** (207-338-1160; youngslobsterpound.webs.com), Fairview St. (posted from Rt. 1 just across the bridge from downtown Belfast), East Belfast. Open in-season 7:30–8, and year-round (winter closing at 4) for live and cooked lobsters, crabs, clams, and mussels, or take-out. A pound with as many as 30,000 lobsters and seating (indoor and outdoor) to accommodate 500 with a beautiful view of Belfast across the Passagassawakeag River. They pick the lobster meat here fresh every day for the lobster rolls.

an amenity for the Comfort Inn to which it's attached, this spot is a local favorite given the view, the service, and the menu, which ranges from chicken and broccoli Alfredo with fettuccine to surf and turf. Entrées $10–28. Children's menu.

Darby's Restaurant and Pub (207-338-2339), 155 High St., Belfast. Open daily for lunch and dinner. A storefront café with tin ceilings and local artwork. A reasonably priced dinner might include pecan haddock with mojito sauce, or a black bean enchilada "smothered in cheddar and Ranchero sauce." Soups, salads, and sandwiches are served all day. Entrées $8–22.

🎣 **Anglers** (207-548-2405), Rt. 1, Searsport. Open daily 11–8. Buddy Hall's Maine-style diner serves seafood that ranges from chowder to fried and broiled fish dinners to lobster every which way. "Land Lovers" get chicken Parmesan, BBQ ribs, and prime rib, and the Minnow Menu is for "the smaller appetite" (you don't have to be small). Entrées $7–30.

Bay Wrap (207-338-9757; thebaywrap .com), 20 Beaver St. (off Main), Belfast. Open daily for lunch and dinner, except Sun., closing earlier in winter. An eatery with a next-door coffee shop called the Hub, where you can eat the wraps. On a foggy day we feasted on warm grilled eggplant with roasted red peppers, ricotta and feta cheeses, mint, field greens, and salsa verde ($7.95 for large).

Bell the Cat (207-338-2084), 15G Starett Drive, Belfast. Open 7:30–7:30, Sun. 9–5. Set inside a spacious upfront corner of Mr. Paperback, this is the local, very casual favorite for designer sandwiches, from breakfast sandwiches to a fat Reuben. Also good for salads, soups, and ice cream. Coffees and teas. This little café has a cult-like following—among adults.

Seng Thai (207-338-0010), 139 Searsport Ave. (Rt. 1), Belfast. Open daily (except Mon.) from 11:30. Not your ordinary Thai. Residents warn you not to try level-five spiciness. Entrées $9–14.

CHEESE Eat More Cheese (207-358-9701; eatmorecheese.me), 33 Main St. Eating more cheese is a delightful experience with Eat More Cheese's selections. Salami goes nicely, too. Sample to your heart's content.

ICE CREAM In Liberty, Maine, on Rt. 3, you will find possibly the best ice cream in the state of Maine at **John's Ice Cream Factory** (207-589-3700), 510 Belfast Augusta Rd. (Rt. 3). This is why you may very well choose to drive to this area via I-95 to Augusta and Rt. 3. Lemon custard; mandarin orange chocolate; strawberry rhubarb; espresso anise swirl.

Nancy English

JOHN'S ICE CREAM, LIBERTY, MAINE

DANNY MCGOVERN, BREWER AT MARSHALL WHARF

BEER Marshall Wharf Brewery Store and Tasting Room (207-338-1707; marshallwharf .com), 2 Pinchy Lane, Belfast. Call for hours. This is the brewery store for Marshall Wharf Brewery, making some of the best beer in Maine and selling tastes, pints, growlers, or half gallons of whatever is on tap.

✳ Entertainment

Marsh River Theater (207-722-4110; marsh rivertheater.com), Rt. 139, Brooks. Community theater performed in historic Union Hall. This group formed in the mid-1990s and has been offering performances ever since.

The Colonial Theater (207-338-1930; colonialtheater.com). The new home of the outsized carved elephants from a local land-mark, Perry's Nut House; three screens with nightly showings in a restored theater in downtown Belfast.

✳ Selective Shopping

ART Don't miss **The Art Alliance Gallery** (207-338-9994), 39 Main St., a cooperative gallery for 7 to 10 very different and interest-ing artists; the **Parent Gallery** (207-338-1553; nealparent.com), 92 Main St., displaying fine black-and-white photographs by Neal Parent, and pastels and oils by daughter Joanne; **High Street Studio and Gallery** (207-338-8990; highstreetgallery.com), 149 High St.,

featuring Susan Tobey White's many-peopled landscapes and amazing doll sculptures. **Waterfall Arts** (207-338-2222; waterfallarts .org), 256 High St., is an arts organization offering classes, residencies, and exhibits in Belfast at Clifford Gallery and Fallout Shelter Gallery.

ANTIQUES Searsport claims to be the Antiques Capital of Maine. **The Searsport Antique Mall**, 149 E. Main St., open more or less daily year-round, is a cooperative of more than 70 dealers spread over two floors. **The Pumpkin Patch Antiques Center** (207-548-6047), 15 W. Main St., a 12-dealer shop in busi-ness since 1975, is run by Phyllis Sommer and is widely respected. Cindy Gallant runs the **Hobby Horse Flea Market** (207-548-2981, 379 E. Main St.), which fills a 3-acre complex with five retail stores. A flea market surrounds it every day but Tue., May–Columbus Day. Two other Searsport flea markets are held week-ends in-season. **Captain Tinkham's Empo-rium** (207-548-6465; jonesport-wood.com), 34 Main St., next to the Penobscot Marine Museum store, is where you can find antique and functional tools as well as books, records, sheet music, and other finds. Open daily in summer, Sat. year-round.

BlueJacket Ship Crafters (207-548-9974 or 1-800-448-5567; bluejacketinc.com), 160 E. Main St. (Rt. 1), Searsport. The to-scale ship models, from starting kits to custom commissions, are made in Maine. Beginners undertaking the *Red Baron*, a Holland 32 lob-ster boat built in Belfast, for instance, will be able to call Charlie Cook if they need advice assembling the kits. The company began in 1904 under the name of the founder, H. E. Boucher. The radio-controlled pond yacht *Osprey* can go for a spin, a voyage that will be guided by Michael de Lesseps's expert, engaging instruction.

BOOKSTORES ♟ Left Bank Books (207-548-6400; leftbankbookshop.com), 109 Church St., Belfast. A cup of tea or coffee is waiting for you here, along with books ranging from great mysteries to Arctic explorations. This handsome and welcoming (with treats for dogs) bookstore also sells vintage cards.

Old Professor's Bookshop (207-338-2006), 99 Main St. Curated used books, rare books, and the best of the new.

Penobscot Books (207-548-6490; penobscotbooks.com), 164 W. Main St., Searsport. Open May–Oct. and Christmas. With art, architecture, and photography books, more than 50,000 titles, this store sells to universities and libraries all over the world.

Victorian House/Book Barn (207-567-3351), 290 Main St., Stockton Springs. Open every day of the year. A landmark collection of 20,000 antiquarian books and a special find for mystery-book buffs.

SPECIAL SHOPS

IN NORTHPORT

Swan's Island Blankets (207-338-9691; swans islandblankets.com), 231 Atlantic Hwy. (Rt. 1), Northport. The old looms are in use in the back room, visible through a window from the elegant showroom, near which a few of the natural sources of dye stand in jars, ready to be used in making these soft, beautiful, expensive blankets. Organic, naturally dyed, imported merino yarn is for sale.

IN BELFAST

Belfast Co-op Store (207-338-2532; belfast .coop), 123 High St. Open daily 7:30 AM–8 PM. Everyone needs something in this store and café with its standout deli and lunches. **Coyote Moon** (207-338-5659), 54 Main St., is a nifty, reasonably priced women's clothing and gift store. **All About Games** (207-338-9984), 78 Main St., is a great place to buy traditional board games; **The Game Loft**, 78A Main, over the store, is a youth center where kids can play nonelectronic games for free. **Colburn Shoe Store** (207-338-1934), 79 Main St., bills itself as the oldest shoe store in America, open since 1832. **Renys** (207-338-4588), Renys Plaza, Rt. 3 just north of the junction with Rt. 1, is one in Maine's chain of distinctive outlet stores. Always worth a stop (good for everything from TVs to socks).

NORTH ALONG RT. 1

Perry's Nut House (207-338-1630), Rt. 1 just north of the Belfast Bridge. Reopened and working on being what it used to be. The nut collection is in the Smithsonian. The man-eating clam cannot be located. **Mainely Pottery** (207-338-1108; mainelypottery.com), 181

Searsport Ave. (Rt. 1), features the work of owner Jamie Oates and carries varied work by 30 other Maine potters.

IN SEARSPORT

Silkweeds (207-548-6501), Rt. 1, Searsport. Specializes in "country gifts": tinware, cotton afghans, wreaths. **Waldo County Craft Co-op** (207-548-6686), 307 E. Main St. (Rt. 1), Searsport Harbor. Open mid-May–mid-Oct. daily 9–5, weekends until Christmas. A showcase for the local extension service.

✳ Special Events

May–October: **Belfast Farmers' Market**, Fri. 9–1 at 256 High St.

June–October: **Friday Night Art Walk**.

July 4: Parade, fairs, and fireworks in Searsport; **Arts in the Park**; and the **Celtic Festival**.

July–August: Free Thu.-night **street concerts** in downtown Belfast.

Nancy English

ORGANIC PRODUCE AT BELFAST FARMERS' MARKET

August: **Searsport Lobster Boat Races** and related events; **Marine Heritage Festival & Boatbuilding Challenge; Harbor Fest**, Belfast.

September: ✪ **Common Ground Fair** in Unity—organic farm products, children's activities, sheepdog roundup, crafts, entertainment, and terrific food.

October: First Sat., **Church Street Festival** and parade (first Sat.); **Fright at the Fort**, when Fort Knox is haunted. **Fling into Fall celebration** (Columbus Day weekend)—parade, bonfire, church suppers.

December: **Searsport Victorian Christmas**—open houses at museums, homes, and B&Bs; **New Year's by the Bay**.

DOWN EAST

EAST PENOBSCOT BAY REGION

Bucksport/Orland Area; Blue Hill Area; Deer
Isle, Stonington, and Isle au Haut; Castine

ACADIA AREA

Mount Desert Island; Acadia National Park;
Bar Harbor and Ellsworth; The Quiet Side of
Mount Desert

EAST HANCOCK COUNTY

WAY DOWNEAST

The Bold Coast: Steuben to Campobello Island
(New Brunswick); Eastport and Cobscook Bay;
Calais and the Downeast Lakes Regions

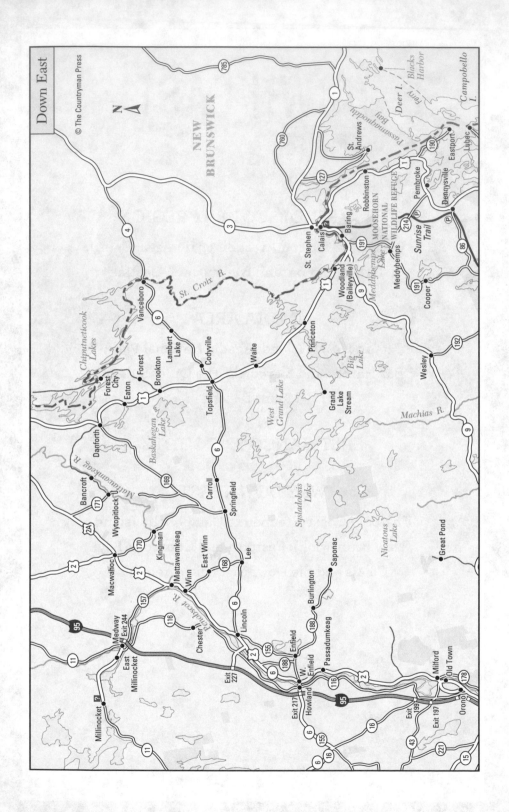

Down East

© The Countryman Press

N

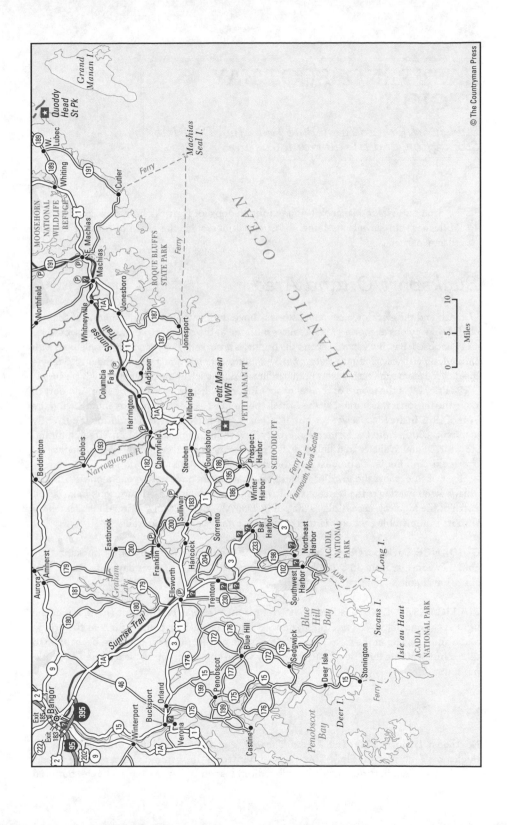

EAST PENOBSCOT BAY REGION

Bucksport/Orland Area; Blue Hill Area; Deer Isle, Stonington, and Isle au Haut; Castine

The dramatic Waldo-Hancock bridge at the Penobscot Narrows links two counties and Midcoast with Downeast Maine. It visually underscores the sense of turning a major coastal corner.

Bucksport/Orland Area

Whoosh and the elevator sets you 45 stories above the Penobscot River, atop one of the two obelisk-like pylons anchoring Maine's newest bridge at the confluence of the Penobscot River and Penobscot Bay. Bucksport, beyond the bridge, is a workaday river and paper mill town with a mile-long walkway along the waterfront, shopping, a choice of restaurants, and a 1916 movie theater/museum showcasing New England films dating back to the turn of the 20th century.

Positioned at the mouth of the Penobscot River, Bucksport was a major shipping port in 1799, the reason it was burned by the British then and was later occupied by them during the War of 1812. In the 1820s it was the largest town in eastern Maine (its population is currently just over 3,800). Note the former Jed Prouty Tavern in the middle of Main Street, a dining stop for Daniel Webster and half a dozen presidents down through the years. Bucksport overlooks New England's biggest fort, dwarfed by its most dramatic bridge.

East of Bucksport the town of Orland offers more than meets the eye along Rt. 1. The village itself overlooks the Narramissic River, and in East Orland, Alamoosook Lake is just north of the highway, accessible to the public from the Craig Brook National Fish Hatchery with its innumerable salmon, visitors center, swimming, and hiking trails.

GUIDANCE **Bucksport Bay Area Chamber of Commerce** (207-469-6818; bucksportbay chamber.com), 52 Main St. Open June–Oct., Mon., Thu., and Fri.; fewer days off-season. Brochures available 24 hours.

PUBLIC RESTROOMS The Bucksport Waterfront Walkway just off Rt. 1 (hang left at the light at the end of the Verona Bridge) offers clean, seasonal restrooms right near the bridge and a short way up at the town landing. This is the perfect place for man and beast alike to take a break after a long ride. Note the doggy waste bags and water bowls as well as drinking fountains.

✳ To Do

Northeast Historic Film/The Alamo Theatre (207-469-0924; oldfilm.org), 85 Main St., Bucksport (entrance on Elm). This 125-seat, vintage-1916 restored theater is open year-round, featuring first-run movies, Dolby digital sound, low prices, and real buttered

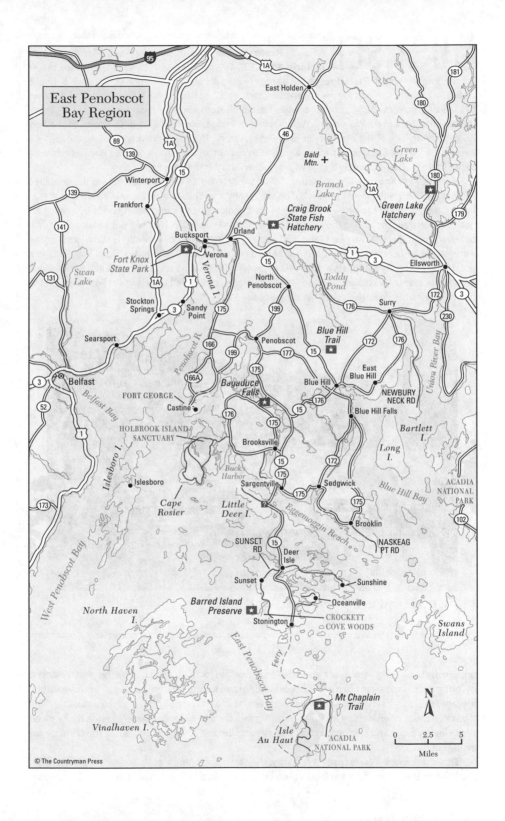

East Penobscot
Bay Region

95

1A

East Holden

181

180

46

Green
Lake

Bald
Mtn.

69

139

15

Branch
Lake

180

1A

Green Lake
Hatchery

179

Winterport

139

Frankfort

Craig Brook
State Fish
Hatchery

Ellsworth

3

1

141

Bucksport
Verona

Orland

15

Fort Knox
State Park

131

Swan
Lake

1A

Verona I.

North
Penobscot

Toddy
Pond

176

Surry

3

172

230

Stockton
Springs

3

1

Sandy
Point

175

199

15

199

177

15

Blue
Hill
Trail

172

176

Searsport

Penobscot R.

166

Penobscot

East
Bluo Hill

3

Belfast

166A

Bayaduce
Falls

175

199

Blue Hill

176

NEWBURY
NECK RD

Union River Bay

52

FORT GEORGE

Castine

176

175

15

Blue Hill Falls

Bartlett
I.

HOLBROOK ISLAND
SANCTUARY

Brooksville

15

172

Long
I.

Islesboro I.

Buck
Harbor

175

Sargentville

Sedgwick

175

Blue Hill Bay

ACADIA
NATIONAL
PARK

Belfast Bay

Cape
Rosier

Little
Deer I.

175

Eggemoggin Reach

1

173

Islesboro

SUNSET
RD

15

Deer
Isle

Brooklin

NASKEAG
PT RD

102

Sunset

Sunshine

West Penobscot Bay

North Haven
I.

Oceanville

Barred Island
Preserve

Stonington

CROCKETT
COVE WOODS

Swans
Island

East Penobscot Bay

Ferry

Mt Chaplain
Trail

N

Vinalhaven I.

Isle
Au Haut

ACADIA
NATIONAL
PARK

0   2.5   5

Miles

© The Countryman Press

MUST SEE

The observatory is open May through Oct., daily 9–5, until 6 in July/Aug. Combo tickets for the observatory/fort are $7 adults ($5 for Maine residents), $3 ages 5–11, $4 for seniors ($2.50 charge for Maine seniors). Nominal admission for the fort only (open in-season until sunset). West of the Waldo-Hancock bridge a traffic light eases access to the Fort Knox grounds, site of the elevator up to the observatory. The elevator whisks you to the top in a minute. Far below, Bucksport is a toy town, and from another window Penobscot Bay sweeps away to the horizon. This is the only bridge with an observatory in the country.

Massive **Fort Knox** itself was built in 1844 as a defense against Canada during the so-called "Aroostook War" with New Brunswick. The war, really a boundary dispute, was ignored in Washington, and so in 1839 the new, lumber-rich state took matters into its own hands by arming its northern forts and mobilizing the militia. The war formally ended in 1842 without a shot being fired, but Maine built this fort two years later, just in case. Though it was never entirely completed, troops were stationed here during the Civil War and again during the Spanish-American War. This is a great fort with plenty of tunnels and turrets to explore. It's a venue for re-enactments, dramas, and a variety of events—including "Fright of the Fort" nights, sponsored by Friends of Fort Knox, on the two weekends before Halloween. Check the website.

William A. Davis

FORT KNOX FROM THE BUCKSPORT WATERFRONT

popcorn. It is also a venue for concerts and live performances. The theater was restored by nonprofit Northeast Historic Film, New England's only "moving-image" archive. Stock footage, technical services, and sales of videos of life in New England are all available. The theater store is open during business hours (weekdays 9–4) as well as weekends in July and Aug. during films and performances. The events line is 207-469-6910; check the website for available films.

The Bucksport Waterfront Walkway. A landscaped brick path stretches a mile from the Verona Bridge to the town landing and on up along the Penobscot River. The **Bucksport**

Historical Society Museum (207-469-3284), open July–Sept., Wed.–Fri. 1–4, Sat. 2–4, is housed in the former waterside Maine Central Railroad Station and is genuinely interesting.

Craig Brook National Fish Hatchery, (207-469-7300), 306 Hatchery Rd., East Orland (marked from Rt. 1). First opened in 1889, this is the country's oldest salmon hatchery. A visitors center (open daily 8–3) offers videos and interactive displays on Maine rivers, watersheds, and salmon. A small Atlantic Salmon Flyfishing Museum exhibits salmon industry memorabilia. There's also a boat launch on Alamoosook Lake, a picnic area and swim beach on Craig Pond, and hiking trails.

✳ Lodging

✪ ✿ ♪ ((ᵠ)) Alamoosook Lakeside Inn (207-469-6393; alamoosooklakesideinn.com), 229 Soper Rd., Orland. Open year-round. A few miles north of Rt. 1, this log lodge—built as a corporate retreat—feels much farther away. Grounds stretch along the lake and you can swim at the beach or push off in a paddleboat or kayak. Innkeeper Gina Bushong likes to help guests explore off the beaten path. The six attractive guest rooms are $95–148 per couple and $10 for each additional person, breakfast included. The lakeside dining room lends itself to weddings and retreats.

Fort Knox Park Inn (207-469-3113; fortknoxparkinn.com), 64 Main St., Bucksport 04416. Open year-round. Built as a modern annex to the old Jed Prouty Inn, it offers rooms with a choice of two double beds, a queen, or king. Request a view of Fort Knox and the dramatic bridge across the mouth of the Penobscot River, well worth the extra $10. $80–150 per couple, depending on the room and season.

✳ Where to Eat

♪ ((ᵠ)) MacLeods (207-469-3963), 63 Main St., Bucksport. Open daily, 4–close, also lunch from 11:30 Tue.–Thu. Dependable dining in a pubby atmosphere with booths. Entrées range from comfort food like baked meat loaf and barbecued ribs to specials like a baked scallop strudel.

♪ Harbor View Grille (207-469-3396), 96 Main St., Bucksport. Open daily 6 AM–8 PM. Sited on the town dock, it overlooks water, Fort Knox, and the bridge. Reasonably priced seafood baskets and specials and a full road-food menu. Kids' menu, too.

♪ Wahl's Dairy Port (207-469-3697), 79 Main St., Bucksport. Open Apr.–late Sept., 11–8. For more than 50 years this old-fashioned ice cream stand has been dishing it up: many flavors of ice cream (Gifford's), also soft serve, frozen yogurt, sherbet, shakes, more.

✳ Selective Shopping

((ᵠ)) Book Stacks (207-469-8992 or 1-888-295-0123; bookstacksmaine.com), 71 Main St., Bucksport. Open Mon.–Sat. 9–6 (later in summer), Sun. 9–4. An inviting full-service bookstore, also selling wine and with a café featuring espresso and WiFi.

h.o.m.e. co-op (207-469-7961; homecoop.net), Rt. 1, Orland. Open daily 9–5. A part of the international Emmaus community, selling crafted coverlets, toys, and clothing; also has a market stand with fresh vegetables, herbs, and other garden produce.

✳ Special Events

Note: Check with Friends of Fort Knox (fortknox.maineguide.com) for colorful events at the fort, staged most weekends Apr.–Oct. Halloween is huge here.

July: Bay Festival (last weekend)—parade, plus a variety of events on the river; at the fort and along the Bucksport waterfront.

August: h.o.m.e.'s Annual Craft & Farm Fair and Benefit Auction (207-469-7961; homecoop.net). A Sat. blueberry pancake breakfast, poetry readings, music, fish-fry supper, street dance, BBQ, children's games, crafts, and more.

October: Ghostport, Bucksport. Held 10–10 Sat. before Halloween—coffin races, lunch with witches, goblins' parade, tent dance, fireworks, much more. Shuttle runs to Fright of the Fort across the river at Fort Knox, held the two weekends before Halloween.

Blue Hill Area

The series of peninsulas and islands defining the eastern rim of Penobscot Bay—an inter-mingling of land and water along ponds and tidal rivers, as well as bays—is a landscape that's exceptional, even in Maine. Scattered over an area webbed with narrow roads thread-ing numerous land fingers are roads leading to studios of local craftspeople and artists. What you remember afterward is the beauty of clouds over fields of wildflowers, quiet coves, some amazing things that have been woven, painted, or blown, and conversations with the people who created them. Getting anywhere takes longer than you'll anticipate, so it's best to allow a few days here.

In Maine, *Blue Hill* refers to a specific hill, a village, a town, a bay, and a peninsula—also to an unusual gathering of artists, musicians, and craftspeople. A shade off the beaten path, one peninsula west of Mount Desert, Blue Hill has its own following—especially among cre-ative people. For many decades the small town of Brooklin was a familiar byline in *The New Yorker* thanks to E. B. White, who also wrote *Charlotte's Web* and *Stuart Little* here at about the time children began to read about Blueberry Hill in Robert McCloskey's *Blueberries for Sal* and about Condon's Garage (still a South Brooksville family-owned landmark) in the 1940s classic *One Morning in Maine*. In the 1950s Helen and Scott Nearing, searching for a new place to live "the Good Life," swung a dowsing pendulum over a map of coastal Maine. It came to rest on Cape Rosier.

Energy lines or not, this peninsula is exceptionally beautiful, with views to the east toward Mount Desert as well as back across Penobscot Bay. Pause at the turnout on Cater-pillar Hill, the height-of-land on Rt. 15/175 (just north of the Deer Isle Bridge), to appreciate the panorama. Then plunge down the hill to an improbably narrow, soaring suspension bridge.

The 1939 bridge spans Eggemoggin Reach, a 10-mile-long passage dividing the Blue Hill Peninsula from Deer Isle but linking Penobscot and Jericho Bays. A century ago this was a busy thoroughfare, a shortcut from Rockland to points Down East for freight-carrying schooners and passenger steamboats. It remains a popular route for windjammers, yachts, and, increasingly, sea kayakers.

GUIDANCE The **Blue Hill Peninsula Chamber of Commerce** (207-374-3242; bluehill peninsula.org), 16B South St. (beside Dunkin' Donuts), Blue Hill, covers the six peninsula towns, publishing a booklet guide. Its year-round information center is open Mon.–Fri. 11–3. Pick up a guide and local map (essential). Also pick up the current free copies of the *Arts Guide* and the *Bay Community Register*, and see **eastpenobscotbay.com**. *The Weekly Packet* lists what's going on each day.

GETTING THERE *By car:* From points south take I-95 to Rt. 295 to I-95 (briefly) to Exit 113: Rt. 3 to Belfast and Rt. 1 to Rt. 15 to Blue Hill. There are many shortcuts through the confus-ing web of roads on this peninsula; ask directions to your lodging.

By air: The nearest commercial airports are **Bangor International** (flybangor.com) and **Hancock County & Bar Harbor Airport** (between Ellsworth and Bar Harbor).

WHEN TO COME Most Blue Hill lodging is seasonal, mid-May through October.

✳ To See

Jonathan Fisher House (207-374-2459; jonathanfisherhouse.org), 0.5 mile south of Blue Hill Village on Rt. 15/176. Open July–Labor Day, Wed.–Sat. 1–4; Fri., Sat. until Columbus Day.

MUST SEE

A dozen miles south of Rt. 1 via Rt. 15, the **Blue Hill Village** (blue-hill.gov) is cradled between its namesake hill and bay. In the center of town you'll find a pillared town hall, a handsome WPA library, two Federal-era historic houses (see *Also See*), shops, and galleries. This is the peninsula hub, but to come this far and no farther would be like walking up to a door and not opening it. The beauty of the peninsula lies beyond—down roads that wander southwest to **Brooksville** (Rt. 15 south to Rt. 176 north to Rt. 176/175) and across the **Bagaduce River** at the **Reversing Falls** (see Bagaduce Lunch in *Eating Out*); head south on Rt. 176 to **Bucks Harbor**. Rt. 176 rejoins Rt. 175 and then Rt. 15; follow it south (right) over **Caterpillar Hill**, where a pullout permits space to enjoy one of the most spectacular panoramas across Penobscot Bay to the Camden Hills. From this height Rt. 15 plunges downhill. Turn left at the bottom, following Rt. 175 as it shadows **Eggemoggin Reach**, through Sargentville, winds up around the Benjamin River in Sedgwick, and down along the Reach again into **Brooklin**, home to **Wooden Boat School** (see *Special Programs*). See *Selective Shopping* for stops along the way.

A house built in 1814 by Blue Hill's first pastor, a Harvard graduate who augmented his meager salary with a varied line of crafts and by teaching (he founded Blue Hill Academy), farming, and writing. His furniture, paintings, books, journals, and woodcuts are exhibited. Antiques show mid-Aug. Admission $5.

Holt House, 3 Water St., Blue Hill. Open July–mid-Sept., Tue. and Fri. 1–4, Sat. 11–2. The Blue Hill Historical Society collection is housed in this restored 1815 Federal mansion near the harbor and noted for its stenciled walls. Don't pass this by if it's open: a lovely old house filled with images and tokens evoking Blue Hill's past.

Blue Hill Library (207-374-5515; bhpl.net), 5 Parker Point Rd., Blue Hill. Open daily except Sun. A handsome WPA building with periodicals and ample reading space; changing art shows in summer.

Bagaduce Music Lending Library (207-374-5454; bagaducemusic.org), 5 Music Library Lane, Rt. 172, Blue Hill. Open Mon.–Fri. 10–4. This Blue Hill phenomenon features roughly 250,000 sheet music titles (instrumental, keyboard, and vocal), some more than a century old and most special for one reason or another—all available for borrowing. The collection includes more than 1,400 pieces about Maine, by Maine composers, or published in Maine. Stop by just to see the mural over the entrance.

The Good Life Center (207-326-8211; goodlife.org), 372 Harborside Rd., Harborside, on Cape Rosier. Open June–Labor Day, Thu.–Mon. 1–4, then weekends until Columbus Day; and by appointment. The grounds are open year-round. **Forest Farm** is a stone home built in 1973 by Scott Nearing when he was in his 90s (d. 1983), along with Helen, then in her 70s. The couple coauthored *Living the Good Life* and seven other books based on their simple, purposeful lifestyle. The grounds include an intensively cultivated organic garden, a greenhouse, and a yurt. Check the website for workshops.

Christina Tree

THE GOOD LIFE CENTER

BUCKS HARBOR IS A SAILING CENTER.

✳ To Do

BOATING Buck's Harbor Marine (207-326-8839), South Brooksville, rents sail- and motor-boats. Inquire about sailing lessons.

Captain Bill Brown offers day sails and longer from Bucks Harbor, Brooksville, in his 30-foot two-masted pinky schooner, *Summertime* (207-326-8485).

Also see *Sea Kayaking, Canoeing.*

FISHING Eggemoggin Guide Service (207-359-2746; eggemogginguideservice.net), Sedgwick. Captain Pete Douvarjo offers half-day trips for striped bass and full-day float trips on the Penobscot River. Fly-fishing and handcrafted fishing rods are specialties.

SEA KAYAKING, CANOEING The Activity Shop (207-374-3600; activityshop.com), 139 Mines Road, Blue Hill. Old Town canoes, kayak, and bicycle rentals. The Bagaduce River north from Walker Pond is a favorite flatwater run for novices, with some popular white-water at Blue Hill Falls, a reversing falls accessible off Rt. 175. Also see *To Do* in "Deer Isle, Stonington" and "Castine."

SPECIAL LEARNING PROGRAMS WoodenBoat School (207-359-4651; woodenboat .com), off Naskeag Rd., south of Brooklin Village. A spinoff from *WoodenBoat* magazine, this seafaring institute of national fame offers summer courses that range from building your own sailboat, canoe, or kayak to navigation and drawing and painting. Accommodations available. The store is a shopping destination in its own right; open weekdays 7:30–6, Sat. 9–5.

Also see **Haystack Mountain School of Crafts** in "Deer Isle, Stonington."

SWIMMING Walker Pond Landing, Sedgwick. From Rt. 175/15 south of the Caterpillar Hill lookout, turn right on Cooper Farm Road, right again on Walker Pond Road. This is a joint Brooksville/Sedgwick-maintained facility with a roped-off swim area and raft, boat launch, and a sand beach with warm, shallow water; great for small children.

✳ Green Space

Blue Hill. Our friends at the Blue Hill Bookstore tell us that this was not the setting for the children's classic *Blueberries for Sal*, by Robert McCloskey—a longtime summer resident of the area. But we choose to disbelieve them. It looks just like the hill in the book and has its share of in-season blueberries. The big attraction, however, is the view of the Mount Desert mountains from the 934-foot summit. From Rt. 172 take Mountain Rd. to the parking area (on your right). It's a mile to the top via the Hayes Trail, a little longer if you loop back down to the road via the Osgood Trail through Blue Hill Heritage Trust land. A trail right from town begins behind the post office.

Holbrook Island Sanctuary State Park (207-326-4012; friendsofholbrook.org), Cape Rosier Road, off Rt. 176 in West Brooksville, is 1,350 acres, including 2.3 miles of shore and 115-acre Holbrook Island. Check the website for a detailed map. A network of old roads and trails leads along the shore and through marshes and forest. This is the gift of Anita Harris, who died in 1985 at age 92. Her will stipulated that her mansion and all the other buildings on Holbrook Island and in the sanctuary be demolished. Birding is exceptional, especially during spring and fall migrations. Great blue herons nest around the pond and the estuary. Bald eagles may also be seen. Guided nature walks in-season.

Blue Hill Heritage Trust (207-374-5118; bluehillheritagetrust.org) is steadily increasing the amount of preserved open space throughout the peninsula.

🖋 **Blue Hill Town Park**. Follow Water St. past the hospital to this pleasant waterside park with picnic tables and great rocks for kids.

THE BEACH AT WALKER POND LANDING

✷ Lodging

INNS AND B&BS

IN BLUE HILL 04614

✪ 🐾 ♿ **Blue Hill Inn** (207-374-2844 or 1-800-826-7415; bluehillinn.com), 40 Union St. The inn is open mid-May–Oct.; the Cape House, year-round. There's a grace to this classic 1830s New England inn on a quiet, elm-lined street in the village. The sitting room and library are stocked with reading material, and innkeeper Sarah Pebworth shows a sure touch and attention to detail in 11 guest rooms, some with sitting room and/or working fireplace. The handicapped-accessible Cape House cottage is divided into two suites with kitchen facilities. Guests may gather for wine and hors d'oeuvres in the evening. A full breakfast with a choice of entrées is served at individual tables in the large, sunny dining room. It's included along with afternoon tea in $195–265 double for rooms in high season, from $145 before July. Suites are $285–375 in-season; from $170 in winter.

The Farmhouse Inn (207-374-5286), 578 Pleasant St. (Rt. 15). Open almost year-round. In 2015 Bill and Ann Rioux reopened the former Blue Hill Farm Country Inn after totally renovating the 19th-century farmhouse and attached barn, reducing guest rooms from 14 to 9. An instant success as a restaurant (see *Dining Out*), its rooms are also now bright and appealing, all with private baths, common

BLUE HILL INN

space, and game rooms. From $150 for a cozy room with a large skylight to $300 for a two-room suite, breakfast included.

ELSEWHERE ON THE BLUE HILL PENINSULA

♂ (())) **Wave Walker Bed & Breakfast** (207-667-5767; wavewalkerbedandbreakfast.com), 28 Wavewalker Lane, Surry 04684. Open year-round. Sited near the tip of Newbury Neck with spectacular views across the bay to Mount Desert Island, this expansive house comes with 20 acres and a 1,000-foot waterfront. The four guest rooms all have views and many comfort perks. $195–290 in-season; from $115 off, three-day minimum, weekly rates. Inquire about weddings and the Guest House.

COTTAGES AND MORE ✪ (())) 🐾 **Oakland House Cottages by the Side of the Sea** (207-359-8521; oaklandhouse.com), 435 Herrick Rd., Brooksville. Few rental cottages have the kind of setting and views these 10 can offer, salted through the woods and along the shorefront near the entrance to Eggemoggin Reach. Each is different, with cooking facilities, living room, and fireplace. Accommodating up to eight, they offer access to an expansive beach, a rec hall with weekly happenings, and 60 mostly wooded acres laced with trails. They are part of former Oakland House resort (check-in is still at the picturesque old hotel), and its "Barn" continues to house weekly events (open to the public) in summer. $150–326 per night in high season, less per week.

Hostel@Acorn by the Sea (207-359-8521; mainehostel.com). Newly opened in a rehabbed annex on the Oakland House property (see above). The six country-comfortable rooms vary from a bunk room to doubles; all share a kitchen, baths, and attractive common rooms, as well as access to the beach and trails. From $30 per person and $40 per room.

✪ 🦞 🐾 ♂ (())) **Hiram Blake Camp** (207-326-4951; hiramblake.com), Cape Rosier, Harborside. Open May–Columbus Day weekend. Well off the beaten track and operated by Deborah Venno's family since 1916, this is the kind of place where you come to stay put. The one- to three-bedroom cottages each have

THE FARMHOUSE INN

a living room with a wood-burning stove, kitchen, shower, porch, and view of Penobscot Bay. In July and Aug. everyone eats in the dining room, which doubles as a library with thousands of books ingeniously filed away by category in the ceiling. There are rowboats at the dock and kayaks for rent, a playground, and a recreation room with table tennis and board games; also trails. In high season, from $1,075 per week with breakfast and dinner for the one-room Acorn Cottage to $3,450 for a three-bedroom cottage (up to five guests). Rates drop during "housekeeping months" (when the dining room closes at the end of Aug.) to $800–1,700 per week plus $20 for linen. Most cottages are reserved by Jan. but it's worth checking.

Peninsula Property Rentals (207-374-2428; peninsulapropertyrentals.com), Main St., Blue Hill 04614. A range of area rentals. Also see **Maine Vacation Rentals** (207-374-2444; mainevacationrentalsonline.com), 105 Main St., Blue Hill.

❋ Where to Eat

DINING OUT

IN BLUE HILL

Arborvine (207-374-2119; arborvine.com), 33 Tenney Hill (Rt. 172), south Blue Hill Village.

Open for dinner Tue.–Sun. in-season, Fri.–Sun. off-season. Few Maine restaurants are as widely acclaimed, and reservations may be necessary a couple of days in advance. Chef-owner John Hikade and his wife, Beth, restored the handsome 1820s Hinckley homestead. The several open-beamed dining rooms with fireplaces are simple and elegant. The menu presents local produce in memorable ways. For starters try Bagaduce River oysters in the half shell with a frozen sake mignonette ($12). Entrées $26–34. The reasonably priced wine list is extensive.

✤ **Barncastle** (207-374-2300), 125 South St. Open daily year-round 3–8, until 9 Fri., Sat. This former mansion is an unlikely but delightful venue for the area's best pizza. The ambience is upscale, the oven is wood-fired, and the pie comes with a choice of more than 30 toppings. The reasonably priced menu also includes crabcakes, ribs, mussels in white wine, also sandwiches and salads featuring local farm ingredients.

The Farmhouse Inn (207-374-5286), 578 Pleasant St. (Rt. 15) , Blue Hill (2 miles north of the village). Open most of the year Wed.–Sat., 3–5 happy hour with a wide selection of tapas and small plates, then a full menu. An open-raftered, nicely rehabbed barn with well-spaced tables and an attractive 10-seat bar, this new restaurant is so popular that it's advisable to reserve for dinner. So many small plates to choose from, maybe crab and smoked gouda or savory bacon and blue cheesecake will strike your fancy. Entrées

Christina Tree

OAKLAND HOUSE

$16-18. Owner Ann Roux is also a local caterer, ably assisted by daughter Megan Rioux.

ELSEWHERE ON THE BLUE HILL PENINSULA

✪ **Buck's Restaurant** (207-326-8688), Buck's Harbor Market, center of South Brooksville, Rt. 176. Open seasonally except Sun. 5:30–8:30; check nights off-season. Reserve. The informal dining room behind the village market is decorated with local sculpture and art and is all about turning local ingredients into tasty dishes. The menu changes daily, but starters might include local mussels with house-made chorizo and grilled swordfish with spicy mango and papaya relish. Entrées $18–32.

✪ **The Brooklin Inn** (207-359-2777; brooklininn.com), 22 Reach Rd. (Rt. 175), Brooklin Village. Reservations advised. Open nightly in summer, closed Mon. and Tue. in winter. This hospitable small-village inn religiously serves only wild fish and produce that's organic and local. Chefs tend to change, but quality has been consistent. Entrées: $22 for chicken Francaise to $56 for a pound ($32 for a half-pound) of pan-seared rib-eye. A three-course prix fixe is $25. There's also a downstairs pub.

🍴 **The Lookout Inn & Restaurant** (207-359-2188; thelookoutinn.biz), 455 Flye Point Rd., Brooklin. Open for dinner Tue.–Sat. mid-June–mid-Oct.; call off-season. Owner Butch Smith was in the kitchen on our last visit, and the sautéed duck breast with raspberry mustard glaze was delicious as was the baked artichoke with kale as a starter. A bit of a local secret, this is one of Maine's oldest family-owned summer hotels and the view is across the sloping meadow to the bay. Entrées $25–30.

Also see *Dining Out* in "Deer Isle, Stonington," and "Castine."

EATING OUT

IN BLUE HILL

🍴 **Boatyard Grill** (207-374-3533), 13 E. Blue Hill Rd. Open June–mid-Sept., Tue.–Sat. for lunch and dinner. Eat inside or out in a pavilion sited in a working boatyard. Chef-owner Annelise Riggall serves up local mussels, clams, and lobster in forms that range from pizza and mac-and-cheese to a shore dinner. Daily specials and all seafood is grilled rather than fried.

🍴 **The Fish Net** (207-374-5240), Blue Hill Village, 162 Main St. (Rt. 172). Open seasonally 11–8, until 9 Fri.–Sat. Known for lobster rolls; also as a place to feast on lobster and steamers or to buy a cooked lobster to take home, plus the usual fried seafood, burgers, and sandwiches. Seating inside and out with a playground for kids.

🍴 **Marlintini's Grill** (207-374-2500), 89 Mines Rd. (Rt. 15/176) south of Blue Hill Village. Local favorite, open for all three meals. There's a sports bar but plenty of space to get away from it. Grilled and fried meat and seafood, hot sandwiches, and nightly specials.

The Deep Water Brew Pub (207-374-2441; arborvine.com), 33 Tenney Hill. Open seasonally, Tue.–Sun. for supper; bar open until 10. No reservations. The attraction is beer (primarily ales) handcrafted in the solar-powered microbrewery in the barn behind Arborvine (see *Dining Out*). The casual pub, created by Tim Hikade and partner Chrissy Allen, offers a reasonably priced menu featuring burgers, ribs, and the like.

Blue Hill Food Co-op Café (207-374-2165), Rt. 172 in Green's Hill Place, a small shopping center just north of the village. Open weekdays 8–7, Sat. 8–6, Sun. 10–5. This attractive café is part of a well-stocked market specializing in organic and local produce as well as

Christina Tree

BOATYARD GRILL

BAGADUCE LUNCH HAS BEEN NAMED "AN AMERICAN CLASSIC" BY THE JAMES BEARD FOUNDATION

wines, vitamins, and premade sandwiches. Organic coffees, teas, wines and a selection of baked goods, soups, sandwiches, and specials.

The Mill Stream Deli, Bakery & BBQ (207-374-1049), 58 Main St. Open Mon.–Sat. 8–5. Breads, pastries, sandwiches, and deli foods, all made from scratch, nitrate-free. Tim and Linda Bingham formerly managed the co-op kitchen.

ELSEWHERE ON THE BLUE HILL PENINSULA

✪ ✄ **El El Frijoles** (207-359-2486; elelfrijoles .com), 41 Caterpillar Hill Rd. (Rt. 15), Sargentville. Open Memorial Day–Sept., Wed.–Sun. 11–8, off-season Wed. and Thu. 11–7. We love the takeoff on L.L. Bean. Michael Rossney and Michele La Vesque serve up California/Mexican food with local ingredients, right down to the black beans. Taco and burrito fillings include grilled veggies and carnitas (slow-braised, shredded pork with chilies, onions, and spices). The house special is spicy lobster. Mini burritos and a PB&J quesadilla for kids. Takeout and a few inside tables, more seating outside at covered and open picnic tables, a play structure, sandbox, and badminton court.

✪ ✿ **Bagaduce Lunch** (207-326-4197), Rt. 176, South Penobscot at the reversing falls and the bridge to North Brooksville. Open seasonally, 11–3 except Wed. This hugely popular lunch stand is a must. Fried seafood baskets are the big draw, and they will spoil you for seafood baskets anywhere else forever. Generous crab and lobster rolls. Picnic tables are scattered over the lawn that slopes to the Bagaduce River.

✄ **Millbrook Company Bakery and Restaurant** (207-359-8344), 160 Snow's Cove Rd. (Rt. 15), Sedgwick. Open year-round, Wed.–Sun. 7:30–2. Attractive dining room, great breads, focaccia, "local chef salad" with locally sourced greens, veggies, and goat cheese, with or without marinated grilled chicken or fish. Daily specials, inside/outside dining.

Buck's Harbor Market (207-326-8683), Cornfield Hill Rd. (Rt. 176), Brooksville Village. Open year-round, 8–6. Soups, deli, baking done here (baked olives too); great picnic fare. The market also has a few tables should you decide to stay and eat.

Tinder Hearth Bread & Pizzas (207-326-8381; tinderhearth.com), 1452 Coastal Rd., West Brooksville. Look for the wood-fired bread and croissants in area shops. The thin-crust pizza, made from organic flour with locally sourced toppings, is available from the bakery Tue., Wed., and Fri. 5–8 PM. Reserve ahead. Inquire about summer music.

✪ **Perry's Lobster Shack** (207-667-1955) 1076 Newbury Neck Rd, Surry. Open May–mid-Oct., but call to check in shoulder months. Near the tip of a long, skinny sliver of land dangling off the peninsula proper in Surry. Picnic tables on the dock below with a view of Acadia. Great lobster and crab rolls, plus local sweet corn and homemade ice cream sandwiches. BYOB.

MILLBROOK COMPANY BAKERY AND RESTAURANT, SEDGWICK

PICNIC FIXINGS Don't waste a nice day by eating inside! For picnic sites, see *Green Space*. Also see **Buck's Harbor Market** in Brooksville and the **Blue Hill Food Co-op**.

✳ Entertainment

New Surry Theatre (207-200-4720; newsurry theatre.org), 18 Union St. (upstairs in the Blue Hill Town Hall). Performances and acting classes throughout the year.

♪ **Kneisel Hall Chamber Music School and Festival** (207-374-2811; kneisel.org), Pleasant St. (Rt. 15), Blue Hill. One of the oldest chamber music festivals in the country (founded 1924). Faculty present string and ensemble music in a series of Sun. afternoon and Fri. evening concerts, June–Aug.; inquire about Young Artist Concerts.

WERU (207-469-6600; weru.org) is a major nonprofit community radio station based in East Orland (89.9 FM) known for folk and Celtic music, jazz, and reggae.

Flash in the Pans Community Steel Band (peninsulapan.org). Mon.-night street dances, Memorial Day–Labor Day, 7:30–9 throughout the Peninsula; check website for schedule.

✳ Selective Shopping

IN BLUE HILL

ART Jud Hartman Gallery and Sculpture Studio (207-374-917; judhartmangallery.com), 79 Main St. Open mid-June–mid-Sept., daily. Hartman exhibits his nationally known realistic bronze sculptures of northeastern Native Americans as well as the work of other well-known local artists.

Randy Eckard (207-374-2510; randyeckard paintings.com), 29 Pleasant St. Open July–Sept., Tue.–Sat. 11–4. Limited-edition prints of the artist's precise, luminous landscapes.

Liros Gallery (207-374-5370; lirosgallery .com), Parker Point Rd., specializes in fine paintings, old prints, and Russian icons; appraisals.

Blue Hill Bay Gallery (207-274-4001; bluehillbaygallery.com), 11 Tenney Hill. Open 10–5 Memorial Day–Labor Day; weekends thereafter. Changing exhibits of 19th-century

BLUE HILL GALLERY   *Christina Tree*

and contemporary art, featuring northern landscapes and the sea.

Cynthia Winings Gallery (207-204-5001; cynthiawiningsgallery.com), 24 Parker Point Rd. Open June–Oct., Tue.–Sat., also Mon. in June, July. A quality contemporary gallery.

✪ **Handworks Gallery** (207-374-5613; handworksgallery.org), 48 Main St. Open Memorial Day–late Dec., Mon.–Sat. 10–5; weekends year-round. A middle-of-town space filled with stunning work by Maine artists and artisans: handwoven clothing, jewelry, furniture, rugs, and blown glass and art.

Rackliffe Pottery (207-374-2297; rackliffe pottery.com), Rt. 172. Open Mon.–Sat. 8–4; also Sun. in July and Aug., noon–4. Since 1968 Phyllis and Phil Rackliffe have produced their distinctive pottery, featuring local clay and their own glazes. Their emphasis is on individual small pieces rather than on sets. Visitors are welcome to watch.

SPECIAL SHOPS

IN BLUE HILL VILLAGE

✪ **Blue Hill Books** (207-374-5632; bluehill books.com), 26 Pleasant St (Rt. 15). Open Mon.–Sat. 10–5:30, also Sun. June–Aug., Blue Hill. A long-established, independent, full-service, two-floor, family-run bookstore with a separate room for children's titles. One of the best bookstores in Maine, with frequent readings by the many local authors.

✪ **Blue Hill Wine Shop** (207-374-2161), Main St. Open Mon.–Sat. 10–5:30. A long-established shop dedicated to the perfect cup of tea or coffee, a well-chosen wine, cheese, and the right blend of tobacco. Also morning coffee and muffins.

⊙ **Black Dinah Chocolatiers** (207-374-5621), 5 Main St., inside the Fairwinds Florist building, Blue Hill. Open Mon.–Sat. 8:30–5, Sun. 10–3. Handcrafted from Venezuelan and Peruvian chocolate, local butter, cream, herbs, fruits, and flowers; signature truffles and artisanal ice cream, chocolate drinks, espresso, and cookies.

ON AND OFF RT. 175 ALONG EGGEMOGGIN REACH

Sedgwick Antiques (207-359-8834), 775 N. Sedgwick Rd. (Rt. 172), Sedgwick. May–Sept., Thu., Fri. 10–4, Sat. 12–4 and by appointment. William Petry runs an old-fashioned shop with a range of furniture, rugs, ceramics, and lighting, emphasis on formal styles.

Handmade Papers Gallery (207-359-8345), 113 Reach Rd., Brooklin. Open summer, Wed.–Sun. noon–5. Virginia Sarsfield fashions exquisite lamp shades and other creations from a variety of fibers, including tufts of cattail. She also carries a selection of striking prints, featuring maritime linocuts by James Dodds, and work in a variety of media, featuring rag rugs by Hillary Hutton.

⊙ **Betsy's Sunflower** (207-359-5030), 12 Reach Rd., Brooklin. A winner. Unusual but

handy kitchen and garden gadgets and other nifty things for cottages and boats; also home furnishings, toys, gifts, books, sailcloth totes, local music, more.

ALONG RT. 176

Tinder Hearth Wood-Fired Bread, (tinder hearth.com) 1452 Coastal Rd., West Brooksville. (See *Eating Out*.)

♂ ♪ **David's Folly Farm** (207-266-6512; davidsfollyfarm.com), 1390 Coastal Rd., West Brooksville. Look for the "Open" flag. A strikingly beautiful 200-year-old working farm. Emma and John Altman practice organic, sustainable methods. Check out the farm store for meat and produce and the website for frequent special events in the barn.

Thomas Hinchcliffe Antiques (207-326-9411), Graytown Rd. (Rt. 176), West Sedgwick. Open most afternoons in-season. Call ahead. Authentic early country furniture, featuring farm tables, decoys, and other nautical and country accessories.

✴ Special Events

Memorial Day–mid-October: **Farmers' Markets**, in **Blue Hill**, Sat. 9–11:30 AM, Blue Hill Fairgrounds, Rt. 15; at Mainescape Garden Shop, Columbus Day–Apr. Crafts, food, and baked goods as well as seasonal produce and flowers. Guest artists in July and Aug. In **Brooklin**, Thu. 3–5 beside Friend Memorial Library. **Brooksville**: Tue. 9–11, Community Center, Cornfield Rd. **Surry**: Sweet Pea Gardens (center of town), Thu. 3–6.

July: **Touring Through Time** (fourth weekend)—all the local historical sites hold open houses. **Blue Hill Bach Festival**, last weekend; (bluehillbach.org).

August: **Academy Antiques Fair** (first weekend), George Stevens Academy, Blue Hill, is big. The **Annual St. Francis Fair** (mid-month), Blue Hill Fairgrounds, is bigger, also about antiques.

Labor Day weekend: **Blue Hill Fair** (207-374-3701; bluehillfair.com) at the fairgrounds—harness racing, a midway, livestock competitions; one of the most color-ful old-style fairs in New England. Best view of the fireworks is from the top of Blue Hill.

Christina Tree

HANDWORKS GALLERY, BLUE HILL

Deer Isle, Stonington, and Isle au Haut

The narrow, half-mile-long suspension bridge across Eggemoggin Reach connects the Blue Hill Peninsula with Little Deer Isle, linked in turn by causeways and bridges to Deer Isle and its wandering land fingers. This intermingling of land and water is characterized by the kind of coves, spruce and lupine-fringed inlets usually equated with "the real Maine." It's divided between the towns of Deer Isle and Stonington, and there are the villages of Sunset, Oceanville, and Sunshine, home of the nationally respected Haystack Mountain School of Crafts. Galleries display outstanding work by dozens of artists and craftspeople who live, or at least summer, in town.

Stonington, 36 miles south of Rt. 1, remains a working fishing harbor, but with more than its share of galleries. Most buildings, scattered on smooth rocks around the harbor, date from the 1880s to the World War I boom years, during which Deer Isle's pink granite was shipped off to face buildings from Rockefeller Center to Boston's Museum of Fine Arts. The Deer Isle Granite Museum depicts Stonington at the height of the granite boom when its population was 5,000, compared with 1,143 in 2010.

In Stonington life still eddies around Billings Diesel and Marine and the commercial pier, home base for one of Maine's largest fishing/lobstering fleets. The tourist season is short but busy enough to support a string of seasonal galleries and visitor-geared shops along waterside Main Street. The restored opera house stages frequent films, live performances, and readings, and the Reach Performing Arts Center is also active year-round. Hundreds of new houses have been built in recent decades, a boon to renters, and the number of nature preserves has also multiplied.

Stonington is departure point for the mail boat to Isle au Haut, a wooded, mountainous island with more than half its acreage preserved as a part of Acadia National Park. The boat makes seasonal stops at Duck Harbor, near the island's southern tip, accessing rugged,

Christina Tree

EGGEMOGGIN REACH BRIDGE

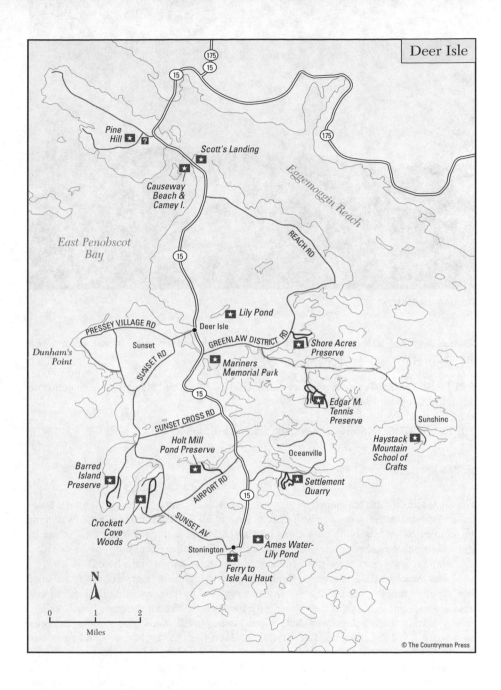

Deer Isle

175
15
15

Pine Hill ★ ?

Scott's Landing ★

Causeway Beach & Camey I. ★

175

Eggemoggin Reach

REACH RD

15

East Penobscot Bay

Lily Pond ★

PRESSEY VILLAGE RD

Deer Isle

Sunset

GREENLAW DISTRICT RD

Shore Acres Preserve ★

Dunham's Point

SUNSET RD

Mariners Memorial Park ★

15

Edgar M. Tennis Preserve ★

SUNSET CROSS RD

Sunshine

Holt Mill Pond Preserve ★

Oceanville

Haystack Mountain School of Crafts ★

Barred Island Preserve ★

AIRPORT RD

15

Settlement Quarry ★

★

Crockett Cove Woods

SUNSET AV

Stonington

Ames Water-Lily Pond ★

Ferry to Isle Au Haut

N

0   1   2
Miles

© The Countryman Press

coastal hiking trails. The remaining half of the island, which supports fewer some 70 year-round residents and an old summer colony, is vividly depicted in *The Lobster Chronicles* by Linda Greenlaw.

GUIDANCE Deer Isle–Stonington Chamber of Commerce (207-348-6124; deerisle.com) maintains an "Information Building" (with facilities) on Rt. 15 at Little Deer Isle, south of the bridge. Open 10–4 mid-June–Labor Day, sporadically after that for a few weeks. Pick up

STONINGTON WATERFRONT

the current map/guide (an outside box is kept stocked) and a copy of *Island Advantages*, Stonington's weekly paper since 1882.

GETTING THERE Follow directions under *Getting There* in "Blue Hill Area"; continue down Rt. 15 to Deer Isle.

PUBLIC RESTROOMS are on the public landing in Stonington.

✳ To See

✐ & **Deer Isle Granite Museum** (207-367-6331), Main St., Stonington. Open Memorial Day–Labor Day on selective days; call to check. This small museum features an 8-by-15-foot working model of quarrying operations on Crotch Island and the town of Stonington in 1900. Derricks move and trains carry granite to waiting ships. Photo blowups and a video also dramatize the story of the quarryman's life during the height of the boom.

✐ **The Penobscot East Resource Center** (207-367-2708; penobscoteast.org), 13 Atlantic Ave. Open seasonally, Mon.–Fri. 10–4. This is a regional fisheries research facility, but visitors are welcome in the Education Room with its touch tank and interactive "touch wall."

✐ **Nervous Nellie's Jams and Jellies and Mountainville Café** (800-77-6845; nervous nellies.com), 598 Sunshine Rd., Deer Isle. Open May–Oct., 10–5. Children of all ages love the whimsical life-sized sculptures Peter Beerits has created over the decades, including a "Nellieville" western-style village peopled by life-sized villains and heroes and a wood full of knights and dragons in Grail Castle, with owls and herons lurking in the shadows and plenty besides the sandbox to please small kids. There's no charge and at every turn the unexpected epitomizes what you come to expect when exploring this area. This all began with Anne and Peter's jams and jellies (wild blueberry preserves, blackberry-peach conserve, hot tomato chutney), cooked up every Mon.-Thu. The Mountainville Café serves tea, coffee, and scones with jams, etc. Three miles off Rt. 15.

The Salome Sellers House (207-348-2897), 416 Sunset Rd. (Rt. 15A), Sunset. Open mid-June–mid-Sept., Wed.–Fri. 1–4. Salome Sellers herself lived to be 108 years old in this snug

MUST SEE

Isle au Haut (pronounced *eye-la-HO*) is 6 miles long and 3 miles wide, a 45-minute boat ride from Stonington. Samuel de Champlain named it "High Island" in 1605, and the highest hill (543 feet) is named for him. It's a quiet, working island with a general store, an inn, and a café. More than half its land is maintained as part of **Acadia National Park,** with an 18-mile network of trails around **Duck Harbor** and along the cliffy southern tip. In summer the **Isle au Haut Ferry** offers round-trip service to Duck Harbor, allowing time to hike the dramatic Western Head and Cliff Trails. The town landing enjoys more frequent (year-round) ferry service, and a well-timed (seasonal) excursion boat also runs (see **Old Quarry Adventures**). From there it's a short walk to the ranger station (207-335-5551), where you can use the facilities and pick up a map, but then it's 6 miles over paved and unpaved roads (see *Bicycle Rentals*) to Duck Harbor. Allow four hours to enjoy the dramatic hiking trails, which are largely pine-needle-carpeted and shaded but demanding with cliffy outcroppings. Camping at Duck Harbor is mid-May–mid-Oct. in the five Adirondack-style shelters (each accommodating six people). Reserve on or as soon after April 1 as possible (207-288-8791, or download a form at nps.gov/acad). Leashed dogs permitted.

1803 red Cape, now the home of the Deer Isle–Stonington Historical Society, displaying ship models, Native American artifacts, and old photos; frequent summer events include music.

LIGHTHOUSES **Pumpkin Island Light**, at the entrance to Eggemoggin Reach, visible from the end of Eggemoggin Rd. on Little Deer Isle, now a private home. **Eagle Island Light** can be viewed from Sylvester Cove in Sunset or, better yet, from the Eagle Island mail boat, from which you can also see the **Heron Neck, Brown's Head**, and **Goose Rocks Lights**. From Goose Cove Lodge in Sunset you can see and hear the now automated **Mark Island Light** (its old bronze bell sits on the resort's lawn); the **Saddleback Ledge Light** is also visible on the horizon. The most extensive lighthouse cruise is offered by **Isle au Haut Ferry Service** (see *Boating*) once a month June–Sept., taking you from East Penobscot Bay through the Fox Islands Thorofare and back up along Vinalhaven and Isle au Haut.

✳ To Do

BICYCLING **Old Quarry Ocean Adventures** rents mountain bikes (see *Boat Excursions*), but we advise using two wheels only on quieter side roads and on Isle au Haut. **Isle au Haut Ferry Service** also rents bikes.

BOATING ☀ ✑ **Isle au Haut Ferry Service** (207-367-5193; isleauhaut.com), end

Christina Tree

NERVOUS NELLIE'S JAMS AND JELLIES

of Seabreeze Ave., Stonington, Twice daily mid-June–mid-Sept. This is the only regularly scheduled service to Duck Harbor (see *Isle au Haut* sidebar) and it's limited to 50 daily passengers, first come/first serve—so buy your ticket at least an hour before the 10 AM departure, then go get some breakfast. $39 roundtrip adults, $19.50 children, $4 pets (must be leashed). The mail boat also serves the island's town dock year-round. It takes kayaks and canoes ($23 one-way) and bicycles ($11 one-way). Check the website for frequent scenic cruises with lobster hauling, also special tours.

Old Quarry Ocean Adventures (207-367-8977; oldquarry.com), 130 Settlement Rd. off the Oceanville Rd., Stonington. Captain Bill Baker offers seasonal 9 AM runs to the Isle au Haut town dock (returning 5 PM), carrying bikes and kayaks gratis ($38.95 roundtrip adults, $20.50 children); guided kayaking around the island is also available. Stay aboard until noon for an ecotour. A variety of other cruises, sailboat rentals and lessons, kayak rentals and lessons, and both half- and full-day guided trips are also offered. The **Old Quarry Campground**, with platform tent sites and camp store, caters to kayakers. The waters off Stonington and Merchant's Row—the many islands just offshore—are among the most popular along the coast, but novice kayakers need a guide; bunkhouses are also available. Inquire about offshore island cottage rentals.

GOLF AND TENNIS **Island Country Club** (207-348-2379), 442 Sunset Rd. (Rt. 15A), Deer Isle, welcomes guests mid-May–mid-Oct. Nine holes; Fairway Café opens Memorial Day for lunch except Mon. Lessons, carts, also **tennis courts** and lessons.

SWIMMING ✪ ✿ ✿ **Lily Pond**, off Rt. 15 north of Deer Isle Village. The beach and access have been preserved and tidied by the Island Heritage Trust. Turn in at Deer Run Apartments; it's a five-minute walk to the pond. The island's freshwater swimming hole offers a shaded, grassy beach that's a great spot for small children, also for long swims.

Sand Beach in Burnt Cove, Stonington. Turn off Rt. 15A on the fire road across from Burnt Cove Market (the sign says NO ENTRANCE AFTER DARK).

Also see **Scott's Landing** in *Green Space*.

✳ Green Space

Island Heritage Trust (207-348-2455; islandheritagetrust.org), 420 Sunset Rd., Deer Isle. Detailed maps of the following walking trails are available from the office, at the visitors center (see *Guidance*), and on the website, which lists walks, talks, and events. Holdings include: **Settlement Quarry**, Stonington. A 0.25-mile walk along an old road to the top of this former working quarry for a view across Webb Cove and west to the Camden Hills. Side trails loop back through woods; **Scott's Landing**. Trails from the causeway web this 24-acre point on Eggemoggin Reach, leading to a vintage-1807 dock and a sandy beach; **Pine Hill Preserve** on Little Deer Isle is a short, rugged climb to a bald summit with a sweeping view; and **Edgar M. Tennis Preserve**, with both wooded and shore trails with shore views, can be found off Sunshine Rd.

Crockett Cove Woods Preserve (a Maine Nature Conservancy property) consists of 100 acres along the water, with a nature trail. From Stonington, take Sunset Rd. through the village of Burnt Cove and turn left onto Whitman Rd.; a right turn at the end of the road brings you to the entrance, marked by a small sign and registration box.

✿ **Barred Island Preserve** is a 2-acre island owned by The Nature Conservancy, accessible only at low tide by a wide sandbar; parking is on the road to Goose Cove Lodge. Owned by landscape architect Frederick Law Olmsted around the turn of the 20th century and

HAYSTACK MOUNTAIN SCHOOL OF CRAFTS

One- and two-week sessions, June–Labor Day, attract some of the country's top artisans in clay, metals, wood, fibers, graphics, and glass. From its beginnings in 1950, Haystack has been equated with cutting-edge design rather than traditional craft. Each session is limited to no more than 90 students, and the workshop topics, like the students, change every two weeks. Each group is carefully balanced to include young (minimum age 18) and old, neophytes as well as master craftsmen; repeaters are kept to a third.

Visitors are welcome to tour the campus, but not classes; tours are offered Wed. at 1 PM and during the "walk-throughs," in which student and faculty work is displayed (7:30 PM on the second Thu. of each session, followed by an 8:15 auction). The public is also welcome in the Gateway Building auditorium for frequent 7:30 PM slide lectures, visiting artists' presentations, and occasional concerts. The campus itself is a work of art: a series of spare, shingled buildings, studios with a central dining hall and sleeping quarters, all weathered the color of surrounding rocks and fitted between trees, connected by steps and terraced decks, floated above the fragile lichens and wildflowers on land sloping steeply toward Jericho Bay. (207-348-2306; haystack-mtn.org), Deer Isle.

bequeathed to The Nature Conservancy by his grandniece, this is a very special place, a good walk with small children.

MORE PUBLIC SPACES **Ames Pond**, east of Stonington Village on Indian Point Rd., is full of pink-and-white water lilies in bloom June–early Sept.

Mariner's Memorial Park, Deer Isle. This is a delightful picnic and bird-watching spot with views of Long Cove. Take Fire Rd. 501 off Sunshine Rd., just east of Rt. 15.

✳ Lodging

INNS AND B&BS

IN DEER ISLE 04627

✪ ☀ (ᵞ) **Pilgrim's Inn** (207-348-6615 or 1-888-778-7505; pilgrimsinn.com), 20 Main St. Open mid-May–mid-Oct. This gracious, four-story, hip-roofed inn stands in the middle of Deer Isle Village yet both fronts and backs on water. According to innkeeper Tina Oddleifson, it was built in 1793 by Ignatius Haskel to house his wife and nine children, and in 1889 Lizzie Haskell turned it into an inn to lodge guests arriving by steamer. Pilgrim's Inn has been lucky in its subsequent owners. The pumpkin pine floors and the 8-foot-wide original fireplaces in the common and tap rooms survive, along with working hearths and paneling in the game room and library, and the original hardware in most of the dozen guest rooms. Tasteful but unfussy

furnishings underscore rather than upstage the 18th-century feel of the space, which has a view of the millpond. On the other hand, jetted tubs and bracing showers are welcome additions. Rooms vary in size, but most have water views; all have private bath and are furnished in antiques. There are also three nicely decorated, two-bedroom cottages with kitchens and living rooms. The Whale's Rib (see *Dining Out*) is open to the public. Inn rooms $139–219 in-season, $119–199 in shoulder months, including full breakfast. $50 charge for pets allowed in cottages, which are $199-259.

✪ ♬ **The Inn at Ferry Landing** (207-348-7760; ferrylanding.com), 77 Old Ferry Rd., RR 1, Box 163. Open year-round. Overlooking Eggemoggin Reach, Jean and Gerald Wheeler's 1840s seaside farmhouse offers magnificent water views, spacious rooms, patchwork quilts, and a great common room with many windows, two grand pianos, and a harpsichord that Gerald plays and uses for summer recitals and spontaneous music sessions. The four guest rooms include a large master suite with a woodstove and skylights. $130–140 for double rooms, $185 for the suite; less off-season. Room rates include a full breakfast; minimum of two nights in high season. The Mooring, a two-story, two-bedroom, fully equipped housekeeping cottage, sleeping five, is $1,500 per week.

IN STONINGTON 04681

✪ ⟨ᵥᵥ⟩ ♿ **The Inn on the Harbor** (207-367-2420 or 1-800-942-2420; innontheharbor .com), 45 Main St. Open year-round. Guest rooms come with binoculars, the better to focus on lobster boats and regularly on the schooners in the Maine windjammer fleet, for which each of the 14 comfortable rooms (private bath, fridge, phone, cable TV) is named. The inn backs on Stonington's bustling Main Street, but most rooms, some with balcony, face the working harbor, one of Maine's most photographed views. Our favorite rooms: the Heritage, with working hearth; the Stephen Taber, a freestanding room retaining its tin ceiling (it used to be a barbershop); and the

American Eagle suite with two bedrooms, an open kitchen, dining area, and living room. A flowery ground-floor café with espresso and expansive deck is shared by all. $151–239 summer, $67–137 off-season, includes continental breakfast. In-room spa services are available.

🐾 ⚓ **Boyce's Motel** (207-367-2421 or 1-800-224-2421; boycesmotel.com), 44 Main St. In the heart of Stonington Village, Barrett Gray has expanded on this appealing motel, run by his family for four decades. This is a bit of a local secret, far bigger than it looks from the street. Most of the 11 units line a quiet lane that angles off Main St. They have queen or twin beds, and there are several efficiency units—one with two bedrooms, a living room, and kitchen. All are clean and comfortable, with in-room coffee, water views from some decks, free long-distance; popular with families and kayakers. $75–160 in high season, $60–135 off-season; $15 per pet per stay.

ON ISLE AU HAUT 04645

The Keeper's House (207-335-2990; keepers house.com), Robinson Point Lighthouse Station. Open June–Columbus Day. The Keeper's

INN ON THE HARBOR

BOYCE'S MOTEL, STONINGTON

House, first opened as a B&B in 1986, has been renovated and reopened by Dr. Marshall Chapman. The seven-room, hip-roofed clapboard house offers four guest rooms, two baths, and another self-contained room in the small Oil House. Off the grid, the complex is powered by photovoltaics, a windmill, and a 30-kilowatt generator. There's a dock for arriving guests; the mail boat from Stonington stops on request. Sited a ways from town and a hike from Duck Harbor. Bikes are available, and the innkeeper frequently offers a lift in his Model T and rides on his vintage-1903 Friendship sloop. $350–400 (two-day minimum) includes three meals. BYOB. Inquire about weekly rental of the Woodshed Cottage.

OFF THE GRID **Deer Isle Hostel** (207-248-2308; deerislehostel.com), 65 Tennis Rd., Deer Isle. Open late May–early Sept. An authentic homesteading endeavor, a three-story 17th-century-style house built from wood harvested on the property, using mostly hand tools. Water is hand pumped and electricity is solar generated. There's an outhouse with a composting toilet and a heated outdoor shower. The hostel sleeps 10 in private as well as dorm rooms. Set in vegetable gardens and woodland. $25 per person in the dorm, $30 per person for a private room, $70 for a secluded hut for two. Rates include dinner (BYO breakfast). Check the website for guided tours, otherwise visitors are not welcome.

VACATION RENTALS Check listings at the chamber website: deerisle.com. Also see Realtors listed for Blue Hill.

✻ Where to Eat

DINING OUT **Whale's Rib Tavern at Pilgrim's Inn** (207-348-5222; pilgrimsinn.com), 20 Main St., Deer Isle Village. Open midMay–Oct., daily 5–9 for dinner; closed Tue. in shoulder seasons. Reservations advised. Co-innkeeper Tony Lawless, a graduate of the Culinary Institute of America, maintains the reliably high-quality dining in this many-windowed old barn on the garden level of the Pilgrim's Inn, overlooking a millpond. We feasted with friends on Deer Isle clams steamed in beer and on locally raised mussels in a butter and cream sauce with roasted garlic and fried leeks, mopped up with freshly baked breads and followed by a seafood stew that included mahogany clams and calamari as well as a half lobster. Daily specials. Entrées $18–30. The wine list is respectable, and there's a choice of Maine microbrews.

Aragosta (207-367-5500), 27 Main St., Stonington. Open seasonally Thu.-Sun. for lunch and happy hour (5–8) on the deck; dinner 5–9 except Wed. Known locally for farm-to-table fare, Devin Finigan is the chef-owner of Aragosta (Italian for *lobster*). Lunch and evening happy hour pub food is served on the large outdoor deck overlooking the harbor and at the small restaurant itself, which is also the venue for a seven-course, locally sourced $75 tasting menu (reserve).

Cockatoo Portuguese Restaurant at Goose Cove (207-348-2300; thecockatoo restaurant.com), marked from Rt. 15 west of Stonington in Sunset, Deer Isle. Open daily in-season, noon–9. The woods road ends in an open green expanse overlooking a beach and the ocean—but that's not the call of seagulls you hear. It's the throaty screech and chatter of Peaches and Mango, Suzen Carter's pet cockatoos. The dining room in this classic old lodge is spacious, with a many-windowed view of the water, and there's dining on the deck. It features the freshest of fish but also meat prepared in interesting ways by Azorean chefs. At lunch try a cup or bowl of Portuguese kale soup; chowder with a scallop roll; or a chorizo and pepper sandwich. The house specialty is Portuguese paella ($40 for one but our waitress says you can add a $5 plate fee to share). If it's on the menu try the authentic bacalhau (shredded codfish with onions, crispy potatoes, and peppers, served with greens), a $15 special. Entrées $18–40 but less for nightly specials.

EATING OUT ✪ ✐ **Harbor Café**, Stonington. Open year-round, Mon.–Sat. 6 AM–8 PM; in summer, open later on Fri. and Sat., plus Sun. 6–2. Spanking clean and friendly; booths and dependable food. Soups and salads. Seafood rolls, sandwiches and subs, fried and broiled seafood. Friday night it's a good idea to reserve for the seafood and fries with free second helpings. Check out the two-for-one lobster specials. Spirits available.

🦞 ✐ **The Fisherman's Friend Restaurant** (207-367-2442), 5 Atlantic Ave., Stonington. Open year-round, 11–9 in summer months, until 10 Sat.; check off-season. This vast waterfront restaurant (next to the quarry-man statue) can seat more than 200 with a second-floor deck. A wide choice of fried and broiled fish, chowders and stews, burgers, and all the usual sandwiches. Lobster many ways. Children's menu.

((•)) **Madelyn's Drive-in** (207-348-9444), 495 N. Deer Isle Rd. (Rt. 15), Deer Isle. A local favorite. Roadside takeout with burgers, fried seafood, hard and soft ice cream. Plenty of picnic table seating, playground for kids.

Stonington Ice Cream Co., next to G. Watson Gallery (68 Main St., Stonington). A seasonal takeout known for its lobster rolls, Gifford's ice cream, daily specials.

✐ **Harbor Ice Cream** (207-348-9949), 11 Main St., Deer Isle Village. A casual oasis good for sandwiches, wraps, Gifford's ice cream, and lobster rolls.

Espresso Bar at the Inn on the Harbor (207-367-2420), 45 Main St., Stonington. Open daily in-season. Espresso, iced drinks, homemade ice cream, and desserts. In good weather this is a must, an excuse to sit a spell on the inn's flower-filled harborside deck.

((•)) **44 North Café**, 70 Main St., Stonington. Open May–Oct., Mon.–Sat. 6:30–5, Sun. 8–2. Housed in the former Eagle Gallery, this sleek new café serves up its locally roasted beans in a variety of hot and cold brews, along with Black Dinah's sipping chocolate, tea from Stonington's Tempest in a Teapot, and locally baked pastries. The beans are sold here or you can climb the stairs in the source, the Deer Isle Roastery and Café (207-348-3403), 11 Church St., Deer Isle Village.

✳ Entertainment

✪ **Stonington Opera House** (207-367-2788; operahousearts.org), School St., Stonington. Open year-round. This shingled building with its skinny, four-story "fly tower" dates to 1912 and was expanded in 2015. It stages an astonishingly full calendar of reasonably priced concerts and original theatrical productions. Movies Fri.–Sun. at 7 PM. Call for schedules of movies (digital!) and live performances.

Reach Performing Art Center (207-348-6301; attthereach.com), 249 N. Deer Isle Rd. at the elementary school, Deer Isle, a venue for theater, dance, and musical performances.

✳ Selective Shopping

ART GALLERIES AND ARTISANS *Note:* Studio crawling is a popular local pastime. Because local galleries feature work by local artists, it's frequently possible to trace a piece to its creator. Handout studio maps and postcards that picture individual artists' works are also readily available. The following is a partial listing.

IN DEER ISLE

Deer Isle Artists Association (207-348-2330; deerisleartists.com), 15 Main St. Open Memorial Day weekend–Columbus Day, daily 10–6; until mid-Dec., noon–5. A stunning, middle-of-the-village cooperative gallery with exhibits changing every two weeks.

Turtle Gallery (207-348-9977; turtlegallery.com), Rt. 15, north of Deer Isle Village. Open daily in summer, year-round by appointment. Artist Elena Kubler's gallery showcases exceptional jewelry as well as biweekly changing shows featuring fine art and contemporary crafts. It's housed in the barn in which Haystack faculty work was first displayed, back when adjoining Centennial House was home to Francis ("Fran") Sumner Merritt, the school's founding director, and his wife, Priscilla, a noted weaver.

LOBSTER

Stonington Lobster Co-op (207-367-2286 or 1-800-315-6625), 51 Indian Point Rd. Since 1948, the largest co-op in Maine of its type, wholesale and retail.

Carter's Seafood (207-367-0900), 24 Carter Lane, off Oceanville Rd. at Webb Cove. Open Mon.–Sat. 10–5. Very fresh fish, clams, lobsters, mussels, and shrimp.

Cold Water Seafood (207-348-3084), 100 N. Main St. (Rt. 15). Open Mon.–Sat. 9–6, call off-season. Fresh fish, local steamers, fresh crab, and house-smoked mussels.

Greene-Ziner Gallery (207-348-2601), 73 Reach Rd. (off Rt. 15 north of the village). Open July–Sept. In a barn surrounded by meadows, iron sculptor Eric Ziner displays his ornate and whimsical creations and potter Melissa Greene, her thrown earthenware pots suggesting Greek amphorae in shape but decorated with designs evoking tribal themes. Their **Yellow Birch Farm Stand** (Tue.–Sat. 10–5) sells fruit, veggies, herbs, eggs, and dairy products.

IN STONINGTON

✪ ♿ **Hoy Gallery** (207-367-2368; jillhoy.com), 80 Thurlow Hill. Open daily July–Columbus Day. Don't miss this big white barn set back from the street, filled with Jill Hoy's bold, bright Maine landscapes.

G. Watson Gallery (207-367-2900; gwatsongallery.com), 68 Main St. Open May–Oct., Mon.–Sat. 10–5, Sun. 1–5. This is a serious gallery, showing contemporary painting and sculpture, featuring prominent East Coast artists.

SPECIAL SHOPS **The Periwinkle** (207-348-5277), in the middle of Deer Isle Village. Open June–Oct., 9–5, closed Sun. Jim and Candy Eaton now run this tiny landmark shop, crammed with toys and games galore, books, cards, and other rainy-day savers, most locally made. Ask Jim about what happened to the store's vintage cash register.

✪ **Dockside Books and Gifts** (207-367-2652), 62 W. Main St., Stonington. Seasonal. Al Webber's waterside bookstore has an exceptional selection of Maine and marine books, also gifts, sweaters by local knitters, and a great harbor view from the deck.

✪ **The Dry Dock** (207-367-5528), Main St. Open daily mid-May–Oct., 9–5. Tempting clothing and craftwork; an outlet for Deer Isle granite products, much more.

✪ **Prints & Reprints** (207-367-5821), 31 Main St. Virginia Burnett's landmark shop featuring framed art, antiquarian books, and unexpected treasures.

V&S Variety Stores (207-367-5570), Rt. 15A, Burnt Cove. The many boutiques and galleries have displaced the basic stuff of life—like groceries and everything a five-and-dime once carried. It's all moved out to Burnt Cove, along with the recycle shop, gas, and plenty of parking. Beside Burnt Cove Market (the supermarket, open daily until 9 PM), this huge but homespun "variety store" stocks everything you forgot to bring.

Also see **Nervous Nellie's Jams and Jellies** under *To See*. The shop is open year-round, producing 15 flavors of jam, chutney, marmalade, and much more.

ON ISLE AU HAUT

((ɣ)) **Black Dinah Chocolatiers** (207-335-5010; blackdinahchocolatiers.com), 1 Moor's Harbor Rd. Closed at this writing while Kate and Steve Shaffer launch their Portland-area facility, which will produce the wildly successful truffles and other confections they began making right here. Call to check because the café is due to return.

✳ Special Events

Note: The weekly *Island Advantages* (island advantages.com) lists and details many more current happenings. Unless otherwise noted the contact is the chamber of commerce: 207-348-6124; deerislemaine.com.

May: **Wings, Waves & Woods**, "birding by land, by sea and by art"—puffin and pelagic trips, walks, lectures, food. **Memorial Day Parade**.

May–October: Fri.-morning (10–noon) **farmers' market** at the Island Community Center (the former elementary school) in Stonington. This is huge.

July: **Independence Day** features island-wide festivities—a parade in Deer Isle Village, fireworks at Stonington Fish Pier. **Lobster boat races** are usually the next Sat. **Fisherman's Day** (slippery cod contest, wacky boat races, and family fun) is the following week, sponsored by the Island Fishermen's Wives Association.

Castine

While the bulk of the Blue Hill Peninsula wanders away to the southeast, one fat finger of land points down along the Penobscot River toward the bay. Rt. 175, the first turnoff from Rt. 1 for the Blue Hill Peninsula, shadows the river, leading to a mini peninsula with Castine at its tip. Sited at the confluence of the Penobscot and Bagaduce Rivers, the town still looms larger on nautical charts than on road maps.

Castine has always had a sense of its own importance. According to the historical markers that pepper its tranquil streets, it has been claimed by four different countries since its early-17th-century founding as Fort Pentagoet. It was an early trading post for the Pilgrims but fell into the hands of Baron de Saint Castine, a young French nobleman who married a Penobscot Indian princess and reigned as a combination feudal lord and Indian chief over Maine's eastern coast for many decades.

Because no two accounts agree, we won't attempt to describe the outpost's constantly shifting fortunes—even the Dutch owned it briefly. Nobody denies that in 1779 residents (mostly Tories who fled here from Boston and Portland) welcomed the invading British. The Commonwealth of Massachusetts retaliated by mounting a fleet of 18 armed vessels and 24 transports with 1,000 troops and 400 marines aboard. This small navy disgraced itself absurdly when it sailed into town in 1779. The British Fort George was barely in the making, fortified by 750 soldiers with two sloops as backup, but the American privateers refused to attack and hung around in the bay long enough for several British men-of-war to come along and destroy them. The surviving patriots had to walk back to Boston, and many of their officers, Paul Revere included, were court-martialed for their part in the disgrace. The town was occupied by the British again in 1814.

Perhaps it was to spur young men on to avenge this affair that Castine was picked (150 years later) as the home of the Maine Maritime Academy, which occupies the actual site of the British barracks and keeps a training ship anchored at the town dock, incongruously huge beside the graceful, white-clapboard buildings from an earlier era.

In the mid-19th century, thanks to shipbuilding, Castine claimed to be the second wealthiest town per capita in the United States. Its genteel qualities were recognized by summer visitors, who later came by steamboat to stay in eight hotels. Many built seasonal mansions. Castine remains one of Maine's most photogenic coastal villages, the kind writers describe as "perfectly preserved." Even the trees that arch high above Main Street's clapboard homes and shops have managed to escape the blight that felled elms elsewhere, and Castine's post office is the oldest continuously operating post office in the country (since 1833). Current population hovers around 1,670, including the 700 Maine Maritime Academy students, but it roughly doubles in summer. Two of the hotels survive, and one baronial mansion is now an inn. The town dock is unusually welcoming, complete with picnic tables, parking, and

CASTINE

restrooms. It remains the heart of this walking town, where you can amble uphill past shops to the impressive Historical Society museum on the common, or down along Perkins St. to the Wilson Museum.

GUIDANCE The **Castine Merchants Association** and Castine Historical Society produce a helpful map/guide, available around town. The seasonal visitors center at 1 Main St. is a welcome addition. Also check **castine.me.us.** For moorings and harbor information call 207-326-9231 or check **castineyachtclub.org.**

PUBLIC RESTROOMS are at the town landing, foot of Main St.

WHEN TO COME Museums are highly seasonal, but the Maritime Academy contributes to the sense of a college town, a pleasant place to stay through October.

✳ To See

Historic District. All of downtown Castine is on the National Register of Historic Places. Pick up the pamphlet *A Walking Tour of Castine*—it's free, available at shops—and walk out along Perkins St. and up along Maine to Battle Ave. Don't miss:

    Castine Historical Society (207-326-4118; castinehistoricalsociety.org), 17 School St. Castine town common. July–Labor Day, Mon.–Sat. 10–4; Sun. 1–4. The permanent exhibit is a multimedia presentation about the 1779 Penobscot Expedition (see chapter introduction), also changing exhibits and the newly opened Grindle House.

    ✪ ✿ **Wilson Museum** (207-326-9247; wilsonmuseum.org), 120 Perkins St. Open daily May 27–Sept. 30, 10–5 weekdays, 2–5 weekends; free. This waterside building houses collections amassed by geologist J. Howard Wilson. These include prehistoric artifacts from North and South America, ancient artifacts from Africa and Oceana, vintage dioramas depicting life in prehistoric and Native American cultures, as well as minerals, stones, shells, early firearms, tools, farm equipment, an 1805 kitchen, and a Victorian parlor. The campus also includes a 19th-century **Blacksmith Shop** and the **John Perkins House**, a pre–Revolutionary War home, restored and furnished. Open July and Aug., Wed. and Sun. 2–5 (admission for Perkins House). Check the website for changing exhibits, demonstrations, and frequent special events.

Fort George, Battle Ave. Open May 30–Labor Day, daylight hours. The sorry tale of its capture by the British during the American Revolution (see the chapter introduction) and again during the War of 1812, when redcoats occupied the town for eight months, is told on panels at the fort—an earthworks complex of grassy walls (great to roll down) and a flat interior.

State of Maine (207-326-4311), town dock. When in port, the training vessel for Maine Maritime Academy is usually open to visitors daily from the second week in July until mid-Aug. Call to check the schedule for tours.

CASTINE HISTORICAL SOCIETY

Christina Tree

✳ To Do

GOLF AND TENNIS **Castine Golf Club** (207-326-8844), Battle Ave. Offers nine holes. To use the **tennis** courts, call 207-326-9548.

SEA KAYAKING **Castine Kayak Adventures** (207-866-3506; castinekayak.com), Sea St., beyond Dennett's Wharf. Half- and full-day trips plus a number of "unique adventures" such as sunrise and phosphorescent paddles, and "intermediate adventures" to the Bagaduce reversing falls and around Cape Rosier. Also overnight camping, B&B tours, and workshops ranging from beginning skills to advanced coastal navigation. This is also the area's source of **bike rentals**.

SAILING **Castine Cruises** (207-701-1421; castinecruises.com), 15 Sea St. Daily departures in-season for two-hour excursions and sunset sails aboard a vintage-1934, 56-foot sailing yacht, limited to six passengers; Capts. Kate and Zander also offer half- and full-day charters.

SWIMMING ⚓ **Back Beach**. This is a long strip of sand backed by parking. Shallow, relatively warm water, great for kids. From Battle Ave., follow Wadsworth Cove Rd. to the end.

✳ Green Space

Witherle Woods is an extensive wooded area webbed with paths at the western end of town. The ledges below **Dyce's Head Light**, also at the western end of town, are great for clambering. The Castine Conservation Commission sponsors nature walks occasionally in July and Aug.; check local bulletin boards.

✳ Lodging

IN CASTINE 04421

✪ ❀ ((ᵗ)) **Pentagoët Inn** (207-326-8616 or 1-800-845-1701; pentagoet.com), 26 Main St., P.O. Box 4. Open May–Oct. A very Victorian summer hotel with a three-story turret, gables, and wraparound porch. Jack Burke and Julie VandeGraaf have restored this vintage-1894 Queen Anne–style building room by room. They've added exceptional food and created an inn with rare warmth and personality. Jack presides behind an oak bar in the **Passports Pub**, papered floor-to-ceiling in photos, paintings, and memorabilia depicting the likes of Lenin, Gandhi, and Queen Elizabeth, collected during this innkeeper's previous life in the foreign service. The 16 guest rooms are variously shaped and furnished in comfortable, period antiques—ornately carved headboards and marble-topped dressers—but good mattresses, serious showers. In all there are 16 guest rooms, most on the second and third floors of the inn, several in the neighboring 18th-century "cottage." There's a cheerful sitting room, a flowery veranda, and a garden. $135–295 during high season with full buffet breakfast. $25 for pets. Amenities include bicycles and a guest computer. (Also see *Dining Out*.)

♂ **Castine Inn** (207-326-4365; castineinn .com), 33 Main St. Open May–Oct. Vintage 1898 with a wide, welcoming hallway with an old-style check-in desk. There's a pleasant sitting room and a pub, both with frequently lit fireplaces. A mural of Castine covers all four walls of the dining room, and French doors open onto a broad veranda overlooking the garden. The village slopes away below, and the 10 rooms on this side of the building all enjoy harbor views. Most 19 second- and third-floor rooms have private bath and have been recently renovated; $125–235 includes full breakfast (open to the public).

❀ ((ᵗ)) **The Manor Inn** (207-326-4861; manor-inn.com), 76 Battle Ave. Open year-round except Christmas–Valentine's Day. This 1890s stone-and-shingle mansion, set off above the village and its own lawns, offers 14 guest rooms. These range widely in size and price, in high season from $125 ($135 on weekends) for twin-bedded Dyces Head to $275 ($290 weekends) for spacious Pine Tree with its king canopy bed, working fireplace, and porch. Innkeepers Tom Ehrman and Nancy Watson are hands-on hosts, with Tom at the front desk or behind the bar and Nancy presiding over the kitchen. The lighthouse is an easy walk; wooded paths lead through neighboring conservation land. Rates include a full breakfast, less off-season. Pets are $25 per stay. (See *Dining Out*.)

Rental cottages are available through **De Raat Realty** (207-326-8448; deraatrealty.com) and **Castine Realty** (207-326-9392).

✳ Where to Eat

ALL LISTINGS ARE IN CASTINE

DINING OUT ✪ **Pentagoët Inn** (207-326-8616; pentagoet.com), 26 Main St. Open for dinner in-season. Reservations advised. The rose-colored dining room glows with candlelight in the evening. White tablecloths and garden flowers dress well-spaced tables, more seating on the veranda. Tables are also set for dinner in **Passports Pub** (see *Lodging*). The focus is on locally sourced seafood and produce. We split a big bowl of rope-cultured mussels followed by seared scallops. House specialties include lobster linguine and lobster bouillabaisse. Entrées $24–28; "bistro plates" $12–16. Don't pass up dessert.

The Manor Inn (207-326-4861), Battle Ave. Open for dinner Valentine's Day–New Year's, Thu.–Sat. off-season. A former enclosed porch has been expanded into an appealing dining room overlooking the sweeping front lawn and gardens. Co-owner Nancy Watson is the chef. The crabcakes are a family recipe, served as an entrée with mustard and aioli sauces. Other choices on the daily changing menu might include seared sesame-marinated hanger steak. Entrées $17–24. Full liquor license and pub food in the appealing **Pine Cone Pub**.

EATING OUT **Dennett's Wharf Restaurant & Oyster Bar** (207-326-9045), 15 Sea St. (off the town dock). Open daily May–Columbus Day, 11–11. An open-framed, harborside structure said to have been built as a bowling alley after the Civil War, this is the town's informal gathering place. There's a big all-day menu with plenty of salads as well as seafood and BBQ back ribs. The home brew is Wharf Rat Ale. Entrées $16–25.

MarKel's Bakehouse (207-326-9510), 26 Water St. Open for breakfast and lunch, dinner to go. Beer and wine. Formerly Bah's Bakehouse, still basically the same great deli counter featuring sandwiches on baguette bread, daily-made soups, salads, and baking.

Dudley's Refresher (207-812-3800), Town Dock. May–Sept., 11–sunset. The owners of El El Frijoles in Sargentville now operate this newly renamed and rebuilt (by the town) take-out on the town dock: fish tacos, burgers, salads and such. With luck, you can dine at the shaded picnic table.

Castine Variety (207-326-9920), corner of Main and Water Sts. Open 7 AM–8 PM. The village gathering spot from early morning on. Oahu native Snow Logan offers unexpected delicacies like "Lokomoko," Japanese chicken salad, miso soup, and combinations like fresh crabmeat and avocado. "The Breeze" sign from her former facility on the dock now hangs above the ice cream take-out window.

T&C Grocery (207-326-4818), 12 Water St. Open 7–9, until 8 Sun. This well-stocked market has a first-rate deli; source of great picnic fixings, liquor.

✳ Selective Shopping

✑ **Compass Rose Bookstore & Café** (207-326-9366 or 1-800-698-9366), 3 Main St. Open Mon.–Sat. 10–6. Sharon Biggie's shop features children's titles, summer reading, nautical, and regional books. The café serves drinks, cookies, and soups.

Four Flags (207-312-8526), 19 Water St. A long-established gift shop with an eclectic mix of Maine-made and exotic gifts.

Lucky Hill (207-326-1066), 15 Main St. Kristin Blanck features family gifts like "gurgle pots" and seriously fine paintings by husband Dan Graziano.

Gallery B. (213-839-0851; gallerybgallery.com), 5 Main St. Open seasonally, showcasing fine art, crafts.

✳ Special Events

May: Memorial Day parade.

June–Oct. **Farmers' Market**, Thu., 7–noon, Castine Common.

July: **Independence Day parade and fireworks**.

ACADIA AREA

Mount Desert Island; Acadia National Park; Bar Harbor and Ellsworth; The Quiet Side of Mount Desert

Mount Desert Island

Mount Desert (pronounced *dessert*) is New England's second largest island, one conveniently linked to the mainland. Two-fifths of its 108 square miles are maintained as Acadia National Park, laced with roads ideally suited for touring by car, more than 50 miles of "carriage roads" specifically for biking and skiing, and 120 miles of hiking trails.

The beauty of "MDI" (as it is locally known) cannot be overstated. Twenty-six mountains rise abruptly from the sea and from the shores of four large lakes. Mount Cadillac, at 1,532 feet, is the highest point on the U.S. Atlantic seaboard; a road winds to its smooth, broad summit for a 360-degree view that's said to yield the first view of dawn (which usually attracts a crowd) in the United States. Sunset, however, attracts a far larger crowd. There are also countless ponds and streams, an unusual variety of flora, and more than 300 species of birds. Mount Desert Island is almost bisected by Somes Sound, the only natural fjord on the East Coast.

Native Americans populated the island for at least 6,000 years before 1604, when Samuel de Champlain sailed by and named it L'Isle de Monts Deserts. In 1613 two French Jesuits attempted to establish a mission on Fernald Point near present Southwest Harbor. They were welcomed by the local Wabanaki chief Asticou but massacred by sailors from an English ship, and for 150 years this part of Maine remained a war zone between French and English. Finally settled in the second half of the 18th century, this remained a peaceful, out-of-the-way island even after a bridge was built in 1836, connecting it to the mainland.

In the 1840s landscape painters Thomas Cole and Frederic Church began summering here, and their images of the rugged shore were widely circulated. Summer visitors began arriving by steamboat, and they were soon joined by travelers taking express trains, bringing guests who filled the dozen huge hotels that mushroomed in Bar Harbor. By the 1880s many of these hotel patrons had already built their own

Nancy English

A TENACIOUS PINE ON THE ROCKY COAST OF MOUNT DESERT ISLAND

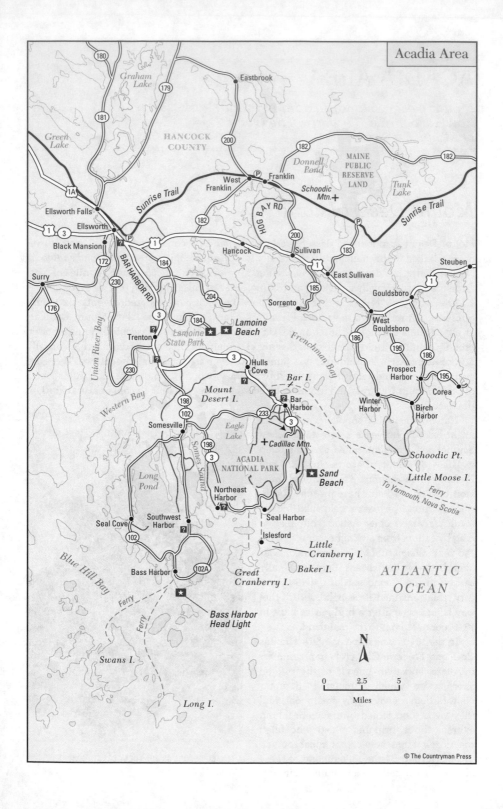

180
179
Eastbrook
181
Graham
Lake
Green
Lake
HANCOCK
COUNTY
200
182
MAINE
PUBLIC
RESERVE
LAND
182
Donnell
Pond
Tunk
Lake
P
West
Franklin
Franklin
Schoodic
Mtn. +
Sunrise Trail
1A
Sunrise Trail
Ellsworth Falls
182
200
P
1
3
Ellsworth
P
183
Steuben
Black Mansion
Hancock
Sullivan
172
1
East Sullivan
Gouldsboro
1
Surry
184
204
185
West
Gouldsboro
230
Sorrento
176
3
184
Lamoine
Beach
186
195
186
Trenton
Lamoine
State Park
Frenchman
Bay
Prospect
Harbor
195
Corea
230
3
Hulls
Cove
Mount
Desert I.
Bar I.
Winter
Harbor
Birch
Harbor
Western Bay
198
Bar
Harbor
102
233
3
Somesville
198
Eagle
Lake
+ Cadillac Mtn.
Schoodic Pt.
3
ACADIA
NATIONAL PARK
Sand
Beach
Little Moose I.
Long
Pond
Northeast
Harbor
To Yarmouth, Nova Scotia
Ferry
Seal Cove
Southwest
Harbor
Seal Harbor
102
Islesford
Little
Cranberry I.
Bass Harbor
102A
Baker I.
Blue Hill Bay
Great
Cranberry I.
ATLANTIC
OCEAN
Ferry
Bass Harbor
Head Light
Ferry
Union River Bay
Somes Sound

N

Swans I.
0   2.5   5
Miles
Long I.

© The Countryman Press

mansion-sized "cottages." These grandiose summer mansions numbered more than 200 before the Depression; many are now inns.

Bar Harbor lost 67 of its 220 summer mansions and five hotels in the devastating fire of 1947, which also destroyed 17,000 acres of woodland, but both the forest and Bar Harbor have recovered in recent decades.

Politically the island is divided into four townships: Bar Harbor, Mount Desert, Southwest Harbor, and Tremont. Northeast Harbor (a village in Mount Desert) and Southwest Harbor, the island's other two resort centers, also enjoy easy access to hiking, swimming, and boating within the park. Compared with Bar Harbor, however, they are relatively quiet, even in July and August, and the several accessible offshore islands are quieter still.

Mount Desert's mountains with "their gray coats and rounded backs look like a herd of elephants, marching majestically across the island," travel writer Samuel Adams Drake wrote in 1891. He was arriving by steamboat instead of traveling down the unimpressive commercial strip that's Rt. 3. Today it's harder to get beyond the clutter and crowds—but not that hard. The memorable march of rounded mountains is still what you see from excursion boats and from Little Cranberry Island.

Acadia National Park

The legacy of Bar Harbor's wealthy "rusticators" is Acadia National Park. A cadre of influential citizens, which included Harvard University's President Charles W. Eliot, began to assemble parcels of land for public use in 1901, thus protecting the forests from portable sawmill. Boston textile heir George Dorr devoted his fortune and energy to amassing a total of 11,000 acres and persuading the federal government to accept it. In 1919 Acadia became the first national park east of the Mississippi. It is now a more-than-47,000-acre preserve, with 30,300 acres and more than another 10,000 in easements encompassing almost half of Mount Desert Island.

Nancy English

Almost two-thirds of the park's more than 2 million annual visitors get out of their cars and hike the park's trails. Many take the free, white-and-blue Island Explorer buses. They usually begin by viewing the introductory film in the Hulls Cove Visitor Center and then drive the 27-mile Park Loop Rd., stopping to see the obvious sites and noting what they want to explore more fully. The park has much more to offer, from simple hikes to rock climbing, horse-drawn carriage rides to swimming, bicycling, canoeing, and kayaking.

Within the park are more than 45 miles of carriage roads donated by John D. Rockefeller Jr. These incredible broken-stone roads take bikers, hikers, joggers, and cross-country skiers through woods, up mountains, past lakes and streams. The paths also lead over and under 17 spectacular stone bridges. In

SEAWALL ON MOUNT DESERT ISLAND

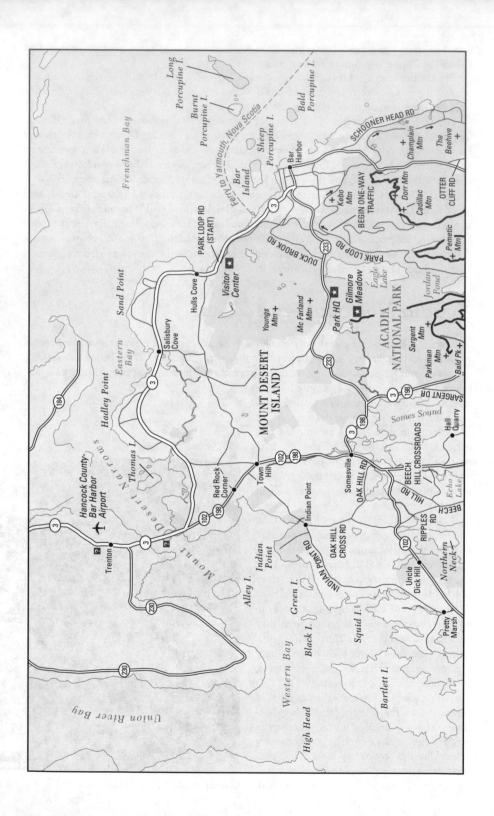

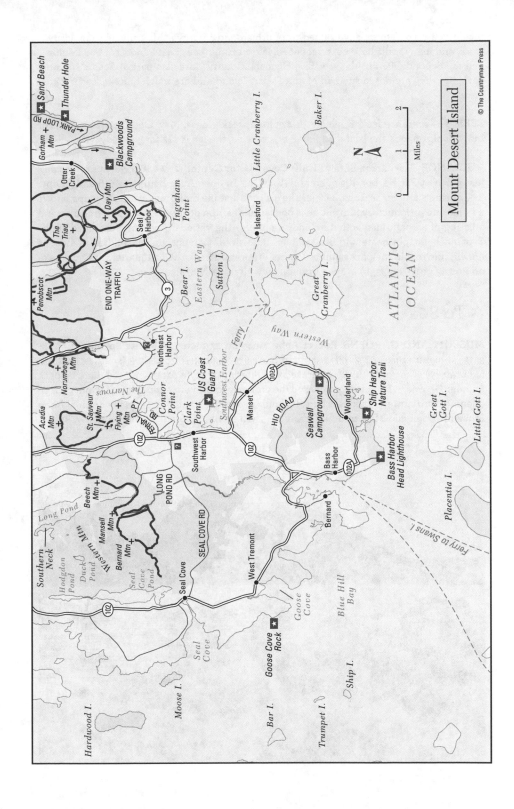

Mount Desert Island

N

0   1   2
Miles

© The Countryman Press

recent years volunteers have rallied to refurbish and improve this truly spectacular net-work, and many trails have been reopened. Isle au Haut (see "East Penobscot Bay Region") and the Schoodic Peninsula (see "East Hancock County") are also part of Acadia National Park, but they are not located on Mount Desert Island and are much quieter, less traveled areas.

FEES The entrance fee for vehicles is $25 for a weekly pass, May–Oct. Free Nov.–Apr. For individuals on foot, the Island Explorer, or a bicycle, the fee is $12 for a weekly pass.

GUIDANCE The park maintains **Hulls Cove Visitor Center** (207-288-3338; nps.gov/acad), just north of Bar Harbor. It's open mid-Apr.–Oct. In July–Aug., hours are 8–6 daily; Sept., 8–5; during shoulder seasons, 8–4:30. The glass-and-stone building, set atop 50 steps, shows a 15-minute introductory film and sells books, guides, and postcards. Pick up a free map and a listing of all naturalist activities, and sign up for the various programs scheduled June–Sept. at the amphitheaters in Blackwoods and Seawall Campgrounds. Children of all ages are eligible to join the park's Junior Ranger Program. The park headquarters at Eagle Lake on Rt. 233 (207-288-3338) is open throughout winter, daily 8–4:30.

✳ To See

MUSEUM AND GARDENS **Robert Abbe Museum at Sieur de Monts Spring** (207-288-3519; abbemuseum.org), 2 miles south of Bar Harbor, posted from Rt. 3 (south of Jackson Laboratory). The spring itself is encased in a Florentine-style canopy placed there by park founder George B. Dorr, who purchased the property to prevent enterprising islanders from opening a springwater business here. It stands in a garden, and beyond is the original **Abbe Museum**, open mid-May–mid-Oct., daily 10–5. On exhibit at Sieur de Monts are Dr. Robert

Nancy English

"THE BUBBLES" AT JORDAN POND

EXCURSIONS

Park Loop Road officially begins at the Hulls Cove Visitor Center but may be entered at many points along the way. Most of the road is one-way, so be alert to how traffic is flowing. Places of interest along the Loop Road include Sieur de Monts Spring, a stop that could include the Wild Gardens of Acadia, Abbe Museum, and Park Nature Center as well as the covered spring itself; Sand Beach, which is actually made up of ground shells and sand and is a great beach to walk down and from which to take a dip, if you don't mind 50- to 60-degree water (there are changing rooms and lifeguards); Thunder Hole, where the water rushes in and out of a small cave, which you can view from behind a railing; Jordan Pond House, popular for afternoon tea and popovers; and Cadillac Mountain. From Cadillac's smooth summit (accessible by car), you look north across Frenchman's Bay, dotted with the Porcupine Islands, which look like giant stepping-stones. Many visitors come at sunrise, but sunset can be far more spectacular.

Abbe's original collections of stone and bone tools, representing the Native American people in Maine from the archaic periods. Admission to this octagonal building, built by Abbe in 1928 and possibly haunted by his spirit, is $3 adults, $1 ages 6–15. The rest of Abbe's collection is exhibited in the downtown Bar Harbor Abbe Museum (see "Bar Harbor"). The park museum is accessible through the **Wild Gardens of Acadia**, where 300 species of native plants are on display. The **Park Nature Center** here (open mid-May–Sept., daily 9–5) has displays on park wildlife.

✳ To Do

BICYCLING The more than 45 miles of broken-stone carriage roads make for good mountain biking. Find outfitters in Bar Harbor.

CAMPING The two campgrounds within the park are Blackwoods, 5 miles south of Bar Harbor, and Seawall, on the quiet side of the island, 4 miles south of Southwest Harbor. Both are in woods and close to the ocean. One vehicle, up to six people, is allowed on each site. No utility hookups, but both have comfort stations, cold running water, a dump station, picnic tables, and fire rings. Showers and a camping store are within 0.5 mile of each. There are also four group campsites at Blackwoods and five at Seawall, for up to 15 people, which must be reserved through the park (207-288-3338).

Blackwoods (207-288-3274, answered May–Oct. only), open all year. Reservations required May–Oct. through the National Recreation Reservation Service (1-877-444-6777; recreation.gov). Cost of sites is $20 per night during the reservation period; fees vary during the off-season, when you need a special use permit and must walk 0.75 mile to the campsite. The road is not plowed.

Seawall (877-444-6777), near Southwest Harbor, open late May–late Sept. First-come first-served sites, and also sites you can reserve in advance. Cost is $30 with a vehicle.

HIKING The park is a mecca for hikers. Several detailed maps are sold at the Hulls Cove Visitor Center. Trails range in difficulty from the **Jordan Pond Loop Trail** (a 3.3-mile path around the pond) to the rugged **Precipice Trail** (1.5 miles, very steep, with iron rungs as ladders). There are 17 trails to mountain summits on Mount Desert. **Acadia Mountain** on the island's west side (2 miles roundtrip) commands the best view of Somes Sound and the islands. The **Ship Harbor** on Rt. 102A (near Bass Harbor) offers a nature trail that winds along the shore and into the woods; it's also a great birding spot.

HORSE-DRAWN CARRIAGE TOURS ✄ **Wildwood Stables** (1-877-276-3622), 0.5 mile south of the Jordan Pond House. One- and two-hour horse-drawn tours in multiple-seat carriages are offered six times a day.

RANGER PROGRAMS A wide variety of programs—from guided nature walks and hikes to birding talks, sea cruises, and evening lectures—are offered throughout the season. Ask at the Hulls Cove Visitor Center for a current schedule.

ROCK CLIMBING Acadia National Park is the most popular place to climb in Maine; famous climbs include the **Precipice**, **Great Head**, and **Otter Cliffs**. See "Bar Harbor" for guide services.

SWIMMING Within Acadia there is supervised swimming at **Sand Beach**, 4 miles south of Bar Harbor, and at **Echo Lake**, a warmer, quieter option 14 miles west of Bar Harbor (see "The Quiet Side").

WINTER SPORTS More than 45 miles of carriage roads at Acadia National Park are maintained as cross-country skiing and snowshoeing trails. Request the *Winter Activities* leaflet from the park headquarters.

Bar Harbor and Ellsworth

Bar Harbor is the island's resort town, one of New England's largest clusters of hotels, motels, inns, B&Bs, restaurants, and shops—all within easy reach of the park's Hulls Cove Visitor Center and Acadia National Park.

Ellsworth is the shire town and shopping hub of Hancock County, a place with a split personality: the old brick downtown blocks along and around the Union River and its falls, and the strip of malls and outlets along the mile between the junctions of Rts. 1A and 1, and Rts. 1 and 3. If you're coming down Rt. 1A from Bangor, you miss downtown Ellsworth, which offers the restored art deco Grand Auditorium as well a sense of the lumbering-boom era in which the Colonel Black Mansion, arguably the most elegant in Maine, was built.

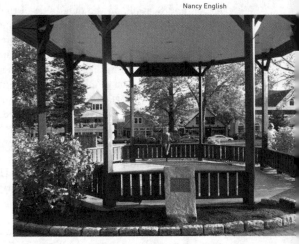
Nancy English

In Bar Harbor itself shops and restaurants line Cottage, Mount Desert, West, and Main Sts., which slope to the Town Pier and to the Shore Path, a mile walk between mansions and the bay. On sunny days most visitors tend to be out in the park or on the water; half an hour before sunset (the time is announced each day in local publications), folks gather on and near the top of Cadillac Mountain.

BAR HARBOR VILLAGE GREEN

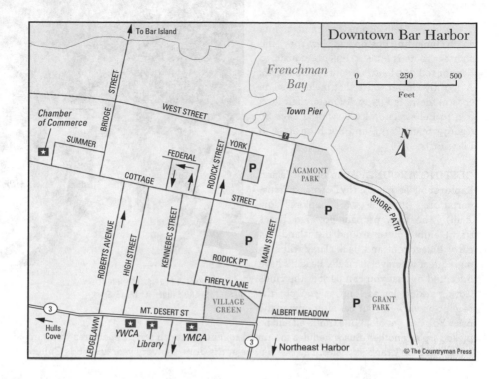

Downtown Bar Harbor

© The Countryman Press

GUIDANCE **Bar Harbor Chamber of Commerce** (year-round 207-288-5103 or 1-888-540-9990; barharbormaine.com), 1201 Bar Harbor Rd., Trenton 04605, also maintains a year-round information center on the corner of Cottage and Main Sts. in Bar Harbor.

Mount Desert Island Information Center (207-288-3411) is open daily mid-May–mid-Oct. (8:30–6 during high season) on Thompson Island, just after Rt. 3 crosses the bridge. This is the island's most helpful walk-in center, with restrooms and help with lodging reservations on all parts of the island. The in-town **Bar Harbor Information Center** is at the corner of Main and Cottage Sts., open May until the last cruise ship in Oct.

Ellsworth Chamber of Commerce (207-667-5584 or 207-667-2617; ellsworthchamber .org), 163 High St., Ellsworth 04605, is an information center in the Ellsworth Shopping Center on the Rt. 1/3 strip; look for Wendy's.

GETTING THERE *By air:* **Hancock County & Bar Harbor Airport** in Trenton (between Ellsworth and Bar Harbor) is still served by some regional flights out of Boston. Check their website (bhbairport.com) for more information. **Bangor International Airport** (207-947-0384; flybangor.com), 26 miles north of Ellsworth, offers connections to most American cities.

By private boat: For details about moorings, contact the Bar Harbor harbormaster at 207-288-5571.

By bus: **Concord Coach Lines** (1-800-639-3317; concordcoachlines.com) offers unbeatable year-round service from Boston's Logan Airport and South Station (five hours) to Bangor. The **Bar Harbor Shuttle** (207-479-5911; barharborshuttle.com) stops at the Bar Harbor Villager Motel and can pick up passengers by reservation elsewhere. The 10-passenger van provides transportation to and from the airports and the bus depots in Bangor, with other stops in Ellsworth and Somesville.

SELLING SUMMER BERRIES FOR MOUNT
DESERT ISLAND STUDENTS' TRAVELS

By car: From Brunswick and points south (including Boston and New York), the shortest route is I-295 to I-95 in Augusta, to Bangor to I-395 to Rt. 1A south to Ellsworth. A slightly slower route that includes some coastal views is I-95 to Augusta, then Rt. 3 east to Belfast (stop for a swim at Lake St. George State Park), and north on Rt. 1 to Ellsworth.

GETTING AROUND Jump on the **Island Explorer** buses operated by Downeast Transportation (207-288-4573; exploreacadia .com). The free, propane-powered buses travel eight routes around the island and carry bikes front and back. They will stop on request wherever it's safe. Readers have informed us that you can park at the Hulls Cove parking lot as long as you put the receipt on view in your car after buying the pass. You can get off at one trailhead and be picked up at another. Bus schedules are timed to coincide with ferry departures to Swans Island and the Cranberry Isles. The bus service starts June 23 every year and ends Columbus Day.

PARKING Note the lots on our Downtown Bar Harbor map. Much of the lodging is downtown (with parking), and the village is compact. Park and walk.

WHEN TO COME Because this is the most crowded summer place on the coast, everyone who lives nearby, from Portland north, prefers a visit in the off-season, preferably early fall. Although the Island Explorer bus schedule is reduced and the nights are chilly, the scenery is spectacular and the museums are still open. Winter is quiet indeed.

✳ To See

IN BAR HARBOR

✪ ✎ ♿ **Abbe Museum** (207-288-3519; abbemuseum.org), 26 Mount Desert St. Open May–Oct. daily 10–5, off-season Thu.–Sat. 10–4. $8 per adult, $4 ages 6–15, under 6 free. Museum members and Native Americans, no admission fee. The downtown Abbe in the heart of Bar Harbor, facing the village green, is more than eight times the size of its original building and dedicated to showcasing the cultures of Maine's Wabanaki, the 7,000 members of the Penobscot, Passamaquoddy, Micmac, and Maliseet tribes who live in Maine and the Maritimes. The permanent collection of 50,000 objects ranges from 10,000-year-old artifacts to exquisite basketry and crafts from several centuries. The orientation gallery and time line begin with the present and draw visitors back slowly and skillfully through 10,000 years to the core, a circular three-story tower, the "Circle of Four Directions." Exhibits include a fabricated copy of the 1794 treaty between Massachusetts and the Wabanaki that deeded much of Maine to its Native people.

♯ **College of the Atlantic** (207-288-5395; coa.edu), Rt. 3. Housed in the original Acadia National Park headquarters, the **George B. Dorr Museum of Natural History** is a good stop (open Tue.–Sat. 10–5, closed Sun.–Mon.). Admission by donation. Exhibits include a tidal pool tank with marine animals visitors can touch and student-created dioramas of plants and animals of coastal Maine. "Study skins" from animals and birds can be touched as well. The **Ethel H. Blum Gallery** (open Tue.–Sat. 11–4) holds changing exhibits. Founded in 1969, COA is a liberal-arts college specializing in ecological studies. Its waterside acreage, an amalgam of four large summer estates, is now a handsome campus for 350 students.

Bar Harbor Historical Society (207-288-0000; barharborhistorical.org), 33 Ledgelawn Ave. Open June–Oct., Mon.–Sat. 1–4. In winter, open by appointment. A fascinating collection of early photographs of local hotels, Gilded Era clothing, books by local authors and about Bar Harbor, and the story of the big fire of 1947.

IN HULLS COVE

♯ **Hulls Cove Sculpture Garden** (207-288-5126; jonesport-wood.com), 17 Breakneck Rd. This is the Bar Harbor branch of the Davistown Museum in Liberty. Two acres with a path and signage thread through grounds full of work by contemporary Maine artists like Melita Westerlund, who works with polychrome steel, David McLaughlin, who does assemblage art, painter Phil Barter, sculptor Obadiah Buell, and others. A picnic area, tree house, and playhouse for children are all open sunrise to sunset (Rocky Mann's studio is next door). You can also park here to walk into the Breakneck Hollow entrance to Acadia National Park and find a beaver pond.

IN ELLSWORTH

Woodlawn: Museum, Garden & Park (207-667-8671; woodlawnmuseum.org), Surry Rd. (Rt. 172). Open June–Sept., Tue.–Sat. 10–5, Sun. 1–4; May and Oct., Tue.–Sun. 1–4. Audio tours $10 adults, $3 children. The stone walls are shipshape around this outstanding 1824 Federal mansion based on a design by Asher Benjamin and built by John Black, who moved in with his wife and his three youngest children (five older children had already left home). The rooms are furnished as they were when the last Mr. Black and his family lived here. Stroll the formal gardens, walk the 2 miles of walking trails open dawn to dusk year-round, or reserve the croquet court for a match.

Birdsacre/Stanwood Wildlife Sanctuary (207-667-8460; birdsacre.com), Rt. 3. Old homestead and gift shop open May–Oct., daily 10–4; sanctuary open year-round with outdoor shelters that house non-releasable (injured) hawks and owls. This 200-acre nature preserve is a memorial to Cordelia Stanwood (1865–1958), a pioneer ornithologist, nature photographer, and writer. The 1850 homestead contains a collection of Stanwood's photos.

Nancy English

THE GEORGE B. DORR MUSEUM

The Telephone Museum (207-667-9491; thetelephonemuseum.org), 166 Winkumpaugh Rd., marked from Rt. 1A north of Ellsworth. Open July–Sept., Sat. 1–4. $10 adults, $5 children. The evolution of telephone

MUST SEE

There are five Cranberry Isles just southeast of Mount Desert, though we list only the two with year-round residents (cranberry isles.com).

LITTLE CRANBERRY The most visitor-friendly of the islands is 400-acre Little Cranberry (islesford.com), located 20 minutes offshore. The official "sight-to-see" is the incongruously brick and formal **Islesford Historical Museum** (207-244-9224; open daily mid-June–Sept., 9–noon and 12:30–3:30), built in 1928 with funds raised by Bangor-born, MIT-educated summer resident William Otis Sawtelle to house his fascinating collection of local historical objects. Acadia National Park maintains the museum (and restrooms), featuring it as part of a ranger-narrated **Islesford Historical Cruise**. We prefer to come by mail boat, taking our time to explore the island and beating the crowd to **Islesford Dock Restaurant** (see *Dining Out*), the island's gathering spot and a great place to eat. Stop in at the **Islesford Dock Galley** and walk on up the road to Danny and Kate Fernald's **Islesford Artists Gallery** (207-244-3145; islesfordartists.com), specializing in Maine's many excellent island artists. At the dock look for the **Alleyway**, Cari Alley's white truck selling reasonably priced fresh lobster and shrimp rolls (her husband is a lobsterman/shrimper), hot dogs, island desserts, and more. **Winter's Work** showcases island-made crafts, and Marian Baker's **Islesford Pottery** (207-244-5686) is worth a stop. The **Islesford Market** (207-244-7667) has been open sporadically in recent years. Stop by at least to meet island-bred postmistress Joy Sprague, who sells more stamps per year from her window here than any other post office in Maine, despite the fact that Islesford has less than 80 year-round and some 400 summer residents. Requests for Sprague's "Stamps by Mail" come from as far as Fiji, Iceland, and Istanbul—perhaps because with each order she encloses one of her island photos and a monthly newsletter (her address is USPO, Islesford 04646). Sprague also operates **Joy of Kayaking** (207-244-4309), renting one- and two-person kayaks. For a wide choice of summer rentals see islesford.com. To get there see *Boat Excursions*.

GREAT CRANBERRY —the largest of the islands—is a lobstering and boatbuilding island with a year-round population of around 40 that swells to 300 in summer. The **Seawich Café & Cranberry General Store** (207-244-0622) at the ferry landing offers salads, sandwiches, and daily specials. About 0.3 mile down the road is **Cranberry House,** start of the trail to Whistler Cove and home to the **Historical Society Museum** (207-244-7800) and **Hitty's Café** (207-244-7845), serving meals and ice cream on a cheerful deck. Another 0.25 mile farther on is the library in the currently inactive school. Just beyond that look for **The Whale's Rib** (207-244-5153), offering a selection of crafts and art.

service, from 1876 to 1983 (when the museum was founded), is the subject of this quirky museum. Switchboards and phones are hooked up ready for people to place calls—within the museum.

FOR FAMILIES ✈ **Acadia National Park Junior Ranger Programs** (207-288-3338) are the best thing going here for youngsters: First complete the activities in the Junior Ranger booklet, then join a ranger-led program or walk to receive a Junior Ranger patch. Books are for 7 and younger, and 8 and older; the senior ranger book for 18 and older contains much harder activities.

✈ **Family Nature Camp at College of the Atlantic** (see previous page) offers one- and two-week programs, summer field studies for children, and a one-week session for families who live in dorms and spend days on field trips led by naturalists in Acadia National Park.

SWANS ISLAND (swansisland.org). At the mouth of Blue Hill Bay, 6 miles out of Bass Harbor, with frequent car ferry service (see *Getting Around*), this is a large lobstering and fishing island with a year-round population of 300, a library, a general store (no alcohol), seasonal restaurants, quarry pond to swim in, and fine sand beach to walk. With a bike it's a possible day trip, but be forewarned: The ferry dock is 4 hilly miles from **Burnt Coat Harbor,** the picturesque island center with **Hockamock Light** (built in 1872) at its entrance. Swans works better as an overnight, given its choice of places to stay and the beauty of local hiking trails (check out the shore path at the light).

Swans Island is divided into three areas: **Atlantic,** where the ferry docks; **Minturn,** by the quarry pond and grocery store; and **Swans Island Village**, with the beach and lighthouse. The island was named for James Swan, the original owner. Maili Bailey arranges seasonal rentals of cottages, houses and apartments at **Swans Island Vacation** (swansislandvacation.com). **Harbor Watch Motel** (207-526-4563; swansisland.com) is open year-round on Burnt Coat Harbor. The **Island Bake Shop** (207-526-4578) serves breakfast and lunch and is known for its pastries. **Carrying Place Market and Take-out** (207-526-4043) is another welcome place for prepared food; you can buy lobsters and clams from **Trafton's** (207-526-4427).

The Sweet Chariot Festival (sweetchariotmusicfestival.com) gathers folksingers from across the country and starts with a serenade of the boats in the harbor, many of them Maine windjammers, usually in the first week of Aug.

The **Swans Island Library** (207-526-4330) has historic displays and summer speakers; **Swans Island Lobster & Marine Museum** (207-526-4423), open mid-June–mid-Sept., displays ship models, fishing equipment, and photos. **Iverstudio** (207-526-4350) offers weeklong workshops in woodblock printing.

FRENCHBORO The town of Frenchboro (frenchboroonline.com) is composed of 12 islands, but the name is usually applied to Long Island, 8 miles out of Bass Harbor, home to 70 year-round residents (up from 38 in 2000), most in Lunts Harbor. Two-thirds of the island (nearly 1,000 acres) is preserved by the Maine Coast Heritage Trust as the Frenchboro Preserve. A network of hiking trails runs along the shoreline, and the birding is terrific. See *Boat Excursions* for access via the **Maine State Ferry** and **Island Cruises**. The seasonal **Lunt's Dockside Deli** (207-334-2902) serves the basics, from veggie wraps to a lobster dinner; the fish chowder is good. The **Frenchboro Historical Society** (207-334-2932), open daily in-season 12:30–5, displays old tools, furniture, and local memorabilia, and also sells crafted items. *Note:* One day a year (early in Aug.) the island welcomes visitors for the **Annual Lobster Festival**, a lobster feed with plenty of chicken salad and pies.

RT. 3 ATTRACTIONS

⚓ **Mount Desert Oceanarium** (207-288-5005; theoceanarium.com), 1351 Rt. 3, Bar Harbor 04609. Open 9–5 daily, except Sun., mid-May–mid-Oct. $10–12 adults, $6–7 ages 4–12, depending on what you want to see and do. Tour the lobster hatchery and the Thomas Bay Marsh Walk.

Kisma Preserve (207-667-3244; kismapreserve.org), Rt. 3, Trenton. Open mid-May-late fall. $25 adults, under 3 free, but check if allowed. Tours are geared toward adults and more mature children. Make your reservation in advance and consider choosing an animal encounter with a wolf, moose, or primate at this 35-acre nonprofit animal preserve with native and non-native animal species. The moose is a draw for tourists who want to see one, but animals from 60 other species are also living here, many retired, injured, or abused.

🔪 **The Great Maine Lumberjack Show** (207-667-0067; mainelumberjack.com), Rt. 3, Trenton. Mid-June–Labor Day, nightly at 7 rain or shine, in fall on Sat. and Sun. The 1¼-hour show includes ax throwing, log rolling, speed climbing, and more.

✳ To Do

AIRPLANE RIDES **Scenic Flights of Acadia** (207-667-6527; mainecoastalflight.com), Rt. 3, Hancock County Airport, Trenton. Sightseeing flights in a Cessna 172 take four different routes over MDI.

Acadia Air Tours (207-667-7627; acadiaairtours.com), located at both the Hancock County–Bar Harbor Airport and on the pier in downtown Bar Harbor, offers scenic airplane, biplane, and glider flights sunrise to sunset, by appointment, weather permitting. The biplane and the glider flights are extremely popular.

AMUSEMENT PARK 🔪 **Wild Acadia Fun Park** (207-667-3573; wildacadia.com), 233 Bar Harbor Rd., Trenton. Open end of May–Labor Day. Water slides and splash pool, 18-hole mini golf, Indy-style go-carts, 32-foot rock climbing wall, slingshot trampoline, and water wars with water balloons and catapults.

BEER **Atlantic Brewing Company** (207-288-BEER; atlanticbrewing.com), 15 Knox Rd. in Town Hill (across from the Town Hill Market), has re-created an indoor–outdoor European brewery-pub. Daily tours and tastings, Memorial Day–Columbus Day; the barley wine is a wonderful thing to try, and so are the rest of the brews. Try **The Knox Road Grille** for its great BBQ next door; all-you-can-eat Saturdays.

BICYCLING The network of gravel carriage roads constructed by John D. Rockefeller Jr. in 1915 lends itself particularly well to mountain biking. In Bar Harbor, **Bar Harbor Bicycle Shop** (207-288-3886; barharborbike.com), 141 Cottage St., is the oldest bike outfitter in town and still rents only bikes: mountain, tandem, and everything that goes with them. **Acadia Bike** (207-288-9605 or 1-800-526-8615; acadiabike.com), 48 Cottage St., rents mountain and hybrid bikes and offers a full bike shop for sales and service. **Acadia Outfitters** (207-288-8118; acadiaoutfitters.com), 106 Cottage St., offers rentals of mountain and hybrid bikes, sea kayaks, and scooters.

Nancy English

BIRDING **The Natural History Center** (207-801-2617; thenaturalhistorycenter.com), 6 Firefly Lane, Bar Harbor. A snowy owl on Sargent Mountain was one sighting on a bird tour offered by Rich MacDonald and Natalie Springuel, who also run nature tours and other programming.

🔪 **Downeast Nature Tours** (207-288-8128; downeastnaturetours.com), 150 Knox Rd., Bar Harbor. Michael J. Good offers guided bird-watching and nature tours daily.

BOATING **American Cruise Lines** (1-800-814-6880; americancruiselines.com), 741 Boston Post Rd., Ste. 200, Guilford, CT. This cruise company offers an eight-day cruise

ACADIA BIKE

called the Maine Coast and Harbors, with stops in Bar Harbor, Castine, Belfast, Camden, Rockland, Boothbay Harbor, Bath, and Portland.

Bar Harbor Ferry Co. (207-288-2984; barharborferry.com) sails from the Bar Harbor Inn Pier, crossing Frenchman Bay to Winter Harbor several times a day; bring a bicycle and bike around Schoodic. **Lulu Lobster Boat Ride** (207-963-2341; lulu lobsterboat.com), Harborside Hotel and Marina, offers sightseeing (*le capitaine parle français*) on Frenchman Bay, with lobstering demonstrations and seal-watching. **Dive-in-Theater** (207-288-3483; divered .com) operates the *Seal*, an excursion boat from which passengers can watch Diver Ed (through an underwater camera) probe the depths of Frenchman Bay, and then get to touch what he fetches.

Nancy English

VIEW ACROSS BAR HARBOR GREEN AND THE *MARGARET TODD*

CANOEING AND SEA KAYAKING Most ponds on Mount Desert offer easy access. **Long Pond**, the largest lake on the island, has three access points. Boats can be launched at **Echo Lake** from **Ike's Point**, just off Rt. 102. **Seal Cove Pond** is less used and accessible from fire roads north of Seal Cove. **Bass Harbor Marsh** is another possibility at high tide. Canoe rental sources offer suggestions and directions. **National Park Canoe Rentals** (207-244-5854) on Long Pond near Somesville offers tours as well as rentals, including kayaks. In Bar Harbor, **Aquaterra Adventures** (207-288-0007; aquaterra-adventures.com), 1 West St., does guided sea kayak tours and sells gear. **National Park Sea Kayak Tours** (207-288-0342 or 1-800-347-0940; acadiakayak.com), 39 Cottage St., gives guided kayak trips on the remote, west side of MDI. **Coastal Kayaking Tours** (207-288-9605 or 1-800-526-8615; acadiafun.com), 48 Cottage St., operates guided sea kayaking tours 2½–7 hours long and multiday camping excursions. It also rents touring sea kayaks.

GOLF **Kebo Valley Club** (207-288-3000; kebovalleyclub.com), Rt. 233, Bar Harbor. Open daily May–Oct. Eighteen holes. "Eighth oldest golf grounds in America," since 1888. **Bar Harbor Golf Course** (207-667-7505; barharborgolfcourse.com), Rts. 3 and 204, Trenton. Eighteen holes.

FISHING Several charter boats offer deep-sea fishing. **Downeast Windjammer Cruises** (207-288-4585; downeastwindjammer.com) offers a four-hour fishing trip once or twice a day, with bait and tackle provided, leaving from the Bar Harbor Inn pier.

ROCK CLIMBING **Acadia Mountain Guides** (207-288-8186; acadiamountainguides.com), 198 Main St., and **Atlantic Climbing School** (207-288-2521), 67 Main St., offer instruction and guiding for beginner through advanced climbers. (Also see "Acadia National Park.")

SAILING **The *Margaret Todd*** (207-288-4585) sails from the Bar Harbor pier from late May to mid- to late Oct. This 151-foot four-masted schooner, designed and built in 1998 by

Captain Steve Pagels, cruises through Frenchman Bay three times a day in high season, less frequently in late Oct.

SWIMMING ♪ **Lake Wood** near Hulls Cove is a pleasant freshwater beach, ideal for children.

TRAINS **Downeast Scenic Railroad** (1-866-449-7245; downeastscenicrail.org), behind Maine Community Foundation, 245 Main St., Ellsworth. The Calais Branch Line is back in operation—$15 for adults and $8 children 3–12 from Memorial Day weekend to mid-Oct. **Antique rail cars** take passengers down 13 miles of Maine woods and wetlands. Ninety-minute trips leave at 10:30 AM and 1:30 PM every weekend.

WHALE-WATCHING The big operator is **Bar Harbor Whale Watch Co.** (207-288-2386; barharborwhales.com), 1 West St., Bar Harbor, which also offers seal-watching and lobstering tours. Bring a jacket, sunblock, binoculars, and a camera.

✱ Lodging

Reservations are not as crucial as they used to be, with a surge in the number of rooms here, but they're still a good idea. We cannot claim to have inspected every room in town, but we have checked out the most appealing options.

WATER-VIEW B&BS

IN BAR HARBOR 04609

Ullikana Bed & Breakfast (207-288-9552; ullikana.com), 16 The Field. Open May–Oct. This is our top pick in downtown Bar Harbor, steps from both Main Street and the Shore Path, yet with an away-from-it-all feel. Innkeepers Helene Harton and her husband, Roy Kasindorf, combine a rare flair for decorating with a genuine warmth that sets guests at ease. They bought Ullikana, a vintage-1885 Tudor-style summer mansion, in 1990 and transformed it. Breakfast, perhaps a light berry-stuffed soufflé pancake or a Bulgarian feta omelet, is served on the terrace overlooking the water or in Ullikana's attractive dining room, where you will feel as if you've returned to the home you always wished for. Guest rooms all have private bath, air-conditioning; $165–295.

♪ **The Shore Path Cottage** (207-288-0643; shorepathcottage.com), 24 Atlantic Ave. Open May–Oct. Lisabeth Chester Oxman has taken over management of this delightful Bar Harbor "cottage" and comfortable B&B previously run by her mother, Roberta Chester, since 1973. The dining room has a kind of authentic elegance that can't be imitated. Seven guest rooms (just one without with private bath, a few with claw-foot tub) are named for the youngsters who grew up in them. The house is filled with books. Both kosher and vegetarian breakfasts are served, and solo travelers and children are particularly welcome. $140–280 in-season, $110–200 low-season.

♿ **The Bass Cottage Inn** (207-288-1234 or 1-866-782-9224; basscottage.com), 14 The Field, P.O. Box 242. Open mid-May to the end of Oct., this 10-room inn has rooms with whirlpool tubs, gas fireplaces, and TVs with DVD players. Teri Anderholm oversees the cuisine, featuring Maine lobster hash and

AN EARLY-EVENING GATHERING ON THE TERRACE AT ULLIKANA

Nancy English

coconut crunch muffins for breakfast to be eaten on a bright, elegant sunporch, and wine with fine hors d'oeuvres in the early evening. She and her husband, Jeff Anderholm, run things smoothly in the handsome and comfortable inn, where rates range $260–420 in-season, less before and after.

☸ **Balance Rock Inn** (207-288-2610 or 1-800-753-0494; balancerockinn.com), 21 Albert Meadow. The original mansion, built in 1903 for a Scottish railroad tycoon, is augmented by a heated pool. Fourteen rooms, most with ocean view, private balcony, whirlpool bath; some with fireplace. The three suites have a kitchen, living room, and sauna. Rooms and suites, all with breakfast, range $155–635 depending on season. $40 fee for pets.

Saltair Inn (207-288-2882; saltairinn.com), 121 West St. Set on the street that overlooks Frenchman Bay and close to the center of things, Saltair Inn provides traditional accommodations with excellent extras, like the heated travertine tile floor in Sedgwick Room. Stroll down the sweep of green lawn to the seats overlooking the sea and back to enjoy breakfast on a deck close to the inn in fine weather. $95–355.

OTHER DOWNTOWN B&BS

IN BAR HARBOR 04609

Manor House Inn (207-288-3759 or 1-800-437-0088; barharbormanorhouse.com), 106 West St. Open mid-Apr.–Oct. No real water views, but a short walk from Bar Island. Nine comfortable rooms with private bath are in the vintage-1887 "Manor" with its rich woodwork. The full acre of landscaped grounds also includes Acadia Cottage with whirlpool, the Chauffeur's Cottage with three guest rooms and two suites, and two garden cottages with gas fireplace. $83–250 includes full breakfast and afternoon tea.

Seacroft Inn (207-288-4669 or 1-800-824-9694; seacroftinn.com), 18 Albert Meadow. Open mid-May–Oct. Bunny Brown's gracious, many-gabled old "cottage" is sequestered on a quiet street, steps from the Shore Path. Extended stays are the norm; all seven rooms have a fridge and a microwave, or a kitchen. $89–129 in-season, substantially less off-season, with housekeeping $10 extra and a complimentary coffee bar and towel

exchange. A "Breakfast Basket" with fruit, muffin, juice, and yogurt is $5.

Primrose Inn (207-288-4031 or 1-877-TIME-4-BH; primroseinn.com), 73 Mount Desert St. Open mid-May–Oct. This is a spiffy 1878 stick-style "painted lady" Victorian summer cottage owned by Melissa Collier DeVos. The 15 guest rooms are bright with floral wallpaper and Victorian decor; several have a gas fireplace and private balcony. The nicest rooms in the house have a "bubble massage" Kohler bathtub. Every room has a flat-panel TV with DVD player. Rooms are $154–264, depending on season, including a great breakfast and afternoon tea.

The Maples Inn (207-288-3443; maplesinn .com), 16 Roberts Ave. Open May–Oct. Mark Dresser bought this inn in 2005 and has been decorating with his and his family's antiques; his architectural books are a resource at this pleasant 1903 house on a quiet side street within walking distance of shops and restaurants. The six rooms (all with private bath) are crisply decorated, furnished with a high, antique bed and down comforter. Red Oak, under the eaves, has its own tranquil deck. $165–205 per couple; $95–125 off-season, with a fine breakfast.

☸ **Canterbury Cottage** (207-288-2112; canterburycottage.com), 12 Roberts Ave. Open year-round. This architecturally interesting Victorian house (its original owner was the B&M stationmaster, and its architect specialized in railroad stations) has a canine welcome committee. Rooms each hold a private bath and cable TV. One has a small balcony. $145–155 double in-season, $89–99 off-season, includes full breakfast served in the pretty dining room.

Cleftstone Manor (207-288-4951; cleftstone.com), 92 Eden St. Open May–Oct. Located a short drive from downtown, this 1880 mansion once owned by wealthy summer visitors has been an inn for 50 years. One smallish room called Benjamin Stanwood has a huge bathroom; four have a sofa bed. Joseph Pulitzer summered here, and a few of the original antiques are still in place, like two crystal chandeliers in the dining room. Seventeen rooms with private bath, two with whirlpools, five with fireplace. Pool and spa services are shared with neighbor **Bluenose Inn**. In-season rates $130–195, less off-season.

Anne's White Columns Inn (207-288-5357 or 1-800-321-6379; anneswhitecolumns.com), 57 Mount Desert St. Open May–Oct. Built in the 1930s as a Christian Science church, hence the columns. The 10 rooms have private bath, air-conditioning, and cable TV. $110–165 July–mid-Oct. (less off-season), including full breakfast and afternoon wine and cheese.

  ⟁ **Mira Monte Inn and Suites** (207-288-4263 or 1-800-553-5109; miramonte.com), 69 Mount Desert St. Open May–mid-Oct. Bar Harbor native Marian Burns offers 13 comfortable guest rooms and four suites in her gracious 1864 mansion. Many, like Malvern, have a private balcony overlooking the deep, peaceful lawn in back or the gardens on the side. All rooms have private bath, phone, clock-radio, voice mail, and flat-screen cable TV; some have a gas fireplace. Rates include a full breakfast buffet and afternoon refreshments. $188–256 for rooms and suites; $95–165 off-season.

HOTELS AND MOTELS

IN BAR HARBOR 04609

  ⌁ ⟁ **Bar Harbor Inn** (207-288-3351 or 1-800-248-3351; barharborinn.com), Newport Dr. Open Mar.–Nov. With 153 units, this landmark hotel gets its share of groups, but its downtown waterside location is unbeatable. It's a genuinely gracious hotel, with a 24-hour front desk, bellhops, a restaurant, and room service. The hotel-sized lobby with seating near the fire is quite grand. The 51 guest rooms in the Main Inn were the first new hotel rooms available in town after the 1947 fire. Of these, 43 were completely rebuilt in 1998; balconies, jetted tubs, and fireplaces were added. The grounds also include a 64-unit Oceanfront Lodge with private balconies on the bay, and the Newport Building—38 equally comfortable rooms without views. All rooms have phone, cable TV, and access to the pool, Jacuzzi, fitness room, and 7 acres of manicured lawns on the water. $199–379 in-season, continental breakfast included.

  Harborside Hotel & Marina (207-288-5033 or 1-800-328-5033; theharborsidehotel .com), 55 West St. Open May–Oct. Views of the harbor and Porcupine Islands in some rooms. Luxuriously furnished and accented with marble baths and marble-tiled floors,

Nancy English

POOLSIDE AT THE HARBORSIDE HOTEL & MARINA

many rooms and suites are equipped with full kitchens; some have a fireplace in the master bedroom and Jacuzzi on the porch. **La Bella Vita**, a high-end Italian restaurant, lies off the main lobby (and has the same branding as The Samoset's 2011 version in Rockport). The spa is located in the neighboring Bar Harbor Club with its own restaurant. Tennis courts and a saltwater pool. Standard rooms $275–425, suites $399–1,700 in-season; off-season $99–199, $299–800.

  ⌁ **Wonder View Inn** (207-288-3358 or 1-888-439-8439; wonderviewinn.com), 50 Eden St., P.O. Box 25. Open May–Oct. Children are welcome in the 75-unit motel built on 14 acres, the site of an estate once owned by Mary Roberts Rinehart, author of popular mystery stories. Near downtown Bar Harbor, the motel overlooks Frenchman Bay and includes a swimming pool. $109–249 in summer, less off-season. Most rooms have a balcony with an ocean view.

  ⌁ ⌁ **Bar Harbor Villager Motel** (207-288-3211 or 1-888-383-3211; barharborvillager .com), 207 Main St. This reasonably priced motel provides immaculately clean and comfortable rooms within an easy walk of everything Bar Harbor offers, along with a turquoise, heated pool tucked into a back corner of the parking lot. The **Bar Harbor Shuttle** (207-479-5911; barharborshuttle.com) stops here, going to the airports and the bus depot in Bangor. Summer rates $89–$179, depending on season, children 12 and under free.

IN ELLSWORTH 04605

🐾 ✐ **Twilite Motel** (207-667-8165 or 1-800-395-5097; twilitemotel.com), Rts. 1 and 3. In 2007 Chuck and Ariela Zucker took over this charming motel with flowers spilling out in between the 1950s-style, updated rooms, all with private bath and a little outdoor seating area. Children's play area, continental breakfast served in the breakfast room, and coin-operated laundry with games and books for guests to enjoy. Rates $82–123, less off-season.

COTTAGES ✐ **Acadia Cottage Rentals** (207-288-3636; acadiarental.com) offers camps, cottages, private homes, and estates for a minimum of one week (Sat.–Sat.).

✐ **Emery's Cottages on the Shore** (207-288-3432 or 1-888-240-3432; emeryscottages .com), Sand Point Rd., Bar Harbor 04609. Open May–late Oct. In the family since 1969, these 22 cottages and an apartment on Frenchman Bay offer electric heat, shower, and cable TV; 14 have a kitchen. Linens, dishes, and cooking utensils provided. Serene, private pebble beach. Telephone available for local calls. No pets. Hikers like to use these cabins as a launching place from which to set out on day trips in Acadia National Park. $560–1,075 per week late June–late Aug.; $470–820 late Aug.–Oct.; less in May and June.

PUBLIC CAMPGROUNDS **Lamoine State Park** (207-667-4778; campwithme.com), Rt. 184, Lamoine. Open mid-May–mid-Oct. Minutes from busy Rt. 3 (between Ellsworth and Bar Harbor), this 55-acre waterside park offers a boat launch and 62 campsites (no hookups, but hot showers in a bathhouse), two-night reservation minimum, $25 per night for nonresidents in-season, $15 for residents. Neighboring Lamoine Beach is great for skipping stones. *Note:* There are occasionally vacancies here in July and Aug. when Acadia National Park campsites are full, and about 20 sites are on a first-come, first-served basis.

✳ Where to Eat

DINING OUT

ALL LISTINGS ARE IN BAR HARBOR UNLESS OTHERWISE NOTED

The Burning Tree (207-288-9331), Rt. 3, Otter Creek. Open June–Columbus Day 5–10; closed Tue., also Mon. after Labor Day. Reservations recommended. Admired for its fresh fish and its own organically grown produce from five gardens. Dine inside or on a lattice-enclosed porch on a wide choice of seafood, chicken, and vegetable entrées, but no red meat. You might begin with crispy kale and oven-roasted littleneck clams with garlic, pine nuts, and chèvre ($12.50), then dine on a cashew, brown rice, and Gruyère cheese terrine ($23.50) or basil-and-chèvre-stuffed organic chicken breast with homemade tomato jam ($24). Entrées $20–29.

Mache Bistro (207-288-0447; machebistro .com), 321 Main St. Kyle Yarborough has made Mache Bistro a place to count on for vibrant flavors and great cooking. His lobster-stuffed piquillo peppers get dinner started perfectly, and the swordfish with tabbouleh and heirloom tomatoes shows off the summer. Entrées $18–29.

Fathom (207-288-9664; fathombarharbor .com), corner of Cottage, Bridge, and Summer Sts. Inventive dishes that hit the ball out of the park. The lobster and "red snappah" egg roll relies on red-dyed hot dogs, cut into bits, for its umami, and why not when it works this

Nancy English

BAR HARBOR FATHOM

LOBSTER

Lobster pounds are the best places to eat lobster. The easiest to find are the clutch around the Trenton Bridge on Rt. 3. The **Trenton Bridge Lobster Pound** (207-667-2977; trentonbridge lobster.com), open Memorial Day–Columbus Day 8–8, or for live lobsters year-round, has been in George Gascon's family a long time. The view and the aromas are unparalleled.

& **Bar Harbor Lobster Bakes** (207-288-4055; barharborlobsterbakes.com), Rt. 3, Hulls Cove, is a twist on the traditional lobster pound. Reservations are a must. Choices are lobster or steak. Watch the lobsters being steamed with your potatoes and corn in the large steel cookers.

well? Perfectly cooked halibut, grilled salmon done with wild mushroom béarnaise, and more excellent dishes for dinner. Entrées $18–32.

& **Café This Way** (207-288-4483; cafethisway.com), 14½ Mount Desert St. Open seasonally for breakfast and dinner. Tucked just off the village green, this is a winner. Start dinner with a smoked salmon "parcel" that wraps up goat cheese and pickled jalapeños, then try fish-and-chips made with tempura ahi tuna. Entrées $15–26. Reservations a good idea. Breakfast is just as good (see *Eating Out*).

✔ **Jordan Pond House** (207-276-3316; jordanpond.com), Park Loop Rd., Seal Harbor. Open mid-May–late Oct. for lunch and tea 11:30–6 in summer, 5:30 early and late in the season, and for dinner 6–9. Reservations advised. First opened in the 1870s, this landmark was beautifully rebuilt after a 1979 fire, with dining rooms overlooking the pond and mountains. It's best known for popovers and outdoor tea, though in 2015 many popover aficionados were heading to the Asticou in Northeast Harbor. Jordan Pond House is least crowded at dinner, when dishes such as prime rib, fresh fish, and baked scallops are served.

& **Havana** (207-288-CUBA; havanamaine .com), 318 Main St. Open from 5 nightly; reservations suggested. The menu changes weekly, and the accent ranges from the Caribbean to Africa and farther east. Dinners have included braised beef short ribs in soy sauce, apple cider, and brown sugar with avocado guasaca, a spicy Venezuelan spread, and local squash curry. Entrées $19–34.

Sweet Pea's Café (207-801-9078), 854 Rt. 3, Bar Harbor (just north of town). Open seasonally. Wood-fire oven-baked pizza, house-smoked bacon and pastrami, grilled beef

tenderloin, and blueberry pie. The local goats are utterly charming.

Galyn's (207-288-9706; galynsbarharbor .com), 17 Main St. Lunch and dinner. Easy to miss among the shops near the bottom of Main St., but it's bigger than it looks, with dining rooms upstairs and down. Try the crab-cakes or lobster enchilada. Entrées from $16.

McKay's Public House (207-288-2002; mckayspublichouse.com), 231 Main St. Two floors (with live music upstairs) fill up with dedicated local customers at this year-round place. Farm stand salad, Maine étouffée, roasted organic chicken, and brandy-braised pork are possibilities. Entrées $16–21.

✔ **Testa's** (207-288-3327; testas restaurants.com), 53 Main St. Open 8 AM–10 PM, June–Aug., closing earlier off-season (the family moves to its Palm Beach restaurant in Nov.). In Bar Harbor since 1934. Extensive menu, including Italian and seafood specialties. Entrées $17–30.

EATING OUT

IN BAR HARBOR

The Black Friar Pub (207-288-5091; black friarinn.com), across from the Shop and Save, serves winning pub fare, like sweet potato fries, crab fritters, and fish-and-chips. Of course the big beer selection, with many Maine brews on tap, is another draw, along with the best chocolate cakes and fruit pies in town. Meals $10–17.50.

Café This Way (207-288-4483), 14½ Mount Desert St. Open for breakfast 7–11 Mon.–Sat., 8–1 Sun. The menu ranges from scrambled tofu to steak and includes omelets, eggs Benedict with smoked salmon, and many other appetizing dishes.

Lompoc Café (207-288-9392; lompoccafe
.com), 36 Rodick St. Open daily with lunch
11:30–3 in the summer and 5–9:30 for dinner, until 1 for drinks. Billed as the original
home of Bar Harbor Real Ale (the Atlantic
Brewing Company itself has outgrown its
birthplace), this is a congenial oasis with an
open knotty-pine dining room, plus porch
and terrace tables by a bocce court. Entrée
choices include pizzas and salads; live music
on weekends.

Rosalie's Pizza (207-288-5666), 46
Cottage St. Locals head for a booth at Rosalie's when they want excellent pizza. Calzones,
salads, and baked subs are also served.

Morning Glory Bakery (207-288-3041;
morningglorybakery.com), 39 Rodick St.
Open weekdays 7–7, Sat.–Sun. 8–7. Smoothies, espresso, savory and sweet baked goods,
soup, sandwiches. Local meats, produce,
and dairy products on the menu; the bacon
and fresh eggs are local, Smith Family Farm
yogurt, and Sunset Acres Farm goat cheese.

Poor Boy's Gourmet (207-288-4148),
300 Main St. Open for dinner from 4:30
nightly. Count on a decent dining experience
at reasonable prices. Choices range from
vegetarian entrées to a full lobster dinner—
including brownie à la mode. Wine and beer.

Jordan's Restaurant (207-288-3586), 80
Cottage St. Open 4:30 AM–2 PM. Under David
Paine's ownership (since 1976), this remains
an old-style diner: breakfast all day, specializing in blueberry pancakes and muffins and a
wide variety of three-egg omelets. The place
to fuel up for a hike.

IN HULLS COVE

Chart Room (207-288-9740), Rt. 3. Open
for lunch and dinner. A dependable, family-geared waterside restaurant with seafood
specialties; good quiche and Caesar salads.

IN TOWN HILL

Mother's Kitchen (207-288-4403; mothers
kitchenfoods.com), Rt. 102, Town Hill. Fantastic sandwiches, and everything can be served
as a salad. Muffins, scones, pies, and picnic
tables to dine at in good weather, if you are
not hiking to the top of Precipice. Order by
phone ahead of time and skip the wait.

IN ELLSWORTH

The Cellar (207-669-6439), 112 Main St.
A wide array of charcuterie and cheese to
choose from for a starter, then maybe a
cioppino, burger, or flank steak as an entrée.
Brunch and lunch too. $18–23.

Union River Lobster Pot (207-667-
5077; lobsterpot.com), behind Rooster Brothers at the western edge of Ellsworth. Open
daily June–Aug., 11:30–8:30, dinner only
through Oct. Brian and Jane Langley own
this pleasant riverside restaurant and serve a
full menu, including ribs, but the specialty is
lobster and seafood cooked four ways. Leave
room for pie. Beer and wine, and an eagle
overhead at a beautiful setting.

Riverside Café (207-667-7220), 151 Main
St. Open 6 AM–3 PM weekdays, 7–3 Sat., 7–2 Sun.
for breakfast and lunch in expanded, bright,
spacious quarters. Good food and coffees.

Dyon's (207-664-6116; dyonstapas.com),
35 Eastward Ln. A small boîte in the massive
indoor tennis facility, Dyon's serves tapas
or small plates and wine. The waffle falafel,
crispy and warm, works well, along with tape-
nade and house crackers and chicken satay.

AFTERNOON TEA Jordan Pond House

(207-276-3316; jordanpond.com), Park Loop
Rd., Seal Harbor. Tea on the lawn at the Jordan Pond House (served 11:30–6 mid-July–
Aug., till 5:30 mid-May–mid-Oct.) comes with
freshly baked popovers and homemade ice
cream. Reservations suggested.

SNACKS AND ICE CREAM Mount Desert

Island Ice Cream (for information call 207-
460-5515; mdiic.com). Linda Parker started
this business in 2005. Stores are at 7 Firefly
Lane (207-801-4007) and 325 Main St. (207-
801-4006), both in Bar Harbor. Ice cream—
chocolate made with Callebaut chocolate,
vanilla with vanilla beans—and sorbet, like
lemon made with hand-squeezed lemons.
Blueberry basil sorbet and salted caramel ice
cream were both hits.

J. H. Butterfield Co. (207-288-3386), 152
Main St., Bar Harbor. FANCY FOODS SINCE
1887, the sign says, and John Butterfield
preserves the atmosphere of the grocery that
once delivered to Bar Harbor's summer mansions. Now featuring Maine specialty foods.

Morton's Moo (207-266-9671; mortons moo.com), 9 School St., Ellsworth. Devotees to Morton's Moo ice cream are intimately familiar with the high quality of the mint chocolate chip, coffee bean, and double dark chocolate ice cream, as well as many other flavors.

Rooster Brother (207-667-8675; rooster brother.com), Rt. 1, Ellsworth. Just south of the bridge. Gourmet groceries, cheese, fresh-roasted coffee blends, takeout sandwiches.

❋ Entertainment

MUSIC **Bar Harbor Music Festival** (207-288-5744, off-season 212-222-1026; barharbor musicfestival.org), the Rodick Building, 59 Cottage St., Bar Harbor. Late June–late July. For more than 40 years this annual series has brought up-and-coming young artists to the island, with opera, jazz, new composers, the Bar Harbor Festival String Orchestra, and more. The evening concerts are staged at a variety of sites around town.

FILM **Criterion Movie Theater**, Cottage St., Bar Harbor. This vintage-1932, art deco, 700-seat nonprofit performing-arts theater is run by the Bar Harbor Jazz Festival and presents live performances, year-round movies, and modern jazz.

Reel Pizza Cinema (207-288-3811), 22 Kennebec Place, Bar Harbor. Pizza and art, along with foreign and independent films, in a funky setting (beanbag chairs and big sofas). Films at 6 and 8:30 nightly, year-round.

THE CRITERION THEATER IN BAR HARBOR

The Grand (207-667-9500; grandonline .org), Main St., Ellsworth. A classic theater, recently restored, offers live performances, musical theater; live opera from the Met; art and independent films.

THEATER See **Acadia Repertory Theatre** in "The Quiet Side" and **The Grand**, above.

❋ Selective Shopping

ART AND FINE-CRAFTS GALLERIES
Eclipse Gallery (207-288-9048; eclipse gallery.us), 12 Mount Desert St., Bar Harbor. Seasonal. A quality gallery specializing in contemporary handblown American glass, ceramics, and fine furniture; also showing metal sculpture.

Island Artisans (207-288-4214; island artisans.com), 99 Main St., Bar Harbor. Open May–Dec. Featuring Maine artists and crafts-people: textiles, pottery, Native American baskets. Glass, silver, and more.

Alone Moose Fine Crafts (207-288-4229), 78 West St., Bar Harbor. A long-established collection of "made in Maine" crafts, specializing in wildlife sculpture in bronze and wood.

Naturalist's Notebook (207-801-2777; thenaturalistsnotebook.com), 16 Main St., Seal Harbor. One part shop, one part exhibit hall, and one part science program, the Naturalist's Notebook was on hiatus in 2015 but due to reopen. When it does, it will offer riches for anyone alert to flora and fauna on MDI hikes, as well as books and prints by Bernd Heinrich, a past speaker.

The Hulls Cove Tool Barn (207-288-5126; jonesport-wood.com), Hulls Cove. Open Wed.–Sun. year-round, closed in Jan. Owned by Jonesport Wood Company, this store holds a huge selection of hand planes and other old woodworking tools. Books, old postcards, and more are also stocked. The store is next to the Sculpture Garden of the Davistown Museum. (See Liberty Tool Company in the Searsport chapter.)

Rocky Mann Studio Potter and Gallery (207-288-5478; rockymann.com), Breakneck Rd., Hulls Cove. Turn off Rt. 3 at the Hulls Cove General Store. In summer open daily 10–5; off-season 11–4, closed Mon. After Christmas by appointment. Rocky Mann's ever-evolving work is worth a trip, with his

CROQUET AT COLONEL BLACK MANSION

raku and charming frogs and turtles, and the Acadia starry night series. Paintings and cards by Carol Shutt.

Asticou Connection (207-288-2400; asticouconnection.com), 1302 State Highway 102, Town Hill. Intricate baskets, jewelry, and fine furniture share space with fine art with an emphasis on Maine and nature.

BOOKSTORES **Sherman's Bookstore and Stationery** (207-288-3161; shermans.com), 56 Main St., Bar Harbor. Open 9 AM–10:30 PM in summer, 9–6 daily in winter. A great browsing emporium; really a combination five-and-dime, stationery store, gift shop, and well-stocked bookshop.

Big Chicken Barn Books and Antiques (207-667-7308; bigchickenbarn.com), Rt. 1/3 south of Ellsworth. Open daily year-round; call for hours. Maine's largest used-book store fills the vast innards of a former chicken house. Annegret Cukierski has 150,000 books in stock: hardbacks, paperbacks, magazines, and comics; also used furniture and collectibles.

✳ Special Events

Throughout the summer: **Band concerts**, Bar Harbor village green (check current listings); **Ellsworth Harbor Park**, concerts on Friday nights.

June: **Acadia Birding Festival**—lectures, walks, and boat tours. **Working Waterfront**

Celebration (second Sunday) includes the Blessing of the Fleet. **Legacy of the Arts** (midmonth), a week of art and culture with concerts, artists' events, and, at the week's end, **Bar Harbor Chamber of Commerce Art Show**, displaying original work on the Bar Harbor village green (207-288-5103).

July: Bar Harbor Music Festival (see *Entertainment*).

July 4 weekend: **Independence Day**— blueberry pancake breakfast, town parade, seafood festival focused on lobster and mussels, and strawberry shortcake. Live music, kids' games, and fireworks from the pier at night. **Native American Festival**—dances and a big sale by the Maine Indian Basketmakers at the College of the Atlantic (207-288-5744).

August: **Ellsworth Antiques show at Woodlawn**, Ellsworth.

Late September: **Acadia Night Sky Festival** (acadianightskyfestival.com). **Art in the Park** on the Bar Harbor village green throughout a weekend.

October: **Woodlawn Golf Croquet Tournament**, Colonel Black Mansion, Ellsworth.

November: **Shopping in your PJs** downtown for extra discounts, with a parade and fashion show at 9 PM, prize for craziest sleepwear.

December: **Midnight Madness Sale and Village Holidays** (first Friday)—Santa arrives, lights the tree. Discounts from 8 PM to midnight. **Island Arts Association Holiday Fair** (first weekend) sponsored by YWCA (207-288-5008).

COLONEL BLACK MANSION

The Quiet Side of Mount Desert

The Quiet Side has come to refer to the longer, thinner arm of land that's divided by Somes Sound from the part of Mount Desert that's home to Bar Harbor, the Acadia National Park visitors center, and Park Loop Road. The name generally also applies to Northeast Harbor.

Northeast is a yachting village, with a large marina geared to visiting yacht owners, summer residents, and ferries to the Cranberry Islands. A 2008 fire destroyed several Main Street buildings and some priceless art in one of Maine's oldest, most established galleries. Soon, however, the village was bright and humming again. It's flanked by a mile of mansions hidden along Somes Sound. The splendid, public Thuya Gardens are just east of town. The Mount Desert Historical Society in Somesville is well worth a stop. Some of Acadia's best hiking, as well as its best public swimming beach (at Echo Lake) and canoeing (on Long Pond), are found west of Somes Sound.

Southwest Harbor is a boatbuilding center, home of the Hinckley Company—the Rolls-Royce of yacht builders—and a substantial commercial fishing fleet. In the neighboring town of Tremont, Bass Harbor is a classic fishing village. It's also the departure point for Swans, a destination in its own right, and several other islands that were once far busier.

Ironically, back in the 1840s Mount Desert's first summer visitors—artists in search of solitude—headed for the Bar Harbor area precisely because it was then far less peopled than the villages on this western side of the island.

GUIDANCE & (ᵠ) **Mount Desert Chamber of Commerce** (207-276-5040; mountdesert chamber.org), Sea St., Northeast Harbor. A walk-in cottage (with wireless Internet, accessible restrooms, and showers) is open daily Memorial Day–Sept., 9–4, at the town dock.

STEPS ACROSS THE WATER AT ASTICOU GARDEN

Southwest Harbor/Tremont Chamber of Commerce (207-244-9264; acadiachamber .com), 329 Main St. The walk-in info center is open June–Columbus Day, 9–4 daily.

GETTING THERE
Note: **Airport & Harbor Car Service** (207-667-5995) meets planes, buses, and boats; serves the entire area.

By boat: Contact the harbormasters in Northeast Harbor (207-276-5737) and Southwest Harbor (207-244-7913) about guest moorings.

By car: From Ellsworth: Fork right off Rt. 3 as soon as it crosses the Mount Desert narrows; follow Rt. 102/198 to Somesville and Rt. 198 to Northeast Harbor, or Rt. 102 to Southwest Harbor.

GETTING AROUND Beal & Bunker (207-244-3573) offers year-round mail and ferry service from Northeast Harbor to the Cranberry Islands, and the **Maine State Ferry Service** (207-244-4353 or 1-800-491-4883) services Swans Island and Frenchboro.

Island Explorer Bus Service (207-288-4573 or 1-866-282-7558), late June–Columbus Day. Free. This bus stops frequently along the routes from Southwest Harbor to Bernard, up and down both sides of Somes Sound, and into the park and Bar Harbor, connecting with service from Northeast Harbor.

✳ To See

IN NORTHEAST HARBOR

Thuya Garden and Lodge (207-276-5130). Parking is marked on Rt. 3, just east of the junction with Rt. 198. Cross the road and climb the steps, carved in granite beside the Asticou Terraces. These wind up Asticou Hill, offering a splendid view of Northeast Harbor. Thuya Lodge (open late June into Sept., 10–4:30), a botanic library and a lovely spot to read, is the former home of Joseph Henry Curtis, a landscape architect who began this exquisite system of paths and shelters around 1900 and donated the 140-acre property to the public. It is now maintained by the Mount Desert Land and Garden Preserve, to which visitors are asked to donate $3. The 2-acre Thuya Garden was designed by the Asticou Inn's longtime former innkeeper, Charles Savage, who also designed the 2.3-acre **Asticou Azalea Garden** (junction of Rt. 3 and Rt. 198), a spectacular show of azaleas and laurels mid-May–mid-June. Stroll down winding paths and over ornamental bridges. Those not wishing to climb the Asticou Terrace steps can take Thuya Drive (just past the parking lot) up to the garden and lodge. Also note the 1.4-mile **Eliot Mountain Trail** behind Thuya Garden, leading up through blueberry bushes to a sweeping view.

Great Harbor Maritime Museum (207-276-5262; greatharbormaritimemuseum.org), 125 Main St. in the Old Firehouse. Open seasonally, Tue.–Sat. 10–5. $3. The permanent collection is of model ships, small boats, and historical maritime artifacts from Mount Desert Island; there are also notable changing exhibits on a variety of subjects.

Petite Plaisance (207-276-3940; petiteplaisance@acadia.net), South Shore Rd. Open by appointment mid-June–Aug. as well as the first and last two days of this season. The former home of French author Marguerite Yourcenar, where she wrote most of *Memoirs of Hadrian* and also where she died, has long been a destination for her readers.

IN MOUNT DESERT

The tiny white wooden village of **Somesville** at the head of Somes Sound is a National Historic District; be sure to check out **Brookside Cemetery** and the **Somesville Museum**

Christina Tree

THUYA GARDENS

(207-244-5043; mdihistory.org), Rt. 102. Open mid-June–mid-Oct., Tue.–Sat. 1–4 (donation), this lively museum is maintained by the **Mount Desert Historical Society**. Two tidy buildings, one dating back to 1780, connected by a moon bridge, house many artifacts and photographs of the island's vanished hotels and the shipyards for which this village was once widely known. An heirloom garden shows off MDI plants and herbs. The MDI Historical Society's headquarters is on the other side of Somes Sound in the vintage-1892 **School House and Museum**, Rt. 3/198 between Somesville and Northeast Harbor, open June–Sept., Tue.–Sat. 10–4; Sept.–May, weekdays 10–4.

IN SOUTHWEST HARBOR

Wendell Gilley Museum (207-244-7555; wendellgilleymuseum.org), Rt. 102. Open June–Dec., 10–4 (10–5 in July and Aug.), daily except Mon.; Fri.–Sun. only in May, Nov., and Dec. $5 adults, $2 ages 5–12. Wendell Gilley was a local plumber who began hand carving birds as a hobby in the 1930s. Over more than 50 years he carved some 10,000 birds, acquiring a reputation as a master. Friend and patron Steven Rockefeller helped develop the museum, housing more than 200 of Gilley's works.

IN BASS HARBOR

Tremont Historical Society (207-244-9753), Shore Rd. near the Swans Island Ferry. Open July–Columbus Day, Mon. and Wed. 1–4. If you are lucky enough to find this restored country store open, don't pass it by. It's now filled with historic artifacts and photos and sells bargain-priced copies of novels like *The Weir*, *Spoonhandle*, and *Speak to the Winds*, written in the 1940s by longtime local resident Ruth Moore, vividly capturing life on the offshore islands here.

Nancy English

IN SEAL COVE

✒ **Seal Cove Auto Museum** (207-244-9242; sealcoveautomuseum.org), Pretty Marsh Rd. (Rt. 102), between Bass Harbor and Somesville. Open May–Oct., daily 10–5. $6 adults, $5 seniors and teens, and $2 children 12 and under. Squirreled away in a little-trafficked corner of the island across from Cove Pond and Western Mountain, this collection is a real find: more than 50 gleaming

THE 1913 PEUGEOT AT SEAL COVE AUTO MUSEUM

antique cars and 15 motorcycles, including the country's largest assemblage of pre-1915 cars—the lifework of a private collector.

✳ To Do

⚲ **Acadia Ranger Programs**. Pick up a copy of *Acadia's Beaver Log* at Seawall Campground (Rt. 102A). The free handout *Acadia Weekly* also lists programs ranging from guided walks and cruises to evening programs.

BICYCLING The network of gravel carriage roads constructed by John D. Rockefeller Jr. in 1915 lends itself particularly well to mountain biking. The fire roads are also good for mountain biking, as is Swans Island. **Southwest Cycle** (207-244-5856; southwestcycle.com), 370 Main St., Southwest Harbor, rents mountain and touring bicycles, children's bikes, baby seats, car racks, and jogging strollers.

BOATING

FROM BASS HARBOR

Island Cruises (207-244-5785; bassharborcruises.com), Little Island Marine. Mid-June–mid-Sept. Kim Strauss offers daily (weather-dependent) lunch cruises aboard 40-foot *R. L. Gott* to Frenchboro, also afternoon cruises to see wildlife—a wide variety of birds, including several bald eagles, porpoises, and many harbor and gray seals on and around Placentia and Black Islands as well as Great and Little Gott Islands, all depicted in novels by Great Gott native Ruth Moore (1903–89). In *The Weir, Speak to the Winds*, and *Spoonhandle*, Moore describes the poignant ebb of life from these islands in the 1930s and 1940s.

Maine State Ferry (207-244-3254) makes the 40-minute run to Swans Island several times a day, twice weekly to Frenchboro, carrying cars.

FROM NORTHEAST HARBOR

Beal & Bunker (207-244-3575) offers year-round mail-boat and ferry service to the Cranberries and Sutton Island. **Sea Princess Cruises** (207-276-5352; barharborcruises.com) offers seasonal regular cruises with naturalists, including Somes Sound, sunset, and Islesford historical cruises.

FROM SOUTHWEST HARBOR

Cranberry Cove Boating (207-244-5882) offers frequent service to the Cranberries from both Lower Town Dock in Manset and Upper Town Dock on Clark Point Rd., both in Southwest Harbor. **Downeast Friendship Sloop Charters** (207-266-5210; sailacadia.com) offers daysails and private charters. **Schooner *Rachel B. Jackson*** (207-288-2216; downeastsail .com) and **Friendship sloop *Surprise*** both offer daysails from Southwest Harbor.

In Southwest Harbor both **Manset Yacht Service** (207-244-4040) and **Mansell Boat Rental Company** (207-244-5625) rent power- and sailboats and offer sail lesson cruises.

CANOEING AND KAYAKING Long Pond, the largest lake on any Maine island, has three access points. Boats can be launched at Echo Lake on Ike's Point, just off Rt. 102. Seal Cove Pond is less used and accessible from fire roads north of Seal Cove. Bass Harbor Marsh is another possibility at high tide. Canoe rental sources offer suggestions and directions. **National Park Canoe/Kayak Rentals** (207-244-5854; nationalparkcanoerental.com), on Long Pond near Somesville, offers guided paddles and instruction. Guided half- and full-day paddles are offered by **Maine State Sea Kayak** (207-244-9500; mainestatekayak.com), 254 Main St., Southwest Harbor.

GOLF **Causeway Golf Club** (207-244-3780), Fernald Point Rd., Southwest Harbor. Nine-hole waterside course, clubhouse and pull carts, pro shop.

HIKING The highest mountains on the western side of Somes Sound are Bernard and Mansell, but both summits are wooded. The more popular hikes are up Acadia Mountain (3.5 miles roundtrip, off Rt. 102), with an east–west summit trail commanding a spectacular view of the sound and islands. Admittedly we have only climbed **Flying Mountain**, a quick hit with a great view, too. The trail begins at the Fernald Cove parking area. Don't miss **Asticou Terraces** and the **Indian Point Blagden Preserve**. **Ship Harbor Nature Trail** (off

Nancy English

BEES MAKING THE MOST OF A ROSA RUGOSA

Rt. 102A) winds along the shore and into the woods, with good birding. If a sunny Friday is promised, take advantage of the once-weekly service to **Frenchboro** (207-244-5785; see *Boating*) and spend the day hiking in the Frenchboro Preserve.

SAILING **Mansell Boat Rentals** (207-244-5625), Rt. 102A, Manset (near Southwest Harbor), offers sailing lessons; also rents small sailboats. All-day sailing trips offered with Captain Robert Wellborn; bring some wine and cheese and spend the day on the water. Also check **Hinckley Yacht Charters** (207-244-5008), Southwest Harbor, and **Manset Yacht Service** (207-244-4040) in Manset.

SWIMMING **Echo Lake** offers a beach with a lifeguard, restrooms, and parking (Rt. 102 between Somesville and Southwest Harbor). Another favorite spot is known as "the bluffs" or "the ledges." Park in the Acadia Mountain parking area (about 3 miles south of Somesville on Rt. 102). A short path leads down to the lake.

TENNIS The courts at the **Northeast Harbor Marina** are open to the public, and the Mount Desert Chamber of Commerce (see *Guidance*) offers racquets and balls.

✳ Green Space

Indian Point Blagden Preserve, a 110-acre Nature Conservancy preserve in the northwestern corner of the island, includes 1,000 feet of shorefront and paths that wander through the woods. It offers a view of Blue Hill Bay and is a tried-and-true seal-watching spot. From Rt. 198 north of Somesville, turn right on Indian Point Rd., bear right at the fork, and look for the entrance; sign in and pick up a map at the caretaker's house.

Seal Cove. An unpublicized waterside park with picnic tables, a beach at low tide, a kayaking put-in. From Rt. 102 turn at the red buoy onto the waterside extension of Seal Cove Rd.

✳ Lodging

INNS AND B&BS

IN SOUTHWEST HARBOR 04679

The Inn at Southwest (207-244-3835; innatsouthwest.com), Main St., P.O. Box 593. Open May–Oct. Built in 1884 as a Victorian-style annex to a now vanished hotel, this delightful B&B is furnished with comfortable Arts and Crafts antiques. Of the seven guest rooms, all with private bath and named for lighthouses, the third-floor Pemaquid Point suite with its chapel-style window and window seat stands out; Egg Rock was a snug spot for a one-night visit. Dora and Daniel are the warm innkeepers, serving Belgian waffles and a lovely fruit bowl for breakfast, or perhaps eggs and sausages if you prefer. $150–215 per couple in high season.

Lindenwood Inn (207-244-5335 or 1-800-307-5335; lindenwoodinn.com), 118 Clark Point Rd., P.O. Box 1328. This turn-of-the-20th-century sea captain's home set by the harbor among stately linden trees is open Apr.–Nov. 1. Australian-born owner Jim King has a sure decorating touch in the 15 rooms (all with private bath) in the main inn and the Rosebrook House, many with water views, balcony, and fireplace. The pool and hot tub are appreciated after hiking or biking. A full breakfast is served in the paneled dining room. A full bar is also available. $175–295 double in-season, $125–225 in low season.

Harbour Cottage Inn and Pier One (207-244-5738 or 1-888-843-3022; harbourcottageinn.com), 9 Dirigo Rd., P.O. Box 258. Don Jalbert and Javier Montesinos have revamped this old landmark to feature creature comforts and romance. The eight standard rooms are equipped with flat-screen TV; some have whirlpool bath. The Southwester (sleeping six) and Carriage House (sleeping four), both neighboring cottages, have full kitchen. Five skillfully furnished weekly rental units ($1,155–1,715) with kitchens are clustered by the water and are collectively known as Pier One. $179–245 for standard rooms, $199–269 for suites or cottages. Rates include breakfast at separate tables in a sunny dining room and afternoon refreshments.

The Kingsleigh Inn (207-244-5302; kingsleighinn.com), 373 Main St. Open seasonally. The check-in desk is the counter of a large, open kitchen, and the living room has a wood-burning fireplace; wicker chairs fill the wraparound porch, and several rooms have decks to maximize harbor views. We like the Chelsea, Abbott, and Hawthorne Rooms more than the three-room third-floor suite. Innkeepers Pamela Parker and Bryan Stevens offer a multicourse breakfast that's a true event; afternoon tea is another. $170–205 mid-June–mid-Oct., $315 for the three-room, third-floor suite; from $145 off-season.

✐ **Penury Hall** (207-244-7102; penuryhall.com), Main St., P.O. Box 68. Open year-round. This attractive village house with three guest rooms (private bath) was the first B&B on the island. Gretchen Strong takes her job seriously and delights in helping guests figure out what's happening on the island. Breakfast may be blueberry pancakes or a "penurious omelet" (eggs, cheese, and salsa with no meat), served with popovers on Tuesday. $165 May–Oct., otherwise from $120 includes modest use of the fridge, laundry facilities, library, music, games, and sauna. There are also two frisky, friendly black cats; cash or check preferred.

♂ ♂ **The Birches** (207-244-5182; thebirchesbnb.com), Fernald Point Rd., P.O. Box 178. Open year-round. A very special place. Susi Homer's home, built in 1916, offers a waterfront view from its spacious living room. Formal gardens include a croquet court. The three guest rooms (private bath) are furnished in family antiques. $149–189 includes a full breakfast. Inquire about moorings and ski specials.

Moorings Inn (207-244-5523 or 1-800-596-5523; mooringsinn.com), 133 Shore Rd., Rt. 102A, Manset. Overlooking the entrance to Somes Sound, this rambling old inn stands beside the fabled Hinkley boat (as in yacht) yard. Leslie Watson, the fourth generation of her family to run the inn, has made major and tasteful renovations in the Main House, which dates in part to 1784. The inviting living room features a telescope aimed at the spread of mountains and water beyond the picture window. There are 13 rooms in the house itself,

ranging from a couple of small "lawn view" rooms to suites with spectacular views. Three rooms in the Lighthouse Wing have a deck, microwave, and fridge. The complex also includes six cottages, most with a living room, fireplace, and kitchenette. Bikes, canoes, and kayaks are available, and sailing lessons are offered through Mansell Boat Rentals, also on the property. $95–195 for the rooms.

IN NORTHEAST HARBOR 04662

🦞 **Harbourside Inn** (207-276-3272; harbour sideinn.com), P.O. Box 178. Open mid-June–mid-Sept. A gracious 1880s shingle-style inn set on 4 wooded acres, with 11 guest rooms and three suites (two with kitchenette) on three floors, all with phone and private bath, some with kitchen. There are also nine working fireplaces in first- and second-floor guest rooms. This very special place has four generations of the Sweet family living on the premises. Flowers from the garden brighten every guest room. Guests mingle at breakfast over fresh-baked blueberry muffins, served on the sunporch, with all organic ingredients. The Asticou Azalea Gardens, extensive woodland walks, shops, and the town landing with its water excursions are all within walking distance. $150–180 for a room; $250 for a suite with kitchen.

♂ **Asticou Inn** (207-276-3344 or 1-800-258-3373; asticou.com), Rt. 3. Late May–mid-Oct. The inn offers rooms with and without water views, public rooms with Oriental rugs, and a porch overlooking formal gardens and the harbor. The 48 rooms and suites, all with private bath, are divided among the main house and annexes, which include Cranberry Lodge across the road and the Topsider suites in modern water-view cottages. Facilities include a cocktail lounge, tennis courts, and a heated swimming pool. Since the 1960s the inn has been owned by a consortium of summer residents and businesspeople. New management in 2015 made it a popular destination for popovers and brunch on the porch. Along with many of the area's shingle-style "cottages," the inn was designed by Fred Savage, son of A. C. Savage, the original innkeeper. $295–375 per couple in high season, from $155 in shoulder months, plus 5 percent resort fee. Breakfast served but not included in bill. Also see *Dining Out*.

BRUNCH ON THE PORCH OF THE ASTICOU INN, NORTHEAST HARBOR

Nancy English

CLAREMONT HOTEL

Gracious but not stuffy, Mount Desert's oldest hotel has the grace and dignity but not the size of a grand hotel. It also has the best views on the island and has benefited from the fact that, since its 1884 opening, there have been just three owners. Upstairs the original 35 second- and third-floor rooms have been reduced to 24, all with closets and baths, furnished with refinished original pieces and graceful reproductions, all with phones and fresh flowers. Wood floors gleam around thick carpets in sitting rooms, the wraparound porch is lined with rockers, and every table in the dining room has a view. Visitors are welcome to lunch at The Boathouse (see *Eating Out*), to dine at Xanthus (see *Dining Out*), and to attend Thu.-evening lectures (see *Entertainment*). There are large suites in Phillips House, and individual cottages, each with living room and fireplace, all with kitchenette. Facilities include tennis on clay courts, three croquet courts, badminton, and water sports; bicycles and rowboats are available. The Croquet Classic in August is the social high point of the season. The McCue family, current owners, have been summering on Mount Desert since 1871. "We didn't expect to make money, just to keep it going and to improve it" is how the late Gertrude McCue explained what she and her late husband, Allen, were thinking when they bought the hotel in 1968. $145–335 B&B in the hotel; the 12 rooms on the water side are priced slightly higher than those overlooking the tennis courts. Cottages are $180–370 with a three-day minimum. A 15 percent service charge is added. ✪ ⊛ ✒ ☕ (207-244-5036 or 1-800-244-5036; theclaremonthotel.com), 22 Claremont Rd., Southwest Harbor 04679. Open May–mid-Oct.

IN BASS HARBOR 04653

⚲ Bass Harbor Inn (207-244-5157), P.O. Box 326. Open May–Oct. In an 1870 house with harbor views, within walking distance of village restaurants and the ferry to Swans Island, Barbara and Alan Graff offer six rooms ranging from doubles with shared baths to a fabulous top-floor studio with kitchenette. One room with half-bath has a fireplace; two open onto the side deck. $90–135 in-season, $70–115 off-season, including continental breakfast.

Ann's Point Inn (207-244-9595, anns pointinn.com), P.O. Box 398. This secluded, contemporary waterfront home packs some unusual luxuries, like a hot tub, sauna, and 32-by-12-foot indoor pool. The four large rooms have water views and extras like gas fireplace and king bed; three have private terrace. Jeannette and Alan Feuer are hospitable hosts. $295–350 includes a full breakfast with the inn's own vegetables and afternoon nibbles and evening cookies, mid-June–mid-Oct.

MOTELS ✒ ☕ **Kimball Terrace Inn** (207-276-3383 or 1-800-454-6225; kimballterrace inn.com), 10 Huntington Rd., P.O. Box 1030, Northeast Harbor 04662. Open May–late Oct. Replacing its predecessor hotel of the same name, this pleasant motor inn occupies a prime site on the harbor by the Northeast Harbor Yacht Marina. It offers 70 large rooms, 52 with sliding doors opening onto private patio or balcony. Outdoor pool and tennis courts. $155–205 in high season, from $70 single off-season.

⚲ ☺ ✒ Harbor View Motel and Cottages (207-244-5031 or 1-800-538-6463; harborview motelandcottages.com), P.O. Box 701, Southwest Harbor 04679. Open mid-May–mid-Oct. Lorraine and Joe Saunders have owned this

Nancy English

SPACIOUS QUARTERS AT ANN'S POINT INN

20-unit harborside motel for more than 42 years. In July and Aug. rooms with decks right on the water are $116–128, while others are $84–97 including continental breakfast, less in Sept., for solo travelers, and by the week. A third-floor apartment and seven cottages are available in high season by the week.

Seawall Motel (207-244-3020 or 1-800-248-9250; seawallmotel.com), 566 Seawall Rd., Southwest Harbor 04679. Open year-round. Twenty clean, quiet rooms with two queen beds and cable TV, right across the road from the ocean. The free, seasonal Island Express shuttle bus stops outside. From $65 in winter to $115 in high season, when rates include a generous continental breakfast.

OTHER LODGING ✍ **Appalachian Mountain Club's Echo Lake Camp** (207-244-3747; amcecholakecamp.org), AMC/Echo Lake Camp, Mount Desert 04660. Open late June–Labor Day weekend. Accommodations are platform tents; family-style meals are served in a central hall. There is a rustic library and reading room, but more to the point are boats for use on the lake and daily hikes. Reserve on April 1. Rates for the minimum one-week stay (Sat.–Sat.) are inexpensive per person but add up for a family. All meals included.

✍ **Bass Harbor Cottages** (207-244-3460; bassharborcottages.com), 95 Harbor Dr. (Rt. 102A), Bass Harbor 04653. Open year-round. This is a classic old farmhouse with three guest rooms and three more assorted cottages scattered in the meadow below, above the water. It's a great spot for families and kayakers. All accommodations offer housekeeping. $80–175 per couple in the inn, $100–400 daily and $800–3,000 weekly in the cottages. Sorry, no pets.

❋ Where to Eat

DINING OUT

IN THE SOUTHWEST HARBOR AREA

Red Sky Restaurant (207-244-0476; redskyrestaurant.com), 14 Clark Point Rd., Southwest Harbor. Open nightly June–Columbus Day, hours vary the rest of the year; closed Jan. The toast of this restaurant town, a comfortably low-key bistro with locally sourced food to come back for again and again: appetizers like mussels with white wine and Dijon, and crispy polenta with mushrooms and beet greens; entrées like braised baby back ribs and lobster with risotto. Ingredients are all as fresh and local as possible. Owners Elizabeth and James Lindquist are both owners and chefs. Entrées $19–30.

Rogue Café (207-244-7101), 1 Main St. Opened in 2015, this excellent restaurant is the rebirth of Town Hill Bistro, which lost its space and was missed. Be sure to reserve, as careful management allots only a certain number of covers to ensure that the kitchen is in full command. Co-owners Maureen Cosgrove—the chef—and JJ Zeph—a suave master of everything in the front of the house—run the show. If you opt for two small plates and one large, you will be full but not sorry; the pork belly is irresistible, and the fish fresh and perfect; indeed, it's the ingredients themselves that make the dishes stand out. Entrées $21–25.

♿ **Xanthus at the Claremont** (207-244-5036; theclaremonthotel.com), Clark Point Rd., Southwest Harbor. Open for dinner June–Oct. Here most tables have some water view. Both decor and service are traditional, with white tablecloths and wall sconces spilling fresh flowers, the kind of place where it's appropriate (but not required) to dress up. The restaurant is named for Xanthus Smith, who painted the 1885 portrait of the inn hung here. Flash-fried PEI oysters; late summer vegetable soup and pan-roasted scallops are from a September menu. Entrées $24–29.

XYZ Restaurant & Gallery (207-244-5221; xyzmaine.com), end of Bennett Lane off Seawall Rd. (Rt. 102A), Manset. Open nightly for dinner in high season, varying hours shoulder seasons. Ask for directions when you call to reserve. Janet Strong and Robert Hoyt have made XYZ well-loved for its sharp, spicy, complex Mexican dishes (*X* is for "Xalapa," *Y* for "Yucatán," and *Z* for "Zacatecas"). The atmosphere is intimate (just 30 seats) and colorful with Mexican folk art. The fresh lime margaritas are legendary and chiles rellenos a fixed star. Entrées $26.

Café 2 (207-244-4344), 326 Main St., Southwest Harbor. Dinner served Tue.–Sun. 5–9, May–mid-Oct. Reserve a booth. A vintage car dealership transformed into an informal, colorful café with a patio bar offers dishes from pasta to sesame-crusted tuna or rack of lamb. The dinner salads are generous. Entrées $17–26.

Fiddler's Green (207-244-9416; fiddlers greenrestaurant.com), 411 Main St., Southwest Harbor. Open seasonally for dinner except Mon., 5:30–9. Chef-owned with harbor views and a casual decor. Dine on a mix of "small plates" such as salt cod fritters and broiled oysters or on entrées ranging from an Asian vegetable hot pot to a choice of steaks ($16–32). Full bar.

IN NORTHEAST HARBOR

Asticou Inn (207-276-3344), Rt. 3. Open for dinner May–mid-Oct., also for lunch and brunch in July and Aug. Grand old hotel atmosphere with water views. Dinner includes lobster bisque and steak. Entrées $21-30.

Islesford Dock (207-244-7494; islesford dock.com), Islesford. Open mid-June–Labor Day except Mon. for lunch (11–3), dinner (5–9), and Sunday brunch (10–2). Another great reason to come to the Cranberry Islands (see the *Islands* sidebar), this is also a spectacular place to watch the sun set behind the entire line of Mount Desert's mountains. Check the website before making the trip for any dates "closed for a private event." Owners Cynthia and Dan Lief grow herbs and vegetables behind the restaurant and secure most of their seafood and produce from close by or from Maine wonders like Tide Mill Farm far Downeast, an eighth-generation farm. The dinner menu includes the Dock burger (served with fresh-cut fries or a salad) and a crabcake sandwich, "small plates" of Maine mussels or hake sliders, as well as entrées like Gulf of Maine halibut with spinach or duck breast with oyster mushrooms. Save room for blueberry crisp. Entrées $10–42. An attached gallery showcases artists and craftsmen, all with an aesthetic connection to the islands of Maine.

EATING OUT

IN SOUTHWEST HARBOR

Common Good Kitchen Café (207-244-3007; commongoodsoupkitchen.org), 19 Clark Point Rd. Open June to Columbus Day for breakfast. The top "restaurant" in MDI on one tourism website, Common Good started out in a man's kitchen, when Bill Morrison made soup he shared with elderly locals. In 2015, his space with a big kitchen in downtown Southwest Harbor has become a morning destination for popovers with butter and jam, and good coffee—you pay what you wish. Funds raised in the summer pay for weekly winter community dinners. Needless to say, we love the idea as much as we love the food.

Eat-a-Pita (207-244-4344), 326 Main St. Open May–mid-Oct., daily from 8 AM; at dinner this spot turns into Café 2 (see *Dining Out*). A lively, bright café with a patio, soups, salads, pastas, specialty coffees, and pastries, fully licensed.

🎣 **Gilley's Head of the Harbor** (207-244-5222), 433 Main St. This long, diner-shaped place overlooks the harbor. Sharon and Michael Gilley, owners of Thurston's in Bass Harbor, serve thick, creamy seafood chowder studded with scallops, clams, shrimp, and lobster. As at Thurston's, lobster is the big draw; also fried seafood and steaks. Children's menu.

🎣 **Sips** (207-244-4550), 4 Clark Point Rd. Open 7 AM–9 PM in summer, shorter hours off-season. Sips opens early for fresh-brewed coffee, espresso, and full breakfasts, from bagels with homemade spreads to crêpes and all-natural egg omelets. Lunch options include unusual sandwiches and salads. The dinner menu includes crêpes, risotto, vegetarian pastas, and polentas as well classic meat loaf and baked haddock stuffed with crabmeat. Wine and beer. Kids' menu. Entrées $10–24.

Little Notch Café (207-244-3357), 340 Main St. Open late May–Columbus Day 8–8 for coffees, breads, and light meals. The aroma of freshly baked bread is almost impossible to resist. Arthur and Katherine Jacobs specialize in soups and sandwiches like grilled tuna salad with cheddar on wheat; also great pizza. Seating inside and out, take-out.

The Captain's Galley at Beal's Lobster Pier (207-244-3202; bealslobsterpier.net), Clark Point Rd. Open daily Memorial Day–Columbus Day, 11–8. The dining room on this working pier is all about lobster, crabmeat rolls, chowder, fresh fish specialties, and lobster. This is also a place to buy lobster to ship.

The Boathouse at the Claremont Hotel (207-244-3512), Clark Point Rd. Open July–Aug., serving lunch until 2 PM. This informal dockside facility on the grounds of the island's oldest hotel arguably offers the island's best view, east across the mouth of Somes Sound with Acadia's mountains rising beyond. Sandwiches, salads, and burgers; also good for drinks at sunset.

IN NORTHEAST HARBOR

⚓ **The Colonel's Restaurant** (207-276-5147), Main St. Open early Apr.–late Oct. Serving breakfast 6:30–11:30, lunch and dinner 11:30–9. A big, informal eatery rebuilt after the 2008 fire. There's a deli-style storefront section as well as the more formal dining area. Still good for fresh-dough pizzas, burgers, and reasonably priced seafood dinners.

⚓ **Docksider** (207-276-3965), Sea St. Open Memorial Day–Columbus Day, 11–9. Bigger than it looks, with a no-frills, knotty-pine interior and amazingly efficient, friendly waitresses. The light and crispy onion rings are simply the best anywhere; one serving is enough for two. Good chowder and Maine crabcakes; also salads, burgers, clam rolls, and a shore dinner.

IN BASS HARBOR

⚓ **Thurston's Lobster Pound** (207-244-7600; thurstonslobster.com), Steamboat Wharf Rd., Bernard. Open Memorial Day–Columbus Day, daily 11–8:30. Weatherproofed, on a working wharf overlooking Bass Harbor, and just far enough off the beaten path not to be mobbed. Fresh and tender as lobster can be, plus corn and pie, also seafood stew, sandwiches, and blueberry cheesecake. Wine and beer.

⚓ **Seafood Ketch** (207-244-7463; seafood ketch.com), on Bass Harbor. Open mid-May–mid-Oct., daily 11–9. Longtime ownership by Stuart and Lisa Branch has given this place a solid reputation for homemade breads and desserts and fried seafood. Eat inside or out on the new deck. Entrées $19–30.

✳ Entertainment

MUSIC **Mount Desert Festival of Chamber Music** (207-276-3988; mtdesertfestival.org), Neighborhood House, Main St., Northeast Harbor. A series of six concerts presented for more than 48 seasons mid-July–mid-Aug.

Saturday Evening Concerts at the Claremont Hotel (207-244-5036), Claremont Rd., Southwest Harbor. Summer concerts have included the Jerks of Grass and the Gilbert and Sullivan Society of Hancock County.

THEATER **Acadia Repertory Theatre** (207-244-7260; acadiarep.com), Rt. 102, Somesville. Performances during July and Aug., Tue.–Sun. at 8:15 PM; matinees at 2 on the last Sun. of each run. A regional repertory theater group performs in the Somesville Masonic Hall, presenting several popular plays in the course of the season. Tickets are reasonably priced.

The Claremont Hotel Thursday Evening Lecture Series (207-244-5036), Claremont Rd., Southwest Harbor. July and Aug. An impressive array of authorities speak on a variety of topic like "Writing for a Living and Other Mistakes I Have Made" by Alex Beam, as well as talks on jazz, mountain climbing, and Mount Desert history. All lectures are at 8:15.

✳ Selective Shopping

IN NORTHEAST HARBOR

Naturalist's Notebook (207-276-4120; the naturalistsnotebook.com), 115 Main St. A treasure box of books, prints, art, and science for anyone fascinated by 13.8 billion years of earthly nature. The staffer will no doubt be a local naturalist, perhaps Jordan Chalfant, who studied the puffins for several lonely months on a small island far off the coast. **Island Artisans** (207-276-4045; islandartisans .com), 119 Main St. Open mid-June–mid Oct. (also in Bar Harbor), showcasing exceptional work by more than 100 area craftspeople working with textiles, pottery, baskets, paper, wood, glass, silver, metal, and stone. **Artemis Gallery** (207-276-3001; artemisgallery.com), 1 Old Firehouse Lane. Exhibits of skilled MDI artists' work. **Shaw Contemporary Jewelry** (207-276-5000; shawjewelry.com), 126 Main St., open year-round, is an outstanding gallery featuring Sam Shaw's own work but also displaying work by artists from throughout the United States and Europe, genuine eye candy, priced $20–2,000. A village anchor is the **Kimball Shop & Boutique** (207-276-3300; kimballshop.com), an upscale shop geared to summer residents' needs since 1935. Invest some time in the basement and save 50 percent. An amazing trove of home furnishings, gadgets, fine china, and gifts is next door. **McGrath's Store** (207-276-5548), Main St., is an old-fashioned newspaper/stationery store with some surprises, while long-established **Wikhegan Books** (208-276-5079), 117 Main St., is a trove of early history and guidebooks as well as fiction relating to the MDI region, including the legendary Red Book directory of Northeast Harbor summer residents; also nautical titles, Eastern Woodland Indians, poetry, antiques, and much more.

IN SOUTHWEST HARBOR

Aylen & Son Fine Jewelry (207-244-7369; peteraylen.com), 320 Main St. Open mid-Apr.–Oct. Peter Aylen fashions gold, silver, pearl, and Maine gemstone jewelry; Judy Aylen creates bead necklaces and works with a variety of stones.

Carroll Drug Store (207-244-5588), just off Main St. at the north end of the village. A supermarket-sized store with a genuine general-store/five-and-dime feel.

Sawyer's Market (207-244-3315), 344 Main St. This is a great old grocery store with a good deli counter and good soups on tap. **Sawyer's Specialties** (207-244-3317), 353 Main St., sells terrific wine and a good selection of cheeses. Count on good free tastings.

IN BERNARD AND SEAL COVE

Seal Cove Pottery and Gallery (207-244-3602; sealcovepottery.com), Kelly Town Rd., Seal Cove. Marked from Rt. 102. Open Apr.–mid-Nov., 10–5. Lisbeth Faulkner and Ed Davis create handsome, functional pottery (glazes are made from scratch), worth a special trip. Davis is a fifth-generation (both sides) MDI native.

✳ Special Events

July: **Independence Day fireworks** on Somes Sound. **Quietside Festival and Annual Pink Flamingo Canoe Race** at Seal Cove in Tremont (207-244-3713).

Early August: **Sweet Chariot Music Festival** on Swans Island. **Frenchboro Days** in Frenchboro. **Annual Art Show on the Green**, Southwest Harbor (1-800-423-9264).

September: **Mount Desert Island Garlic Festival** (207-288-0269), 20 Main St., Southwest Harbor, at Smugglers Den Campground, with local restaurants, brewers, musicians, and garlic growers.

EAST HANCOCK COUNTY
Hancock, Sullivan, and Schoodic Peninsula

Nowhere in Maine does the coast change as abruptly as along this rim of Frenchman Bay. On the western side of the bay on Mount Desert Island, Acadia National Park draws everyone from everywhere. By contrast, the northern and eastern shores of the bay are a quiet, curving stretch of coves, tidal bays, and peninsulas.

In 1889 the Maine Central's Boston & Mount Desert Limited carried passengers from Boston to a terminal in **Hancock**, connecting with ferries across the bay to Bar Harbor, spawning the area's once large, now vanished, summer hotels. A small seasonal ferry now links Winter Bar Harbor with **Winter Harbor**, gateway to the **Schoodic Peninsula** section of **Acadia National Park.**

This is one place that we suggest taking land over water. The 29-mile **Schoodic National Scenic Byway** offers spectacular views back across the bay to Acadia's high, rounded mountains. It begins on Rt. 1 at the Hancock-Sullivan Bridge, continues to shadow the shore down the Gouldsboro Peninsula, and then makes its way around the loop road within the national park.

The Schoodic Peninsula is one of those just-off-the-beaten-path places that should be busier than it is—and everyone seems grateful that it isn't. **Winter Harbor** and the photogenic fishing villages of **Prospect Harbor** and **Corea** offer several good places to stay and eat. Art and crafts galleries are scattered through the area; in July and early August the **Schoodic Arts Festival for All** offers more than 100 workshops and performances.

Inland there are hidden lakes and high mountains. The **Blackwoods Scenic Byway** (Rt. 182) here links Black and Schoodic Mountains, both offering long views of Mt. Katahdin as well as the Acadia peaks.

GUIDANCE Schoodic Peninsula Chamber of Commerce (acadia-schoodic.org).

GETTING THERE *By car:* For a shortcut to Hancock from Bar Harbor, take Rt. 3 north to Rt. 204, posted for Lamoine State Park. Turn left onto Rt. 184, immediately right at the town hall onto Pinkham Rd., left after a mile or so at the sign for Rt. 1 (Mud Creek Rd.). From points south, see *Getting There* in "Bar Harbor."

By boat: The **Bar Harbor Ferry** (207-288-2984; barharborferry.com) offers frequent service late-June to mid-Sept. across Frenchman Bay between Bar Harbor and Winter Harbor, connecting with the free *Island Explorer* that makes stops in Winter, Birch, and Prospect Harbors as well as the park. Bring your bike or rent at either side.

Water Taxi & Boat Rentals (207-963-7007; winterharbortaxitours.com), 22 Harbor Rd., Winter Harbor. Capt. Wesley Shaw offers 30-minute service to Bar Harbor, also rents small boats.

GETTING AROUND Island Explorer (exploreacadia.com). Late June–Aug. this fabulous, free bus meets the Bar Harbor Ferry and makes an hourly circuit from Winter Harbor around Schoodic Point and back through Birch and Winter Harbors. Bicycles are a great way to explore the park itself.

EXCURSIONS

Schoodic Scenic Byway (see the description in this chapter's introduction and at byways.org). Federal funding has improved signage and turnouts along this breathtakingly beautiful 29-mile stretch of coast with views back across the bay to Acadia's mountains.

Blackwoods Scenic Byway (Rt. 182; blackwoodsbyway.org). Rt. 182 is the mostly wooded, inland shortcut from Hancock to Washington County (you save 9 miles vs. Rt. 1). The 12.5 easternmost miles—between **Franklin** and **Cherryfield** (see the Washington County chapter)—is a state scenic byway, meaning better signage and turnout areas, and boat launches to access the more than 14,000 acres of woods and water now maintained by the **Donnell Pond Public Reserved**. It includes **Tunk Lake**, **Donnell Pond**, and **Spring River Lake** and hiking trails up **Schoodic Mountain** and **Black Mountain** (see *Hiking*).

Christina Tree

✳ To Do

BIKING The 12-mile loop from Winter Harbor around Schoodic Point is a popular bike route. Rentals available from **SeaScape Kayaking** (below). Also check out the **Down East Sunrise Trail** (sunrisetrail.org), a converted railbed that begins at Washington Junction in Hancock and runs east across this area.

BOATING Bar Harbor Ferry (see *Getting There*).
  Robertson Sea Tours (robertsonseatours.com), departing from Milbridge Marina (see *To Do* in "Washington County"), cruises the 50 miles east of Schoodic.

FISHING Donnell Pond is known for salmon; **Tunk Lake** and **Spring River Lake** are good for trout. Look for launch sites along Rt. 182.

KAYAKING Hancock Point Kayak Tours (207-422-6854; hancockpointkayak.com), 58 Point Rd., Hancock. Antonio Blasi offers guided paddling in Frenchman and Taunton Bays, also overnight camping and guided snowshoeing.

MUST SEE

ACADIA NATIONAL PARK, SCHOODIC PENINSULA (nps.gov/acad). Accessed from Rt. 186 just east of Winter Harbor, this is a one-way shore road, 6 miles of it within the park. **Frazer Point Picnic Area** (with comfort station) is a good first stop, a place to unload bikes if you want to tour on two wheels. It's said to have been an Indian campsite for thousands of years.

Farther along this stretch note the turnouts with views of the **Winter Harbor Light** (1856) and across Frenchman Bay to Cadillac Mountain.

A little more than 2.5 miles farther along, the unmarked, unpaved road up to **Schoodic Head** may or may not be open. Visitors are clearly encouraged to access the long views from this rocky 400-foot summit via hiking trails (see *Hiking*).

Bear right at the intersection for Schoodic Point (this portion of the road is two-way). You can pick up a map and hiking advice at the **visitors center** at the **Schoodic Education and Research Center** (207-288-1310; shoodicinstitute .org) campus. Housed in hand-some, 1930s Rockefeller Hall, the staffed center includes displays

PICK UP A MAP AND HIKING ADVICE AT THE NEW SERC VISITOR CENTER

on the park's history and ecology, and on the radio and cryptologic operations carried on here between 1935 and 2002. The former U.S. Navy base is now managed jointly by Acadia National Park and SERC, a private nonprofit organization. Try your hand at typing Morse code. Check the website for year-round lectures, discussions, and ranger-led programs. Limited lodging is also available.

Schoodic Point (plenty of parking) thrusts into the Atlantic, and on sunny days tidal pools invite clambering. On stormy days surf and spray can shoot as high as 40 feet, a popular spectacle. That surf can be deadly, so be careful. Bear right along the drive to the **Blueberry Hill Parking Area** (about a mile beyond Schoodic Point) with its views of Moose and Schoodic Islands and access to most of the area's hiking trails. Continue along the drive 2 more miles to Rt. 186 in the village of Birch Harbor.

SCHOODIC POINT IS PART OF ACADIA NATIONAL PARK

SeaScape Kayak & Bike (207-963-5806; seascapekayaking.com), 18 E. Schoodic Dr., Birch Harbor. Kayak and canoe rentals, good for quiet coves and lakes only, along with guided tours of Flanders Bay and the Corea area, more.

GOLF **Grindstone Neck Golf Course** (207-963-7760), Gerrishville. A nine-hole course dating to 1895 as part of this summer colony; open to the public June–Sept.

Blink Bonnie Golf Course (207-422-3930), Rt. 185, Sorrento. A nine-hole walking course with an open layout and views of Flanders Bay. Golf cart rentals.

HIKING **Acadia National Park, Schoodic Peninsul**a (see *To See*), offers several short hikes, all best accessed from the Blueberry Hill Parking Area. The gentle 0.6-mile **Alder Trail** leads to the steeper 0.6-mile **Schoodic Head Trail** to the summit of Schoodic Head (440 feet), a vantage point also accessed by the relatively demanding 1.1-mile **Anvil Trail**. While it's not marked, another popular hike at low tide is out on Little Moose Island. Check the tide and pick up a map at the Schoodic Gatehouse.

Schoodic Mountain, off Rt. 183 north of Sullivan, provides one of eastern Maine's most spectacular hikes, with 360-degree views. Maine's Bureau of Parks and Lands (207-287-5936) has improved the parking area and trail system here. Take the first left (it's unpaved) after crossing the **Sunrise Trail** (sunrisetrail.org) on Rt. 183; bear left at the Y and in 2 miles reach the parking lot (outhouse facility). The hike to the top of Schoodic Mountain (1,069 feet) should take around 45 minutes; a marked trail from the summit leads down to sandy **Schoodic Beach** at the southern end of **Donnell Pond** (good swimming and half a dozen primitive campsites). Return to the parking lot on the old road that's now a footpath (0.5 mile). From the same parking lot, you can also follow a dirt path down to Donnell Pond or hike to the bluffs on **Black Mountain**, a mesmerizingly beautiful hike with summit views north to Tunk Lake and east across Washington County. Another trail descends to **Schoodic Beach**. This is now part of 14,000 acres known as **Donnell Pond Public Preserved Land**, which also includes Tunk and Spring River Lakes and primitive campsites. **Tucker Mountain** rewards a mile's hike with panoramic views. The trail begins on old Rt. 1, across from the Long Cove scenic turnout on Rt. 1 in Sullivan.

SWIMMING **Jones Beach** on Jones Pond in West Gouldsboro offers a family playground, swimming and picnic areas, changing rooms, and a boat launch. Take Recreation Rd. off Rt. 195 just south of Rt. 1. Along Rt. 183 there's **Flanders Pond** (turn left 2.9 miles north of Rt. 1); **Little Tunk Lake** offers a sandy beach. Look for a blue FBC sign on your left at 4.7 miles (it's 0.4 mile to the beach). Ask locally about **Molasses Pond** in Eastbrook. Also see **Donnell Pond** under *Hiking*.

✳ Green Space

The **Schoodic** section of **Acadia National Park** is detailed under *To See*. In addition, the **Frenchman Bay Conservancy** (frenchmanbay.org) maintains many outstanding preserves; check out SHORT HIKES on their website and look for their blue diamond-shaped trail sign. Outstanding: **Tidal Falls**, formerly a popular lobster pound, is now a great picnicking site from which to watch eagles, herons, seals, and kayakers playing in the whitewater of the reversing falls in the Taunton River. From Rt. 1 turn right just before the Hancock-Sullivan bridge on Eastside Rd., then left on Tidal Falls Rd. (0.7 mile down).

Corea Heath is an excuse to drive, as everyone should, out scenic Corea Rd. (Rt. 195); look for the FBC sign beyond the junction with Rt. 186 and park in the National Wildlife Refuge lot a short distance beyond on the right. The path loops around a peat bog and beaver flowage. Great for bird-watching, as is the adjoining 600-acre wildlife refuge, formerly owned by the Navy, which includes Grand Marsh and Grand Marsh Bay.

Also see *Hiking* and *Swimming* for more about the 14,000-acre mountain- and lake-spotted **Donnell Pond Public Preserved Land**, maintained by the **Maine Bureau of Parks and Lands**.

✳ Lodging

INNS AND B&BS ✪ ❀ ✐ ♿ (🐾) **Crocker House Country Inn** (207-422-6806 or 1-877-715-6017; crockerhouse.com), 967 Point Rd., Hancock Point 04640. Open daily May–Oct., weekends Nov.–New Year's Eve. Billed as "a little out of the way and out of the ordinary," this handsome, shingled inn is midway between the sections of Acadia National Parks on Mount Desert and Schoodic Point. Sited at the center of a charming 1880s summer colony, complete with a chapel, tiny post office, octagonal library, and tennis courts, it's the lone survivor among several once-larger hotels. Since 1980 it's been owned by Richard and Elizabeth Malaby, and the welcome is genuine. There are nine antiques-furnished rooms in the inn itself, two in the Carriage House, all with private bath and phone, and in addition to the inn's parlor, there's a den with TV (adjoining a room with a hot tub) in the Carriage House. The inn is set among flowers and trees, but water is a short walk in most directions. $125–165 mid-June–mid-Oct., $100–130 off-season, $10 more Fri., Sat. rates include a full breakfast. Moorings are available, and a few touring bikes are kept for guests. The restaurant is a major draw (see *Dining Out*).

(🐾) **Ironbound** (207-422-3395; ironboundinn .com), 1513 Rt. 1, Hancock 04640. Open mid-May–late-Oct. Known for decades as Le Domaine, primarily a dining destination. The restaurant (see *Dining Out*) remains the draw, and the three attractive rooms and two suites are still a bit of a secret. Sited at the back of the building (away from Rt. 1) are decks overlooking acres of landscaped garden. All are brightly, comfortably furnished with king or queen beds, art, and antiques. Bathrooms are luxurious, and the suites have a gas fireplace and cathedral ceilings. A breakfast of fresh fruit, bagels, cream cheese, and locally smoked salmon is included in $145–185.

Acadia View Bed & Breakfast (1-866-963-7457; acadiaview.com), 175 Rt. 1, P.O. Box 247, Gouldsboro 04607. Aerospace engineers in a previous life that took them many places, Pat and Jim Close have designed and built this mansion specifically as a B&B. The Great Room, with its wood-burning fireplace, and two of the four guest rooms (private bath) all share splendid views across Frenchman Bay to Acadia. All rooms have private deck with water views. $155–185 in high season, otherwise from $135, includes a full breakfast.

z ✐ ✐ ♿ ✐ **Acadia's Oceanside Meadows Inn** (207-963-5557; oceaninn.com), P.O. Box 90, Prospect Harbor 04669. Open May–Oct., off-season by special arrangement. This 1860s sea captain's home and neighboring 1820s farmhouse offer a total of 15 guest rooms, most overlooking well-named Sand Cove. Sonja Sundaram and Ben Walter are passionate conservationists, and their 200 acres of woods and meadows are webbed with trails, good for spotting wildlife ranging from moose to eagles. $139–189 for rooms, $189–209 for suites July–Labor Day weekend, including Sonja's multicourse breakfasts, which might begin with sweet sorrel soup. Less off-season. Also see *Entertainment*.

Christina Tree

OCEANSIDE MEADOWS INN OVERLOOKS SAND COVE IN PROSPECT HARBOR

ELSA'S INN ON THE HARBOR

🐾 𝒫 **Three Pines B&B** (207-460-7595; threepinesbandb.com), 274 Eastside Rd., Hancock 04640. Open year-round. Turn in at this organic farm and follow a private road down through 40 acres of woods and meadow to the shore. Here Ed and Karen Curtis have built a shingled, timber-frame, passive solar dream house with a separate wing housing two delightful B&B guest rooms, each with a sitting room and water view. Breakfast includes eggs from the farm's chickens, and frequently home-grown vegetables and fruit, too. Farm animals also include sheep, ducks, and roosters. $100–125 per couple, $15 per extra person.

♺ 🐾 𝒫 ♿ **Elsa's Inn on the Harbor** (207-963-7571; elsasinn.com), 179 Main St., Prospect Harbor 04669. This gabled, mid-1800s house overlooks a working harbor. Six bright, spiffy guest rooms with handmade quilts, private bath, and water views, as well as a comfortable living room, veranda, and patio. In all, 16 guests can bed down. $120–165 June 15–Oct. 15, from $115 off-season, including a full breakfast. Shared space includes a back patio as well as the bright, comfy living room and long veranda with rockers.

♂ 🐾 𝒫 ((ᵠ)) **Bluff House Inn** (207-963-7805; bluffinn.com), 57 Bluff House Rd., South Gouldsboro 04607. Open year-round. This contemporary lodge offers a dining room with floor-to-ceiling windows, a screened porch overlooking the water, and a comfortable sitting area by a stone hearth. The eight guest rooms line the upstairs hall; three have water views. It's set off by itself above the pink

granite shore; there's a road down to a beach from which you can launch a kayak onto Frenchman Bay. Inquire about Sat.-night lobster dinner. $125–150 in high season includes a continental breakfast. From $85 off-season.

Schoodic Woods Campground (207-288-3338; acadia_information@nps.gov) Open by reservation late May through Sept., this large new facility is adjacent to the park entrance. Its 90 campsites include hike-in, drive-in tent, electric hook-up, and water hook-up.

✳ Where to Eat

DINING OUT **Ironbound Restaurant** (207-422-3395; ironboundmaine.com), 1513 Rt. 1, Hancock Village. Open daily 5–9. Patrons of the former Le Domaine will recognize the Provençal-style dining rooms, but the vibe is now casual—a handsome bar and outdoor seating have been added. Named for an island in Frenchman Bay, Ironbound's menu is varied, moderately priced, and locally sourced. Specialties include fish smoked next door at Sullivan Harbor Salmon, and other dinner options include a roll with Maine seaweed, shrimp burger, and locally smoked Finnan Haddie. Also good: hamburgers, jerk pork ribs, tender duck breast. Entrées $10–29. Music Thu.–Sat, 5–6:30.

♺ **Crocker House Country Inn** (207-422-6806; crockerhouse.com), Hancock Point. Open nightly Apr.–Jan., weekends off-season, for dinner 5:30–9. The main dining room, with its 19th-century leaded-glass windows, is the setting for reliably fine dining. Frequent menu changes take advantage of local produce and fish. Staples include Crocker House scallops and farm-raised semi-boneless roast duckling with Grand Marnier ginger sauce. Entrées $26–34, include fresh baked bread, salad, starch, and a fresh vegetable. Don't pass on the Crocker House mousse (layered white and dark chocolate, laced with Myers's rum).

Salt Box (207-422-9900; saltboxmaine .com), 1166 Rt. 1, Hancock. Open for dinner Thu.–Sun., Sun. brunch., Wed. tasting menu. Reserve for dinner. Chef Mike Poirier has a strong local following and this is his latest restaurant, tucked into a corner of a large Rt. 1 commercial building. The menu features exotic meals made from scratch, and it's constantly changing. Check the website. Entrées

$24–29; the nine-course tasting menu is $45. Cash only, on-site ATM. Wine and beer are served.

Raven's Nest Restaurant (207-963-2234; ravensnestrestaurant.com), 10 Newman St., Winter Harbor. Open seasonally for light breakfast and lunch Mon.–Fri., dinner nightly; Sun. brunch. Built and operated by Roxanne Quimby, Raven's Nest is both a convenient source of lunch and local information (maps and brochures), plus diners have the chance to sample Roxanne's own wood-fired pizza (Thu.–Sat. evenings). In 2015 the restaurant shifted focus to Italian-inspired, locally sourced destination dining, orchestrated by Richard Hanson, former chef-owner of widely celebrated Cleonice in Ellsworth. The menu might include lobster fra diavalo ($33) and Frutti di Mare ($15 half-portion, $27 full).

Fisherman's Inn Restaurant (207-963-5585), 7 Newman St., Winter Harbor. Open seasonally Tue.–Sun. 4:30–8:30. Chef-owner Carl Johnson's booth-filled restaurant is pleasant, with a full menu from pasta to char-grilled filet mignon. Seafood is the specialty. Signature dishes: lobster several different ways, a Winter Harbor seafood casserole, and haddock in a creamy lobster sauce. Entrées $17–30 (burgers, $11); early-bird specials 4:30–5:30.

Also see **The Pickled Wrinkle** in *Eating Out* listings.

EATING OUT

HEADING EAST ALONG RT. 1

Ruth & Wimpy's Kitchen (207-422-3723), Rt. 1, Hancock. Open year-round. Look for "Wilbur the Lobster." Wimpy Wilbur is a former long-haul truck driver, and this family-run mainstay is decorated with his collection of miniature trucks, license plates, beer bottles, and more. The menu includes burgers and steaks, overstuffed sandwiches, and seafood, including lobster with all the fixings.

Chester Pike's Galley (207-422-8200), 2336 Rt. 1, Sullivan. Open 6–2 Tue.–Sat.; also 4:30–8:30 Fri., 7–2 Sun. The nicest kind of roadside diner, ideal for a Maine crabmeat and cheese omelet, strawberry rhubarb pie, or cream-cheese-stuffed French toast. There's also a sardine salad.

ON THE SCHOODIC PENINSULA

The Pickled Wrinkle (207-963-7916; the pickledwrinkle.com), 9 East Schoodic Drive, Birch Harbor. Kitchen open 11–9, pub until 11 PM daily, year-round, with frequent live music. Some of the best food around is to be found in this neighborhood gathering spot (formerly the Nautica Pub) in a small shopping plaza. "Wrinkle" is a local name for a sea snail, better known as a whelk. Patrons can sample it as a starter—it's worth splitting the order. Don't pass up the seafood chowder or onion rings, either. Kudos for the crab salad on local greens. The menu ranges from clam dinners to rib eye (Wed. only; reserve), and there are also a variety of pizzas.

&. **J. M. Gerrish** (207-963-7000), 352 Main St., Winter Harbor. Open Memorial Day–Columbus Day, 8–4 daily in July, Aug.; otherwise closed Wed. Long established as an old-style ice cream parlor beloved by generations of summer residents, this is the place for breakfast, lunch, and pastries as well as ice cream.

Corea Wharf Gallery & Grill (207-963-8888), 13 Gibbs Lane, Corea. Open June–Sept. for lunch and dinner, weather permitting. On a sunny day you can't beat the view or experience. In the village turn left after the post office at the sharp bend in Rt. 195. Joe Young puts a sign at this spot if he's open. The real deal: reasonably priced stone crab claws, grilled cheese, lobster rolls, and more, served on the wharf. There's also a gallery displaying work by Joe's mother, Louise, a pioneer photographer.

🦞 🍴 **Chase's Restaurant** (207-963-7171), 193 Main St., Winter Harbor. Open all year for all three meals. A convenient local hangout on Rt. 186 near the entrance to the park. Booths, fried lobsters and clams, good chowder; will pack a picnic.

✽ Entertainment

Schoodic Arts for All (207-963-2569; schoodicartsforall.org), Hammond Hall, 427 Main St., Winter Harbor. This grassroots nonprofit sponsors music, art, crafts, dance, theater, and film through most of the year. Check the website for ongoing events such as Fri.

concerts, coffeehouses, community theater, and a summer chorus. See *Special Events* for the **Schoodic Arts Festival**.

Pierre Monteux Memorial Concert Hall (207-422-3931; monteuxschool.org), off Rt. 1, Hancock. In June and July the internationally respected Pierre Monteux School for Conductors, founded in 1943, hosts a series of symphony concerts (Sun. at 5) and chamber music concerts (Wed. at 7:30) presented by faculty and students in the school's Forest Studio.

Also check sercinstitute.com for frequent programs at the **Schoodic Education and Research Center** and frenchmanbay.org for **Mon.-evening concerts at Tidal Falls** in Hancock, sponsored by the **Frenchman Bay Conservancy**.

Also see *Special Events*.

✳ Selective Shopping

ART

LISTED GEOGRAPHICALLY, MORE OR LESS, HEADING EAST ALONG RT. 1

Gull Rock Pottery (207-664-3576), Eastside Rd. (1.5 miles off Rt. 1 at 103 Gullrock Rd.), Hancock. Open year-round, Mon.–Sat. 9–5. Akemi Wray maintains this fabulously sited

Christina Tree

PHILIP BARTER STUDIO & GALLERY IS WORTH A DETOUR

gallery known for wheel-thrown stoneware and now, too, for Japanese glazes. The sculpture garden offers a spectacular view of Frenchman Bay and seats to enjoy it from.

✪ **Philip Barter Studio & Gallery** (207-422-3190; bartergallery.com), 318 Taunton Bay Rd., Sullivan. Open July into Sept., Tue.–Sat. 10–5, or by appointment. Posted from Rt. 1 at Sullivan's common just east of the bridge. Maine native Phil Barter's bold, deeply colored paintings hang in museums and fetch big money in the best galleries. His own studio/gallery adjoins the small house that he built and in which he and his wife Priscilla raised seven children. It's easily the most colorful gallery in Maine, but remote enough to keep browsers and buyers to a trickle. Here, added to dozens of distinctive Barter mountains, houses, and harbors, are off-the-wall pieces and wood sculptures.

Lunaform (207-422-0923; lunaform.com), 66 Cedar Lane, marked from Rt. 1 at the Sullivan common. Open year-round, Mon.–Fri. 9–5; closed 12–1. Striking handmade, steel-reinforced concrete garden urns (some are huge) as well as pots and planters are made in this former granite quarry.

Christina Tree

PHILIP BARTER IN THE BARTER FAMILY GALLERY, SULLIVAN

ALSO WORTH A DETOUR

✪ **Hog Bay Pottery** (207-565-2282; hogbay
.com), 245 Hog Bay Rd. (Rt. 200, 4 miles
north of Rt. 1), Franklin. Open Apr.–Nov.; call
off-season. This shop/studio is a find, the kind
of place patrons return to again and again.
Susanne Grosjean's bright, multicolored,
hand-dyed and -woven, award-winning rugs
complement distinctive table- and ovenware
by Charles Grosjean (great seconds).

Spring Woods Gallery (207-442-3007;
springwoodsgallery.com), Rt. 200, 0.25 mile
off Rt. 1, Sullivan. Open May–Oct., Mon.–Sat.
10–6. This gallery features work by *National
Geographic* cartographer and illustrator Paul
Breeden, paintings by Ann Breeden, as well as
work by other members of the Breeden family.
The garden alone is worth a stop.

ON THE PENINSULA

Lee Art Glass Studio (207-963-7280; leeart
glass.com), Rt. 186, 3 miles south of Rt. 1.
Open June–Oct., 10–4. It's difficult to describe
this fused-glass tableware, which incorporates
ground enamels and crocheted doilies or
stencils. Wayne Taylor has acquired the secret
of creating these distinctive pieces, which
he makes and sells in a former post office in
South Gouldsboro.

✪ **Works of Hand & Winter Harbor
Antiques** (207-963-7900), 424–426 Main St.,
Winter Harbor. Open June–Oct., daily 10–5.

WORKS OF HAND GALLERY, WINTER HARBOR

Set back in a flowery, visitor-friendly garden,
Roger Fisher's two-floor gallery showcases
work by more than 50 artists and craftsmen
in a wide range of media, and a selection of
author-signed books. Check out the jewelry
and the adjoining antiques shop.

Littlefield Gallery (207-838-2156;
littlefieldgallery.com), 145 Main St., Winter
Harbor. Open seasonally, 11–6. Sited just before
the turnoff for the park, this is an exceptional
contemporary Maine gallery, housing a mix of
paintings and pieces by prominent sculptors.

U.S. Bells and Watering Cove Pottery
(207-963-7184; usbells.com), Rt. 186, Prospect
Harbor. Open weekdays 9–5, Sat. 9–2, and
by appointment. Richard Fisher designs and
casts bells that form musical sculptures, and
Liza Fisher creates wood-fired stoneware and
porcelain.

✪ **Chapter Two** (207-963-7269), 611 Corea
Rd., Prospect Harbor. Open year-round, Thu.–
Mon. 11–4.; daily July, Aug. Rosemary's hand-
hooked designs and Gary's extraordinary
accumulation of books are a winning combination. Many local products, from jewelry to
soap; frequent workshops.

SMOKED SALMON ✪ **Sullivan Harbor
Salmon** (1-800-422-4014; sullivanharborfarm
.com), 1542 Rt. 1, Hancock Village. Open 9–5
Mon.–Sat.; weekdays only off-season. Maine's
premier, award-winning artisanal smoked
salmon. Only salmon from within 60 nautical
miles is used, and it's processed within hours
of harvesting. In the smokehouse attached to
the Rt. 1 store, it's cured in small batches,
hand rubbed with a blend of salt and brown
sugar, then rinsed in springwater and slowly
smoked over a smudge fire of hickory shav-
ings. No preservatives or additives. The store
also sells day boat scallops from Nova Scotia,
smoked mussels, rainbow trout, salmon
bacon, pâtés, and Maine-made items. Tasty
samples.

Grindstone Neck of Maine (207-963-7347;
grindstoneneck.com), 311 Newman St. (Rt.
186), Winter Harbor. A source of smoked
mussels, oysters, scallops, and seafood
spreads as well as salmon.

WINE AND SPIRITS ✪ ♿ **Bartlett Winery
and Spirits of Maine** (207-546-2408; bartlett
winery.com), just off Rt. 1, Gouldsboro. Open
for tastings ($5) June into Oct., Tue.–Sat. 11–5

AWARD-WINNING SULLIVAN HARBOR SALMON IS SMOKED, SAMPLED, AND SOLD IN ITS RT. 1 SHOP, HANCOCK

and by appointment. Before Bob and Kathe Bartlett could open Maine's first winery back in 1982, they had to get the law changed. "Prohibition began in Maine," Bob Bartlett will remind you. An architect by training, he designed this low-slung winery sequestered in firs. Over a dozen wines, which utilize Maine fruit and honey as well as regional pears and peaches, continue to win top honors in national and international competitions, as do such spirits as Rusticator Rum, pear eau de vie, and Calvados-style apple brandy. Call before coming for handicapped directions.

Shalom Orchard Organic Farm and Winery (207-565-2312; shalomorchard.com), 158 Eastbrook Rd. (Rt. 200 north of Rt. 182). The peaceful old hilltop farm includes a 1,000-plus apple orchard, also blueberries, cherries, and raspberries that are all made into organic wines. The farm store sells eggs, meat, and homespun yarns as well as tanned pelts and fleece from Rambouillet sheep.

SPECIAL SHOPS ✿ **Darthia Farm** (207-963-2770; darthiafarm.com), 51 Darthia Farm Rd. off Rt. 186 (east), Gouldsboro. Open June–late Sept. Mon.–Fri. 8–5, Sat. 8–noon. A 150-acre organic farm on West Bay with resident sheep, pigs, and turkeys, where much of the farmwork is powered by drafthorses. Cynthia and Bill Thayer's farm stand is justly famed for its vinegars, jams, salsas, and cheeses; Hattie's Shed, a weaving shop also at the farm, features coats, jackets, scarves, shawls, and Cynthia Thayer's well-respected, locally set novels.

✪ **Winter Harbor 5&10** (207-963-7927; winterharbor5and10.com), 349 Main St., Winter Harbor. Open daily, year-round. Peter Drinkwater will tell you it isn't easy operating a genuine, old-style five-and-dime these days. While it sells some souvenirs, this is the genuine article with just about everything you come looking for; also the local stop for keys, photo developing, digital printing, UPS, a copier, fax, and newspapers.

✳ Special Events

Late June–Labor Day: **Winter Harbor Farmers' Market**, Tue. 9–noon, corner of Rt. 186 and Main St.

July–August: **Frenchman Bay Conservancy Mon.-night concerts** at Tidal Falls Preserve, Hancock (207-422-2328; frenchman bay.org; also see *Green Space*).

Late July–mid-August: ♿ The **Schoodic Arts Festival** (schoodicarts.org), held annually the first two weeks in August, is a destination extravaganza with dance, theater, visual arts, writing and crafts workshops, and evening performances staged throughout the area, but otherwise the venue is Hammond Hall—renovated, heated, and handicapped-accessible. **Sullivan Daze** (first Saturday) is a daylong celebration in Sullivan. The **Winter Harbor Lobster Festival** (second Saturday; acadia.schoodic.org) is the biggest day of the summer here: crafts fair, lobster-boat races, a parade, live music, and a huge lobster feed.

WINTER HARBOR 5&10

WAY DOWNEAST

The Bold Coast: Steuben to Campobello Island (New Brunswick); Eastport and Cobscook Bay; Calais and the Downeast Lakes Region

Travel Down East as far as you can in this country and you get to a coastline that harbors some of the most dramatic cliffs and deepest coves—certainly the highest tides—on the eastern U.S. seaboard. Lobster boats and trawlers far outnumber pleasure craft.

A fraction of Maine's visitors get this far, but those who do find access to the area's natural beauty. On **Machias Seal Island** you can watch puffins, auks, and arctic terns close-up or view them from excursion boats off **Petit Manan Wildlife Refuge**. In summer there's no shortage of whales or ways to see them; seals ride the tides in narrows and tidal rivers. Hiking trails rim the cliffs along the **Bold Coast** in Cutler and on up to **West Quoddy Light**. Fishing guides lead the way to landlocked salmon and smallmouth bass in the vast chain of **Downeast Lakes**. Bald eagles are everywhere.

Created in 1789 by order of the General Court of Massachusetts, this is **Washington County**, as large as the states of Delaware and Rhode Island combined. Yet it's home to less than 32,000 people, widely scattered among fishing villages, logging outposts, Native American reservations, and saltwater farms. Many people—not just some—survive here by raking blueberries, lobstering, clamming, digging sea worms, harvesting sea cucumbers, diving for sea urchins, and making Christmas wreaths. It's the world's largest source of wild blueberries.

This is former lumbering country. Maine writer Wayne Curtis has noted that here the North Woods meets the shore, and "you can set off in search of moose and whales on the same hike." More than a million acres of former commercial woodland have been preserved as trail- or water-accessed conservation land.

Wherever you explore in Washington County—from the old sardine-canning towns of **Eastport** and **Lubec** to the coastal fishing villages of **Jonesport** and **Cutler**, you find a Maine you thought had disappeared decades ago.

You don't drop off the end of the world beyond **Calais** or **Campobello Island**, despite the boundary drawn across the face of **Passamaquoddy Bay** in 1842. From Calais it's 19 miles to **St. Andrews**, the Bar Harbor of New Brunswick. In summer it is lovely crossing the bay, either via passenger or car-ferries. We also include the magnificent island of **Grand Manan**, which lies 12.5 miles off Maine's Bold Coast but is in New Brunswick, accessible by a 20-mile car-ferry ride from Blacks Harbour, NB

With the border tightening after 9/11 the international flow of tourists ebbed for several years, but it's on the rise again, with an ever-increasing number of websites and pamphlets promoting a "Two Nation Vacation," encompassing Passamaquoddy Bay.

For exploring purposes, we divide this area into three distinct regions.

(1) The **Bold Coast and Passamaquoddy Bay,** from Steuben to Lubec via Rt. 1 (with many more miles of wandering coastline), across the bridge to **Roosevelt Campobello International Park,** and on across the bay to **St. Andrews** and **Grand Manan, NB**.

(2) **Eastport and Cobscook Bay**

(3) **Calais, The Saint Croix Valley and the Downeast Lakes**, the lake-splotched backwoods largely accessible from Rt. 1 and Grand Lake Stream.

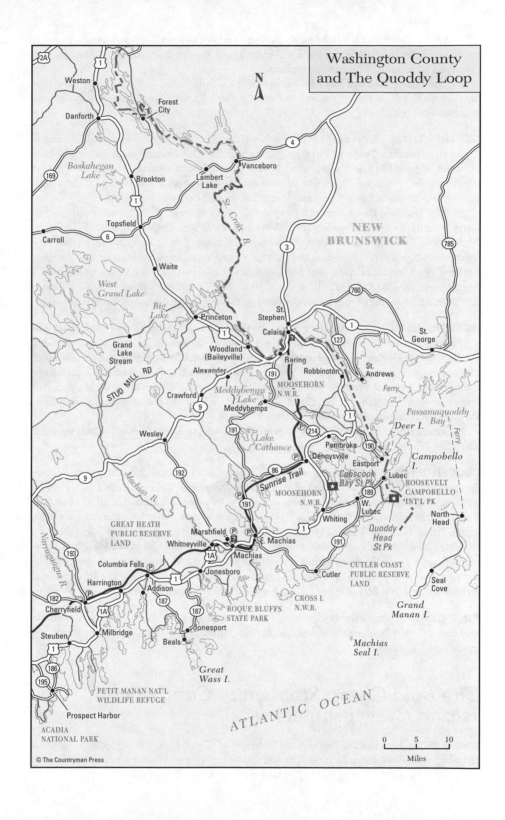

N

2A
1
Weston
Forest
City
Danforth
4
Vanceboro
169
Baskahegan
Lake
Brookton
Lambert
Lake
1
Topsfield
6
NEW
785
BRUNSWICK
Carroll
Waite
3
St.
Croix
R.
West
Grand Lake
760
Big
Lake
St.
Princeton
Stephen
St.
127
George
Grand
Lake
Calais
Stream
1
Woodland
Baring
(Baileyville)
St.
Alexander
191
Robbinston
Andrews
MOOSEHORN
STUD MILL RD
N.W.R.
Ferry
Crawford
Meddybemps
Passamaquoddy
9
Lake
Deer I.
Bay
Meddybemps
Wesley
Lake
Pembroke
190
Campobello
191
Cathance
I.
P
192
86
Dennysville
Eastport
Sunrise Trail
Cobscook
9
MOOSEHORN
Bay St Pk
Lubec
P
N.W.R.
ROOSEVELT
191
189
CAMPOBELLO
W.
'INT'L PK
GREAT HEATH
Whiting
Lubec
North
PUBLIC RESERVE
Marshfield
P
Head
LAND
Machias R.
P
E. Machias
Quoddy
Whitneyville
P
Head
1A
191
St Pk
193
Machias
CUTLER COAST
Columbia Falls
P
1
PUBLIC RESERVE
Seal
Harrington
Addison
Jonesboro
Cutler
LAND
Cove
182
187
Narraguagus R.
CROSS I.
Grand
Cherryfield
1A
187
ROQUE BLUFFS
N.W.R.
Manan I.
STATE PARK
Steuben
Milbridge
Jonesport
Machias
Beals
Seal I.
1
186
Great
Wass I.
195
PETIT MANAN NAT'L
ATLANTIC OCEAN
WILDLIFE REFUGE
Prospect Harbor
ACADIA
0   5   10
NATIONAL PARK
© The Countryman Press
Miles

GUIDANCE DownEast & Acadia Regional Tourism (1-888-665-3278; downeastacadia.com) is the umbrella tourism promotion for Hancock and Washington Counties. Also see the chambers of commerce for specific regions.

(((•))) **The Maine Tourism Association** maintains a full-service visitors center (207-454-2211) at 39 Union St. (the Wabanaki Cultural Center), Calais. Open June–Oct., daily 8–6, otherwise 9–5:30.

GETTING THERE *By air:* See "Bar Harbor" and "Bangor Area" for scheduled airline service.

By bus: **Concord Coach** (1-800-639-3317; concordcoachlines.com), best service to Bangor from Augusta, Portland, and Boston. **West's Coastal Connection** (1-800-596-2823; westbusservice.com) offers daily service year-round between Bangor Airport and Calais, with stops in Machias and Perry, flag-down stops (call ahead) between.

By car: The **Bold Coast Scenic Byway** designates 125 miles of Rt. 1 from Milbridge to Eastport with detouring loops along Rt. 187 and Rt. 191/189 to Cutler and Lubec.

Practical Tips: From points south take I-95 to Rt. 295 to I-95 to Bangor. For the westernmost towns take Rt. 1A to Ellsworth, then Rt. 1. For coastal points east of Harrington, you save 9 miles by cutting inland on Rt. 182 from Hancock to Cherryfield, but for most easterly points from Bangor, take the Airline Highway (Rt. 9) from which many roads connect to coastal communities. Rt. 9 runs for 90 miles, straight through the blueberry barrens and woods, to Calais.

GETTING AROUND The Quoddy Loop (quoddyloop.com) refers to a rewarding way of touring the Passamaquoddy Bay area on both sides of the border by both land and water. See **East Coast Ferries** (eastcoastferriesltd.com) in the **Bold Coast** section for details about car/passenger service from Eastport and Campobello Island to Deer Island and on across the bay to the New Brunswick mainland. We suggest spending the night in St. Andrews, known as "the Bar Harbor of New Brunswick" (see sidebar). It's just 19 miles (25 km) from Rt. 1 once you've crossed the border in Calais.

Lubec-Eastport passenger ferry service is offered late June to mid-September Tue.-Sun., The Wharf (207-733-4400), 69 Johnson St., Lubec.

CROSSING THE BORDER Passports or NEXUS cards are required for re-entry to the United States from Canada by land. For details check **getyouhome.gov**. Children 15 and under need a birth certificate. For questions about pets and what you can bring back and forth, see **cbp.gov**. U.S. Immigration in Lubec (207-733-4331) can also answer questions about the crossing there and in Calais. Canadian citizens are also required to present a passport or a NEXUS card.

Note: Do not bring a radar detector into Canada; they are illegal in the Maritime Provinces. Also, if you're driving a vehicle other than your own, you must have the owner's written permission. The Calais crossing has been eased since the opening of the International Avenue crossing on Rt. 1 north of town. There is also a Milltown crossing.

TIME CHANGE Cross the bridge from Lubec and you lose an hour. Atlantic Canada is an hour ahead of Maine during daylight saving months, especially significant if you are catching a Canadian ferry.

The Bold Coast: Steuben to Campobello Island (New Brunswick)

GUIDANCE The Machias Bay Area Chamber of Commerce (207-255-4402; machiaschamber.org). A walk-in information center in the town's newly restored Railroad Station (across from Helen's Resturant) is open 10–3 weekdays, also Sat. in-season.

For **Lubec** check the websites **visitlubecmaine.com, cobscookbay.com,** and **westquoddy** **.com.** The **West Quoddy Head Light Keepers Association Visitor Center** (207-733-2180; westquoddy.com) at the lighthouse is open daily Memorial Day weekend to mid-Oct., 10–4.

The **Campobello Welcome Center** (506-752-7043) is open daily May–Columbus Day. Also New Brunswick tourist information at 1-800-561-0123; tourismnbcanada.com.

WHEN TO GO **The Down East Birding Festival** (downeastbirdfest.org) is held Memorial Day weekend, and the best months to view puffins on Machias Seal Island are May–early July. **Milbridge Days,** last weekend in July, and the **Wild Blueberry Festival** in Machias, third weekend in Aug., are the big summer events. September brings the clearest weather. From mid-Sept. to early Oct. the blueberry barrens turn red, adding their brilliance to Maine's fall foliage.

GETTING AROUND
By land: **The Bold Coast Scenic Byway** begins on Rt. 1 in Milbridge and loops down Rt. 187 to **Jonesport** (continue across the bridge to Beals Island and continue to the hiking trails on Grand Wass). Beyond **Machias,** the byway detours from Rt. 1 down Rt. 191 to **Cutler** and on up toward **Lubec.** If time permits, bear right on Boot Cove Rd. in South Trescott and follow the unpaved road along the real "Bold Coast" to **West Quoddy Light.**

By water: **Lubec-Eastport passenger ferry service** runs late June to mid-Sept., Tue.–Sun.; contact **The Wharf** (207-733-4400), 69 Johnson St., Lubec.

Fundy Passenger Ferry (877-346-2225), 727 Friars Bay Beach, Welshpool, Campobello Island. In-season, Brandon Flynn offers frequent service from Campobello to St. Andrews in his 32-foot weatherproofed lobster-style boat, leaving 9 AM and returning late afternoon.

East Coast Ferries Ltd. (506-747-2159 or 1-877-747-2159; eastcoastferriesltd.com) runs a seasonal car ferry from Eastport and Campobello Island to Deer Island. From there the free ferries run by the New Brunswick Department of Transportation (506-453-3939) cross Passaquoddy Bay to L'Etete, NB, handy to St. Andrews and to Blacks Harbour. The harbor is a departure point for ferries to Grand Manan (see sidebars). The ferry is a tug with long, hydraulically operated arms linked to a barge. Passengers and bikes, cars, and even buses board on ramps lowered to the beach. It's 100 miles shorter from Campobello to St. Andrews by water than land, but the two trips may take the same amount of time. On a beautiful day, however, there's no comparison.

✳ To See

LISTED GEOGRAPHICALLY, HEADING EAST
Steuben, the first town in Washington County, is known as the site of the **Maine Coastal Islands Refuge.** See *Green Space.*

Milbridge (visitmilbridge.com). A Rt. 1 town of less than 1,300 residents, with a wandering coastline, is the administrative home of Jasper Wyman and Sons, one of the oldest wild blueberry processors. **McClellan Park** (207-546-2422), overlooking Narraguagus (pronounced *nair-a-GWAY-gus*) Bay, offers picnic tables, fireplaces, campsites, restrooms, and drinking water. The **Milbridge Historical Museum** (207-546-4471; milbridgehistorical society.org) is open in summer Tue. and Sun. 1–4. It's a delightful window into the past of this spirited community. **Milbridge Days,** in late July, features a codfish relay race.

Cherryfield (pop. 1,080). A few miles up the Narraguagus River, Cherryfield bills itself as the Blueberry Capital of Maine (there are two processing plants in town), but its very early, stately houses (see *Lodging*) were built with the proceeds of lumbering. The

Cherryfield-Narraguagus Historical Society, 88 River Rd., is generally open summer Saturdays, 1–4. The small village offers rewarding *Selective Shopping*.

Columbia Falls (pop. 560) is a picturesque village with one of Maine's most notable houses at its center: **Ruggles House** (207-483-4637; 0.25 miles off Rt. 1; open June–mid-Oct., Mon.–Sat. for guided tours, 9:30–4, Sun. noon–4; $5 adults, $2 children 6–12) is a Federal-style mansion built by wealthy lumber dealer Thomas Ruggles in 1818. It is a beauty, with a graceful flying staircase, a fine Palladian window, and superb woodwork. Legend has it that a woodcarver was imprisoned in the house for three years with a penknife. South of Ruggles House veer left at the fork. Also note: Behind the town offices is where you can find the **Wreaths Across America Museum** (1-877-385-9504; wreathsacrossamerica.org). Housed in the back of the former elementary school and open daily 9–4, this museum is dedicated to the U.S. military and chronicles the story of the

CHERRYFIELD IS AN ANTIQUES CENTER   Christina Tree

movement, begun by local wreath-maker Morrill Worcester, to place Christmas wreaths on veterans' graves in some 840 locations around the world. Just off Rt. 1 note the sign for the **Wild Salmon Research Center** (207-483-4336; mainesalmonrivers.org), open weekdays 8–4.

Jonesport (townofjonesport.com; pop. roughly 1,400) is at the tip of a 12-mile-long peninsula facing Moosabec Reach, which is, in turn, spanned by a bridge leading to **Beals Island** (pop. 600, known for the design of its lobster boats). Both communities are all about fishing. Together these towns are home to eastern Maine's largest lobstering fleet, and the bridge is a popular viewing stand for the July 4 lobster boat races. Beals Island, populated largely by Alleys and Beals, is connected to **Great Wass Island**, a hiking destination with trails through a 1,579-acre Nature Conservancy preserve with good picnicking on the rocky shore. The neighboring **Downeast Institute for Applied Marine Research and Education** (207-497-5769; downeastinstitute.org; open to the public year-round, daily 9–4) produces millions of seed clams annually for local clam flats, also thousands of lobsters; check out the lobster tanks in the Education Center.

Back in Jonesport, the **Peabody Memorial Library** offers WiFi, restrooms, and art exhibits. It's home to the **Jonesport Historical Society** (207-497-2395; jonesporthistoricalsociety.org) with computer access to visual and oral histories of over 65,000 residents (present, past, and related). Heading north from the village on Rt. 187, be sure to stop if the open sign is out at Ronnie Peabody's **Maine Coast Sardine History Museum** and farther along at Buzz and Helen Beal's **Maine Central Model Railroad** (call ahead: 207-497-2255; Mon.–Sat. 10–6), where 380 cars traverse 3,000 feet of tracks that wind through hand-built miniature replicas of local towns and scenery.

Jonesboro (pop. roughly 600), judging from Rt. 1, is just blueberry barrens, a church, and a post office. The beauty of this town is its shoreline, which wanders in and out of points and coves along the tidal Chandler River and Chandler Bay on the way to **Roque Bluffs**

State Park, 6 miles south of Rt. 1. A public boat launch with picnic tables is five minutes south of Rt. 1 on Roque Bluffs Rd. (right on Evergreen Point Rd.).

Machias (pop. 2,221). Early in the 19th century, Machias was second only to Bangor among Maine lumber ports. The opera house, two newspapers, three hotels, and trotting park are long gone, but Machias remains a must-stop. The Machias River runs down along the back of Main Street and over the **Bad Little Falls**. Look for picnic tables in the park by the falls and for **Burnham Tavern** (207-255-6930; burnhamtavern.com), 14 Colonial Way (open mid-June–Sept., Mon.–Fri., 10–3). A 1770s gambrel-roofed tavern, it's filled with period furnishings and tells the story of British man-of-war *Margaretta*, captured on June 12, 1775, by townspeople sailing the small sloop *Unity*. This was the first naval battle of the American Revolution. Unfortunately, the British retaliated by burning Portland.

At the opposite eastern end of downtown, across from **Helen's Restaurant**, note the Machias Chamber's **1898 Station** (information center) and the access point to the multi-use **Sunrise Trail** along the Middle River. The neighboring "**Dike**," a land bridge between Machias Bay and Middle River, is a frequent venue for vendors selling everything from fish to antiques. The **University of Maine at Machias** (207-255-1200), just south of downtown, enrolls roughly 1,000 students on a 43-acre campus; check umm.maine.edu for art gallery hours and use of the fitness center and pool. Machias is best known for its **Wild Blueberry Festival** (third weekend in August), but the summer organ concerts in its 1836 Congregational church are also a major attraction.

Machiasport (pop. 1,071). Take Rt. 92 at Bad Little Falls Park in Machias. This picturesque village includes the **Gates** and **Cooper Houses** (open July and Aug., Tue.–Fri. 12:30–4:30, free), Federal-style homes with maritime exhibits and period rooms. Neighboring **Fort O'Brien** consists of earthen breastworks with cannons and includes the grass-covered remains of the ammunition powder magazine used during the American Revolution and the

JONESPORT

War of 1812. Continue on down this road to the fishing village of Bucks Harbor and on to **Jasper Beach**, so named for the wave-tumbled and polished pebbles of jasper and rhyolite that give it its distinctive color. The road ends with great views and a beach to walk in the part of town known as **Starboard**.

Cutler (pop. less than 650). From East Machias, follow Rt. 191 south to this small, photogenic fishing village that's happily shielded from a view of the U.S. Navy communications station's 26 antenna towers (800 to 980 feet tall), which light up red at night and can be seen from much of the county's coast. A portion of this former base is now Beachwood Bay Estates, a housing development with an enterprising general store. The **Little River Lighthouse** (see *Other Lodging*) at the mouth of its harbor has been restored. This area was initially about lumbering, not fishing. In 1835 Massachusetts investors built a dam across the upper part of the harbor and a tidal mill to turn spruce into laths and shingles. However, fires destroyed what was left of the original forest in the 1850s and the area's economy shifted to fishing. Cutler is a departure point for **Bold Coast puffin cruises** to **Machias Seal Island**, 9.7 miles offshore (see *Birding*). Beyond the village, Rt. 191 follows the shoreline through moorlike blueberry and cranberry country, with disappointingly few views from the road but splendid panoramas from the **Bold Coast Trails** (see *Hiking*).

In South Trescott bear right onto Boot Cove Rd. instead of continuing north on Rt. 191 and follow the coast, keeping an eye out for the **Hamilton Cove Preserve**, with a walk to a cobble beach. Continue on to **West Quoddy Light** (next page), one of the jewels of the entire Maine coast. Take time to hike and/or get out on the water.

Lubec (pop. 1,508). The direct route from Machias to **Quoddy Head State Park** (207-733-0911) in South Lubec is via Rt. 1 to the marked Rt. 189 turnoff. The 532-acre park is open mid-May–mid-Oct., sunrise to sunset, with a staffed visitors center (&) in the **Light Keepers' House** (207-733-2180; westquoddy.com), open Memorial Day–mid-Oct., 10–4. Displays tell the story of the lighthouse, which dates back to 1858, and of local industries; there's also a gift shop and a gallery with changing art exhibits. Despite its name, the red candy-striped

William A. Davis

WEST QUODDY LIGHT

West Quoddy Head Lighthouse marks the easternmost tip of the United States (see the *Campobello Island* sidebar for the **East Quoddy Head Lighthouse**). There are benches for those who come to be among the first in the United States to see (fog permitting) the sunrise, a pleasant picnic area, and a fine view of **Grand Manan Island** (see sidebar). Best of all is the spectacular 2-mile **Coastal Trail** along the cliffs to Carrying Place Cove. Between the cove and the bay, roughly a mile back down the road from the light, is an unusual coastal, raised-plateau bog with dense sphagnum moss and heath.

In **downtown Lubec**, Water Street is transitioning from sardine cannery row to a lively lineup of shops, restaurants, and galleries. Don't miss **McCurdy's Herring Smokehouse** (207-733-42197), 50 Water St., restored to evoke the era in which Lubec was

Christina Tree

MCCURDY'S HERRING SMOKEHOUSE, LUBEC

home to 20 canneries. Stop by the old town landing with its public boat launch, breakwater, and a view of **Mulholland Point Light** just across on Campobello Island. The tide rushes in and out through the narrows here, and frequently you can see seals playing and fishing in the water. **Lubec Channel Light**, for obvious reasons better known as "the Sparkplug," can be viewed from **Stockford Park**, along the water south of the bridge. **SummerKeys** (see *To Do*) offers musical, writing, art, and photography workshops and a series of free Wed.-evening concerts all summer long. The **Lubec Historical Society Museum** (207-733-2274), 135 Main St. (Rt. 189), fills the old Columbian Store with photos and memorabilia from the days when Lubec was home to 14 sardine canneries. See *Hiking* for trails that access scenic stretches of the town's widely wandering shoreline.

Christina Tree

LUBEC HISTORICAL SOCIETY MUSEUM

✳ To Do

BICYCLING **Down East Sunrise Trail** (sunrisetrail.org). An 85-mile railbed, paralleling Rt. 1 as far as East Machias then turning inland, has been surfaced to serve wide-wheel bicyclists, ATVs, and pedestrians. Best access: from Cherryfield off Rt. 193 at Matthews Grocery; in Columbia Falls: off Rt. 1 on Tibbettstown Rd. north; in Machias: at the boxcar just south of the Dike (causeway); in East Machias: off Rt.1 on Willow St. next to the gas station and on Rt. 191, 7 miles north of Rt. 1. Ideal for mountain bikes. **Bicycle rentals** are available from **The Wharf** (207-733-4400), Lubec.

BOATING AND PADDLING **Robertson Sea Tours Adventures** (207-483-6110; cell phone, 207-461-7439; robertsonseatours.com).

MUST SEE

CAMPOBELLO ISLAND Campobello Island, New Brunswick, is easily accessible from Lubec via the FDR Memorial Bridge. You have to pass through Canadian and U.S. Customs, but there's rarely a wait. Franklin D. Roosevelt's "Beloved Island" (the family summered here for six decades) is 9 miles long with some 925 year-round residents living primarily in the fishing villages of Wilson's Beach, Welshpool, and North Road. Granted to Captain William Owen in the 1760s, much of the island remained in the family until 1881, when a large part was sold to Boston developers who built three large (long-gone) hotels. Another major real estate development in the 1980s and '90s by the same Arkansas-based company that developed Whitewater (the Clintons were not involved in this one) failed.

✒ **Roosevelt Campobello International Park** (506-752-2922; fdr.net), Welshpool, Campobello Island, New Brunswick. Open Sat. before Memorial Day weekend–mid-Oct., daily 9–5 EDT (10–6 Canadian Atlantic Daylight Time). This manicured 2,800-acre park with a Visitor Centre and shingled "cottages" is the number one sight to see east of Bar Harbor. The house in which Franklin Delano Roosevelt summered as a boy has disappeared, but the airy 34-room **Roosevelt Cottage**, a wedding gift to Franklin and Eleanor, is sensitively maintained just as the family left it, charged with the spirit of the dynamic man who was felled by polio here on August 25, 1921. (They are quick to tell you that he had contracted it several weeks before at a Boy Scout jamboree in New York.) The house is filled with many poignant objects, such as the toy boat FDR carved for his children. During his subsequent stints as governor of New York and then as president of the United States, FDR returned only three times. Neighboring **Hubbard Cottage**, with its oval picture window, gives another slant on this turn-of-the-20th-century resort. Afternoon **"Tea with Eleanor"** is offered here twice daily (free but tickets required); you can also reserve ($12) a seat for tea at the Wells-Sober Cottage. For information about **Road Scholar programs** (roadscholar.org) offered in the Victorian cottages and nearby Campobello venues, contact the Atlantic Leadership Center (207-853-6036). The park's **Visitor Centre** offers excellent historical exhibits and a 15-minute introductory film. Beyond stretch more than **8 miles of trails** to the shore and then inland through woods to lakes and ponds. There are also 15.4 miles of **carriage road drives** modified from the network that the wealthy "cottagers" maintained on the island. Detailed trail maps and advice are available at the Visitor Centre. A short but rewarding walk leads to **Friar's Head**. We recommend the coastal trails from **Southern Head to the Duck Ponds** and from **Raccoon Beach to Liberty Point**. Seals frequently sun on the ledges off Lower Duck Pond, and loons are

Christina Tree

ROOSEVELT COTTAGE

Captain Robertson offers a variety of cruises on a 30-foot lobster boat from Milbridge, including whale-watching and island lobster bakes. The focus is on the 50 miles of coast west to Schoodic.

Downeast Coastal Cruises (207-546-7720; downeastcoastalcruises.com), Milbridge Town Landing. Mid-May–mid-Oct., Captain Buzzy Shinn offers 1½- to 3-hour cruises, which can include an island lobster feast.

Coastal Cruises (207-598-7473; cruisedowneast.com), 117 Kelley Point Rd., Jonesport. Captain Laura Fish and her brother Harry, whose family has been in this area since 1773, are

Christina Tree

HEAD HARBOUR LIGHT, CAMPOBELLO

often seen off Liberty Point. Along this dramatic shoreline at the southern end of the island, also look for whales July–Sept. The international park has recently acquired the **Adams Lodge** (formerly Lupine Lodge) and has renovated the restaurant. Neighboring 1,049-acre **Herring Cove Provincial Park** (506-561-7010), open mid-May–mid-Nov., also offers trails, a beach, a **restaurant** (open 8–8), and a **golf course** with nine holes, a clubhouse, and rentals. There's also a **campground** with 76 campsites, 40 hook-ups.

Head Harbour Light, as it's known in Canada (in the U.S. it's **East Quoddy Head Lighthouse**) is a 51-foot-high tower built in 1829, at the northern tip of the island. Its wooden, shingled exterior, painted white with a distinctive red cross, has recently been restored, thanks to its "Friends." The cast-iron lantern is vintage 1887. This is a popular whale-watching station but demanding to reach and accessible only at low tide, then only if you are physically fit. Beware the incoming tide. There's a great viewing spot from just across the narrow channel. From the international park follow Rt. 774 to the end. There's WiFi and Internet access at the **Campobello Public Library & Museum** (open Tue.–Fri.), car-ferry service via Deer Island to mainland New Brunswick, and direct passenger ferry service to St. Andrews (see *Getting Around*).

WHALE-WATCH CRUISES Campobello is a prime departure point for seasonal whale-watching. Both **Capt. Riddle's Whale Watch Cruises** (1-877-FINBACK; finback.com), tickets: 727 Friar's Bay Rd., and **Island Cruises** (1-888-249-4400; bayoffundywhales.com), from **Head of Harbour Wharf**, offer several cruises.

themselves seasoned guides to Moosabec Reach and its islands. Their cabin cruiser *Aaron Thomas* accommodates up to six passengers on three- and five-hour cruises. Special charters and dive trips are also offered.

Pleasant River Boat Tours (207-483-6567; pleasantriverboattours.com), South Addison Town Landing. Captain Paul Ferriero offers coastal tours on his 34-foot lobster boat, the *Honey B.* Six people max. Seals, eagles, maybe puffins or a whale are all possible.

✪ **Bold Coast Charter Co.** (see *Birding*). Puffins up close are Captain Andy's specialty, but he also offers coastal sightseeing cruises and nature/hiking tours.

✪ **Sunrise Canoe and Kayak Tours** (207-255-3375; sunrisecanoeandkayak.com), at 68 Main St. (Rt. 1 just north of the Dyke), Machias. Rob Scribner offers kayak rentals and guided tours out in Machias Bay. Conditions permitting, tours visit petroglyphs, the Bold Coast, and the Wass Island Archipelago. Shuttles and logistical support offered.

Sunrise Expeditions International (sunrise-exp.com) offers multiday canoe expeditions on the Machias and St. Croix Rivers. Rigorous spring Whitewater Weekends or Weeks With Wilderness camping are Bangor-based Martin Brown's specialty.

Wharf Rentals (207-773-4400), 69 Johnson St., Lubec, offers full- and half-day kayak and bike rentals.

Downeast Charter Boat Tours (207-733-2009; downeastcharterboattours.com), 31 Johnson St., Lubec. Tours of Passamaquoddy, Cobscook, and Fundy Bays.

Also see **Getting Around** for ferries across Passamaquoddy Bay and the **Campobello Island** sidebar for more whale-watching tours.

FISHING Sea-run Atlantic salmon, long the draw for fishermen to the Narraguagus and Machias Rivers, are currently illegal to catch and will be until stocks have been replenished. Landlocked salmon are, however, still fair game and can be found in **Schoodic Lake** (8 miles north of Cherryfield), **Bog Lake** in Northfield on Rt. 192 (10 miles north of Machias), **Gardner Lake** in East Machias (look for the new boat ramp and parking area), and **Cathance Lake** on Rt. 191 (some 18 miles north of East Machias with a nice boat landing). Trolling lures, streamer flies, or bait from a boat are the most popular ways to catch landlocked salmon. Brook trout can be caught in May and June in local rivers and streams, but in warm weather they move to deeper water like **Six Mile Lake** in Marshfield (6 miles north of Machias on Rt. 192), **Indian Lake** along Rt. 1 in Whiting, and **Lily Lake** in Trescott. Brown trout are found in **Simpson Pond** in Roque Bluffs (park in Roque Bluffs State Park), as well as in the lakes listed above.

Saltwater or tidewater fishing is usually for striped bass or mackerel. For information about licenses, guides, and fish, check with the regional headquarters of the **Inland Fisheries and Wildlife Department** in Milbridge (207-546-2124).

GOLF **Great Cove Golf Course** (207-434-7200), 387 Great Cove Rd., Roque Bluffs, offers nine holes, water views, a clubhouse, rental clubs, and carts.

Barren View Golf Course (207-434-7651), Rt. 1, Jonesboro. This new course offers nine holes with views of the blueberry barrens and boasts Maine's largest sand trap. Facilities include a clubhouse plus rental carts and clubs. Also see the **Campobello Island** sidebar.

HIKING Within the past 15 years the number of coastal hiking options has increased dramatically. See *Green Space*.

PICNICKING **McClellan Park**, in Milbridge, 5 miles south of town at Baldwin Head, overlooks the Atlantic and Narraguagus Bay (from Rt. 1, follow Wyman Rd. to the park gates). It's a town park on 10.5 acres donated in 1926 by George McClellan, a onetime mayor of New York City. There's no charge for walking or picnicking.

Roosevelt Campobello International Park's large natural area on Campobello Island, **Quoddy Head State Park** in Lubec, and **Roque Bluffs State Park** also all have picnic areas.

SPECIAL PROGRAMS (ADULT) ✪ **SummerKeys** (207-733-2316; in winter, 973-316-6220; summerkeys.com), 6 Bayview St., Lubec. Mid-June–Labor Day. In 1992 New York piano teacher Bruce Potterton began offering weeklong programs in Lubec. The program has ballooned to cover a wide variety of instruments, but especially piano for beginners to

PUFFIN-WATCHING AND OTHER BIRDING

This region is said to have northern forest habitat, from thick stands of boreal softwood to marsh and bog wetlands, clam flats, rocky cliffs, meadows, and blueberry barrens. Thinly populated, it also has two national wildlife refuges and is home or a migratory stop for hundreds of species, many now rare (see mainebirdingtrail.com/Downeast). The **Annual Down East Spring Birding Festival**, Memorial Day weekend (downeastbirdfest.org), with an associated **Road Scholar** (roadscholar.org) program, is growing year by year; more than 171 species of birds are usually spotted. By far the area's most famous bird is the puffin, and the place to see it is Machias Seal Island, 9.7 miles off Cutler.

PUFFINS CAN BE VIEWED UP CLOSE ON MACHIAS SEAL ISLAND

Puffins are alcids, seabirds that come to land only to breed. Just about 12 inches tall, these colorful "sea parrots" converge in spring on 15-acre **Machias Seal Island**, a rodent-free outcropping of rocks with crevices seemingly designed for birds to lay and nurture eggs. On the June day we visited, Captain Andy Patterson estimated it was home to 3,000 pairs of nesting puffins, 2,000 pairs of razorbills, 300 arctic terns, and 800 common murres. Visitors are strictly limited to formal groups and herded into blinds, which tend to be surrounded by birds. It's an unforgettable sight—and sound (a chorus of puffins sounds just like a chain saw). The birds are pretty much gone by late August. Although it's just 9 miles off Cutler, Canada maintains and staffs a lighthouse station as well as the wildlife refuge. Reservations are usually required well ahead of time with any of the two outfits that have landing permits for the island.

Bold Coast Charter Company (207-259-4484; boldcoast.com), Cutler, offers the only U.S.-based access to the island itself. Captain Patterson's five-hour puffin-watching trips (weather permitting) are late May–mid-Aug. His partially enclosed 40-foot passenger vessel *Barbara Frost* also cruises the Bold Coast, the stretch of high, rocky bluffs east of Cutler. **Sea Watch Tours** offers tours to Machias Seal Island from Grand Manan (see *To Do* in that chapter).

Also see *Boating and Paddling*. For any of these trips, come prepared with windbreakers, hats, and mittens for the early-morning ride out, usually in fog.

CAPTAIN ANDY ABOARD *THE BARBARA FROST*

advanced students. Plein-air summer art workshops are now also offered, along with writing and photography. Lodging is at local B&Bs.

Road Scholar (formerly Elderhostel; roadscholar.org) offers weeklong programs on varied subjects on Campobello Island, geared to groups of 24 with lodging in the International Park cottages.

SWIMMING ♪ **Roque Bluffs State Park**, Roque Bluffs (6 miles off Rt. 1). The pebbly ocean beach is frequently windy, but a sheltered sand beach on a freshwater pond is good for children—though the water is cold. Tables, grills, changing areas with toilets, and a playground.

Sandy River Beach in Jonesport (off Rt. 187), marked by a small sign, is a rare white-sand beach—but the water is frigid. On Beals Island, the Backfield Area, Alley's Bay, offers equally bracing saltwater swimming.

Gardner Lake, Chases Mills Rd., East Machias. Freshwater swimming, a picnic area, and a boat launch. **Six Mile Lake**, Rt. 192 in Marshfield (north of Machias), is also good for a dip.

WHALE-WATCHING **The Wharf** (207-733-4400; theinnatthewharf.com), 69 Johnson St. Lubec is the departure point for the 26-passenger *Tarquin*, specializing in whale-watching in Passamaquoddy Bay. Also see the *Campobello Island* sidebar.

✳ Green Space

LISTED GEOGRAPHICALLY, HEADING EAST, AND CONTINUED UNDER *GREEN SPACE* IN THE NEXT TWO SUBCHAPTERS

Pigeon Hill and Petit Manan. From Rt. 1 in Steuben turn onto Pigeon Hill Rd.; after some 5 miles, look for a small graveyard on your left. Stop. The well-trod path up Pigeon Hill begins across the road. The climb is fairly steep in places, but it's nonetheless a pleasant 20-minute hike, and the view from the summit reveals a series of island-filled bays that stretch away to the east, as well as mountains inland. Drive another mile down Pigeon Hill Rd. and past the sign announcing that you have entered a 2,166-acre preserve, part of **Maine Coastal Islands Refuge** (fws.gov/northeast/mainecoastal), which includes two other parcels and 47 offshore islands. There are two loop trails, and you can drive to the parking lot for the second. This is a varied area with pine stands, cedar swamps, blueberry barrens, marshes, and great birding (more than 250 species have been identified here). Maps are posted at the parking lots. A 0.5-mile shore path hugs the woods and coastline.

✪ **Great Wass Island.** The Maine chapter of The Nature Conservancy owns this 1,579-acre tract at the southern tip of the Jonesport-Addison peninsula. Trail maps are posted at the parking lot (simply follow the island's main road to its logical end). The interior of the island supports one of Maine's largest stands of jack pine and is a quite beautiful mix of lichen-covered open ledge, wooded path, and coastal peatland. Roughly a third of the 5-mile loop is along the shore. Little Cape Point is a great picnic spot. Wear rubber-soled shoes.

Middle River Park and Machias River Preserve, both maintained by Downeast Coastal Conservancy (207-255-4500), have recently greatly expanded river access right in Machias. Access to 100-acre Middle River Park is via Kilton Lane (across from Helen's Restaurant) and parking for the 900-acre preserve is on Rt. 1A.

Western Head, off Rt. 191, 11 miles south of East Machias, is maintained by the Maine Coast Heritage Trust, Brunswick (207-276-5156). Take the first right after the Baptist church onto Destiny Bay Rd. and follow it to the sign. The 3- to 4-mile loop trail is through mixed-growth woods and spruce to the shore, with views of the entrance to Cutler Harbor and high ledges with crashing surf, large expanses of open ocean, as well as the high, sheer ledges of Grand Manan to the northeast and Machias Seal Island to the southeast.

✪ **Bold Coast Trails.** Look for the trailhead marked CUTLER COAST UNIT TRAILS some 4 miles east of Cutler Harbor on Rt. 191. Maine's Bureau of Parks and Lands (207-287-4920) has constructed inner and outer loop trails (one 5 miles, one 10 miles) from the road to the rugged cliffs and along the shore overlooking Grand Manan Channel. The **Coastal Trail** begins in deep spruce-fir forest, bridges a cedar swamp, and 1.5 miles from the parking lot climbs out of the woods and onto a promontory, continuing to rise and dip along the cliffs to Black Point Cove, a cobble beach. (Note: The cliffs are high and sheer, not good for children or shaky adults.) Bring a picnic and allow at least five hours. The trail continues from Black Point Cove to Fairy Head, site of three primitive campsites.

The Quoddy Regional Land Trust (207-733-5509; qrlt.org), with the help of the Maine Coast Heritage Trust, publishes a thick, ever-expanding booklet titled *Cobscook Trails: A Guide to Walking Opportunities Around Cobscook Bay and the Bold Coast*. It's available locally and from the trust. Descriptions include trails in Lubec to Morong Cove, Mowry Beach to Horan Head, and trails in the Pike Lands, in the Hamilton Cove and Boot Head Preserves, and to Commissary Point in Trescott.

✪ **Quoddy Head State Park, Lubec** (follow signs from Rt. 189). The candy-striped lighthouse and visitors center (see *To See*) are as far as most people come, but the Coastal Trail, along the cliffs, is one of the most dramatic in Maine. The views from the trail and from well-placed benches are back to the lighthouse, down the coast, and across to the sheer cliffs of Grand Manan 7 miles offshore. Bring a picnic.

✳ Lodging

INNS AND B&BS

LISTED GEOGRAPHICALLY, HEADING EAST.

🌸 **The Englishman's Bed and Breakfast** (207-546-2337; englishmansbandb.com), 122 Main St., Cherryfield 04622. This is a beautifully restored four-square 1793 Federal-style mansion (on the National Register) set above the Narraguagus River, with a wide back deck and screened gazebo. Kathy and Peter Winham offer two guest rooms (1½ baths) in the house itself and a delightful Carriage House unit with a fridge, microwave, toaster, and hot plate. A full breakfast is served by the 18th-century hearth in the dining room. Teas and cream teas are also available on request. Per-couple rates: $80–100 for rooms; $95–155 for the Carriage House (pets permitted); less for singles.

✪ ♂ (ᵞₚ) **Pleasant Bay Bed & Breakfast** (207-483-4490; pleasantbay.com), 386 West Side Rd., P.O. Box 222, Addison 04606. Open year-round. We can't say enough about this special place! After raising six children and

a number of llamas in New Hampshire, Leon and Joan Yeaton returned to Joan's girlhood turf, cleared this land, and built this gracious house with many windows and a deck and porch overlooking the tidal Pleasant River. A living room is well stocked with puzzles and books for foggy days; there's also a

Christina Tree

PLEASANT BAY BED & BREAKFAST

MICMAC FARM GUESTHOUSES, MACHIASPORT · Christina Tree

more formal library with fireplace and a big screened porch. But the heart of the house is the open kitchen and dining area, overlooking grounds that slope to the water. Amazing breakfasts—maybe individual herbed egg soufflés, sourced from the house hens and herb garden—are served at a common table overlooking the water. There are horses and angora goats and wooded trails through more than 100 acres of woods and meadow, down to the bay. The four upstairs guest rooms with views include one family-sized room with private bath and a lovely two-room suite with a living room, kitchenette, and deck overlooking the water. There are moorings for guests arriving by water. $55–110 per couple ($10 per child); $160 for the suite.

Chandler River Lodge (207-434-2540; chandlerriverlodge.com), 654 Rt. 1, Jonesboro 04648. Open year-round, this comfortable old house welcomed guests in decades past, and it's nice to see it restored. Set back in its grounds from Rt. 1, it offers four rooms, one with a king-sized bed and spa bath, the others with queens and private bath, although one is down the hall. $125–150 in-season includes a continental breakfast. There is no common space, as the first floor is a restaurant (see *Dining Out*).

✪ ✿ ✾ ☙ ✐ **Micmac Farm Guesthouses and Gardner House** (207-255-3008; micmacfarm .com), 47 Micmac Lane, Machiasport 04655. Open Memorial Day to Columbus Day weekends. This classic Cape, built by Ebenezer Gardner above the Machias River in 1776, is the oldest house in Machias and a real treasure. Ebenezer Gardner was born in Roxbury, MA, and went to Nova Scotia in 1763, but because he sided with the Americans in the Revolution he had to move back down the coast. The house he built there is now home to Anthony Dunn, Bonnie, his wife, and their small daughter; in summer they occupy a separate wing and offer guests the large downstairs bedroom off the library. Very private—with a deck overlooking the river and a bath with whirlpool tub—it's furnished in family antiques, a desk, and a life's collection of books. $125 includes breakfast. Three comfortable, well-designed guesthouses ($95 daily, $595 per week). Children and pets are welcome in the cabins and kayaks can easily be launched here.

Captain Cates (207-255-8812; captain cates.com), 309 Port Rd. (Rt. 92), Machiasport 04655. Open year-round. This 1820s sea captain's house overlooks the tidal river and offers guests six cheerful, antiques-furnished rooms on the second and third floors, sharing three baths. Downstairs there is a lilac-colored front parlor, a library, and a dining room. Rick and Mary Bury offer hospitality with a southern accent: The library now features portraits of Confederate generals and battlefield prints as well as cable TV, books, and games. From $75 with full breakfast that may well include grits.

✪ **Riverside Inn** (1-888-255-4344; riversideinn-maine.com), Rt. 1, East Machias 04630. Open year-round. The heart of this vintage-1805 house—actually the first thing guests see—is the kitchen. Innkeepers Ellen McLaughlin and Rocky Rakoczy will probably be there preparing for the evening meal (see *Dining Out*). We recommend one of the two suites (one with a living room, bedroom, and kitchen facilities; the other with two bedrooms) in the Coach House, nearer the river and with decks. The Downeast Sunrise (recreation) Trail passes below the inn, by the river. There are also two nicely decorated upstairs guest rooms with private bath in the house. $89–135 includes a full breakfast.

West Quoddy Station (1-877-535-7414; quoddyvacation.com), P.O. Box 98, Lubec 04652. The former U.S. Coast Guard station within walking distance of Quoddy Head State Park has been transformed into six attractive units, nicely furnished with antiques, fitted with phones and TV; upstairs units have a sea view. From $95–130 per day and $700 per week for a one-bedroom to $1,900 per week for the five-bedroom Station House.

 ♿ (((•))) **Peacock House** (207-733-2403; peacockhouse.com), 27 Summer St., Lubec 04652. Open May–Oct. A gracious 1860s house on a quiet side street, home to four generations of the Peacock family, owners of the major local cannery. There are three carefully, comfortably furnished guest rooms and four suites, one handicapped accessible. The most luxurious suite, the Peacock, is especially spacious and has a gas fireplace. Innkeepers Dennis and Sue Baker have the right touch. Children ages 7 and up are welcome. Rates, which include a full breakfast served at the dining room table, are $103–149.

   Whiting Bay Bed & Breakfast (207-733-2402; whitingbaybb.com), 1 Cobscook Way, Whiting 04691. A contemporary house on the water's edge, designed and built by owner Brenda Gay. Open year-round but check off-season. The three rooms vary in size: A sunny room has a double bed and shared bath ($80 single, $100 double); the master bedroom features a private bath and a king-sized bed; a suite, which can sleep a family, also has private bath. $139–149 double. A full breakfast is included.

   Home Port Inn Bed and Breakfast (207-733-2077 or 1-800-457-2077; homeportinn .com), 45 Main St., P.O. Box 50, Lubec 04652. Open mid-May–mid-Oct. Happily, this long-established inn is flourishing under owners Dave and Suzannah Gale. The large, raspberry-colored living room is a great space to read or watch TV, and each of the seven guest rooms (private bath) has been tastefully decorated. We like Room 5, melon-colored with a canopy bed. $99–135 per couple; $30 per extra person.

   Inn on the Wharf (207-733-4400; theinn onthewharf.com), 69 Johnson St., Lubec 04652. Open May–Oct. 20. Victor and Judy Trafford have transformed the town's last surviving sardine-processing plant into a waterside inn with 12 spacious suites and 3 two-bedroom, two-bath apartments (suitable for four). There's a common gathering space with a kitchen, dining areas, and two-level deck. Suites $100, apartments $150 daily; inquire about weekly rates.

   ✪ ✐ **The Owen House** (506-752-2977; owenhouse.ca), 11 Welshpool St., Welshpool, Campobello, New Brunswick, Canada E5E 1G3. Open late May–mid-Oct. This delightful inn is reason enough to come to Campobello. Built in 1835 by Admiral William Fitzwilliam Owen, son of the British captain to whom the island was granted in 1769, this is probably the most historic house on the island, and it's a beauty, set on a headland overlooking Passamaquoddy Bay. Joyce Morrell, a watercolor artist who maintains a gallery here, inherited the house from her parents and with an able assist from Jan Meiners maintains the B&B beautifully. The nine guest rooms (seven with private bath) are furnished with friendly antiques, handmade quilts, and good art. Room 1 is really a suite with a single bed in the adjoining room; Room 2, the other front room, is a favorite. Guests gather around the formal dining room table for a full breakfast and around one of several fireplaces in the evening. Paths lead through the 10-acre property to the water, and the Deer Island ferry leaves from the neighboring beach. From $110 (Canadian) for the shared-bath third-floor rooms to $210 for the water-view suite; $115–178 for a private room with bath, plus 13 percent tax.

COTTAGES Summer rentals with water views in this area abound. We describe only those that offer one-night lodging but heartily recommend renting for a week, something we have done many times here, taking advantage of local seafood, wild blueberries, and other produce. Check chamber listings under *Guidance*.

   Robinson's Log Cottages (207-726-9546; robinsonscottages.com), 231 King St., off Rt. 86, Edmunds Township 04628. Open spring–Thanksgiving. These are fourth-generation sporting-camp-style cottages on the Dennys River, fully equipped, heated, most with stone fireplace, canoes, and direct access to the multiuse Sunrise Trail, good for mountain biking. $90–115 per night, from $511 per week. Inquire about the Guide Service.

MOTELS ✿ ✐ **Machias Motor Inn** (207-255-4861; machiasmotorinn.com), Rt. 1 next to Helen's Restaurant, Machias 04654. Larry Barret maintain a two-story, 35-unit motel; most rooms are standard units, each with two double, extra-long beds, cable TV, coffee, fridge, microwave, and phone. Rooms feature decks overlooking the Machias River. $124–129 double, more for efficiencies; from $83 off-season. Dogs (no cats) are $10 per night each.

🐾 🏔 ✨ 🚭 ♿ ((ᵞ)) **The Eastland Motel** (207-733-5501; eastlandmotel.com), 385 County Rd., Lubec 04652. Open year-round. Current owners have breathed new life into this classic motel. Rooms are brightly, thoughtfully furnished and spanking clean, each fitted with a fridge, microwave, coffeemaker, and TV, as well as phones with free service in the U.S. $90 double includes a continental breakfast with fresh fruit and homemade doughnuts. Dogs are $10; from $68 off-season,

CAMPGROUNDS **McClellan Park**, marked from Rt. 1, Milbridge. Open Memorial Day–Columbus Day. This waterside town park is free for day use; a nominal fee is charged to stay at one of the 14 campsites (showers available). For details, call the town hall at 207-546-2422.

Also see **Cobscook Bay State Park** under *Lodging* in "Eastport."

OTHER LODGING **Little River Lighthouse** (207-259-3833; littleriverlight.org). This 1847 lighthouse is set on a 15-acre trail-webbed island at the mouth of Cutler Harbor. Three guest rooms in the 1888 keeper's house can be reserved mid-June through Aug, $150–225 per night (two guests maximum per room). Transport is included but it's BYO linens, towels, sleeping bag, food, beverages, and bottled water.

HELEN'S RESTAURANT, MACHIAS

✳ Where to Eat

DINING OUT ✪ ✨ **44 Degrees North** (207-546-4440; 44-deegrees-north.com), 17 Main St., Milbridge. Open daily 11–9 in season, Mon.–Sat. 11–8 in winter. Bright, attractive, affordable, this is a great road-food stop. Soups and salads, burgers and slow-roasted prime rib, Bourbon Street chicken, grilled swordfish, beer-batter-fried shrimp, pasta, daily specials, homemade pies, and a full bar (blueberry martinis). However, if you order grilled or baked fish and don't like it dry, say so. Children's menu.

Chandler River Lodge (207-434-2540; chandlerriverlodge.com), Rt. 1, Jonesboro. Open by reservation for dinner July–Sept., Wed.–Sat. 5–8; off-season, Thu.–Sat.; closed Mar.–Apr. Chef-owner Beth Foss is well known locally, having honed her skills at her family-owned Bluebird Ranch Restaurant in Machias. Two candlelit dining rooms with white-clothed tables are the setting for a fine dining menu. Entrées $29–38.

✪ ✨ **Helen's Restaurant** (207-255-8423; helensrestaurantmachias.com) 111 E. Main St., Machias. Open 6 AM–8:30 PM, Fri. and Sat until 9; Sun. 7–3. The town's landmark restaurant since 1950 burned to the ground in 2014, but energetic owners David and Julie Barker managed to reopen for the 2015 season. The new Helen's is airier, filled with natural and recessed light, with nicely designed open spaces, which means that most tables now have water views. Improvements also include a bar and heated floor, but the menu is thankfully unchanged. The fish chowder is made daily with haddock, onions, Maine potatoes, butter, and cream. Options range from a (local) goat cheese or crabmeat salad to a hot roast beef sandwich on homemade bread; also from hot dogs, burgers, and pot roast to rib-eye steak and lobster dinners. Whatever you do, don't pass up a piece of pie. Fully licensed. Children's plates.

Frank's Dockside (207-733-4484), 20 Water St., Lubec. Open year-round for lunch and dinner, daily except Wed. in summer. Check days off-season. Seafood chowders, soups, and baskets at lunch; Italian menu at dinner, plenty of pasta and veal dishes plus chicken Leanna, baked with seasoned crabmeat. There's a welcoming feel and reliably

FRANK'S DOCKSIDE, LUBEC

good taste to this place, with its cheery dining room and back deck overlooking the water. Moderately priced.

Water Street Tavern & Inn (207-733-2477; watersttavernandinn.com), 12 Water St., Lubec. Open 7 AM–8 PM. A prime spot with a great water view. It's a frequently changing and varied menu: From Southwest chicken egg rolls to scallop po'boys and turkey with cranberries at lunch; tavern pie, duck with a berry sauce, and Brazilian seafood stew at dinner. Moderately priced. Inquire about rooms and the Narrows Suite.

Fisherman's Wharf Seafood & Restaurant (207-733-4400; theinnonthewharf.com), 68 Johnson St., Lubec. Open May–Oct., 11:30–8. Reservations suggested for dinner in high season because the dining room is relatively small, with windows overlooking the water. There's also a deck. Lobster, steamers, and local seafood are the specialties, also available for take-out. Moderately priced.

Fireside Restaurant, (506-752-6055) 610 Rt. 774, Campobello Island. Open seasonally Sun.–Wed. 12–5, Thu.–Sat. 12–9. Owned and managed by the Roosevelt International Park, this large log lodge was the centerpiece of a vintage-1913 estate and sits atop a bluff with views across the bay. Reserve if you want a seat near the window or hearth. The interior and the atmosphere are casual, comfortable for families. Specialties include local salmon and scallops but there's plenty to choose from. Don't pass up the raspberry cobbler. Entrees: $15–28.

Herring Cove Clubhouse (506-752-1092), Herring Cove Road (end). May–Oct., 8 AM–9 PM daily. A lovely setting with a water view, good for fried fish, soups, salads, tortilla

chips with lobster salsa, and house-made pies including wild berry and coconut cream. Local brews. Moderately priced.

EATING OUT

LISTED GEOGRAPHICALLY, HEADING EAST

✐ **Joshy's Place**, Rt. 1, Milbridge. Good seasonal take-out. Having researched crab rolls up and down the coast, we think Joshy's rates an 8 on a scale of 1–10. Gifford's ice cream.

🐾 **Vazquez Mexican Food**, 38 Main St., Milbridge. Open May–late July (closed Sun.). Chimichangas, chorizo, tacos, and much more are served up by a Mexican family who know how to cook. Still just picnic tables, but this enterprise has evolved from a backstreet bus serving Mexican blueberry harvesters, and rumor has it a real dining area is in the offing.

Milbridge House Restaurant (207-546-4454; milbridgehouse.com), 20 Main St. Open Tue.–Sun., 6–2. This middle-of-the-village diner is a find! Serious breakfasts and a big lunch, local produce and seafood—scallop, crab, and lobster stew—house-made coleslaw and baking. Don't pass on the pie.

Bayview Takeout (207-497-3301) is just over the bridge from Jonesport on Beal's Island (by the co-op). The best bet around for a lobster or crab roll, deep-fried seafood, and ice cream.

Christina Tree

BAYVIEW TAKEOUT, BEAL'S ISLAND

IN MACHIAS

((ᵖ)) **Salt Water Café** (207-255-8855), 4 Colonial Way. Open year-round, Mon.–Sat. 11–2. A spacious, window-side café in Whole Life Natural Market, with espresso bar and baked goods, also full menu including grilled panini, many veggie choices, daily soups, and specials.

🍴 🦞 **Blue Bird Ranch** (207-255-3351), Lower Main St. (Rt. 1). Open year-round for all three meals. Family-owned with a diner atmosphere and good food. Plenty of fried fish and steak choices, fresh-made chowders and seafood stews, burgers and sandwiches, pies and puddings. Fully licensed.

Skywalkers Bar & Grille (207-259-6001), 86 Main St., corner of Rt. 1, south of the Dike. Open daily 11:30 AM–1 AM. A Tex-Mex menu plus extensive cocktail and beer selections, live music Fri. and Sat. nights, open mic Wed. nights.

Riverside Take-Out (207-263-7676), 273 Main St. (Rt. 1, north of the Dike). Open 11–7, weather permitting. A local favorite for all the basics and known for its monster haddock burger, crab and lobster rolls, fried seafood, and homemade blueberry iced tea.

IN LUBEC

Uncle Kippy's Seafood Restaurant (207-733-2400), Rt. 189. Open daily 11–8. Closed Mon.; also Tue. off-season, when hours are 11–7. A local dining landmark known for steak, seafood, and the area's best pizza.

Atlantic House Coffee Shop (207-733-0906), 52 Water St. Open seasonally, daily 7–7. Check out the back deck on the water: pastries, pizza, lobster rolls, stromboli, calzones, sandwiches, 30 flavors of ice cream.

Lubec Brewing Company (207-733-4555), 41 Water St. Open 11–7 Thurs.–Sun. This new brewpub opened for business in 2015. Have a seat on their velveteen couches and try a flight of four beers for $10.

ON CAMPOBELLO ISLAND, NB

Family Fisheries (506-752-2470), Rt. 774, Wilson's Beach. Open from 11:30 through at least 8:30 daily off-season; until 10 local time (an hour later than Lubec) June–Oct. Eppy and Carol Joy employ four generations of their family, including the fishermen who supply their kitchen, the source of the island's best chowders, fish-and-chips, fried clams, chowder, and lobster—boiled outside over a wood fire, served an amazing number of ways. Eat-in or take-out, BYOB.

((ᵖ)) **Jocie's Porch** (506-752-9816), 724 Rt. 774, Welshpool. Open seasonally 7–7. Robert Calder presides at this spacious way station on Friar's Bay (Jocie is his young daughter), a good stop any time of day for fresh-roasted coffee, gluten-free pies and sweets, or soup and a sandwich. Open Mon.–Thu. 9–6, Fri. 9–7, Sat. 9–5. Closed Sun.

✳ Entertainment

MUSIC **Machias Bay Chamber Concerts** (207-255-3889), Center Street Congregational Church, Machias. A series of six chamber music concerts, July–early Aug., Tue. at 7:30 PM. Top groups such as the Kneisel Hall Chamber Players and the Vermeer Quartet are featured.

Mary Potterton Memorial Piano Concerts (summerkeys.com), Lubec Congregational Christian Church. Mid-June–Aug., Wed. at 7:30 PM. Free. Featuring SummerKeys faculty and guest artists. See *Special Programs*.

✳ Selective Shopping

ENTRIES ARE LISTED GEOGRAPHICALLY, HEADING EAST

✪ **A&M Chain Saw Sculptures** (207-546-3462), 232 Rogers Point Rd., Steuben. Arthur Smith's wooden animals are truly amazing and exhibited in widely respected galleries for many times the price that he sells them for from his roadside house-gallery. Marie Smith is responsible for painting the sculptures.

Milbridge Farmers' Market, 29 Main St. parking lot, June–Oct., Sat. 9–noon.

IN CHERRYFIELD

4 Main Street Antiques (207-546-2664), 4 Main St. Open mid-June–mid-Oct., Tue.–Sat. 10–5. Two floors, an eclectic mix including furniture, large architectural and garden items.

Cherryfield General Store (207-546-8006), 7 Main St. Open seasonally, Tue.–Sun.

Zita Leonard stocks mainly Maine-made products and local produce. Art is upstairs.

Riverlily (207-546-7666), 2 Wilson Hill Rd. (at the Rt. 1 bridge). Open May–Christmas, Tue.–Sat. 10–5. Billed as "A shop for your senses," with a wide selection of cards, scarves, Christmas ornaments, great gifts.

Catherine Hill Winery (207-546-3426; cathillwinery.com), 661 Blackwoods Rd. (Rt.182). Open Wed.–Fri. and Sun. Now with a shop in Bar Harbor, but the wine is made here and has names like "Black Fly Special."

Intervale Farm (207-546-2589; intervale blueberryfarm.com). In Cherryfield head north on Rt. 193 for 2.2 miles; it's No. 199. A family farm growing and packing certified organic wild blueberries, jam, and chutney.

ON AND OFF RT. 1

✪ **Columbia Falls Pottery** (207-483-4075 or 1-800-235-2512; columbiafallspottery.com), 150 Main St., Columbia Falls (0.5 mile off Rt. 1). Open June–Oct., daily 10–5; otherwise call ahead. Striking bright, sophisticated pottery featuring lupines and other wildflowers; custom Delft-style bird- and sea-themed tiles, lamps, and tide clocks by April Adams; sculpture by Dana McEacharn.

Wild Blueberry Land (207-483-3583), Rt. 1, Columbia Falls. The blue geodesic dome suggests a squashed blueberry and houses an assortment of berries—fried, in freshly made pies, jam, syrup, juice, frozen (will ship), and actual blueberries beyond the usual season.

Nelson Decoys Gallery and Gifts (207-497-3488), Cranberry Lane, Jonesport. Open

RIVERLILY, A BOUTIQUE IN CHERRYFIELD

May–Dec., sells prizewinning decoys, local art, and Maine-made gifts.

Downeast Quilting & Interiors (207-497-2251; downeastquilting.com), 178 Main St., Jonesport. Sarah Davis sells quilts, also makes draperies and much more.

IN MACHIAS

Note: A **Machias First Friday Art & Craft Walk** is held year-round, 5–8, first Friday of the month.

Machias Bay Antiques and Fine Art (207-255-0686), 1 Water St. Specializing in 17th-through 19th-century American furniture and decorative arts, vintage and contemporary Maine paintings.

Columbia Falls Pottery (207-255-2716), 4 Water St. Open Tue.–Sat. 10–5, less off-season. See the Columbia store for details about this shop's appealing pottery and tiles. This in-town branch showcases the work made in Columbia Falls.

✪ **Woodwind Gallery** (207-255-3727), 23 Main St. Open July–Aug., Tue.–Sun., closed Sun. off-season. Holly Gran Jackson's gallery showcases some 40 local sculptors and artists. Work includes glass, pottery, photography, paintings, and metal; art supplies too. This is also home base for the **Maine Blackfly Breeder's Association** and an info source for all things cultural in the area.

Machias Hardware Co. (207-255-6581), 25 Main St. An old-fashioned hardware store that's also an unexpected source of reasonably priced herbs and spices in 2-ounce and

APRIL ADAMS AT COLUMBIA FALLS POTTERY

WILD BLUEBERRY LAND, RT. 1, COLUMBIA FALLS

1-pound packages. Also local products like those by Look's Gourmet Food (see below).

(ɯ) **Whole Life Natural Market** (207-255-8855), 80 Main St., Machias. Open year-round; summer hours Mon.–Sat. 9–6, Sun. 10–2. Finally, a first-class market featuring organic and local produce and environmentally safe products, beauty aids, and supplements. There's also a resource/lending library and café with wireless Internet (see *Eating Out*).

Machias Valley Farmers' Market (machiasvalleyfarmersmarket.com), Rt. 1 across from Helen's Restaurant, May–Oct., Fri., Sat. 9–1.

BACK ON AND OFF RT. 1, HEADING EAST

Connie's Clay of Fundy (207-255-4574), Rt. 1, East Machias. Open year-round. Connie Harter-Bagley's combination studio-shop is filled with her distinctive glazed earthenware in deep colors. Bowls, pie plates, platters, lamps, and small essentials like garlic jars and ring boxes, also "healing spiritual jewelry."

Maine Sea Salt Company (207-255-3310; maineseasalt.com), 11 Church Lane, Marshfield, 2 miles up Rt. 192 from downtown Machias. Salt is produced in shallow pools of seawater inside greenhouses. Tours are offered daily. Open 8–6 most days, salt tastings.

Look's Gourmet Food Co. (207-259-3341 or 1-800-962-6258), Rt. 191 south of East Machias. Retail shop open year-round, weekdays 8–4. Said to be the first company to successfully can crabmeat and the first to bottle

clam juice, Look's now produces a whole line of specialty products under both the Atlantic and Bar Harbor labels.

A2Z General Store (207-259-3800), Beachwood Bay Estates, Rt. 191, Cutler. Open 10–2. This much-needed general store has opened in the former Cutler Naval Base. In addition to groceries, pizza, sandwiches, and gas, it carries local products.

IN LUBEC

✪ **Monica's Chocolates** (207-733-4500 or 1-866-952-4500; monicaschocolates.com), 100 County Rd. (Rt. 189). Open daily. Monica Elliott, a native of Peru, pioneered (so to speak) chocolate-making in Lubec, where she now creates truffles, crèmes, and bonbons with her father's special recipes.

Northern Tides Art and Gift Gallery (207-733-2500), 24 Water St., Lubec. Debra and Larry Kasunic's attractive shop features original prints, locally woven, carved, and otherwise produced art and crafted work.

Campobello Island Gift Shop (506-752-2233), Rt. 774, Welshpool. The specialty of the house is New Brunswick and Celtic folk music CDs, but there's plenty of everything else, from souvenirs (especially lighthouse stuff) to books and local crafts, especially jewelry.

CHRISTMAS WREATHS More than half of Maine's Christmas wreaths are made in Washington County. You can order in the fall and take delivery of a freshly made wreath right before Christmas. Prices quoted include delivery. **The Wreath Shoppe** (207-483-4598), Harrington (wreaths decorated with cones, berries, and reindeer moss), and **Flo's Wreaths** (1-800-321-7136; floswreaths.net), Marshfield, are a couple among dozens of purveyors. The big ones are **Whitney Wreaths** (whitneywreath.com) and **Worcester Wreaths** (www.worcesterwreath.com).

✳ Special Events

Memorial Day weekend: **Down East Birding Festival**—guided hikes, cruises, lectures (downeastbirdfest.org).

June: ♿ **Bay of Fundy International Marathon** (bayoffundymarathon.com) from

West Quoddy Lighthouse in South Lubec, across the FDR Memorial Bridge to Campobello in Canada and out to Head of Harbor Lighthouse.

Margaretta Days (margarettadays.com), held on the second Sat., celebrates Machias's role in the American Revolution with a parade, re-enactments, and more.

July: **Independence Day** celebrations in **Jonesport/Beals Island** (lobster boat races, easily viewed from the bridge); **Cherryfield** (parade and fireworks); and **Steuben** (firemen's lobster picnic and parade); **Lubec** goes all-out with a grand parade, contests, and fireworks;

Cutler and **Machias** also celebrate. Campobello celebrates **Canada Day** (July 1) in a big way. Also see the **Eastport** section for the state's biggest celebration. **Milbridge Days** (last weekend; visitmilbridge.com) includes a parade, dance, lobster dinner, and the famous codfish relay race. **Campobello** stages a five-day **Fog Fest**, end of July.

August: **Wild Blueberry Festival and Machias Craft Festival** (third weekend) in downtown Machias—concerts, food, a major crafts fair, and live entertainment.

September: **Lights Across the Border** is a day of activities at all the area's lighthouses.

Eastport and Cobscook Bay

Eastport is just 3 miles north of Lubec by boat but 43 miles by land around Cobscook Bay. That's 15 minutes via the seasonal water taxi and a good hour by car. *Cobscook* is said to mean "boiling water" in the Passamaquoddy tongue, and tremendous tides—a tidal range of more than 25 feet—boil in through this passage and slosh up deep inlets divided by ragged land fingers. In Pembroke, tides funnel through a narrows at 6 to 8 knots, alternately filling and draining the smaller bays beyond. For several hours the incoming tide actually roars through these "Cobscook Reversing Falls."

The force of the tides in Passamaquoddy Bay on Eastport's eastern and northern shores is so powerful that in the 1930s President Roosevelt backed a proposal to harness this power to electrify much of the northeast coast, including Boston. More modest attempts continue.

The sardine-canning process in Maine began in Eastport in 1875 and a boom era quickly followed, but today the population of this island "city" has dropped to below 1,400 (from more than 5,000 in 1900). Still, Eastport—which once rivaled New York in shipping—remains a "city" and a working deepwater port, the deepest on the U.S. East Coast. Large freighters regularly dock, loading cows bound for Russia and pulpwood for China. Federal-style homes here are reminders that by the War of 1812 this was already an important enough port for the British to capture and occupy it.

Today there are many gaps in the old waterfront, now riprapped in pink granite to form a walkable seawall. With its flat, haunting light, Eastport has an end-of-the-world feel and suggests an Edward Hopper painting. It's a landscape that draws artists, and there are a number of galleries along Water Street.

Eastport consists entirely of islands, principally Moose Island, which is connected to Rt. 1 by Rt. 190 via a series of causeways linking other islands. Frequently there are whales to be seen, and always there's Old Sow, a whirlpool between Eastport and Deer Island said to be the largest in the Western Hemisphere. Thanks to the extreme tides and currents, marine life is more varied than in other places. Nutrients that elsewhere settle to the bottom shoot here to the surface and nourish some forms of life that exist nowhere else. The fact that you can see only a short distance down into the water around Eastport is due not to pollution but to this rich nutrient life.

Rt. 190 runs through the center of Sipayik (pronounced *zeh-BAY-igh*), the **Pleasant Point Indian Reservation**, home to some 2,000 members of the Passamaquoddy Indian tribe. The three-day Indian Ceremonial Days in early August fully celebrate Passamaquoddy culture.

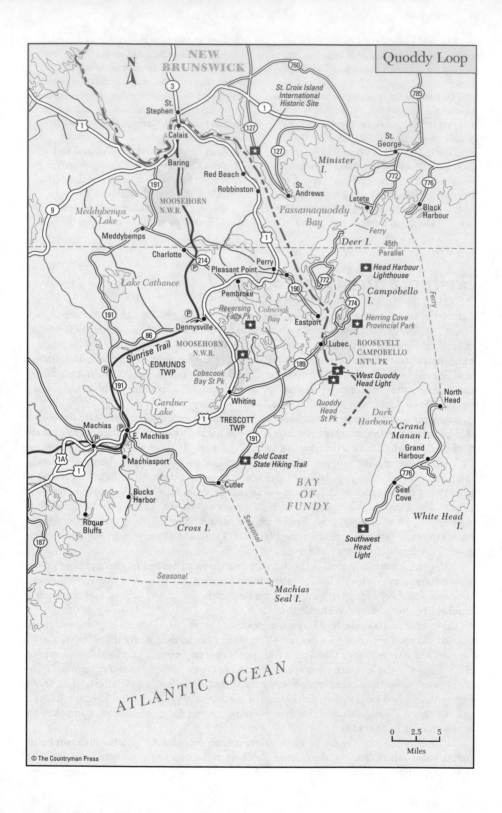

Unfortunately, the 20 miles of Rt. 1 between Whiting (turnoff for Lubec) and Perry (turnoff for Eastport) offer few glimpses of Cobscook Bay. We recommend the short detour into Cobscook Bay State Park and, time permitting, into the village of Pembroke to find your way to the Reversing Falls Park.

GUIDANCE **Eastport Chamber of Commerce** (205-853-4644; eastportchamber .net), operates a **Visitors Center** in the Eastport Port Authority Building (restrooms) at the head of the breakwater. Open daily, 9–5; manned 10–3 Memorial Day and Columbus Day weekends.

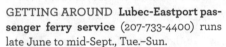

FISHERMAN STATUE, EASTPORT

GETTING AROUND **Lubec-Eastport passenger ferry service** (207-733-4400) runs late June to mid-Sept., Tue.–Sun.

East Coast Ferries Ltd. (506-747-2159 or 1-877-747-2159; eastcoastferries.ltd.com) **to Deer Island**, departing hourly late June to mid-Sept., weather permitting, from beside the Chowder House, 167 Water St., Eastport. This is a small car ferry (no reservations). See *Getting Around* in the Bold Coast introduction. It connects with the larger, free Canadian ferry to the New Brunswick mainland, not far from St. Andrews, NB.

Quoddy Loop (quoddyloop.com) describes routes circling both sides of Passamaquoddy Bay, by land and, in summer, by ferry. Check to see whether the Eastport Ferry to Deer Island is working.

Artsipelago (artsipelago.net), published by the **Tides Institute and Museum of Art** (tidesinstitute.org), is a free map/guide to cultural and specifically local sites and festivals on both sides of Passamaquoddy Bay.

EASTPORT WATERFRONT

✳ To See

○ **The Tides Institute and Museum of Art** (207-853-4047; tides.institute.org), 43 Water St., Eastport. Open seasonally Tue.–Sun. 10–4. In 2002 the city's ornate, vintage-1887 bank building came up for sale and seemed in danger of demolition. Still evolving, it's now an impressive cultural center committed to collecting and exhibiting art, photography, and archival pictures of local architecture and landscape, focusing particularly on the region surrounding Passamaquoddy Bay on both sides of the border. The institute is also committed to creating new work and has installed letterpress and printmaking facilities, offering a series of workshops. Check the website for lectures, workshops, and changing exhibits, also culturepass.net for arts events around the bay. The permanent collection is on the second floor.

✪ **Raye's Mustard Mill and Pantry** (207-853-4451 or 1-800-853-1903; rayesmustard.com), Rt. 190 (Washington St.), Eastport. Open daily 9–5 in summer, 10–4 off-season. Closed Sun. off-season. In business since 1900, this company is the country's last stone-ground mustard mill. Washington County's sardines were packed in this mustard and are sensational. Sample many varieties. Mill tours year-round, daily.

Quoddy Dam Museum, 72 Water St., Eastport, open Memorial Day–Sept., usually open daily 10–4. A 14-by-16-foot concrete model of the Passamaquoddy Tidal Power Project (see the introduction). The storefront also houses a crafts cooperative and information center. Inquire here about the nearby **Barracks Museum** (borderhistoricalsociety.com), originally part of Fort Sullivan and occupied by the British during the War of 1812.

Seawall Walk. This flowery walk runs behind the commercial blocks, from the Waco Diner to the Quoddy Tides office. Note the amphitheater, scene of seasonal concerts and happenings, including Fri.-night movies.

Waponahki Museum and Resource Center (tribal office 207-853-2600; waponahkimuseum.org), 59 Passamaquoddy Rd. off Rt. 190, Pleasant Point in the Sipayik Youth Center. Open Mon.–Thu. 1–4 and alternate Saturdays. Baskets, beaded artifacts, historical photos, and crafts.

Reversing Falls Park. Turn off Rt. 1 at Rt. 214 into the village of Pembroke; follow the slight jog in the road, then Leighton Point for 3.3 miles, and turn right onto Clarkside Cemetery Rd. (the sign may or may not be there), then left at the T. This last road turns to dirt before it ends at a parking area for a town park with two short trails to the water. Try to time your visit to coincide with the couple of hours before the height of the incoming tide, which funnels furiously through the gap between Mahar's Point and Falls Island. As the salt water flows along at 6 to 8 or more knots, it strikes a series of rocks, resulting in rapids. At low water this is a great place to hunt for fossils, and it's well worth finding anytime.

Old Sow. Billed as the largest whirlpool in the Western Hemisphere, this is 230 feet in diameter, sited between the tips of Moose and Deer Islands. It's said to be produced by 70 billion cubic feet of water rushing into Passamaquoddy Bay, much of which finds its way around the tip of Deer Island and an underwater mountain at this narrow point. The area's smaller whirlpools are called Piglets. See *Boating* for viewing.

✲ To Do

BIRDING **Moosehorn National Wildlife Refuge** (see *Green Space*) is a prime spot for spotting bald eagles. Vast tidal flats in Eastport are good places to watch migrating plovers, sandpipers, and other shorebirds. For details about the late-May **Down East Spring Birding Festival**, see downeastbirdfest.org, and for puffin-watching on Machias Seal Island see boldcoast.com.

BOATING **Eastport Windjammers** (207-853-2500; eastportwindjammers.com), 104 Water St., Eastport. Mid-June–Oct. No windjammers at this writing, but Butch Harris and his crew offer frequent seasonal lobster/whale-watching cruises.

Fundy Breeze Charters (207-853-4660), 109 Water St., Eastport. Captain Skip Harris specializes in deep-sea fishing charters.

WALKS **Shackford Head State Park** (posted from Rt. 190 near downtown Eastport) is a 90-acre peninsula with several trails including a roughly 0.7-mile path from the parking lot to a 173-foot-high headland overlooking Campobello Island and Lubec in one direction and Cobscook Bay in the other. Another 0.25-mile-long trail leads down the headland and permits access to the shore. Views are of the bay with its floating salmon pens. Look for fossils at low water.

SPECIAL LEARNING PROGRAMS **Eastport Arts Center** (see *Entertainment*) offers a variety of arts workshops ranging from outdoor painting to storytelling and soap making. **The Tides Institute** (see *To See*) offers workshops in printmaking, letterpress, and photography.

✳ Green Space

The Quoddy Regional Land Trust (207-733-5509) publishes *Cobscook Trails* (see *Green Space* in the Bold Coast subchapter).

Moosehorn National Wildlife Refuge (fws.gov/northeast/moosehorn) consists of two divisions. Trails in the first—the Baring section (Unit 1)—are maintained; see "Calais." The second division, the Edmunds, is threaded by Rt. 1 between Dennysville and Whiting. Some 7,200 acres are bounded by Whiting and Dennys Bays and the mouth of the Dennys River. North Trail Rd. is 2.5 miles long and leads to a parking area from which canoes can be launched into Hobart Stream. South Trail Rd. covers 0.9 mile and leads to a parking area for a 10-mile unmaintained trail network.

♻ **Cobscook Bay State Park** (207-726-4412), S. Edmunds Rd., just off Rt. 1 between Dennysville and Whiting. The 880-acre park includes a 2-mile nature trail with water views and a 0.5-mile Shore Trail. Wildlife and birds are plentiful. The campground is open mid-May–mid-Oct.; there are 150 campsites, most of them for tents and many with water views. It also offers a boat-launch area, picnic benches, and a hiking and cross-country ski trail. Birding is superb.

Gleason's Point State Park, Perry. On Rt. 1 look for Shore Rd., across from the New Friendly Restaurant. After a short way turn right on Gleason Cove Rd. This is a great place for walking, sunbathing, and picnics (tables provided).

✳ Lodging

IN EASTPORT 04631

INNS AND B&BS ♻ 🐾 (𝖜) **Kilby House Inn** (207-853-0989 or 1-800-853-4557; kilbyhouse inn.com), 122 Water St. Open year-round. This Queen Anne–style house is on the quiet end of the waterfront, an easy walk from shops and restaurants. The double parlor with a fireplace and grand piano invites you to sit down and read. Innkeeper Gregg Noyes's passions include playing the Estey reed organ, refinishing antiques, and sharing Eastport and Kilby family history. He clearly relishes his role as full-time innkeeper after many years of also teaching. The four pleasant antiques-furnished upstairs guest rooms (private baths) include a sunny master with a four-poster canopy bed and water view. The interior of the neighboring coach house has been crafted with a woodworker's eye to detail as well as comfort. Guests gather around the dining room table for very full breakfasts. $95–110; inquire about the carriage house.

🐾 ☀ ✒ 🚻 **Todd House** (207-853-2328), 1 Capen Ave. Open year-round. A restored and expanded 1775 Cape, the oldest house in Eastport, with water views. In 1801 men met here to charter a Masonic order, and in 1861 the house became a temporary barracks. Three large double rooms with kitchenettes, also one double room with twin beds. Our favorites are the ground-floor Cornerstone Room and the Masonic Room, with a working fireplace. Grandmotherly innkeeper Ruth McInnis presides in the living room, welcoming well-behaved children and pets; her own pets include three cockatiels. $70–110 in-season, otherwise from $50.

☘ ✐ **The Milliken House** (207-853-2955 or 1-888-507-9370; eastport-inn.com), 29 Washington St. Mary Williams is the owner of this 1840s house, which retains Victorian charm with a large double parlor, ornate detailing, and some original furniture. There are six guest rooms, all with private bath. $90–100 year-round includes a full breakfast.

The Commons (207-853-4123; thecommon seastport.com), 51 Water St., P.O. Box 255. Two second-floor, two-bedroom upscale units in a lovingly restored 1887 brick waterfront building in the walkable waterfront historic district. $770–1,150 per week.

Cobscook Property Management (207-853-6179; cobscookpm.com), based in Eastport, offers a wide selection of weekly and monthly rentals.

Note: A number of weekly cottage rentals are available; check eastportchamber.net.

✳ Where to Eat

IN EASTPORT UNLESS OTHERWISE NOTED

✪ ❀ **Quoddy Bay Lobster Co.** (207-853-6640), 7 Sea St. Open daily in-season 10–6, Sun. 11–4. It's well worth finding your way down to this fish store/eatery. The rewards are fresh fish and lobster rolls drizzled with butter, great homemade chowder and coleslaw, and fried clam rolls so thick you have to eat them with a fork. Try a grilled seared scallop roll with garlic pepper seasoning (scallops are the local specialty). This family operates four fishing boats, and both the quality and prices reflect a lack of middlemen. Picnic tables, sheltered pavilion overlooking Passamaquoddy Bay, limited seating in the fish store.

1887 Landmark Grill & Ale House (207-853-7074), 32 Water St., Eastport. Open seasonally, Thu.–Sun. for lunch and dinner, Mon., Tue. for dinner from 4. Pleasant ambiance and a menu ranging from burgers, salads, and pizzas to steak and seafood, specials.

✐ **Eastport Chowder House** (207-853-4700), 167 Water St. Open seasonally, daily 11–9. A good location on what's said to be the site of the country's first fish and sardine

cannery. The downstairs pub on Cannery Wharf is informal, and it's possible to get take-out (and thus park in line) for the ferry that departs from the adjacent beach. The restaurant is barnlike and can be noisy; the outside deck is a blessing. The reasonably priced menu runs from fried haddock and eggplant Parmesan to lobster.

Localz Tavern & Grill (207-853-2080), 33 Water St., Eastport. Open daily 11–9, bar closes later. Jim and Sherrie Wolfer try to keep things fresh, with fish tacos and chowder, home-grown burgers, local brews, and bands. Nightly specials.

WaCo Diner (207-853-4046; wacodiner .com), 47 Water St. Open year-round; 6 AM–8 PM in summer. Billed as the oldest diner in Maine, a local landmark with a great view from its Schooner Room and a deck.

✐ **The Happy Crab Downeast Grill and Sports Bar** (207-853-9400), 35 Water St. Open daily 11:30–8:30. There are two sides to this place, one family-geared with a selection of burgers, pizza, seafood baskets, and sandwiches, all made with the specially flavored house mayo. The other is a sports bar with a pool table, popular dining with a deck.

((•)) **Moose Island Bakery** (207-853-3111; mooseislandbakery.com), 75 Water St. Open year-round, 7–5. Cream puffs, carrot cakes, coffees, drinks, a great deck with water views.

((•)) **Dastardly Dick's** (207-853-2090), 62 Water St. Open 7–3 (or later); Sun. 9–1. Espressos, teas, frappés, smoothies, snacks, and sweets, a welcome gathering spot in the middle of town.

Rosie's Hot Dog Stand at the breakwater. Local institution open seasonally for decades.

✪ ❀ ✐ **The New Friendly Restaurant** (207-853-6610), Rt. 1, Perry. Open daily 11–8. Great road food. A homey restaurant with booths. Fish stews and chowders, basics like liver and onions, not-so-basics like crab salad and plenty of lobster in a lobster sandwich. Desserts include Grape-Nuts pudding as well as pies. Beer and wine served.

More Food: Part of the appeal of a vacation rental around here is the plethora of local seafood, produce, and locally produced staples; check out the **Eat Local Eastport Co-op** (207-853-7138), 49 Water St., open year-round Thu.–Sat., as well as the **Eastport Farmers' Market** (207-853-0800), 149 Water St., Sat. 11–1.

✳ Entertainment

Eastport Arts Center (207-853-5803; eastport artscenter.com), 36 Washington St., Eastport. The vintage-1837 Washington Street Baptist Church has been restored and fitted with a new heating system as home to six arts organizations, including the **Northern Lights Film Society** (Thu.-evening films at 7 on a large screen, great sound) as well as frequent performances by the **Passamaquoddy Bay Symphony Orchestra** and other concerts, performances by **Stage East** (stageeast.org), a terrific community theater, plus puppetry, and more. Check the website for the current schedule.

✳ Selective Shopping

IN DOWNTOWN EASTPORT

ART **The Commons** (207-853-4123; the commonseastport.com), 51 Water St. Open year-round; in summer, Mon.–Sat. 9–6, Sun. 1–5, otherwise Mon.–Sat. 10–6. An outstanding gallery displaying the work of more than 90 Passamaquoddy Bay area artists and artisans: botanical and wildlife paintings, fabric art, carved burl bowls, jewelry, hand-knit sweaters, wooden ware, pottery, and Passamaquoddy sweetgrass baskets.

🐚 **The Eastport Gallery** (207-853-4166; eastportgallery.com), 74 Water St. Open early June–Oct. 1, daily 10–5, Sun. noon–5. Eastport's oldest art gallery, a cooperative representing local artists.

Crow Tracks (207-853-2336; crowtracks .com), 11 Water St. Open year-round. R. J. LaVallee carves a variety of birds, whales, and fantasy figures, from decoys to Christmas ornaments.

✪ **Breakwater Gallery** (207-853-4773; eastportbreakwatergallery.com), 93 Water St. Cynthia Morse is a talented artist and her husband, Little Cranberry Island native Michael Morse, is a talented (not your traditional) bird carver. This is a serious gallery, with paintings, sculptures, much more.

SPECIAL SHOPS **Port O'Call** (207-853-0800; portocalleastport.com), 54 Water St. An

enticing shop with a great mix of cards, alpaca gifts, PJs, jewelry and bags, books and toys.

Quoddy Crafts. Sharing space with the Quoddy Dam Museum (see *To See*), a local crafts outlet worth checking out.

S. L. Wadsworth & Sons (207-853-4343; slwadsworth.com), 42–44 Water St. Opened in 1818 by Samuel Wadsworth, son of General Peleg Wadsworth and uncle of poet Henry Wadsworth Longfellow, this is billed as the country's oldest ship chandlery. It remains marine-geared but also carries hardware and "nautical gifts." Buy a rod and fish from the breakwater (you don't need a license).

Sweeties Downeast (207-853-3120; sweetiesdowneast.com), 80 Water St. Sweet!

Seaside Salts (207-853-7008), 103 Water St. These salts are mined in the foothills of the Himalayas and turned into lamps that are good for you.

ALONG RT. 1, HEADING NORTH FROM WHITING

✪ **Tide Mill Farm** (207-733-2551; tidemill farmorganicfarm.com), 91 Tide Mill Rd., Edmunds. This 200-year-old working farm on Whiting Bay and Crane Mill Stream has been in the Bell family since 1765. It is set on 1,600 acres with 6 miles of shorefront. Terry and Cathy Bell are maintaining the property as a working organic farm with Hereford cattle, chickens, pigs, and an organic dairy herd. The seventh through ninth generations raise organic produce and animals, with milk, vegetables, and eggs available in summer season. Check the website to order winter wreaths and for current open farm days and farm stand hours.

Mainely Smoked Salmon Company (207-853-4794; mainelysmokedsalmon.com), 555 South Meadow Rd., Perry. Hot and cold smoked salmon.

✪ **45th Parallel** (207-853-9500), "Halfway between the Equator and the North Pole," Rt. 1, Perry. Open seasonally. Filled from floor to 12-foot-high ceilings with an eclectic mix of gifts and home decor accents and furnishings: stained glass and antique beds, a stuffed lion, drawer pulls and lamps, jewelry, bird feeders, much more.

✳ Special Events

Memorial Day weekend: **Down East Birding Festival**—guided hikes, boat tours, presentations (downeastbirdfest.org).

July: **Independence Day** is celebrated for an entire week in Eastport, with parades, a military flyover, and fireworks. Eastport's is the first flag in the United States to be raised on July 4 at dawn (eastport4th.com).

Mid-August: **Annual Indian Ceremonial Days**, Pleasant Point Reservation—a celebration of Passamaquoddy culture climaxing with dances in full regalia (wabanaki.com).

September: **Eastport Salmon and Seafood Festival** (Labor Day weekend; eastportsalmonfest.com) celebrates Eastport's salmon industry with great food, boat tours of area fish farms, walking tours, live entertainment, games, concerts. **Eastport Pirate Festival** (eastportpiratefestival.com), a weeklong celebration climaxing the following weekend.

December: **New Year's Eve** is huge in Eastport, the first American city to welcome in the new year. A sardine slides down the pole.

Calais and the Downeast Lakes Region

Calais (pronounced *Callus*), the largest city in Washington County, is a major point of entry into the United States from Canada, just across the St. Croix River from St. Stephen, New Brunswick. The two communities are inextricably linked, celebrating a nine-day International Homecoming Festival together in August.

The city's present population is less than 3,000, far fewer than in the 1870s, when its fleet of sailing vessels numbered 176 and the brick downtown was rebuilt after a fire. The wooden residential district retains many older, handsome sailing-era houses. At the center of town the **Wabanaki Cultural Center**, showcasing the history and culture of the Passamaquoddy Nation, hidden away downstairs in the Visitors Center, is a must-see. Exhibits are drawn from the Passamaquoddy reservations north of Calais, divided between Princeton and Peter Dana Point on Big Lake.

William A. Davis

North of Calais you enter the Downeast Lakes area of Maine, seemingly as watery as anywhere along the coast and a sportsman's paradise. The village of Grand Lake Stream, a community of some 100 residents scattered along neighboring lakes, is the hub of this region. The town's namesake stream links Big Lake with West Grand Lake, which flows into Pocumcus Lake and on into Sysladobsis, with water links to Junior and Scraggly Lakes on the north and to Wabassus and Third Machias Lakes on the south. Big Lake links to Long Lake, which links to Lewy Lake, which links to Grand Falls, and so on. Fishermen are lured by landlocked salmon, lake trout, smallmouth bass, pickerel, and white perch.

The lakes are ringed by a wooded shorefront owned for more than a century by timber companies with no interest in developing them. In the 1990s, however, these companies began selling off woodland. Georgia-Pacific sold almost half a million

WABANAKI CULTURAL CENTER, CALAIS

acres surrounding the village to a holding company. A David-versus-Goliath fight ensued as residents rallied to raise funds to buy the land along the river and subsequently formed the Downeast Lakes Land Trust (downeastlakes.org), which has worked with other conservation groups to protect some 445 miles of shorefront along 60 Maine lakes and more than a million contiguous acres on both sides of the border.

The symbol of Grand Lake Stream remains the Grand Laker, an unusually long canoe with a distinctive square stern, designed to hold a small outboard motor that can be easily flipped up when the paddling gets rough or shallow. The community continues to boast the state's largest concentration of fishing guides. Its fishing lodges and camps are typically open from ice-out through hunting season. In July and August they cater to families. Inquire about hiking and guided kayaking. The Grand Lake Stream Folk Festival in late July draws visitors from far and wide.

The St. Croix River actually rises in another chain of lakes to the north and forms the boundary with Canada as it flows south 110 miles. It's one of the East's great paddling rivers.

GUIDANCE (((•))) **Maine Tourist Information Center** (207-454-2211), 39 Union St., Calais. Open year-round; June–Oct. 15, daily 8–6, otherwise 9–5:30. This center, staffed by the Maine Tourism Association, has information for all of Maine as well as the local area; public restrooms. Note the three-dimensional map of Washington County and the Passamaquoddy Bay area, the diorama of a local shipyard, and the touch tank for kids. Also **visitstcroix valley.com** and, for the **Grand Lake Stream area**, grandlakestream.org and downeast lakes.org.

GETTING THERE *By car:* The direct route to Calais from Bangor and points west of Washington County is Rt. 9, the Airline Highway. From the Machias area, take Rt. 191. The slower but more scenic **Bold Coast Byway** (boldcoastbyway.com) follows Rt. 1.

CROSSING THE BORDER See the "Way Downeast" introduction. *Note*: If the crossing in the middle of town is backed up, there are two alternatives: Rt. 1 north of town and the Milltown crossing.

✱ To See

Wabanaki Cultural Center (207-454-2126), 39 Union St., Calais. Open daily, same hours as the Maine Tourist Information Center (it's downstairs). Created in 2004 to celebrate the 400th anniversary of the settling of nearby St. Croix Island, the first European settlement north of Florida, but focused on telling the story Maine's native tribes. The numerous exhibits are about the local Passamaquoddy tribe and include a vintage 1872 canoe, exquisite basketry, and more.

St. Croix International Historic Site Overlook, Rt. 1, 8 miles south of Calais in Red Beach. A **visitors center** (restrooms) is open mid-May–Columbus Day weekend, 9–4:30 (closed Tue.–Wed. through June). The island itself is a ways offshore. A path leads to a bronze replica of the settlement. Along the way you encounter half a dozen haunting, life-sized bronze statues, here an elaborately dressed Frenchman, there a young Passamaquoddy girl. The French expedition came for the fur trade, and its leader, Pierre Dugua, Sieur de Monts, retained Samuel de Champlain as his mapmaker and chronicler. They chose a 6½-acre island for their settlement in June 1604 and set about building a storehouse and dwellings, despite the black flies. The waters teemed with fish, and the Native inhabitants were friendly—but the first snow came in early October, the river froze, and 35 of the 79 settlers died. Finally, on June 15, supply vessels arrived, and Dugua sailed eventually to Port Royal, Nova Scotia, seeding French culture in Canada.

Dr. Holmes Cottage/Museum (stcroixhistorical.com), 527 Main St. Open July through mid-Aug. The oldest existing house in Calais, restored to its 1850 look. Pick up a *Walking Tour Guide to the Calais Residential Historic District,* which includes several Gothic Revival gingerbread houses on S. Main St.

Whitlock Mills Lighthouse. The northeastern-most lighthouse in the country is best viewed from the Pike Woods Rest Area on Rt. 1, 3 miles south of Calais.

✳ To Do

BIRDING **Moosehorn National Wildlife Refuge** is a prime birding center with some 190 species recorded, as well as resident bald eagles (see *Green Space*).

FISHING The Downeast Lakes are famed for their abundance of landlocked salmon, square-tailed trout, and some of the finest smallmouth bass fishing in Maine. Best May–mid-June. When ice is out in spring, trolling starts on **West Grand Lake, Big Lake**, and **Pocumcus Lake. Grand Lake Stream** itself, fast-flowing water linking West Grand and Big Lakes, is one of the country's premier fly-fishing spots for landlocked salmon. Fishing licenses covering three days to a full season (also necessary for ice fishing) are available, along with lodging and supplies, in the village of Grand Lake Stream (**grandlakestream .org**), the focal point of the region and base for the state's largest concentration of fishing guides (**grandlakestreamguides.com**). Princeton, on the way to Grand Lake Stream, also offers access to Big Lake and Grand Falls Lake. Both once ran freely into the St. Croix River, but thanks to a series of 19th-century industrial dams they're now known for their shallows and flowage, great for trout as well as moose-watching and canoeing. Within **Moosehorn National Wildlife Refuge** (see *Green Space*), several lakes and streams are open for fishing.

GOLF **St. Croix Country Club** (207-454-8875), River Rd., Calais. A tricky nine-hole course on the banks of the St. Croix River.

PADDLING **Cobscook Hikes & Paddles** (207-726-4776; off-season, 207-454-2130). Registered Maine Guides Stephen and Tess Forek, based in Robbinston, offer guided two- and three-hour kayaking paddles from Whiting to Calais. Also see *Lodging* entries for Princeton and Grand Lake Stream; all fishing camps offer boat rentals.

OUTDOOR PROGRAMS **Washington County Community College** (207-454-1060), 1 College Dr., Calais. Year-round programs open to the public: hiking, kayaking, camping, cross-country skiing; inside climbing wall also available.

SWIMMING **Red Beach** on the St. Croix River is named for the sand on these strands: pulverized deep red granite. There is also swimming in dozens of crystal-clear lakes. Round Pond in Charlotte has a free beach and boat launch. North of Calais, follow the Charlotte Rd. 8 miles to the pond.

✳ Green Space

Moosehorn National Wildlife Refuge (207-454-7161; moosehorn.fws.gov). This area is the northeast end of a chain of wildlife and migratory bird refuges extending from Florida to Maine and managed by the U.S. Fish and Wildlife Service. The 23,000-acre refuge is divided into two sections some 20 miles apart. The larger, 17,200-acre area is in Baring, 5 miles north of Calais on Rt. 1. Look for eagles, which nest each spring at the intersection of Char-lotte Rd. and Rt. 1. The Edmunds Division is found by heading south on Rt. 1 from Calais, between Dennysville and Whiting (see "Eastport"). This 7,200-acre area lies on the border of the tidal waters of Cobscook Bay. Volunteer-dependent programs—guided hikes, bike tours, and van tours, which sometimes take you down roads you wouldn't be able to explore on your own—are offered late June–Aug.

Downeast Lakes (downeastlakes.org). Evolving preservation efforts safeguard some 370,000 forested acres, one of the largest wilderness areas in the East (see the introduction to this section). It's best explored by canoe or kayak with a guide (readily available at local lodging places), but there are also trails (see *Walks*, below). Look for loons, bald eagles, herons, ruffed grouse, and many kinds of warblers as well as fish.

WALKS

IN THE CALAIS AREA

Calais Waterfront Walkway. A 1.5-mile path follows a former railbed along the river, begin-ning at city landing parking lot. It's the northern terminus of the East Coast Greenway, with land from Key West, FL, embedded in it (there's a piece of Red Beach granite embedded at the Key West end). A good venue from which to appreciate the daily 25-foot tidal changes.

Devil's Head. A trail leads to a promontory, said to be the highest point east of Cadillac Mountain; great views. Look for the sign on Rt. 1 south of Heslin's Motel.

DOWNEAST LAKES (DOWNESASTLAKES.ORG)

Little Mayberry Trail begins in the village of Grand Lake Stream and runs some 2.5 miles along the western shore of West Grand Lake. **Pocumcus Lake Trail** offers a choice of 1.3- or 3.6-mile loops to the shoreline. Look for the trailhead 7.5 miles west of Grand Lake Stream. This is a rough footpath. Hikers can expect to hear vireos, thrushes, and warblers as well as loons. Watch for bear and moose. **Wabassus Mountain Trail** is a 1-mile, moderately steep path which climbs to the summit following a small brook, with views of surrounding lakes. The trailhead (yellow blazes) is on Wabassus Mountain Rd.

Little Mayberry Cove Trail begins at the Grand Lake Stream dam and runs 2.5 miles along the lake. Follow yellow blazes.

✳ Lodging

IN THE CALAIS AREA

✪ **Greystone Bed & Breakfast** (207-454-2848; greystonecalaisme.com), 13 Calais Ave. This 1840s Greek Revival mansion is set back on a quiet street, within walking distance of downtown shops. Alan and Candace Dwelley offer two attractive upstairs guest rooms with private bath and TV; common space includes a double parlor with black marble fireplace mantels and Corinthian columns separating the two rooms. Breakfast is served at 8 at the dining room table. $95 ($130 for a two-room family suite with shared bath) includes break-fast; $89 off-season.

🐾 ⚯ (ʻɪʻ) **The International Motel** (207-454-7515 or 1-800-336-7515; theinternational motel.com), 626 Main St. The best lodging views in town are from the 19 Riverview units in this 61-unit motel owned and operated by three generations of the Thomas family. From $75, $80 per couple for water views, more for efficiency units with whirlpool tubs. Dogs accepted but not in Riverview rooms. Meals are next door at the Wickachee (see *Eating Out*).

🐾 ⚯ **Calais Motor Inn** (1-800-439-5531; calaismotorinn.com), 663 Main St. A friendly, locally owned 70-unit motel with a licensed restaurant (see *Where to Eat*). $79 per couple in-season, from $59 off-season.

Bellmard Inn (207-796-2261), 86 Main St. (Rt. 1), Princeton 04668. This big, rambling

ST. ANDREWS, NEW BRUNSWICK

During the 1890s the Maine towns along Passamaquoddy Bay were all about sardine fishing and canning. The summer hotels—attracting as many Americans as Canadians—were on Campobello Island and on the New Brunswick mainland at St. Andrews. The canneries and most of the hotels are long gone now, but the grand old *Algonquin Resort* sits enthroned like a queen mother above St. Andrews.

Street names like Queen, King, and Princess Royal date to the town's 1783 founding by American colonists who so strongly opposed breaking with the mother country that they left the new United States . . . and settled in what they thought was Canada, only to find out when the border was finally determined that they were actually in Maine! Loyally they moved again and an appreciative British government responded by granting them a superb site. British army engineers dug wells, built a dock, constructed a fort, and laid out the town on its present grid. Each loyalist family was also given a house lot twice the usual size. The result is an unusually gracious-looking town. The focal point remains Market Wharf, where the first settlers stepped ashore—now the cluster point for outfitters offering whale-watching, sailing, and kayaking tours—and Water Street, lined with shops.

St. Andrews is the Bar Harbor of New Brunswick, but with distinctly Anglo-Canadian attractions like the *Kingsbrae Horticultural Garden* (506-529-3335; kingsbraegarden.com) a 27-acre floral extravaganza. Built on the grounds of several long-gone estates, it weaves long-standing cedar hedges, flower beds, and old-growth forest into magnificent designs. There are display gardens with rare and native plants, a fantasy garden with animals made from moss, demonstration gardens, a woodland trail through the old-growth forest, a therapy garden, bird and butterfly gardens, and much more. Housed in the original manor home, the gracious art-hung *café* is a pleasant place for lunch and afternoon tea. Come evening it's Savour in the Garden (506-529-4055; chefalexhaun. com), set for fine dining (by reservation) with white-clothed tables, candles reflected in the long windows. and delicacies prepared by celebrated Chef Alex Haun. Wednesdays are Pump Nights: light menu, patio dining, and live music

St. Andrew's grandest surviving estate is **Ministers Island Historic Site** (506-529-5081; ministersisland.net), built around 1890 on an island accessed by a "tidal road" at low tide; otherwise by shuttle boat or kayak. Built for Sir William Van Horne, the driving force in construction of the Canadian Pacific Railway, the 50-room mansion has 17 bedrooms, a vast drawing room, a bathhouse, and a gigantic livestock barn.

Be sure to visit *Huntsman Marine Science Centre* (506-529-1200; huntsman marine.ca), Lower Campus Rd. (off Rt. 127), a nonprofit aquaculture and research center that showcases the bay's sea creatures, big and small. It features a 20,000-square-foot aquarium and a display dramatizing the magnitude of the Fundy tides. **Ross Memorial Museum** (506-520-5124; rossmemorial-museum.ca), an 1824 mansion at King and Montague Streets, displays an exceptionally fine decorative art collection.

Christina Tree

THE ALGONQUIN RESORT IS ONE OF NORTH AMERICA'S GREATEST HOTELS

KINGSBRAE

St. Andrews is a true resort town. The 18-hole, waterside **Algonquin Resort Golf Course** (algonquinresort.com) is legendary. The other big draw is whale watching in Passamaquoddy Bay and beyond via fast hurricane boats (fundytiderunners.com), traditional tours, and sailing vessels (jolly breeze.com). You can also *kayak or canoe* (easternoutdoors.com) and swim in relatively warm water at Katy's Cove (506-529-3433).

Open year-round, **The Algonquin Resort** (506-529-8823; in the U.S., 1-855-529-8693; algonquinresort.com) is the last of the truly grand 19th-century coastal resorts in northeastern America. The 233-room (including suites), Tudor-style hotel is staffed in summer by about 200 employees—some in kilts. Amenities include tennis courts and an outdoor pool. The hotel was recently totally renovated, and new amenities include an indoor water slide, full spa, and a fitness center. Rack rates from $189.

Other St. Andrews lodging options include **Kingsbrae Arms Relais & Chateaux** (506-529-1897; kingsbrae.com), a luxurious 1897 shingled mansion adjoining Kingsbrae Gardens, and the **Treadwell Inn** (1-888-529-1011; treadwellinn.com) and **St. Andrews Motor Inn** (506-529-4571; st.andrewsmotorinn.com), both on Water St. overlooking the bay.

Rossmount Inn (506-529-3351; rossmountinn.com), east of town, is a boxy three-story hilltop period piece with 18 charmingly furnished rooms, a swimming pool, and walking trails up Chamcook Mountain, the highest point on this side of Passamaquoddy Bay. Thanks to Swiss-born and -trained chef-owner Chris Aerni, the many-windowed dining room is the premier place to dine. Another favorite is **Niger Reef Tea House** (506-529-8005; nigerreefteahouse.com), 1 Joe's Point Rd. Good for either lunch or dinner, it occupies a 1926 waterside summer cottage that served for many years as a meetinghouse for the Daughters of the Empire, local equivalent of the Daughters of the American Revolution.

The **St. Andrews Blockhouse** (506-529-4270), erected during the War of 1812, is in neighboring Centennial Park. Last but not least, the town's best WiFi and caffeine source is **Honeybeans** (506-529-4888), 157 Water St. Open year-round, Mon.–Sat. 7:30–6. Serious teas as well as locally roasted beans. Angela and Matthew Honey also serve up scones and other fresh-baked treats.

Christina Tree

THE ROSSMOUNT INN OFFERS LEGENDARY FINE DINING

19th-century house, a tourist home since 1951, is now a bed & breakfast run by Andrea Smith and Doug Clements. Guests share the dining room and sitting room; there's one guest room on the ground floor, four on the second, both shared and private baths. From $40 for one person, $50 double with private bath. Add $11 for full breakfast, $22 for dinner.

IN GRAND LAKE STREAM 04637

Leen's Lodge (207-796-2929 or 1-800-995-3367; leenslodge.com). Open May–Oct. This traditional sporting camp faces West Grand Lake. According to guide and owner Charles Driza, this area represents the best woodcock hunting in the United States. July and Aug. are family season, a good time just to fish, kick back, and relax by the lake. Lights are doused by 9 PM, the better to see the amazing sky. The nine cabins (50 beds) are scattered along the wooded shore, ranging in size from one to eight bedrooms, each with a full bath, fireplace or Franklin stove (with gas heat as a backup), and fridge. The dining room overlooks the water. The Tannery, a pine-paneled gathering space with a picture window, is equipped with games, books, and a TV. BYOB. $150 per person per day double occupancy, $180 per person single occupancy includes all meals. Less in spring and fall. Cabin rentals (no meals) also offered; boat rentals and guide service are extra.

✪ 🦌 🐾 ♪ (📶) **Grand Lake Lodge** (207-796-5584; grandlakelodgemaine.com), P.O. Box 8. Open from ice-out to Oct. 20. Six classic Maine camp-style, well-equipped housekeeping cottages are nestled under the pines on the shore of West Grand Lake, just above the headwaters of Grand Lake Stream. Each is different (some with lofts), but all have electric heat, good showers, and screened porches from which to take in the expanse of lake and listen to the loons. Chris and Lindsay Wheaton welcome guests on the big sun porch, equipped with rockers and a computer. Fishing/hunting licenses and guides, boats and bikes are available. We weathered a hurricane comfortably in Cabin 1 (it sleeps seven). $50 single, $45 per person for two or more, half price under 12 years. $500–725 per week in July and Aug.

🐾 ♪ **Chet's Camps** (207-796-5557; chetscamps.com), 140 Chet's Camp Rd. Open late Apr.–Nov. deer season. Al and Sue Le Plante's lakeside cabins and a central lodge overlook Big Lake. They serve as a base for fly-fishing workshops and canoe expeditions as well as laid-back family vacations. Cabins can accommodate four to 10 people, each with a screened porch and dock. They can be booked on a housekeeping basis ($55 per person, minimum $165) with meals available. Inquire about guided backcountry canoe trips, flat- and whitewater canoeing and kayaking workshops, boats, licenses, and guides.

🐾 ♪ **The Pines** (207-557-7463; off-season, 207-825-4431; thepineslodge.com), P.O. Box 158. Open May 15–Oct. 1. Twelve miles and a century in atmosphere away from Grand Lake Stream on Lake Sysladobsis, part of the Grand Lake Stream chain. It's the oldest sporting camp in the area; past guests include Andrew Carnegie and Calvin Coolidge. There are five cabins, also two housekeeping cottages on small islands. The oldest cabin dates to 1883 and the large, double-porched white clapboard house, to 1884. The cabins are heated by woodstoves and have gas lights and a chemical toilet. The main house (which offers flush toilets) and bathhouse are electrified. Cabins are $95 per person per night with three meals, including a packed lunch, $75 for children 3–10. Housekeeping cottages are $700 per week for four or less, $172 per day. Steve and Nancy Norris have managed The Pines for the past 25 years.

🐾 ♪ ♿ **Weatherby's** (207-796-5558; in winter 207-926-5598; weatherbys.com), open early May–Nov. Fly-fishing is what this place is about. Jeff McEvoy and Elizabeth Rankin are the owners of this historic sporting camp, a rambling white 1870s lodge surrounded by 15 cottages, each with screened porches, a bath, and a Franklin stove or fireplace. In high season $189 per person double occupancy (family rates available) includes three meals. Motorboats are $50 per day; a guide begins at $300 for two people. Inquire about scheduled fly-fishing schools for novices and women as well as pros. Pets are $10 per day. Kayaks and canoes available. Housekeeping plans from $180 per day.

WHERE TO EAT Z Crumbs Café & Bake Shoppe (207-454-8996), 257 Main St., Calais. Open 7:30–7 Tue.–Fri., 9–5 Mon. An inviting café with varied seating, homemade soups and chowders, a wide choice of paninis, several kinds of grilled cheese, as well as sandwiches and pastries, all breads baked from scratch on site.

✦ **Wickachee** (207-454-3400), 282 Main St. (Rt. 1), Calais. Open year-round 6 AM–10 PM. Steak and seafood, a big salad bar, specials. Spacious, clean, and friendly.

Nino's, Calais Motor Inn Restaurant (207-454-7111), 293 Main St. (Rt. 1), Calais. Open for lunch and dinner. A large, comfortable dining room, known for steak and seafood.

❊ Selective Shopping

✪ **Calais Bookshop** (207-454-1110), 405 Main St., Calais. This is Washington County's only genuine bookstore and it's a treasure. Carol Heinlein stocks new, used, and rare titles and serves a wide circle of loyal patrons. Maine titles make this a destination for far and near, but so does the pile of well-chosen novels, both current and classic.

Urban Moose (207-454-8277), corner of North and Main Sts., Calais. Open May–Dec. An enticing, smaller version of the owner's 45th Parallel, south on Rt. 1 in Perry.

Marden's (207-454-1421), 189 Main St. and Rt. 1, Calais. Two representatives of the chain of Maine discount centers, which has been doing business in the state since 1964. Big-time bargains can be found here, from furniture to fabrics, housewares to clothing.

Pine Tree Store (207-796-5027), Water St., Grand Lake Stream. Open year-round, 6 AM–8 PM. Leslie Severance and Brinda Leighton offer one of the largest selections of fishing flies in Maine; also tackle, clothing, hunting and fishing licenses, groceries, a selection of wines, plus pizza and full menu, eat-in as well as take-out.

Christina Tree

PINE TREE STORE, GRAND LAKE STREAM

❊ Special Events

Last weekend of July: **Grand Lake Stream Folk Art Festival**—bluegrass and folk music, woodsmen's skills demonstrations featuring canoe building, crafts, dinner cooked by Maine Guides. See **downeastlakes.org** for lectures and other events in Grand Lake Stream throughout the summer.

August: **International Festival**, Calais and St. Stephen, NB—a week of events on both sides of the border, including pageants, a parade, entertainment, and more.

GRAND MANAN (NEW BRUNSWICK)

Grand Manan (grandmanannb.com) is Canada's southernmost island, far enough at sea to be very much its own place, a rugged outpost at the mouth of the Bay of Fundy.

Right whales, the rarest of whales, gather offshore in summer months, feeding on krill and other nutrients in the tide-churned waters. Some 360 species of birds have been identified on the island itself. Birders find their way along 45 miles of hiking trails that in many places hug cliffs varying from 100 to almost 400 feet. From mid-June to early Aug. Seal Cove is also departure point for tours to see puffins up close on Machias Seal Island (seawatchtours .com; 1-877-662-8552).

Fishing boats line Grand Manan wharves the way they used to in New England. The hundreds of herring smokehouses for which the island was known are long gone, but salmon farming remains big, along with harvesting lobster and clams, periwinkles, and that Grand Manan delicacy: dulse (rolandsdulse.com), a mineral-rich seaweed that's sold worldwide.

The island's population (2,460) clusters in the sheltered harbors and coves along its gentle Bay of Fundy shore. In contrast, the northern and southern "heads" of the island are soaring cliffs, and the western shore is a mirror image of Maine's Bold Coast, clearly visible 10 miles offshore from Dark Harbour. Trails and boats lead to isolated beaches and coves.

Grand Manan is all about getting out and enjoying the island's rare beauty, which you don't see by simply driving the 15-mile length of grandiosely numbered Rt. 776, the island's one main road. Begin by visiting the Swallowtail Light in North Head and be sure to walk the spectacular cliff paths at Southwest Head Light. Take a kayak or a whale-watch tour.

Grand Manan remains as out-of-the-way and unspoiled as it was during the 20 summers (1922–42) that Willa Cather spent here, working on some of her most famous novels, including *Death Comes for the Archbishop*. Her beautiful cottage at Whale Cove (whalecovecottages.ca) remains much the way she knew it. The novelist's typewriter and desk are in The Grand Manan Museum (506-662-3524; grandmananmuseum.ca), which also showcases one man's collection of more than 300 mounted birds and documents the island's smoked herring industry in paintings, photographs, memorabilia, and much more.

Coastal Transport (506-662-3724; coastaltransport.ca) operates ferries on the 20-mile sail between Blacks Harbour (35 miles from Calais, ME) and the mainland. Car ferries run year-round, every two hours beginning at 7:30 AM in high season. Plenty of comfortable seating, food, and computer plug-ins plus WiFi. Roundtrip reservations are strongly advised for vehicles. Pedestrians and bicyclists have no problem getting on, and for an overnight you might not want to leave your car parked (free) in the ferry lot. Whale-watching and sea-kayaking tours, and rental bikes within walking distance of the ferry terminal in North Head. The Compass Rose (compassroseinn.com) is a gem of an inn within walking distance of the ferry, and the Marathon Inn (marathoninn.com) is also in North Head. A car, however, is essential for longer stays. There's camping at The Anchorage Provincial Park (1-800-561-0123) and at Hole in the Wall Park & Campground (1-866-662-4489; grandmanancamping.com).

GUIDANCE The Grand Manan Tourism Association maintains a seasonal information center at 130 Rt. 776 in North Head. It also publishes *Grand Manan Trails* and *Grand Manan Guide*, available in most island stores. The island website is excellent.

Note: Prices are in Canadian dollars.

WESTERN MOUNTAINS AND LAKES REGION

∎

SEBAGO AND LONG LAKES REGION

OXFORD HILLS AND LEWISTON/
AUBURN

BETHEL AREA

RANGELEY LAKES REGION

SUGARLOAF AND THE
CARRABASSETT VALLEY

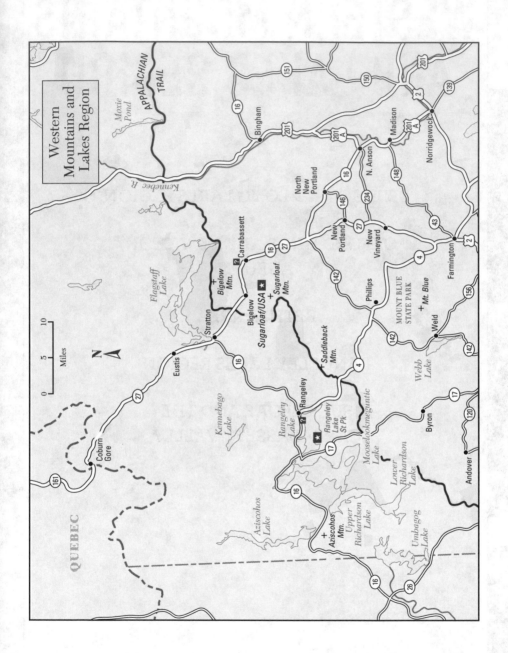

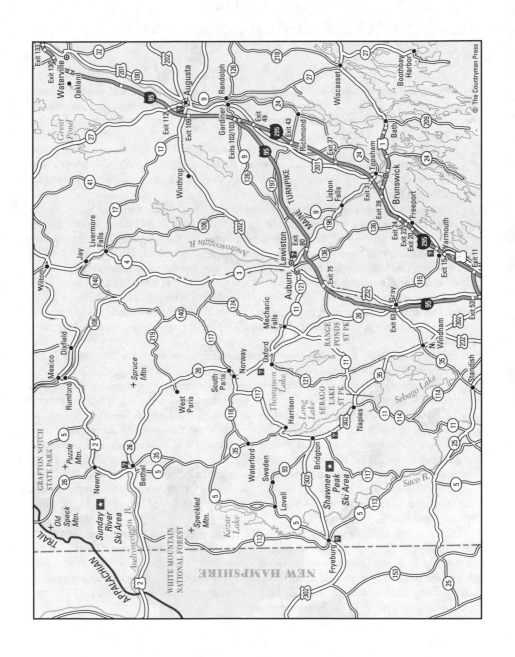

WESTERN MOUNTAINS AND LAKES REGION

Larger than Vermont and New Hampshire combined, inland Maine is composed of several distinct and unique regions and distinguished by a series of almost continuous mountain ranges, more extensive than New Hampshire's White Mountains and higher than Vermont's Green Mountains.

In contrast to the coast, inland Maine was actually more of a resort area a century ago than it is today. By the 1880s trains connected Philadelphia, New York, and Boston with large resort hotels in Rangeley and Greenville, and steamboats ferried "sports" to "sporting camps" in the far corners of lakes.

Today inland Maine seems even larger than it is because almost a third of it lies beyond the public highway system, a phenomenon for which we can blame Massachusetts and its insistence that Maine sell off the "unorganized townships" (and divide the profits) before it would be permitted to secede in 1820. In the interim most of this land has been owned and managed by lumber and paper companies. Debate currently rages about the future of these woodlands (somewhere between a third and almost half of inland Maine); many environmental organizations would like to see a Maine North Woods National Park, but locals remain adamantly against such an initiative. The reality of the way public roads run—and don't run—continues to physically divide Maine's mountainous interior into several distinct pieces.

One of these pieces is the Western Mountains and Lakes Region, extending from the rural farmland surrounding the lakes of southwestern Maine, up through the Oxford Hills and into the foothills of the White Mountains and the Mahoosuc Range around Bethel, then on into the wilderness (as high and remote as any to be found in the North Woods) around the Rangeley Lakes and the Sugarloaf area—east of which public roads cease, forcing traffic bound for the Moosehead Lake region to detour south into the Lower Kennebec Valley.

The five distinct areas within the Western Mountains and Lakes Region are connected by some of Maine's most scenic roads. Many of these views are not generally appreciated because the area is best known to skiers, accustomed to racing up to Sunday River and Sugarloaf (Maine's most popular ski resorts) by the shortest routes from the interstate. But the roads around Rangeley offer views so spectacular, stretches of two of them (Rts. 4 and 17) are a National Scenic Byway.

In summer and fall we suggest following Rt. 113 through Evans Notch or heading north from Bridgton to Bethel by the series of roads that threads woods and skirts lakes, heading east along Rt. 2, continuing north to Rangeley via Rt. 17 through Coos Canyon and over the spectacular Height o' Land from which you can see all five Rangeley Lakes and the surrounding mountains. From Rangeley it's just another 19 scenic miles on Rt. 16 (better known as Moose Alley) to the Sugarloaf area.

SEBAGO AND LONG LAKES REGION

Fifty lakes can be seen from the summit of Pleasant Mountain, 10 within the town of Bridgton itself. These lakes are what draw summer visitors, who swim and fish, fish and swim, cruise out in powerboats, or paddle canoes and kayaks. On rainy days they browse through the area's abundant antiques and crafts stores. In winter visitors ski, downhill at Shawnee Peak (alias Pleasant Mountain) or cross-country almost anywhere.

Before the Civil War visitors could actually come by boat all the way to Bridgton from Boston. From Portland, they would ride 20 miles through 28 locks on the Cumberland & Oxford Canal, then across Sebago Lake, up the Songo River, Brandy Pond, and Long Lake to Bridgton. The first hotel atop Pleasant Mountain opened in 1850, and in 1882 the "2-footer" narrow gauge opened between Hiram and Bridgton, enabling summer visitors to come by train as well.

The Naples Causeway is the base for water sports and the departure point for cruises on Long Lake and through the only surviving canal lock. Sebago, Maine's second largest lake, is its most popular waterskiing area. But this southwestern corner of the state offers hiking, golf, tennis, mineral collecting, and such fascinating historic sites as Willowbrook in Newfield.

Fryeburg, just west of the lakes in the Saco River Valley, is the site of the state's largest agricultural fair. It is also headquarters for canoeing the Saco River. Sandy-bottomed and clear, the Saco meanders for more than 40 miles through woods and fields, rarely passing a house. There is usually just enough current to nudge along the limpest paddler, and the ubiquitous sandbars serve as gentle bumpers. Outfitters rent canoes and provide shuttle service.

In summer most families come for a week to stay in lakeside cottages—of which there seem to be thousands. Motels, inns, and B&Bs fill on weekends with parents visiting their children at camps—of which there seem to be hundreds. As more travelers discover the beauty and tranquility of the region, the number of these types of lodgings is expanding every year.

GUIDANCE **Greater Bridgton Lakes Region Chamber of Commerce** (207-647-3472; mainelakeschamber.com), 101 Portland Rd. (Rt. 302), P.O. Box 236, Bridgton 04009. The chamber maintains a walk-in information center.

Sebago Lakes Region Chamber of Commerce (207-892-8265; sebagolakeschamber .com), 747 Roosevelt Trail (Rt. 302), Windham 04062, is open year-round (call for hours); there's also a seasonal information bureau next to the Naples Village green on Rt. 302. The chamber publishes an information guide that covers the towns of Casco, Gray, Naples, Raymond, Sebago, Standish, Limerick, Limington, New Gloucester, and Windham.

Cornish Association of Businesses (207-625-8083; cornish-maine.org), P.O. Box 573, Cornish 04020. The website lists lodging, dining, shopping, and events, and relates the history of the town.

Fryeburg Information Center (207-935-3639; mainetourism.com), Rt. 302, Fryeburg 04037. The Maine Tourism Association staffs this spacious facility with AC and restrooms 500 feet from the New Hampshire line. Information on the entire state, with directions to every destination.

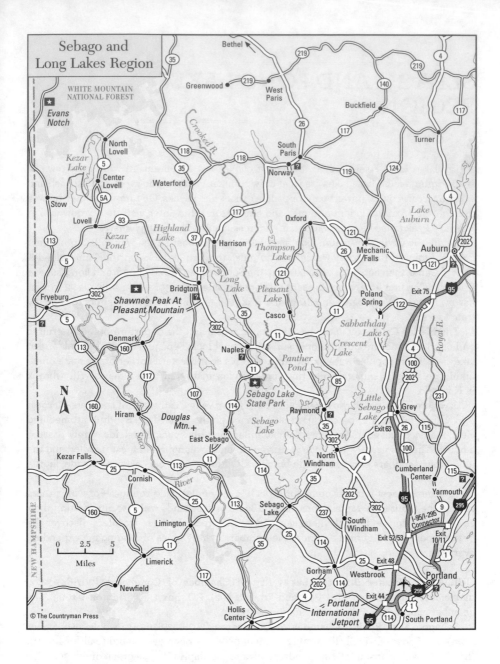

Sebago and Long Lakes Region

© The Countryman Press

GETTING THERE *By air:* The **Portland International Jetport** is a 30- to 60-minute drive from most points in this area.

By bus and train: **Concord Coach Lines** (207-828-1151 or 1-800-639-3317; concordcoach lines.com) bus lines and **Amtrak's Downeaster** (1-800-USA-RAIL; amtrak.com) serve the Portland area at its rail–bus station on Congress St. in Portland.

By car: From New York and Boston, take I-95 to the Westbrook exit (Exit 48), then Rt. 302 to the lakes region. For Newfield and south of Sebago area, take Rt. 25 from I-95 at Westbrook (Exit 48).

WHEN TO COME With some inns and B&Bs open year-round and good cross-country skiing available, this can be a place for a winter retreat. Ice fishing is another winter pastime some people love. Still, the big time is summer.

✳ Villages

Bridgton has a plethora of antiques shops, making it a good way stop for browsers. Take time for a lovely hike on the trails newly developed inside Pondicherry Park (described under *Green Space*).

Cornish. The colonial and Victorian homes lining Main and Maple Sts. were moved here by teams of about 80 oxen in the 1850s after the arrival of a new stagecoach route. It's halfway between Portland and the Mount Washington Valley in New Hampshire.

Fryeburg is an interesting town that sees its share of traffic as travelers pass through en route to North Conway, NH, and the White Mountains. The traffic clog during the Fryeburg Fair (Maine's largest, most popular agricultural fair) can back up for more than an hour. Canoe trips down the Saco originate here.

✳ To See

MUSEUMS 19th Century Willowbrook Village (207-793-2784; willowbrookmuseum.org), off Rt. 11, Newfield. Open Memorial Day–Columbus Day, Thu.–Mon. 10–5. Admission $15 adults, $12 seniors; student discount. Devastated by fire in 1947, the village was almost a ghost town when Donald King began buying buildings in the 1960s. The complex now includes 20 buildings displaying more than 10,000 items: horse-drawn vehicles, tools, toys,

Nancy English

THE LIMINGTON RAPIDS

a vintage-1894 carousel, and many other artifacts of late-19th-century life. Linger in the ballroom, ring the schoolhouse bell, or picnic in the area provided.

Rufus Porter Museum (207-647-2828; rufusportermuseum.org), 67 N. High St. (Rt. 302), Bridgton (but see the end of this description). Open mid-June–mid-Oct., noon–4 Wed.–Sat. $8 adults, $7 seniors, 15 and under free. Dedicated to Rufus Porter, a multitalented man, this house contains his 1828 original murals, an icon of folk art. Porter founded the *Scientific American* magazine and invented the Colt revolver; he patented a churn, corn sheller, fire alarm, and cheese press, among many other inventions, and in his spare time he painted murals in homes all over New England. A signed set of murals from Westwood, MA, can be seen (by appointment only) in the historic Wales and Hamblen building, renovated in 2007, 260 Main St., Bridgton. The museum will move to 121 Main St. once renovations are complete; call or visit the website for up-to-date information.

HISTORIC BUILDINGS AND MUSEUMS Daniel Marrett House (207-882-7169; historic newengland.org), Rt. 25, Standish. Tours on the first and third Sat. of the month beginning at 11, June–mid-Oct. Admission charged; colonial garden free. Money from Portland banks was stored in this Georgian mansion for safekeeping during the War of 1812. Built in 1789, it remained in the Marrett family until 1944; architecture and furnishings reflect the changing styles over 150 years.

Narramissic (207-647-9954, summer only), Ingalls Rd. (2 miles south of the junction of Rts. 107 and 117), Bridgton. Open late June–Labor Day. Donation suggested. A Federal-period home and a Temperance Barn in a rural setting, this interesting site includes a working blacksmith shop and is the scene of frequent special events; check with the **Bridgton Historical Society Museum** (207-647-3699; bridgtonhistory.org), Gibbs Ave., which also maintains a former fire station built in 1902. The collection (open July and Aug., call for hours) includes slide images of the old narrow-gauge railroad.

Naples Historical Society Museum (207-693-4297), village green, Rt. 302, Naples. Open summer weekends and by chance. The brick complex includes a rooftop brake coach and great memorabilia on the Cumberland & Oxford Canal, photos of and information on the Sebago and Long Lake steamboats and the Songo Locks, and artifacts from vanished hotels, like the Bay of Naples Hotel.

Hopalong Cassidy in the Fryeburg Public Library (207-935-2731), 98 Main St., Fryeburg. Open Mon.–Thu. 8–5, Sat. 9–noon. The library is housed in an 1832 stone schoolhouse and is decorated with many paintings by local artists. It also contains a collection of books, guns, and other memorabilia belonging to Clarence Mulford, creator of Hopalong Cassidy. The **Fryeburg Historical Society** (207-697-2044), 511 Main St., has a museum in the village and a research library in North Fryeburg on Rt. 113, open Wed. and Fri. 9–noon, Thu. 1–4.

Harrison Historical Society and Museum (207-583-2213), 121 Haskell Hill Rd., Harrison. Open July and Aug., Wed. 1–4 and by appointment; May–Dec., open the first Wed. of the month at 7 PM. The public is welcome at this small museum full of artifacts, cemetery records, town histories, and news-clipping scrapbooks.

DANIEL MARRETT HOUSE AND GARDEN, STANDISH

Nancy English

Raymond-Casco Historical Museum
(207-655-8668; raymondcascohistory.org),
Rt. 302, Casco. Open Memorial Day–
Columbus Day, free. Exhibits of Victoriana,
carriages, and old photographs are a few of
the sights in the simple red building with a
60-foot mural on its side depicting 1800s
summer visitors arriving on the Sebago
Lake steamer and the Concord Coach—
which was a horse-drawn covered carriage
long before it was a bus.

OTHER HISTORIC SITES **Songo Locks**,
Naples (2.5 miles off Rt. 302). Open May–
Oct. Dating to 1830, the last of the 27
hand-operated locks that once allowed people to come by boat from Portland to Harrison still enable you to travel some 40 watery
miles. Boat traffic is constant in summer.

Nancy English

HARVEST AT APPLE ACRES FARM,
SOUTH HIRAM

✳ To Do

APPLE PICKING **Five Fields Farm** (fivefieldsski.com), 720 S. Bridgton Rd. (Rt. 107), South
Bridgton. Fresh cider and seven varieties of apples for picking, with pumpkins for sale. In
winter, cross-country ski trails lace through the 450 acres.

    Apple Acres Farm (207-625-4777; appleacresfarm.com), 363 Durgintown Rd., South
Hiram. Pick your own and check out the farm store at this pretty orchard near Cornish Village. Pumpkins, fresh cider, fudge, and more—like their own invention, Apple Crackle, fruit
brittle that is simply delicious.

    Douglas Mountain Orchard (207-787-2745), 42 Orchard Rd., Sebago. Apples, pears, and
pumpkins.

    And see Dole's Orchard and Libby U-Pick, below.

BLUEBERRY (AND MORE) PICKING **Crabtree's Pick-Your-Own Highbush Blueberries**
(207-787-2730; crabcoll.com), 703 Bridgton Rd., Rt. 107, Sebago. The multiple varieties of
blueberries here make the picking season long—mid-July to the first frost, which can be as
late as Oct. 15.

    Dole's Orchard (207-793-4409; dolesorchard.com), 187 Doles Ridge Rd., Limington.
Blueberries, strawberries, raspberries, tart cherries (unless Allagash Brewery buys the
whole crop for cherry lambic!), apples, plums, and peaches are pick-your-own. Call first to
learn what's ripe and available. Fall hayrides and live music.

    Libby & Son U-Picks (207-793-4749; libbysonupicks.com), Limerick. This popular
inland spot for highbush blueberry picking grows more than 7,500 bushes. Even so, call
in advance to make sure it's not closed for a day to let more berries ripen. In fall the apple
orchard opens for picking, and there's berry picking into Oct. Freshly pressed cider and
pumpkins, too.

BOATING ♦ ♿ **Songo River Queen II** (207-693-6861), Naples Causeway. Operates daily
July–Labor Day; reduced schedule in spring and fall. The *Queen* is a replica of a Mississippi

SONGO RIVER QUEEN II DEPARTING IN NAPLES

River stern paddle-wheeler, with accommodations for 300 passengers, a snack and cocktail bar, and restrooms. One-hour Long Lake cruises and moonlight charters are popular during good weather.

CANOEING AND KAYAKING **Saco River Canoe and Kayak** (207-935-2369; sacoriver canoe.com), 1009 Main St. (Rt. 5), Fryeburg (across from the access at Swan's Falls). Fred Westerberg, a Registered Maine Guide, runs Saco River Canoe and Kayak with the help of his wife, Prudy, and daughters, Beth and Chris. They offer shuttle service and canoe and kayak rentals, which come with a map and careful instructions geared to the day's river conditions.

Saco Bound (603-447-2177; sacobound.com), Rt. 302, Center Conway, New Hampshire (just over the state line, west of Fryeburg). The largest canoe outfitter around. With its sister company Northern Waters, Saco Bound offers rentals, guided day trips, and white-water canoeing on the Androscoggin River in summer, a campground at Canal Bridge in Fryeburg, and a shuttle service. Its base is a big glass-faced store stocked with kayaks and canoes, trail food, and lip balm.

KAYAKING ON LONG LAKE

Sebago Kayak Company (207-935-4763; sebagokayakcompany.com), Naples Causeway. Canoes and kayaks rented by the day or week, with free delivery for multiday rentals.

Sportshaus (207-647-3000), 103 Main St., Bridgton. Rents canoes and kayaks by the day or week.

Woodland Acres (207-935-2529; wood landacres.com), Rt. 160, Brownfield. Full-facility camping, canoe rentals, and a shuttle service.

River Run (207-452-2500; riverruncanoe .com), P.O. Box 190, Brownfield. Canoe rentals, a shuttle, and parking Memorial Day–Labor Day weekends. They also have camping—see *Lodging*.

FISHING Licenses are available at town offices and online at mefishwildlife.com; check marinas for information. Salmon, lake trout, pickerel, and bass abound.

GOLF AND TENNIS **Bridgton Highlands Country Club** (207-647-3491; bridgtonhighlands .com), Highland Rd., Bridgton, has an 18-hole course, snack bar, carts, a resident golf pro, and tennis courts. Also 18-hole **Lake Kezar Country Club** (207-925-2462; lakekezargolf .com), Rt. 5, Lovell; and 18-hole **Naples Golf and Country Club** (207-693-6424; naplesgolf course.com), Rt. 114, Naples.

Point Sebago Golf Resort (1-800-530-1555; pointsebago.com), 261 Point Sebago Rd., Casco. This 18-hole, par-72 course on 500 acres of white birch forest was judged southern Maine's top course in *Golf Digest*, May 2003.

HIKING **Douglas Mountain**, Sebago. A Nature Conservancy preserve with great views of Sebago and the White Mountains. The trail to the top is a 20-minute walk, and there's a 0.75-mile nature trail at the summit; also a stone tower with an observation platform. Take Rt. 107 south from the town of Sebago and turn right on Douglas Mountain Rd.

Pleasant Mountain, Bridgton. Several summits and interconnecting trails, the most popular of which is the Firewarden's Trail to the main summit: a relatively easy 2.5-mile climb from base to peak through rocky woods.

✓ **Jockey Cap**, Rt. 302, Fryeburg. Starts near the Jockey Cap Country Store and Motel under a small arch. A 15-minute climb up the path (steep near the top) accesses a bald, garnet-studded summit with a sweeping view of the White Mountains to the west, lesser peaks and lakes to the east and south, all ingeniously identified on a circular bronze monument designed by Arctic explorer Admiral Peary.

HORSEBACK RIDING **Secret Acres Stables** (207-693-3441), 185 Lambs Mill Rd. (1 mile off Rt. 302), Naples, offers trail rides and lessons.

✓ **Carousel Horse Farm** (207-627-4471; chfmaine.com), 69 Leach Hill Rd., Casco. Takes beginning through advanced riders on trail rides with views of lakes and the White Mountains.

MINI GOLF ✓ **Steamboat Landing** (207-693-6782; steamboatlandingminigolf.com), Rt. 114, Naples (0.25 mile off the causeway). Open Memorial Day weekend–Labor Day, daily 10–10. A lovely 18-hole course with a Maine theme in a wooded setting. Ice cream parlor with Gifford's ice cream, and game room for pinball and family-oriented video games.

✓ **Seacoast Fun Park** (207-892-5952; seacoastfunparks.com), Rt. 302, Windham. Open May–Oct. Elaborate mini golf, go-carts, bumper boats, arcade, hillside tubing, Ferris wheel, disk golf, trampoline, 32-foot rock climbing wall, and a 100-foot-plunge sky swing.

SAILING **Sportshaus** (in winter, 207-647-3000; in summer, 207-647-9528), 103 Main St., Bridgton, rents Sunfish and Rhumbas by the week.

SWIMMING ✓ **Sebago Lake State Park** (Memorial Day–Labor Day, 207-693-6613; otherwise, 207-693-6231; maine.gov), off Rt. 302 (between Naples and South Casco). A great family beach with picnic tables, grills, boat ramp, lifeguards, and bathhouses. Day use only; there is a separate camping area (see *Lodging*). No pets. **Tassel Top Beach**, just off Rt. 302 on Sebago Lake, is run by the town of Raymond. Picnic tables, 900 feet of sandy beach, nature trail, and roped-off swim area. Changing rooms but no lifeguards. The town of Bridgton maintains a tidy little beach on **Long Lake** just off Main St., another on **Woods Pond** (Rt. 117), and another on **Highland Lake**. The town of Fryeburg maintains a beach, with float, on the **Saco River**, and **Casco** maintains a small, inviting beach in its picturesque village.

✽ Winter Sports

CROSS-COUNTRY SKIING ✐ **Five Fields Farm Cross-Country Ski Center** (207-647-2425; fivefieldsski.com), Rt. 107, 6 miles south of Bridgton. Open daily 9 AM–dusk. Trails loop around the 70-acre working apple orchard and connect to logging roads. You can snowshoe to the top of Bald Pate Mountain for spectacular views. Full- and half-day rates, rentals, warming hut. Mushers' Bowl, a dogsled race with 70 teams, is held here every year.

    Sebago Lake State Park (207-693-6231), off Rt. 302 (between Naples and South Casco). Six miles of groomed trails open to the public, $1.50 per person, pay on the honor system at a trail "iron ranger."

DOWNHILL SKIING ✐ **Shawnee Peak** (207-647-8444; shawneepeak.com), Rt. 302, Bridgton. An isolated 1,900-foot hump 6 miles west of the center of town. Maine's oldest ski area has a vertical drop of 1,300 feet and offers 40 trails with 98 percent snowmaking capacity, a double, two triples, and a quad lift, plus a surface lift. Open until 9 PM (until 10 Fri. and Sat.), and night skiing is big here. Glades and freestyle terrain park. Ski and snowboard instruction, rentals, child care, and base lodge with pub. Rooms in a variety of lodging options.

    Sportshaus (207-647-5100; sportshausski.com), rental facility on Rt. 302, also at 103 Main St., Bridgton, rents skis, snowshoes, and snowboards by the day or week.

✽ Green Space

Pondicherry Park (207-647-4352; lelt.org) is a 66-acre park that surrounds Bridgton, with 5 miles of trails that loop through the woods. Loon Echo Land Trust is in charge, with plans for a covered pedestrian bridge to access the parkland from downtown Bridgton. No pets, no bikes.

    The **Lakes Environmental Association** (LEA; 207-647-8580; mainelakes.org), 102 Main St., Bridgton, has been working since 1970 to preserve the clear, unsullied lakes in western Maine from development, invasive species such as milfoil, and overuse. Trails and a boardwalk lead through the ✐ **Holt Pond Preserve**, a watershed with a bog, a river, and other wetlands, and a boardwalk over a quaking bog full of sphagnum moss and orchids. The **Stevens Brook Trail** follows the water body from Highland Lake to Long Lake. Tour the LEA's **Harry & Eunice Bradley Lake Center**, 230 Main St., Bridgton, to see the water-testing lab, buffer gardens, and educational displays.

    Sebago Lake Land Reserve (207-523-5421; pwd.org), Sebago Lake Ecology Center at Rts. 237 and 35, Standish. Wetlands, lakeside trails, and forests account for 1,700 acres under protection in this reserve. Sign in at any of 11 visitors permit kiosks at trailheads. The Ecology Center offers free lake maps that explain permitted uses; swimming is not allowed anywhere in the 2-mile shorefront of this reserve except one spot—where there is no fence. Camping, campfires, ATVs, and motorcycles are not allowed on the land of this watershed, which supplies Greater Portland with clean water.

    Mountain Division Trail (mountaindivisiontrail.org) is a rail-trail under development. The Windham–Gorham–Standish section is completed from Rt. 202 in South Windham to Otter Ponds in Standish, with a 6-mile, unpaved section from Otter Ponds to Johnson Field on Rt. 35 in Standish, where you can park. On the other end, 4 miles of trail start at the Fryeburg Visitors Center on Rt. 302 by the state line and head to Porter Rd., south of town on Rt. 113, with parking at both ends and views of Burnt Meadow Mountains and the White Mountains.

    Kezar Falls, reached from Lovell Rd. off Rt. 35, is a small, pretty waterfall on the Kezar River.

The Wilson Wing Moose Pond Frog Preserve, formerly Sucker Brook Preserve, has 0.5-mile signed, interpretive trails, one for adults and one for children, and is part of the **Greater Lovell Land Trust** (207-925-1056; gllt.org), 208 Main St., Center Lovell. A view platform looks over the bog, and an evening program in March uses the platform to call owls—which usually respond. **The Heald Pond Preserve** and **Bradley Pond Reserve** total 801 acres in Lovell, with 7 miles of trails. The **Kezar Outlet Fen** in Lovell, a 250-acre wetland perfect for eagle-watching, has no vehicle access. Access by canoeing or kayaking. Trail maps are easy to download from the website.

✳ Lodging

RESORTS ✐ ♿ **Migis Lodge** (207-655-4524; migis.com), off Rt. 302, P.O. Box 40, South Casco 04077. Open Father's Day–Columbus Day weekend. This classic Maine lakeside resort takes excellent care of its guests, tucking them under hand-sewn quilts at night, with arrival-day fresh flowers. A comforting fire burns constantly in the Main Lodge, fed from fences of stacked firewood that frame the paths. Deluxe accommodations include six rooms in the two-story Main Lodge and 35 cottages with names like Skylark and Tamarack on 147 acres. All cottages have a fireplace, with daily wood deliveries (and ice for the ice bucket). A private beach, tennis,

PADDLEBOARDING AND KAYAKING AT MIGIS LODGE

Nancy English

waterskiing, sailboats, canoes, paddleboards, kayaks and boat excursions, massage and yoga while away the days. Children 5 and under eat in a family dining room and are offered supervised dining and playtime 6–9 PM (afternoon camp included in rates); older children are welcome to join in. $199-415 per adult per night (cottages) includes three meals. $209-454 per single adult in the lodge rooms, less if double. Fifteen percent service charge.

✐ **Quisisana** (207-925-3500; off-season 914-833-0293; quisisanaresort.com), Lake Kezar, Center Lovell 04016. Mid-June–Aug. One-week minimum stay in high season. This unique lodging was founded in 1917 as a place for music lovers to relax in the pines by one of Maine's clearest lakes. Each evening staff, many from music conservatories, perform in the lakeside hall, including perhaps the tenor who is the longtime business manager. The 75 guest quarters in one- to three-room pine-paneled cottages (some with fireplace) are scattered through the woods or near the soft beach. The lack of phone or TV in the cabins means more time for waterskiing, boating, fishing, croquet, tennis, and swimming. The white-frame central lodge includes a bar with tables on a deck, and the dining room to enjoy lobster and local produce. $180-255 per person double occupancy includes all meals.

B&BS ✿ ♂ ✐ **Noble House Inn** (207-647-3733 or 1-888-237-4880; noblehouseinn.com), 81 Highland Rd., Bridgton 04009. Open year-round. Cindi Hooper is the innkeeper at this former senator's manor. Eight guest rooms (all with private bath) are divided between the original house and the former carriage house, with luxurious linens and beds in each one; several have a semi-private deck overlooking the gardens. Highland Lake's public beach is 0.2 miles up the road. $145-275 includes breakfast, use of the canoe or

NOBLE HOUSE INN

snowshoes. Intimate house concerts are an inn specialty.

✪ ✔ **Center Lovell Inn** (1-800-777-2698; centerlovellinn.com), Rt. 5, Center Lovell 04016. Open most of the year. In 2015, essay contest winners and new innkeepers Prince and Rose Adams took over this striking old inn with a cupola and busy restaurant in-season (see their Caribbean-inspired entry in *Dining Out*). The inn features four guest rooms on the second floor (the two with shared bath can be a suite), nicely furnished with antiques and art. In the 1835 Harmon House there are five cozy rooms, three with private bath. $149–245 includes breakfast.

✔ **Oxford House Inn** (207-935-3442 or 1-800-261-7206; oxfordhouseinn.com), 548 Main St., Fryeburg 04037. Open year-round, but call first. Jonathan Spak and Natalie Knickerbocker Spak are in charge of this gracious 1913 house in the middle of Fryeburg, with its idyllic view across corn and potato fields and the placid Saco River to the White Mountains in New Hampshire. Four rooms are large, two with in-room sinks and one with a luxurious rain shower and a magnificent view. $129–195 includes breakfast, perhaps butternut squash bread French toast, or crêpes.

✔ **Main Street Bed & Breakfast** (207-935-7171; mainstbandb.com), Fryeburg 04037. Margaret Cugini has transformed this 1820 farmhouse in the heart of Fryeburg into a stunning and luxurious B&B, with the original woodwork, pumpkin pine floors in the hallway, and oak balustrade. The inn's five guest rooms, three with immaculately tiled private

bath, one with a 6-foot Jacuzzi, are furnished with antiques, updated beds, and lovely linens. Full breakfast and afternoon tea included. $109–219.

🐾 **Admiral Peary Inn** (207-935-3365 or 1-877-423-6779; admiralpearyinn.com), 27 Elm St., Fryeburg 04037. Named for Robert E. Peary, Maine's famed Arctic explorer, this house holds seven well-appointed rooms; each has a private bath and air-conditioning, three have a gas fireplace. There's a friendly dog and cat. $139–189 includes a full breakfast. Ten percent military discount; complimentary rooms on Veterans Day.

🐾 ✔ ♿ **Sebago Lake Lodge** (207-892-2698; sebagolakelodge.com), White's Bridge Rd., P.O. Box 110, North Windham 04062. A homey white inn opened in the mid-1980s, set on a narrows between Jordan Bay and the Basin, seemingly surrounded by water. There are also 12 cottages. An inviting beach, picnic tables, and grills; fishing boats, kayaks, canoes, and motorboat rentals. Pets are allowed in cottages rented by the week. $88 for a room in high season, $165–185 in the main lodge, continental breakfast.

Greenwood Manor Inn (207-583-4445; greenwoodmanorinn.com), 52 Tolman Rd., Harrison 04040. Open year-round. A former carriage house on 108 hillside acres sloping down to Long Lake, the inn features seven guest rooms and two suites, some with a gas log fireplace, some with whirlpool tub, and all with private bath. The dining and living areas overlook a landscaped garden. $140–245 in-season includes a full breakfast. *Note:* Although this B&B is technically in Harrison, much of its property lies in the town of Bridgton, and it is thus much closer to the Sebago/Long Lakes area than to the Oxford Hills.

✔ **The Olde Saco Inn** (207-925-3737; theoldesacoinn.com), 125 Old Saco Lane, Fryeburg 04037. Set in a grove of tall pines along the quiet, meandering Old Saco River, this secluded inn holds eight rooms and one suite, Heather's Loft, with a deck. Its pub is open to guests every night, open to the public and serving "Pub Grub" Fri.–Sat. only. Dessert one night was a South African malva pudding with apricots. Owners Pete and Sandi MacLauchlan are from South Africa and left behind LA's IT world. Trails for snowshoeing, cross-country skiing, and hiking, and kayaks and canoes are available for guests. Rates $95–180, including breakfast.

MOTELS 🐾 **The Midway Country Lodging** (207-625-8835; mainemidwaylodging.com), Rt. 25, Cornish 04020. Clean rooms, views of the mountain, a TV, mini fridge, and microwave, outdoor pool, gardens, and deluxe room with (heart-shaped) whirlpool, all at reasonable and low rates, add up to a find off the beaten track in western Maine. Rates $64–99.

🐾 🗲 ♿ **Jockey Cap Motel and Country Store** (207-935-2306), 116 Bridgton Rd., Fryeburg 04037. Open year-round. Located at the trailhead for Jockey Cap Mountain, this simple place is run by Allyson and Robert Quinn. Four rooms hold two doubles, and three have queens; all have private bath with tub and shower, air-conditioning, cable TV. $69–79.

OTHER LODGING 🐾 🗲 ♿ **Point Sebago Resort** (207-655-3821 or 1-800-655-1232; pointsebago.com), 261 Point Sebago Rd., Casco 04015. Open May–Oct. One hundred sites for RV hook-ups on a 775-acre lakeside site, plus hundreds of small, manufactured "park homes" for rent, some with linens and others empty, requiring you to stock the basics.

Beach, marina, pavilion, children's activities, excursion boats, soccer and softball fields, horseshoe pitches, 18-hole championship golf course, 10 tennis courts, video-game arcade, and combination restaurant/nightclub with DJs and teen dances. $200–250 for a park home per night.

CAMPGROUNDS See *Canoeing and Kayaking* for information about camping along the Saco River. In addition, the Appalachian Mountain Club maintains a campground at Swan's Falls. The Maine Camping Guide, available from the **Maine Campground Owners Association** (207-782-5874; campmaine.com), 655 Main St., Lewiston 04240, lists private campgrounds in the area.

🐾 🗲 **Sebago Lake State Park** (Memorial Day–Labor Day, 207-693-6613; otherwise, 207-693-6231), off Rt. 302 (between Naples and South Casco). Open through Oct. 15. Visitors return year after year to these 1,300 thickly wooded acres on the northern shore of the lake, so make your reservations early. The camping area (with 250 campsites, many on the water) comes with its own beach, hot showers, a program of evening presentations such as outdoor movies, and nature hikes. For

Nancy English

SEBAGO LAKE STATE PARK

reservations, call 1-800-332-1501, or 207-624-9950 from outside the state. Go to camp withme.com to make reservations online. Ninety-five sites have water and electricity.

River Run (207-452-2500; riverruncanoe .com), Denmark Rd., P.O. Box 190, Brownfield 04010. Memorial Day–Labor Day, camp on more than 100 acres, with sites in the woods and along the Saco River. Amenities include public phone, group tenting area, swimming beaches, fire rings, picnic tables, and firewood and ice for purchase. $10 per person per night.

❊ Where to Eat

DINING OUT **Oxford House Inn** (207-935-3442; oxfordhouseinn.com), 548 Main St., Fryeburg. Open nightly for dinner May–Oct.; closed Mon. otherwise. Reservations suggested. The most romantic spot in western Maine when you sit in the dining room's back porch, with sunsets and wildlife sightings of an albino woodchuck and passing deer. The CIA-graduate chef Jonathan Spak worked at The Water Club in New York City, and according to his wife and business partner really loves what he does. Sherman's Farm Stand is responsible for a lot of the sides in-season; Maine lobster carbonara or salmon pad Thai salad might be on the excellent menu. Jonathan's in the stone-lined cellar is perfect for dinner in the dark of winter. Entrées $14–34.

Center Lovell Inn (207-925-1575), Rt. 5, Center Lovell. Open for dinner daily in summer; check for hours off-season. Call for reservations. A daily ceviche, curried crab dip on tostones, and jerked duck wing drumlettes were on the starter list; pork tenderloin with spiced rum guava BBQ sauce looked awfully good among the entrées. Entrées $19–29.

❂ **Krista's** (207-625-3600; kristas restaurant.com), 2 Main St., Cornish. Open Thu. 11:30–8, Fri. 11:30–9, Sat. 7 AM–9 PM, Sun. 7–8, different off-season. The portions at dinner are simply incredible—unless you are conducting a survey, one entrée will do the trick. Prime rib, pork chops, seared shrimp, and scallops all come with a small salad, great mashed or other potatoes, and vegetables. Breakfast is homemade muffins and scones, and perhaps Nutella-stuffed French toast. Entrées $18–26.

❂ **Ebenezer's Restaurant & Pub** (207-925-3200; ebenezerspub.net), 44 Allen Rd. Lovell. Seasonal; call first. Thirty-five beers on tap and more than 1,000 bottled beers from an incredible cellar make this a destination pub for the beer aficionado—according to *BeerAdvocate* magazine, it the best beer bar in America. Burgers, one with Stilton garlic cream cheese, cheese steak, battered and fried cod in a sandwich, or fish-and-chips—the frites are made here—make it a destination for hungry folks anywhere.

The Galley Restaurant & Pub (207-693-1002; thegalleyseafoodpub.com), 327 Roosevelt Trail, Naples. If you are not up for the Surf and Turf Suicide Challenge, which involves a timed consumption of wings and shrimp in "Revenge Sauce," you have to pay—but the lobster rolls are extolled by locals and visitors alike, and you can customize yours just as you like it. Perhaps with bacon? Or try the "plain Jane." Lobster bisque, clam chowder, a huge variety of wings, burgers, pasta, wraps, and more.

Venezia Ristorante (207-647-5333), Bridgton Corners, Rts. 302 and 93, Bridgton. Open for dinner Tue.–Sun. 5–9 in summer, Wed.–Sun. in winter. Dependable, moderately priced Italian dishes.

Black Bear Café (207-693-4770; theblack bearcafe.com), 215 Roosevelt Trail (Rt. 302), Naples. Open daily in summer, closed Tue. and Wed. off-season. Susan Bohill has expanded from her popular breakfasts and lunches, with lobster Benedict and burgers, to dinners of pizza and lasagna and dinner specials that take flight, like lobster risotto croquettes with lemon caper aioli, or pork tenderloin with blueberry chutney. Entrées $8–19.

🦞 **Tom's Homestead** (207-647-5726), Rt. 302, Bridgton. Lunch and dinner are served in this 1821 historic home (closed Mon.). The dining room may be a little tired, but the chef in the kitchen is making everything from scratch and diners consistently praise the food. House sausages makes the lunch a great deal, or you might find fried squash blossoms in summer.

EATING OUT **Bray's Brew Pub** (207-693-6806; braysbrewpub.com), 678 Roosevelt Trail, Rts. 302 and 35, Naples. Open year-round for lunch and dinner daily. Mike Bray and brewer Rob Prindall brew excellent

American ales using grains and malted barley, Oregon yeast, and Washington hops; a beer garden with a hops vine is a pleasant place on warm nights. The dinner menu runs from grilled salmon to BBQ baby back ribs and smoked beef brisket; pub menu served till 9:30 PM.

Beth's Kitchen Café (207-647-5211; beths kitchencafe.com), 82 Main St., Bridgton. Open daily 7–3. Salads and sandwiches and perfect lobster salad on greens for lunch. Breakfast includes Belgian waffles, quiche, fruit, and more.

Standard Gastropub (207-647-4100), 233 Main St., Bridgton. Pulled pork sandwiches, smoked wings, and double cheeseburgers enjoyed at painted picnic tables inside a converted gas station, surrounded by glass-door coolers. Respectable mac-and-cheese, lots of cool beer.

Depot Street Tap House (207-803-8064), 18 Depot St., Bridgton. Pub food in a tap house that has a following for its fine cocktails. "Beer, Booze, Darts" reads the sign in front; and they do a mac-and-cheese here too.

Chao Thai (207-647-4355), 112 Main St., Bridgton. This is the best Thai food that some customers have ever tasted—and they have been trying it all over. High praise indeed.

Center Lovell Market (207-925-1051), Rt. 5, Center Lovell. This place combines the best of an old-fashioned general store (clothing, groceries, Maine-made items) with a deli and café. Pizza, salads, and more served to go or to eat in the pleasant dining area.

Route 160 Ice Cream and Hot Dog Stand, north of Kezar Falls on Rt. 160. Locals swear by the dogs here, as well as the hamburgers and ice cream. A good place to stop for lunch when traveling between Cornish and Fryeburg.

The Good Life Market (207-655-1196; thegoodlifemarket.com), 1297 Roosevelt Trail (Rt. 302), Raymond. Sandwiches like a classic Reuben or a steak-house wrap, salads, great coffee, and fine fresh-baked goods, with tables outside. Also wine, some local produce, and gourmet foods in the market.

SPECIALTY FOODS **Weston's Farm & Sugar House** (207-935-2567; westonsfarm .com), 48 River St., Fryeburg. Open mid-May–Dec. 24, daily 9–6. Fresh fruit and vegetables grown here, jams made from the farm's fruit, cider, and syrup made with the sap of the trees all around you. "Sustainable Agriculture Since 1799" is the motto at this seventh-generation farm. Cut your own bouquet outside.

❄ Entertainment

FILM **The Magic Lantern** (207-647-5065; magiclanternmovies.com), 9 Depot St., Bridgton. Originally built in the 1920s, this old theater had to be torn down, but it was rebuilt and reopened in 2009 to the delight of the town. Three theaters show first-run and independent films, and **The Tannery** serves pub food. **Bridgton Drive-In** (207-647-8666), Rt. 302, shows movies in summer.

MUSIC **Sebago–Long Lake Region Chamber Music Festival** (207-583-6747), Deertrees Theatre and Cultural Center, Deertrees Rd., Harrison. A series of five world-class concerts held mid-July–mid-Aug.

The Saco River Festival Association (207-625-7116; sacoriverfestival.org) holds a chamber music festival in Cornish in July and Aug., and sponsors bandstand concerts in Parsonsfield in July.

Leura Hill Eastman Performing Arts Center at Fryeburg Academy (207-935-9232; fryeburgacademy.org), 745 Main St., Fryeburg. Opened in 2009, this new arts center with 400 seats hosts live broadcasts of Metropolitan Opera performances and concerts along with musicals performed by Fryeburg Academy students.

THEATER See **Deertrees Theatre and Cultural Center** in "Oxford Hills."

❄ Selective Shopping

ANTIQUES SHOPS Rt. 302 is chockablock with antiques shops, so stop anyplace that looks interesting. Cornish has also grown into an antiques haven, where you can relish the lack of crowds.

The Smith Co. (207-625-6030), 24 Main St., Cornish. Specializes in country-store fixtures and memorabilia—including old Coca-Cola collectibles and advertising signs.

Cornish Trading Company (207-625-8387; cornishtrading.com), 19 Main St., Cornish.

MUST SEE

Stone Mountain Arts Center (1-866-227-6523; stonemountain artscenter.com), 695 Dugway Rd., Brownfield. Musician Carol Noonan's 200-seat hall in Brownfield "literally picked up, moved and plopped onto a new foundation," as she describes it online. It's a phenomenon she wonders about sometimes. Though grateful to be able to stay home after growing weary of the road, she looks this gift horse in the mouth. "People are driving three hours to see a show," Noonan writes. "Why? There is something here bigger than me that drives this train."

Sold-out shows are held year-round in the open-raftered building, and dinner is served first if you can snag a dinner ticket, too. The meals are served quickly, with choices from a small menu like gourmet pizzas; salads with shrimp, salmon, or chicken; and chowder or chili. Beer and wine are served, but all service stops at 8 when the music starts. "It's a listening room first and foremost," says Katy Noonan, Carol's sister.

The business is booking a lot of shows, and some performers include Enter the Haggis, Robert Cray, Suzanne Vega, and Shemekia Copeland, national acts that found the way up the hilly road. At Stone Mountain's live concerts, Carol Noonan and the Stone Mountain Band host performers like Scottish master fiddler Alasdair Fraser.

The hall is in Brownfield, 20 miles east of Conway, New Hampshire. Whatever you do, do not use GPS to find it. Follow the precise directions available on the website. GPS and Google Maps will put you on rough roads.

Open Apr.–Oct., Wed.–Mon. 10–5; in Nov., Fri.–Sun. 10–5. A multidealer antiques shop with Americana, Persian carpets, garden sculpture, and more.

BOOKSTORES **Bridgton Books** (207-647-2122), 140 Main St., Bridgton. More than 20,000 titles, new and used books, books on tape, cards and stationery, as well as music.

SPECIAL SHOPS **Harvest Gold Gallery** (207-925-6502; harvestgoldgallery.com), Rt. 5, Center Lovell. Crafts and original art, garden sculpture like a flock of pale fish, and lovely jewelry made by the owners.

Cornish Vintage Faire (207-625-7700), 51 Main St., Cornish. Three floors of vintage clothes and a few house goods, with fantastic examples of '50s and '60s styles, much of it very reasonably priced.

Kedar Quilt Gallery (207-693-5058; kedarquilts.com), 966 Roosevelt Trail (Rt. 302), Naples. This gallery sells quilts of all sizes made by Maine quilters. Orders taken for custom quilts, too.

The Cool Moose (207-647-3957), 108 Main St., Bridgton. Handmade belts and leather goods and other well-made and quirky inventory.

Craftworks (207-647-5436), 67 Main St., Upper Village, Bridgton. Open daily. Fills a former church. Selective women's clothing, shoes, pottery, books, linens, handmade pillows, crafted jewelry, Stonewall Kitchen–prepared foods, and wines from all over the world.

Blacksmiths Winery (207-655-3292; black smithswinery.com), 967 Quaker Ridge Rd., South Casco. May–Dec. 31, daily 11–6, tastings end at 5:30; Jan.–Apr., Fri.–Mon. 11–5, tastings end at 4:30. Visitors sample the surprisingly good Cabernet Sauvignon, Chardonnay, and blueberry wines, along with an ice wine made with Ontario grapes.

✳ Special Events

January: **Mushers' Bowl**, a dogsled race at the Fryeburg Fairgrounds with participants from all over the United States. Includes sleigh rides, crafts, dancing, stargazing, ice skating, snowshoeing, ice fishing, and more.

March: **March Maple Syrup Sunday**, with tapping and sugaring-off demonstrations around the area, including Pingree Maple Syrup and Highland Farms Sugar Works, both in Cornish, and Grampa Joe's Sugar House, Rt. 107, Sebago, among many.

April: **Sheepfest**, Denmark—demonstrations of spinning, carding, combing, knitting, dyeing, sheep shearing, hoof trimming, and more.

June: **Windham Summer Fest** (third weekend)—parade, contests, and food vendors. **Naples Blues Fest**, growing every year. **Wheels and Water Antique Transportation**, with chicken BBQ.

July: Independence Day is big in Bridgton and Naples, with fireworks, a parade, and the **4 on the Fourth Road Race**—a 5K walk/run/wheelchair race around Bridgton. In **Naples** the fireworks over the lake are spectacular. Harrison and Casco also hold their **Old Home Days** this month, and check out the **Waterford World's Fair**. **Strawberry Festival**, Thompson Park, Cornish.

August: In Lovell the **Annual Arts and Artisans Fair** (midmonth) is held at the New Suncook School—a juried crafts fair. The **Spinners and Weavers Show** at Narramissic has grown in popularity in recent years (see *To See*).

September: **Chili Cook-Off and Road Race**, Waterford. **Cornish Apple Festival**, including crafts booths, food vendors, quilt show, antique auto parade, apple pie contest, and the **Apple Acres Bluegrass Festival**. **Brew Fest** at Point Sebago Resort, Casco, offers tastes from microbreweries; look at lakesbrewfest.com for details.

October: **Fryeburg Fair**, Maine's largest agricultural fair, is held for a week in early Oct., climaxing with the Columbus Day weekend.

November: **Early-Bird Shopping**, discounts at local retail shops, and **Snowflake Trail**, local crafts and open houses in Newfield, Limerick, and Limington.

Late November–early December: **Christmas in Cornish**—open houses, concerts, Cornish Historical Society Walking Tour, horse-drawn carriage rides, children's story time, poinsettia display, and caroling. **Bridgton's Festival of Lights**—a candlelight parade culminates with Santa Claus and tree lighting.

December: **Christmas Open House** and festivals in Harrison.

OXFORD HILLS AND LEWISTON/AUBURN

A rolling gem- and lake-studded swatch of Oxford County is known as the Oxford Hills. Technically made up of eight towns, the region seems to stretch to include many of the stops along Rt. 26, the region's traffic spine, as visitors pass through from Gray (an exit on the Maine Turnpike) to Bethel, an area with both summer attractions and winter ski resorts.

Its commercial center is the community composed of both Norway and South Paris, towns divided by the Little Androscoggin River but joined by Rt. 26. Off Rt. 26 is a quiet part of the Western Lakes and Mountains Region, with startlingly beautiful villages like Waterford and Paris Hill, and genuinely interesting places to see, such as the country's last living Shaker community at Sabbathday Lake.

The area's bedrock is a granite composed of pegmatite studded with semiprecious gemstones, including tourmaline and rose quartz. Several local businesses invite visitors to explore their "tailings," or rubble, and take what they find.

Otisfield is renowned for a unique summer camp devoted to healing the wounds of war, called Seeds of Peace Camp. It began with Palestinian and Israeli children, and now includes campers from Afghanistan, India, Pakistan, Iraq, and Iran, who spend the summer getting to know children they might have encountered otherwise only as enemies.

Lewiston and Auburn (Maine's "L/A"), just east of the Oxford Hills, are the "cities of the Androscoggin," but for most visitors are seen as "the cities on the turnpike," the exits accessing routes to the Rangeley and Sugarloaf areas. By the 1850s mills on both sides of the river had harnessed the power of the Androscoggin's Great Falls, and the Bates Mill boomed with the Civil War, supplying fabric for most of the Union army's tents.

Today Lewiston is best known as the home of prestigious Bates College (founded in 1855), an attractive campus that's the summer site of the nationally recognized Bates Dance Festival. It's also the home of a growing number of Somali immigrants, who are bringing their own cultural flair to the region. The Bates Mill is now a visitor-friendly complex housing a museum and restaurants, and both Lewiston and Auburn offer a number of colorful festivals—some, like Festival de Joie, reflecting the rich diversity of the residents.

GUIDANCE **Oxford Hills Chamber of Commerce** (207-743-2281; oxfordhillsmaine.com), 4 Western Ave., South Paris 04281, publishes a comprehensive directory to the area.

Androscoggin County Chamber of Commerce (207-783-2249; androscoggincounty .com), 415 Lisbon St., P.O. Box 59, Lewiston 04243.

GETTING THERE For the Sabbathday Lake–Poland Spring–Oxford area, take I-95 to Gray (Exit 63) and Rt. 26 north. Auburn is Exit 75 and Lewiston is Exit 80 off the Maine Turnpike.

WHEN TO COME This is lovely country in winter, but dinner choices can be limited to weekends in the countryside. We love the Lilac Festival at the McLaughlin Garden on Memorial Day weekend.

✱ Villages

Harrison. Once a booming lakeside resort town, Harrison is now a quiet village resting between two lakes. Main Street has a popular restaurant and restored clock tower. In the 1930s many of the country's most popular actors came to perform at the Deertrees Theatre, which is again offering theater, dance, music, and children's shows to the area.

Norway. Making up part of the commercial center of the region, the downtown is quiet and quaint. L. M. Longley's hardware store has items from days gone by, the town is home to Maine's oldest newspaper, and there are interesting art exhibits held by the Western Maine Art Group in the Matolcsy Art Center.

Paris is a town divided into sections so different, they don't feel like the same town at all. Paris Hill has views of the White Mountains and a number of historic houses and buildings, including the Hamlin Memorial Library.

Oxford. Home of the Oxford Plains Speedway, which attracts stock-car-racing fans throughout the season, and the Oxford County Fairgrounds (host to several annual events), and now the Oxford Casino, Oxford is also the largest manufacturing base in the area, including manufactured homes, information processing, textiles, and wood products.

✱ To See

The International Sign. At the junction of Rts. 5 and 35 in the village of Lynchville, some 14 miles west of Norway, stands Maine's most photographed roadside marker, pointing variously to Norway, Paris, Denmark, Naples, Sweden, Poland, Mexico, and Peru—all towns within 94 miles of the sign.

FOR FAMILIES ✎ ♿ **Maine Wildlife Park** (207-657-4977), Rt. 26, Gray. Open Apr. 15–Nov. 11, daily 9:30–4:30 (no one admitted after 4 PM). $7 adults, $5 ages 61-plus and ages 4–12, and free for those 3 and under. What started as a pheasant farm in 1931 has evolved into a wonderful haven for injured animals and other creatures that cannot live in the wild. It's a great opportunity to see more than 30 species of native Maine wildlife you might otherwise never glimpse. The park allows visitors to observe animals as they live in the wild. Nature trails and picnic facilities round out the experience. Animals include moose, lynx, deer, black bears, red foxes, mountain lions, and eagles.

✎ **Beech Hill Farm & Bison Ranch** (207-583-2515; beechhillbison.com), 630 Valley Rd. (Rt. 35), Waterford. Call for hours. Doretta and Ted Colburn are raising a breeding herd of North American bison here and operate a shop with bison meat, buffalo hides, and a variety of gifts. For

Nancy English

THE INTERNATIONAL SIGN

the most part the herd is visible, and you might see Chief Chadwick, who has produced champions.

HISTORIC BUILDINGS **Poland Spring Museum** (207-998-7143; polandspring.com), 115 Preservation Way, Poland Spring. Open Memorial Day–Columbus Day. Free admission. The original bottling plant from the early 1900s and springhouse for the well-known bottled water, Poland Spring, is its own branch in Preservation Park, with 4 miles of trails. The old spa had a renowned visitor list, and photos of some are displayed in the gallery here, like Mae West and Babe Ruth.

Maine State Building (207-998-4142; polandspringps.org), Rt. 26, Poland Spring. Open July and Aug., Tue.–Sat. 9–4, fewer hours off-season. Admission. A very Victorian building that was brought back from the 1893 World's Columbian Exposition in Chicago to serve as a library and art gallery for the now vanished Poland Spring Resort (today the water is commercially bottled in an efficient, unromantic plant down the road). Peek into the **All Souls Chapel** next door for a look at its nine stained-glass windows and the 1921 Skinner pipe organ.

Hamlin Memorial Library and Museum (207-743-2980), Hannibal Hamlin Dr. off Rt. 26, Paris Hill, Paris. Open seasonally, call for hours. The old stone Oxford County Jail now houses the public library and museum. Stop to see the American primitive art; also local minerals and displays about Hannibal Hamlin (who lived next door), vice president during Abraham Lincoln's first term; and the setting, a ridgetop of spectacular early-19th-century houses with views of the White Mountains.

MUSEUMS **Sabbathday Lake Shaker Community and Museum** (207-926-4597; maine shakers.com), 707 Shaker Rd. (just off Rt. 26), New Gloucester (8 miles north of Gray). Open Memorial Day–Columbus Day for six 75-minute tours daily (except Sun.), 10–4:30; $6.50 adults, $2 ages 6–12. Self-guided tours of Spin House exhibits. The Sabbathday Lake Shaker Community was formally organized in 1794. Founded by Englishwoman Ann Lee in 1775, Shakers numbered 6,000 Americans in 18 communities by the Civil War. Today, with only two Shaker Sisters and one Brother, this village is the only one in the world that still functions as a religious community. The Shakers here continue to follow the injunction of Mother Ann Lee to "put your hands to work and your heart to God." Guided tours are offered of some of the white-clapboard buildings; rooms are either furnished or filled with exhibits to illustrate periods or products of Shaker life.

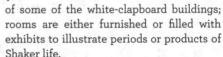

The **Shaker Store** and **Shaker Museum Reception Center**, a bookshop and exhibit area, sells Shaker-made goods, including oval boxes, knitted and sewn goods, home-made fudge, yarns, souvenirs, antiques, Shaker-style furniture, and Shaker herbs. During warm-weather months services are held at 10 AM on Sunday in the 18th-century meetinghouse just off Rt. 26, when Shakers speak in response to the psalms and gospel readings. Each observation is affirmed with a Shaker song—of which there are said to be 10,000. This complex includes an extensive research library housing Shaker books, writings, and records.

SHAKER VILLAGE

SHAKER VILLAGE STORE

Nancy English

Museum L-A, Museum of Labor and Industry (207-333-3881; museumla.org), 35 Canal St., Box A7, Lewiston. Open Mon.–Sat. 10–4. $5 adults, $4 seniors and students. A 50-foot drop in the Androscoggin River powered the mills built alongside; in its heyday Lewiston had seven mills turning out elegant bedspreads for Bates Mills. George Washington spreads, matelassé spreads that sandwich fibers inside the weave, were one of their best products. Shoes and bricks were also made, and the mills prospered until cheaper electricity and labor moved the textile industry to the South in the mid-20th century. One last company still operates in the mills; the Maine Heritage Weavers throws are also for sale in the gift store. Don't miss the jacquard loom, a model for early computers studied by IBM employees for functionality.

Franco-American Collection, The University of Southern Maine Lewiston-Auburn College (207-753-6545; usm.maine.edu/lac /franco), 51 Westminster St., Lewiston. Hours vary; call for appointment. The curators of this collection research and promote interest in the French roots of many of the region's inhabitants.

Bates College Museum of Art, Olin Arts Center (207-786-6158; batescollege.edu), 75 Russell St., Lewiston. Open Tue.–Sat. 10–5. Hosts a variety of performances, exhibitions, and special programs. The museum also houses fine artworks on paper, including the Marsden Hartley Memorial Collection. Lovers of the artist won't want to miss this small but excellent collection of bold, bright canvases by Hartley, a Lewiston native.

Finnish-American Heritage Society of Maine (207-743-5677), 8 Maple St., West Paris. Open in July and Aug., Sun. 2–4, or by appointment; closed Jan.–Mar. A museum, library, and gift shop focused on the Finnish settlers in this area.

STOCK-CAR RACING **Oxford Plains Speedway** (207-539-8865; oxfordplains.com), Rt. 26, Oxford. Weekend stock-car racing, late Apr.–Oct.

✳ To Do

APPLE PICKING ☙ **Ricker Hill Orchards** (207-225-5552; rickerhill.com), Turner. Maps show you where your favorite varieties can be picked in the big orchard here. Cranberries for sale at the farm stand, along with apple butter, fresh doughnuts, and, in-season, the best corn of the summer. In fall a corn maze can be explored. A petting "ranch" brings you close to goats, pigs, cows, donkeys, and horses.

BALLOONING **Dream Song Ballooning** (207-713-6578; dreamsongballooning.org), Reservoir Ave., Lewiston. Dave Gagnon, a licensed commercial pilot, offers a printout of the ground track of your flight path; weekend trips by reservation.

Androscoggin Balloon Adventures (207-783-4574), 169 Ferry Rd., Lewiston. Jim Rodrigue, a licensed commercial pilot, offers weekend balloon rides by reservation.

EXCURSIONS

ALONG RT. 26 The following sights are described in order of appearance, heading north:

Sabbathday Lake Shaker Community and Museum, New Gloucester (8 miles north of Gray), just off Rt. 26, is a must-stop (see *Museums*).

State of Maine Building from the 1893 World's Columbian Exposition in Chicago (see *Historic Buildings*). An abrupt right, up through the pillars of the old Poland Spring Resort.

🎿 In Oxford two exceptional **farm stands** make ice cream from their own cows' milk. Northbound, don't miss hilltop **Crestholm Farm Stand and Ice Cream** (on your right; 207-539-8832), which has a petting zoo (sheep, goats, pigs, ducks, and more) as well as cheeses, honey, and great ice cream; also a nice view. Southbound, it's **Smedberg's Crystal Spring Farm** (see *Where to Eat—Snacks*).

Across from Ripley Ford, look for the **McLaughlin Garden** (see *Green Space*).

Paris Hill is posted just beyond the second light in South Paris. The road climbs steadily up to Paris Hill common, a spacious green surrounded on three sides by early-19th-century mansions, with the fourth commanding a panoramic view of hills and valley and the White Mountains in the distance. Look for **Hamlin Memorial Library and Museum** (see *Historic Buildings*).

Christian Ridge Pottery (see *Special Shops*) is marked from Christian Ridge Rd., a way back to Rt. 26.

🎿 **Snow Falls Gorge**, 6 miles south of the center of West Paris on Rt. 26, left as you're heading north. A great picnic and walk-around spot, a rest area with tables and a trail by a waterfall that cascades into a 300-foot gorge carved by the Little Androscoggin.

🎿 **Trap Corner**, an area in West Paris (at the junction of Rts. 219 and 26) is rockhounding central.

Greenwood Shore Rest Area, Rt. 26 just north of Bryant Pond. A good waterside spot for a picnic.

BIRDING **Sabattus Pond**, Sabattus. The mudflats of autumn bring migrating ducks, sandpipers, and waterfowl, including American golden plovers. The boat access and beach at Martin's Point on the pond is the access point. See also Thorncrag Nature Preserve in *Green Space*. Birding hot spots are listed at its sponsor's website, stantonbirdclub.org.

CASINO **Oxford Casino** (207-539-6700; oxfordcasino.com), 777 Casino Way (on Rt. 26), Oxford. Come and gamble your money at Maine's second casino, with 850 slot machines and table games, open 24 hours a day, seven days a week.

GOLF **Paris Hill Country Club** (207-743-2371), Paris Hill Rd., Paris, nine holes, founded in 1899, is the epitome of old-shoe; rental carts, snack bar. **Norway Country Club** (207-743-9840; norwaycountryclub.com), off Rt. 118 on Norway Lake Rd., nine holes, long views. Fourteen holes as well at **Summit Springs Golf Course** (207-998-4515), 292 Summit Spring Rd., Poland. **Spring Meadows Golf Club** (207-657-2586; springmeadowsgolf.com), 59 Lewiston Rd., Gray. An 18-hole golf course with rentals and clubhouse.

HIKING 🎿 **Streaked Mountain**. This is a short, occasionally steep hike with a panoramic view, good for kids. From Rt. 26, take Rt. 117 to the right-hand turnoff for Streaked Mountain Rd. and look for the trailhead on your left. The trail follows a power line up to an old fire tower at just 800 feet. A round-trip, 1-mile hike takes about 1½ hours, longer to eat the blueberries in-season.

Singepole Mountain. Also off Rt. 117, nearer South Paris (see the *Maine Atlas and Gazetteer*, published by DeLorme), is a 1.5-mile walk up a dirt road (bear left) through the woods to a summit with a view of Mount Washington and the Mahoosuc Mountains.

MOUNTAIN BIKING **Paris Hill Area Park**, near the common. You can bike the ridge roads radiating from here.

ROCKHOUNDING **Rochester's Eclectic Emporium** (207-539-4631), 403 Main St. (Rt. 26), Oxford. Nicholas Rochester has some of the finest mineral and crystal specimens you can see; he can steer you to local mines.

SWIMMING ✍ & **Range Pond State Park** (207-998-4104), Empire Rd., features a beach perfect for spreading out a picnic blanket. Lifeguards, playground, ball field, changing rooms, bathrooms, boat launch, swimming, and fishing, plus 2 miles of easy walking trails. The pond has a 10-horsepower limit—kayakers love it here. **Pennesseewassee Lake** in Norway is well off the road, but public and equipped with lifeguards.

❄ Winter Sports

CROSS-COUNTRY SKIING **Carter's X-C Ski Center** (207-539-4848; cartersxcski.com), 420 Main St. (Rt. 26), Oxford. Extensive acreage used to grow summer vegetables is transformed into a ski center in winter. Equipment rentals, lessons, 30 kilometers of groomed trails, and food. Disc golf in summer.

DOWNHILL SKIING **Lost Valley Ski Area** (207-784-1561; lostvalleyski.com), Lost Valley Rd., Auburn. With 21 trails and two chairlifts, this small mountain is a favorite for schools and families. Night skiing every night until 9 except Sun. at 5. Weekend adult lift tickets are $45, junior $33, less for fewer hours on the slopes.

SNOW TUBING ❄ ✍ **Oxford Plains Snow Tubing** (207-539-2454; oxfordplains.com), Rt. 26, Oxford. A lighted 1,000-foot slope open Sat.–Sun. plus school vacation days. Tubes, helmets, and a T-bar are the ingredients of this low-tech, low-cost sport. Snowmaking keeps it open.

❄ Green Space

The McLaughlin Garden (207-743-8820; mclaughlingarden.org), 97 Main St., South Paris. Garden open daily May–Oct., 8–7. Free admission. Historic house and gift shop open year-round, Mon–Sat. 10–5. In 1936 Bernard McLaughlin, who had no formal horticultural training, began planting his farmstead; now lilacs and established garden beds flourish next to stone walls and a massive barn. After his death in 1995, a nonprofit organization formed to preserve the home, barn, and 5-acre floral oasis. In lilac season, with more than 100 varieties, the annual Lilac Festival is a sensual delight. The gift shop is open year-round, and the **café** serving light lunches—including Provençal panini with prosciutto, artichoke hearts, and pesto—is open Memorial Day weekend–Labor Day, Wed.–Sun. 11–3.

Thorncrag Nature Sanctuary in Lewiston is a 372-acre wildlife sanctuary, owned and managed by Stanton Bird Club (207-782-5238; stantonbirdclub.org). Six nature trails cross through meadows, forest, wetlands, and vernal pools, all good for bird-watching or walking and jogging. This preserve is accessible through two gates, one at the end of East Ave., the other on Montello St.

The Ordway Grove, Pleasant St., Norway. These old-growth white pines, some 12 feet around and 140 feet or more tall, have been protected since 1789. The grove is a left turn heading north on Rt. 118 as you pass Lake Pennesseewassee. The grove of 250-year-old trees became a preserve in 1931.

✳ Lodging

INNS AND B&BS 🐾 ✎ **The Waterford Inne** (207-583-4037; waterfordinne.com), turn off Rt. 37 at Springer's General Store, Box 149, Waterford 04088. This striking 1825 farmhouse with its double porch is sequestered up a back road, set on 25 quiet acres of fields and woods. Barbara Vanderzanden opened her inn in July 1978; her unobtrusive style will appeal to those who prefer privacy. Four spacious rooms in an addition and four upstairs, six with private bath, include The Chesapeake Room with a second-story porch. A full breakfast is included. $125–200 per room; dinner is available by reservation (see *Dining Out*) at an additional cost. Pets are accepted; $15 fee.

✎ ♿ **King's Hill Inn** (207-744-0204; kingshillinn.com), 56 King Hill Rd., South Paris 04281. Five suites, and some offer both a great view of the White Mountains and a gas log fire. Enjoy blueberry pancakes in the morning before a tour of the perennial gardens spreading out on the lawn. $119–149 per night, depending on season.

✎ **Bear Mountain Inn** (207-583-4404; bearmtninn.com), Rts. 35 and 37, South Waterford 04081. Open year-round. This 150-year-old farmhouse is set on 52 gorgeous acres next to Bear Pond. Eleven rooms and suites, most with private bath. Each has its own bear—Minnesota, Polar, and Polo are three. Sugar Bear Cottage has a fireplace, kitchenette, claw-foot tub, and terrific views. $120–325 per room includes a full breakfast.

Wolf Cove Inn (207-998-4976; wolfcoveinn.com), 5 Jordan Shore Dr., Poland 04274. Open year-round. A romantic, quiet lakeside hideaway holds 10 accommodations, each named for a flower or herb and nicely decorated. Eight rooms have private bath; three have whirlpool tub and gas fireplace. Kayaks and canoes are available. $100–250 in-season includes a full breakfast. Light-filled sunporch or the grand room are the site of blueberry pancakes and pecan waffles for breakfast.

OTHER LODGING ✎ ♿ **Papoose Pond Resort and Campground** (207-583-4470; papoosepondresort.com), 700 Norway Rd. (Rt. 118), Waterford 04088 (10 miles west of Norway). Family-geared for 40 years, this facility is on 1,000 wooded acres with 0.5 mile of sandy beach on mile-long Papoose Pond. Cabins with or without bath, housekeeping cottages, bunkhouse trailers, tent and RV sites (some with electricity, water, and sewer); rates in high season range from $36 per night for a tent site and from $252 for a cottage. Amenities include a recreation hall, store, café, movie tent, canoes, rowboats, paddleboats, kayaks, fishing equipment, and a 1916 merry-go-round.

✳ Where to Eat

DINING OUT **Fuel** (207-333-3835; fuelmaine.com), 49 Lisbon St., Lewiston. Open for dinner Tue.–Sat. from 4:30. Fuel and an art gallery are now inside the renovated Lyceum Hall. The restaurant feeds appreciative locals bistro-style steak frites and braised short ribs, buttermilk-brined Cornish game hen and roasted scallops. Great wine list and elegant bar area with bar menu. Entrées $18–26.

Marché Kitchen and Wine Bar (207-333-3836; marchemaine.com), 40 Lisbon St., Lewiston. Good cocktails to start, perhaps also with the charcuterie plate, then segue nicely to blackened salmon with a glass of Ardèche Chardonnay from Louis Latour. Entrées $12–15.

76 Pleasant Street (207-744-9040; 76pleasantstreet.com), 76 Pleasant St., Norway. Charcoal duck comes with port raisin sauce; salmon with an eggplant compote. Count on thoughtful dishes and a tranquil evening at this beautiful old house. $23–28.

DiSanto's Italian Restaurant (207-428-4300; disantosrestaurant.com), 322 West Gray Rd, Gray. A vibrant marinara makes the Italian classics served here wonderful, and count on good veal and steaks, too. The house sausage is perfectly seasoned and can be enjoyed in an appetizer, but save room for the excellent cannoli and spumoni for dessert. Entrées $17–29.

Fish Bones American Grill (207-333-3663; fishbonesag.com), 70 Lincoln St., Lewiston. Grilled fish in a spacious room with exposed brick and lively people. Seafood fra diavolo and linguine with clams, or blueberry-glazed roast pork tenderloin. Entrées $17–26.

The Waterford Inne (207-583-4037; waterfordinne.com), Waterford (turn off Rt. 37 at Springer's General Store). Open by reservation only. Come and enjoy a surprisingly sophisticated meal in this classic country inn. A four-course prix fixe dinner ($45) might include salmon with walnut crust, carrots Vichy, or pork à la Normande with apples and Calvados. BYOB.

Sedgley Place (207-946-5990; sedgley place.com), off Rt. 202, Greene. Reservations required. A Federal-style house with a well-known dining room. Five-course dinners with entrées that change weekly but always include prime rib, fish, poultry, and a fourth selection. Prix fixe $19–29 includes salad and dessert, with greens, vegetables, meat, and berries from local farms.

Mother India (207-333-6777; motherindia maine.com), 114 Lisbon St., Lewiston. A draw for Indian-food lovers from all over the state.

EATING OUT ○ **Nezinscot Farm Store and Cafe** (207-225-3231; nezinscotfarm.com), 284 Turner Center Rd., Turner. Food served Mon.–Fri. 7–4, Sat. 7–4, closed Sun., and also on Mon. Oct.–June. Exceptional cheeses, jams, pickles, organic meats, eggs, and vegetables sold, and a café with a perfect organic hamburger on toasted, homemade bread. Gloria Varney, her husband, and her large family run this farm,

providing eggs for omelets, organic cheese for lunch. The Tea House in the garden, with tea with clotted cream and scones, is open mid-May–Oct. amid the strolling chickens.

Bresca and the Honey Bee (207-926-3388; brescaandthehoneybee.com), 106 Outlet Rd., New Gloucester, on Outlet Beach. Open Memorial Day–Labor Day, Wed.–Sun. 11–4 for food, until 6 for ice cream. The former owner of one of Portland's best restaurants now runs a "food shack" next to a beach on Sabbathday Lake, where swimming can be enjoyed for an admission fee ($5 adults, $3 children, $4 seniors). The business also rents boats. No credit cards. Pastries, burgers, hot dogs, sandwiches, maybe a buckwheat crêpe with goat ricotta and ice cream, which might be passion fruit, perhaps unmatched in the state of Maine.

The Café Nomad (207-739-2249; cafe nomad.com), 450 Main St., Norway. Open early AM though lunch and for summer weekend dinners. Scott Berk serves invigorating coffee drinks. Local produce and meat are on the menu, with breakfast burritos, omelets, weekend pancakes, along with a great caprese sandwich and soups. Chicken salad is a multi-day process starting with marinade. Wine, beer, and more for sale.

Chick-A-Dee (207-225-3523; chickadee lewiston.com), Rt. 4, Turner. Closed Tue. A longtime local favorite for lunch and dinner. Specialties include seafood like fried clams and beef. Entrées $6–20.

☙ **Olde Mill Tavern** (207-583-9077; olde milltavern.com), Main St., Harrison. Open daily for dinner at 4. Popular with local residents and families. Chorizo burritos, chicken Parmesan, shrimp stir-fry with soba noodles, pasta, and burgers, among many other things on the varied menu. Entrées $9–24.

Cyndi's Dockside Restaurant (207-998-5008; dockside.me), 723 Maine St., Poland. Boat rentals in-season, open year-round. Enjoy an outside deck and outdoor pavilion on Middle Range Pond in good weather. Local beef burgers, fried clams, pulled pork sandwiches. Entrées $6–19.

☙ **Cole Farms** (207-657-4714; colefarms .com), 64 Lewiston Rd. (Rt. 100/202), Gray. Open Sun.–Thu. 6 AM–9 PM, Fri. and Sat. until 9:30. No credit cards; checks accepted with ID. Maine family recipes, including fried seafood, hot chicken sandwiches, Indian

NEZINSCOT FARM STORE

Nancy English

pudding, and daily specials like New England boiled dinner. No liquor. Playground with swings, and gift shop.

🐾 **Melby's Market** (207-583-4447), 927 Valley Rd. (Rt. 26), North Waterford. Open 6 AM–9 PM except the last week of March. Paul and Kay Legare have run Melby's (formerly Tut's) for more than 20 years, making fresh bread and pastries, selling local honey and preserves, and cooking a fine buffalo burger. Breakfast served all day.

🖉🔥 **Val's Root Beer** (207-784-5592), 925 Sabattus St., Lewiston. Open daily mid-Apr.–mid-Sept., 11–8 except Sun., when they open at noon. A 1950s-style drive-in with carhops and a *Happy Days* theme. Greasy burgers, great onion rings, hot dogs, and the like, and their specialty, homemade root beer. Popular summer hangout among locals.

SNACKS 🖉 **Crestholm Farm Stand and Ice Cream** (207-539-2616), Rt. 26, Oxford. Open in-season. Farm stand, cheeses, honey, ice cream, and a petting zoo: sheep, goats, pigs, ducks, and more.

Forage Market (207-333-6840; foragemarket.com), 180 Lisbon St., Lewiston. Open daily. A market for good produce; a bakery for fresh bread, like ciabatta and rustic rye; and a kitchen for sandwiches to go, like one with Papou's falafel from Maine and Israeli chopped salad, or ham and salami on that ciabatta.

Greenwood Orchards (207-225-3764; greenwoodorchards.com), 174 Auburn Rd., Turner. Open July–Dec. Fresh cider in fall, apples, house jams and jellies, and a bakery making pies and bread—100 percent whole wheat is one. Local produce fills this shop through the growing season.

Smedberg's Crystal Spring Farm (207-743-6723; smedbergfarm.com), Rt. 26, Oxford, sells its One Cow Ice Cream (there is actually a herd of beef cattle here); also jams, honey, maple syrup, fruits and vegetables, cheese, berries, home-baked pies, and homegrown grass-fed beef, pork, and lamb. Open-house country festival with a pig roast, free roast pork, and samples, first Sun. of Nov.

Marta's Bakery (207-583-2250; martasbakery.com), 684 Valley Rd., Waterford. This Czechoslovakian baker catered to dignitaries in Boston—and retired to Waterford, where she makes cakes to order and much more. Call to be sure it's open.

Nancy English

OUTLET BEACH BESIDE BRESCA AND THE HONEY BEE

✳ Entertainment

🖉 **Celebration Barn Theater** (207-743-8452; celebrationbarn.com), 190 Stock Farm Rd. (off Rt. 117 north of South Paris). In 1972 theater and mime master Tony Montanaro founded a performing-arts school in this red racing-horse barn on Christian Ridge. Summer workshops in acrobatics, mime, voice, clowning, and juggling by resident New Vaudeville artists from around the world in summer.

🔥 **Deertrees Theatre and Cultural Center** (207-583-6747; deertreestheatre.org), Deertrees Rd., Harrison. A 300-seat historic theater, built as an opera house in 1936, saved from being used as an exercise for the local fire department in the 1980s, and restored to its original grandeur complete with perfect acoustics. The nonprofit performing arts center, run by the Deertrees Foundation, is host to the Sebago–Long Lake Music Festival concert series (see below) and the venue for dance, music, and theatrical productions through the summer, as well as children's shows. Assisted audio for the hard of hearing. Fine arts and sculpture in the **Backstage Gallery**, open an hour before showtime.

Sebago–Long Lake Region Chamber Music Festival (207-583-6747), Deertrees Theatre and Cultural Center, Deertrees Rd., Harrison. Five world-class concerts held Tue., mid-July–mid-Aug.

The Public Theatre (207-782-3200; thepublictheatre.org), 2 Great Falls Plaza, Auburn. Professional Equity theater featuring high-quality productions of Broadway and off-Broadway shows.

L/A Arts (207-782-7228; laarts.org), 221 Lisbon St., Lewiston. A local arts agency bringing exhibitions, community arts outreach, dance and musical performances, and award-winning educational programs to the area. **Gallery 5**, 49 Lisbon St., has themed, group exhibits that change every six weeks.

The Maine Music Society (207-782-1403), 215 Lisbon St., Lewiston, is home to both the Maine Chamber Ensemble and the Androscoggin Chorale. A variety of performances throughout the year.

Bates Dance Festival (207-786-6381), Schaeffer Theater, Bates College, Lewiston. Mid-July–mid-Aug. Student, faculty, and professional performances at one of the best dance festivals in the country.

✷ Selective Shopping

ANTIQUES **Orphan Annie's Antiques** (207-782-0638; metiques.com/catalog/orphan.html), 96 Court St., Auburn. Open Mon.–Sat. 10–5, Sun. noon–5. If you're looking for art deco and art nouveau objects, this is the place. Tiffany, Steuben, Fiestaware, Depression glass, and much more. The vintage fashions are worth a long journey. Three-floor warehouse sale every Mon. 10–1.

BOOKSTORES ✐ **Books N Things** (207-739-6200; bntnorway.com), 430 Main St., Norway. Billing itself as "Western Maine's Complete Bookstore," this is a fully stocked shop with a good children's section. Coffee, Stonewall Kitchen products, and author events.

The Maine Bookhouse (207-743-9300; themainebookhouse.com), 1545 Main St. (Rt. 26), Oxford. A new- and used-book store in a charming, mustard-yellow building, with more than 13,000 well-organized titles. Specializing in Maine books, first editions, rare and out-of-print books, and children's classics. Coffee and tea are available. Check out the small art gallery, too.

GALLERIES **Western Maine Art Group-Matolcsy Arts Center** (207-739-6161), 480 Main St., Norway. May–Dec., the Western Maine Art Group presents visual arts exhibits with fine arts, artisan crafts, and sculpture; classes are offered throughout the year, run by executive director Aranka Matolcsy.

The Frost Farm Gallery (207-743-8041; frostfarmgallery.com), 272 Pike's Hill Rd., Norway. Exhibits of area artists and special events.

The Commons Art Collective (207-743-9579; faresharecoop.org), 445 Main St., Norway. Exhibits of member artists; open during Fare Share Market hours and some weekends.

The Painted Mermaid (207-743-7744; paintedmermaid.com), 6 Briggs Ave., South Paris. Brenda Ellis Sauro's paintings and Michael Sauro's sculpture are on display.

SPECIAL SHOPS **United Society of Shakers Store or Museum Reception Center** (207-926-4597), Rt. 26, New Gloucester. Open Mon.–Sat. 10–4:30, Memorial Day–Columbus Day. Sells Shaker herbs, teas, poultry seasoning, mulled cider mix, pumpkin pie spices, and handcrafted items.

The Barn on 26 (207-657-3470; barnon26.com), 361 Shaker Rd., Gray. Set inside a restored, 1870 Shaker-built barn, this business owned by Alice E. Welch features furniture, quilts, hoosiers, and more.

Fiber & Vine (207-739-2664; fiberandvine.com), 402 Main St., Norway. Wool yarns and hand-dyed wools for rug hooking and roving, wool for spinning. Classes in rug hooking, knitting, and spinning. And a wide selection of wine, including unusual rosés.

Rough & Tumble (207-739-2186; roughandtumbledesign.com), 414 Main St., Norway. Handsome, finely crafted bucket bags in Italian leather for women, wallets, clutches, and more, all made here in the studio with its lovely scent of leather.

Christian Ridge Pottery (207-743-8419; applebaker.com), 210 Stock Farm Rd., South Paris (marked from Rt. 26 and from Christian Ridge Rd.). Open Memorial Day weekend–Dec., daily 10–5, except Sun. noon–5. Known for its functional, distinctive stippleware in microwave-safe designs, Christian Ridge Pottery makes coffee- and teapots, apple-baking dishes, and more.

Creaser Jewelers (207-744-0290 or 1-800-686-7633; creaserjewelers.com), 145 Main St., South Paris. Open daily 9–5; Jan.–June 1, Mon.–Sat. Original designs using Maine tourmaline and amethyst. A small room holds specimens of different gems and crystals.

Kedar Quilts (207-583-6182; kedarquilts.com), 18 Valley Rd., Waterford 04088.

UNSPUN WOOL AT FIBER AND VINE IN NORWAY

Margaret Gibson began making quilts as a child in England. Now she makes them for this quaint shop.

OUTLETS **Bates Mill Store** (207-784-7626 or 1-800-552-2837; batesmillstore.com), 41B Chestnut St., Lewiston. Bedspreads, towels, and sheets, as well as blankets made by Maine Heritage Weavers are sold only over the phone and Internet. But go to the Museum of Labor and Industry (see Museum L-A in *To See*) to buy them in person.

 Marden's Discount (207-786-0313; mardens.com), Northwood Park Shopping Center, Rt. 202, Lewiston. Like Renys (see "Damariscotta/Newcastle"), this is a Maine original, the first store in a Maine chain. The founder died in 2002, but the legend lives on. A mix of clothing, staples, furnishings—whatever happens to have been purchased cheaply, after a hurricane like Katrina, or, memorably, after 9/11, when designer clothes here were going at 90 percent off.

 Oxford Mill-End Store (207-539-4451), 971 Main St. (Rt. 26), Oxford. Open Mon.–Fri. 9–4, Sat. 9–1. First-quality woolen and quilting fabric store; flannel and fleece, too.

 New Balance Factory Store (207-539-9022), Rt. 26, Oxford. Mon.–Sat. 9–7, Sun. 9–5. The running shoes you love at major discounts.

✳ Special Events

February: **Norway-Paris Fish and Game Ice Fishing Derby**, on Norway Lake. City

of Auburn and Lost Valley **Winter Festival**, Auburn.

 May: **Maine State Parade** (first Saturday), Lewiston—the state's biggest parade; theme varies annually. **Lilac Festival** at McLaughlin Garden.

 Summer: **First Friday Gallery Hop** includes The Lajos Matolcsy Arts Center (207-739-6161; thewmag.org), 480 Main St., Norway, The Frost Farm Gallery (207-743-8041; frostfarmgallery.com), 272 Pike's Hill Rd., Norway, The Commons Art Collective (207-743-9579; faresharecoop.org), 445 Main St., Norway, The Painted Mermaid (207-743-7744; paintedmermaid.com), 6 Briggs Ave., South Paris, The Café Nomad (207-739-2249; cafenomad.com), 450 Main St., Norway, McLaughlin Garden (see *Green Space*), and Norway Library (207-743-5309; norway.lib .me.us), 258 Main St., Norway.

 July: **The Oxford 250 NASCAR Race** draws entrants from throughout the world to the Oxford Plains Speedway; Harrison celebrates **Old Home Days. Founders Day** (midmonth) on Paris Hill. **The Moxie Festival** (second weekend), downtown Lisbon, features live entertainment, plenty of food, and Moxie (Maine's own soft drink). **The Norway Sidewalk Art Show** has more than 100 exhibitors.

 July–August: **Sebago–Long Lake Music Festival** at Deertrees Theatre, Harrison.

 August: **Deertrees Theatre Festival**, award-winning plays with Equity casts and student acting workshops for all four weeks of the month (207-583-6747; deertreestheatre .org). **Gray Old Home Days** (beginning of the month)—parade, contests, and public feeds. **Festival de Joie** (first weekend), Lewiston—music, dancing, and cultural and crafts displays. **Great Falls Balloon Festival** (fourth weekend), Lewiston—music, games, hot-air launches.

 September: **Oxford County Agricultural Fair** (usually second week), West Paris—horse pulls, 4-H shows, fiddling contests, apple pie judging, and a midway.

 November: **The Biggest Christmas Parade in Maine**, Thanksgiving Saturday in South Paris and Norway.

BETHEL AREA

Bethel may just be Maine's most multiseason inland destination. A summer retreat for city people since trains from Portland to Montreal began stopping in 1851, it's now better known for winter skiing. Spring brings fly-fishing for trout in the Androscoggin River, while fall is prime time for hiking in the White Mountains and Mahoosucs.

Nineteenth-century families stayed the summer in big farmhouses, feasted on home-grown food, then walked it off on nearby mountain trails. The White Mountain National Forest comes within a few miles of town, and trails radiate from nearby Evans Notch. Just 12 miles northwest of Bethel, Grafton Notch State Park also offers short hikes to spectacles such as Screw Auger Falls and to a wealth of well-equipped picnic sites.

In winter skiers file through town on their way to Sunday River Resort, 6 miles to the north. Claiming "the most dependable snow in New England" and "the largest choice of slope-side lodging in the East," Sunday River is justifiably one of New England's most popular ski mountains. Mt. Abram Ski Area, a few miles south of the village, remains an old-fashioned family ski area. Serious dogsledding expeditions offered by two prominent local outfitters are yet another winter draw.

These hills were once far more peopled—entire villages have vanished. Hastings, now just the name of a national forest campground, was once a thriving community complete with post office, stores, and a wood alcohol mill that shipped its product by rail to Portland, thence to England.

The Bethel Inn Resort, born of the railroad era, is still going strong. Opened in 1913 by millionaire William Bingham II and dedicated to a prominent neurologist who came to Bethel to recuperate from a breakdown, it originally featured a program of strenuous exercise—one admired by the locals who gleefully watched wealthy clients paying the doctor to chop down his trees. The inn is still known for two forms of exercise—golf and cross-country skiing.

For Bethel, tourism has remained the icing rather than the cake. Its mill and various wood-product businesses manufacture pine boards, furniture, and more. Farm stands include the seven-generation Middle Intervale Farm. Brooks Bros. is still the name of the hardware store, not a men's clothier. The town is also home to Gould Academy, a coed prep school with a handsome campus.

A FIELD OF SUNFLOWERS NEAR RUMFORD

GUIDANCE Bethel Area Chamber of Commerce (207-824-2282 or 1-800-442-5826; bethelmaine.com) publishes an excellent area guide and maintains a large walk-in information center with restrooms in the depot-style Bethel Station, off Lower Main St. (Rt. 26). Open year-round, weekdays 9–5, varying hours on weekends.

White Mountain National Forest Service (603-466-2713; fs.usda.gov/whitemountain). The office is in Gorham, NH, so call for information about camping, hiking, and

Nancy English

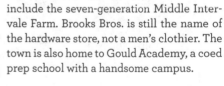

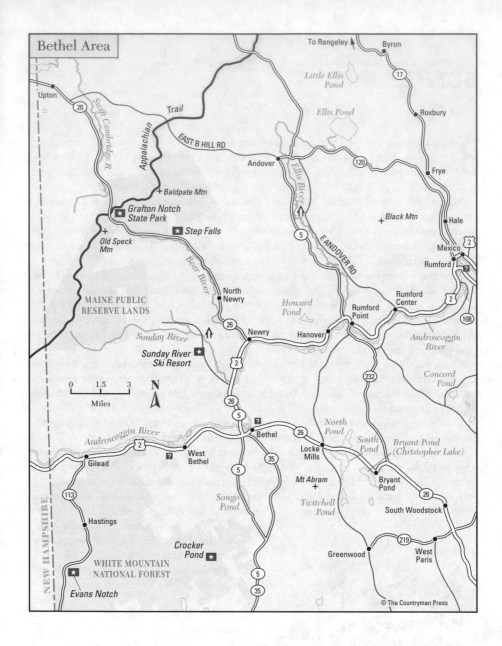

other outdoor activities in the national forest and other nearby natural areas. You can pick up a pass for trailhead parking within the White Mountain National Forest at Pleasant River Campground (207-836-2000; pleasantrivercampground.com), Rt. 2, West Bethel (see Camping).

GETTING THERE *By air:* The **Portland International Jetport**, served by several carriers, is 75 miles from Bethel. All major car rentals are available at the airport (see "Portland"). The **Bethel Airport** (207-824-2669) has a paved 3,818-foot runway, open year-round. **Stagecoach**

Shuttle Service (srstage.com) and **Northeast Charter & Tour** (northeastchartertour.com) pick up from Portland and Manchester airports, offer local service.

By car: Bethel is a convenient way stop between New Hampshire's White Mountains and the Maine coast (via Rt. 2). From Boston, take the Maine Turnpike to Gray, Exit 63; Bethel is 52 miles north on Rt. 26.

GETTING AROUND Mountain Explorer. Just before Christmas weekends through the first weekend in April, this free 28-passenger van connects Sunday River with Bethel shops and inns.

WHEN TO COME The ski season, especially Christmas and February vacations, is high season here; given Sunday River's famous snowmaking, snow is fairly dependable through March. May and June offer great trout fishing in the Androscoggin. Summer is beautiful, with golf, hiking, swimming, horseback riding, mountain and road biking, canoeing, and kayaking. Fall is even more beautiful, the best season for hiking.

✻ To See

HISTORIC HOMES AND MUSEUMS ✪ The Museums of the Bethel Historical Society (207-824-2908; bethelhistorical.org), 10 Broad St., Bethel. Open year round, Tue.–Fri. 10–4 and posted on the website. No charge. Built in 1821, the O'Neil Robinson House was remodeled in the Italianate style in 1881 and also houses the museum shop. Next door is the **Dr. Moses Mason House** (open July and Aug., Tue.–Sat. 1–4). Ambitious, fascinating exhibits are on display in this exquisite Federal-style mansion built in 1813, proof of the town's early prosperity. Restored to its original grandeur, it has magnificent Rufus Porter–style murals in the front hall. Guided tours are $3 adults, $1.50 children.

COVERED BRIDGES Artist's Covered Bridge, Newry (across the Sunday River, 5 miles northwest of Bethel). A weathered town bridge built in 1872 and painted by numerous 19th-century landscape artists, notably John Enneking. A great spot to sun and swim. Other swimming holes can be found at intervals along the road upstream of the bridge.

Lovejoy Covered Bridge, South Andover, roughly 0.25 mile east of Rt. 5. Built across the Ellis River in 1867, another local swimming hole (it's more than 7 miles north of Rt. 2).

✻ To Do

BIRDING Birders will encounter waterfowl in the Patte Marsh area of **White Mountain National Forest**, and in **Grafton Notch State Park** (see *Hiking* for both areas) look for Philadelphia vireos near the Appalachian Trail parking lot, along with many more species.

BICYCLING/WALKING The **Bethel Pathway** offers a nearly 3.5-mile round-trip along the Androscoggin River beginning in the Davis Park picnic area and playground on the eastern edge of town off Rt. 26., where you walk through a replica of the Artists' Covered Bridge (maps available at the Bethel Area Chamber). *✎* **Baker Mountain Bikes** (207-824-0100; barkermountain.com), 53 Mayville Rd. (Rt. 2 North), Bethel. Bicycles sold, rented, and repaired.

CAMPING In the **Evans Notch area** of White Mountain National Forest there are five campgrounds: **Basin** (21 sites), **Cold River** (14 sites), **Crocker Pond** (seven sites), **Hastings**

MAINE MINERALS TO SEE, TO FIND, AND TO BUY IN AND AROUND BETHEL

More than a third of the world's mineral varieties can be found here. Gems include amethyst, aquamarine, tourmaline, and topaz. Mining around here began in 1821 when tourmaline was discovered at Mount Mica.

Maine Mineral and Gem Museum (207-824-3036; mainemineralgemmuseum.org), 99 Main St., Bethel. Open in late 2015, this nine-years-in-the-making project has collected some of the best mineral discoveries in Maine in one building in Bethel. A Hall of Gems displays more than 200 gemstones. One of the stars of the museum is the largest flawless 154-carat morganite gemstone, cut from the 50-pound "Rose of Maine." Specimens from the Smithsonian National Museum of Natural History and the Harvard Museum of Natural History are included in the collection. Geological history displays tell the story of the creation and mining of the luminous stones found in the mountains around Bethel.

Maine Mineralogy Expeditions at Bethel Outdoor Adventure and Campground (207-824-4224; rocksme.biz), 121 Mayville Rd. (Rt. 2), Bethel. Late May–Columbus Day. Buy a bucket and fill it with mine tailings, then sluice it clean in search of gems. Tourmaline is the most exciting discovery, along with mica, rose and smoky quartz, and pretty lepidolite, according to Jeff Parsons, an owner.

✒ **Western Maine Mineral Adventures** (207-890-3953; digmainegems.com), 1413 S. Main St. (Rt. 26), Woodstock. May–Oct., Zoltan and Jody Matolcsy invite you to dig for up to 74 minerals at area mines, mostly closed locations. Call ahead to check available times.

The **Annual Gem, Mineral, and Jewelry Show** (second weekend in July) is a mega mineral event with guided field trips to local quarries.

Sunday River Gems (207-824-3414), 251 Sunday River Rd., Bethel, is open daily 10–6, and sells local jewelers' one-of-a-kind pieces set with Maine gems, along with other gold and silver jewelry. Prospecting equipment also sold.

(24 sites), and **Wild River** (12 sites). All except Crocker Pond and Wild River, which take campers first come, first served, accept reservations mid-May–mid-Oct. through the National Recreation Reservation Service (1-877-444-6777; recreation.gov), but sites are often available without reservations. Also see *Campgrounds* under *Lodging*.

CANOEING AND KAYAKING The **Androscoggin River** has become far more accessible in recent years, with 10 put-in points mapped and shuttle service offered between Shelburne on the New Hampshire line and the Rumford boat landing (androscogginrivertrail .net); the **Sunday River** (beginning at the covered bridge) is also good for whitewater trips in spring. A chain of water connects **North**, **South**, and **Round Ponds** and offers a day of rewarding paddling, with swimming holes and picnic stops en route.

Bethel Outdoor Adventure and Campground (207-824-4224; betheloutdooradventure .com), 121 Mayville Rd. (Rt. 2), sited on the Androscoggin River in Bethel, offers shuttle service, canoe and kayak rentals, guided trips.

Pleasant River Campground (207-836-2000; pleasantrivercampground.com), Rt. 2, West Bethel, rents canoes and kayaks and offers shuttles. **Mahoosuc Guide Service** (207-824-2073; mahoosuc.com), 1513 Bear River Rd., Newry 04261. One- to 10-day canoe trips, including a trip down the Allagash River in fall and spring, a trip with Cree Indians in Quebec, and western U.S. trips, too.

FISHING Fly-fishing for brown, brook, and rainbow trout is a growing sport here, especially along the Androscoggin. World-class bass fishing can be found below Rumford Falls.

EXCURSIONS

Evans Notch. Follow Rt. 2 west to Gilead and turn south on Rt. 113, following the Wild and then the Cold River south through one of the most spectacular mountain passes in northern New England.

Grafton Notch State Park. A beautiful drive even if you don't hike. Continue on beyond Upton for views of Lake Umbagog; note the loop you can make back from Upton along the old road (East B Hill Rd.) to Andover (look for the vintage-1867 Lovejoy Covered Bridge across the Ellis River), then south on Rt. 5 to Rt. 2.

Patte Brook Auto Tour, a 4-mile, self-guided tour with stops at 11 areas along Patte Brook near the national forest's Crocker Pond campground in West Bethel. The tour begins on Forest Rd. No. 7 (Patte Brook Rd.), 5 miles south of Bethel on Rt. 5. A glacial bog, former orchards and homesites, and an old dam and pond are among the clearly marked sites.

Rangeley and Weld loops. You can access both by following Rt. 2 north from Bethel along the Androscoggin River, but back-road buffs may prefer cutting up the narrow rural valleys threaded by Rumford Rd. or Rt. 232 from Locke Mills (Greenwood); both join Rt. 2 at Rumford Point.

Temporary nonresident licenses are available at the Bethel, Newry, and Woodstock town offices; also at **Bethel Outdoor Adventure** (207-824-4224; betheloutdooradventure.com), 121 Mayville Rd. (Rt. 2), and **Sun Valley Sports** (207-824-7533; sunvalleysports.com), 129 Sunday River Rd., both of which offer guided fishing, as does **Bethel Bait, Tackle & More** (207-824-4868; bethelbait.com), 7 Mechanic St. We can recommend **Locke Mountain Guide Service** (207-381-7322) and **Orion Outfitters** (603-401-1802; orionoutfitters.net).

GOLF **Bethel Inn Resort** (207-824-2175; bethelinn.com), 21 Broad St., Bethel. An 18-hole, 6,700-yard course and driving range. Mid-May–Oct. the Guaranteed Performance School of Golf (PGA) offers three- and five-day sessions (classes limited to three students per PGA instructor); golf-cart rentals are available.

Sunday River Golf Club. See the Sunday River sidebar for details about this 18-hole course top-rated by *Golf Week* and *Golf Digest*.

HIKING **White Mountain National Forest**, although primarily in New Hampshire, includes 41,943 acres in Maine. A number of the trails in the Evans Notch area are spectacular. Trail maps for the Baldface Circle Trail, Basin Trail, Bickford Brook Trail, and Caribou Trail are available from the **Bethel Area Chamber of Commerce** (207-824-2282 or 1-800-442-5826; bethelmaine.com).

Grafton Notch State Park, Rt. 26, between Newry and Upton. From Bethel, take Rt. 2 east to Rt. 26 north for 7.8 miles. Turn left at Newry Corner and drive toward New Hampshire for 8.7 miles. **Screw Auger Falls** is 1 mile farther—a spectacular area at the end of the Mahoosuc Range. Other sights include **Mother Walker Falls** and **Moose Cave**, a 0.5-mile nature walk. The big hike is up **Old Speck**, the third highest mountain in the state; round-trip is 7.8 miles. Also see *Green Space* for the new 35-mile Grafton Loop Trail.

Wight Brook Nature Preserve/Step Falls can be found just before the entrance to Grafton Notch State Park. From Newry Corner, drive 7.9 miles. On your right will be a sign for Step Falls.

In Shelburne there are hiking trails on **Mount Crag, Mount Cabot**, and **Ingalls Mountain,** and there are more trails in **Evans Notch**. For details, check the Appalachian Mountain Club's *White Mountain Guide* (subscribe online for $15 at outdoors.org) and John Gibson's *50 Hikes in Coastal and Inland Maine: From Burnt Meadow Mountains to Maine's Bold Coast* (Countryman Press).

Mount Will Hiking Trail. Developed by the Bethel Conservation Commission, this 3.25-mile loop is a good family trip; many people choose to climb only to the North Ledges

(640 vertical feet in 0.75 mile), yielding a view of the Androscoggin Valley, which only gets better over the next 1.5 miles—climbing over ledges 1,450 feet and then descending the South Cliffs. The trailhead parking lot is opposite the recycling center on Rt. 2, just 1.9 miles east of the Riverside Rest Area (which is just beyond the turnoff for Sunday River Resort).

HORSEBACK RIDING **Deepwood Farm** (207-824-2595; deepwoodfarm.com), Albany, offers trail rides and summer camps. **New England Riding and Driving** (207-731-6888; newenglandridinganddriving.com), Telemark Inn, Mason. Leo Joost and Steve Crone offer "Learn to Carriage Drive" packages and riding instruction, as well as therapeutic riding and driving for special-needs children.

SWIMMING There are numerous lakes and river swimming holes in the area. It's best to ask the chamber of commerce about where access is currently possible. Reliable spots include:

Angevine Park and Swim Pond (207-824-2669). The town of Bethel has a swimming pond open to all free of charge. It is located on North Rd., 2.2 miles from Rt. 2 (turn in at Big Adventure Center and the Norseman Inn & Motel). Open daily 10–7, summer only.

Artists' Covered Bridge. Follow SUNDAY RIVER SKI RESORT signs north from Bethel, but bear right at two Y-intersections instead of turning onto either of the ski-area access roads. Look for the covered bridge on your left. Space for parking, bushes for changing.

Wild River in Evans Notch, Gilead, offers some obvious access spots off Rt. 113, as does the **Bear River**, which follows Rt. 26 through Grafton Notch.

✳ Winter Activities

DOWNHILL SKIING See the sidebar for Sunday River Resort.

🐾 ⚘ **Mt. Abram Ski Area** (207-875-5000; mtabram.com), Locke Mills (Greenwood). Open 11–7 Thu.–Fri., 9–4 weekends and holidays. With 54 trails and slopes, this is a great place to learn to ski—but there are also a number of black-diamond trails. Ski terrain comprises 560 acres, and you'll find small crowds and lots of local tradition. A lightning strike and fire destroyed the base lodge in 2011, and the temporary structure adds to the down-home charm. The vertical drop is 1,150 feet, but well-designed trails create the sense of a big mountain. Facilities include two double chairlifts, T-bars, and a magic carpet. The ski area offers tubing on Fri. nights and weekends. Fri.-night Town League Race Series and live music help make Mt. Abram a community-focused ski area. There's a PSIA ski school with snowboard and telemark instruction. $49 adults, $39 seniors and juniors on weekends and holidays, $79 per car load on Fri., $25 Thu. Those over 80 and 5 and under ski free.

CROSS-COUNTRY SKIING ⚘ **Bethel Nordic Ski Center** (207-824-2175; caribourecreation .com), Bethel Inn, Bethel. More than 30 km of groomed trails, most wide enough for skating, begin on the inn's golf course and meander off through woods and fields with some beautiful mountain views. Rental equipment, lessons, food and drink available.

Carter's X-C Center (207-539-4848; cartersxcski.com), 781 Intervale Rd. (off Rt. 26 south of the village), Bethel. Open daily during winter. The Carters, one of Bethel's oldest families, maintain 55 km of wooded trails on 1,000 acres, meandering from 600 up to 1,800 feet in elevation; an easy loop runs along the Androscoggin River. Sales and rentals, lessons, lodging; additional center on Rt. 26 in Oxford with 40 km of trails.

The Outdoor Center (theoutdoorcenter.net), Sunday River, Newry. Cross-country and snowshoeing trails with picnic areas; equipment rentals available.

DOGSLEDDING **Mahoosuc Guide Service** (207-824-2073; mahoosuc.com), 1513 Bear River Rd., Newry 04261. Polly Mahoney and Kevin Slater have been offering combination skiing and mushing trips for more than 20 years. From Mahoosuc Mountain Lodge they offer two-day trips in the Mahoosucs and three days that include Umbagog Lake, also four-day "Northern Classic" trips from wilderness lodge to lodge near Moosehead Lake.

New England Dogsledding (207-731-6888; newenglanddogsledding.com), 591 Kings Hwy., Mason Township. Steve Crone is a competitive dogsledder with decades of experience. Leo Joost has a special empathy with their extensive team. Based at the Telemark Inn, a rustic lodge built in 1898 as a lumber baron's retreat and surrounded by woodland, they offer multiple-day "Learn to Dogsled" packages in nearby areas, including 60 miles of groomed, high trails in the Umbagog National Wildlife Refuge. One- to three-hour rides are also available.

ICE SKATING **Bethel Inn Resort** loans skates and offers skating at no charge. Also see the **Sunday River Resort** sidebar.

SLEIGH RIDES The **Bethel Inn Resort** (see *Lodging*), Bethel, hosts sleigh rides on Sat. night. **Deepwood Farm** (207-824-2595; deepwoodfarm.com), Albany, offers sleigh rides winter days and evenings.

SNOWMOBILING Contact the Bethel Area Chamber of Commerce for information on where to get maps of the trail system. Maine and New Hampshire also maintain 60 miles of trails in the Evans Notch District. **Northeast Snowmobile and ATV Rentals** (1-800-458-1838; northeastsnowmobile.com), 121 Mayville Rd. (Rt. 2), Bethel, rents snowmobiles.

✳ Green Space

The Mahoosuc Land Trust (207-824-3806; mahoosuc.org), P.O. Box 981, Bethel 04217. Formed in 1988 to preserve land in the Mahoosuc Range and the Androscoggin Valley, the trust owns islands, shoreland, and floodplain land, along with easements on land in the eastern foothills and on the banks of a large pond. Grafton Loop Trail, a trail about 35 miles long, is a collaborative partnership on land trust land with Maine Appalachian Trail Club (matc.org). It can be accessed at the Grafton Loop Trailhead on Rt. 26, or at the Appalachian Trail parking lot in Grafton Notch State Park. The Rumford Whitecap Mountain Preserve was purchased in 2007; the 2.5-mile trail is a popular day trip, and is accessed off East Andover Rd. in Rumford. A map of the 42-mile Androscoggin Canoe Trail is available.

✳ Lodging

ALL LISTINGS ARE IN BETHEL 04217 UNLESS OTHERWISE NOTED

INNS ✪ ☃ ✿ ☞ ♿ **The Bethel Inn Resort** (207-824-2175 or 1-800-654-0125; bethelinn.com). The 49 rooms in the inn and guesthouses vary widely in size and view (request a larger room in back, overlooking the mountains), but all main inn rooms have air-conditioning, flat-screen TV, and private bath; some have a fireplace. Families opt for one of the 60 one-, two-, and three-bedroom town houses on the golf course and on Mill Hill Rd. Indoor–outdoor pool (heated to 92 degrees in winter); also two saunas, an exercise room, a game room, and a lounge. The 18-hole golf course, with seven holes dating to 1915 and 11 more added by Geoffrey Cornish, is a big draw, with golf-school sessions offered throughout the season. Other facilities also include a Har-Tru tennis court, a boathouse with canoes, and a sandy beach on Songo Pond, as well as an extensive cross-country ski and snowshoe

SUNDAY RIVER RESORT

Powered by its snow guns (powered in turn by snowmaking ponds fed continuously by the Sunday River), the family-geared Sunday River Resort is known for the dependability and quality of its snow. Six miles north of Bethel, this rambling resort can now accommodate 6,000 visitors on-mountain on any given day, and to fill all those beds now offers year-round activities. (207-824-3000; sundayriver.com), Newry 04261.

Courtesy of Sunday River Resort

SUMMER/FALL

CHAIRLIFT RIDES The Chondola operates in summer and fall for rides to the North Peak, offering spectacular views of the Mahoosuc

THE CHONDOLA LIFT RUNS SUMMER, FALL, AND WINTER

Mountains; Old Speck Mountain, the third highest peak in Maine, is visible from the summit. You can choose to ride up in an enclosed cabin or an open chair, and hike down on a trail.

GOLF Sunday River Golf Club is top-rated by *Golf Week* and *Golf Digest*. Designed by Robert Trent Jones, the 18-hole championship course has gracefully situated, wide fairways with views of surrounding mountains. Lessons, clinics, and New England Golf Camp for ages 12–17.

MOUNTAIN BIKING The Sunday River Bike Park offers 25 miles of terrain for all levels: dirt roads, singletrack trails with jumps, bridges, and berms. The bike park is accessed by the Chondola lift; trails cover North and South Peaks. Bike rentals, lessons, and events.

Courtesy of Sunday River Resort

MOUNTAIN BIKING AT SUNDAY RIVER

SKIING AT SUNDAY RIVER

WINTER

DOWNHILL SKIING ⊕✦ A total of 132 trails and glades now lace eight interconnected mountain peaks, from an easy 3-mile run from the top of Barker Mountain to White Heat off White Cap, considered one of the premier bump runs in the East. The trails are served by 15 lifts including a Chondola (a hybrid chair/gondola): nine quad chairlifts (four high-speed detachable), three triple chairlifts, one double, and two surface lifts. The vertical descent is 2,340 feet, and the top elevation is 3,150 feet. Snowmaking covers more than 95 percent of the non-gladed terrain. The six terrain parks range from beginner to advanced, including—new for the 2014 season—a 15-acre park with a 500-foot superpipe. Facilities include three base lodges and a Peak Lodge, ski shops, several restaurants, and 6,000 slope-side beds (see *Lodging*). The Perfect Turn Ski & Snowboard School offers Guaranteed Learn-to-Ski in One Day and specialty clinics, **Tiny Turns** (ages 3 and 4), **Mogul Munchkins** (4–6), **Mogul Meisters** (7–14), and the Gould Academy Competition Programs. Day care for ages 6 weeks to 6 years. Night skiing on weekends and select holidays. Sunday River is also home to Maine Adaptive Sports and Recreation. A Mountain Trolley connects the mountain base lodges and lodging properties; the **Mountain Explorer** links the mountain with Bethel shops, restaurants, and lodging.

ICE SKATING (207-824-3000). The lighted rink is free and open every day and evening that weather permits at Snow Cap Lodge.

YEAR-ROUND

ZIPLINE TOURS Cross back and forth high above a deep ravine and streambed near the ski trails of Sunday River from a series of six lines from 100 to 300 feet long. Reservations are recommended for the tours, offered in summer, fall, and winter. The six-zipline tour takes about 2½ hours.

THE ZIPLINE OPERATES SUMMER, FALL, AND WINTER.

network. From $50 per person double occupancy in the inn including breakfast; town houses, $110. Spa and concierge center offering fly-fishing, sleigh rides, and canoe and kayak trips.

♂ ♿ **Mill Hill Inn** (207-824-3241; millhillinn.com), 24 Mill Hill Rd. Lee and Woody Hughes have done a superb job of renovating this old carriage-barn-turned-longtime-inn. Its six rooms (private bath) and two suites are comfortably, tastefully decorated. Game room with a pool table and two saunas. Studio Bistro bar (see *Dining Out*). Rooms $99–109, suites (with kitchen facilities and sleeping up to six) $129–159.

🐾 **Sudbury Inn** (207-824-2174; thesudburyinn.com), 151 Main St., P.O. Box 369. A restored village inn built in 1873 to serve train travelers (the depot was just down the street). There are 11 guest rooms ($106 double in-season) and six suites ($139). All have a private bath, TV, and air-conditioning, and two suites have whirlpool. The dining room is popular (see *Dining Out*). Suds Pub (see *Eating Out*) is a year-round evening gathering spot. Pets are accepted only in the Carriage House for $15 a night. The town house accommodates six, $475 during ski season.

The Briar Lea Inn at the Jolly Drayman Pub (207-824-4717 or 1-877-311-1299; briarleainn.com), Rt. 2/26. Open year-round. One mile west of town, 5 miles east of Sunday River. Cindy Coughenour and Fred Seibert are innkeepers at this 1850s farmhouse, an attractive inn whose six rooms feature private bath, flat-screen TV, phone, and eclectic antique decor, all updated in 2011. The pub is open to the public (see *Dining Out*). The sitting area with a fireplace is particularly attractive, a great place to enjoy a drink. $85–140.

♪ **Telemark Inn** (207-731-6888; newenglanddogsledding.com), 591 Kings Hwy., Mason Township 04217. A rustic 1890s lodge off the beaten track, surrounded by national forest. Longtime innkeeper and outdoorsman Steven Crone and his hospitable partner Leo Joost offer outdoor adventures featuring their 70 huskies in snow season and horseback riding/carriage driving in summer. Five comfortable guest rooms share two baths; rates begin at $125–145 per couple with breakfast.

B&BS Holidae House Bed and Breakfast (207-824-3400 or 1-877-224-3400; holidae

house.com), P.O. Box 1248, 85 Main St. A gracious turn-of-the-century Victorian built by a local lumber baron, freshly refurbished and repainted under new owners John and Jeanette Poole. Seven rooms are furnished in comfortable antiques, with cable TV, private bath, and air-conditioning. $125–139 double, including a full breakfast made to order.

☉ **Bethel Hill Bed & Breakfast** (207-824-2461; bethelhill.com), 66 Broad St. Renovated with the needs of a B&B in mind, Scott and Carol Gould host three suites with whirlpool bath and cable TV, ceiling fans and air-conditioning, and soundproofing in the walls. $139–169 depending on season, includes complimentary pair of bikes. Scott Gould, a certified staff trainer and Level III ski pro at Sunday River, can provide ski-tuning lessons. Inquire about the Lake House.

♪ **Chapman Inn** (207-824-2657 or 1-877-359-1498; chapmaninn.com), 1 Mill Hill Rd. Sandra Frye brings years in the hospitality business to this rambling white wooden inn on the common. Eight comfortable units have private bath and two share; there's cable TV and air-conditioning in all rooms, and a phone in all, too. Common space in the barn includes a game room with a pool table and two saunas. $79–119 for rooms, $89–139 for suites; $35 per person for the dorm, breakfast included, with fresh fruit, muffins, and omelet of the day.

SKI LODGES AND CONDOS ♪ **Sunday River Resort** maintains its own toll-free reservation number, 1-800-543-2SKI, good nationwide and in Canada; the service is geared toward winter and condo information. It offers more than 6,000 slope-side beds.

The 230-room **Grand Summit Hotel** has both standard and kitchen-equipped units, a health club with a pool, and conference facilities; it offers rooms and studios as well as one-, two-, and three-bedroom efficiency units. The 195-room **Jordan Hotel** is off by itself but linked by ski trails as well as a road, circled by the mountains of the Jordan Bowl; facilities include a health club, a swimming pool, and restaurants. Hotel prices start at $69. In winter, condo units are based on ski packages, from $69 per night or $359 per person for five days. Most winter lodging rates include a lift ticket and a ski school lesson.

Nine condominium complexes range from studios to three-bedroom units. Each complex has access to an indoor pool, Jacuzzi, sauna, laundry, recreation room, and game room; **Cascades** and **Sunrise** offer large common rooms with fireplaces. **Merrill Brook Village Condominiums** have fireplaces, and many have a whirlpool tub. **South Ridge** also offers a fireplace in each unit, ranging from studios to three bedrooms. The 68-room **Snow Cap Inn** has an atrium with fieldstone fireplaces, an exercise room, and an outdoor Jacuzzi; it also offers reasonably priced bunks.

MOTELS ✪ 🐾 🛏 **The Inn at the Rostay** (207-824-3111 or 1-888-754-0072; rostay.com), 186 Mayville Rd. Kathy and Al Thrall's motel consists of units ranged behind a 19th-century house, with 19 rooms accommodating one to four people, including a two-room suite. Number 26 is a surprisingly cozy room in the older but nicely renovated 1950s section, with a queen bed and a sofa. All rooms have phone, heat, TV and VCR, refrigerator, and microwave. Heated pool in summer and outdoor hot tub year-round. Hot chocolate and cookies après ski. A full breakfast with a menu is served ($9 extra). The house has a guest parlor that doubles as a showcase for locally made quilts, sold in a quilt store in back. $69–135 for rooms, $160–250 for two-bedroom suites.

🔋 (((•))) **Bethel Village Motel** (207-824-2989; bethelvillagemotel.com), 88 Main St. A real find! A 10-room, middle-of-the-village, family-owned motel with nicely decorated rooms, AC, TV, phones, and coffee in the friendly office. $149.80 for two nights includes tax.

🛏 **The Norseman Motel** (207-824-2002 or 1-800-824-0722; norsemaninn.com), 134 Mayville Rd. (Rt. 2). The 22 spacious motel units are in a renovated barn. Guests can sit by the common room's fireplace, made from local stones, in the old farmstead where continental breakfast is served. Amenities include a laundry room and game room, deck, and walking trails. $68–158 depending on season.

CAMPGROUNDS 🐾 🛏 **Littlefield Beaches** (207-875-3290; littlefieldbeaches.com), 13 Littlefield Lane, Greenwood 04255. Open mid-May–Sept. Arthur and Lisa Park run a clean, quiet family campground surrounded by three connecting lakes. Full hook-ups, a

laundry room, miniature golf, a game room, swimming, kayak rentals.

✪ 🐾 🛏 **Bethel Outdoor Adventure and Campground** (207-824-4224; betheloutdoor adventure.com), Rt. 2. Jeff and Pattie Parsons offer RV and tent sites with a camp store on the Androscoggin River (where you can swim), within walking distance of downtown.

🛏 **Pleasant River Campground** (207-836-2000; pleasantrivercampground.com), 800 West Bethel Rd. (Rt. 2). Wooded sites, restrooms, pool, playground, and many recreational possibilities. In addition to camping, Mike and Michelle Mador offer canoe and kayak rentals, Androscoggin River access, shuttle service, and lobster boils, pig roasts, and barbecues. $22–30 daily.

✪ 🐾 **Stony Brook Recreation** (207-824-2846; stonybrookrec.com), 42 Powell Place, Hanover 04237. Open year-round with open and wooded sites.

🐾 **Grafton Notch Campground** (207-824-2292; campgrafton.com), near the Bear River in Newry 04261. Open May–Oct. The closest campground to Grafton Notch State Park. $25 a day.

Also see **Papoose Pond Resort and Campground** in "Oxford Hills." For campgrounds in the White Mountain National Forest, see *To Do—Camping*.

SPECIAL LODGING ✪ 🛏 **The Maine Houses** (1-800-646-8737; themainehouses .com), Bryant Pond, are four houses located on or near Lake Christopher, good for small groups or large reunions.

✳ Where to Eat

ALL RESTAURANTS ARE IN BETHEL UNLESS OTHERWISE NOTED

DINING OUT **22 Broad Street** (207-824-3496), 22 Broad St. This handsome inn holds an elegant dining room with an Italian-inspired menu that starts with carpaccio, escarole and bean soup, and more. A lovely primo, first course, might be the ravioli amatriciana with pancetta, onions, and herbs. Among secondi there is osso buco, braised veal shank, and braciole alla Siciliana—beef rolls simmered in tomato sauce. Screened porch for summer dining, with 20-plus tables, plus a martini bar. Entrées $12.50–24.

✪ **The Bethel Inn Resort** (207-824-2175 or 1-800-654-0125), Bethel Common. Serves breakfast and dinner. An elegant formal dining room with a Steinway, hearth, and large windows overlooking the golf course and hills, plus a year-round veranda. The menu offers a choice of a dozen entrées that might include Maine lobster, Tuscan veal chop, and prime rib. Entrées $17–32.

Cho Sun (207-824-7370; chosunrestaurant .com), 141 Main St. Open Wed.–Sun. 5:30–9. Pleasing atmosphere and authentic Japanese and Korean cuisine from owner Pok Sun Lane. Sample Korean classics like savory and spicy beef bulgogi, kimchee stew, and teriyaki steak.

Mill Hill Inn (207-824-3241), 24 Mill Hill Rd. Open Thu.–Sun. for dinner. The tapas and small-plate menu is a delightful discovery in this pleasant dining room; a couple might split several plates, perhaps Thai fish cakes with savory orange-ginger sauce ($8.50), seared tuna with ginger sesame sauce ($16), or falafel with yogurt cilantro sauce, pita, and spinach salad ($8.75). Full bar. Frequent weekend music.

Sudbury Inn & Bistro 151 (207-824-2174; sudburyinn.com), Main St. Open for dinner 5:30–9 Tue.–Sun. year-round, but check. Attractive, traditional dining rooms and a sunporch in a 19th-century village inn. Menu changes seasonally with local ingredients. Try the veal Piccata with mushrooms, white wine, and capers. Entrées $13–31.

🍴 **Jolly Drayman Pub at the Briar Lea Inn** (207-824-4717), Rt. 2/26. The inn's welcoming dining room serves dinner daily. This English pub serves classics like fish-and-chips and bangers and mash along with Indian specialties including kormas, tikka masala, and vindaloos. Fine selection of draft and bottled beers. A reliably good and reasonably priced place for dinner. Entrées $10–20.

S. S. Milton (207-824-2589), 43 Main St. Open for dinner 5–9, lunch in summer. Entrées ($16–23) might include scallops Nantucket with white wine, lemon, and cheddar cheese topped with Ritz crackers, or Boothbay fettuccine with Maine lobster, scallops, and shrimp in a white cream wine sauce.

Sunday River Resort operates several "fine-dining" restaurants, namely **Camp**

DICOCOA'S MARKET & BAKERY

Nancy English

(207-824-5858; sundayriver.com) at the Grand Summit Resort Hotel and **Sliders** (207-824-5000) at the Jordan Hotel. Inquire about **Dinners on North Peak**, offered Sat. evening late Dec.–late Mar. and once a month in summer on the Sat. nearest the full moon.

The Phoenix (207-824-2222; phoenix houseandwell.com), Skiway Rd., just before South Ridge Base Lodge at Sunday River. With windows on a great view, pick from a list of pastas and sauces. A pub atmosphere but also special beer-pairing dinners. Live music in winter. Entrées $16–22.

EATING OUT ✪ 🍴 **DiCocoa's Market & Bakery** (207-824-6386; cafedicocoa.com), 125 Main St. A market and café with breakfast and lunch items; an ethnic dinner is served some Sat. by reservation only, BYOB. Cathi DiCocco's cheerful eatery specializes in vegan and vegetarian dishes. Full bakery, juice and espresso bars, and wonderful pain au chocolat. A calzone with cheese was crisp and savory, and stir-fry with tofu and bell peppers delicious.

✪ 🍴 **Suds Pub** (207-824-6558 or 1-800-395-7837), downstairs at the Sudbury Inn, 151 Main St. Open year-round, from 4:30 PM daily; lunch served in summer and between Thanksgiving and mid-Apr. A friendly pub with 29 beers on tap and a reasonably priced pub menu with a wide choice of pizzas. Burgers, soups and salads, ribs, lobster rolls, and pasta.

Black Diamond Steakhouse (207-824-4044; blackdiamondsteakhouse.com), 96

Sunday River Rd., Bethel. Angus beef and seafood fresh local in-season produce, and chicken, burgers, pasta dishes, and hearty salads.

Milbrook Tavern and Terrace (207-824-2175; bethelinn.com) at the Bethel Inn Resort. The big inn has a comfortable barroom and outside terrace, serving pub food and basic dinner.

Rooster's Roadhouse (207-824-0309; roostersroadhouse.com), 159 Mayville Rd., Rt. 2. Popular with locals and visitors alike, this roadhouse serves lunch and dinner all year round. Owners Steve Etheridge and Gary Szpara preside at this pub and family-style eatery. Entrées up to $28.

Funky Red Barn (207-824-3003; funkyredbarn.com), 19 Summer St. The Funky Burger is served on a huge Thomas' English muffin. Nasty Nachos include black olives and jalapeños to get the digestive turmoil up to speed. Try the last-Thursday-of-the-month $8.50 prime rib dinner.

Crossroads Diner (207-824-3673), 24 Mayville Rd. (Rt. 2). Breakfast, lunch, and dinner. A local hangout.

Sunday River Brewing Co. (207-824-4ALE; sundayriverbrewpub.com), junction of Sunday River Rd. and Rt. 2, North Bethel. Open from 11:30 for lunch and dinner daily, with a build-your-own burger, pizza, and gourmet hot dogs. Live entertainment.

Matterhorn Ski Bar (207-824-6271; matterhornskibar.com), Sunday River Rd., ski season only, offers entertainment and steak, seafood, and brick-oven pizza.

Kowloon Village Chinese Restaurant (207-824-3707), Lower Main St. Simon and his wife are from Kowloon, and their Chinese food is good. Eat in or take-out.

Smokin' Good BBQ (207-824-3754), in the parking lot of the **Good Food Store** (goodfoodbethel.com), Rt. 2. Cooked low and slow for up to 16 hours. "You Don't Need Teeth to Eat Our Beef," says the motto.

Homeslice Pizza of Bethel (207-824-3637), 188 Main St. New York-style pizza, burgers, subs, and salads. Delivery beginning at 4 PM.

FARMERS' MARKET AND FARM STANDS **Bethel Farmers' Market**, summer Sat. 9–1 at the junction of Rt. 2 and Parkway; also Farmers at the Market on Wed. afternoons. Call DiCocoa's (see *Eating Out*) to

check. **Middle Intervale Farm** (207-824-2230), 758 Intervale Rd., Bethel. Open May–Dec. 1. Apples, salad greens, hot peppers, many varieties of garlic, and much more, in-season. **Swain Family Farm** (207-824-2949), 185 West Bethel Rd., corn, apples, veggies.

✳ Entertainment

The Mahoosuc Arts Council (207-824-3575; mahoosucarts.org) presents the Mahoosuc Arts Council Summer Bandstand Series, Sun.-afternoon Aug. concerts on the Bethel common. Music begins at 4 PM.

✳ Selective Shopping

ALL ENTRIES ARE IN BETHEL UNLESS OTHERWISE NOTED

ANTIQUES **Steam Mill Antiques** (207-824-0844; steammillantiques.com), 155 West Bethel Rd. (Rt. 2). Owner Jay Boschetti sells a huge range of antiques, with china, glass, art, furniture, and antique signs just a few categories of items for sale.

Peabody Tavern Antiques and Collectibles (207-836-2422), 695 Gilead Rd. (Rt. 2), Gilead, is set across from Bog Trail in a red house.

ART ✪ **Bonnema Potters** (207-824-2821; bonnemapotters.com), Lower Main St. June–Oct., Thu.–Tue. Destination shopping! Since

Nancy English

THERE ARE 29 BEERS ON DRAFT AT THE SUDS PUB IN THE SUDBURY INN

1975 Garret and Melody Bonnema have attracted a loyal following for their distinctive stoneware and porcelain: lamps, dinnerware, and—more recently—Melody's stunning tiles subtly depicting local landscapes, all produced and sold in Bonnema's big barn. Seconds are available.

Elements Art Gallery (207-357-0189; elementsartgallerymaine.com), 162 Main St. Open daily 10–5. Paintings, jewelry, pottery, photographs, and more, all handmade locally.

SPECIAL SHOPS **Brooks Bros. Inc.** (207-824-2158), 73 Main St. All kinds of old-fashioned hardware along with up-to-date products and fine service.

Maine Line Products (207-824-2522; mainelineproducts.com), 23 Main St. Made-in-Maine products and souvenirs, among which the standout is the Maine Woodsman's Weatherstick. We have one tacked to our back porch, and it consistently points up to predict fair weather and down for foul. A second store, an expanded version of this old landmark, is open in Locke Mills/Greenwood: even more pine furniture, toys, wind chimes, buckets, birdhouses.

S. Timberlake (1-800-780-6681; stimberlake.com), 158 Mayville Rd. (Rt. 2 east). The showroom has windows on the woodworking shop, where tours are offered and everything is hand built. Shaker furniture is a specialty.

Ruthie's Boutique (207-824-2989), Main St. From elegant little cocktail dresses to smooth sweaters in jewel colors.

✳ Special Events

March: **Maine Adaptive Sports & Recreation Ski-A-Thon** (third weekend). **The Annual**

Dumont Cup (Sunday River Resort), started after Bethel native Simon Dumont broke the quarterpipe record in 2008.

June: **Androscoggin River Canoe/Kayak Race.**

July: **Bethel Historical Society Fourth of July Celebration. Bethel Annual Art Fair** (first Saturday). **Strawberry Festival** (date depends on when strawberries are ready; announced in local papers), Locke Mills Union Church. **Annual Gem, Mineral, and Jewelry Show** (second weekend) at Telstar High School in Bethel—exhibits, demonstrations, and guided field trips to local quarries. **Mollyockett Day** (third weekend)—features road races, a parade, and fireworks honoring an 18th-century medicine woman who helped the first settlers.

August: **Andover Old Home Days** (first weekend). **Annual Maine State Triathlon Classic** (second weekend), Bethel, and the Saturday before, **Kids' Triathlon. Sudbury Canada Days** (second weekend), Bethel—children's parade, historical exhibits, old-time crafts demonstrations, bean supper, and variety show.

Third weekend of September: **Bethel Harvest Fest and Chowdah and Apple Pie Contest. Upper Andro Two-Fly Contest** and **Drift Boat Championship.**

Columbus Day weekend: **Fall Festival at Sunday River Resort** includes the now world-famous **wife-carrying championship**—U.S. version started here—free chairlift rides, wine tasting, crafts, and much more.

Day after Thanksgiving: **Local Craft and Wares Fair.**

December: A series of Christmas fairs and festivals climaxes with a **Living Nativity** on the Bethel common the Sunday before Christmas. Free horse-drawn wagon rides on Sat.

RANGELEY LAKES REGION

Rangeley Lake itself is only 9 miles long, but the Rangeley Lakes Region includes 112 lakes and ponds, among them vast sheets of water with names like Mooselookmeguntic, Cupsuptic, and Aziscohos.

The scenery is so magnificent that segments of the two roads leading into Rangeley, Rts. 4 and 17, have been designated National Scenic Byways. In summer be sure to approach the town of Rangeley via Rt. 17 and pull out at the Height of Land. Below you, four of the six major Rangeley Lakes glisten blue-black, ringed by high mountains. Patterned only by sun and clouds, uninterrupted by any village or even a building, this green-blue sea of fir and hardwoods flows north and west to far horizons.

A spate of 1863 magazine and newspaper stories first publicized this area as "home of the largest brook trout in America," and two local women ensured its fishing fame through ensuing decades. In the 1880s Phillips native Cornelia "Fly Rod" Crosby pioneered the use of the light fly rod and artificial lure and in 1897 became the first Registered Maine Guide; in 1924 Carrie Stevens, a local milliner, fashioned a streamer fly from gray feathers and caught a 6-pound, 13-ounce brook trout at Upper Dam. Stevens took second prize in *Field & Stream*'s annual competition, and the Gray Ghost remains one of the most popular fishing flies sold.

The Rangeley Lakes Historical Society is papered with photographs and filled with mementos of the 1880s through the 1930s, an era in which trainloads of fishermen and visitors arrived in Rangeley every day throughout the summer. In the 1940s and 1950s hotels closed and burned, and in the 1980s many sporting camps were sold off as individual "condominiums."

Landlocked salmon now augment trout in both local lakes and streams, and fly-fishing equipment and guides are easy to come by. Moose-watching, kayaking, and canoeing, as well as hiking and golf, are big draws; shops and restaurants, events, and entertainment are as lively again as they were in the 1930s. Rangeley is a town of 1,500 year-round residents, and "downtown" is a short string of single-story frame buildings along the lake. The village of Oquossoc, 7 miles west, is just a scattering of shops and restaurants on a peninsula between Rangeley and Mooselookmeguntic Lakes. The summer population zooms to 6,000, but both year-round homes and camps are hidden away by the water, and much of that water is itself sequestered in woodland. Saddleback, Rangeley's 4,120-foot, 66-trail mountain, is one of New England's best ski resorts, with huge investments in trails, condominiums, and amenities in the past few years. Because the area's snow is so dependable, a separate and well-groomed cross-country system has also evolved.

Within the past dozen years hundreds of square miles have been protected through cooperative ventures involving state agencies, timberland owners, and the Rangeley Lakes Heritage Trust.

GUIDANCE **Rangeley Lakes Region Chamber of Commerce** (207-864-5364 or 1-800-MT-LAKES; rangeleymaine.com), P.O. Box 317, Rangeley 04970. Open year-round, Mon.–Sat. 10–4. The chamber maintains a walk-in information center in the village and publishes a handy *Accommodations and Services Guide*; *Who, What, Where & When*; as well as an indispensable map. The *Rangeley Hiking Trail Guide* put out by TRAC, Trails for Rangeley Area Coalition, is also sold here.

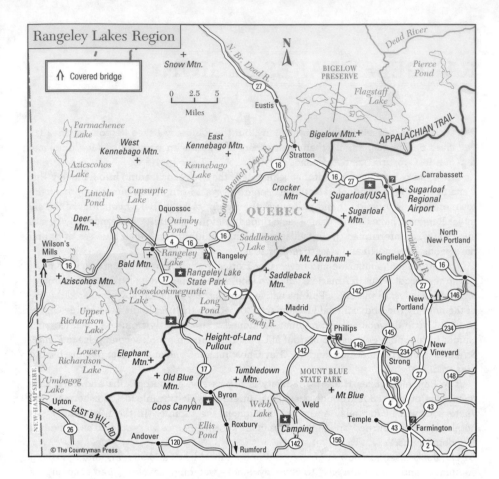

GETTING THERE *By car:* From points south, take the Maine Turnpike to Exit 75 (Auburn), then take Rt. 4 to Rangeley. In summer the slightly longer (roughly half an hour) but more scenic route is to turn off Rt. 4 onto Rt. 108 in Livermore, follow it to Rumford, and then take Rt. 17 to Oquossoc. From the Bethel area, take Rt. 17 to Rumford. From New Hampshire's White Mountains, take Rt. 16 east.

By bus: **Northeast Charter & Tour** (1-888-593-6328; northeastchartertour.com) is a charter and tour bus operator that runs a door-to-door bus service to and from the Portland International Jetport; Boston's Logan Airport; Manchester, New Hampshire; and all of New England.

WHEN TO COME Rangeley's water is the focus of fishermen and -women in summer and fall, and its hills have good trails. Saddleback Mountain makes this a winter destination as well, as skiers are discovering the charms of a place still off the radar.

✳ To See

MUSEUMS ✪ Rangeley Lakes Region Historical Society (207-864-2333), 2472 Main St., Rangeley. Open late June–Aug., Mon.–Sat. 11–2, or when the flag is out. This is a great little museum occupying a former bank building in the middle of town. It features photographs and local memorabilia from Rangeley's grand old hotels, sporting camps, trains, and lake steamers. Note the basement jail cell and the bird egg collection, coveted by the Smithsonian Museum.

✒ **Wilhelm Reich Museum** (207-864-3443; wilhelmreichtrust.org), Dodge Pond Rd., off Rt. 4/16 between Rangeley and Oquossoc. Open July and Aug., Wed.–Sun. 1–5; in Sept., Sat. 1–5. $6 adults, 12 and under free. The 175-acre property, Orgonon, is worth a visit for the view alone. Wilhelm Reich (1897–1957) was a pioneer psychoanalyst with controversial theories about sexual energy. A short documentary video profiles the man and his work. The museum occupies a stone observatory that Reich helped design; it contains biographical exhibits, scientific equipment, paintings, and a library and study that remain as Reich left them. The wooded trails on the property are open daily year-round 9–5; leashed pets welcome.

✒ **Rangeley Lakes Region Logging Museum** (207-864-3939 or 207-864-5595), Rt. 16, 1 mile east of Rangeley Village. Open late May–early Sept., Wed.–Sun. 11–5; Sept.–early Oct., Thu.–Sun. 11–4 or by appointment. Founded by woodsman and sculptor Rodney Richard, the museum features paintings about logging in the 1920s by local artist Alden Grant.

Rangeley Outdoor Sporting Heritage Museum (207-864-3091; rangeleyoutdoor museum.org), corner of Rts. 4 and 17, Oquossoc Village. Open July–Aug., Wed.–Sat. 10–2; June and Sept., Fri.–Sat. 10–2. Built in 2009–10, this museum focusing on outdoor sports has an authentic 1890s sporting camp as an entry room, its birch-bark ceiling laced with thin branches is a work of art. It features native Carrie Stevens, originator of the Gray Ghost fly; 150 of the flies that she tied are on display, including the last one she made, and flies she tied herself, duplicates of ones on display, are for sale. Fish mounts and paintings by Herb Welch, 1879–1960, like his unusual grouping of seven brook trout under a glass bubble, are exhibited. *White Nose Pete*, a carving by Shang Wheeler, portrays a fish credited with stealing many a fisherman's flies.

Phillips Historical Society (207-639-3111), Pleasant St., P.O. Box 216, Phillips 04966. Open June–Sept., first and third Sun. 1–3, and the third week in Aug. for Old Home Days; also by appointment. The historical society is based in an 1820 house in the middle of the village. Exhibits include a significant Portland Glass collection, Fly-Rod Crosby memorabilia, as well as pictures of the town's own resort era, when it had three hotels, and the Sandy River Rangeley Lakes Railroad.

Weld Historical Society (207-585-2542), Weld Village. Open July and Aug., Wed. and Sat. 1–3, and by appointment. The 1842 house is filled with period furniture, clothing, and photographs. The original Town House (1845) features farming, logging, and ice-cutting tools. Other buildings include Dr. Proctor's 1880s office (containing his equipment), a spruce gum shop that became a library around 1900, and a reconstructed garage/workshop filled with tools, artifacts, and school and post office equipment.

✲ To Do

AIR TOURS **Acadian Seaplanes** (207-864-5307; acadianseaplanes.com), Rangeley. A 30-minute tour of fall foliage and the lakes was $99 a person in 2015, and "Sights on a Shoestring," which lasts 15 minutes, was $65. Moose tours, history tours, regional tours, and more are available in this Cessna 180 seaplane piloted by Keith Deschambeault, who has a commercial pilot's license.

BIRDING Birders can often see Bicknell's thrushes and perhaps blackpolls, boreal chickadees, and more above 2,500 feet at the peak of Saddleback Mountain, and the base lodge

EXCURSIONS

PHILLIPS/WELD/BYRON/OQUOSSOC/RANGELEY LOOP

Rt. 4 to Phillips and Rt. 142 to Weld. Follow Rt. 4 from Rangeley 12 miles south to **Small's Falls** and on to Phillips, once the center of the Sandy River–Rangeley Lakes "2-footer" line, now a quiet residential area. Plan to come the first or third Sun. of the month, or on foliage weekends, to ride the rails behind the steam train. Stop at the **Phillips Historical Society** and ask directions to **Daggett Rock**, a massive 50-foot-high boulder that glaciers deposited several miles from town (off Rt. 142), having knocked it off Saddleback Mountain (the nearest place that matches it geologically). It's a pleasant mile's walk and has been the local sight to see in Phillips for more than a century. From Rt. 4 near Phillips, it's 12 miles on Rt. 142 to **Weld**, a quiet old lake village with several good hiking options, including **Tumbledown Mountain** and **Mount Blue**. You can also swim in **Lake Webb** at **Mount Blue State Park**.

Weld to Byron. From Weld, it's 12 miles to Byron. Drive 2 miles north on Rt. 142 to the STATE BEACH sign; turn left, go 0.5 mile, and turn right on the first gravel road. This is Byron Rd., well packed. Soon you follow the Swift River (stop and pan for gold) down into **Coos Canyon**; the picnic area and waterfalls are at the junction with Rt. 17. This is said to be the first place in America where gold was panned.

Rt. 17 to Oquossoc. From the picnic area, drive north on Rt. 17 for 10 miles to the **Height of Land** (the pullout is on the other side of the road), from which the view is a spectacular spread of lakes and mountains; the view from the **Rangeley Lake Overlook** (northbound side of the road, a couple of miles farther) offers another panorama.

From Oquossoc, it's a beautiful drive west along the lakes on Rt. 16 to Errol. Roughly 20 miles west of Rangeley, be sure to detour 0.3 mile to see the **Bennett Covered Bridge** (1901–85) spanning the Magalloway River in Wilson's Mills; follow signs to the Aziscohos Valley Camping Area.

THE VIEW FROM HEIGHT OF LAND ON ROUTE 17

has a hiking map available. Check the stand of spruce near the parking lot at Hunter Cove, cared for by the Rangeley Lakes Heritage Trust, for boreal chickadees as well. The same organization's Boy Scout Rd., a dead-end dirt road, is home to gray jays. Bald Mountain, in between Rangeley and Mooselookmeguntic Lakes, is another good place for boreal bird species.

BOATING Check with the chamber of commerce about the 13 places in town that rent motorboats, canoes, sailboats, and kayaks. **River's Edge Sports** (207-864-5582), Rt. 4, Oquossoc, rents canoes and kayaks and offers shuttle service. **Saddleback Marina on Rangeley Lake** (207-864-3463 or 207-864-5496), Rt. 4, Oquossoc, offers the largest choice of motorboats. **Lakeside Marina** (207-864-9004), 2582 Main St., Rangeley, is another resource.

Oquossoc Lady (207-670-8391), Rt. 17, Oquossoc. Daily one-hour cruises Memorial Day–Columbus Day take visitors by Naramantic Island, Rangeley Lake State Park, and more, with narration about Rangeley region history by Captain Kevin Sinnett. $25 adults, ages 10 and under $10.

BOWLING **Moose Alley** (207-864-9955; moosealleymaine.com), 2809 Main St., Rangeley. Open Sat., Sun. noon; weekdays 3 PM. Bowling on 10 lanes with electronic scoring in a bright, social space that turns into a music venue and late-night pub in the evening.

CAMPING Wilderness camping is a part of what this area is about. The **Stephen Phillips Preserve** (207-864-2003), Oquossoc, maintains 70 campsites with fireplaces, picnic tables, and toilet facilities; $16 per site per couple, $8 teenagers or extra person, $5 children. Also see **Rangeley Lake State Park** under *Green Space*. **Aziscohos Valley Camping Area** (207-486-3271), in Wilson's Mills, has 34 sites and offers easy canoe or kayak access to Magalloway River.

CANOEING AND KAYAKING Rangeley is the departure point for an 8-mile paddle to Oquossoc. On Lake Mooselookmeguntic a 12-mile paddle south to Upper Dam is popular; many people portage around the dam and paddle another 8 miles down Upper Richardson Lake and through the Narrows to South Arm. Kayaks can be rented from **River's Edge Sports** (207-864-5582), Rt. 4 in Oquossoc. They are also available from **Ecopelagicon, A Nature Store** (207-864-2771; ecopelagicon.com) in the village of Rangeley, which offers guided tours and kayaking instruction.

A section of the 700-mile **Northern Forest Canoe Trail**, which follows the ancient water route of Native Americans traveling from New York to Fort Kent, comes through Umbagog Lake, the Richardson Lakes, and Mooselookmeguntic and Rangeley Lakes before hitting a long portage to the South Branch of the Dead River. This section takes two to five days to complete. A map, produced by **Native Trails Inc.** (P.O. Box 240, Waldoboro 04572), is available for $5.95 from the Rangeley Lakes Heritage Trust (207-864-7311) and from Ecopelagicon in Rangeley.

FISHING As noted in the chapter introduction, fishing put Rangeley on the map. Both brook trout and landlocked salmon remain plentiful, and while early spring and Sept. remain the big fishing seasons, summer months now also lure many anglers with fishfinders, downriggers, rods, and reels. Rangeley has, however, always been best known as a fly-fishing mecca, and both local sporting stores, **River's Edge Sports** (207-864-5582), Rt. 4 in Oquossoc, and **Rangeley Region Sport Shop** (207-864-5615), Main St., Rangeley, specialize in fly-tying equipment; they are also sources of advice on where to fish and with whom (a list of local guides is posted). Request a list of members of the **Rangeley Region Guides & Sportsmen's Association** (rangeleyguidesandsportsmen.org), P.O. Box 244, Rangeley

04970. The group traces its origins to 1896. The current chamber of commerce guide also lists local Registered Maine Guides as well as camps that specialize in boats, equipment, and guides. Nonresident fishing licenses, sold at sporting stores, are $11 per day, $43 for seven days.

FITNESS CENTER **Rangeley Region Physical Rehab and Wellness Pavilion** (207-864-3055; rangeleyhealth.org), Dallas Hill Rd., Rangeley. This community facility offers exercise equipment and daily exercise classes including yoga.

GOLD PANNING **Coos Canyon**, on Rt. 17, 23 miles south of Oquossoc, is said to be the first place in America where gold was panned. The Swift River churns through a beautiful natural gorge. Free gold-panning demonstrations are offered, and equipment can be rented or bought at the **Coos Canyon Rock & Gift Store** (207-364-4900).

GOLF **Mingo Springs Golf Course** (207-864-5021), Proctor Rd. (off Rt. 4), Rangeley. A historic (since 1925) par-71, 18-hole course with lake views; instruction, carts, and club rentals.

   Evergreen Golf Club & Golf School (207-864-9055), 528 Dallas Hill Rd., Rangeley. This nine-hole course built in 2002 has spectacular views, with five tees on each hole so everyone can play.

GUIDE SERVICE See **Rangeley Outdoor Sporting Heritage Museum** or the chamber, above, to obtain advice on guide services.

HIKING **The Rangeley regional map** published by the chamber of commerce outlines more than a dozen well-used hiking paths, including a portion of the Appalachian Trail that passes over **Saddleback Mountain.** The most popular is the trail to the summit of **Bald Mountain** (3 miles roundtrip) with sweeping views of lakes, woods, and more mountains. Other favorites are Bemis Stream Trail up **Elephant Mountain** (six hours round-trip) and the mile walk in to **Angels Falls**—which is roughly 4 miles off Rt. 17 and listed in the *Rangeley Hiking Trail Guide* sold at the chamber of commerce.

   In Weld the tried-and-true trails are **Mount Blue** (3.25 miles) and **Tumbledown Mountain**, a particularly varied climb with a high elevation.

MOOSE-WATCHING **Rt. 16 north from Rangeley to Stratton** is a good bet for seeing moose at dusk, but drive with caution.

SUMMER PROGRAMS **Rangeley Parks and Recreation Department Summer Programs** (207-864-3326), open to everyone vacationing in town, include lessons in fly-casting and -tying, golf, canoeing, swimming, tennis, and much more.

SWIMMING **Rangeley Lake State Park** offers a beautiful, secluded grass beach and

MINGO SPRINGS GOLF COURSE, RANGELEY

swimming area plus scattered picnic sites. Day-use fee; free under age 12. There is also a town beach with lifeguards, picnic tables, and a playground at **Lakeside Park** in the village of Rangeley.

Mount Blue State Park also has a nice swimming area.

Coos Canyon, Rt. 17, Byron. It's terrifying to watch kids jump from the cliffs and bridge here, but there are several inviting pools among the smooth rocks and cascades.

TRAINS ✐ **Sandy River & Rangeley Lakes Railroad** (207-778-3621; srrl-rr.org), Phillips. Runs on the first and third Sun. of each month, June–Columbus Day; runs continuously through Phillips Old Home Days in late Aug. and Fall Foliage Days in late Sept. and early Oct., and on other special occasions (check the website). $6 adults, $1 ages 7–13, free 7 and under. From 1873 until 1935 this narrow-gauge line spawned resort and lumbering communities along its 115-mile length. Begun as seven distinct lines, it was eventually acquired by the Maine Central. Shops and a large roundhouse were built by railroad companies in Phillips. Since 1969 volunteers have been working to rebuild a part of the railroad, producing a replica of the old steam locomotive and the roundhouse and laying 0.6 mile of track so that you can rattle along in an 1884 car just far enough to get a sense of getting around Franklin County "back when." Seven original railroad buildings remain—including Sanders Station and a freight shed.

❅ Winter Sports

CROSS-COUNTRY SKIING **Rangeley Lakes Trail Center at Lower Saddleback Mountain** (207-864-4309), 524 Saddleback Mountain Rd., Rangeley. More than 55 km of groomed trails with a skating lane and a track for classic skiing, 4 miles from downtown Rangeley.

Mount Blue State Park (207-585-2347), off Rt. 156, Weld, offers extensive cross-country skiing trails.

DOGSLEDDING **Rangeley Region Sled Dog Adventures** (rangeleydogsled.com) and **Morningsong Wilderness Tours** (207-864-5002) both offer a chance to drive as well as ride a sled through woodland. In the Rangeley Lakes area.

SNOWMOBILING is huge in this region. The **Rangeley Snowmobile Club** (rangeleysnow mobile.com), subsidized by the town, maintains hundreds of miles of well-marked trails connecting with systems throughout Maine and Canada. Snowmobile rentals are available from **Polaris Snowmobile Rentals from River's Edge Sports** (207-864-5582).

SNOWSHOEING Ask for more information at the Rangeley Lake Region Chamber of Commerce (207-864-5364).

❅ Green Space

Lakeside Park, in the middle of the village of Rangeley, is a great spot with picnic tables, grills, a playground, new restrooms, and a boat launch.

✐ **Rangeley Lake State Park** (207-864-3858) covers more than 700 acres, including 117 acres on the shore. Open May 15–end of Sept. There are scattered picnic sites and barbecue grills near the swimming area, an idyllic swimming area, a boat launch, and a children's play area; $4.50 nonresident adults, $1 ages 5–12.

SADDLEBACK MOUNTAIN

This is a very big downhill ski area with a fiercely loyal following, on the verge of wider popularity under a new owner making a huge investment but still seeking additional support. Saddleback itself, 4,120 feet high with a vertical drop of 2,000 feet, forms the centerpiece in a semicircle of mountains rising above a small lake. Top-to-bottom snowmaking augments more than 200 inches of annual snowfall to keep the slopes open from the end of November into April. Expansion here was blocked for 26 years by an impasse with the National Park Service over the segment of the Appalachian Trail that passes over Saddleback, but former President Clinton's 11th-hour moves to expand national park holdings cleared the way. ✎ **Saddleback Mountain** (207-864-5671; snow phone, 1-800-458-7502; saddleback-maine.com), off Dallas Hill Rd., Rangeley.

SKIING AT SADDLEBACK MOUNTAIN

Trails and slopes total 66, including a 44-acre glade and a 2.5-mile beginner trail, and an above-tree-line snowfield in spring. Intermediate runs such as Gray Ghost and Green Weaver are memorable cruising lanes. Experts will find plenty of challenge on Tight Line, Warden's Worry, and the Nightmare Glades, and there's a snowboard park with a 200-foot half-pipe.

Lifts: Two quad chairlifts, two double chairs, and one T-bar.

Facilities include a three-story lodge with cafeteria, lounge, ski school, shop, rentals, nursery, and mountain warming hut. About 40 condominium units can be rented through the mountain's main telephone number at a range of $125–220 a night.

Lift tickets: 2014–2015, $69 adults, $59 ages 7–18 and college students; 6 and under free.

Mount Blue State Park (207-585-2261), off Rt. 156, Weld. Open May 30–Sept. 30, but center open until mid-Oct., and trail open through the fall. This 6,000-acre park includes Mount Blue itself, towering 3,187 feet above the valley floor, and a beachside tenting area (136 sites) on Lake Webb. The lake is 1.5 miles wide, 7 miles long, and provides good fishing for black bass, white and yellow perch, pickerel, trout, and salmon. There are boat rentals and a nature center complete with fireplace. Despite its beauty and the outstanding hiking, this is one of the few state camping facilities ($25 for nonresidents) that rarely fills up, except on August weekends. Day-use fee $6 per person for nonresidents, $4 for Mainers, children 5–11 $1.

✎ **Small's Falls**, Rt. 4, 12 miles south of Rangeley. The Sandy River drops abruptly through a small gorge, which you can climb behind railings. A popular picnic spot. You can follow the trail to **Chandlers Mill Stream Falls**, equally spectacular.

Hunter Cove Wildlife Sanctuary, off Rt. 4/16, 2.5 miles west of Rangeley Village (across from Dodge Pond). A 95-acre Rangeley Lakes Heritage Trust preserve with color-coded trails leading to the cove (boat launch). Bring insect repellent, waterproof footwear, and a picnic (tables are near the parking lot and benches are scattered throughout).

Rangeley Lakes Heritage Trust (207-864-7311; rlht.org), Rt. 4/16, Oquossoc, open weekdays 9–4:30, Sun. 9–1. Since the trust's founding in 1991, more than 12,300 acres have been preserved, including 45 miles of lake and river frontage, 15 islands, and a 2,443-foot mountain. Request the map/guide and inquire about the guided hikes and nature-study programs offered.

Hatchery Brook Preserve is easily accessible, just 0.5 mile north of town on Rt. 4 (take a left on Manor Brook Rd. and look for the trailhead on your right in another 0.25 mile). We were lucky enough to hike this easy, rewarding loop in blueberry/raspberry season. Yum. This 50-acre Rangeley Lakes Heritage Trust property was at one time slated for a 50-lot subdivision.

The Stephen Phillips Memorial Preserve Trust (207-864-2003) has preserved many miles of shore on Mooselookmeguntic and maintains a number of campsites (see *To Do—Camping*).

Also see *Lodging—Campgrounds*.

SMALL'S FALLS, RANGELEY

Nancy English

✳ Lodging

INNS AND LODGES ✪ ✦ ⟁ **Kawanhee Inn** (207-585-2000; maineinn.net), 12 Anne's Way, Weld 04285. Open Memorial Day–Columbus Day. This Maine lodge set atop a slope overlooking Lake Webb has a paneled lobby and dining room, moose and deer presiding over the stone fireplaces, and birch trunks standing in for columns. Four lodge rooms share a bath, eight have private bath. Eight cabins (one-, two-, and three-bedroom) sit by the lake, six with kitchenette and two with full kitchen. The restaurant (see *Dining Out*) serves excellent meals. Rooms $110–165 B&B; cabins $1,350–1,750 per week.

⟁ **The Loon Lodge Inn and Restaurant** (207-864-5666; loonlodgeme.com), 16 Pickford Rd., P.O. Box 676, Rangeley 04970. Log exterior walls and indoor pine paneling, a large stone fireplace, and the moose-antler chandelier in **Pickford Pub** create a mountain lodge ambience. The upstairs can be hot in summer, despite the ceiling fans. Nine rooms, two with detached bath and three that share a bathroom, include two suites for families. Two rooms with king bed are on the ground floor, with picture windows looking at the lake, an exterior entrance, and private bath. Dinners are recommended (see *Dining Out*); guests are on their own for breakfast. $110–165.

⟁ **The Rangeley Inn** (207-864-3341 or 1-800-666-3687, therangeleyinn.com), Rt.

THE FRONT PORCH OF THE KAWANHEE INN LOOKS OUT ON WEBB LAKE

Nancy English

4, Rangeley 04970. Open year-round. This blue-shingled, three-story landmark, on the site of a vanished grand hotel that stood across the road overlooking the lake, is owned by Travis Ferland, who took charge in August 2013. The classic hotel lobby dates to 1907 and the massive caribou (or elk?) supervises from above the fireplace. More than 30 guest rooms are in the main building, some with water views, all comfortably furnished and old-fashioned with oak furniture and good beds; 15 units are in the motel overlooking Haley Pond. $125–225.

☃ ♿ **Country Club Inn** (207-864-3831; countryclubinnrangeley.com), Rt. 4, P.O. Box 680, Rangeley 04970. Open year-round except Apr. and Nov. This friendly retreat offers the best views of Rangeley Lake of any lodging in the region. The 20 old-fashioned rooms, all with private bath, have picture windows framing water and mountains. Although set by the Mingo Springs Golf Course, only half its summer patrons even play golf; it was built by millionaire sportsmen as a private club in the late 1920s. Owner-manager Margie Jamison is the second generation of her family to run the inn; her husband, Steve, is chef in the restaurant (see *Dining Out*). In winter you can cross-country ski from the door, and in summer there's an outdoor pool. $139–169.

☃ ♿ **Bald Mountain Camps** (207-864-3671; baldmountaincamps.com), Bald Mountain Rd., P.O. Box 332, Oquossoc 04964. Open year-round. This is a surviving American Plan (all three meals) fishing resort that dates to 1897. Fireplaces are in 15 cabins, all remodeled to include an efficiency or complete kitchen; step out of the porch rocker and into Mooselookmeguntic Lake, and enjoy the hospitality found under long-term ownership of Stephen and Fernlyn Philbrick. $125–250 without meals, less for children and during May and June; one-week minimum in July and Aug., but occasionally there are a few days open. Some pets accepted.

B&BS Pleasant Street Inn Bed & Breakfast (207-864-5916; pleasantstreetinnbb.com), 104 Pleasant St., Rangeley 04970. Rob and Jan Welch offer expertise in hiking and skiing, including quiet spots for cross-country skiing. Shuttling cars for hikers, making reservations, and pickups after a dinner are part of their services. The well-appointed B&B has beds with adjustable firmness, only one item on the checked-off list. Five quiet rooms, each with tile-floored private bath and TV. Early risers can enjoy muffins and cereals; a full breakfast, perhaps shirred eggs, is served between 8 and 9. Rates $155–175, with discounts for multiple nights.

MOTELS ☃ ♿ Rangeley Saddleback Inn (207-864-3434; rangeleysaddlebackinn.com), 2303 Main St., Rangeley 04970. On the Interconnected Trail System (ITS) beloved by snowmobilers and near Saddleback Mountain, this inn has new, comfortable beds, flat-screen TVs, and an indoor pool and Jacuzzi. There are 40 rooms, most with two queen beds; all have private bath, microwave, mini fridge, and a view of Rangeley Lake. Rooms $125–160.

SPORTING CAMPS ☃ ♦ Bosebuck Mountain Camps (207-670-0013; bosebuck.com), Wilson's Mills 03579. Open year-round, except Apr. Accessible by boat or a 14-mile private gravel road, the camps are sited at the remote end of Aziscohos Lake and on ITS 84. Wendy and Michael Yates bought this site in 2007. A wilderness navigation seminar is offered in June and Aug.; women's groups and artists come here, too. The lodge dining room overlooks the water. The 12 cabins have a woodstove, electric lights, flush toilet, and shower. Powered by a generator that never shuts off. Three full meals, with prime rib on Sat., are included. July and first two weeks of Aug., $119 per person per night, with 15 percent gratuity, distributed to staff, added at checkout; $150 before and after high summer, during hunting and fishing seasons.

🐾 🎣 **Lakewood Camps** (207-243-2959; lakewoodcamps.com), Middle Dam, Lower Richardson Lake, P.O. Box 1275, Rangeley 04970. Open after ice-out through Sept. Owners are Whit and Maureen Carter. Specialty fly-fishing for landlocked salmon and trout in 5 miles of the Rapid River. Twelve truly remote cabins; meals feature fresh-baked breads, cakes, and pies. Access is by boat from Andover. This is very much the same area described in Louise Dickinson Rich's *We Took to the Woods*. $170 per person (two-day minimum), double occupancy, includes three full meals; $120 children 12–16, $70 6–11, age 5 and younger free. $22 pets, 15 percent gratuity not included. No credit cards; cash or check only.

COTTAGES AND CONDOS **Clearwater Sporting Camps** (207-864-5424; clearwater campsmaine.com), Bald Mountain Rd., Oquossoc 04964. Open from ice-out through Oct.

Four cottages, all different, are scattered on private waterfront ledges along Mooselookmeguntic Lake; the fronts of two of the cottages open out almost completely onto the lake. This is a very private, beautiful spot. A year-round log home is for rent as well. Michael and Tina Warren also offer boat rentals, a boat launch, swimming, and guide service, specializing in fly-fishing. Cabins $150 per day double; $950 per week. Log home $1,400. No pets.

Mooselookmeguntic House Cabin Rentals (207-864-2962; mooselookmegunticrentals .com), Haines Landing, Oquossoc 04964. Open ice-out to Columbus Day. The grand old hotel is gone, but the eight log cabins are well maintained and occupy a great site with a beach and marina. Many of the one- and two-bedroom cabins are on the water and have fireplace or woodstove. $600–800 per week.

North Camps (207-864-2247; northcamps .com), P.O. Box 341, Oquossoc 04964 (write to E. B. Gibson). Open May–Oct. Twelve cottages on Rangeley Lake among birches on a spacious lawn, with fireplace or woodstove, modern bath, screened porch, and access to the beach, tennis, sailboats, fishing boats, and canoes. In July and Aug., weekly rentals preferred. $595–895 weekly, $85–195 per night for two to eight people.

Nancy English

LAKESIDE SEATING AT BALD MOUNTAIN CAMP, OQUOSSOC

Hunter Cove on Rangeley Lake (207-864-3383; huntercove.com), 334 Mingo Loop, Rangeley 04970. Open year-round. Chris and Ralph Egerhei offer eight nicely equipped one- and two-bedroom lakeside cabins with loft, full kitchen, one with hot tub. $170–200 per night; $1,050–1,200 per week.

CAMPGROUNDS For reservations in the following state parks, call in-state 1-800-332-1501, out-of-state 207-624-9950.

✔ Rangeley Lake State Park, between Rts. 17 and 4, at the southern rim of Rangeley Lake. Some 50 campsites are well spaced among fir and spruce trees; facilities include a secluded beach and boat launch, picnic sites, three shower buildings, one new, with hot showers at no extra charge, and a children's play area. One group camping site has a shelter. $20 for nonresidents. Some wilderness sites on Mooselookmeguntic Lake are accessible only by boat; inquire at the chamber of commerce.

Mount Blue State Park (207-585-2347), Weld. Campsites here ($20) tend to fill up later than those in better-known parks.

Coos Canyon Campground (207-364-3880; cooscanyoncabins.com), on Rt. 17, 445 Swift River Rd., Byron, 23 miles south of Oquossoc, is only about half an hour from Rangeley, but at these sites you feel as though you're in the middle of the woods. Swimming holes and riverside camping, with kids jumping off the cliffs during the day. At $16 per night, plus tax, the rates can't be beat. There's a small store and a shower house. Two fully equipped units in a log cabin are $120 per night for two adults and two children under 12.

✻ Where to Eat

DINING OUT ✪ **Kawanhee Inn** (207-585-2000; maineinn.net), 12 Anne's Way, Weld. Open Memorial Day–Columbus Day. Dining is lovely on the screened porch in good weather, or by the fire when it's cold. Entrées $16–28.

The Loon Lodge Inn and Restaurant (207-864-5666; loonlodgeme.com), 16 Pickford Rd., Rangeley. Dining on the deck overlooking Rangeley Lake on a summer night is the way life should be. Spanish duck with a wonderful spicy flavor was one entrée on a recent dinner menu, and seafood and steaks with or without shrimp or scallops are more good choices. Dates wrapped with bacon with slices of chorizo hit a home run. Entrées $22–31.

Rangeley Tavern (207-864-3341; rangeley inn.com), 2443 Main St. The comfortable tavern at the Rangely Inn might have the grilled mango, feta, blueberries, and greens summer salad, a Cubano, or a bacon burger with sambal aioli and cheddar. The brined double pork chop was a favorite from one menu. Entrées $23–32.

✔ The Gingerbread House (207-864-3602; gingerbreadhouserestaurant.net), Rt. 4/16, Oquossoc. Open for breakfast, lunch, and dinner year-round, fewer days in winter, closed Nov. and Apr. An ice cream parlor since the turn of the 20th century, preserved and expanded by the Kfoury family. Breakfast might be blueberry waffles, and lunch crabcakes or chicken pesto salad. For dinner, the ribs are long-braised and coated with blueberry chipotle barbecue sauce (with a goat cheese fritter to start). In the winter, watch the deer feeding behind the enclosed porch while you dine. Entrées $16–29.

Forks in the Air Mountain Bistro (207-864-2883; forksintheair.com), 2485 Main St., Rangeley. You can't go wrong starting with the chop salad and a glass of good wine; entrées like paella and grilled hanger steak may be satisfying next courses, and count on fruit for dessert, perhaps in a pie or cobbler. Entrées $14–28.

Country Club Inn (207-864-3831; country clubinnrangeley.com), Rangeley. Open for dinner Wed.–Sun. in summer and fall; weekends in winter by reservation. The inn sits on a rise above Rangeley Lake, the dining room windows maximize the view, and the food is good. Chef Steve Jamison's menu changes frequently but might include veal Gruyère; roast duck with bing cherry sauce is available every night. Entrées $15–32, including a salad.

Bald Mountain Camps (207-864-3671; baldmountaincamps.com), Bald Mountain Rd., Oquossoc. Serving during the summer months. Dinner by reservation is available to nonguests in this classic sporting camp dining room by the lake. The set menu varies with the night; you might find pork chops with a tangy honey sauce or summer ratatouille pasta.

THE DINING ROOM AT THE COUNTRY CLUB INN, RANGELEY

EATING OUT 🍴 Rangeley's Moose Loop Café, Bakery & Rental Shop

Rangeley's Moose Loop Café, Bakery & Rental Shop (207-864-3000; campdowhatyouwanna.com), 2419 Main St. (next to Rangeley Inn). Breakfast on good baked goods—and rent a snowmobile.

Red Onion (207-864-5022), Main St., Rangeley. Open daily for lunch and dinner. A friendly Italian American dining place with a sunroom and biergarten; fresh-dough pizzas and daily specials. Recommended by locals—even if the menu doesn't spell Parmesan right.

Parkside & Main (207-864-3774), 2520 Main St., Rangeley. Open daily, with later hours in summer. An attractive dining room with plenty of windows and a deck overlooking the lake, great for a drink. Large menu with burgers, good homemade chowders, seafood, pastas, and daily specials.

The Four Seasons Café (207-864-2020; fourseasonscafe.com), Rt. 4, Oquossoc. Open for breakfast, lunch, and dinner, closed part of April. A woodstove, tables with checked green cloths, and a big menu with Mexican dishes, salads, good soups, sandwiches, and vegetarian specials all make this a good place to eat. Fresh-dough pizzas are also a specialty. Fish, lobster, clams, and scallops are served as well. Prime rib on Fri. night, house pies. Entrées $17–29. Two-for-one dinners Thu.

Moosely Bagels and Scoops Ice Cream (207-864-5955), 2588 Main St., Rangeley. Open for breakfast, lunch, and ice cream Mon.–Sat. 5:30–8:30, Sun. 6:30–6. Call for hours off-season. Great lakeside location and good bagels; enormous, family-sized, tender

blueberry muffins; and an array of coffee choices. For lunch: soup, salad, and a lot of vegetarian options. Fridays come in for fresh fish.

🍴 **Pine Tree Frosty** (207-864-5894), 2459 Main St., Rangeley. Gifford's ice cream.

Lakeside Convenience (207-864-5888), Main St., Rangeley. Great fried chicken on weekdays only, usually in at 9 AM and sold out by 2 PM.

Scotty's Pound (207-864-2493), 17 Rumford Rd. (Rt. 17), Rangeley, in Oquossoc Village. Call ahead, and give an hour's notice, to order cooked lobsters, 5 PM and 5:30 PM pickup; lobster rolls are made to order with 4 ounces of knuckle and claw lobster meat.

COFFEE Inner Eye (207-864-5100), 2487 Main St., Rangeley. This coffee shop was inspired by a love of photography. Transform your photos into postcards in the print kiosk. Write the postcard, buy a stamp, and mail it, all in the café, while enjoying coffee, espresso, baked goods, and doughnuts baked at sister business Moose Alley (see *To Do*).

A MENAGERIE INSIDE THE RESTAURANT AT BALD MOUNTAIN CAMP, OQUOSSOC

✻ Entertainment

⚓ **Lakeside Rangeley Theater** (207-864-5000), Main St., Rangeley. A renovated landmark that offers first-run films; matinees on rainy days when the flag is hung out. Off-season shows on weekends.

Rangeley Friends of the Performing Arts sponsors a July–Aug. series of performances by top entertainers and musicians at local churches, lodges, and the high school. For the current schedule, check with the chamber of commerce.

✻ Selective Shopping

Alpine Shop (207-864-3741), Main St., Rangeley. Open daily year-round. The town's premier clothing store, with name-brand sportswear and Maine gifts.

✪ **Bog Pond Pottery** (207-639-5327; robsieminski.com), 63 Bog Pond Rd. (just off Rt. 4), Phillips. Rob Sieminski makes outstanding pottery at this farmhouse surrounded by flowers; the raku work is fired in a wood-burning kiln for 24 hours or more. Sieminski's work is in the Philadelphia Museum of Art; with deeply textured surfaces and wood-ash glazing, it resembles stone or wood.

Books, Lines, and Thinkers (207-864-4355), Main St., Rangeley. Open year-round;

BOG POND POTTERY, PHILLIPS

Nancy English

hours vary depending on season. Wess and Pongsiri Connally offer a good selection of books, including a customer-recommended shelf, and music. The store also sponsors a regular book discussion group; the next meeting's selection is featured by the cash register.

⚓ **Ecopelagicon, A Nature Store** (207-864-2771), 3 Pond St., Rangeley. In the middle of town but with windows on Haley Pond. Kites, life jackets, camping stuff, and wonderful things for nature lovers, from bird and reptile guides to books on mountain trails and good maps. Also kayak rentals, instruction, and tours (see *Canoeing and Kayaking*).

The Gallery at Stoney Batter Station (207-864-3373), Oquossoc. Open Memorial Day–mid-Oct., daily 10–4; Thu.–Sun. in winter. Art shares the space with rustic furnishings, from stick benches to birchbark frames. Ceramics, lamps with custom shades, antique furniture, local art, and much more.

✻ Special Events

ALL EVENTS ARE IN RANGELEY UNLESS OTHERWISE NOTED

January: **Rangeley Snodeo**—snowmobile rally and cross-country ski races.

February: **New England Pond Hockey**.

May: **House and Garden Showcase** (Memorial Day weekend).

July: **Independence Day** parade and fireworks, silent auction, cookout; **Strawberry Festival**; **Old-Time Fiddlers Contest**; and **Logging Museum Festival Days. Heritage Day Fair** (final Saturday) in Weld Village.

August: **Sidewalk Art Show; Annual Blueberry Festival; Outdoor Sporting Heritage Days; Phillips Old Home Days** (third week). **Oquossoc Day**—dog show, sailing race, dinner, and more.

Third Sunday of September: **Saddleback Day Fall Festival**.

First Saturday of October: **Rangeley Lakes Logging Museum Apple Festival**.

December: **Walk to Bethlehem Pageant; Mountain Holly Days; Parade of Trees**, Main St.

SUGARLOAF AND THE CARRABASSETT VALLEY

The second highest mountain in the state, Sugarloaf faces another 4,000-footer across the Carrabassett Valley—a narrow defile that accommodates a 17-mile-long, unusual town.

In 1972, when Carrabassett Valley was created from Crockertown and Jerusalem townships, voters numbered 32. The school and post office are still down in Kingfield, south of the valley; the nearest chain supermarket and hospital are still in Farmington, 36 miles away. There are now just 761 full-time residents, but more than 5,000 "beds." Instead of "uptown" and "downtown," people say "on-mountain" and "off-mountain."

On-mountain, at the top of Sugarloaf's 2-mile access road, stands one of New England's largest self-contained ski villages: a handful of shops and more than a dozen restaurants, a seven-story brick hotel, and a church. A chairlift hoists skiers up to the base lodge from lower parking lots and from hundreds of condominiums clustered around the Sugarloaf Inn. More condominiums are scattered farther down the slope, all served by a chairlift, and from all you can also cross-country ski down to the extensive town-owned Sugarloaf Outdoor Center.

More than 800 condominiums are scattered among firs and birches. To fill them in summer, the town of Carrabassett has built an outstanding 18-hole golf course, which Sugarloaf leases, and maintains the country's top-rated golf school. It also promotes rafting, mountain biking, and hiking, and even seriously attempts to eliminate black flies.

Spring through fall the focus shifts off-mountain to the backwoods hiking and fishing north of the valley. Just beyond the village of Stratton, Rt. 27 crosses a corner of Flagstaff Lake and continues through Cathedral Pines, an impressive sight and a good place to picnic. The 30,000-acre Bigelow Preserve, which embraces the lake and great swatches of this area, offers swimming, fishing, and camping. Rt. 27 crosses the Canadian border 29 miles north of Eustis at Coburn Gore, a popular route for Mainers heading to Montreal.

A woodland to the east that separates the Carrabassett Valley from the Upper Kennebec has long been traversed by the Appalachian Trail—and now the Maine Huts and Trails system offers a hiking/cross-country ski link there, with three comfortable lodges to break your trek along the way.

Kingfield, at the southern entrance to the Carrabassett Valley, was founded in 1816. This stately town has long been a woodworking center and produced the first bobbins for America's first knitting mill; for some time it also supplied most of the country's yo-yo blanks. It is, however, best known as the onetime home of the Stanley twins, inventors of the steamer automobile and the dry-plate coating machine for modern photography. The Stanley Museum includes fascinating photos of rural Maine in the 1890s by Chansonetta, sister of the two inventors.

The Carrabassett River doesn't stop at Kingfield. Follow it south as it wanders west off Rt. 27 at New Portland, then a short way along Rt. 146, to see the striking vintage-1841 Wire Bridge. Continue on Rt. 146 and then west on Rt. 16 if you're heading for The Forks and the North Woods; to reach the coast, take Rt. 27 south through Farmington, a gracious old college town with several good restaurants, shops, and an opera museum.

EXCURSIONS

Rt. 142 from Kingfield to Phillips (11 miles) runs through farmland backed by Mount Abraham. Stop at the **Phillips Historical Society** and **Daggett Rock** and continue to **Mount Blue State Park**; return to Kingfield via New Vineyard and New Portland, stopping to see the **Wire Bridge**.

Rt. 16 though North New Portland and Embden is the most scenic as well as the most direct route from Kingfield to the Upper Kennebec Valley and Moosehead Lake.

THE WIRE BRIDGE NEAR FARMINGTON IS ALSO THE LOCATION OF A GOOD SWIMMING SPOT.

GUIDANCE **Maine's High Peaks** (eustismaine.com) is an umbrella name for the Kingfield/Stratton/Eustis area. Look for the volunteer-staffed info center on your right, heading up Rt. 27 from Kingfield to Sugarloaf.

GETTING THERE *By air:* **Portland International Jetport** (207-779-7301), 2½ hours away, offers connections to all points. **Rental cars** are available at the airport.

By car: From Boston it takes at least four hours to reach the Carrabassett Valley. From Maine Turnpike Exit 75 (Auburn), take Rt. 4 to Rt. 2 to Rt. 27; or take I-95 to Augusta, then Rt. 27 the rest of the way. (We swear by the latter route, but others swear by the former.)

By van: **Northeast Charter & Tour** (1-888-593-6328; northeastchartertour.com) is a charter and tour bus operator that runs a door-to-door bus service to and from the Portland International Jetport; Boston's Logan Airport; Manchester, NH; and all of New England. **All Points Transportation** (207-329-3482) also picks up from Portland and Logan as well as offering local transport, including drop-off and pickup from the huts (see *To Do*).

GETTING AROUND In ski season the **Valley Ski Shuttle Bus** runs from the Sugarloaf base lodge to the Carrabassett Valley Ski Touring Center and Rt. 27 lodges. Also see *By van*.

WHEN TO COME Summer hikes and winter skiing trips work in this area, with its year-round accommodations and restaurants. Sporting camps run from spring ice-out to late fall. Whitewater rafting is at its prime in spring.

✳ To See

MUSEUMS ✪ ✎ **Stanley Museum** (207-265-2729; stanleymuseum.org), 40 School St., Kingfield. Open June–Oct., Tue.–Sun. 1–4; Nov.–May, Tue.–Fri. 1–4. Admission. Housed in a stately wooden school donated by the Stanley family in 1903, this is a varied collection of inventions by the Stanley twins, F. O. and F. E. (it was their invention of the airbrush in the 1870s that made their fortune). Exhibits also include evocative photographs and hand-colored glass lantern slides by their sister, Chansonetta Emmons, including her portraits of Henry Wadsworth Longfellow and William Cullen Bryant. There are also violins made by the brothers and their nephew, Carlton, as well as the steam car for which the Stanleys are best known.

Ski Museum of Maine (207-265-2023; skimuseumofmaine.org), upstairs at 265 Main St., Kingfield. Open July–Apr. 15, daily 9–5; otherwise by appointment. Visitors are welcome to look around at exhibits illustrating the history of skiing in Maine. There are made-in-Maine wooden skis and other equipment, photos of wooden ski jumps, mementos from Maine members of the World War II 10th Mountain Division, great posters, and much more. This is also the Maine Ski Hall of Fame.

Nordica Homestead Museum (207-778-2042), 116 Nordica Lane on Holley Rd. (off Rt. 4/27), north of Farmington. Open June–mid-Sept., Tue.–Sat. 10–noon and 1–5, Sun. 1–5. This 19th century farmhouse is the unlikely repository for the costumes, jewelry, personal mementos, and exotic gifts given to the opera star Lillian Norton, who was born here (she later changed her name to Nordica).

Nowetah's American Indian Museum (207-628-4981; mainemuseums.org), 2 Colegrove Rd., just off Rt. 27, New Portland. Open daily 10–5; no admission charge. Nowetah Cyr—a descendant of St. Francis Abenaki and member of the Paugussett Nation—and her husband, Tom Cyr, display Native American artifacts from the United States, Canada, and South America, with a focus on the Abenaki of Maine. More than 600 Native American Maine baskets and bark containers are displayed in one room, and quill-work baskets, arrowheads, a birch-bark canoe, and a dug-out canoe are on display in another.

HISTORIC SITES **Kingfield Historical House** (207-265-4032; kingfield-maine.gov), 45 High St., Kingfield. Open June–Sept. Wed. 10–2, Sun. 1–4, during Kingfield Days in July, and by appointment. Built in 1890, this high-Victorian house museum operated by the Kingfield Historical Society is full of period furnishings and the personal possessions of Maine's first governor, William King (where Kingfield got its name), and photographer Chansonetta Stanley Emmons.

Dead River Historical Society (207-246-2271), Rts. 16 and 27, Stratton. Open weekends in summer 11–3. A memorial to the "lost" towns of Flagstaff and Dead River,

NOWETAH'S AMERICAN INDIAN MUSEUM

Nancy English

THE MAINE HUTS AND TRAILS SYSTEM

This vibrant nonprofit organization has built four splendid off-the-grid "huts" along an 80-mile trail linking the Carrabassett and Upper Kennebec Valleys. Each hut is actually a soundly and ecologically built lodge accommodating 32 to 40 people. Guests come in summer and fall for hiking, mountain biking, fishing, swimming, and paddling; in winter, for snowshoeing and cross-country skiing. During the winter (late Dec.–late March) and summer/fall seasons (June–late Oct.) breakfast, dinner, and a trail lunch (almost all local and organic) are included in $94 per adult weekdays, $109 weekends in a shared bunk room; $54 per child, $64 weekends; private rooms $279 double weekdays, $329 weekends. Less for members. Note that if shared bunk rooms are not full, the per-person rate gets you a whole room. Beer and wine are available, as are guided treks and hikes. $25 fee for baggage transport. Self-catering between seasons is $35 per night for nonmembers. (207-265-2400; mainehuts.org), 396C Main St., Kingfield.

STRATTON BROOK HUT A many-windowed lodge completed in 2013 sits at an elevation of 1,880 feet above the Carrabassett Valley with views of Sugarloaf and the Bigelow Range. It's just 3 miles from the trailhead on Rt. 27 (BYO sleeping bag or linens), first along the Narrow Gauge rec path (frequented by dog walkers) and then up and up well-named Newton's Revenge. A gentler 4.2-mile trail from the Poplar Stream hut (see below) has since been built, and we recommend it. The lodge itself is a beauty whose spacious common room features radiant heat as well as solar and a woodstove. Bunk rooms are in a separate building, across a breezeway. Washrooms (male and female), with composting toilets and token-operated showers (six minutes a token) are in the lodge.

Courtesy of Maine Huts and Trails

CROSS-COUNTRY TRAILS LINK FOUR OFF-THE-GRID HUTS.

flooded in 1950 to create today's 22,000-acre, 24-mile Flagstaff Lake. Artifacts include carpentry and logging tools, china, and glass. When the water is low foundations and cellars, including one of a round barn, rise out of Dead River.

Wire Bridge, on Wire Bridge Rd., off Rt. 146 (not far) off Rt. 27 in New Portland. Nowhere near anywhere, this amazing-looking suspension bridge across the Carrabassett River has two massive shingled stanchions. The bridge is one of Maine's 19th-century engineering feats (built in 1864–66 and renovated in 1961). There's a good swimming hole just downstream and a place to picnic across the bridge.

✳ To Do

BOATING See *Fishing* for rental canoes, kayaks, and motorboats.

FLAGSTAFF LAKE HUT

POPLAR STREAM FALLS HUT Seven rooms accommodate four, eight, and 12 people 2.4 miles from Gauge Rd. in the Carrabassett Valley, nestled in the woods at 1,322 feet. We're told that trails are groomed and tracked, appropriate for novice and intermediate skiers. It's 11.3 miles on to Flagstaff Lake Hut.

FLAGSTAFF LAKE HUT is on a remote shore of its namesake lake, a great summer location for using the available canoes and kayaks and stand-up paddleboards. Its 10 bunk rooms accommodate between four and 12 people. It's just 1.8 miles to the nearest trailhead on paved Long Falls Dam Rd., 31 miles from Rt. 27 in Kingfield and 23 miles from Rt. 16 in New Portland.

GRAND FALLS HUT Sited above the banks of the Dead River and 1.7 miles below Grand Falls, this is the most remote hut: 14 miles from the trailhead off Rt. 201 in The Forks, 11.5 miles from Flagstaff Hut. The eight rooms here accommodate either two, four, or six people. In winter it's accessed by car from the Long Falls Dam Road, 4 miles beyond the Flagstaff trailhead (see above), from which it's an easy 7.8-mile ski.

CANOEING AND KAYAKING The **Carrabassett River** above East New Portland is a good spring paddling spot, with Class II and III whitewater. The north branch of the **Dead River** from the dam in Eustis to the landing after the Stratton bridge is another good paddle, as is the upper branch of the **Kennebago River**.

FISHING **Northland Cash Supply** (207-246-2376) is a genuine backwoods general store that also carries plenty of fishing gear: "We've got everything, clothing, souvenirs, wine, the Lottery." In Eustis, **Tim Pond Wilderness Camps** is a traditional fishing enclave. In Farmington, **Aardvark Outfitters** (207-778-3330) offers a wide selection of fly-fishing gear. Inquire about fly-fishing schools at Sugarloaf. Also see the Sugarloaf sidebar.

GOLF See the Sugarloaf sidebar.

SUGARLOAF RESORT

Sugarloaf Mountain Corporation was formed in the early 1950s by local skiers, and growth was steady but slow into the 1970s. Then came the boom decades, producing one of New England's largest self-contained resorts, including a base village complete with a seven-story brick hotel and a forest of condominiums. Given its distance from the coast and major cities—it's more than five hours from Boston—most skiers come for more than a weekend. Unlike Katahdin, Maine's highest mountain—which actually is shaped like a loaf—Maine's second highest mountain slopes away on all sides from its rounded bald pate (snowfields in winter). The combination of elevation, snowmaking, and snowfall usually ensures skiing into May, with spring skiing on the snowfields (the only lift-serviced above-tree-line skiing in the East). The mountain can be windy, and January can be frigid. Our favorite ski month here is March, but we're not alone—you need to book far ahead. One of New England's top golf courses is the summer and fall draw here, along with hiking and mountain biking. 5093 Access Rd., Carrabassett (207-237-2000 or 1-800-THE-LOAF 843-5623; sugarloaf.com).

SUMMER

CHAIRLIFT RIDES Fri.–Sun. 9–5 on the Sugarloaf SuperQuad.

FISHING Through Guided Adventures at Sugarloaf, spring and summer fly-fishing lessons with a Maine guide.

FOR FAMILIES Sugarloaf Outdoor Adventure Camp (207-237-6909), Riverside Park, Rt. 27, Carrabassett Valley. Runs weekdays July–mid-Aug. Begun as a town program and now operated by Sugarloaf. Open to visitors (reservations required); designed for ages 4–13: archery, swimming, biking, golf, climbing, camping, fly-fishing, and arts and crafts.

GOLF Sugarloaf Golf Club (207-237-2000), Sugarloaf. This spectacular 18-hole, par-72 course, designed by Robert Trent Jones Jr., is ranked among the nation's best, as is its golf school. Junior Golf Camp (five midweek days), designed for ages 12–18, is offered several times between June and Aug.

MOUNTAIN BIKING See *To Do*.

WHITEWATER RAFTING Sugarloaf partners with Northern Outdoors (1-800-765-RAFT), providing rafting trips and packages May–Oct.

ZIPLINE Sugarloaf Zipline Tours are offered in summer season from the top of the Skidway lift: seven 200-foot lines, about 30 feet off the ground.

THE 11TH HOLE AT THE SUGARLOAF GOLF CLUB.

SNOW AND FOLIAGE SEASON OVERLAP AT SUGARLOAF

YEAR-ROUND

ON-MOUNTAIN LODGING ✍ ⅋ **Sugarloaf Inn and Condominiums** (207-237-2000 or 1-800-THE-LOAF; sugarloaf.com), Carrabassett Valley 04947. More than 250 ski-in, ski-out condominiums are in the rental pool. Built gradually over more than 20 years (they include the first condos in Maine), they represent a range of styles and sites; when making a reservation, you might want to ask about convenience to the base complex, the Sugarloaf Sports and Fitness Club (to which all condo guests have access), or the golf club. The 42-room Sugarloaf Inn offers attractive standard rooms and fourth-floor family spaces with lofts; there's a comfortable living room with fireplace and a solarium restaurant and bar called The Shipyard Brew Haus. The front desk is staffed around the clock, and the inn is handy to the health club as well as to the mountain. Packages $69–299 per person in winter, from $99 in golf season.

✍ ⅋ **Sugarloaf Mountain Hotel & Conference Center** (1-800-527-9879), RR 1, Box 2299, Carrabassett Valley 04947. So close to the base complex that it dwarfs the base lodge, this is a massive, seven-story, 120-room brick condominium hotel with a gabled roof and central tower. Rooms feature a small refrigerator and microwave. Request a view of the mountain or you might get stuck overlooking the less attractive back of the hotel. A pair of two-bedroom suites come with a living room and kitchen. Each of the two palatial tower penthouses holds three bedrooms, three baths, and a hot tub. Health club with two hot tubs (open at noon) and sauna and steam room. Midwinter $109–159 per night for a one- or two-bedroom, $224–650 for suites; less in summer; multiday discounts.

SPORTS & FITNESS CENTER (207-237-2000), Mountainside Rd. Offers an indoor swimming pool, indoor and outdoor hot tubs, an exercise room, racquetball/volleyball courts, a sauna, and a café with Internet service.

WINTER

DOWNHILL SKIING/SNOWBOARDING  Sugarloaf (207-237-2000; snow report, ext. 6808; on-mountain reservations, 1-800-THE-LOAF; sugarloaf.com).

Trails number 153, including 28 glades, and add up to the largest acreage of any ski area in the East; 24 double black diamond, 39 black diamond, 49 intermediate. The 34 easy trails include the 3.4-mile Tote Road.

Vertical drop is a whopping 2,820 feet, from a summit elevation of 4,237.

Lifts: 15: five quads, one triple, six double chairs, a T-bar, and two surface lifts.

Terrain parks: Three parks vary in difficulty.

Snowmaking covers 618 acres, including much of the alpine cap; snowfall averages 197 inches.

Facilities include a **Perfect Turn Development Center**, a ski shop, rentals, a base lodge, cafeteria, nursery (day and night), game room, and no less than 12 bars and restaurants.

Kids: The nursery is first-rate; there are children's programs for 3- to 12-year-olds; also mini mountain tickets for beginners. Tubing is also offered for kids under age 12.

Lift tickets: In the 2015–16 season two-day lift rates were $158 adults, $132 young adults 13–18, $112 juniors 6–12 and seniors. Also multiday, early- and late-season, and packaged rates. Lifts are free for kids 5 and under. Single-day lift tickets are $86, or less if you purchase in advance online.

CROSS-COUNTRY SKIING Sugarloaf Outdoor Center (207-237-6830), Rt. 27. Open in-season 9 AM–dusk. Ninety kilometers of trails, including race loops (with snowmaking) for timed runs. Rentals and instruction are available and are free with a downhill lift ticket. The center itself includes the **Bull Moose Bakery**, which serves soups and sandwiches, and provides space to relax in front of a fire with a view of Sugarloaf. Trails are well groomed and varied but badly marked.

ICE SKATING Sugarloaf Outdoor Center (207-237-6830) maintains an Olympic-sized, lighted rink and rents skates.

Courtesy of Sugarloaf Resort

SKIING THE BACKSIDE

HIKING There are a number of 4,000-footers in the vicinity, and rewarding trails lead the way up **Mount Abraham** and **Bigelow Mountain**. The APPALACHIAN TRAIL signs are easy to spot on Rt. 27 just south of Stratton; popular treks include the two hours to **Cranberry Pond** or four-plus hours (one-way) to **Cranberry Peak**. The chamber of commerce usually stocks copies of the Maine Bureau of Parks and Lands' detailed map to trails in the 35,000-acre **Bigelow Preserve**, encompassing the several above-tree-line trails in the Bigelow Range. (The trails are far older than the preserve, which dates to 1976 when a proposal to turn these mountains into "the Aspen of the East" was defeated by a public referendum.)

  ❧ **West Mountain Falls** on the Sugarloaf Golf Course is an easy hike to a swimming and picnic spot on the South Branch of the Carrabassett River. Begin at the Sugarloaf Clubhouse.

  Poplar Stream Falls is a 51-foot cascade with a swimming hole below. Turn off Rt. 27 at the Valley Crossing and follow this road to the abandoned road marked by a snowmobile sign. Follow this road 1.5 miles.

  Check in at the **Sugarloaf Outdoor Center** on Rt. 27, then head up **Burnt Mountain Trail**, a 3-mile hike to the 3,600-foot summit. At the top you'll have a 360-degree view of mountains, Sugarloaf's snowfields, and Carrabassett Valley towns. The trail follows a streambed through soft- and hardwoods.

MOOSE-WATCHING (207-237-4201) vans leave from the Sugarloaf Mountain Hotel in summer months.

MOUNTAIN BIKING The **Sugarloaf Outdoor Center** (207-237-2000), Rt. 17, is the hub of a trail system designed for cross-country skiers that also serves bikers well. The more adventurous can, of course, hit any number of abandoned logging roads. More information is available at the Carrabassett Valley Recreation Department (207-237-5566). **Narrow Gauge Pathway**, a 6-mile recreational trail that follows the Carrabassett River along a former railbed, is also popular. Check locally for access to the 19.5-mile loop from Rt. 27 at Carriage Rd. into the **Bigelow Preserve** on double- and singletrack logging roads.

SWIMMING ❧ **Cathedral Pines**, Rt. 27, Stratton. Just north of town, turn right into the campground and follow signs to the public beach, with changing rooms and a playground, on Flagstaff Lake. Free.

  ❧ **Riverside Park**, Rt. 27, 0.5 mile south of Ayottes Country Store, is among the Carrabassett River's popular swimming holes. It features a natural water slide and a very small beach, ideal for small children. Look for a deeper swimming hole off Rt. 27, 0.5 mile south of Riverside Park on the corner of the entrance to Spring Farm.

  Also see **Wire Bridge** under *Historic Sites*.

TENNIS **Riverside Park**, Rt. 27, Carrabassett Valley. This municipal park along the Carrabassett River also features volleyball, basketball, a playground, and bathroom facilities.

❄ Winter Sports

See the sidebars on Maine Huts and Trails, and on Sugarloaf Resort.

SNOWMOBILING Snowmobile trails are outlined on many maps available locally; a favorite destination is **Flagstaff Lodge** (maintained as a warming hut) in the Bigelow Preserve. **Flagstaff Rentals** and **T&L Enterprises** (207-246-4276), Stratton, rent snowmobiles.

☀ Lodging

INNS AND B&BS ✪ **Three Stanley Avenue** (207-265-5541; stanleyavenue.com), Kingfield 04947. Designed by a younger brother of the Stanley twins, now an attractive B&B with six Victorian-inspired rooms (three with private bath, three sharing two baths) next to the ornate restaurant One Stanley Avenue, also owned by Dan Davis (see *Dining Out*). A breakfast of granola and eggs or blueberry pancakes is included in $70–119 double. Also single rates.

✪ 🐾 **The Mountain Village Inn** (207-265-2030; mountainvillageinn.com), 164 Main St., Kingfield 04947. This 1850s farmhouse has been carefully updated, and the six tastefully decorated guest rooms—all with private bath, some with whirlpool tub and cedar shower—have antique or cottage beds and good mattresses. Call in your arrival time, and the two dogs will be kept inside. Innkeeper Lisa Standish is a warm, knowledgeable host who offers guided hikes geared to women. ("Even local women hesitate to walk alone," she explains.) For breakfast count on organic oatmeal, organic granola, and eggs from the chickens kept in the enormous white barn. $89–125.

Nestlewood Inn (207-237-2077; nestlewoodinn.com), 3004 Town Line road, Carrabassett Valley. Spacious, clean rooms in a new log lodge show off with modern simplicity, pine paneling, and comfortable beds; count on a good breakfast. Rates $130–255 depending on season.

Tranquillity Lodge (207-246-2122; tranquillitylodge.com), 310 Rt. 27 on Flagstaff Lake, Stratton 04982. This converted 1850s barn is north of Stratton with a broad lawn bordering the lake and a view of mountains beyond. The nine nicely decorated rooms each have private bath, and there's a spacious common room. From $65 single, $98 double.

🐾 **The Herbert Grand Hotel** (207-265-2000 or 1-888-656-9922; herbertgrandhotel .com), 246 Main St., Kingfield 04947. Open year-round. This three-story Beaux Arts–style hotel was billed as a "palace in the wilderness" when it opened in 1918 in the center of Kingfield. The sink on the dining room wall is where stagecoach customers used to clean up before dining. The 26 rooms (including four suites) are furnished with antiques and cable TV, AC, and private bath. From $79. Pets are welcome for a fee.

MOTEL 🐾 🐾 **Spillover Motel** (207-246-6571), P.O. Box 427, Stratton 04982. An attractive, two-story, 20-unit (16 nonsmoking) motel just south of Stratton Village. Spanking clean, with two double beds to a unit, cable TV, and phone. From $89 double ($69 single), including continental breakfast; inquire about condo unit.

SPORTING CAMPS 🐾 🐾 **Tim Pond Wilderness Camps** (207-243-2947; in winter, 207-897-4056; timpond.com), Eustis 04936. Open May–Nov. Located on a pond where there are no other camps and down a road with gated access, with 11 log cabins, each with a fieldstone fireplace or woodstove. This is one of the oldest sporting camps in Maine. The specialty is fly-fishing, but there's deer and moose hunting, mountain biking, hiking, swimming, or canoeing at this clear, remote lake surrounded by 4,450 acres of woodland. $195 single per night (plus 15 percent gratuity) includes meals, cabin, boat and motor. Ten percent discount July–Aug. Pets $10. Dinner by reservation for people who want just a meal July–Sept.

CAMPGROUNDS 🐾 🐾 **Cathedral Pines Campground** (207-246-3491; gopines camping.com), Rt. 27, Eustis 04936. Open mid-May–Sept. Three hundred town-owned acres on Flagstaff Lake, with 115 wooded tent and RV sites set amid towering red pines. Recreation hall, beach, playground, and canoe and paddleboat rentals. Rates $27–35.

🐾 🐾 **Deer Farm Camps & Campground** (207-265-4599 or 207-265-2241; deerfarm camps.com), Tufts Pond Rd., Kingfield 04947. Open May–mid-Oct. Fifty wooded tent and RV sites near Tufts Pond (good swimming); facilities include a store, playground, and hot showers. $18 tent sites, $22 with water and electric; hook-ups available.

☀ Where to Eat

DINING OUT ✪ **One Stanley Avenue** (207-265-5541; stanleyavenue.com), Kingfield. Open mid-Dec.–mid-Apr. 5–9:30, except Mon.

Reservations recommended. Dan Davis has been chef-owner of the area's best restaurant for 40 years and he has his menu down pat. "If I changed something, people would be furious with me," he says—and we see his point. We have great memories of the rabbit with raspberry sauce, which wasn't available on our most recent visit. Dates next to each dish indicate when it first appeared on the menu. Our roast duck with rhubarb glaze (1979), served with wild rice and a mix of seasonal veggies, was exceptional. $21–35 includes fresh bread, salad, vegetables, starch, coffee, and tea, but it's difficult to pass on the wines and desserts.

Hug's Italian Cuisine (207-237-2392), 3001 Town Line Rd. (Rt. 27), Carrabassett Valley. Open mid-July–mid-Oct., Wed.–Sun. for dinner, closed through Nov.; open every night for dinner in winter. The green metal roof and board-and-batten siding keep this restaurant looking modest—but inside you'll find some great northern Italian food. Past the shrine to pasta, among festoons of grapevines, you can enjoy wild mushroom ravioli with Gorgonzola, fresh tomato, and spinach sauce accompanied by great pesto bread—or chicken, veal, and seafood. All entrées can be altered, our good waiter told us.

Coplin Dinner House (207-246-0016), 8252 Carrabassett Road, Stratton. Rack of lamb, fantastic meat loaf, and seafood au gratin made with proper attention to detail bring devotees back again and again. Wild blueberry tart to finish in blueberry season, of course. Five courses for $55; two-for-one nights with two entrees for $28. All-you-can-eat fish-and-chips might be offered in the pub.

45 North (207-237-4220 or 237-2451), Sugarloaf Mountain Hotel. Open for breakfast and dinner. The decor evokes a local farmhouse. Upscale, locally sourced fare with the executive chef's German accent.

Bullwinkle's at Night (1-800-THE-LOAF), at the top of Bucksaw chair. On Sat. night (and special nights by appointment) this place converts from a daytime ski cafeteria into a charming on-mountain full-service restaurant featuring a six-course candlelit feast. Reserve early. We were lucky enough to ride up in the Sno-Cat during a lovely snowstorm. Soups like lobster and corn bisque were spectacular, and the venison and lobster filled us up nicely after a day on the slopes.

Have a drink in the **Widowmaker Lounge** at the base of the mountain before or after, watching the powder collect on the runs you'll ski the next morning.

EATING OUT ✪ ✆ **Gepetto's Restaurant** (207-237-2192), Sugarloaf Village. Open for lunch and dinner. Recently acquired by Sugarloaf, hopefully this spot will retain the warm atmosphere and quality enjoyed for 35 years under the previous ownership. The expansive menu ranges from pizza to steak with jumbo salads and from-scratch soups at lunch; there's a nightly sushi selection, full bar, Sat. music.

((ᵠ)) **The Orange Cat Café** (207-265-2860; orangecatcafe.com), The Brick Castle, 329 Main St., Kingfield. Open 7–5 in winter, 7–3 in summer. Good coffee and homemade scones are served under a map of the world; you can also get great lunch dishes, like a fantastic quiche; best hot chocolate in the valley. In summer count on ice cubes made with coffee for iced coffee.

🍴 ✆ **Longfellows Restaurant** (207-265-4394), 247 Main St., Kingfield. Open year-round for lunch from 11 and dinner 5–9. An attractive, informal dining place in a 19th-century building decorated with photos of 19th-century Kingfield. A find for budget-conscious families, with reasonably good food and two-for-one dinners Tue. Deck overlooking the Carrabassett River. Entrées $7–17.

✆ ♿ **Tufulio's Restaurant & Bar** (207-235-2010), Rt. 27, Carrabassett (6 miles south of Sugarloaf). Open for dinner 5–9:30 daily; happy hour begins at 4. A pleasant dining room with large oak booths, specializing in pasta, pizza, seafood, steaks, and microbrews. Children's menu and game room.

✆ **The Woodsman** (207-265-2561), Rt. 27, Kingfield (north end of town). Open Mon.–Sat. for breakfast and lunch; Sun. for breakfast only. Pine-paneled, decorated with logging tools and pictures, this is a friendly barn of a place. Good for stacks of pancakes, omelets, homemade soups, and local gossip.

The Rack (207-237-2211; therackbbq.com), Sugarloaf Access Rd., Carrabassett. BBQ and pulled pork are the focuses but there are other options, from fresh fish to pasta. Seth Wescott, co-owner of this restaurant, thrilled Maine both times he won the snowboard cross gold medal in the Winter Olympics, in 2006 and 2010. Entrées $15–25. Live entertainment.

The Bag & Kettle (207-237-2451), Sugarloaf Village. Wood-fired brick-oven pizza, the "Bag Burger," frequent music, a fixture since '69.

The Sugar Bowl (207-235-3300), 1242 Carrabassett Valley. American jerk chicken, nachos, poutine make sure famished skiers recoup their strength; there's also lobster rolls, pizza, and a brownie sundae for dessert.

Java Joe's Carrabassett Coffee (207-127-3330), Sugarloaf Village and Rt. 27, Kingfield (where beans are roasted). Open daily at 7 AM. Espresso, latte, and cappuccino; also tea, hot chocolate, bagels, muffins, and pastries.

White Wolf Inn & Restaurant (207-246-2922), Main St. (Rt. 27), Stratton. Ten miles north of the Sugarloaf access you are out of the glitz zone. Nothing fancy here but a good bet for lunch or dinner, from burgers and pizza to slow flying crispy duck with crab-apple glaze, or venison with wild mushrooms. $15–29.

IN FARMINGTON

✪ **Soup for You! Cafe** (207-779-0799), 222 Broadway. Open Mon.–Sat. 10:30–7. Be sure to get there before noon for lunch because a line starts forming. This small restaurant offers homemade soups, salads, and a large choice of terrific sandwiches that bear the names of *Seinfeld* characters and other whimsical monikers like Don Quixote and Barking Spider. On a winter day the potato bacon soup and a chicken/avocado wrap hit the spot. Smoothies, cappuccino, and espresso, too.

The Homestead Kitchen Bar Bakery (207-778-6162), 186 Broadway (Rt. 43). Open Mon.–Sat. 8 AM–9 PM, Sun 8–2 for brunch. Dinner choices include steaks, seafood, chicken, and vegetarian options, like vegetable ravioli in vodka sauce, as well as Cajun-spiced duck diavolo. The eggs Benedict with lobster or crabmeat are delicious at brunch. Entrées $15–24.

Thai Smile (207-778-0790), 103 Narrow Gauge Square. This fine Thai restaurant serves sushi and Thai specialties; 30 beers on tap and great curries plus barbecued eel.

✻ Selective Shopping

IN KINGFIELD-STRATTON

Kingfield Art Walk, first Fridays 5–8, Nov.–Apr. and during Kingfield Pops in late June, highlights a rough dozen venues in town.

Stadler Gallery (207-265-5025; stadlergallery.com), 225 Main St., Kingfield. Ulrike Stadler Kozak runs her wide-ranging gallery with the vision of an artist—which she is. Her own work is here and so are new exhibits every summer, all worthy of contemplation.

Schoolhouse Gallery (207-939-6518), 266 Main St. Housed in a renovated 1874 schoolhouse and featuring work by nature photographers John and Cynthia Orcutt, also paintings, glass, jewelry, furniture, and more by local craftspeople and artists.

The Reinholt Gallery (207-624-9824), 245 Main St., features work by woodworker Ian Reinholt, also other local artists, craftspeople.

Hugh Verrier Gallery (207-246-6694; birds-in-flight.com), 991 Arnold Trail (Rt. 27), Eustis. Extraordinary woodcarvings.

IN FARMINGTON

✪ ✎ **Devaney, Doak & Garrett Booksellers** (207-778-3454; ddgbooks.com), 193 Broadway. Open daily. A bookstore worthy of a college town and one with a good children's section. Comfortable seating invites lingering. Readings from local and Maine authors.

✪ **Renys** (207-778-4631; renys.com), 200 Broadway. Filling a former silent-movie house, the statewide chain of fine discount goods has a popular store here that features a restored stage and balconies.

Twice-Sold Tales (207-778-4411), 155 Main St. Specializing in Maine history, Maine literature, and nonfiction, but carrying mysteries and more, this eclectic collection is well organized.

Sugarwood Gallery (207-778-9105; sugarwoodgallery.com), 248 Broadway. A cooperative gallery showing the work of local artisans, mostly woodwork, stained glass, and pottery.

Mainestone Jewelry (207-778-6560), 179 Broadway. Ron and Cindy Gelinas craft much of the jewelry here—made from Maine-mined gems—but some is made by local craftspeople.

✳ Special Events

January: **White White World Week**—snow sculpture contest, annual Dummy Jump, and discounts at Sugarloaf.

February: **Polar Blast**, Eustis/Stratton—a snowmobile jump, cribbage tournament, and chowder/chili cook-off.

April: **Reggae Festival at Sugarloaf**—held for 25-plus years, "the biggest party in ski country."

June: **Family Fun Days**, Eustis/Stratton—games and children's events, parade, fireworks. **Kingfield Pops** (last weekend; kingfieldpops.com) with the Bangor Symphony, art walk, crafts fair.

Mid-July: **Kingfield Days Celebration**—four days with parade, art exhibits, potluck supper.

August: **Wilton Blueberry Festival**, Wilton.

Third week of September: **Farmington Fair**, with popular harness racing and live-stock exhibits.

October: **Corn Maze and Pumpkin Patch** (sandyriverfarms.com), Rts. 2 and 27, 3 miles south of Farmington at Sandy River Farms. A 10-acre fall extravaganza with food, hayrides, and some haunting.

December: **Yellow-Nosed Vole Day**, Sugarloaf Mountain. **Chester Greenwood Day**, Farmington, honors the local inventor of the earmuff with a parade and variety show.

THE KENNEBEC VALLEY

AUGUSTA AND MID-MAINE

Including the Belgrade Lakes Region

THE UPPER KENNEBEC VALLEY AND MOOSE RIVER VALLEY

Including The Forks and Jackman

AUGUSTA AND MID-MAINE
Including the Belgrade Lakes Region

ugusta was selected as the nascent state's capital in 1827 because then, as now, so many travelers come this way, whether headed up or down the coast, into or out of Maine's interior. First I-95 and now the Rt. 3 connector make it all too easy, however, to bypass the city.

If time permits, approach Augusta via the Kennebec instead of the highway. Follow Rt. 201, the old river road, at least for the 6 miles from Gardiner up through Hallowell's mid-19th-century Water Street, lined with antiques and specialty shops and restaurants. However you come, don't skip the Maine State Museum, which does an excellent job of showcasing Maine's natural history and traditional industries, as well as tracing human habitation back 12,000 years.

Augusta and neighboring Hallowell both mark the site of Native American villages. In 1625 the Pilgrims came here to trade "seven hundred pounds of good beaver and some other furs" with the Wabanaki for a "shallop's load of corn." They procured a grant for a strip of land 15 miles wide on either side of the Kennebec, built a storehouse, and with the proceeds of their beaver trade were soon able to pay off their London creditors. With the decline of the fur trade and rising hostilities with the Wabanaki, the tract of land was sold to four Boston merchants. It wasn't until 1754, when the British constructed Fort Western (now reconstructed), that serious settlement began.

The statehouse, designed by Charles Bulfinch and built of granite from neighboring Hallowell, was completed in 1832 (it's been expanded and largely rebuilt since). During the mid-19th century, this area boomed: Some 500 boats were built along the river between Winslow and Gardiner, and river traffic between Augusta and Boston thrived.

This Lower Kennebec Valley was the site of numerous, now vanished 19th-century summer hotels and boardinghouses and still is home to many summer camps. The Belgrade Lakes Region, just north of Augusta, remains a low-key *On Golden Pond* kind of resort area with old-style family-geared "sporting camps." East of the city, the China Lakes area is another old low-profile summer haven. Art lovers find their way to the stellar Colby College Museum of Art in Waterville, and the Maine International Film Festival draws cinephiles to town in July. Long-established summer theater continues to thrive in Monmouth and Skowhegan.

The latter town, sited at one of the major drops in the Kennebec River, holds walking bridges across the gorge and a gem of a small museum and research center honoring the late U.S. Senator Margaret Chase Smith, "the Lady from Maine."

Nancy English

THE OLD GRANITE BLOCK ON AUGUSTA'S MAIN STREET

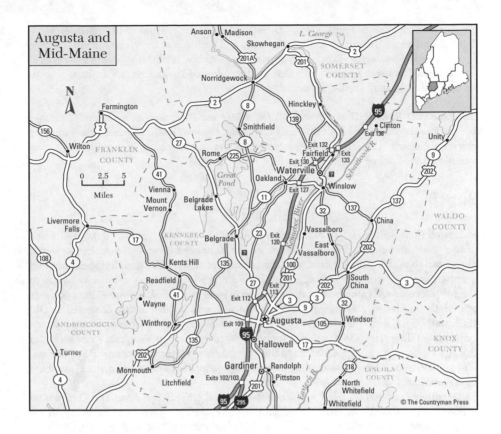

Augusta and Mid-Maine

Embden (just across a bridge from Solon), is the site of petroglyphs that are evidence of a Native American culture that dates back several thousand years.

GUIDANCE **Kennebec Valley Chamber of Commerce** (207-623-4559; augustamaine.com) runs a website worth checking for current updates.

Mid-Maine Chamber of Commerce (207-873-3315; midmainechamber.com) covers Belgrade and China Lakes as well as Waterville. Its office, 50 Elm St., Waterville, is open weekdays 9–5.

Belgrade Lakes Region Business Group, Inc. (207-495-2744; belgradelakesmaine.com) maintains a good website and a seasonal information booth on Rt. 27 in Belgrade.

Skowhegan Chamber of Commerce (207-474-3621; skowheganchamber.com), 23 Commercial St., is open year-round 9:30–5:30 weekdays. Rt. 201 snakes through downtown right by this office.

GETTING THERE *By air:* **Augusta State Airport** (augustaairport.org) is served by **Cape Air** (capeair.com) to Boston. Check the website for car rentals and taxis.

By bus: **Concord Coach Lines** (1-800-639-3317; concordcoachlines.com) offers service from Portland and Boston, stopping at the **Augusta Transportation Center** (207-622-0808, ext. 450), 9 Industrial Dr., just off I-95 Exit 112 (head north on Rt. 8/27). Open 5:30 AM–7:45 PM. Taxis are available. Also long-term parking spaces (free for two weeks).

Greyhound (207-622-1601) stops at the airport in Augusta; also stops in Waterville.

By car: From points south, Rt. 295 is both quicker and cheaper than I-95 (the Maine Turnpike). The two merge just south of Augusta, and both access the West Gardiner Service Plaza. Note the connector (Exit 113) bypassing Augusta and facilitating access to Rt. 3 east. For Rt. 3 via downtown Augusta take Exit 112; for Belgrade Lakes, Exit 127; for Rt. 201 north through Hinkley and Skowhegan, Exit 133.

SUGGESTED READING *A Midwife's Tale*, a Pulitzer Prize winner by Laurel Thatcher Ulrich, vividly describes life in this area 1785–1812. *Empire Falls*, a Pulitzer Prize–winning novel by Richard Russo, describes current life in a town resembling Waterville; the movie was filmed in Skowhegan.

✳ Villages

Hallowell (hallowell.org). Two miles south of Augusta, this "city" (pop. 2,467), with its line of two- and three-story brick buildings along the Kennebec River, looks much the way it did at the time this, not Augusta, was the region's commercial center. Shipbuilding and granite quarrying were the big industries here, along with ice. The city's revival dates to the 1970s. A road-widening proposal threatened to level most of Water Street, but residents rallied; the anniversary of their protest, the last weekend in July, is now observed as **Old Hallowell Day**. Note the **"Museum in the Streets"** consisting of 19 archival photos and captions on buildings along Water and neighboring streets. Walk in **Vaughan Woods**, part of the city's most historic estate, dating to the 18th century. **Water Street**, now all a National Historic District, is lined with quality, individually owned shops (no chain stores) and the best restaurants around.

    Gardiner (pop. 6,100). Sited at the confluence of the Kennebec River and Cobbossee-contee Stream, this old industrial (shoe, textile, and paper) town has been hovering on the verge of renaissance for more than a decade. It was home to Pulitzer Prize–winning poet

DOWNTOWN HALLOWELL

Edwin Arlington Robinson (1869–1935), best known for his poem "Richard Cory" and collection of *Tilbury Town* poems; check earobinson.com for his life story and a Tilbury Town walking tour. The **A1 Diner** and **Reny's** are a draw for travelers and locals alike, as are performances at the **Johnson Hall Performing Arts Center**.

Waterville (pop. 15,970). The thinly disguised subject of Richard Russo's novel *Empire Falls*, this old mill town is 25 miles upriver from Augusta. It's home to a major art museum and some interesting restaurants. **Colby College** (207-872-3000; colby.edu) is the pride of the city. Founded in 1813, it enrolls some 1,800 students at its 714-acre campus, with ivy-covered brick buildings, a 128-acre arboretum and bird sanctuary (with nature trails and a picnic area), and the 274-seat **Strider Theater**, offering performances throughout the year. The newly expanded **Colby College Museum of Art** is now the largest art museum in the state and drawing art lovers from afar (see *To See*). Whether you reach the city from I-95 Exit 127 (Rt. 137) or Exit 130 (Rt. 104), access to the college is well marked, as is the way to "Downtown," literally down by the river.

The **Waterville-Winslow Two Cent Bridge** on Front St. is one of the only known toll footbridges in the country (now free). The **Redington Museum and Apothecary** (207-872-9439; redingtonmuseum.org), 64 Silver St. (open seasonally, Tue.–Sat. 10–2), houses the local historical collection.

Belgrade Lakes (belgradelakesmaine.com). There is no Belgrade Lake per se; the towns here are Rome, Oakland, Smithfield, and Mount Vernon as well as Belgrade. There are seven lakes, with Great Pond, at the center, flanked by Long Pond to the west, Salmon Lake (connected to) McGrath Pond and Messalonskee Lake on the west, North Pond to the north, and East Pond to the northeast. **Belgrade Lakes Village** at the center sits astride Rt. 27 on a narrow land bridge between Long and Grand Ponds; many customers of **Day's Store** (the region's epicenter; see *Selective Shopping*) come by boat. The lakeshores are dotted but not lined with summer cottages. There are several traditional, full-service family-geared "camps," the kind that have since vanished from all of Maine save the North Woods. The area offers an 18-hole golf course and the Belgrade Lakes Community Center with an indoor pool as well as beach. This was the area that inspired Ernest Thompson's play and then movie, *On Golden Pond*. Thanks to the **Belgrade Regional Conservation Alliance** (belgrade lakes.org), the 6,000-acre Kennebec Highlands have been preserved. There's a trail up Blueberry Hill that families have hiked for generations.

Winthrop (pop. 2,980). A proud town with 12 lakes and many summer cottages within its boundaries, Winthrop seems to be thriving despite closure of the woolen mill.

Skowhegan (pop. 8,875). In Wabanaki the name is said to mean "watch for fish." This, one of the major falls in the Kennebec River, has long been harnessed to generate power for both textile and woodworking mills. Skowhegan is also shire town of Somerset County and a major north–south (Rt. 201) and east–west (Rt. 2) crossroads. Stop downtown (there's parking behind the Water St. shops and restaurants) to view the gorge from one of two pedestrian bridges or from **Coburn Park** on the eastern edge of town. If it's a hot day, **Lake George Regional Park** (see *Swimming*) is worth the detour. The Kennebec doglegs west here and Rt. 201A follows it up through **Norridgewock** (see the *Wabanaki Cultural Landmarks* sidebar), rejoining Rt. 201 in **Solon**. Whichever way you go, be sure to stop by the riverside **Margaret Chase Smith Library Center**. This is really an outstanding small museum (see *To See*). On the way check out the **Skowhegan History House** (skowhegan historyhouse.org; 66 Elm St.), open Memorial–Columbus Day, Tue.–Sat. 1–4. Skowhegan is also home to **Gifford's Famous Ice Cream**, the **Skowhegan State Fair**, and the **Skowhegan Lakewood Theater** on Lake Wesserunsett, billed as America's Oldest Summer Theater. The prestigious **Skowhegan School of Painting and Sculpture** (skowheganart.org) holds an intensive nine-week summer residency program, squirreled away on a 300-acre campus 4 miles from town, and also opens its evening lectures to the public.

✳ To See

IN AUGUSTA

✪ ⚲ ♿ **Maine State Museum** (207-287-2301; mainestatemuseum.org), housed in the State Library/Archives building in the State House Complex, marked from Sewall St., also accessible from State St. (Rt. 201/27). Open Tue.–Fri. 9–5, Sat. 10–4. Closed holidays and state government holidays. Maine's best-kept secret, this is a superb and extensive museum, just a few blocks off the interstate but badly posted. It's well worth finding, especially if there are children along. It's a great way to break up a long drive.

The *Back to Nature* exhibit features animals such as the lynx and snowshoe rabbit, deer, moose, beaver, and birds in their convincingly detailed habitats (the trout are real) with plenty of sound effects. The *Maine Bounty* exhibits depict the way the state's natural resources have been developed through fishing, agriculture, granite quarrying, ice harvesting, shipbuilding, lumbering, and more. Exhibits include a gigantic wagon used to haul stone from quarries and the equally huge Lombard Log Hauler and 1846 narrow-gauge locomotive Lion, used to transport lumber. Archival films such as *From Stump to Ship* bring the era to life. *Made in Maine* depicts more than a dozen 19th-century industrial scenes: textile mills and shops producing shoes, guns, fishing rods, and more, again with sound effects. Don't miss the fourth floor with its *At Home in Maine* galleries depicting domestic life from the 1800s through 1960s.

Yet another outstanding exhibit, *12,000 Years in Maine*, traces the story of human habitation in the state from the Paleo Indians up through the "ceramic period" (3,000 B.C.–A.D. 500) with genuine artifacts and reproductions of petroglyphs. It also dramatizes early European explorations and displays 19th-century Penobscot and Passamaquoddy craftsmanship, from highly decorative bent-birch boxes to birch-bark canoes. Check the website for current special exhibits and don't miss the gift store.

Directions: From I-95 Exit 109 follow Western Ave. (Rt. 17/202) and turn right at the light across from the armory (posted for the capitol complex). Follow signs for the State House until you see the museum posted (a right turn onto Sewall St.). The museum is in the low-slung modern building that also houses the state library and archives.

Tours of the State House (by reservation weekdays 9–1 through the museum). The governor's 1830 mansion, Blaine House (blainehouse.org), is no longer open regular hours, but visitors willing to procure security clearance may see it.

Fort Western (207-626-2385; oldfortwestern.org), City Center Plaza, 16 Cony St., Augusta. Open late May–Columbus Day, weekdays 10–4 (closed Tue. except July and Aug.), weekends 11–4. $10 per adult, $6 ages 6–14. The original 16-room garrison house has been restored to reflect its use as a fort, trading post, and lodge from 1754 to 1810. The blockhouse and stockade are reproductions, but the main house (barracks and store) is original. The fort, a National Historic Landmark, is the oldest surviving wooden fort in New England. Costumed characters answer questions and demonstrate 18th-century domestic activities.

Fort Halifax, Rt. 201 (1 mile south of the Waterville–Winslow Bridge at the junction of the Kennebec and Sebasticook Rivers). Just a blockhouse remains, but it's original, built in 1754—the oldest in the United States. There's also a park with picnic tables here.

ALONG RT. 201 NORTH

⚲ **L. C. Bates Museum** (207-238-4250; gwh.org), Rt. 201, Hinckley. A few miles up Rt. 201 from I-95, Exit 133. Open Wed.–Sat. 10–4:30, Sun. 1–4:30; closed Sun. off-season, but look for the OPEN flag; it's frequently staffed on "closed" days. *Note:* The museum is unheated.

MUST SEE

○ ♿ **Colby College Museum of Art** (207-859-5600; colby.edu/museum), Colby College, 5600 Mayflower Hill Dr. Open Tue.–Sat. 10–5, Sun. noon–5, Thu. until 9 during the academic year. Free. Closed Mon. and major holidays. In 2013 this already substantial teaching museum added a three-story glass-walled wing, the Alfond-Lunder Family Pavilion. It displays Peter and Paula Lunder's significant 500-piece collection of largely American and contemporary art, also select collections of Chinese antiquities and European works. Founded only in 1959, the museum has been amazingly lucky in not only the generosity of its donors but also the quality of their gifts. With 8,000 works and five wings totaling 38,000 square feet of exhibition space, it is now Maine's largest art museum.

Highlights of the collection include 200 prints by James McNeill Whistler, paintings by Edward Hopper and Georgia O'Keeffe, and sculptures by Augustus Saint-Gaudens and Alexander Calder. The Lunders (Peter is Colby '56 and past president of Dexter Shoe Co.) had previously donated a 13-gallery wing to display more of the college's own collection, with its particular strength in American contemporary art, including significant Maine-based works by Marsden Hartley, John Marin, George Bellows, and Rockwell Kent. The Paul J. Schupf Wing rotates more than 700 paintings, ranging from modest-sized to huge, as well as prints and works on paper by Alex Katz. There are also unexpected treasures like Duane Hanson's sculpture, *Old Man Playing Solitaire*.

Major special exhibits, also frequent gallery talks, performances, and receptions throughout the year are listed on the website. The museum sounds trickier to find than it is. It's minutes off I-95 Exit 127. Head toward downtown Waterville on Rt. 127 and follow the blue COLBY signs. Turn left at the light opposite Inland Hospital on First Rangeway, and at the T turn left onto Mayflower Hill Dr. The building is beyond the main campus quad, with easy parking both in front of the building and behind the Bixler Fine Art Building.

THE TRAPPER BY WINSLOW HOMER

$3 adults, $1 ages 17 and under. Across the road from the Kennebec River, one in a lineup of brick buildings that are part of the campus of the Good-Will Hinckley School (founded in 1889 for "disadvantaged chidden"), this ponderous Romanesque building houses a large and wonderfully old-fashioned collection, with stuffed wildlife, dioramas by noted American impressionist Charles D. Hubbard, and some significant Wabanaki craftsmanship ranging from several thousand years old to early-20th-century items. Allow at least an hour. The annual summer art exhibit, usually incorporating work by faculty and/or students at the nearby Skowhegan School of Painting, is a bonus. The 2,540-acre campus includes many miles of walking and biking trails, an arboretum, and a picnic area.

Margaret Chase Smith Library Center (207-474-7133; mcslibrary.org), 54 Norridgewock Ave., Skowhegan (turn left at the first traffic light heading north out of town). Open year-round Mon.–Fri. 10–4. Free. Set in 15 acres above the Kennebec, this expanded version of Senator Smith's home is a major museum to an era as well as to a stateswoman who voted her conscience in the face of overwhelming opposition. She is credited with putting an end to the reign of national paranoia instigated by Senator Joseph R. McCarthy. Well worth a stop for the exhibits. This research and conference center houses over 300,000 documents relating to "the Lady from Maine," as Margaret Chase Smith (1897–1995) was known during her years as a U.S. representative (1940–49) and senator (1949–73).

Also see the **South Solon Meeting House** in the Upper Kennebec Valley chapter.

FOR FAMILIES ♂ **Children's Discovery Museum** (207-622-2209; childrensdiscovery museum.org), 171 Capitol St. (next to Harvest Time Natural Foods), Augusta. Open Tue.–Thu. 10–4, Fri. and Sat. 10–5, Sun. 11–4; extended hours during school vacations and summer. Admission $6. A hands-on museum, with a stage for performing skits, a puppet theater, construction area, computer games, double train tracks, nature center, music area, supermarket, and more.

♂ **DEW Haven** (207-293-2837; dewhaven.com), 918 Pond Rd. (Rt. 41), West Mount Vernon. Open June–Labor Day, 10–5 except Mon.; Sept.–mid-Oct. and May to mid-June weekends 10–5. $15 ages 13–64; $10 ages 4–12 and 65-plus; free for children 3 and under. Julie and Bob Miner stress that this is a "farm," not a "zoo." But what began as a traditional farm with pigs and cows has evolved into the most exotic menagerie in New England: more than 200 animals contained within chain-link pens on 43 wooded acres. It is both a sanctuary for animals no longer wanted at zoos and a resource for local wildlife rehabilitation. What's striking is the way the animals relate to Julie and Bob, who have raised most from birth. Cougars and lions nuzzle them. A female lynx offers her tail to be pulled. The tigers lumber up to be hugged. Eddie the Camel offers slurpy kisses to visitors as well. A wallaby baby peeks from its mother's pouch. You can feed the several kinds of goats, but this isn't a petting farm—just a place to marvel at animals that are native (deer and black bear) or fairly familiar (ostrich and llamas), and also those you may have only read about—from badgers to black leopards and a white tiger.

Nancy English

A DEW HAVEN TIGER YAWNS WHILE VISITORS ADMIRE HIM

♂ **Norlands Living History Center** (207-897-4366; norlands.org), 290 Norlands Rd., Livermore. From Rt. 4 take Rt. 108 east for 1.2 miles, then travel 1.6 miles up Norlands Rd. Open in summer months for guided tours Tue., Thu., and Sat. 11–4; also for seasonal events and school programs. Live-in programs also available. This 455-acre complex includes a restored Victorian mansion, farmer's cottage, church, granite library, and one-room schoolhouse. A fire destroyed the large barn, and fund-raising is paying for its reconstruction. These buildings and grounds provide the backdrop for rural late-19th-century living history experiences—hear the story of the Washburn family and their 11 sons and daughters, or take part in the daily chores of the 1870s.

✻ To Do

BICYCLING AND WALKING **The Kennebec River Rail Trail** (kennebecriverrailtrail.org) runs 6.5 miles along the river most of the way from Augusta (best parking near Waterfront Park and Capitol Park) through Hallowell to Gardiner (at the Hannaford parking lot). It's popular with bicyclists, runners, and strollers.

BOATING **Great Pond Marina** (207-495-2213; greatpondmarina.com), Belgrade Lakes Village, operates the **Mail Boat** on Great Pond. Also moorings, boat rentals (canoes, sailboards, sailboats, fishing boats), and service. **Belgrade Boat Canoe & Kayak Rental** (207-495-3421; belgradeboatrentals.com) rents small fishing boats, canoes, and kayaks; free delivery and pickup.

FISHING The **Belgrade Lakes** are a big lure for anglers. The seven ponds and lakes harbor smallmouth bass, brook, pickerel, and landlocked salmon, among many other species. The sporting camps listed under *Lodging* all offer rental boats and cater to fishermen, especially in May, June, and Sept. **Day's Store** (207-495-2205) in Belgrade Lakes Village is a source of fishing licenses and devotes an entire floor to fishing gear.

GOLF AND TENNIS **Belgrade Lakes Golf Club** (207-495-GOLF; belgradelakesgolf.com), Belgrade, is a relatively new, highly rated 18-hole golf course designed by renowned English golf architect Clive Clark. Just off Rt. 27 with views of both Great and Long Ponds. Fees vary with season. Restaurant open to the public.

    Augusta Country Club (207-623-9021; augustacountryclub.org), 19 Hammonds Grove, Manchester. Eighteen holes, the back nine with views of Lake Cobbosseecontee; reserve tee time two days in advance.

    Natanis Golf Club (207-622-3561), Webber Pond off Rt. 201, Vassalboro, offers a 36-hole course and tennis courts. **Waterville Country Club** (207-465-9861), Waterville (off I-95), 18 holes, clubhouse with restaurant, carts, and caddies. **Lakewood Golf Course** (207-474-5955; lakewoodgolfmaine.com), off Rt. 201A, Madison, 18 holes on the west side of Lake Wesserunsett.

KAYAKING AND CANOEING **Maine Wilderness Tours** (207-465-4333; mainewildernesstours.com), guided canoe and kayak trips on the Belgrade Lakes and down the Kennebec as well as fishing, moose-watching, and rafting farther afield. Also see *Boating* for rentals. Mercer Bog is a great spot for kayaking.

ROLLER SKATING **Sunbeam Roller Rink** (207-362-4951), 830 Village Rd. (Rt. 8), Smithfield in the Belgrade Lakes, next door to Sunset Camps on the shore of North Pond. Open seasonally; call for hours.

SPA **The Senator Inn & Spa** (207-622-3138; senatorinn.com), 284 Western Ave., Augusta. The three-story spa wing contains a fitness center, saltwater lap pool, aerobics and yoga studio, hot tub and steam room, and outdoor pool. Full menu of spa services.

WABANAKI CULTURAL LANDMARKS

Wabanaki heritage is particularly strong along this stretch of the Kennebec River. Your clue might be the 62-foot-high Skowhegan Indian, billed as "the world's largest sculptured wooden Indian." Carved by sculptor Bernard Langlais in 1969 and restored in 2015, he stands in newly landscaped Langlais Park, visible (and accessible) from Rt. 201. Finding genuine evidence of longtime Indian habitation, however, requires some sleuthing. There are two sites, one commemorating an early-18th-century Indian mission village and the second consisting of genuine Indian petroglyphs. To find the first from Skowhegan, follow Rt. 201A along the Kennebec for just a few miles to Norridgewock. If you are interested only in the petroglyphs, you can remain on Rt. 201 into Solon.

THE 62-FOOT TALL "SKOWHEGAN INDIAN"

French Jesuit Sebastian Rasle established the mission in Norridgewock, insisting that Native American lands "were given them of God, to them and their children forever." Rasle and his mission were wiped out by the English in 1724. **Norridgewock Oosoola Park** features a totem pole topped by a frog (this is a good picnic spot and boat-launch site). The site of the village itself is marked by a pleasant riverside picnic area in a pine grove.

The petroglyphs are in Embden on an arrowhead-shaped rock that juts into the Kennebec. From Rt. 201 in Solon, turn at the sign for the Evergreens Campground and Restaurant. Cross the Kennebec and turn south on Rt. 201A. The trail to the river is just down the road; it's not marked, but it's easy to see. If you are coming from the mission village site, continue straight ahead; the road hugs the river all the way to Solon. Also see the L. C. Bates Museum in *To See*.

SWIMMING 🏊 **Peacock Beach State Park,** Richmond (just off Rt. 201, 10 miles south of Augusta). A small, sand beach on Pleasant Pond; lifeguards and picnic facilities. $3 adults, free under age 12.

On the southern edge of **Belgrade Lakes Village, Long Pond Public Beach** is on Lakeshore Dr. (off West Rd.), **Oakland Town Beach** on Messalonskee Lake, and **Rome Town Beach** on Great Pond (Frederick Lane off Rt. 225). The **Belgrade Community Center** (207-495-3481), 1 Center Dr. (off Rt. 27 south of the village), offers lakefront and a pool.

Lake George Regional Park (lakegeorgepark.org), Rt. 2, 8 miles east of Skowhegan. Open seasonally with two sand beaches on either side of the lake; changing rooms, restrooms, boat launch, and picnicking facilities. (Also see *Green Space.*)

Lake St. George State Park (207-589-4255), Rt. 3, Liberty. A pleasant, clean, clear lake with a sandy beach and changing facilities; a perfect break if en route from Augusta to the coast. $4 day-use fee.

✳ Green Space

Capitol Park, across from the State House Complex, is a good place for a picnic. Also located here is the Maine Vietnam Veterans Memorial, three triangular structures with a cutout section in the shape of soldiers that visitors can walk through.

Viles Arboretum (207-621-0031; vilesarboretum.org), 153 Hospital St., Augusta. (At Cony Circle—the big rotary across the bridge from downtown Augusta—turn south along the river; it's a short way down on the left, across from the Augusta Mental Health Institute.) Open daily dawn to dusk. Visitors center open 8–4 weekdays. There are 224 acres, with trails through woods and fields, which share a history as productive farmland worked by inmates of the state hospital. More than 600 trees and shrubs (including rhododendrons and lilacs as well as hostas and a rock garden). Cross-country ski trails and sculpture, too.

Jamies Pond Wildlife Management Area, Meadow Hill Rd., Hallowell. These 800 acres of woodlands, managed by the Maine Department of Inland Fisheries and Wildlife, include 6 miles of trails good for walking and cross-country skiing, and a 107-acre pond perfect for a swim off the boat launch. There is a small parking lot and a launch ramp.

Lake George Regional Park (207-474-1292), Rt. 2, 8 miles east of Skowhegan. This 320-acre lakeside park, site of a 19th-century mineral spring resort, then a summer camp, was acquired by the state in 1992 and is maintained by a nonprofit group for year-round use. Ten kilometers of trails for mountain biking and cross-country skiing. Inquire about an evolving museum. Nominal admission charged in summer; see *Swimming*.

Coburn Park, Water St. (Rt. 2 east) on the edge of downtown Skowhegan. This riverside park with a lily pond and formal landscaping hosts a regular concert series in July and Aug.

Kennebec Land Trust (tklt.org) has protected more than 3,200 acres of land in the Kennebec River and Lakes region with most properties open to visitors, including **Vaughan Woods** in Hallowell. In 1791 Charles Vaughan settled in the town named for his grandfather, Benjamin Hallowell; in 1797 his brother Benjamin arrived and built himself a fine house here, transforming the property into an agricultural showplace. Seven generations later, 152 acres have been granted as a conservation easement to the Kennebec Land Trust. Vaughan Woods represents the largest acreage open to the public, and it's beautiful: webbed with footpaths through mixed forest and open fields. The best entrance is from Litchfield Rd. at the end of Middle St. Park at the stone wall—look for the path.

Belgrade Regional Conservation Alliance (207-495-6039; belgradelakes.org) publishes detailed maps to its major holdings. Check the website for details about hiking the **French Mountain**, **Mount Philip**, and the **Kennebec Highlands** trails. Pick up the Belgrade Lakes Region free map at the visitors booth or Day's Store to locate these trailheads as well **Blueberry Hill** with its great view of Long Pond. There's a state-maintained overlook. Also note the small park just north of Day's Store in Belgrade Lakes Village, a handy picnic spot.

✳ Lodging

IN THE AUGUSTA AREA

✪ ♂ ✎ ♿ **Maple Hill Farm Inn & Conference Center** (207-622-2708 or 1-800-622-2708; maplebb.com), 11 Inn Rd. (off the Outlet Rd.), Hallowell 04347. The innkeepers of this hilltop farmhouse with modern additions and amenities, near the turnpike and downtown Augusta, have been offering attentive hospitality since 1992 along with wooded trails adjoining an 800-acre wildlife reservation (see Jamies Pond, above). Scott Cowger, a veteran of 10 years in the state legislature, is the inn's outgoing meeter and greeter; Vincent Hannan is the skilled chef. Together they have created the first place in Maine to be certified as a green lodging, with solar electricity and hot

MAPLE HILL FARM, HALLOWELL

water. Guests' names are posted on their doors. All eight tastefully furnished rooms have cable TV, DVD, air-conditioning, and private bath (four with whirlpool tub). Guests enter through the former kitchen, now an informal pub with local brews. A sauna and outdoor hot tub are popular. The Gathering Place seats up to 135 people, and surrounding lawns make this a pretty place for a wedding. In winter trails are available for cross-country skiing and snowshoeing. Llamas and chickens (which contribute eggs for breakfast) are in residence. A full breakfast with menu choices is included in $115–219 high season, $95–169 off.

🐾 ♿ **Senator Inn and Spa** (207-622-5804 or 1-877-772-2224; senatorinn.com), 284 Western Ave., Augusta 04330. A longtime gathering spot for Maine politicians, this property, with 122 guest rooms and suites, extends far back from the road and offers one of the area's best restaurants and a full-service spa featuring a glass-walled, Grecian-columned saltwater lap pool, hot tub, and fitness center (see *Dining Out*). Lodgings include attractive suites with fireplace, writing area, jetted tub, and fridge. You'll also find an inviting little bar. $88–209, from $188 for spa suites. $9 per pet.

IN THE BELGRADE LAKES REGION

🐾 ♂ ♿ **Village Inn and Tavern** (207-495-3553; villageinnducks.com), 157 Main St. (Rt. 27), Belgrade Village 04918. Better known as a

restaurant (see *Dining Out*) and newly refurbished, this middle-of-the-village, two-story '60s motel is attached to the inn, angled to face the garden, and some of the eight rooms overlook Great Pond. No minimum stay. $135 for rooms, $240 for a two-room suite with deck. Rates includes a fruit, yogurt, and muffin breakfast.

♿ **Wings Hill Inn** (207-495-2400 or 1-866-495-2400; wingshillinn.com), Rt. 27 and Dry Point Dr., Belgrade Lakes 04918. Open year-round. This 200-year-old white-clapboard farmhouse rambles across a knoll above its lawns just north of the village of Belgrade Lakes, overlooking Long Pond. The name recalls a onetime owner, U.S. Air Force general Edmund "Wings" Hill. Current innkeepers Christopher and Tracey Anderson met in culinary school, and the inn is known for fine dining (see *Dining Out*). The six guest rooms, all with private bath (one with a Jacuzzi), have been individually decorated. $115–195 includes a three-course breakfast and afternoon tea.

The Pressey House Lakeside Bed & Breakfast (207-465-3500; presseyhouse.com), 32 Belgrade Rd., Oakland 04963. Open year-round. This 1850s octagonal house with an ell and attached barn on Messalonskee Lake holds five suites, each with its own bedroom, bath, living room with TV, and kitchen. Henry and Sharon Wildes provide a canoe, paddleboat, and two kayaks, or you can swim off the dock. Just 2.5 miles off I-95. Open year-round. $125–240 including breakfast.

FAMILY-GEARED SPORTING CAMPS 🐾 ♂
Alden Camps (207-465-7703; aldencamps .com), 3 Alden Camps Cove, Oakland 04963. Founded by A. Fred Alden in 1911 with just one rental unit, it's still in the family with 18 one- to three-bedroom log cabins with screened porch and woodstove or Franklin fireplace, scattered among the pines on the shores of East Pond. Meals are served in a wonderfully rambling old clapboard house with a big dining room, sitting area, and long porch. Activities include fishing, golf nearby, swimming, waterskiing, boating, tennis, hiking, and several playing fields. Children are welcome, and pets can be accommodated for an extra fee. $103–194 per person per day, and $760–1,162 per person per week, includes all three meals. Children's rates.

THE CABINS AT BEAR SPRING CAMP IN ROME

🛶 ♿ **Bear Spring Camps** (207-397-2341; bearspringcamps.com), 60 Jamaica Point Rd., Rome 04957. Open mid-May–Sept. Ron and Peg Churchill are the fourth generation to run this very special family resort and fishing spot, set on 400 acres of woods and fields on Great Pond. It's been in Peg's family since 1910. Writer E. B. White summered here as a kid and would certainly recognize the rambling white farmhouse with all those rockers on the porch. Serious anglers come in early May for trout and pike, and in July there are still bass. The 32 cabins, each different, are strung along the shore of Great Pond, two to

four bedrooms, each with a bathroom, hot and cold water, a shower, heat, an open fireplace, and a dock. There's a tennis court, a golf driving range, and a variety of lawn games. The swimming is great (the bottom is sandy). Meals are served in the farmhouse set a ways back across open lawns from the lake. "People get sleepy and tend to take a nap after lunch, then get going again," Peg explains. Weekly rates July–Labor Day: $1,045–1,205 per couple includes all meals; special children's rates. Motor and pontoon boats, kayaks and canoes available; off-season weekend stays are allowed.

Taconnet on Great Pond (1-800-588-7024; taconnetongreatpond.com), Joyce Island. Set in the north end of Great Pond, this camp has a short season but a loyal following. Fifteen cottages with decks or porches and indoor baths, some with sleeping lofts; all have a private dock with a canoe or kayak and are set along the edge of this wooded island. Tennis courts, the main lodge, and the dining hall are within a few minutes' walk; children's activities on weekdays. Guests park in the business's lot and are ferried to their cabins. $1,150 per week per person, less for children, covers the minimum stay that begins and ends on Sat.

🛶 **Castle Island Camps** (207-495-3312; castleislandcamps.com), P.O. Box 251, Belgrade Lakes 04918. Open late Apr.–mid-Sept. John

THE DOCK ACROSS THE STREET FROM CASTLE ISLAND CAMPS

and Rhonda Rice are the owners of this great old family compound: a dozen comfortable cottages clustered on a small island (connected by bridges) in 12-mile Long Pond. The camps have been in Rhonda's family since 1929. Geared to fishing (the pond is stocked; rental boats are available). Three daily meals are served in the cozy central lodge, where guests also gather around an open fireplace. $164 per couple per day, $1,150 per week children's rates.

♥ ✐ **Whisperwood Lodge and Cottages** (207-465-3983; whisperwoodlodge.com), 102 Taylor Woods Rd., Belgrade 04917. Open mid-May–late Sept. Doug and Candee McCarthy host another traditional sporting camp, this one seriously fishing-focused. Tidy one- and two-bedroom cottages with screened porches overlook Salmon Lake, known for its largemouth and smallmouth bass fishing. Late May–late Aug. $60 per person (double) per day (three-day minimum), $595 per week, children's rates; less off-season. This includes three meals as well as use of kayaks, canoes, game room, swim area and firewood. Fishing licenses.

COTTAGES Many seasonal rentals are available. See Belgrade Reservation Center (belgraderental.com).

B&BS The **Pleasant Street Inn** (207-680-2515; 84pleasantstreet.com), 84 Pleasant St., Waterville 04901, within walking distance of downtown. The seven guest rooms, five with a private bath, are bright and cheery with TV, AC, and beds covered by colorful quilts. Guests have access to a common area that includes kitchen, dining room, and a living room with TV/DVD. $60–95.

✐ **Home-Nest Farm** (207-897-4125; home nestfarm.com), 76 Baldwin Hill Rd., Fayette 04349. Open year-round. The main house, built in 1784, offers a panoramic view of the White Mountains. Lilac Cottage (1800) and the Red Schoolhouse (1830) are available for rent as separate units. The property has been in the Sturdevant family for seven generations. House rates are $140 daily, $700 weekly for one- to three-bedroom units with kitchens; all include breakfast. Two-night minimum stay July–Oct.

♿ **A Rise and Shine Bed and Breakfast** (207-933-9876; riseandshinebb.com), 19

Moose Run Dr. (Rt. 135), Monmouth 04259. Ten miles west of Augusta, with a distant view of Lake Cobbosseecontee, this rambling house with its even larger stables was for many years a racehorse farm, part of a 2,000-acre spread belonging to the Woolworth family. Locals Tom Crocker and Lorette Comeau have replaced 76 windows, used up some 300 gallons of paint, and installed gas- or pellet-fired hearths in many of the eight guest rooms. The Sunshine Room, the former master bedroom, has a king-sized bed, hearth, and steam shower. $100–150 includes a full breakfast. Cottage $300 a night.

✳ Where to Eat

DINING OUT

IN AUGUSTA/HALLOWELL

❂ **Slates** (207-622-9575; slatesrestaurant .com), 163 Water St., Hallowell. Open Tue.–Sat. for lunch and dinner, Sun. for brunch. Reserve if possible. First opened in 1979, renovated and reopened in 2008 after a devastating fire, this is a special place that chef-owner Wendy Larson describes as a mix of music, art, and great food. The several rooms are all brightly painted and display local art. Lunch on a crêpe for two, stuffed with fresh crabmeat, artichoke hearts, and Jarlsberg cheese ($15). Dine on pesto and goat cheese pizza, flatiron steak or pasta primavera (pasta is made here). Entrées $20–24. Check out the

Nancy English

A COLORFUL CORNER TABLE AT SLATES IN HALLOWELL

THE BAR AT SLATES, HALLOWELL

website for the names, some of them nationally known, playing in Mon.-night concerts (8:15).

Hattie's Chowder House (207-621-4114; hattieslobsterstew.com), 103 Water St., Hallowell. Open daily for lunch and dinner. Spacious and pleasant, this is a great spot for chowders and lobster stew. Harriett Schmidt markets her lobster stew nationally, but it was the light, nicely herbed haddock chowder that really got our attention. We pleaded with Harriett until she revealed the secret: "A little sherry." Pasta, meat, and chicken dishes as well as seafood fried, baked, and stuffed.

Gagliano's Italian Bistro (207-213-4708), 287 Water St., Augusta. A welcome addition to downtown Augusta, Gagliano's serves house pasta bow ties with salmon, linguine with sausages, and panna cotta from its Italian menu.

✐ **Cloud 9 at the Senator Inn & Spa** (207-622-0320), 284 Western Ave., Augusta. Open daily 6:30 AM–9 PM; lounge 11–11. Some of the region's best dining can be found just off I-95 in "the Senator," the capital's prime gathering spot. Cloud 9 is a large but artfully divided restaurant with a contemporary bistro decor. Lobster is served up many ways. A Sunday brunch buffet (11–2).

IN THE BELGRADE LAKES REGION

Wings Hill Inn (207-495-2400; wingshillinn .com), Rt. 27, Belgrade Lakes Village. Open for dinner May–Sept. (five-course prix fixe), Thu.–Sun.; Oct.–Dec., Fri. and Sat. (three-course option); seatings at 6 and 8. Reservations requested. Chef-owner Christopher Anderson and his wife, Tracey (who makes the desserts), trained at the Culinary Institute of America. Together they orchestrate seasonal five-course prix fixe menus served to a maximum of 16 diners seated in adjoining rooms. An evening's feast might begin with a sirloin and white bean chili, move to a Caesar with anchovies, then to pork tenderloin with morels, ending with lemon cheesecake. Diners bring their own wine, served by the staff at the table (no corking fee); an 18 percent service fee is added to the $67 prix fixe bill. Inquire about three-course $45 "Bistro Nights."

✪ **The Village Inn** (207-495-3553; village innandtavern.com), Rt. 27, Belgrade Lakes. Open Easter–mid-Oct., daily 5–9 in-season, Thu.–Sun off-season. This is a large, old-fashioned dining landmark with a lake view and a mural depicting the 19th-century Belgrade Hotel, one of several summer inns once here. The Village Inn, dating to 1921, is the last link with that era, and in 2015 new owners redecorated with tradition in mind—tearing out the wall-to-wall carpeting, for example. The specialty is duckling, roasted for up to 12 hours and served with a choice of sauces, including brandied black cherry or Madagascar green peppercorn. You might begin with lobster and corn fritters or oysters Rockefeller updated as "Oysters Rock." Entrées $19–30.

✪ **Riverside Farm Market & Café** (207-465-4439; riversidefarmmarket.com), 291 Fairfield St. (Rt. 23), Oakland. Lunch Tue.–Sat., 11–3, dinner Tue.–Sat 5:30–8:30, brunch Sun. 10–2. Just off the beaten track, a handsome little restaurant with a deck overlooking a vineyard that slopes to a pond. Begun as a farm stand in 1990, the complex also includes a market. The creative dinner menu might feature grilled local tofu ($16), and porchetta ($18).

Sadie's Boathouse Restaurant (207-495-4045), 25 Marina Drive. An upstairs deck and dining room overlooks Great Pond. Penobscot Bay salmon with local cantaloupe, arugula, and spinach salad, or a lobster roll on brioche make the view of the plate pretty good too. Chocolate pecan pie, if you're lucky.

IN WATERVILLE

The Last Unicorn (207-873-6378), 8 Silver St. Open daily 11–9, until 10 Fri. and Sat.; Sun. brunch until 2:30. Colorful and conveniently sited right off the central parking lot. There are usually 15 different dinner specials; soups, desserts, and most dressings and spreads are made here. You might dine on sautéed veal Marsala with spinach, apples, and grapes. Entrées $18–23. Also a great, reasonably priced lunch option, seasonal street-side café.

EATING OUT

IN AUGUSTA

Riverfront Barbeque & Grill (207-622-8899), 300 Water St. Open daily for lunch and dinner. An offshoot of Bath's famous Beal Street Barbeque and considered to be just as good: slow-smoked chicken and ribs, daily made soups with corn bread, chili, seafood and sausage jambalaya, and more.

Sweet Chilli Thai (207-621-8575; sweetchillime.com), 75 Airport Rd. Tucked away at the small airport, this Thai restaurant makes an excellent pad Thai, as well as other Thai noodle dishes and an array of vibrant coconut milk curries.

Downtown Diner (207-623-9656), 204 Water St. Open 5–2 weekdays, 6–2 Sat., 7–1 Sun. Mike and Kim Meserwy own this bright spot in downtown, handy to Fort Western. Serious all-day breakfasts include steak and eggs and porkers in a blanket (sausages wrapped in small, fluffy pancakes); also freshly made soups, burgers, meat loaf, and pies. The bright room and wide counter amplify your welcome.

IN HALLOWELL

♪ **Slates Bakery and Deli** (207-622-4101), 165 Water St. Open weekdays 8–6, Sat. 9–6, Sun. 10–4. $3 children's menu. Neighboring **Slates** restaurant (see *Dining Out*) is great for a more leisurely lunch. This combination café-bakery is all about freshly baked breads, cakes, and pies as well as morning muffins and croissants. It's a good source of ready-made sandwiches, wraps, and burritos to take to the riverbank or Vaughan Woods.

Liberal Cup (207-623-2739), 115 Water St. Open for lunch and dinner, Fri. and Sat. until 10. Mid-Maine's brewpub, noisy on the bar side, less so in the dining room. Half a dozen good brews (crafted here) on tap. Live music Thu.–Sat. evenings. Most menu items, including sandwiches, are served all day, along with shepherd's pie, fish-and-chips, and drunken pot roast.

The Maine House (207-621-1234; the mainehouse.net), 119 Water St. A craft cocktail lounge with a menu of small plates that includes three little lobster dishes and chicken teriyaki, the better to enjoy the drink—like the Maine Accent, with rye, lemon, herbal syrup and nero d'avola.

Joyce's (207-512-8433; joycesinhallowell .com), 192 Water St. Grilled chicken with roasted garlic pesto and pot roast with gravy are entrées; a tent by the water in good weather is a lovely place to dine and enjoy a cocktail. Entrées $14–17.

Café de Bangkok (207-622-2638), 232 Water St. Just south of the village with river views, this is a highly respected local dining option. The menu includes the usual tom yum and miso soups, a softshell crispy crab salad with hot chili lime sauce on lettuce, "pad" and fried rice dishes. Entrées $10–25. Don't overlook the best local sushi, also on offer.

Lucky Garden (207-622-3465), 218 Water St. A popular Chinese restaurant offering Mandarin, Szechuan, and Cantonese dishes. House specialties include General Tso's chicken, crispy shrimp, and Peking duck. Entrées $8–25. The dining room has a river view. Lunch buffet $7.95 adult, $3.95 children under 10.

IN GARDINER

The A1 Diner (207-582-4804; a1diner.com), 3 Bridge St. Open Mon.–Sat. for all three meals, brunch only on Sun. (8–1:30). A vintage-1946 Worcester diner with plenty of Formica, blue vinyl booths, blue and black tile, and a 14-stool, marble-topped counter. In addition to typical diner fare there are some surprises. The breakfast menu may include banana almond French toast. The specials and freshly made soups are worth trying, but there is always meat loaf, baked beans, and a choice of salads and veggie options. Herbal tea, beers and wines. The restroom is outside and in through the kitchen door.

THE A-1 DINER IN GARDINER

IN WATERVILLE/WINSLOW

Jorgensen's Café (207-872-8711), 103 Main St., Waterville. An inviting café with at least a dozen flavored coffees, as well as tea and espresso choices. The deli serves quiche, soups, salads, and sandwiches. Coffee and tea supplies.

✪ **Barrels Community Market** (207-660-4844; barrelsmarket.com), 74 Main St., Waterville. A great addition to downtown, a community-owned market and café showcasing local, sustainable produce, meats, milk, cheeses, also crafts and food products. Great salad bar and breads by Black Crow Bakery.

✪ **Selah Tea Café** (207-660-9181; selahteacafe.com), 177 Main St., Waterville. Open Mon.–Sat. 7 AM–10 PM. A sunny café with soothing colors and comfortable seating, a wide choice of loose-leaf teas and coffees; you'll also find yummy caffeine-free Belgian chocolate latte, and Crio Brü cocoa from roasted and ground cocoa beans. A veggie breakfast sandwich as well as meaty specials. Specialty sandwiches include a vegan wrap, salads, flat-bread pizza, baked Brie, more.

The Villager Restaurant (207-872-6231), 40 W. Concourse, Waterville. An old-fashioned coffee shop with reasonably priced sandwiches (cream cheese and olive for $3.70), also lasagna, mac-and-cheese, and Italian-style potato salad plates. Most dinner items are under $10.

Lobster Trap & Steakhouse (207-872-0529), 25 Bay St. (Rt. 201), Winslow. Open daily 11–9. Just across the bridge if you follow Rt. 137 from downtown over the Kennebec. Since 1986, this is the local place to eat lobster, preferably on the deck picnic tables overlooking the river. Seafood fried, baked, and stuffed. Reasonable prices.

Pad Thai Too (207-859-8900; padthaitoo .com), 400 Kennedy Memorial Dr. (Rt. 137), Waterville. Open for lunch and dinner, Tue.–Sat.; from 4 Sun.–Mon. Loved locally for the freshness of ingredients and quality of a standard Thai restaurant menu.

IN THE BELGRADE LAKES REGION

& **The Sunset Grille** (207-495-2439), 4 West Rd., Belgrade Lakes Village. Open year-round, Mon–Thu. 7–9, Fri.–Sat. 7–midnight. Hopping in the summer, casual family fare served waterside. Sat.-evening karaoke.

Alden Camps (207-465-7703; aldencamps .com), 3 Alden Camps Cove, Oakland. Non-guests are welcome by reservation—and if you can't stay at one of the local sporting camps, you should sample the atmosphere. The from-scratch food is generous, varied, and good, too. Set price.

The Old Post Office Café (207-293-4978; oldpostofficecafe.com), 366 Pond Rd., Mount Vernon Village. Open daily 7–2:30. Check the website for dinner/music nights. A chef-owned local gathering spot with a screened porch overlooking the lake.

Hello, Good Pie Bakery & Gourmet Kitchen (207-485-2323), 39b Main St., has been welcomed to town with enthusiastic

THE INTERIOR OF A-1 DINER, A 1946 WORCESTER DINER

customers clamoring for the pies, pastries, savory salads, breads, and more, not to mention coffee ice cubes for the iced coffee, which goes so well with one of the oatmeal raisin cookies—all of it worth whatever the price happens to be. Dine under an umbrella on the front lawn or take-out.

IN CHINA

✪ ✎ **The China Dine-ah** (207-445-5700; chinadine-ah.com), 281 Lakeview Dr. (Rt. 202, 1.5 miles off Rt. 3). Open Tue.–Sat. 7 AM–dinner, until 3 Sun., closed Mon. A new owner in 2014 sustained the feel of a landmark establishment. A good road-food break for motorists heading Down East, serving generous portions, a good dried haddock sandwich with house-made tartar sauce with great crabcakes, and a loaded sirloin steak and cheese.

IN SKOWHEGAN

Heritage House Restaurant (207-474-5100; townemotel.com), 182 Madison Ave. (Rt. 201). Open for lunch (buffet Tue.–Fri.) and for dinner daily. A popular restaurant with a strong local following. The large menu always includes six fresh seafood entrées (such as sea scallops tempura with apricot mustard dip), medallions of beef with brandied mushroom sauce, and Cajun chicken breast with wine, lemon, capers, and mushrooms. Most entrées $15–20.

✪ **Old Mill Pub** (207-474-6627; oldmillpub .net), 39 Water St. Open daily for lunch and dinner in summer; check off-season. It's just where you may want to stop en route: a picturesque old mill building set back from the main drag with a seasonal deck overlooking a gorge in the Kennebec, with views downriver as well as of the dam. A friendly bar and scattered tables; sandwiches (a good Reuben), quiche, and specials for lunch; spinach lasagna or stir-fried shrimp for dinner; music on Thu. and Sat.

✪ **The Pickup Café** (207-474-0708; thepickupcsa.com), 42 Court St. Currently open Fri., Sat. 4–9 for dinner; Sat., Sun. 7–2. Housed in the Somerset Grist Mill, the town's former jail that's been turned into Maine's first gristmill to operate in many decades. Amber Lambke, executive director of the Maine Grain Alliance, found the mechanism to stone-grind grains in Austria and had it installed here to turn grains from 12 area farms into flour. You can buy it in the attractive café, which features wood-fired pizza as well as a blackboard menu; it also serves as a CSA pickup stop and a venue for live music during Sat.-morning farmers' markets.

The Bankery (207-474-2253; thebankery .com), 87 Water St., makes bread and pastries with the Somerset Grist Mill's flours and makes the pizza dough used for pizza in the Pickup Café. Soups, chowders, breakfast pastries, and more.

✎ **Ken's Family Restaurant** (207-474-3120; kensfamilyrestaurant.com), 411 Madison Ave. (Rt. 201). Open Mon.–Thu. 10:30–8; Fri. 10:30–9; Sat. 7–9; Sun. 7–8. Family-run (by the Dionne family) and -geared since 1972. Children's menu. Known for seafood but generally a good bet.

✪ **Gifford's Famous Ice Cream** (207-474-2257; giffordsicecream.com), Upper Madison Ave. (Rt. 201 north; look for the big plastic moose). Proudly served throughout Maine, century-old, family-owned Gifford's is made in Skowhegan, and this is its prime local outlet, a classic ice cream stand serving 50 flavors, including Lobster Tracks and Maine Birch Bark, in cones, cups, parfaits, frappés, sodas, more. Limited picnic tables out back overlook a mini golf course.

IN WINTHROP

✎ **Sully's** (207-377-5663), corner of Union and Main Sts. Open Mon.–Sat. for lunch and dinner, Sun. dinner noon–7. Set back from Main St. with plenty of parking to accommodate its local following. Salads as well as burgers and sandwiches for lunch; seafood dishes, like a seafood medley that includes lobster and salad.

✳ Entertainment

LIVE PERFORMANCES ✎ **Theater at Monmouth** (207-933-2952; theateratmonmouth .org), Main St., Monmouth. Summer/fall season shows July–Oct. Housed in Cumston Hall, a striking turn-of-the-20th-century building designed as a combination theater, library, and town hall. A resident nonprofit company specializes in Shakespeare but also presents more contemporary shows throughout the season, including, in 2015, *The Turn of the Screw*.

✐ **Lakewood Theater** (207-474-7176; lakewoodtheater.org), off Rt. 201, 6 miles north of Skowhegan on Lake Wesserunsett, billed as America's Oldest Summer Theater. A resident company performs Memorial Day–mid-Sept., Thu.–Sat. at 8, alternate Sun. and Wed. matinees. The restaurant specializes in pre-theater dinners.

Waterville Opera House (207-873-7000; operahouse.org), 93 Main St., Waterville, presents a number of shows throughout the year, including music performances and theater productions. It's also a prime venue for the 10-day Maine International Film Festival (see *Film*).

Snow Pond Center for the Arts (207-465-3739; snowpond.org), 8 Goldenrod Lane, Sidney. Summer concerts, recitals, and theater are presented at this burgeoning cultural center, a year-round arts education facility and the site of the New England Music Camp. Weekend concerts are free.

Gaslight Theater (207-626-3698; gaslighttheater.org), City Hall Auditorium, Hallowell. This community theater stages productions throughout the year.

Johnson Hall Performing Arts Center (207-582-7144; johnsonhall.org), 280 Water St., Gardiner. A restored historic space where workshops, dances, and other performances occur frequently.

FILM **Maine International Film Festival** (207-861-8138; miff.org), 177 Maine St., Waterville. In existence for more than a decade, this weeklong, mid-July festival has evolved into a major event screening scores of films from around the world—although always including some made in Maine—and attracting noted actors, directors, and screenwriters as speakers and lecturers.

Railroad Square Cinema (207-873-4021; railroadsquarecinema.com), Main St., Waterville. From I-95 Exit 130 head toward downtown; turn left between Burger King and the railroad tracks. Art and foreign films, and in mid-July home of the Maine International Film Festival.

Skowhegan Drive-in (207-474-9277), Rt. 201 South. A genuine 1950s drive-in with nightly double features "under the stars" in July and Aug.; weekends in June.

Strand Cinema (207-474-3451; strandcinema.net), Court St., Skowhegan. A 1929 jewel, recently lovingly revamped with nightly films, reasonable prices.

✳ Selective Shopping

IN HALLOWELL

ANTIQUES **Brass and Friends** (207-626-3287), 154 Water St. (look for the gargoyles atop the building), is a large trove of antique lighting fixtures. **Josiah Smith Antiques** (207-622-4188), 168 Water St., specializes in Asian and British ceramics and early glass. **Johnson-Marsano Antiques** (207-623-6263), 172 Water St., sells Victorian, art deco, and estate jewelry.

ELSEWHERE

ANTIQUES **Fairfield Antiques Mall** (207-453-4100; fairfieldantiquesmall.com), Rt. 201, Hinckley. Open daily 8:30–5, with three floors of antiques under one roof, the largest group shop in central Maine. **Hilltop Antiques** (1-800-899-6987), 52 Water St., Skowhegan. Two floors (16 rooms) filled with "fresh picked merchandise."

BOOKS **Merrill's Bookshop** (207-623-2055), 134 Water St., on the second floor because this side of Water St. still occasionally floods in spring. This is an antiquarian bookshop among antiquarian bookshops. Particular emphasis on Americana, Maine books, history—including a large Civil War collection—and literature. There is also a room filled with books for a buck.

Barnes & Noble Booksellers (207-621-0038), the Marketplace at Augusta, directly across from the Augusta Civic Center. A full-service bookstore with music and computer software sections as well as a café.

GALLERIES **Harlow Gallery** (207-622-3813; harlowgallery.com), 160 Water St., Hallowell. The place to visit to catch up on Maine artists like Britta Konau and owner Robin Harlow's own poetic images.

SPECIAL STORES **Renys** (207-582-4012), 185 Water St., Gardiner, and at 73 Main St. in

Madison. Open weekdays 9–5:30, Fri. until 8, Sat. 9–5, Sun. 10–4. Don't pass up this amazing Maine discount department store, good for quality clothing and shoes, peanut butter, art supplies, and a range of everything in between.

Marden's Discount Store (207-873-6112), 458 Kennedy Memorial Dr., Waterville. Maine's salvage and surplus chain with 10 stores. The Waterville outlet is well worth checking.

New Balance Outlet Store (207-858-6551; newbalance.com), 12 Walnut St. (Rt. 201, south of the bridge), Skowhegan. Open Mon.–Sat. 9–6, Sun. 11–5. Housed in a former school, this is a major outlet with a wide selection of athletic gear as well as shoes made in town.

The Green Spot (207-465-7242), 818 Kennedy Dr. (Rt. 137), Oakland. Open May–Columbus Day, daily 9–7; closed Tue. A quarter mile or so west of I-95 look for a small yellow store on the left. Locally loved as a source of amazing daily fresh breads, organic produce, fine wines, and terrific deli items, Tanya and Brenda Athanus's small store on the way from Waterville to Oakland is well worth seeking out.

Johnny's Selected Seeds (207-861-3900; johnnyseeds.com), 955 Benton Ave., Winslow. Open Mon.–Sat. in-season, selective days off-season. A catalog seed company with more than 2,000 varieties.

Day's Store (207-495-2205; go2days.com), 180 Main St., Belgrade Lakes Village. Open daily 7 AM–8 PM, until 9 in summer: groceries, liquor, fishing licenses, boots, gas, pizza, soups, and sandwiches at this true center of the Belgrade Lakes.

Maine Made & More (207-465-2274; mainemadeandmore.com), Maine St., Belgrade Lakes Village, and 93 Main St., Waterville. Sweatshirts, cards, souvenirs; the "more" is a concession to who makes those sweatshirts, T-shirts, etc., these days.

Stoney End Farm (207-397-4214), 441 Mercer Rd., Rome. A great farm stand with veggies, honey, eggs, maple syrup, strawberries, raspberries, blueberries, quilted items, and two donkeys to feed.

✳ Special Events

June–July: During its nine-week sessions the prestigious **Skowhegan School of Painting and Sculpture** (207-474-9345) sponsors a lecture series on weekday evenings that's free and open to the public.

July: Beginning the last week in June, **The Whatever Family Festival** (kennebec valley.org) climaxes July 4 and entails many events—children's performances, soapbox derby, Learn the River Day, entertainment, carnival, and more. **Maine International Film Festival** (midmonth) in Waterville (miff.org). **Old Hallowell Day** (third weekend)—parade and fireworks, crafts and games. **Pittston Fair**, Pittston.

August: **Skowhegan State Fair**, one of the oldest and biggest fairs in New England—harness racing, a midway, agricultural exhibits, big-name entertainment, tractor and oxen pulls. **China Community Days**, China. Public supper, fishing derby, scavenger hunt. In late Aug., **Father Rasle Days** (madison.com) is a weekend of festivities commemorating the 18th-century Jesuit priest and native village destroyed by the British. **Windsor Fair**, Windsor, runs the last week through Labor Day.

September: **Oosoola Fun Day**, Norridgewock (Labor Day), includes the state's oldest frog-jumping contest (up to 300 contestants) around a frog-topped totem pole; also canoe races, crafts fair, flower and pet contests, live music, and BBQ. **Litchfield Fair**, Litchfield. **Common Ground Country Fair**, Unity, a celebration of rural living sponsored by the Maine Organic Farmers and Gardeners Association.

THE UPPER KENNEBEC VALLEY AND MOOSE RIVER VALLEY

Including The Forks and Jackman

The Kennebec River is a north–south corridor linking northern woodlands with mid-Maine mills and farms. Skowhegan, the crossroads for Rts. 201 and 2, is the gateway, and Solon is the divide; Bingham, 8 miles north, has the feel of the woodland hub that it is.

The 78-mile stretch of Rt. 201 north from Solon to the Canadian border is officially the **Old Canada Road Scenic Byway**, with a granite marker at its gateway on Robbins Hill. From this rise the valley rolls away north with the blue peaks of Sugarloaf and the Bigelow Range clearly visible to the northwest. Along the way interpretive panels at scenic way stops tell the story of this magnificent but haunting valley.

The Kennebec River itself rises in Moosehead Lake and flows south, as did most 19th-century traffic along this route. More than a million French Canadian and Irish families came looking for work in New England logging camps, farms, and factories. This stretch of Rt. 201 is now also a link in the 233-mile Kennebec-Chaudiere International Corridor, stretching from Quebec City to Bath near the mouth of the river. Whatever its titles, this remains a busy, twisty, two-lane road, and traffic flows both ways far too quickly. It's also frequented by both lumber trucks and lumbering moose. Drive carefully!

Once upon a time, the river was the highway. For more than 140 years beginning in 1835, logs were floated down from the woods to the mills. Then in 1976 fishing guide Wayne Hockmeyer discovered the rush of **riding the whitewater through dramatic Kennebec Gorge**, deep in the woods, miles northeast of Rt. 201. On that first ride Hockmeyer had to contend with logs hurtling all around him, but as luck would have it, 1976 also marked the year in which environmentalists managed to outlaw log drives on the Kennebec.

Rafting companies currently vie for space to take advantage of up to 8,000 cubic feet of water per second released every morning from late spring through mid-October from the Harris Hydroelectric Station. In and around **The Forks**, a community (pop. 60) at the confluence of the Kennebec and Dead Rivers, whitewater rafting has spawned lodging and dining facilities that also cater to snowmobilers, hunters, hikers, and travelers passing through—many of whom spend an extra day or two here once they discover the accessibility of this valley's waterfalls and summits, its remote ponds for fishing and kayaking, and its woods roads for biking.

Hikers, snowshoers, and cross-country skiers can take advantage of the new Maine **Huts and Trails** facilities between Dead River and Sugarloaf; the Appalachian Trail and snowmobile trails also traverse this backcountry.

Empty as it seemed when rafting began, this stretch of the Upper Kennebec was a 19th-century resort area of sorts. A 100-room, four-story Forks Hotel was built in 1860, and the 120-room Lake Parlin Lodge soon followed. Caratunk, The Forks, and Jackman were all railroad stops; "rusticators" came to fish, hike, and view natural wonders like 90-foot Moxie Falls. Increasingly whitewater rafting outfitters are styling themselves "adventure companies," offering a choice of rock climbing, moose safaris, bicycle and kayak rentals, and more.

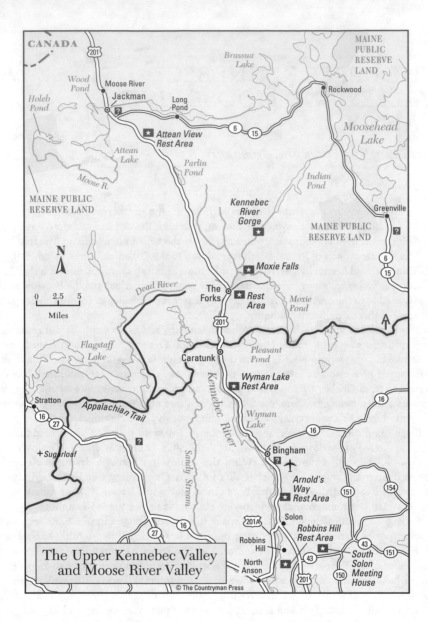

The Upper Kennebec Valley
and Moose River Valley

© The Countryman Press

Bingham (pop. 1,200), 23 miles south of The Forks, is the only town along the Upper Kennebec and it's small. Just north of town a 155-foot-high hydro-dam walls up the river, raising it more than 120 feet and creating wide, shimmering 13-mile-long Wyman Lake.

At The Forks, Rt. 201 itself forks off from the Kennebec River, heading northwest through lonely woodland. Don't fail to stop at the **Attean View Rest Area** south of Jackman, with its spectacular panorama of Attean Lake and the mountains beyond. Joseph Attean was a governor of the Penobscot tribe who served as Thoreau's guide on his 1853 North Woods trip.

Jackman and Moose River form a community (divided by a short bridge) on Big Wood Lake, offering restaurants and reasonably priced camps. Named for the man who built the

Canada Road from the border down to The Forks, Jackman boomed after the Canadian Pacific Railroad arrived in 1888, setting the lumbering industry into high gear. The former rail junction is now a major hub of snowmobiling and ATV trails. Winter is actually high season and snow softens the severity of this shrunken old border community.

If you aren't heading for Quebec from Jackman, turn off Rt. 201 onto Rt. 15/6, a lonely 31-mile road that follows the Moose River east to Rockwood on Moosehead Lake. Otherwise it's a roughly three-hour drive to Quebec City.

GUIDANCE The Forks Area Chamber of Commerce (forksarea.com) has an excellent website, as does the **Jackman-Moose River Region Chamber of Commerce** (207-668-4171 or 1-888-633-5225; jackmanmaine.org); this group also maintains a Rt. 201 seasonal welcome center near the lakeside town park.

GETTING THERE *By car:* The obvious route from points south and west is I-95 to Exit 133, then Rt. 201 north all the way to The Forks. The approach from the Rangeley and Sugarloaf areas, Rt. 16, is also a beautiful drive.

WHEN TO COME Whitewater rafting and fishing commence in April, but we prefer paddling in warmer months. June is buggy. July through mid-October are glorious, with fall bringing plenty of color. Hikers should check the "seasons" described under *Hunting.* Snow usually begins in November but has been more plentiful in recent years during late February and March.

CROSSING THE BORDER Jackman is 17 miles from the Canadian border. For a detailed list of requirements for both U.S. and Canadian citizens, see the "Washington County" introduction.

✳ To See

LISTED SOUTH TO NORTH ALONG RT. 201

Note: See the **L. C. Bates Museum** and the **Margaret Chase Smith Library Center** in the previous chapter; both are rewarding stops along Rt. 201 south of Solon.

Old Canada Road rest areas have interpretive panels (and outhouses). Just north of the junction with Rt. 43 look for **Robbins Hill**. Access is over the brow of the hill (heading north); there are picnic tables, a 0.5-mile trail with interpretive panels, and the spectacular view described in the chapter intro. Twenty panels in all are scattered along Rt. 201 in pullouts and rest areas between this point and Jackman. At **Arnold's Way Rest Area**, on the Bingham town line, panels chronicle the 1775 saga of Colonel Benedict Arnold and his more than 1,000 men traveling this way in a heroic but luckless attempt to capture Quebec.

The **Lake Wyman Rest Area** is a pine-shaded and carpeted lakeside spot with

Christina Tree

LAKE WYMAN REST AREA

picnic tables; panels tell of Indian habitation and the 1932 creation of the lake. **The Forks** pullout is just below the bridge at the actual fork in the river. Panels describe 19th-century lumbering and river runs while logging trucks rumble over the bridge.

Moxie Falls is said to be the highest falls (90 feet) in New England. From The Forks rest area on Rt. 201, it's 1.8 miles down Lake Moxie Rd. to the badly marked parking area. The well-maintained but sometimes buggy trail to the falls is 0.8-miles; continue straight ahead at the junction with other trails. The pools below are a popular swimming hole.

More Old Canada Road rest areas: Note the pullout at **Parlin Pond**, one of the spots where you are most likely to see moose, the subject of its interpretive panels. **Attean View**, the next pullout, is a must-see. The view is splendid: **Attean Lake** and the whole string of ponds linked by the Moose River, with the western mountains as a backdrop. There are picnic tables and restrooms. Note the trail leading to **Owls Head** (see *Hiking*).

✳ To Do

AIR TOURS Jackman Air Tours (207-668-4461), 7 Attean Rd., Jackman. Jim Schoenmann offers scenic air tours of the entire area.

ATVS This is a mecca for people who love to ride their all-terrain vehicles, with 400 miles of trails. Bingham and Jackman are both hubs. Rentals are available from **Northern Outdoors** (see *Whitewater Rafting*).

BIKING AND MOUNTAIN BIKING Local terrain varies from old logging roads to tote paths. Rentals are available from many whitewater rafting outfitters. A 12-mile multiuse (ATV/walking/biking) **Kennebec Valley Trail** now follows the old railbed along the river from Solon to Bingham. The 16.8-mile road from Pleasant Pond to Moxie Falls is also a favorite among mountain bikers. **Maine Huts and Trails** (mainehuts.org) is still evolving as a mountain biking facility (see *Hiking*). In **Jackman** check with the chamber of commerce for details about the **Sandy Bay Loop** north of town.

CANOEING AND KAYAKING The **Moose River Bow Trip** is a Maine classic: A series of pristine ponds forms a 34-mile meandering route that winds back to the point of origin, eliminating the need for a shuttle. The fishing is fine, 21 remote campsites are scattered along the way, and the put-in is accessible. One major portage is required. Canoe rentals are available from a variety of local sources. Several rafting companies rent canoes and offer guided trips, but the kayaking specialists here are Registered Maine Guides. **Cry of the Loon Outdoor Adventures** (207-668-7808; cryoftheloon.net), east of Jackman, offers a fully outfitted and guided Moose River Bow Trip as well as one- to seven-day tours throughout northwestern Maine. They also offer canoe and kayak rentals and shuttle services.

FISHING is what the sporting camps (see *Lodging*) are all about. The catch includes landlocked salmon, trout, and togue. Rental boats and canoes are readily available. Camps supply guides, and a number are listed at jackmanmaine.org.

GOLF Moose River Golf Course (207-668-5331), Rt. 201, Moose River (just north of Jackman). Mid-May–mid-Oct.; club rental, putting green, nine holes.

HIKING *Note:* The **Appalachian Trail** (AT) crosses Rt. 201 in Caratunk and climbs Pleasant Pond Mountain (below).

MUST SEE

South Solon Meeting House (207-643-2555 or 207-643-2721), South Solon. Turn east off Rt. 201 onto Rt. 43, continue 1.5 miles to Meeting House Rd. and north to the meetinghouse at the crossroads in South Solon. Open daily year-round. The classically plain, white-clapboard exterior of this 1842 Greek Revival building belies its colorful interior. The walls and ceiling were almost entirely frescoed in the 1950s by artists from the nearby Skowhegan School (skowheganart.org), still one of the country's most prestigious summer arts programs. The building is maintained by the South Solon Historical Society (SSHS), a small, all-volunteer group that includes descendants of the church's original congregation. The center of a rural community from 1842 until 1900, the building was abandoned as population shifted south to Skowhegan's mills. It was restored 35 years later as a venue for summer services. Vincent Price was among actors from the nearby Lakewood Theater (lakewoodtheater.org) who read scripture here. World War II interrupted this pattern, but in the 1950s a wealthy student at the Skowhegan School envisioned the building's blank interior walls as a showcase for fresco artists. She funded a national competition for fellowships to be awarded over the five summers needed for the project. Winners included several nationally recognized artists.

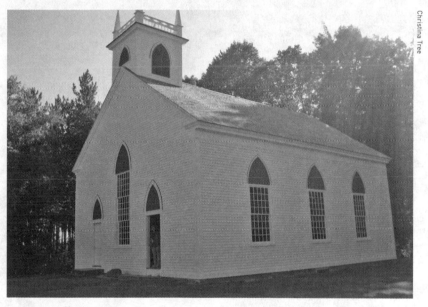

Christina Tree

SOUTH SOLON MEETING HOUSE

Maine Huts and Trails (1-877-634-8824; mainehuts.org). Four huts and 37 miles are completed of an evolving hiking/mountain biking/skiing trail that runs from Flagstaff Lake (near Sugarloaf) along the Dead River, each spaced one day's hike or ski from the next. The "huts" are really lodges, fully staffed during the summer, fall, and winter seasons, serving three daily meals. The **Grand Falls Hut** is 14.2 miles from the trailhead in West Forks, a long day's hike, so plan an early start if you want to spend the night there. The trail, which follows the Dead River into this wilderness area, is free of ATVs.

Coburn Mountain is the site of the former Enchanted Mountain ski area. The gravel access road off Rt. 201 begins about 10 miles north of Berry's Store. The Forks snowmobile

WHITEWATER RAFTING

T he 12-mile run down the Kennebec River from Harris Dam begins with 4 miles of Class II and IV rapids—notably Magic Falls early in the trip—and after that it's all fun and a beautiful ride through the Kennebec River gorge. The slightly more challenging run on the Dead River, available less often (releases are less frequent), is also offered by most outfitters. The safety records for all outfitters are excellent, or they wouldn't be in this rigorously monitored business.

Apr.–Oct. rates include a river ride and a chance to view (and buy) slides of the day's adventures, also usually a steak and chicken BBQ. The minimum suggested age is 10 on the Upper Kennebec and 8 on the lower section, compared with 15 on the Dead River.

River trips begin between 8 and 10 and end between 3 and 4, so it makes sense to spend the night before at your outfitter's base camp.

Variables: The time of the morning put-in, whether you eat along the river or back at camp afterward, the size and nature of the group you will be rafting with, and the comfort level of the lodging. Note that some outfitters are on lakes or ponds, good for kayaking and canoeing. Some outfitters also offer additional activities: overnight camping trips, rock climbing, and more.

Note: Children, seniors, and others who want to experience smaller rapids can join the trip later in the day. Midweek trips are generally more family-geared. Weekends draw a younger, wilder crowd. Although whitewater rafting began as a big singles sport, it's now popular with families, who frequently combine it with a visit to Quebec City. Minimum age requirements vary, but weight is often a consideration (usually no less than 90 pounds). We identify the outfitters who cater to kids.

Cost: Prices vary with the day and package, but current day trips on the Kennebec are $140–180 per person. On the Penobscot it's $80–130 per person, and on the Dead, $90–140. Wet suit and water shoe rentals are extra.

✪ 🏕 ✂ ((•)) **Northern Outdoors** (207-663-4466 or 1-800-765-7238; northernoutdoors.com), 1771 Rt. 201, The Forks. Open year-round. The first and still the largest rafting company of the Kennebec, Northern Outdoors anchors The Forks area. It claims to have rafted some 400,000 people since 1976—in the process evolving into "Maine's first and premier adventure resort." Rafting on all three rivers remains the prime adventure May–Oct., but float trips on the Lower Kennebec, ATV-only trails and rentals, guided fishing, and hiking are also on offer. Suzie Hockmeyer, who began running trips on the Kennebec in 1976 (see the chapter introduction), the Penobscot in 1977, the Dead in 1980, and was the first female licensed Registered Maine Guide in Whitewater, is still a hands-on member of Northern's management team. Many of the old photos on the lodge dining room wall depict her grandfather's North Woods logging camp. In winter snowmobiling (rentals) is the big draw, but cross-country skiing and snowshoeing, partnering with Maine Huts and Trails (see *Hiking*), is growing once more.

Courtesy of Northern Outdoors

RAFTING THROUGH MAGIC FALLS ON THE KENNEBEC

PLAY AREA AT NORTHERN OUTDOORS LODGE

This is a genuine resort with well-built and comfortable log cabins salted over the wooded hillside above an expansive, open-timbered lodge with its huge hearth, comfortable seating, and a cheerful dining room. The **Kennebec River Pub & Brewery** (see *Where to Eat*) is the central gathering place for much of the valley. There are still a few rooms in the lodge, along with nearby "logdominiums" (condo-style units with lofts and a kitchen/dining area), a riverside campground, and assorted other rentals, some quite luxurious. Amenities include outdoor play areas (giant hot tub, pool, basketball court), and a private pond with kayaks and canoes. Inquire about Northern's Family Adventure, which welcomes children (from age 8) and their parents. Lodging rates from $81 for a lodge room to $411 for a cabin sleeping 10 to 12. Cabin tents start at $15 per person per night. There are also a number of large (10-12 guest) cabins 3 miles south on Lake Wyman ($380–730 per night).

OTHER OUTFITTERS WITH LODGING ✪ ✐ Magic Falls Rafting (1-800-207-7238; magicfalls .com), P.O. Box 9, West Forks 04985. Owned by Dave and Donna Neddeau since 1989, with an attractive base on the Dead River in the The Forks. Lodging includes the ♿ **Dead River Lodge**, with nicely decorated double and family rooms, each with half-bath and, downstairs, a living room with big-screen TV. A renovated farmhouse sleeps up to 16, and there's a campground; amenities include inflatable kayaks, a climbing tower, and recreation pavilion. In addition to rafting trips on the Kennebec and Dead Rivers, they offer "Cheap Thrills" ($44 rafting trips limited to the Upper Gorge) and "Outback" camping adventures.

✐ **Adventure Bound** (1-888-606-7238; adv-bound.com), Rt. 201, a 20-acre site in Caratunk 04925. A family- and kids-geared outfitter. Facilities include an outdoor pool, indoor climbing wall, and ice cream bar. It has its own base lodge and cabin-tent village.

Courtesy of Northern Outdoors

club maintains a trail to the summit of the mountain along the old ski area service road. At 3,750 feet, it's the highest groomed snowmobile trail in Maine and can be hiked in summer. The 360-degree view from the open summit and its tower includes Mount Katahdin (68 miles to the northeast) and Sugarloaf Mountain (30 miles southwest).

Owls Head, Jackman. A 0.75-mile hike begins at the Attean View pullout on Rt. 201 (see *To See*) south of Jackman Village. This is one of Maine's most amazing, easily accessible panoramas, stretching to the Canadian border and encompassing Big Wood Lake, Slide Down Mountain, and Spencer Valley. The trail begins at the north end of the picnic area.

Moxie Falls is the area's easiest and most famous hike (see *To See*).

HUNTING Deer season runs late Oct.–Nov. Moose hunting usually begins the second week in Oct. (by permit only); bears are hunted Aug.–Nov. and partridge, Oct.–Dec.

MOOSE-WATCHING The best time to see a moose is at dawn or dusk. Favorite local moose crossings include Moxie Rd. from The Forks to Moxie Pond; the Central Maine Power Company road from Moxie Pond to Indian Pond; the 25 miles north from The Forks to Jackman on Rt. 201; and the 30 miles from Jackman to Rockwood on Rt. 6/15. Drive these stretches carefully; residents all know someone who has died in a car–moose collision. Moose safaris are offered May–Oct. by most outfitters.

✳ Winter Sports

SNOWMOBILING is huge in this region, with **The Forks** and **Jackman** serving as hubs for hundreds of miles of the Interconnecting Trail System (ITS) over mountains, rivers, and lakes and through woods with connections to the Rangeley and Moosehead areas, and to Canada (for which trail passes must be purchased). Rentals and guided trips are available from most major rafting companies.

Northern Outdoors (northernoutdoors.com) offers rentals, guided tours, and packages. Also check with the Jackman Region Chamber of Commerce (jackmanmaine.org) for the extensive trail network in that area.

CROSS-COUNTRY SKIING **Maine Huts and Trails** (see *Hiking*). In winter the trail from West Forks to Grand Falls Hut is groomed for both classic and diagonal stride. Not recommended for novices. If you don't want to go all the way, this is still the area's best wilderness ski trail, free of snowmobile traffic.

✳ Lodging

Note: See the *Whitewater Rafting* Sidebar. **Northern Outdoors** offers by far the greatest range of accommodations as well as the most amenities.

LODGES & CABINS (𝖎) **Sterling Inn** (207-672-3333; mainesterlinginn.com), 1041 Rt. 201, Caratunk. This white-clapboard inn appears like a friendly ghost along a lonely stretch of highway, a vintage-1816 stage coach stop. It's been lucky in its owners through the decades, and innkeepers Eric and Jason Angevine offer a sense of both history and comfort. There's an old-fashioned parlor with wing chairs; in the new addition, a cathedral-ceilinged great room invites relaxing. The 17 rooms vary in size and shape, sharing six baths. From $80 double with breakfast.

Inn by the River (207-663-2181; innbythe river.com), 2777 Rt. 201, West Forks. Open year-round. A contemporary lodging, built to resemble a 19th-century inn, sits across the road from the river, high on a bluff on a major

WOOD CARVINGS AT HAWK'S NEST LODGE, WEST FORKS

snowmobile trail. There are 10 nicely decorated guest rooms with private bath, some with whirlpool tub and private porch; many have river views. There's a big fireplace in the living room, plus a cozy pub. Three meals are served. $80–129 includes breakfast. The two-bedroom, housekeeping Carriage House is $249 for four.

Hawk's Nest Lodge (207-663-2020; hawksnestlodge.com), Rt. 201, West Forks. A whitewater rafting guide, Peter Doste has settled in and built this three-story post, beam, and glass construct with a restaurant/lounge and some amazing chain-saw sculptures both inside and out. The five suites are each different, $60 per person.

♂ **Lake Parlin Lodge** (207-688-9060 or 1-888-668-9060; lakeparlinlodge.com), 6003 Rt. 201, Lake Parlin. The one-time community here (between the Forks and Jackman), which once included a hotel, has about disappeared. Still, it's one of the prettiest sites around, with six contemporary one- and two-bedroom log cabins with full kitchen, living room, and propane fireplace spaced above the swim pond. The central lodge offers rooms, lounge, and restaurant, but it's currently open just Dec. 26–Mar. 31 for snowmobiling season. Cabins $150–200 per night, two-night minimum.

Cabins and lodge can also be rented for weddings.

IN JACKMAN

Cozy Cove Cabins (207-608-5931; cozycovecabins.com), 3 Elm St. Tami and Steve Cowen maintain nine shingled cottages on Big Wood Lake, accommodating two to six; full kitchen, some with screened or glassed-in porch. Kayaks, canoes, and aluminum boats for rent. $75–115 for two (two-night minimum); additional person, weekly rates.

✳ Where to Eat

LISTINGS ARE IN GEOGRAPHIC ORDER ALONG RT. 201, SOUTH TO NORTH

In this remote area the line between "eating out" and "dining out" blurs—and if you're between rafting, hunting, and snowmobiling seasons, it comes down to what's open. See *Eating Out* in Skowhegan in the previous chapter for suggestions between I-95 and the Canada Road.

IN BINGHAM

⊙ **Thompsons** (207-672-3820), 348 Main St. Open Mon.–Wed. 7–3; Tue, Thu.–Sat. 7–7; Sun. 7–3. One of our favorite road-food stops. In business off and on since 1929, it has deep booths and friendly waitresses who greet you with hot coffee. Stoke up on homemade soups,

Christina Tree

THOMPSON'S RESTAURANT, BINGHAM

ATTEAN LAKE LODGE

Sited on Birch Island in 5-mile-long Attean Lake, accessed by shuttle from the end of Attean Rd., off Rt. 201. Surrounded by mountains, this is one of Maine's premier family-run and family-geared sporting camps. It was established in 1903 when the lake was a flagstop on the Canadian Pacific Railroad. The 18 traditional peeled spruce log cabins are a mix of old and new, all genuinely rustic, with light from gas and kerosene lamps and heat from Franklin stoves, but baths are full and sparkling, linens and beds, comfy. The mountain and lake views from each deck are so splendid that you want to just to sit until it all soaks in. Families with young children opt for the cabins near the dock and sandy beach; others cluster in the pines at the end of a wooded path. (Be sure to bring flashlights!) Second-generation owner Brad Holden designed and largely constructed the current spacious, open-timbered lodge after the original burned to the ground. Before and after meals, Brad or Andrea can usually be found behind the check-in desk with the canoe suspended above it, while guests play cards and board games or check their computers in the many-windowed, comfortable corners of the central lodge room. There's also a library and children's playroom. During the day visitors scatter in motorboats, canoes, kayaks, and sailboats to explore this pristine, mountain-ringed lake—spotted with 22 islands—and trails that lead to moose meccas and summit views. For serious fishermen, guides can arrange multiday trips, sleeping in backwoods cabins. One way or another guests work up an appetite for the generous breakfasts and dinners (wine and beer available) and box lunches included in the rates: July–Aug. $367 per day for the first two adults, $150 for the third, $100 per child 6–12, $50 under 6; weekly rates, less in shoulder months. ✪ ♂ 🐾 ✐ **Attean Lake Lodge** (207-668-3792; atteanlodge.com), Jackman. Open Memorial Day weekend–Sept.

Courtesy of Attean Lake Lodge

VIEW FROM THE PORCH OF A CABIN AT ATTEAN LAKE LODGE

doughnuts, sandwich bread, and pies. Wine and beer served.

IN THE FORKS

✪ ✎ **Kennebec River Pub & Brewery** (207-663-4466), **Northern Outdoors**, Rt. 201. Open daily year-round for all three meals. This is an inviting brewpub with half a dozen beers ranging from light summer ale to robust stout. The pine-sided dining room, hung with archival photos of The Forks, is the venue for burgers, salads, and baskets, also dinner entrées ranging from stuffed portobello mushrooms to a full rack of Class V Stout BBQ ribs. Kids' meals all include Gifford's ice cream. Entrées $15–24.

Riverside Restaurant & Pub (207-663-2181), 2777 Rt. 201, The Forks. Open June–Aug., Jan.–Mar. to the public for breakfast, lunch, and dinner. The dining room at the **Inn by The River** (see *Lodges & Cabins*) is the nearest The Forks comes to fine dining. There's a fireplace, and windows overlook the river. Specialties include lazy lobster pie and beef tenderloin, but there's also a pub menu for the small, separate pub. Entrées $14–27. Breakfast and lunch also served, but call to check.

((ᵗ)) **Hawk's Nest** (207-663-2020; hawksnestlodge.com), Rt. 201, West Forks Village. Open daily for lunch and dinner during rafting and snowmobiling seasons. Hard-crust pizza is the specialty, also burgers, sandwiches, salads, linguine, pub food. Specials.

IN JACKMAN

✪ **Mama Bear's** (207-668-4222), Rt. 201. Open 4 AM–8 PM, from 6 AM on weekends. We like the warmly colored walls, pine booths, and a genial little bar in back. We also like the great daily specials and a menu ranging from poutine to scallops in white wine. Soups are from scratch.

Four Seasons Restaurant (207-668-7778), 417 Main St. Open 6 AM–PM. Newly renovated, a spacious room with wooden booths and a welcoming atmosphere. Pizzas and a big menu. Steak is the specialty: bourbon-style steak tips, steak salad, rib eye. There's also a back lounge with a deck.

Mike's Jackman Moose Crossing (207-668-2077), 766 Main St., Moose River. Open Wed.–Fri. from 4 PM, Sat. from 11:30, Sun. 8–8:30. Mike is from the coast and this large, newly renovated restaurant features seafood along with the usual staples.

✳ Selective Shopping

General stores in Solon and on up through Jackman are frequently the only stores. Our favorite is **Berry's in The Forks** (open 4:30 AM–7:30 PM), a source of fishing/hunting licenses and liquor, lunch, flannel jackets, rubber boots, and groceries, as well as gas. Stuffed birds and other wildlife are scattered throughout the store, most of them shot by Gordon Berry, who has been behind the counter for more than 40 years. Son Sam is more often there now, and on our last visit we were sorry to see less stock, a sign of the flattening whitewater trade.

Jackman Trading Post (207-666-2761), 281 Main St. (Rt. 201 south of the village). Open May–Thanksgiving, 8–6. A peerless selection of Far North T-shirts and souvenirs, tchotchkes, tacky jewelry, joke gifts (for people you don't like), toys, fishing flies, and much more, along with a wide range of ice cream flavors, restroom.

✳ Special Events

March: **Northeast Sled Dog Races,** Jackman—a three-day professional race.

November: **West Forks Fish & Game Annual Hunter's Supper** (207-663-2121).

MAINE HIGHLANDS

■

BANGOR AREA

THE NORTH MAINE WOODS

MOOSEHEAD LAKE AREA

KATAHDIN REGION
Including Gulf Hagas, Lower Piscataquis,
and Lincoln Lakes

AROOSTOOK COUNTY

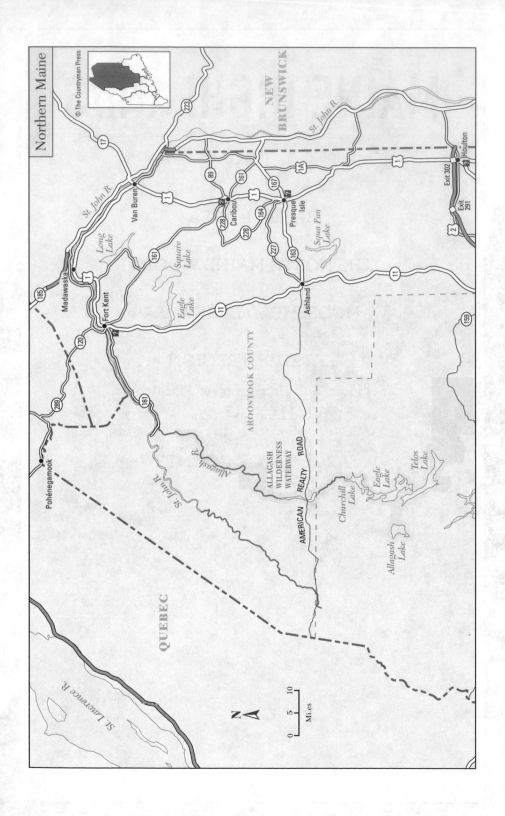

Northern Maine

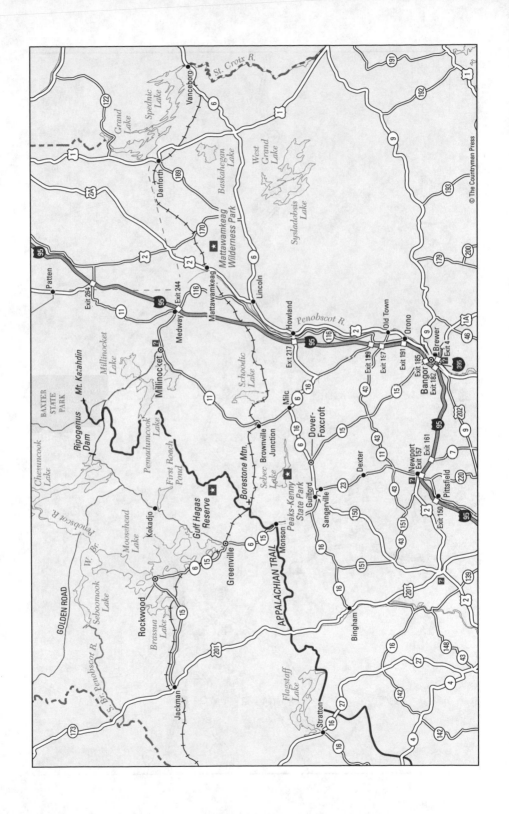

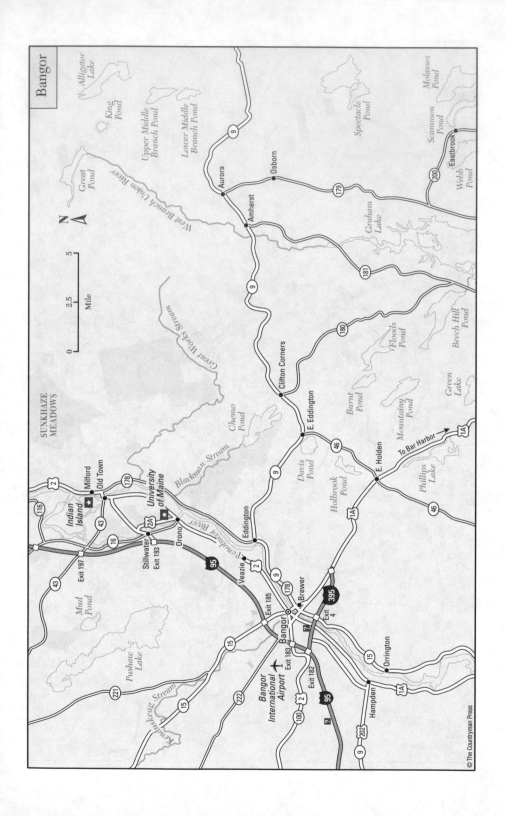

Bangor

BANGOR AREA

Bangor is both the natural gateway to much of central, northern, and eastern Maine and the largest city in the region, hosting famous performers like Lil Wayne at Darling's Waterfront Pavilion. It makes a good layover spot for those venturing into either the Baxter State Park region, the Moosehead Lake region, or the vast expanse of Aroostook County. With Brewer on the other side of the Penobscot River, and Orono, home of the main campus of the University of Maine, the Bangor metropolitan area is a vibrant commercial and cultural hub. Bangor International Airport (referred to locally as BGR) is a departure point for flights to every corner of the globe.

Bangor hosts the American Folk Festival every year, celebrating the richness and variety of American culture through music, dance, traditional storytelling, a "craft row" with handmade goods, beer gardens, and food.

Residents will tell you wistfully that the city's real glory days were in the mid-19th century, when the pine tree was arboreal gold and Bangor was the most important lumber port in the world. Local lumber barons built grandiose hilltop mansions, sparing no expense. After a long winter's work in the woods, the loggers who labored for them spent their hard-earned money, roistering in the bars and brothels of the city's notorious red-light district, known as "the Devil's Half-Acre," most of which was wiped out in a 1911 fire. The outsized symbol of Bangor's romantic timber boom era is native son Paul Bunyan. The mythical lumberjack superhero was conceived in tall-tale-swapping sessions in the logging camps of northern Maine and the saloons of the Devil's Half-Acre. A 21-and-older tour guided by

Nancy English

DOWNTOWN BANGOR

Nancy English

THE COURTHOUSE IN BANGOR

the Bangor Museum and History Center, in partnership with the Greater Bangor Convention & Visitors Bureau, brings the district back to (imaginary) life (information at visitbangormaine.com). Paul Bunyan is still very much a presence here: A 31-foot-high fiberglass statue of the great logger, wearing a red-and-black-checked shirt and carrying a huge ax, stands in a city park named for him—and casts a long shadow just across the street from Hollywood Casino Hotel & Raceway.

The Bangor of today has recovered some of its notoriety with the enormous Hollywood Casino Hotel & Raceway, the first slot machine gaming floor in the state (now also featuring poker and blackjack). Its hours, from 8 AM to 3 AM, reveal the lure for both in-state and out-of-state travelers. But walking tours of the historic districts are a good diversion, and far less risky.

The West Market Square Historic District is a mid-19th-century block of downtown shops. West Broadway holds a number of even more ornate homes, including the turreted and thoroughly spooky-looking Victorian home of author Stephen King, with its one-of-a-kind bat-and-cobweb wrought-iron fence.

GUIDANCE **Greater Bangor Convention and Visitors Bureau** (207-947-5205 and 1-800-991-6673; visitbangormaine.com) operates staffed, year-round information centers at 330 Harlow St., Bangor and operates kiosks at both Bangor International Airport and the Harbormaster's Office on the waterfront in the summer. Its website is the source for information about walking tours for the Devil's Half-Acre, Mount Hope, and Ghostly Bangor.

Bangor Region Chamber of Commerce (207-947-0307; bangorregion.com), 208 Maine Ave., Bangor 04401. Contact GBCVB above with tourism inquiries.

Maine Tourism Association maintains two rest areas/information centers on I-95 in Hamden between Exits 175 and 180: northbound (207-862-6628) and southbound (207-862-6638).

GETTING THERE *By air:* **Bangor International Airport** (BGR; 207-992-4600; flybangor.com) is served by Delta, Allegiant Air, United, and American Airlines. **Rental cars** are available at the airport.

By bus: **Greyhound** (207-942-1700), **West Transportation** (207-546-2823), and **Cyr Bus Line** (207-827-2335 or 1-800-244-2335) offer daily bus service. Cyr Bus Line provides daily trips all the way to Fort Kent, with stops in between. **Concord Coach Lines** (207-945-5000 or 1-800-639-5150) has express trips, complete with movies and music, daily from Portland and Boston.

By car: I-95 north from Augusta and south from Millinocket; Rt. 9 from Calais; Rt. 1A from Bar Harbor.

WHEN TO COME The American Folk Festival draws a lot of folks at the end of August, but the Penobscot Nation Museum on Indian Island, a unique home brewing shop, and great restaurants downtown suggest a visit anytime.

✳ Villages

Hampden. Adjacent to Bangor, but offering a more rural setting. The academically excellent Hampden Academy is found here.

Orono. A college town housing the University of Maine, but still a small town where almost everyone knows everyone else. Downtown there are some nice shops and local dining landmarks.

Old Town. Definitely a mill town, but also the home of the famous Old Town Canoe factory. There's a great little museum worth visiting.

Winterport. An old river town, once home of many sea captains and now a quiet little area with a historic district. Walking-tour brochure available from area businesses.

✳ To See and Do

CANOEING AND KAYAKING Sunrise International (207-942-9300 or 1-888-490-9300; sunriseexpeditions.com), 4 Union Plaza, Suite 2, Bangor, is one of the state's best river expedition, guided-kayaking and -canoeing businesses. Martin Brown started Sunrise County Canoe Expeditions, a traditional Maine guiding business, in 1973, and it is now Maine's oldest river guide and outfitter service. Brown has taken his customers out west and far north. But the St. Croix, St. John, and Machias Rivers, as well as other eastern and northern Maine waterways, are explored in scheduled trips every year from May–Oct.

Kayaks can also be rented from **University Inn–Orono, Maine** (universityinnorono.com; 207-866-4921), which is on the Stillwater River.

MUSEUMS Cole Land Transportation Museum (207-990-3600; colemuseum.org), 405 Perry Rd. (near junction of I-95 and I-395), Bangor. Open May 1–Nov. 11, daily 9–5. $7 adults, $5 seniors, under 19 free. A collection of 200 antique Maine vehicles going back to the 19th century: snowplows, wagons, trucks, sleds, rail equipment, and more. A World War II memorial, Korean Veterans Memorial, Vietnam Veterans Memorial, and Purple Heart Memorial are all on-site.

Hose 5 Fire Museum (207-945-3229), 247 State St., Bangor. Open by appointment. A working fire station until 1993, now a museum with firefighting artifacts from the area. Three fully restored fire engines, wooden water mains, and plenty of historical pictures on display.

University of Maine Museums, Rt. 2A, Orono. **Hudson Museum** (207-581-1901), in the **Collins Center for the Arts** (open Mon.–Fri. 9–4, Sat. 11–4), is an exceptional anthropological collection including a special section on Maine Native Americans and Maine history. **Page Farm Home Museum** (207-581-4100; umaine.edu/pagefarm), on the University of Maine–Orono campus, is open Tue.–Sat. 9–4; closed Sun., Mon., and holidays. Free. Historical farm implements and household items from 1865 to 1940.

Nancy English

COLE LAND TRANSPORTATION MUSEUM

University of Maine Museum of Art (207-561-3350; umma.umaine.edu), 40 Harlow St., Bangor, shows a fraction of its 4,500-work collection, which includes an extensive selection of 19th- and 20th-century European and American prints by Goya, Picasso, Homer, and Whistler, as well as modern American paintings by George Inness, John Marin, Andrew Wyeth, and others. The museum also hosts four exhibitions a year of modern and contemporary art. Open Mon.–Sat. 10–5.

Old Town Museum (207-827-7256; theoldtownmuseum.org), 353 Main St., Old Town. Open early June–Oct. 12, Fri.–Sun. 1–4. St. Mary's Catholic Church houses a great little museum with exhibits on the Penobscot tribe and local logging, early area photos, an original birch-bark canoe, and well-informed guides.

Maine Forest and Logging Museum at Leonard's Mills (207-974-6278; leonardsmills .com), Leonard's Mills, off Rt. 178 in Bradley (take Rt. 9 north from Brewer; turn left onto Rt. 178 and watch for signs). Open during daylight hours. Varying admission. "Living History Days" on two weekends, one in mid-July and another in Oct., feature people in period attire with horses or oxen. Located on the site of a 1790s logging and milling community, this museum includes a covered bridge, water-powered sawmill, millpond, saw pit, barn, and trapper's line camp.

HISTORIC HOMES AND SITES **Bangor Museum and History Center** (207-942-1900; bangormuseum.org), 159 Union St., Bangor. Open May–Mar., Tue.–Sat. 10–4. $7 adults, children and members free, but fee depends on program. The museum is located in the Thomas A. Hill House. The downstairs of the Hill House has been restored to its 19th-century grandeur with Victorian furnishings and an elegant double parlor. The *Edgar Allan Poe et al.* exhibit in fall is highly recommended. **Mount Hope Cemetery** in Bangor is one of the nation's oldest garden cemeteries, designed by noted Maine architect Charles G. Bryant. Abraham Lincoln's first vice president, Hannibal Hamlin, is buried here.

FOR FAMILIES ✿ **Maine Discovery Museum** (207-262-7200; mainediscoverymuseum .org), 74 Main St., Bangor. The largest children's museum north of Boston, with three floors of kid-oriented displays and activities. Science and music exhibits on the third floor include a giant body to climb through and the Recollections Room, with lights that follow movement. The second floor has exhibits about world trade with a cargo ship, warehouses, and an airplane. $7.50 per person, 12 months and older.

GAMBLING **Hollywood Casino Hotel & Raceway** (207-561-6100 or 1-877-779-7771; hollywoodslots.com), 500 Main St., Bangor. Open daily 8–3. You must be 21 to enter and use the gaming floor. Younger people can enter the restaurant and the hotel, but no one under 21 can enter the slot machine area (except licensed employees). Revenues from Hollywood Slots, shared with the state, the city of Bangor, and other entities, have exceeded predictions: It grossed more than $30 million in January 2015 alone (totals listed at maine.gov/dps/GambBoard/Financial.html). The business comprises 1,000 slot and video poker machines, 16 gaming tables, a 152-room hotel, a 1,500-car parking garage, a lounge with live entertainment on weekends, a simulcast theater for off-track betting, a buffet, and a snack bar.

GOLF **Bangor Municipal Golf Course** (207-941-0232; bangorgc.com), Webster Ave., Bangor; 27 holes. **Penobscot Valley Country Club** (207-866-2423), Bangor Rd., Orono; 18 holes. **Hermon Meadow Golf Club** (207-848-3741; hermanmeadow.com), 281 Billings Rd., Hermon; 18 holes.

SWIMMING ✿ **Jenkins' Beach**. Popular beach on Green Lake for families with children. Store and snack bar.

MUST SEE

Indian Island In 1786 the Penobscot tribe deeded most of Maine to Massachusetts in exchange for 140 small islands in the Penobscot River. An 18th-century agreement (discovered in the 1970s) detailed that Indian Island (much of it now valuable) belonged to the tribe and brought the island a new school and a large community center, which attracts crowds to play high-stakes bingo (call 1-800-255-1293 or visit penobscotbingo.com for the schedule). Today the Indian Island Reservation, the Penobscot homeland for more than 5,000 years, and connected by bridge to Old Town, is occupied by about 500 tribal members. At 12 Down St., the Penobscot Nation Museum (207-827-4153; penobscotnation.org) is open year-round Mon.–Wed. 9–4 and Thu.–Sat. 9–1. The museum occupies the former Indian agent's office, the fifth building on the right after crossing the bridge. Museum coordinator James Neptune greets visitors, explaining that the birch table was made by the legendary Passamaquoddy craftsman Tomah Joseph (who taught Franklin Roosevelt to paddle a canoe) and that the beaded deerskin dress belonged to Indian Island's Molly Spotted Elk, a dancer, actress, and writer known around the world in the late 1930s. Most items in this authentic and informal collection—which includes a 200-year-old birch-bark canoe and some exquisite beaded works, war bonnets, war clubs, and basketry—have a human story. The island is accessible from Rt. 2, marked from I-95 exit 197.

Hudson Museum, University of Maine-Orono

A FANCY BASKET BY CLARA NEPTUNE KEEZER

Violette's Public Beach and Boat Landing (207-843-6876), Dedham (between Ellsworth and Bangor). $4 admission. Also on Green Lake, a popular spot for college students and young adults. Swim float with slide, boat launch, and picnic tables.

Beth Pancoe Aquatic Center (207-992-4490; bangormaine.gov), run by the Bangor Parks and Recreation Department. An outdoor Olympic-sized pool with a waterslide, this facility has a slow slope into the water, easy on the old and young, and was built with a gift from Stephen King, Bangor's best-selling novelist. Open end of June–Aug. $2 children, $3 resident adults; $3 children, $5 adults from away.

DOWNHILL AND CROSS-COUNTRY SKIING **Hermon Mountain Ski Area** (207-848-5192; skihermonmountain.com), Newburg Rd., Hermon (3 miles off I-95 from Exit 173, Carmel; or off Rt. 2 from Bangor). Popular local downhill skiing area, with a chairlift and a T-bar and 20 runs (the longest is 3,500 feet); rentals available; base lodge, night skiing, snowboarding. A tubing park, with a lift, runs Wed.–Sun. ($12 tickets). Day passes for adults $25, 12 and under $20.

See also **Sunkhaze Meadows** under *Green Space*.

✳ Green Space

Sunkhaze Meadows National Wildlife Refuge, Milford. Unstaffed. Contact the Maine Coastal Islands Wildlife Refuge Milbridge office (207-546-2124; sunkhaze.org) for information. Just north of Bangor, this 11,500-acre refuge includes nearly 7 miles of Sunkhaze

THE ORONO BOG WALK

Stream and 12 miles of tributary streams. Recreation includes canoeing, hiking, hunting, and fishing—contact refuge staff for regulations. Also excellent bird-watching and cross-country skiing.

The *Greater Bangor Region* guidebook is available at the Greater Bangor Convention & Visitors Bureau visitors center and lists all trails for biking, walking, picnicking, running, hiking, cross-country skiing, and other outdoor activities. Maps are also available.

✪ **The Orono Bog Walk and the Rolland F. Perry Bangor City Forest** (207-581-1697 for Jim Bird, director of Orono Bog Boardwalk; oronobogwalk.org), located 1.5 miles north of the intersection of Stillwater Ave. and Hogan Rd. at Bangor Mall, on Tripp Dr., Bangor. Open May–late Nov., this 1-mile looping boardwalk winds into a carpet of peat moss, and signs help you identify the fascinating vegetation that thrives in acidic dampness. Guided walks are offered on Sat.; check the website for the schedule and subject matter. Another 9 miles of trails lace Bangor City Forest. Birders are on the prowl for yellow-rumped warblers, black-throated green warblers, and many others that migrate through.

✳ Lodging

Hollywood Casino Hotel & Raceway (207-561-6100; hollywoodcasinobangor.com), 500 Main St., Bangor 04401. With 152 rooms ready for guests who like to gamble and play the slots, roulette, blackjack, and three-card poker, and 42-inch TVs, this hotel is a destination for many visitors to Bangor. Rates run around $129–159.

🐾 **Fireside Inn and Suites** (207-942-1234; firesideinnbangor.com), 570 Main St., Bangor 04401. A 51-room hotel that is clean, comfortable, and convenient. Next door to Hollywood Casino, this place is busier than ever. All the basic conveniences, including mini fridge, microwave oven, and cable TV. **Geaghan's**, the on-site restaurant with a microbrewery, serves decent food, with Irish specials. $90–150, including continental breakfast. Children under 18 stay free.

♿ **The Charles Inn** (207-992-2820; thecharlesinn.com), 20 Broad St., Bangor 04401. A historic art gallery hotel on West Market Square, a vest-pocket park in the heart

Nancy English

THE LOBBY OF THE CHARLES INN IN BANGOR

of downtown Bangor, is a perfect location for getting to know the city. New ownership in late 2015 promises changes; 36 large rooms are simple, some with solid mahogany or cherry beds. All have private bath, air-conditioning, and TV. A continental kosher or nonkosher breakfast is included. $79–139. Count on good cocktails at the hotel bar.

Country Inn at the Mall (207-941-0200 or 1-800-244-3961; countryinnatthemall.net), 936 Stillwater Ave., Bangor 04401. Despite the name, this is essentially a 96-room motel—but brighter and better decorated than most. There's no restaurant, newsstand, or gift shop, but with the Bangor Mall (largest in northern Maine) right next door that's not an inconvenience. $75–111 with continental breakfast.

🐾 ♿ **The Lucerne Inn** (207-843-5123 or 1-800-325-5123; lucerneinn.com), 2517 Main Rd., Holden 04429. An 1812 mansion on Rt. 1A, overlooking Phillips Lake in East Holden. Best known as a restaurant (see *Dining Out*), it also has 31 rooms with private bath (whirlpool), working fireplace, heated towel bars, phone, and TV. Outdoor heated pool. $119–219 in-season includes continental breakfast. Lower rates off-season.

Howard Johnson's Hotel (207-942-5251; hojo.com), 336 Odlin Rd., Bangor 04401. Just plain, clean rooms—starting at $72 and five minutes from the airport.

Note: Bangor also has many hotels and motels, mainly located by the mall and near the airport. Contact the **Greater Bangor Convention and Visitors Bureau** (207-947-5205 or 1-800-991-6673; visitbangormaine.com) for more information.

✻ Where to Eat

DINING OUT **Thistles Restaurant** (207-945-5480; thistlesrestaurant.com), 175 Exchange St., Bangor. Open for lunch Tue.–Sat. 11–2:30 and dinner 4:30–9. A fine-dining place that does many things perfectly, the Argentinean dishes in particular. Chef-owner Alejandro Rave puts together tangy chimichurri sauce for steaks and empanadas. Spanish paella is served in paella pans, with fresh seafood and chicken. Half portions fit a smaller appetite and cost $10–15. Entrées $17–28.

The Fiddlehead (207-942-3336; thefiddleheadrestaurant.com), 84 Hammond St., Bangor. Open Tue.–Sun. Depending on the season, the menu holds bouillabaisse with calamari, shrimp, scallops, haddock, and tomato and roasted red pepper rouille; pork chop with char siu and Japanese fried rice; and spinach and wild mushroom Wellington with goat cheese cream and 18-year balsamic. Beginning with a cocktail like the Gin and the Giant Peach is recommended by Maine.Eater.com.

Massimo's Cucina Italiana (207-945-5600; massimoscucinaitaliana.com), 96 Hammond St., Bangor. Zuppa di cozze, mussels with white wine and garlic, or spinach salad with Gorgonzola makes a wonderful introduction to dinner at Massimo's; then head right to the linguine alla carbonara or tortellacci stuffed with beef and veal. Seared rib eye or lamb chops are served as secondi. $10–25. **Massimo's Breads** next door sells fantastic pizza by the slice.

11 Central (207-922-5115; 11centralbangor.com), 11 Central St. Prosciutto and goat cheese on ciabatta toast or a smoked salmon plate start dinner; then try chorizo gnocchi and duck stir fry. $18–36.

Evenrood's (207-941-8800), 25 Broad St. Excellent crab cakes are served in this modern restaurant in an old bank space in the Circular Building in downtown Bangor. The name comes from a mispronounced character's name in *The Rescuers*—and this business and others like it are in the process of rescuing the downtown from a long sleep. Scallops, French onion soup, and more.

EVENROOD'S AT 25 BROAD STREET, BANGOR

The Lucerne Inn (207-843-5123 or 1-800-325-5123; lucerneinn.com), 2517 Main Rd., Rt. 1A, East Holden (11 miles out of Bangor, heading toward Ellsworth). Open for dinner daily, as well as a popular Sunday brunch, at this grand old mansion with a view of Phillips Lake serving Belgian waffles and chicken cordon bleu. Entrées start at $20; more than $29 for a steamed lobster or filet mignon.

Reverend Noble's Pub (207-942-5180) and **Ipanema Bar and Grill** (207-942-9339), 10 Broad St., Bangor. Steve Parlee owns these two businesses. The pub is on the second floor, serving burgers and pub food. Ipanema offers Caribbean food like skewers of double jerk chicken or steak with coffee bourbon sauce. Live entertainment.

Luna Bar & Grill (207-990-2233; lunabar andgrill.net), 49 Park St., Bangor. Open Tue.–Sat. for dinner. Grilled burgers, seared duck with caramelized onion flan and cherry compote, filet osso buco, and miso-glazed sea bass with jasmine rice and bok choy. $9–32. Bar is open until 1 AM, with bar menu available.

Nocturnem Draft Haus (207-907-4380; nocturnemdrafthaus.com), 56 Main St., Bangor. This is a can't-miss for every beer lover when in Bangor. Simple delicious foods, locally supplied, locally grown, made in Maine whenever possible.

EATING OUT **Tesoro's** (207-942-6699), 114 Harlow St., Bangor. Located across from the Bangor Public Library, this family-run restaurant serves good Italian American food—like chicken Parmesan and veal and peppers—in generous portions and is famous for its pizza. Cash only; ATM nearby.

Paddy Murphy's Irish Pub (207-945-6800; paddymurphyspub.com), 26 Main St., Bangor. Hungarian mushroom soup and hot pulled pork sandwich. Colcannon, Guinness beef stew, bangers and mash with pork sausages. Entrées $9–23.

Giacomo's (207-947-3702; giacomos bangor.com), 1 Central St., Bangor. Open Mon.–Fri. 7–6, Sat. 8–4, Sun. 11–3. Brett Settle has run Giacomo's since Sept. 2009. His kitchen turns out "vegetable antipasta"— focaccia stuffed with roasted red peppers, artichoke hearts, olives, and Fontina, for example. Wine and fine coffee served.

✍ **Governor's** (207-947-3113; governors restaurant.com), 643 Broadway in Bangor; and 963 Stillwater Ave. in Old Town (207-827-4227). Open all day. The Stillwater restaurant is the original in a statewide chain and has a breakfast menu, but this place is also popular for hamburgers, specials like shepherd's pie, fresh strawberry pie, and amazing whoopie pies from its bakery.

🍴 **Dysart's** (207-942-4878; dysarts.com), Coldbrook Rd., Hermon (I-95, Exit 180). Open 24 hours. Billed as "the biggest truck stop in Maine," but it isn't just truckers who eat here. Known for great road food, good prices, and a 1-pound burger.

Pat's Pizza (207-866-2111), 11 Mill St., Orono. A local landmark, especially popular with high school and university students and families. Now franchised throughout the state, this is the original with booths and a jukebox, back dining room, and downstairs taproom. Pizza, sandwiches, Italian dinners.

Java Joe's Café (207-990-0500), 98 Central St., Bangor. Breakfast, lunch, and the all-important morning latte. Mon.–Fri. 8–4, Sat. 9–2, with bagels, eggs, sandwiches, salads and wraps, and Thai specialties.

Sea Dog Brewing Company (207-947-8004; seadogbrewing.com), 26 Front St., Bangor. Open 11:30–1 AM daily. Microbrews and a long menu of seafood, burgers, and steaks. A great deck next to the Penobscot River, and the winter view is good, too.

SNACKS ✍ **The Store Ampersand** (207-866-4110), 22 Mill St., Orono. Mon.–Sat. 7–7, Sun.

9–4. A combination health food store, coffee bar, and gift shop. Great for snacks (try the big cookies) and specialty items. Wine and cheese.

Friar's Bakehouse (207-947-3770; franciscansofbangor.com), 21 Central St., Bangor. Open Tue.–Thu. 7–3, Fri. until 6, Sat. 8–2, give or take four minutes. This bakery run by the Franciscan Brothers of Hungary, a Roman Catholic order from Brewer, makes and sells muffins, chocolate chip cookies, whoopie pies, and lots of bread. A chapel up the stairs is always open for prayer and meditation. A brewhouse is a 2013 addition.

Bagel Central (207-947-1654; bagelcentralbangor.com), 33 Central St., Bangor. Open Mon.–Fri. 6–6, Sat. and Sun. 6–2. Bagels, bialys, and spinach knish at this kosher deli. We hear the leek and potato soup is perfect in winter; avocado vegetable sandwich, great in summer. There is a line out the door every Sunday.

❋ Entertainment

⚓ **Collins Center for the Arts** (207-581-1805; box office, 207-581-1755; collinscenterforthearts.com), at the University of Maine in Orono, has become the cultural center for the area. It hosts a wide variety of concerts and events, from classical to country-and-western, children's theater, and dance. Many performances are held in Hutchins Concert Hall, Maine's first concert hall.

⚓ **Penobscot Theatre Company** (207-942-3333; penobscottheatre.org), 131 Main St., Bangor. This company has been putting on quality shows since 1973. Performing in the Bangor Opera House, the company presents a variety of plays during the season; *Ink*, a world premiere, was a recent production. In summer the company sponsors the Northern Writes New Play Festival, dedicated to the development of new work.

The Maine Masque (207-581-1792; umaine.edu/mainemasque), Hauck Auditorium, University of Maine, Orono. Classic and contemporary plays presented Oct.–May by University of Maine theater students.

Cross Insurance Center (207-561-8300; crossinsurancecenter.com), 515 Main St., Bangor. Home to the Bangor State Fair and Raceway, which features Hollywood Casino's

live harness racing, the CIC has an 8,000-seat arena and is Bangor's newly constructed arena and convention center. (Go to the website for a schedule of events.)

Bangor Symphony Orchestra (207-581-1755; bangorsymphony.com). The symphony began in 1895 and is still going strong, with performances at the Collins Center for the Arts Oct.–May.

❋ Selective Shopping

BOOKSTORES

IN BANGOR

Antique Marketplace & Café (207-941-2111; antiquemarketplacecafe.com), 65 Main St. Open daily. Seventy dealers sell antiques, jewelry, furniture, rugs, tin ads, and, from four book dealers, books of all kinds. **Sarah Faragher**'s stock includes secondhand editions of great books, with an emphasis on Maine, history, travel, poetry, and literature, and you can also find books from **W. J. Lippincott**.

BookMarcs Book Store (207-942-3206; bookmarcs.com), 78 Harlow St. A first-rate, full-service downtown bookstore with new, used, and discounted books. Particular specialties are books about Maine and by Maine authors. Java Joe's Café is connected to the store.

⚓ **The Briar Patch** (207-941-0255), 27 Central St. A large and exceptional children's bookstore, with creative toys, puzzles, and games.

Top Shelf Comics (207-947-4939; tcomics.com), 115 Main St. All the newest comics, as well as old comics, and coins and paper money.

CANOES **Old Town Canoe Visitors' Center and Factory Outlet Store** (207-827-1530; old-towncanoe.com), 125 Gilman Falls Ave., Old Town. Open daily Apr.–Sept.; closed Sun.–Mon. Oct.–Mar. Varieties of canoes and kayaks sold include polyethylene, wood, and Royalex. Factory-tour video shows how canoes are made. Memorabilia and museum-quality wooden canoes and a birch-bark canoe are on display, not for sale.

SPECIAL SHOPS **Winterport Boot Shop** (207-989-6492), 264 State St., Twin City Plaza,

Brewer. Largest selection of Red Wing work boots in the Northeast. Proper fit for sizes 4–16, all widths.

Valentine Footwear (207-907-2128; valentinefootwear.com), 115 Main St., Bangor. Opened in 2011 by the daughter of the owner of Winterport Boot Shop, Valentine Footwear was embraced with open arms. "Well-made, comfortable-yet-cute shoes" selected by a woman brought up in the business are on sale here.

Antique Marketplace & Café (207-941-2111; antiquemarketplacecafe.com), 65 Main St., Bangor. Booths display antiques (also see *Books*), and the café serves tea, coffee, sandwiches, salads, and pie.

One Lupine Fiber Arts (207-992-4140; onelupine.com), 170 Park St., Bangor. Open Mon. 10–5, Tue. 10–7, Wed.–Thu. 10–6, Fri.–Sat. 10–5. Felting, scrollwork ornaments, and chiffon scarves in beautiful colors, as well as coats, balls, and other felt items, many made with Maine-based yarns and fibers, also available for sale. American-made fine handwork from jewelry to pottery and painting.

Central Street Farmhouse (207-992-4454; centralstreetfarmhouse.com), 30 Central St., Bangor. The spiritual center of homebrewing, with "Maine's largest selections of grain and hops." Maple syrup, feed-bag shopping bags, and fine local products for sale.

✳ Special Events

February: **Brewer Waterfront Winterfest. Maine Chef Challenge.**

April: **Kenduskeag Stream Canoe Race.**

All summer: **Waterfront concerts** at Darling's Waterfront Pavilion, **free outdoor movies**, Pickering Square; **Cool Sounds** concerts; **Tommyknockers and More Bus Tour**, the only Stephen King literary tour in the world.

June: **Bangor's Beer Festival.**

July: **Bangor State Fair**, Bass Park—agricultural fair with harness racing.

August: **WLBZ Sidewalk Art Festival**, downtown Bangor. **American Folk Festival** (last weekend), Bangor—a celebration of American culture through song, dance, storytelling, and food. Free. **KahBang Music, Film & Art Festival**.

Weekend after Labor Day: **Bangor Car Show: Wheels on the Waterfront**—more than 300 cars.

October: **Fright at the Fort**, Fort Knox.

New Year's Eve: **Downtown Countdown** in Bangor centers on a beach ball wrapped in Christmas lights that gets thrown off a tall building.

THE NORTH MAINE WOODS

L ike "Down East," the "North Maine Woods" may seem a bit of a mirage, always over the next hill. Much of this land lies within the area already described in this book as the "Western Mountains and Lakes Region," and extends east into Aroostook County. However, the one particular tract of forest that tends to be equated with "the Maine Woods" is the section bordered on the north and west by Canada, the one for which highway maps show no roads. This is the largest stretch of unpeopled woodland in the East, but wilderness it's not.

Private ownership of this sector, technically part of Maine's 10.5 million acres known as the unorganized townships, dates to the 1820s when Maine was securing independence from Massachusetts. The mother state, her coffers at their usual low, stipulated that an even division of all previously undeeded wilderness be part of the separation agreement. The woods were quickly sold by the legislature for 12¢ to 38¢ per acre.

Pine was king, and men had already been working this woodland for decades. They lived together in remote lumber camps such as the one Thoreau visited in 1846 at Chesuncook. They worked in subzero temperatures, harvesting and hauling logs on sleds to frozen rivers. They rode those logs through the roaring spring runoffs, driving them across vast lakes and sometimes hundreds of miles downstream to mills. These were lumberjacks, the stuff of children's stories and adult songs, articles, and books. They were the cowboys of the East, larger than ordinary men.

What's largely forgotten is that by the second half of the 19th century, this North Maine Woods region was more accessible and popular with visitors than today. By 1853 *Atlantic Monthly* editor James Russell Lowell could chug toward Moosehead on a cinder-spraying train; by 1900 Bostonians could ride comfortably to Greenville in a day, while Manhattanites could bed down in a Pullman and sleep their way to the foot of Moosehead Lake. The Bangor & Aroostook Railroad published annual glossy illustrated guidebooks to Moosehead and its environs.

By 1882 the Kineo House, with 500 guest rooms and half a mile of verandas overlooking Moosehead Lake, was said to be the largest hotel in America. In Greenville, Sanders & Sons, the era's L.L. Bean, outfitted city "sports" with the clothing, firearms, and fishing gear with which to meet their guides and board steamers bound for far corners of the lake, frequently continuing on by foot and canoe to dozens of backwoods "sporting camps."

With the advent of World War I, the Depression, and the switch from rails to roads, the North Woods dimmed as a travel destination. In the 1920s the steamboat *Katahdin*, once the pride of the Moosehead fleet, was sold to a logging company as a towboat, and the Maine state legislature refused to protect woodland around Mount

Liam Davis

LUMBER TRUCKS RULE ON THE GOLDEN ROAD

MOUNT KATAHDIN

Katahdin, the state's highest mountain. Governor Percival Baxter bought the core of current **Baxter State Park** with his own money. In 1938 the Kineo House burned to the ground.

In ensuing decades the wisdom of Governor Baxter's purchase became increasingly apparent. Mount Katahdin, as the terminus of the 2,190-mile Appalachian Trail from Georgia, attracted recognition and serious hikers from throughout the world. Hunters and fishermen continued to make spring and fall trips to their fathers' haunts, and families still found their way to reasonably priced lake camps. In 1966 a 92-mile ribbon of lakes, ponds, rivers, and streams running northwest from Baxter State Park was designated the **Allagash Wilderness Waterway**, triggering interest among canoeists—though only a very narrow corridor was actually preserved because the state owns only 400 to 800 feet from the high-water mark. Still, it can control activities up to a mile on each side of the river.

Meanwhile the timber industry was transforming. This woodland was harvested initially for tall timber, but in the late 19th century the value of less desirable softwood increased when the process of making paper from wood fibers was rediscovered. (It seems that the method first used in A.D. 105 had been forgotten, and New England mills had been using rags to make paper.) By the turn of the 20th century many pulp and paper mills had moved to their softwood source. The city of Millinocket boomed into existence around the mammoth mills built by Great Northern Company Paper, which also maintained far-flung farms to support more widely scattered lumber camps.

In 1900 it's said that some 30,000 men worked seasonally in the Maine woods. By 1970, however, just 6,500 loggers were working year-round; by 1988 this number fell to 3,660. On the other hand, the total wood harvest in Maine doubled between 1940 and 1970, and again by the mid-1980s. These numbers mirror technological changes, from axes to chain saws, skidders, and ultimately mammoth machines unselectively cutting thousands of trees per day, creating clear-cuts as large as 8 miles square. Today the Maine Forest Practices Act does not allow clear-cuts larger than 75 acres.

Changes in North Woods ownership in recent years have been cataclysmic. Through most of the 20th century large timber companies assumed much of the management responsibility and taxes as well as the cost of building hundreds of miles of roads (log drives ended in the 1970s) in this area. They also accommodated limited recreation, maintaining campsites and honoring long-term leases for both commercial and private camps. In recent decades, however, mergers and sales have fragmented ownership, and much of this "working forest" has been bought by firms without local ties, and not just by timber companies but by investment businesses as well.

North Woods ownership continues to shift and splinter. On the one hand, the organization RESTORE: The North Woods has advocated creation of a North Woods National Park. On the other, park opponents have argued that a national park would destroy the traditional economy and lifestyle in the region. Maine's Bureau of Parks and Lands has quietly acquired large tracts, and major nonprofit groups such as The Nature Conservancy, The New England Forestry Foundation, The Forest Society of Maine, and the Appalachian Mountain Club have secured thousands of acres outright and over 1 million acres in easements that permit timber management.

Forms of recreation have also significantly altered in recent decades, notably with the popularity of snowmobiling and whitewater rafting, thanks to the area's relatively reliable snow cover and even more reliable whitewater releases on the West Branch of the Penobscot River. Many visitors also now use ATVs on woods roads. The resurgence of the moose population has sparked these animals' popularity as something to see rather than shoot. Fly-fishing, kayaking, dogsledding, hiking, and cross-country skiing all contribute to the rediscovery of the beauty of these magnificent woods.

To date the effect of increased visitation has been limited. In the lake-studded area around Millinocket and Mount Katahdin, rafting outfitters have established bases and lodging options. East of Moosehead Lake the **Appalachian Mountain Club** (AMC) has acquired more than 70,000 acres and three historic, full-service sporting camps dedicated to hiking, biking, fly-fishing, paddling, cross-country skiing, and snowshoeing. The country's oldest nonprofit outdoor recreation and conservation group, the AMC is working to maintain an extensive, 80-mile trail system, open for use by the public.

North Maine Woods, a long-established nonprofit cooperative organization of landowners, maintains some 300 widely scattered campsites and operates staffed checkpoints at entry points to industrial logging roads (visitors pay a day-use and camping fee). These roads have themselves altered the look and nature of the North Woods. Many remote sporting camps, for a century accessible only by water, and more recently by air, are now a bumpy ride from the nearest town. However, many of the sporting camps themselves haven't changed since the turn of the 20th century. They are Maine's inland windjammers, holdovers from another era and a precious endangered Maine species, threatened by competition from the region's new second-home owners as well by land sales and access.

GETTING THERE There are four major approaches to the North Woods. The longest, most scenic route is up the Kennebec River, stopping to raft in The Forks, and along the Moose River to the village of Rockwood at the dramatic narrows of Moosehead Lake, then down along the lake to Greenville, New England's largest seaplane base.

From Rockwood or Greenville you can hop a floatplane to a sporting camp or set off up the eastern shore of Moosehead to the woodland outpost of Kokadjo and on up to the **Golden Road** (see sidebar), through uninterrupted forest to Millinocket. As Thoreau did in the 1850s, you can canoe up magnificent Chesuncook Lake, camping or staying in the outpost of Chesuncook Village. With increased interest in rafting down the West Branch of the Penobscot River through Ripogenus Gorge and the Cribworks, this stretch of the Golden Road has become known as the West Branch Region.

The second and third routes, leading respectively to Greenville and Millinocket, both begin at the I-95 exit in Newport and head up through Southern Piscataquis County, itself an area of small villages, large lakes, and stretches of woodland that here include Gulf Hagas, Maine's most magnificent gorge.

GOLDEN ROAD

This legendary 96-mile road is the privately owned high road of the North Maine Woods, linking Millinocket's paper mills on the east with commercial woodlands that extend to the Quebec border. Its name derives from its multimillion-dollar cost in 1975, but its value has proven great to visitors heading up from Moosehead Lake, as well as from Millinocket to Baxter State Park. It's also used by the whitewater rafting companies on the Penobscot River and the Allagash Wilderness Waterway, and for remote lakes like Chesuncook. Expect to pull to the side to permit lumber trucks to pass. Much of the road is now paved, graded, and well maintained, even (especially) in winter. Be sure to bring along your Maine atlas or another detailed map. Silas Hill, part of the Greenville Road link to the Golden Road, is the roughest part but there's a bypass. If you are heading from Greenville to Millinocket, ask advice. You should have a high-clearance car and try to keep to 20 MPH or less. Hazards include moose as well as washouts and potholes.

For those who come this distance primarily to climb Mount Katahdin and camp in Baxter State Park, or to raft the West Branch of the Penobscot, the quickest route is up I-95 to Medway and in through Millinocket; it's 18 miles to the Togue Pond Gatehouse and Baxter State Park.

While I-95 has replaced the Penobscot River as the highway into the North Maine Woods, it has not displaced Bangor, sited on both the river and I-95 (25 miles east of Newport and 60 miles south of Medway) as the area's commercial hub and gateway. A recent effort promotes the two counties—Penobscot and Piscataquis, which include Moosehead Lake, Baxter State Park, Bangor, and a good portion of the North Maine Woods—as a distinct region named "the Maine Highlands."

Contrary to its potato-fields image, Aroostook County to the north is also largely wooded and includes a major portion of the Allagash Wilderness Waterway. Northern reaches of Baxter State Park and the lakes nearby are best accessed from the park's northern entrance via Patten. Both Ashland and Portage are also points of entry, and Shin Pond serves as the seaplane base for this northernmost reach of the North Maine Woods.

GUIDANCE **North Maine Woods** (207-435-6213; northmainewoods.org) publishes maps/guides that show logging roads with current checkpoints, user fees, campsites, and a list of outfitters and camps licensed and insured to operate on the property. The website is excellent, but it's wise to secure the print versions, too.

Maine Bureau of Parks and Lands (207-287-3821; parksandlands.com). The bureau publishes a map/guide identifying holdings, but what's golden here is the website. It details specific areas such as Nahmakanta Public Reserved Land—43,000 acres of backcountry hiking trails and remote campsites.

Maine Sporting Camp Association (mainesportingcamps.com) maintains an excellent website.

SUGGESTED READING *Northeastern Wilds: Journeys of Discovery in the Northern Forest*, photography and text by Stephen Gorman (Appalachian Mountain Club Books). *The Maine Woods*, by Henry David Thoreau (Penguin Nature Library).

The Wildest Country: Exploring Thoreau's Maine, by J. Parker Huber (Appalachian Mountain Club Books). *The Maine Atlas and Gazetteer* is essential for navigating this region.

MOOSEHEAD LAKE AREA

As Rt. 15 crests Indian Hill, you see for a moment what Henry David Thoreau described from this spot in 1858: "A suitably wild looking sheet of water, sprinkled with low islands . . . covered with shaggy spruce and other wild wood." After a sunset by the shore of Moosehead Lake you also see what he meant by: "A lake is the Earth's eye, looking into which the beholder measures the depth of his own nature."

Moosehead is Maine's largest lake—40 miles long, up to 20 miles wide, with some 400 miles of shoreline—and its surface is spotted with more than 50 islands. Greenville at its toe is the only "organized" town (population: 1,646). Rockwood, with fewer than 300 residents, is halfway up the western shore.

A while back Maine's Land Use Regulatory Commission (LURC) approved the request by Seattle-based Plum Creek Timber Company for rezoning to permit major residential development near Rockwood and two resorts on the lake. Little has visibly developed since and, thanks to ensuing easements secured by conservation organizations and timber companies, more than 800,000 continuous acres east of Moosehead Lake have now been conserved as a mix of responsible forestry practices and recreation.

Greenville began as a farm town, but the best crops turned out to be winter lumbering and summer visitors. Immense and flanked by mountains, Moosehead Lake possesses majestic beauty and offers the widest lodging choices in the North Woods—rustic camps to family-owned motels to luxurious inns. Greenville remains a lumbermen's depot with a salting of souvenir and offbeat shops. It's also a seaplane base, with flying services shuttling guests to remote camps and campsites deep in the woods.

Rockwood is a cluster of sporting camps and marinas on the lake's western shore at its narrows, across from its most dramatic landmark: **Mount Kineo**. Native Americans revered Kineo, using its large deposits of rhyolite—a flint-like volcanic rock—for arrowheads. The Mount Kineo House opened in 1847 at the foot of this outcropping and eventually evolved into one of the largest hotels in America, maintaining its own farm as well as a golf course and stables. The golf course survives and most of the island-like Kineo peninsula is now owned by the state. Trails to its summit yield one of the most spectacular 360-degree views in Maine.

East of Greenville the **Appalachian Mountain Club** (AMC) has restored three classic "wilderness lodges" and is offering lodge-to-lodge skiing, snowshoeing, and dogsledding as well as hiking and mountain biking, adding substantially to the numbers who discover the nonmotorized appeal of this backcountry. An 80-mile-long protected corridor, stretching from the Katahdin Iron Works north to Baxter State Park, includes many lakes, ponds, and majestic mountains.

Courtesy of the Maine Office of Tourism

MALE MOOSE

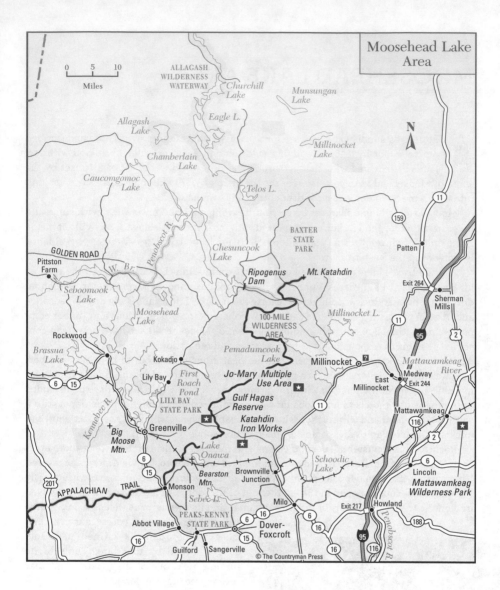

Moosehead Lake Area

North of Greenville along Moosehead's eastern shore, **Lily Bay State Park** offers a beach and campsites, and continuing northeast there's the outpost village of Kokadjo, prime moose-watching country. It's another dozen miles north to the legendary **Golden Road** to Millinocket.

GUIDANCE **Moosehead Lake Region Chamber of Commerce** (207-695-2702 or 1-888-876-2778; mooseheadlake.org) maintains a walk-in information center at the DOT rest area, 2 miles south of town on Rt. 15, open year-round, Mon.–Sat. 10–4.

The Piscataquis Chamber of Commerce (207-564-7533; piscataquischamber.com) maintains an info center at the junction of Rts. 7 and 15 in Dover-Foxcroft. It covers Monson as well as the Lake Sebec area.

AIR TOURS ARE THE BEST WAY TO EXPERIENCE THE REGION

GETTING THERE *By car:* Greenville is 54 miles north of I-95 Exit 157, at Newport. Follow Rt. 7 to Dexter, Rt. 23 to Sangerville (Guilford), and Rt. 15 to Greenville. The longer, more scenic route is up Rt. 201 (I-95 Exit 133) through **The Forks** (see "Upper Kennebec Valley"). From Rt. 201 in **Jackman**, take Rt. 5/15 east to Rockwood.

GETTING AROUND *By air:* **Currier's Flying Service** (207-695-2778; curriersflyingservice .com), Greenville Junction, offers day trips, scenic flights, and service to remote camps. **Jack's Air Service** (207-695-3020), May–Oct. 1, caters to Allagash canoe trips, fly-ins to housekeeping cottages, and sightseeing flights. John Willard at **The Birches** in Rockwood (207-534-7305) specializes in scenic flights as does **Fletcher Mountain Aviation** (207-299-8220).

By car: If you plan to venture out on the area's network of private roads, be forewarned of occasional gate fees and the need for a car with high clearance.

WHEN TO COME Greenville's seasons begin with spring fishing. June can be uncomfortably buggy (black flies). The busy season is July 4 through the mid-September annual "fly-in" of floatplanes from all over. Deer season begins in mid-November. With snow comes snowmobile season. March brings bright blue days and dependable snow cover; it's our favorite month for ski treks in this region.

✳ To See

Eveleth-Crafts-Sheridan House (207-695-2909; mooseheadhistory.org), 444 Pritham Ave., Greenville. Carriage house open year-round; house tours offered June–Sept., Wed.–Fri. 1–4. $5 adults, $3 children under 12. The Moosehead Historical Society maintains a 19th-century home with an 1880s kitchen and displays on the region's history, including postcards and photos picturing early hotels and steamboats. There are changing exhibits about the town's resort history, a fine collection of Indian artifacts and lumbering tools, and a one-room schoolhouse. The related **Center for Moosehead History**, 6 Lakeview Ave., Greenville,

MUST SEE

♂ & The **S. S. *Katahdin*** and **Moosehead Marine Museum** (207-695-2716; katahdincruises.com), Greenville. Call ahead to confirm sailings scheduled Tue.–Sat., late June–Columbus Day on a fairly complicated schedule. Three-hour cruises are the most popular ($33 adults, $29 seniors, $18 ages 11–16, $3 ages 10 and under). One of 50 steamboats on the lake at its height as a resort destination, the vintage 1914 *Katahdin* was the last to survive, converted to diesel in 1922 and in the 1930s modified to haul booms of logs, which she did until 1976, the year of the nation's last log drive. This graceful 115-foot, 225-passenger boat was restored through volunteer effort and re-launched in 1985. The Louis Oakes Map Room depicts the lake's resort history from 1836.

Moose. Don't leave the area without seeing at least one. Chances are you can spot the lake's mascot any dawn or dusk at local hangouts like the DOT site on Rt. 15, 4.5 miles south of Indian Hill, or the road from Rockwood to **Pittston Farm** and **Lazy Tom Bog** in Kokadjo, 18 miles north of Greenville.

If you want to leave the guiding to someone else, the **Birches Resort** (207-534-7305) in Rockwood offers moose cruises aboard pontoon boats. **North-woods Outfitters** (207-695-3288) in Greenville also offers moose-watching cruises and excursions by kayak or canoe.

Mount Kineo is an island-like peninsula with several trails to the summit of the cliff that rises 763 feet above the water. Below is the apron of land once occupied by the Kineo House, one of the country's largest resorts. Most of the 8,000-acre peninsula is now state-owned. Take the moderately difficult 0.9 mile **Indian Trail**, which heads straight up over ledges that are a distinct green. Continue to the summit for one of Maine's most spectacular 360-degree views. The **Bridle Trail** is easier for the descent. Seasonal access from Rockwood Landing (off Rt. 15) is via the **Kineo Shuttle**, a pontoon boat departing on the hour (8–6). It's operated by the **Mount Kineo Golf Club** (207-534-9012; see *Golf*); no need to hike or play golf to enjoy walks on Kineo's shore paths. Lunch at the golf club or bring a picnic.

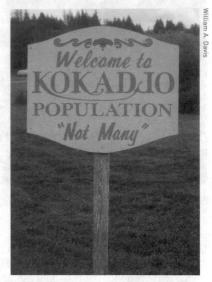

William A. Davis

KOKADJO IS 18 MILES NORTH OF GREENVILLE.

William A. Davis

THE S.S. *KATAHDIN* SETS OUT FROM GREENVILLE

housed in a former Universalist church, is open Thu.–Sun. 10–4 with exhibits of Native American artifacts, local aviation history, and changing displays.

✻ To Do

AIRPLANE RIDES See *Getting Around.*

ATV TOURING The region offers 300-plus miles of trails. **Moosehead ATV Riders** (207-695-8928), the local club, also maintains a well-marked trail system on the west side of Moosehead Lake; **Northwoods Outfitters** (207-695-3288) and **Moose Mountain Inn** (207-695-3321) rent ATVs.

BIRDING Warblers and many elusive species, including the boreal chickadee, gray jay, black-backed woodpecker, Bicknell's thrush, and white-winged crossbill, are found in local bogs and woodland. Also see *Hiking.* The **Appalachian Mountain Club** offers birding programs at its Little Lyford Lodge and Cabins and Medawisla Wilderness Lodge and Cabins (see *Lodging*). **Borestone Mountain Audubon Sanctuary** (see *Hiking*) rents its classic old lodges to groups (207-781-2330).

BOATING See S/S *Katahdin* under *To See.* That's the big one.
The **Birches Resort** (207-534-7305) offers pontoon-boat cruises around Mount Kineo. The **Mount Kineo Shuttle** (see *To See*) has hourly service from Rockland Landing. **Northwoods Outfitters** (1-866-223-1380) also has cruises to Mount Kineo.

CANOE AND KAYAKING RENTALS These are available in Greenville from **Northwoods Outfitters** (1-866-223-1380; maineoutfitter.com) and **Indian Hill Trading Post** (207-695-2104); in Rockwood from **The Birches Resort** (207-534-75305; birches.com). See mooseheadlake.org for a more extensive list.
Note: Flying services will ferry canoes into remote backcountry.

CANOEING AND KAYAKING We recommend **Allagash Canoe Trips** (207-237-3077; allagashcanoetrips.com), based in Greenville, May–Oct. A family business since 1953, this is the oldest continuously running guided canoe trip service in Maine. It's now operated by third-generation guide Chip Cochrane and specializes in weeklong expeditions into the Allagash Wilderness Waterway, on the West Branch of the Penobscot, and on the St. John River. **Northwoods Outfitters** (northwoodsoutfitters.com) also offers four- to seven-day Allagash guided canoe trips.
Also see *To Do* in the Katahdin Area and Aroostook chapters.

FISHING This region is a famed source of eastern brook trout, lake trout, blue-back trout, landlocked salmon, and smallmouth bass. Aside from its centerpiece lake (75,000 acres), the region includes 600 lakes and ponds, 30-plus miles of main-stream rivers, and more than 3,000 miles of tributaries. Rental boats and boat launches are too plentiful to list (see mooseheadlake.org). Two prime sources of fishing information: the state's **Inland Fisheries and Wildlife office** (207-695-3756), Greenville, and the **Maine Guide Fly Shop and Guide Service** (207-695-2266), 34 Moosehead Lake Road, Greenville. Dan Legere sells 314 different flies and a wide assortment of gear; he also works with local guides to outfit you with a boat and guide or to set up a river float trip or a fly-in expedition. Also see *Lodging—Sporting Camps* and fishing guides listed at mooseheadlake.org. **Ice fishing** usually begins

CHESUNCOOK VILLAGE

Chesuncook Village is the surviving example of a 19th-century North Maine Woods lumbermen's village, now on the National Register of Historic Places. In summer you can paddle or motor up Chesuncook Lake from the landing on the Golden Road, and in winter there's snowmobile access farther west along the road. Today there's a church with a regular summer service and a loggers' graveyard, relocated from the shore to a hollow in the woods when Great Northern raised the level of the lake. Several stone markers for gravestones read NAME UNKNOWN. A cluster of camps near the state landing and the lodge at the other end of the island are all that remain of the village that once included stores and a school and was home for 250 people in the 1920s. **Chesuncook Lake Lodge** (see *Lodging*), where Henry David Thoreau is said to have stopped in 1853, offers rooms and cabin rentals (chesuncookvillage.org).

Christina Tree

in January and ends in March. Icehouse rentals are available locally. See **mooseheadlake .org** for a list of locally based Registered Maine Guides. Also check **maineguides.org**.

GOLF **Mount Kineo Golf Course** (207-534-9012; in winter, 207-236-2906). A spectacularly sited nine-hole course at Kineo, accessible by frequent boat service from Rockwood; carts and club rentals; the clubhouse sells subs and snacks. Dating from the 1880s, this is one of the oldest golf courses in New England.

HIKING The area's must-do hike is **Mount Kineo** (see *Must See/Do*).
   Gulf Hagas, billed as the "Grand Canyon of Maine," is described in the Katahdin chapter. It's also accessible from Greenville via Airport Rd. When the pavement ends it's another 12.6 miles to the Hedgehog Gate, where you pay a toll and can pick up a map. It's another 2

miles to the trailhead parking lot. In winter it's also accessible by snowshoe or ski from the AMC's **Little Lyford** and **Gorman Chairback Wilderness Lodges** (see *Lodging*).

Big Moose Mountain. The trail leaves Rt. 15 north of Greenville. This a challenging three- to four-hour hike to the summit at 5,267 feet. The trail is well marked.

⚘ **Borestone Mountain Audubon Sanctuary** (207-781-2330, ext. 215; maineaudubon .org). A good hike for families. From Rt. 6/15 in Monson turn north onto Elliotsville Rd. Follow the chickadee signs 8 miles and cross the bridge over Big Wilson Falls. Bear left, uphill over railroad tracks. Park in lot on your left, across from the sanctuary gate. At 1.5 miles the little **Moore Nature Center** houses interpretive displays. Connected trails lead 2.5 miles to Borestone's rocky West Peak; a blazed trail continues another 0.5 mile to the East Peak (elevation 2,000 feet) for a 360-degree view.

The Appalachian Trail (appalachiantrail.org) is most easily accessed in this area from the parking area on Rt. 15 in Monson. The 100-mile wilderness segment north of this spot is one of the most popular, most scenic—and most difficult.

Check local sources for details about hiking **Little** and **Big Spencer Mountains** and **Elephant Mountain**.

MARINAS Big Lake Equipment Marina (207-695-4487), 25 Lakeview St., Greenville, offers slips, fuel, and supplies. **Beaver Cove Marina** (207-395-3526; beavercovemarina.com), 8 miles north of Greenville on the eastern side of the lake, offers slips, boat launch, fuel, repairs.

MOUNTAIN BIKING Rentals are available from **Northwoods Outfitters** (207-695-3288) in Greenville and from **The Birches Resort** (207-534-7305) in Rockwood, which maintains an extensive trail network on its 10,000 wooded acres.

The Appalachian Mountain Club (outdoors.org/mwi) maintains an ever-increasing network of bike/ski trails around its backwoods lodges and cabins.

SWIMMING Lily Bay State Park (207-695-2700), 8 miles north of Greenville, offers a sandy beach, a grassy picnicking area, and separate camping area. It's a superlatively beautiful spot. $4.50 nonresidents, $3 residents, $1.50 all seniors day-use fee.

Red Cross Beach, halfway between Greenville Village and the Junction, is a good beach on the lake, with lifeguards.

WHITEWATER RAFTING AND KAYAKING Moosehead Lake is equidistant from Maine's two most popular rafting routes—**Kennebec Gorge** and **Ripogenus Gorge**. See "Upper Kennebec" and "Katahdin Region."

❋ Winter Sports

CROSS-COUNTRY SKIING AND SNOWSHOEING Groomed trails aside this region's vast network of snowmobile trails and frozen lakes constitute splendid opportunities for backcountry skiing.

❂ **The Appalachian Mountain Club** (outdoors.org) maintains 80 miles of groomed trails connecting four sporting camps and facilitates lodge-to-lodge skiing. See the sidebar for details about the three AMC **Wilderness Lodges** and **West Branch Pond Camps**. We have been and can vouch for the improved access the AMC has brought to one of the most splendid cross-country experiences in New England. Whether you ski from lodge to lodge or stay at just one, the AMC, working with Northwoods Outfitters, offers rentals (and shuttle service).

✪ **Birches Ski Touring Center** (207-534-7305), Rockwood, rents equipment, offers lessons, and maintains an extensive network of trails, taking advantage of an 11,000-acre forested spread across the neck between Brassua and Moosehead Lakes; you can spend the night in yurts spaced along the trail. You can also ski to Tomhegan, 10 miles up the lake, or out past the ice-fishing shanties to Kineo. Rentals and instruction; snowshoes, too.

DOGSLEDDING **Song in the Woods** (207-876-4736; songinthewoods.com), Abbot. Stephen Medera and his team of huskies offer sled rides ranging from two hours to multiday adventures.

ICE FISHING usually begins in January and ends with March. Icehouse rentals are available locally. Inquire at the chamber.

SNOWMOBILING is huge in this area, with 500 well-maintained miles of snowmobile trails. **Moosehead Riders Snowmobile Club** offers a 24-hour trail-condition report (207-695-4561) on the 166-mile trail circumnavigating the lake. The club also sponsors guided tours. Interconnecting Trail System (ITS) Rts. 85, 86, and 87 run directly through the area, and there are many locally groomed trails as well. The 100-mile Moosehead Trail circles the lake. Rt. 66 runs east–west from Mount Kineo to Kokadjo. Snowmobile rentals and guided tours are available from **Northwoods Outfitters** (207-695-3288) and **Moosehead Motorsports** (207-695-2020) in Greenville; in Rockwood **The Birches Resort** (1-800-825-9453) rents and offers guided tours. Northeast of the lake **Kokadjo Trading Post** (207-695-3993) offers rentals, cabins, and food at the hub of a trail system. See mooseheadlake.org for additional rental listings.

❋ Green Space

Katahdin Iron Works Property falls between the Katahdin and Moosehead Lake areas, a 37,000-acre tract of forest maintained by the **Appalachian Mountain Club** (outdoors.org) with more than 55 miles of trails for hiking, snowshoeing, skiing, and mountain biking. Local snowmobile clubs also maintain 17.5 miles of groomed trails, including the east–west ITS route connecting Greenville and Brownville. Campsite reservations can be made through the **KI Jo-Mary Multiple Use Forest** (207-965-8135). Hunting, fishing, and trapping are allowed, but to protect the integrity of the headwaters of the West Branch and Pleasant Rivers, the surrounding area is closed to motorized traffic; 113 miles of logging roads remain open. The AMC maintains **Little Lyford Lodge and Cabins** and **Gorman Chairback Lodge and Cabins** in this area (see *Lodging*). **Moose Point Cabin** is available for rent. The AMC maintains an office in Greenville (207-695-3085). The **Appalachian Trail** traverses this area, and the **Gulf Hagas** section (detailed under *Green Space* in the Katahdin chapter) is spectacular. The **Chairback Mountain** section of the AT (16 miles east of Greenville) is also a popular hike.

WATERFALLS See **Gulf Hagas** (see *Green Space* in "Katahdin Region") and **Moxie Falls** (*To See* in "Upper Kennebec Valley"), both accessible from the Greenville area.

✳ Lodging

INNS ✪ ♂ (◌) **The Blair Hill Inn** (207-695-0224; blairhillinn.com), 351 Lily Bay Rd., Greenville. Open mid-May–Oct. An airy Victorian mansion overlooking Moosehead Lake from high atop Blair Hill, this is Maine's most gracious inland inn. The view can be enjoyed from comfortable wicker on the veranda, deep armchairs by the hearth in the living room, or tables in the dining room or pub. The mansion has been sensitively restored to its original grandeur—and then some—by Dan and Ruth McLaughlin. Upstairs eight guest rooms all offer a sitting area, a featherbed, fine linens, and flat-screen TV, DVD, and CD player. Seven rooms overlook the lake (four have a wood-burning fireplace), and there is a two-room suite, good for families (children must be 10 or older); a ground floor suite features a tiled fireplace and French doors opening onto a private balcony. $298–495 includes a multi-course breakfast served on the sunporch. A five-course prix fixe dinner is served Thu.–Sat. (see *Dining Out*).

🐾 ♿ **The Lodge at Moosehead Lake** (207-695-4400 or 1-800-825-6977; lodgeatmoose headlake.com), 368 Lily Bay Rd., Greenville. Open except Apr., Nov. Set above the lake, this rustic mansion has five themed guest rooms. Carved four-poster beds depict each theme (moose, bear, loon, totem). All rooms have cable TV, gas fireplace, air-conditioning, and bath with Jacuzzi tub. There are four more suites, each with double Jacuzzi and private deck, in the Carriage House. Common space includes a living room and an informal downstairs pub with a pool table. Dinner is served weekends in-season; drinks available in Chloe's pub. $250–695 includes full breakfast.

✪ ♂ ♿ (◌) **Greenville Inn** (207-695-2206 or 1-888-695-6000; greenvilleinn.com), Norris St., Greenville. Open all year (B&B Nov.–May). A lumber baron's mansion set atop a hill with a view of Moosehead Lake. Rich wood paneling, embossed walls, working fireplaces, and leaded glass all contribute to the sense of elegance. Terry and Jeffrey Johannemann have added air-conditioning. A master suite with a fireplace in a separate sitting room has a lake view, and there are four more attractive

THE GREENVILLE INN IS A LUMBER BARON'S MANSION

second-floor rooms in the mansion itself, two more spacious suites (one good for a family of six) in the Carriage House, and six cottages that sit high behind the inn, each tastefully decorated. A separate Tower Suite, painted valentine red, has been designed for romance with an in-room, two-person Jacuzzi. Rooms $160–198, suites $265–279, cottages $189–249, buffet breakfast included; many packages. Also see *Dining Out*.

CABINS

Note: Check **mooseheadlake.org** for a larger list of traditional cabins and individual rentals. Here are our top picks.

✪ 🐾 ♂ (◌) **The Birches Resort** (207-534-7305 or 1-800-825-WILD; birches.com), 281 The Birches Rd. Open year-round. Location! Not your usual resort, this is a 1930s sporting camp that's been in John Willard's family since 1969, and he has expanded it to include 11,000 wooded acres. We love the 17 original rustic cabins, spaced among birch trees along the narrows in Moosehead Lake overlooking Mount Kineo. But be forewarned, as their prices suggest, these are traditional hand-hewn log "camps." If its lakeside luxury you want, that too is available here in a choice of contemporary homes farther along the shore with up to four bedrooms, four baths, and a hot tub. The central lodge features an open-timbered dining room (see *Dining Out*) and a pub with tree-stump stools. Upstairs are the four guest rooms (shared bath); there are also "Kozy Kabins" near the lodge and several yurts scattered along wooded cross-country skiing/biking trails. There's an outside hot tub and sauna near the lodge and a fitness center out by the marina. Moose cruises, guided kayak tours, and biking tours are offered, along with fly-fishing, whitewater rafting, family paddling at East Outlet, and scenic floatplane rides. Sailboats, kayaks, canoes, fishing boats, and mountain bikes are available. In winter there are 38 miles of maintained cross-country trails (overnights in trailside yurts available). Snowmobiles are rented and there's ice fishing within walking distance of the cabins. High season: $85–128 for lodge rooms; $180–207 per night, $1,080–1,240 per week for one-bedroom "rustic" cabins; $480 per night for a luxury four-bedroom cabin sleeping eight. Kozy Kabins begin at $85 per first person per night, $15 per additional person; yurts begin at $75. Pets are $10 per night; rafting, canoeing, and other packages.

EASILY ACCESSIBLE CAMPS ✪ 🐾 ✒ Gray Ghost Camps (207-534-7362; grayghost camps.com), Jackman Rd., Rockwood. A dozen nicely renovated 1950s fishing camps on the Moose River, with access to

Moosehead Lake. In the same family for 40 years, now ably managed by Steve and Amy Lane. One- to four-room cabins, each with a full kitchen, bath, living room, TV, VCR, and CD. From $100 per night; $600 per week including tax, use of kayaks, canoes, and water facilities. Extras: boat rentals, laundry facilities, docking. Pets are $5 per day.

🐾 **Wilson Pond Camps** (207-695-2860; wilsonpondcamps.com), 51 Lower Wilson Pond Rd., Greenville. Open year-round. Bob and Martine Young are the owners of five modern waterfront cottages (most with wood-stove) and two cottages overlooking 7-mile-long Lower Wilson Pond, 3.5 miles from downtown Greenville. A remote cottage called Top Secret Lodge, on Upper Wilson Pond, accepts pets. The housekeeping cottages offer one to three bedrooms, fully equipped kitchen, and screened-in porch. Boats and motors, kayak and canoe rentals are available. From $150 a day for two in-season.

REMOTE FULL-SERVICE SPORTING CAMPS All require a four-wheel-drive or high-clearance vehicle, and in winter possibly either snowmobile or nonmotorized access; inquire about fly-in access.

THE BIRCHES RESORT

Christina Tree

✪ ⚭ 🐾 ♿ **West Branch Pond Camps**
(207-695-2561; westbranchpondcamps.
com), P.O. Box 1153, Greenville 04441. An
easy 10-mile drive off the Lily Bay Road, also
accessible by floatplane. Open after ice-out
through Sept., and Jan. 21–Mar. 21. This is
a magical place and prime moose-viewing
spot. Eric Stirling is the fourth generation of
his family to run this classic cluster of nine
weathered, waterside log sporting camps and
lodge, with a view across the lake to majestic
White Cap Mountain. The family now owns
the property outright, after a century of
leasing the land, and an easement protects
the surrounding woodland and White Cap
itself from development. All nine cabins
(total capacity 36) have woodstove, electricity (6–9 PM), and bathrooms in summer;
a shower house (with toilets) in winter. The
furnishings are comfortable, with some rare
"rustic" pieces. Food is hearty New England
fare with a set menu—prime rib on Thu. and
turkey dinner on Sun.—with fresh vegetables
and greens from the organic garden and
vegetarian fare on request. The 15 km of
trails Eric maintains for nonmotorized use
connect with the AMC network, and in winter dogsledding as well as cross-country and
snowshoeing treks are offered in conjunction
with the AMC. It's a way to sample the differ-
ence between the nonprofit's rehabbed "Wilderness Lodges" and a proudly preserved,
historic sporting camp. Eric is a stickler for
authenticity, constantly upgrading but with
an eye to preserving the look and feel of
the cabins (two date to the 1880s) and the
trophy-filled lodge. Summer dining is on a
sunporch overlooking the lake, and in winter
it's family-style in the big country kitchen.
Summer rates ($120 MAP per person, $175
single, $50 per child 5–11) include three
meals, firewood, and use of a rowboat or
canoe. In winter it's $125 per adult with two
hot meals and a bag lunch; BYO sleeping
bag. Two-day minimum stay.

🐾 ⚭ **Spencer Pond Camps** (207-745-
1599; spencerpond.com), 806 Spencer Pond
Rd., Greenville. Open May–mid-Nov. This
long-established cluster of six waterfront
housekeeping camps (sleeping 2–12) is off
the grid. This is in a beautiful spot, 14 miles
from the closest neighbor. Registered Maine
Guides Christine Howe and Dana Black, along
with their two daughters, are carrying on a

hospitable family tradition. Fly in or drive, 34
miles north of Greenville via a logging road
from Lily Bay Rd. Each camp is different, but
all have a screened porch from which to chill
and listen to the loons. Guests are welcome to
fresh vegetables from the gardens. There are
kerosene lights, water is hand-pumped, and
cottages are furnished with handmade quilts
and rocking chairs; each has a private shower
room (sunshower) and outhouse. The camp
library is stocked for rainy days. $62 per adult
per night, less for students and teens (free
under 12), includes use of canoes, kayaks,
mountain bikes, and a sailboat.

**OTHER REMOTE WOODLAND DESTINA-
TIONS Chesuncook Lake House and Cabins**
(207-745-5330; greatnorthernvacations.com).
Open year-round by reservation. While the
postal address is Greenville, this farmhouse/
boardinghouse was built in 1846 in the middle
of the North Woods (see the *Chesuncook Village* sidebar) to serve as a lumbering outpost.
David and Luisa Surprenant offer four guest
rooms (shared baths) and three housekeeping
cabins. With its braided rugs, patterned tin
walls and ceilings, comfortable furnishings,
and woodstoves, this is a peaceful, pleasant
place. You can paddle, drive, hike, fly, ski, or
snowmobile in. $150 per person includes
three meals and use of canoes and kayaks.
Cabins are $200–300 per night for four peo-
ple, $40 per extra person. $10 per dog.

🏕 **Historic Pittston Farm** (207-280-0000;
pittstonfarm.com), 20 mile Road, Rockwood.
Overlooking Seboomook Lake, 20 rough
miles north of Rockwood via dirt road, also
accessible by seaplane. A century ago Great
Northern Paper Company built the clapboard
lodge and barns here as a base for woodland
operations. It's currently owned by Jen and
Guy Mills, who cater to summer birdwatch-
ers, fall moose and bear hunters, and winter
snowmobilers. You are definitely in the North
Woods here, with plenty of mounted game
in the dining and living rooms. The complex
is powered by its own wind turbine. There
are homey lodge rooms with shared baths
and two large bunk rooms, also seven pine-
paneled motel-style units in the carriage
house, and a campground with RV hook-ups.
$80–120 for lodging; $40 per person with
three hearty meals, famed for from-scratch
baking.

AMC MAINE WOODS INITIATIVE

Founded in 1876 to blaze and map trails through the White Mountains, the Boston-based Appalachian Mountain Club (outdoors.org; reservations, 603-466-2727 or 207-358-5187) is best known for its lodges and high huts catering to hikers in New Hampshire's White Mountains. More recently the AMC has focused on the "100-Mile Wilderness Region" east of Moosehead Lake. It currently conserves 66,500 acres, working with local partners to foster recreation and sustainable forestry. It maintains 120 miles of trails for nonmotorized recreation and has renovated three historic "wilderness lodges." In summer and fall the focus is on hiking, paddling, fly-fishing, birding, and the family program; in winter options include lodge-to-lodge cross-country skiing, guided dogsledding, and snowshoeing. We can vouch for the beauty of skiing from **West Branch Pond Camps** (see *Lodging*) to **Little Lyford** with the AMC guides and shuttle service. The three AMC lodges are fully staffed. Open late Dec.–mid-Mar.; mid-May–late Oct. Towels and linens are provided at Gorman Chairback. Guests supply their own towels and linens at the other lodges. Also see *Hiking*, *Cross-Country Skiing*, and *Green Space*.

✪ ✐ **Little Lyford Lodge and Cabins**, 16 miles east of Greenville on the Katahdin Iron Works logging road. Open late Dec.–mid-Mar. and mid-May–late Oct. Reservations are required. Sited in a sheltered alpine valley, these camps were built in the 1870s as a logging company camp on a "tote road." The nine log cabins (including one that's ADA-accessible) have no plumbing or electricity but feature woodstoves and gas lamps, with cold running water in summer and fall. They sleep from one to six, and each has a private outhouse. A bunkhouse sleeps 12. The central lodge houses the dining room and space to relax. A spiffy bathroom/shower house is open year-round, and there's a sauna in winter. **Gulf Hagas** (see *Green Space* in "Katahdin Region") is a 7-mile roundtrip hike or ski and snowshoe, and six trails begin at the camp. In winter you can ski, dogsled, or hitch a snowmobile shuttle (along with your gear) to the camps. Spring, summer, and fall offer fly-fishing for wild brook trout in the two Little Lyford ponds, the West Branch Pleasant River, and surrounding remote ponds. From the camps, it's a short walk through the woods to a small pond where canoes and kayaks are stashed. Paddle across and follow a short path to the larger pond. Guests get trail lunches after breakfast and off they go. The camp is 4.5 miles off the Appalachian Trail. $105–151 per person in the cabins, $78–117 in the bunkhouse, includes all meals; less for youths (ages 13–17), children (2–12), and AMC members (save 20 percent), also for three- and five-night stays. There's a charge for the snowmobile shuttle and gear shuttle.

♿ **Gorman Chairback Lodge and Cabins**, 20 miles on logging roads east of Greenville, 15 west of Rt. 11 in Brownville. Open late Dec.–mid-Mar. and mid-May–late Oct. Also accessible by floatplane. Twelve cabins on secluded Long Pond, around 5 miles from Little Lyford. This is

MOTEL Chalet Moosehead Lakefront Motel (207-695-2950; mooseheadlodging.com), 12 North Birch St., Greenville Junction. Family owned for 20 years, this complex is away from the main drag, set in grassy lakeside grounds with grills and picnic tables, easy access to swimming and boating. All rooms have lakeside views; those in the two-story newer building have private balconies, whirlpool tub, and more amenities. $89–165 depending on room and season.

RENTALS Private camp rentals are listed with the chamber of commerce at moosehead lake.org. Also check listings at moosehead rentals.com.

CAMPGROUNDS ♿ **Lily Bay State Park** (207-695-2700). Open May–Oct. 15. Nine miles north of Greenville on the east shore of Moosehead Lake, this 925-acre park contains 92 well-spaced sites, many along the shore. Two are wheelchair-accessible; facilities include a shower house, boat launch, and beach. $25 nonresidents, $15 for Maine residents. It's advisable to reserve online at maine.gov/parks/reservations.

another classic sporting camp, dating from 1867. There are four new cabins with private bath (including one that's ADA-accessible) and eight renovated lakefront cabins, with woodstoves and gas lights, sleeping up to five. The standout here is Number 8, a late-1800s log octagon said to have been built by a one-armed Civil War veteran. Shelves on three walls are lined with books. A separate bunkhouse sleeps 10. Hot showers and composting toilets are in the spacious new LEED-registered central lodge, which is solar powered and offers a wood-fired sauna in winter. There's a sandy beach, good swimming; also free use of kayaks and canoes for guests. From here, it's also a 2.1-mile hike to Gulf Hagas with several water crossings. Regular cabin $120–179, deluxe cabin with private bath $151–221. Bunkhouse $78–117 (year-round). Fees include linens and towels as well as three meals. Less for youths (ages 13–17), children (2–12), and AMC members (save 20 percent), also for three- and five-night stays. There's a charge for the snowmobile shuttle and gear shuttle.

(**Medawisla**, a lodge sited on Second Roach Pond, is currently closed for renovations.)

Courtesy of Appalachian Mountain Club

GORMAN CHAIRBACK HAS RECENTLY BEEN RESTORED BY THE AMC

✳ Where to Eat

DINING OUT Blair Hill Inn (207-695-0224; blairhill.com), Lily Bay Rd., Greenville. Open to the public late June–mid-Oct., Thu.–Sat. Reservations recommended. A five-course menu with a choice of three entrées, served in the dining room or on the side porch with lake views. Guests tend to come early for a cocktail in the bar by the fire or to settle in with a drink on the porch and watch the sunset. The menu changes each week, using the freshest produce available. It might include poached lobster with fresh corn, baby turnips, a homemade spinach and ricotta manicotti, and a mixed berry vol-au-vent with pastry cream and white wine glaçage. $60 prix fixe. Figure $200 per couple with wine, tax, and tip.

Greenville Inn (207-695-2206 or 1-888-695-6000), Norris St., Greenville. Dinner served late June–mid-Oct., Mon.–Sat. Reservations requested. The oval-shaped dining room in this classic lumber baron's mansion is charming, with views up the lake. Currently you might dine on wild mushroom risotto,

LAKE WATCHING AT THE BIRCHES

Dijon chicken, or cheese ravioli with sautéed lobster. The seasonal fall soup was butternut squash with gingered pumpernickel croutons. There's always a vegan option. Entrées $24–33.

The Birches Resort (207-534-2242), Rockwood. Open year-round: daily in summer, check otherwise. The log-sided dining room (see *Lodging*) has a many-windowed wall overlooking the lake, a massive stone hearth, and a canoe turned upside down in the open rafters. The food is family-geared and -priced. The baby back ribs could feed two. Entrées come with salad, a veggie, and starch: $14–24. Reservations suggested. There's also an inviting pub. Lunch soups, sandwiches, and salads. Part of the fun here is watching patrons paddle, sail, motor, and fly up to the dock.

🦌 **Maynard's Dining Room** (207-534-7703), off Rt. 6/15, Rockwood. Open year-round but check for meals, in-season dinner 5–7:30 Fri. and Sat.; otherwise from 5:30. Dine as your grandparents would have in the traditional old lodge dining room overlooking the Moose River. Choices vary with the night; $21.95 includes entrée, juice or soup, salad, choice of potato or veggie, bread, dessert, and beverage. BYOB. Friday draws a knowing crowd for the prime rib, Saturday for baby back ribs, and Sunday for the roast turkey dinner. You can also stay at this classic sportsmen's camp,

maintained by the Maynard family since 1919. Overlooking the Moose River, a short walk from Moosehead Lake, its 14 tidy moss-green cabins contain dark Edwardian furniture, much of it from the grand old Mount Kineo Hotel. The lodge is filled with mounted fish, birds, and other trophies.

Historic Pittston Farm (207-280-0000; pittstonfarm.com), Rockwood. Open year-round 7–7. Destination dining. The food is hearty and fresh, featuring from-scratch baking. See *Lodging* for more about this wilderness outpost, built in the early 1900s as a major hub of Great Northern's logging operations. Breakfast is ready by 4:30 AM during hunting season; otherwise, 7 AM. Lunch includes a make-your-own sandwich bar, fish stews, and burgers. The buffet all-you-can-eat dinner is 5–7 every night. BYOB.

EATING OUT

IN GREENVILLE

✂ **Kelly's Landing** (307-695-4438; kellysat moosehead.com, 13 Rockwood Rd. (Rt. 15), Greenville Junction. Open daily 11:30–8:30. Hidden away by the water (look for the sign by the RR trestle), this is a big, friendly dining room with deep booths, water views, and a fireplace, plus a long, umbrella-shaded deck by the water. Fresh soups and salad bar, great burgers and onion rings at lunch, and a big dinner menu featuring prime rib, nightly specials. Sunday brunch menu. Easy parking and docking.

Rod 'n' Reel Café (207-695-0388), 44 Pritham Ave., Greenville. Open year-round for dinner, usually lunch in summer (call to check). Newly renovated, air-conditioned. Fish and seafood, chowders and salads are the specialties, but a full menu includes prime rib specials. Fully licensed with reasonable wine prices.

Flatlander's Pub (207-695-3373), 39 Pritham Ave. Open daily (except in winter when it's closed on Wed.) from 11 AM "until closing." The specialty is "broasted" chicken; other choices include hamburgers, seafood, and homemade desserts. Reasonable prices.

Jamieson's Market/Jamo's Pizza (207-695-2201), Pritham Ave. and West St. This is a downtown source of fast, good, reasonably priced take-out ranging from breakfast sandwiches through subs, wraps, and pizza; also groceries, beer, wine, and crawlers.

Claudine Crêpe, lakefront, downtown Greenville. Look for this classic food truck, open daily in-season except Sun., 11–6. Savory as well as sweet crêpes—maybe opt for the spinach and goat cheese with caramelized onions.

BEYOND GREENVILLE

Kokadjo Trading Post (207-695-3993; kokadjo.com), Kokadjo. Open 7 AM–closing; earlier during hunting season. Fred and Marie Candeloro offer a cozy dining room with a large fieldstone fireplace and a view of First Roach Pond. Terrific fish sandwich at lunch, custom-cut Black Angus steaks at dinner. Inquire about cabins.

ON THE WAY TO GREENVILLE

Note: Blink and you are through **Monson**—but don't miss two great places to eat.

Spring Creek Bar-B-Q (207-997-7025), Rt. 15, Monson. Open Thu.–Sun. 10–6 or when the food is gone; also open Mon. seasonally. Closed Dec. and Apr. Ribs are the big specialty here, but you might want to reserve (you can call days ahead), because they run out toward the end of the day. Also good for standard road food.

Lakeshore House Pub & Eatery (207-997-7069; lakeshore-house.com), 9 Tenney Hill Rd. (Rt. 15), Monson. Open for lunch and again in the evening for light fare. Geared to AT hikers with six rooms upstairs, this place also has a great rep for reasonably priced food, with the option of the back deck overlooking Lake Hebron, weather permitting. Sunday afternoon music. Children's menu.

FOR DOVER-FOXCROFT SEE KATAHDIN AREA CHAPTER

✷ Selective Shopping

IN GREENVILLE

Indian Hill Trading Post (207-695-3376), Greenville. Open daily year-round, Thu. until 9. Huge—a combination sports store, supermarket, and general store, stocking everything you might need for a week or two in the woods.

Moosehead Indian Store at Kamp Kamp (207-695-0795; kampkamp.com) 3 Lily Bay Rd. Greenville. Downtown Greenville's most

Christina Tree

JOE BOLF, WOOD CARVER EXTRAORDINAIRE

colorful store, now an amalgam of the old Indian Store, stuffed with North Woods souvenirs, toys, and gadgets; upscale rustic furniture; clothing and decorative items; plus taxidermy, maybe a mounted "koyote."

Northwoods Outfitters (207-695-3288), selling sporting gear and wear, now occupies the space vacated by Greenville's other old commercial landmark, Sanders Store. It includes a small cyber café.

The Corner Shop (207-695-2142), corner of Main and Pritham (across from Great Eastern Clothing), Greenville. Gifts, books, magazines, and fudge.

Moosin' Around Maine (207-695-3939), Pritham Ave., downtown Greenville. Pottery, jewelry, blown glass from Maine and beyond.

Joe Bolf Woodcarver (207-695-0380), 11 Minden St., Greenville. Off Moosehead Lake Road near the downtown junction. Check out these woodcarvings, large and small.

Book Nook (207-695-3696), 13 Moosehead Lake Rd. (Rt. 15). Open year-round, 9–5. An inviting store with nicely arranged "pre-owned books" in almost-new condition.

See also the **Maine Guide Fly Shop** under *Fishing*.

✳ Special Events

January: **Ice fishing derby**, Greenville.

February: **Snofest**, Greenville—snowmobile events, 100-mile sled dog race.

Late May–mid-June: **Moosemainea** month (mooseheadlake.org) throughout the area.

July: The **Fourth of July** is big in Greenville, with a crafts fair, food booths, music, parade, fireworks, and street dance. **Thoreau-Wabanaki Festival. Friday Night Concert Series** at the gazebo.

August: **Forest Heritage Days**, Greenville—crafts fair and many forestry-related events.

Second weekend of September: **International Seaplane Fly-In Weekend**, Greenville.

KATAHDIN REGION

*Including Gulf Hagas, Lower Piscataquis,
and Lincoln Lakes*

Mile-high Mount Katahdin rises massively from a vast green woodland sea, mirrored in nearby lakes and clearly visible from a surprising distance. Maine's highest mountain and the northern terminus of the Appalachian Trail, it's been synonymous with hiking since Henry David Thoreau described his first climb to the top in 1846.

The trails leading to the summit still represent the most popular hikes in the state, but climbers can also choose from several less-trafficked mountains within the surrounding 204,733 acres of Baxter State Park, all with views of Katahdin itself. In all the park offers hiking on 300 miles of trails, as well as fishing on remote lakes and ponds.

Hiking is just one of the many ways to accomplish what's described locally as "getting out," which is what this area is about. Fishing and hunting have long been a way of life; more recently whitewater rafters have been plunging down the West Branch of the Penobscot River through Ripogenus Gorge, the ultimate rafting run in the Northeast.

Early-morning and evening moose-watching is another ritual. Organized excursions are offered, but there are also many well-known spots where you're likely to see moose at sunset. Scenic flights are another popular way of moose-spotting and circling Katahdin, and floatplanes ferry guests to remote sporting camps and fishing spots. The winter months are predictably snowy, and there's a big commitment to maintaining snowmobile, cross-country skiing, and snowshoeing systems. Dogsledding and ice fishing are also draws.

The nearest town to Katahdin is Millinocket, a lumbering outpost that boomed into existence around the Great Northern Paper Company mills. The population skyrocketed from two families to 2,000 people between 1888 and 1900, and to 5,000 in 1912.

As recently as the 1980s the company's two mills—the second in East Millinocket—employed more than 4,500 workers, which is roughly the same number of residents left in town these days. Both mills have been closed in the past few years and the economic focus is shifting to attracting more outdoors-minded visitors. Local support for the establishment of a national park east of Baxter State Park is gaining momentum.

Currently most visitors head for Baxter State Park's Togue Gate, 18 miles northwest of Millinocket, stopping by the causeway separating pristine Lake Millinocket, separated by a narrow and Ambajejus Lake. Within walking distance here you can board a floatplane or cruise boat and stock up on supplies, food, and lodging.

Southwest of Millinocket, lower Piscataquis County is largely woodland traversed (north–south) by Rt. 11, the old road to Millinocket before the advent of I-95. This is a slice of "the real Maine," with Dover-Foxcroft (pop. roughly 4,200) as its big town. The relatively little-known treasures here are 13-mile-long Sebec Lake, site of **Peaks-Kenny State Park**, **Gulf Hagas**, billed as "Maine's Grand Canyon," and the Lincoln Lakes region to the southwest.

GUIDANCE **Katahdin Area Chamber of Commerce** (207-723-4443; katahdinmaine.com), 1029 Central St. (Rt. 11/157), Millinocket. Open weekdays. This staffed information center is the source of the *Katahdin Area Visitors Guide*, maps, and brochures.

The **Baxter State Park Headquarters** (207-723-5140; baxterstateparkauthority.com), 64 Balsam Dr., Millinocket, is open Memorial Day–Columbus Day, daily 8–4; otherwise weekdays. Just off Rt. 11/57 on a service road (next to McDonald's), it's the park's prime source of maps and guides; there are also picnic tables and restrooms (see the *Baxter State Park* sidebar).

Piscataquis County Chamber of Commerce (207-564-7533; piscataquischamber.org), 1033 South St. (Rt. 7), Dover-Foxcroft. This log information center is open Wed.–Fri. 9–2, when volunteers are available. The website lists rental camps and lodging options.

GETTING THERE The most direct route from points south is I-95 to Exit 244 in Medway (73 miles northeast of Bangor) and 12 miles into Millinocket. From here, it's about 10 miles to Millinocket Lake, and from there another 8 miles to the Togue Pond entrance to Baxter State Park. Alternately exit I-95 in Newport and follow Rt. 11/7 north to Dover-Foxcroft for **Peaks-Kenny State Park**, on up through Milo and Brownville Junction (the turnoff for **Gulf Hagas**). From the Midcoast the shortest way to this area is Rt. 220 north from Waldoboro to Newport, a beautiful drive in its own right.

From the Moosehead Lake area: Millinocket is 70 miles northeast of Greenville via the **Golden Road**. Check conditions locally before setting out. It's not wise to exceed 20 MPH; lumber trucks have the right of way.

GETTING AROUND *By air:* **Katahdin Air Service Inc.** (207-723-8378 or 1-866-359-6246; katahdinair.com), Millinocket. Available May–Nov. to fly in to remote camps and shuttle in canoes and campers; will drop hikers at points along the Appalachian Trail. Also scenic flights, ranging from a 15-minute trip along the base of Mount Katahdin to a day exploring remote lakes, also fly-in fishing trips and fly-and-dine packages. **West Branch Aviation LLC** (207-723-4375), based at the Millinocket Municipal Airport (16 Medway Rd.), also offers scenic flights and shuttle service using both sea- and standard planes.

By road: **Woods & Waters Scenic Byway**. This 89-mile circuit begins (or ends) at Baxter State Park's Togue Pond Gate, runs up Rt. 11 to Patten, and veers off on Rt. 159 to Shin Pond. Highlights include the view from Ash Hill in Stacyville, the Patten Lumberman's Museum, and Shin Pond.

WHEN TO COME Spring draws fishermen; May and June bring moose-watching and black flies; July and August are great for swimming, canoeing, and rafting; September and early October are best for hiking and foliage. Snowfall is dependable February into April.

✱ To See

KATAHDIN Maine's Mount Fuji, this is the region's number one year-round sight to see, not just to climb. Check out the **Baxter State Park** sidebar. Don't miss a sunset! At dusk locals and visitors alike gather at nearby lakes to watch the big sky as well as big mountain change hues. If you come no nearer than the interstate, don't pass up I-95's **A. J. Allee Scenic Overlook**, some 15 miles northeast of the Medway exit. Katahdin is impressive even at that distance.

Ambajejus Boom House (moreairphotos.com/boomhouse), Ambajejus Lake. Open year-round. Accessible via boat or snowmobile, or even by walking if you don't mind getting your feet wet. Riverman Chuck Harris has single-handedly restored this old boom house, former quarters for log drivers, as a museum about life during the river drives. Exhibits include tools, paintings, and photographs among the artifacts of the river-driving years.

Katahdin Scenic Cruises at Big Moose Inn (207-723-8391) and **Maine Quest Adventures** (207-447-5011; mainequestadventures.com) offer access.

Patten Lumbermen's Museum (207-528-2650; lumbermensmuseum.org), Shin Pond Rd. (Rt. 159), Patten. Open Memorial Day–June, Fri.–Sun. 10–4; July–Columbus Day, Tue.–Sun. 10–4. $8 adults, $7 seniors, $3 children. The museum, which encompasses more than 4,000 displays, is housed in nine buildings with exhibits ranging from giant log haulers to "gum books," the lumberman's scrimshaw: intricately carved boxes in which to keep spruce gum, a popular gift for a sweetheart. There are replicas of logging camps from different periods, dioramas, machinery, and photos as well as a bateau, more.

❋ To Do

AIR RIDES See *Getting Around.*

BOAT CRUISES **Katahdin Scenic Cruises** (207-723-2020) offers wildlife cruises on Millinocket and Ambajejus Lake daily June–Oct.

CANOEING/KAYAKING Rentals and Shuttles are offered by **Maine Quest Adventures** (207-447-5501; mainequestadventures.com). Only expert paddlers should attempt the East or West Penobscot Rivers, but many other options are described in the free *Hiking and Paddling Guide* published by the Katahdin Chamber of Commerce (katahdinmaine.com).

CAMPING AND CANOEING/KAYAKING EXPEDITIONS This area is often used as a starting point for trips on the **Allagash Wilderness Waterway**. There is also challenging canoeing on the East and West branches of the Penobscot River as well on the area's many lakes. **Katahdin Outfitters** (207-723-5700; katahdinoutfitters.com) specializes in trips up the Allagash, and **Maine Quest Adventures** (207-447-5011; mainequestqdvntures.com) offers Allagash as well as less ambitious tours. **New England Outdoor Center** (207-723-5438; neoc.com) offers two-day guided tours on the East branch of the Penobscot.

In Southern Piscataquis, **Peaks-Kenny State Park** (see *Green Space*) rents canoes to use on Sebec Lake.

FISHING **Dolby Flowage** is good for bass fishing, and the West Branch of the Penobscot River offers good salmon and trout angling. Check out the **Maine Department of Inland Fisheries and Wildlife**'s excellent website (mefishwildlife.com) for Katahdin area fishing spots and much more. **Maine Quest Adventures** (207-447-5011; mainequestadventures .com) offers customized fishing trips, from half a day to three days. Licenses are available at the **Millinocket municipal office** on Penobscot Ave. and at many of the area's stores, including the **North Woods Trading Post** on Millinocket Lake. For a complete list of guide services, contact the **North Maine Woods office** (207-435-6213; northmainewoods.org) in Ashland and the **Katahdin Area Chamber of Commerce** (207-723-4443; katahdinmaine .com) in Millinocket.

GOLF **Highlands Golf Course** (207-794-2433), Town Farm Rd., Lincoln; 18 holes with full-service clubhouse, rental carts, and clubs. **Green Valley Golf Course** (207-732-3006), Rt. 2, West Enfield. Eight holes. **Hillcrest Golf Course** (207-723-8410), 59 Grove St., Millinocket. Nine holes with full-service clubhouse, rental carts, and clubs.

HIKING See Baxter State Park and Gulf Hagas under *Green Space*.

MUST SEE

Baxter State Park (207-723-5140; baxterstateparkauthority .com; see *Guidance*). Like Acadia National Park, Baxter State Park's acreage was amassed privately and given to the public as a gift. In this case it was the gift of one individual: Percival Baxter (1876–1969). In 1921, at age 44, Baxter became one of the state's youngest governors; he was then re-elected for another term. He was unsuccessful, however, in convincing the Maine legislature to protect Katahdin and surrounding lands. Instead, in 1930 he himself paid $25,000 to buy 6,000 acres that included Maine's highest mountain. For the remainder of his life he continued to negotiate with paper companies and other landowners to increase the size of the park. Thanks to his legacy, it continued to grow even after his death and currently encompasses 209,501 acres.

While nominally a state park, it receives no state funds, and the Baxter State Park Authority operates under its own unique and complicated rules, dedicated to ensuring that this preserve "Shall forever be kept and remain in the Natural Wild State." Camping and even day-use admissions to the park are strictly limited. Rental canoes are available at several locations in the park.

There are only two entry points: Togue Pond Gate, 18 miles northwest of Millinocket, by far the most popular; and Matagamon Gate, in the northeast corner of the park. Both are open 6 AM– 10 PM, May 15–Oct. 15. After the close of the camping season on Oct. 15, the gates are open for day visitors only from 6 AM–7 PM until Nov. 30. Vehicles with Maine plates are admitted free, but others pay a $14 day-use fee.

The list of rules governing the park is long and detailed. No motorcycles, motorized trail bikes, ATVs, or pets are allowed in. Bicycles can be used on maintained roads only. Snowmobiles are allowed only on the ungroomed main Tote Road in the park. And so forth; the park goes through periodic reviews of the regulations, so pick up a current copy at headquarters or the visitors center, or check the website before heading in.

The park is open daily, but note the restricted camping periods and the special-use permits required Dec.–Mar. Vehicular access is not possible once snow blocks the roads—whether roads are blocked is determined on a day-to-day basis by the park director, so call ahead. Also note that prohibition on collecting any park plants, animals, or artifacts is strictly enforced unless you have applied to the BSP Research Committee at least six months in advance (see the website for guidelines) and have been approved by the director.

Ever since the 1860s—when Henry David Thoreau's account of his 1846 ascent of "Ktaadn" began to circulate—the demanding trails to Maine's highest summit (5,267 feet) have been among the most popular in the state. Climbing Katahdin itself is considered a rite of passage in Maine and much of the rest of New England. The result is a steady stream of humanity up and down the Katahdin trails, while other peaks, such as 3,488-foot Doubletop, offer excellent, less crowded hiking and views of Katahdin to boot.

Day-trippers should be aware that the number of vehicles allowed at specific trailheads is finite; when the parking lots fill, people are directed to other options for hiking. Eighty percent of day-trippers head for lots in the southern end of the park, with access to the most popular trails—but with 42 miles of road, 46 mountain peaks, and 205 miles of trails, there's plenty of room for everyone.

It's possible to reserve a trailhead parking space at some of the most popular trailheads— Roaring Brook, Abol, and Katahdin Stream; check the BSP website. There is still some room for first-come, first-served arrivals, though. All Day Use Parking Registration (DUPR) vehicles must be through the gate at 7 AM. Only then will the first-come, first-served vehicles be allowed in on the chance that a DUPR vehicle did not make it.

The climb to Katahdin's summit and back takes 8 to 12 hours. If you are determined to access the Roaring Brook Campground parking area for the Knife's Edge Trail (the legendary narrow link between Baxter and Pamola Peaks) via the Chimney Pond Trail, arrive early to give yourself enough time. Sleep in if you're heading to a mountain other than Katahdin; later in the day, there's rarely a line. Remember, all parties wishing to hike to Katahdin's summit, whether from Abol, Katahdin Stream, or Roaring Brook campground trailheads, must be through the gate by 7 AM with DUPR, or waiting in line earlier without.

The pamphlet *Day Use Hiking Guide*, available at the Togue Pond Visitors Center (located a short way before the Togue Pond Gate), locates and describes 32 trails. Park staff, here and at both gates, suggest appropriate trails given conditions and the time of day. Arriving midafternoon on a July Sunday we were advised to take the Hunt Trail (a popular way to the peak) only as far as Katahdin Stream Falls.

Another popular hike is **Sentinel Mountain** from the Kidney Pond Trailhead. The trail traverses moderate wooded terrain until the very end, when it abruptly ascends to a series of excellent vantage points with views in several directions. A flat alternative is the **Daicey Pond Nature Trail**, 1.7 miles around Daicey Pond. **Doubletop Mountain** offers a full day hike with several mileage options: 9.6 miles round-trip hiking up and down from Kidney Pond Trailhead, 6.6 miles round-trip from the Nesowadnehunk Trailhead, and 7.9 miles hiking from Kidney to Nesowadnehunk Trailhead or vice versa. **South Turner Mountain Trail** from Roaring Brook via Sandy Stream Pond (4 miles round-trip) is a good wildlife-watching trail. Many hikers base themselves at Chimney Pond Campground and tackle Katahdin from there on one of several trails. A wide selection of retail maps and trail guidebooks is available at park headquarters in Millinocket. Pick up *Katahdin: A Guide to Baxter State Park*, edited and compiled by BSP.

CAMPING RESERVATIONS Camping is permitted May 15–Oct. 15 and Dec.–Apr. 1. Summer reservations for sites throughout the park are on a rolling reservation system. Space can be reserved four months in advance by mail, phone, in person, or online. Download the form at baxterstateparkauthority.com. All campsite reservations can be made online except Chimney Pond, Russell Pond, Davis Pond, Wassataquoik Lake Island, bunkhouse spaces, group sites, and ADA-accessible sites. The 10 campgrounds are widely scattered; there are no hook-ups, and you carry out what you carry in. Two campgrounds, Daicey Pond and Kidney Pond, offer **traditional cabins** with beds, gas lanterns, firewood, and tables and chairs; $55 a night for a two-bed cabin, $75 for three-bed cabins, $100 for a four-bed cabin, and $150 for a six-person cabin. Six more campgrounds, accessible by road, offer a mix of **bunkhouses, lean-tos,** and **tent sites** (in summer bunkhouses cost $11 per person per night; lean-tos and tenting sites are $30). Two other popular campgrounds, **Chimney Pond** and **Russell Pond**, require hiking in. Several individual backcountry sites are available by reservation for backpackers. Check restrictions before planning your trip. Ideally, allow three to five days at a campground like Trout Brook Farm, in the northern wilderness area of the park, or base yourself at Russell Pond (a 7- or 9-mile hike in from the road, depending on where you begin) and hike to the Grand Falls and Lookout Ledges.

Payment must accompany the reservation request. The mailing address is Baxter State Park, 64 Balsam Dr., Millinocket 04462. Enclose a stamped, self-addressed envelope for confirmation. July through mid-Aug. weekends fill quickly, but tent sites midweek and earlier or later in the season are possible. For a current update on this rolling reservation system, contact the park directly (see *Guidance*) or visit its website.

MOOSE-WATCHING

IN AND AROUND MILLINOCKET

Maine Quest Adventures (207-447-5011; mainequestadventures.com) offers canoe and kayak moose-spotting paddles, also moose cruises via pontoon boat on Katahdin Lake. **New England Outdoor Center** (1-800-634-7238; neoc.com) offers moose tours primarily by pontoon boat. Alternatively, ask locally about likely moose-watching spots.

SWIMMING ♦ **Medway Recreation Complex** in Medway and Jerry Pond in Millinocket offer family-geared beaches, picnic areas, and playgrounds. **Ambajejus Lake** has a public boat landing and also offers a small public beach. **Mattawamkeag Wilderness Park** (207-736-4881), off Rt. 2 in Mattawamkeag (11 miles southeast of I-95's Medway exit), offers a sand beach on the river, also picnic tables, hot showers, a recreation hall, and a playground. Nominal day-use fee.

Peaks-Kenny State Park (207-654-2003), Rt. 156, six miles northeast of Dover-Foxcroft, is a great family beach with lawns, playground, and a roped-in swimming area. Hiking trails and camping; day-use fee.

Note: Swimming opportunities abound in Baxter State Park and the many lakes around Millinocket.

WHITEWATER RAFTING The West Branch of the Penobscot represents the most challenging commercial whitewater rafting in Maine (you must be at least 15). Rafters are bused from their base camps to the put-in below McKay Station from which point the river drops more than 70 feet per mile—seething and roiling through **Ripogenus Gorge**—and continues another 12 miles, with stretches of relatively calm water punctuated by steep drops like the Cribworks and on to Nesowadnehunk Falls. Trips run late Apr.–mid-Oct., but we suggest midsummer through early foliage season. Rates are lower midweek than on weekends.

✪ **New England Outdoor Center** (207-723-5438 or 1-800-634-7238; neoc.com). This is the most established outfitter in this area and offers a variety of rafting trips, from high adventure to family float trips, also a range of lodging options, from tent and cabin sites at the **Penobscot Outdoor Center** (penobscotoutdoorcenter.com) on Pockwockamus Pond cabins to ecologically designed "guest houses" with views of Katahdin at **Twin Pine Camps** on Millinocket Lake (see *Lodging*)

Northern Outdoors (1-800-765-7238; northernoutdoors.com), New England's oldest whitewater rafting company, is based in The Forks on the Kennebec River, but has also been a longtime operator on the Penobscot. It's currently based at **Abol Bridge Campground and Store** (see *Campgrounds*) with sites on the Penobscot and a full-service restaurant, also bunkhouses and housekeeping cabins at Rip Dam.

❄ Winter Sports

CROSS-COUNTRY SKIING AND SNOWSHOEING **Millinocket Municipal Cross-Country Ski Area** is the name of the community's free, 40 km-plus network of groomed cross-country ski trails (20 km novice, 10 km intermediate, and 10 km expert terrain). These are divided between two distinct areas, linked by a 5-mile wooded trail. The **Bait Hole Area** is well marked 2.7 miles south of town on Rt. 11; the **Northern Timber Cruisers Clubhouse** (see *Snowmobiling*) on Baxter State Park Rd. is the departure point for the second network. Many skiers also continue on Baxter State Park Rd. and ski Periphery or Telos Rds. Within Baxter State Park, the road to the Hidden Springs campground is maintained for skiers.

Note: **Katahdin Lake Wilderness Camps** cater to cross-country skiers, offering spectacular backcountry trails, and are accessible only by skis. See *Lodging.*

DOGSLED TOURS **Maine Dogsledding Adventures** (207-731-8888; mainedogsledding .com). Don and Angel Hibbs have traveled more than 40,000 miles by dogsled. They offer half- and full-day dogsled runs in the forest and lakes just south of Baxter State Park.

SNOWMOBILING This region offers more than 350 miles of groomed trails, and more than 10 snowmobile clubs in the area to consult. A snowmobile map available at the Katahdin Area Chamber of Commerce shows the Interconnecting Trail System (ITS) trails. **The Northern Timber Cruisers Antique Snowmobile Museum** (northerntimbercruisers.com), on Baxter State Park Rd. next to the group's clubhouse, traces the history of snowmobiling in the region. It's open winter weekends.

New England Outdoor Center (207-723-5438 or 1-800-634-7238; neoc.com) has the area's largest rental fleet at Twin Pines (see *Lodging*). They offer half-day, full-day, and overnight guided snowmobile excursions, multiday packages, a complete shop, gas for sleds, clothing, and an ITS 85/56 trailside restaurant.

✳ Green Space

Gulf Hagas Reserve is a remote part of the Appalachian Trail corridor, jointly owned and managed by the Appalachian Trail Conference and the National Park Service. It's best accessed (3.1 miles) from the Katahdin Iron Works, marked from Rt. 11 in Brownsville. At the North Maine Woods Gate ($10 nonresidents, $9 residents) you should purchase a trail map. The parking area for the trailhead is at Hay Brook. Billed as the "Grand Canyon of Maine," this 2.5-mile-long gorge with walls up to 40 feet high was carved by the West Branch of the Pleasant River. At the beginning of the trail you will need to cross the river in ankle- to calf-high water. The trail threads a 35-acre stand of virgin white pines, some more than 130 feet tall, a landmark in its own right known as **The Hermitage** and preserved by The Nature Conservancy. The trail then follows the river along the Appalachian Trail for a ways, but turns off along the rim of the canyon toward dramatic **Screw Auger Falls** and on through **The Jaws** to **Buttermilk Falls**, **Stair Falls**, and **Billings Falls**. The trail winds through the woods, almost always moving either up or down. Turnouts offer views of the falls and the gorge. The hike back is flatter, and logs cover mud in some spots. Many visitors come only as far as the first waterfall for a swim and a picnic. Allow six to eight hours for the hike, and plan to camp at one of the waterside campsites within the **Jo-Mary Lake Campground** (see *Camping*) or at one of the two nearby **AMC Wilderness Lodges** (see sidebar in the Moosehead chapter).

Peaks-Kenny State Park (207-564-2003), Sebec Lake Rd., Dover-Foxcroft. The centerpiece of this park is Sebec Lake (13 miles long, 3 miles wide), with its popular beach, but there are also 9 miles of hiking trails and campsites.

MULTI-USE TRAILS **Katahdin Region Multi-Use Trail** (KRMUT). Park on the State Road to Baxter State Park from Millinocket to hike this 16.5-mile trail, which runs south, paralleling Rt. 11, before connecting with ATV and snowmobile networks. It's also suited to mountain bikes and cross-country skiers.

Newport/Dover-Foxcroft Rail Trail. This 17-mile, multiuse trail begins in Newport, running from the north side of Rt. 7 in Newport to Fairview St. in Dover-Foxcroft, threading woods, farms, and wetlands along Sebasticook Lake, Corundel Lake, and the Sebasticook and Piscataquis Rivers.

✳ Lodging

Christina Tree

BIG MOOSE INN

❂ (ᵥ) 🐾 ✑ **New England Outdoor Center** (1-800-634-7238; neoc.com), P.O. Box 669. Sited on Millinocket Lake with a great view of Katahdin, 20 cabins of different sizes and shapes are scattered in the pines, and a number of newer "guest houses" are set back in a wooded area. The latter are "green built," using recycled, nontoxic, and local materials, warmed with radiant heat, and have living rooms with cathedral ceilings. All share a rec lodge with a hot tub, satellite TV, table tennis, and ample outdoor space that includes a swim dock and small beach. Canoes and kayaks are available for guests; paddleboats and motorboats can be rented. Most guests are here for packages ranging from canoe camping and whitewater rafting to snowmobiling (see *To Do*). Base high-season rates are $245–529 for cabins that sleep four to six. **The River Driver's Pub** (see *Dining Out*) serves all three meals in high seasons, dinner year-round. NEOC also maintains the **Penobscot Outdoor Center Campground** (see *Camping*).

♿ **5 Lakes Lodge** (207-723-5045; 5lakeslodge.com), 46 Marina Dr., South Twin Lake, Millinocket. Open year-round. Debbie and Rick LeVasseur, both locally born and raised, have created a luxury lodge on a narrow point of land on South Twin Lake, surrounded by water with a superb view of Katahdin. Windows maximize the views. The five spacious guest rooms feature log bed, gas fireplace, cathedral ceiling, and Jacuzzi. Both Debbie and Rick are active outdoorspeople who know the local waters and woods and enjoy tuning their guests in to the best that this region offers. $175–275, depending on the day and season, includes a full breakfast. Free use of kayaks and canoes. Motorboat rentals.

❂ (ᵥ) **Big Moose Inn, Cabins & Campground** (207-723-8391; bigmoosecabins.com), Baxter Park Road, 8 miles west of Millinocket. Open May–Oct. Sited between Millinocket and Ambajejus Lakes with access to swimming, this classic 1830s cedar-shake inn has been run by Laurie Boynton-Cormier's family since 1974. We love the old-fashioned lobby with the moose above the hearth. The lodging options vary: seven comfortable guest rooms with double or twin beds sharing three baths, and eight suites with private bath. There are

also 18 cabins—including six large enough for groups and several right on the lake—as well as 35 tent sites and six lean-tos. $56 per person for inn rooms and $140–199 per couple for the suites; $49 per person for cabins ($90 minimum); $11 per person per campsite, $14 for lean-tos. Canoe and kayaks available. Breakfast is available to inn guests. This is also the base for **North Country Rivers** and **Penobscot Adventures** (see *Whitewater Rafting*) and **Katahdin Scenic Cruises** (see *Air Rides*). Also see *Dining Out*.

❂ **Mountain Glory Farm** (1-800-219-7950; mountaingloryfarm.com), 199 Happy Corner Rd., Patten. Open year-round. This 1890s farmhouse with its spectacular view of Katahdin is divided into two comfortable, tastefully furnished duplex apartments, well-stocked with books about the area and the Amish. Owned by Christina Shipps (see Inn on the Harbor, Stonington), the 170-acre farm–replete with an orchard, cultivated fields, grazing meadows, and livestock—is maintained by an Amish family who have rebuilt the large barn. Guests are asked to respect the family's privacy but are free to walk the farm's grassy trails. A short drive north from Millinocket, this is rolling, open country, paced to that of the Amish horse-drawn carriages that traverse it. Shin Pond and the Metagamon Gate to Baxter State Park are a short ride away. $105 for the one-bedroom, $110 for the two-bedroom per night; $660/665 per week.

IN SOUTH PISCATAQUIS COUNTY

Brewster Inn (207-924-3130; brewsterinn
.com), 37 Zion's Hill Rd., Dexter 04930. Open
year-round. Dexter is a proud old Maine
town, and this is its proudest house, built in
the 1930s for Governor (later Senator) Ralph
Owen Brewster by noted architect John
Calvin Stevens. Brits Mark and Judith Ste-
phens offer nine guest rooms and two suites.
$79–159 includes a full breakfast.

REMOTE SPORTING CAMPS *Note:* Also
see *Remote Sporting Camps* in the preceding
and following chapters.

🐾 🦌 **Frost Pond Camps** (207-852-4700;
frostpondcamps.com). Open May to Nov. Off
the Golden Road (35 miles from Millinocket,
45 miles from Greenville), drive across Ripogenus Dam to Frost Pond—3 miles in and
you'll feel you've taken a step back in time.
Gene Thompson and Maureen Raynes, both
Registered Master Maine Guides, are the
owners of these seven waterside cabins and
10 campsites along the shore of Frost Pond.
Rustic cabins are off-grid with gas lights,
refrigerator, cooking stove, and heated by a
woodstove in spring and fall. Water is carried
from a nearby well and each has a clean pit
toilet. One cabin has plumbing, a shower, and
toilet. $102 per couple per cabin, $51 for each
additional adult, children 15 and under are
$15. Also bunkhouses, rental boats, canoes,
and kayaks. Best contact is by email: info@
frostpondcamps.com.

✪ **Katahdin Lake Wilderness Camps**
(207-837-1599; katahdinlakewildernesscamps
.com). Privately owned but on land owned
by and accessed through Baxter State Park,
these legendary 1880s camps offer the view
of Mount Katahdin depicted by artists from
Frederick Church to Marsden Hartley and
James Fitzgerald. Spring through fall you can
fly in, or hike the 3.3-mile trail from Roaring
Brook Rd. in the park. Dec.–Mar. the camps
welcome those hardy souls who ski the 9.3
miles from the Togue Gate (gear is trans-
ported by snowmobile from the Abol Bridge
Store). Ten log cabins (one to eight people per
cabin) and a main lodge (with a library and
dining room) are built on a bluff overlooking
the lake. All have a woodstove and propane
lights; some are housekeeping. Facilities
include a spring, outhouses, a beach, dock,
and canoes. The lake yields native brook
trout. No access for snowmobilers. The camps

VIEW OF KATAHDIN FROM MOUNTAIN GLORY FARM

Christina Tree

are currently owned by Charles FitzGerald and managed by Bryce and Holly Hamilton. $125 per adult, $55 per child per day includes linens and towels, breakfast, dinner, and a trail lunch. Winter rates are slightly higher, and guests are advised to bring sleeping bags. No credit cards.

☀ **Nahmakanta Lake Camps** (207-731-8888; nahmakanta.com). Founded in 1872, this is a remote set of nine lakefront cabins (accommodating two to eight people) with picture windows, screened porch, woodstove, gas lights, and fridge, plus six shower houses with hot water and flush toilets behind the cabins. Guests can choose from housekeeping at $85 per person per day, $118 MAP (breakfast and dinner), or $150 per person with all meals (packed lunch); special children's rates. All plans include use of rowboats and canoes; guide service and dogsled tours in winter are the house specialties. Nahmakanta is within walking distance of the Appalachian Trail.

☀ ✎ **Bowlin Camps** (207-528-2022; bowlincamps.com), Patten. Open year-round, a classic Maine sporting camp with 10 cabins (private baths) with gas light and wood heat, one dating to 1895. Some have cooking facilities, but three meals are served in the central lodge. Not far from the Northern Gate of Baxter State Park, the camps are on the East Branch of the Penobscot River with trails to ponds and waterfalls, and rental canoes for an easy paddle (shuttle service offered). Families are welcome in July, Aug.; otherwise this is a serious fishing and hunting base, equally popular with snowmobilers. Twelve miles of cross-country trails. $150–200 per person includes three meals.

CAMPGROUNDS **Penobscot Outdoor Center Campground** (neoc.com/penobscot outdoorcenter). Owned by the New England Outdoor Center (1-800-634-7238) on Pockwockamus Pond, this is a whitewater rafting base and the closest commercial campground to Baxter State Park. Lodging is in cabin tents and cabins as well as campsites. Facilities include the Paddle Pub, a hot tub, game rooms, canoes, and kayaks.

Chewonki Big Eddy Cabins and Campground (207-882-7323, 207-882-7323 Apr. 1–Oct. 15; bigeddy.org). Open mid-May through Sept., on the Golden Road just outside Baxter State Park's south entrance. Chewonki is a long-established, Wiscasset-based nonprofit offering family-geared outdoor experiences. Sited on Penobscot at Big Eddy, a famed spot for landlocked salmon, it offers 75 riverside primitive campsites, three cabins, and a limited number of RV sites, also camping gear, canoe rentals, and shuttles.

Abol Bridge Campground and Store (207-447-5803; abolcampground.com), 18.5 Golden Rd. Open May 1–Thanksgiving. Location! Location! The 36 campsites are on the Penobscot River and Abol Stream with access via the AT to Baxter State Park, a sandy beach, and a marina. There are also 12 new bunkhouses (up to four people per), bath and shower houses, and the **Northern Restaurant**, open year-round for all three meals. This is now the Penobscot base for **Northern Outdoors** (see *Whitewater Rafting*). Lodging options also include RV sites and the housekeeping cabins at nearby **Rip Dam Sporting Camps**.

Jo-Mary Lake Campground (207-723-8117), open mid-May–Oct. 1. On the south shore of Jo-Mary Lake, some 15 miles south of Millinocket and 5 miles west of Rt. 11 in **KI Jo-Mary Multiple Use Forest**, a 200,000-plus-acre tract of commercial forest harboring fine fishing, hunting, and access to Gulf Hagas (*Hiking*). There are 60 campsites, flush toilets, and hot showers. See northmaineoods.org.

Peaks-Kenny State Park (207-564-2003), off Rt. 153, 6 miles northeast of Dover-Foxcroft. Open mid-May through Sept., with 56 campsites on Sebec Lake. Reservations are a must.

The **Department of Conservation** (parks andlands.com) Northern Region Office in Ashland (207-435-7963) can supply information and pamphlet guides to campsites in the Penobscot River Corridor and other nearby holdings.

✳ Where to Eat

ALL ENTRIES ARE IN MILLINOCKET UNLESS OTHERWISE NOTED

DINING OUT ♻ ✎ ♿ **River Driver's Pub** (207-723-5523), 30 Twin Pines Rd. off State Park Rd., 8 miles east of Millinocket (turn onto Black Cat Rd. at the 35 MPH sign). An attractive space in the reception center for New England Outdoors (neoc.com), sited with a view from the dining room and patio of Katahdin Lake and its namesake mountain. All three meals are served, but check in off-season. Crab stuffed haddock roulade is a specialty. Burgers and sandwiches always available. Entrées $10–29.

♻ ♿ **Fredericka's at Big Moose Inn** (207-723-8391), 8 miles west of Millinocket on Baxter State Park Rd. Open for dinner Wed.–Sat., June–early Oct.; also Sun. July–Aug. Hot breakfast is served Sat.–Sun. in-season to B&B guests. Dinner reservations suggested. Accessible by boat. Laurie Cormier tells us that the restaurant is named for her mother and that everything is made from scratch, including the risotto and gnocchi. It's a pleasant dining room. The menu ranges from chicken to flatiron steak to duck in a fennel blueberry reduction. Entrées $18–22. The **Loose Moose Bar and Grill** (open Thu.–Sat), with good pub grub and live music, is usually jammed.

EATING OUT ♻ (((ᵒ))) **Appalachian Trail Café** (207-723-6720), 210 Penobscot Ave. Open 5 AM–8 PM daily, year-round. A beloved landmark, good burgers, omelets, doughnuts (try the pumpkin), pies, home cooking, and reasonable prices. The walls and back counter are filled with AT photos and memorabilia. Owners Paul and Jamie Renaud literally walked into town after completing the trek from Georgia. They were puzzled by the café's name, given its lack of any obvious link to the trail. They didn't mean to buy it, but it came with the lodge down the street. They kept the cooks, just rehabbed the kitchen and redecorated the café. Between meals, stop by with a couple of friends for a Summit Sundae (the ultimate banana split: 14 scoops of ice cream). Check out the new **Hiker Cafe** upstairs (May 15–Oct. 15, 8–4), geared to AT hikers with a computer, WiFi, and showers; also souvenirs, books, and more.

✍ **Pelletier Loggers Family Restaurant Bar and Grill** (207-723-6100; americanloggers .com), 57 Penobscot Ave. Open year-round Wed.–Sat. 11–9, Sun. 11–8. The logging truck jutting from its facade gets your attention. Seems that the Discovery Channel's *American Loggers* reality show features the Pelletier family, local loggers who spent $1 million transforming the former

Downtown Restaurant and Laundromat into a pine-paneled lounge and grill with a large stone fireplace and decor that includes moose and deer heads and chain saws. The menu is large and so are the portions. Don't pass on the onion rings.

✍ **Scootic In Restaurant** (207-723-4566; scooticin.com), 70 Penobscot Ave. Open Mon.–Sat. 11–10, Sun. 4–10. George and Bea Simon are third-generation owners. The menu choices include fresh-dough pizza, calzones, pasta entrées, seafood, and smoked baby back ribs.

Sawmill Bar and Grill (207-447-6996), 9 Millinocket Lake Rd. A former convenience store is now a way stop between town and park. Reasonably priced pizzas, soups, subs, and sandwiches named for local landmarks. Try the hefty Baxter BLT.

ROAD FOOD ✍ **The Nor'easter Restaurant** (207-564-2122), 44 North St., Dover-Foxcroft. Open daily lunch–dinner. Road food includes "broasted" chicken with fries and slaw.

Bear's Den Restaurant & Tavern (207-564-8733), 73 North St., is the place for breakfast.

In **Newport** road-food and fuel sources cluster around the I-95 exit. Check out **Anglers** (207-368-3374; anglersseafood restaurant.com), 542 Elm St. (Rt. 7/100 near the junction with Rt. 2), one in a small chain of Maine restaurants featuring fresh fish, great onion rings.

Christina Tree

PELLETIER LOGGERS FAMILY RESTAURANT, MILLINOCKET

✳ Entertainment

Center Theatre for the Performing Arts (207-564-8943; centertheatre.org), 20 E. Main St., Dover-Foxcroft. A vintage movie theater that's been restored as a venue for live performance and film. Check the website for current listings.

✳ Selective Shopping

IN MILLINOCKET

✪ **North Light Gallery** (207-723-4414; art northlight.com), 356 Penobscot Ave. Open year-round, Mon.–Sat. 10–6. Marsha Donahue has worked in Maine's leading coastal galleries and knows the state's leading artists. This gallery showcases some two dozen artists and sculptors as well as her own exceptional work, all focusing on interior Maine. Crafted items, prints, framing, and many other reasons to stop.

Moose Prints (207-447-6906; markpicard .com), 58 Central St., Millinocket. This gallery showcases wildlife photography by Mark Picard. Inquire about guided photographic tours, workshops, and seminars.

Katahdin General Store (207-723-4123), 160 Bates St., is a source of hunting and fishing licenses, gas, live bait, groceries, cold beer, camping permits, and the largest selection of camping and sporting gear in the area.

((ɣ)) **North Woods Trading Post** (207-723-4326), Baxter State Park Rd. Open May–Oct., 7 AM–9 PM. The nearest store to Baxter State Park offers WiFi, clothing and tech gear, wine, fishing licenses, books and maps, ice cream, pizza, and more, as well as sound advice from owners Sandy and Matt Bell.

✳ Special Events

February: **Winterfest** in Millinocket—snowmobile parade, antique snowmobile display, bonfire, cross-country skiing.

July: **4th of July Festival**, Millinocket—parade, music, vendors, fireworks, usually two to three days' worth of activities. **Summerfest**, East Millinocket, a weekend full of activities and a fireworks display.

Mid-September: **Trails End Festival** (trailsendfestival.org) features music, water and kids' activities, plenty of food, a car show, more.

October: **Fly-in and car show** at Millinocket Airport.

AROOSTOOK COUNTY

roostook is Maine's least populated county but the largest in area—it's the size of Connecticut and Rhode Island combined. Bounded by Canada on two sides, it's definitely off the beaten track. Portland is as far from Fort Kent, the northern end of Rt. 1, as it is from Manhattan. But contrary to its image as one flat potato field, The County (as it's simply known) is largely wooded, and much of the open farmland is a rolling patchwork of varied crops.

Aroostook divides into four visibly distinct regions. The broad western swath is an extension of the **North Maine Woods**, and a number of visitors actually paddle into The County along the north-flowing **Allagash Wilderness Waterway**. To the east the lake-spotted **St. John Valley** forms the northeastern corner of Maine (and the country). It's bounded on the north as well as east by the St. John River, which forms as much of a bond as a border between French-speaking Acadians, who have preserved their distinctive culture through a tortuous 400-year-long, widely wandering history. Note the many homes and barns decorated with five-pointed stars, a proud symbol of Acadian heritage. To the south, **Central** and **South Aroostook** are narrow (less than 40 miles wide), comprised of mostly agricultural land, bordered by woodland to the west and New Brunswick on the east.

For decades American and Canadian settlers disputed the border in this area, and in 1839 Maine mobilized 10,000 solders, building military roads to the blockhouses at Fort Kent and Fort Fairfield. The bloodless **Aroostook War** that ensued brought a population boom to **Central Aroostook**. Many of the soldiers, who were from rocky coastal farms, noted the region's superior soil and took advantage of generous land grants that followed the 1842 Webster/Ashburton Peace Treaty.

Another distinctive wave of immigrants arrived in Central Aroostook after the Civil War, thanks to Lincoln's ambassador to Sweden, which was suffering at the time from famine. A Portland man, he was instrumental in obtaining an 1870 federal land grant that bestowed 100 acres of woodland to each Swedish family; 1,400 had arrived by 1895. The story is beautifully told today in the **New Sweden Historical Museum**.

Beginning in the 1990s, The County has been welcoming yet another distinctive group. In South and Central Aroostook, **Amish families** continue to arrive, bringing their horse-drawn wagons and breathing new life into old farm buildings and soil that had begun to lie fallow. The first families settled in Smyrna, west of Houlton in Southern Aroostook, an area in which their stores and carriages are most visible. New groups continue to arrive, maintaining the big old farmhouses and distinctive hip-roofed and sunken-looking potato barns.

Christina Tree

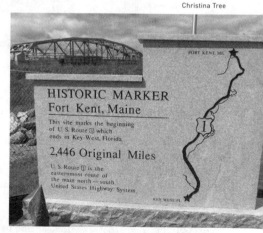

A MEMORIAL MARKS THE BEGINNING OF THE FIRST MILE OF RT. 1 IN THE UNITED STATES

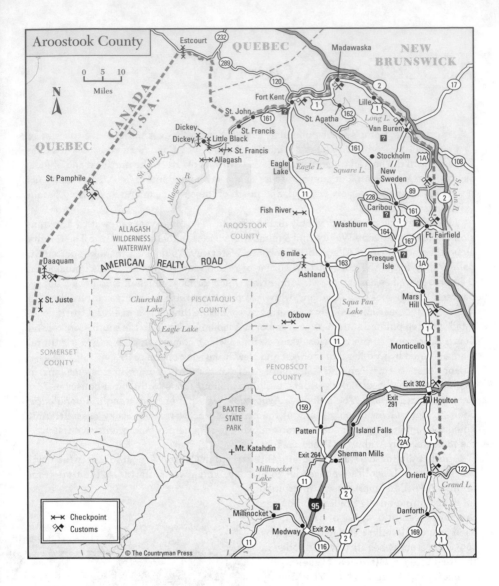

Aroostook County

The Amish are helping ensure the biggest attraction of all in South and Central Aroostook: A European-style agricultural landscape that's a patchwork of cultivated fields and forest. There are still plenty of potatoes (early Irish and Scotch Irish settlers are credited with introducing it), but broccoli, canola, and grains are now important.

Ask locally for directions to the best places to walk, ski, swim, and fish; feast on fiddleheads, ployes (buckwheat crêpes), and poutine (fries with cheese and gravy).

GUIDANCE Aroostook County Tourism (1-800-427-8736; visitaroostook.com) publishes an exceptional guide that's worth securing before a visit.

Maine State Visitors Center (207-532-6346), just off I-95 Exit 302 at the intersection of Rt. 1 in Houlton, offers friendly advice and a wealth of print material about this area. It's open daily 9–5:30, in summer 8–6. Restrooms open 24 hours.

Greater Houlton Chamber of Commerce (207-532-4216; houltonchamber.com), 109-B Main St. is in the **Aroostook County Historical Museum**, and **Caribou Area Chamber of Commerce** (207-498-6156; cariboumaine.net), 393 Main St., is in **The Nylander Museum** (see *To See*). Also note: The **Greater Fort Kent Area Chamber of Commerce** (207-834-5354; fortkentchamber.com), 291 W. Main St.; **Greater Madawaska Area Chamber of Commerce** (207-728-7000), 356 Main St.; and **Central Aroostook Chamber of Commerce** (207-834-5343), 3 Houlton Rd., Presque Isle.

North Maine Woods (207-435-6213; northmainewoods.org) maintains a terrific website and an information office posted from Rt. 1, Ashland. Check with them about gates and fees within the commercial woodlands. This is a prime source of information about day use and camping.

Tourism New Brunswick (1-800-561-0123; tourismnewbrunsick.ca) maintains visitors centers just across the border from Houlton, Fort Fairfield, Van Buren, Madawaska, and Fort Kent. Bring your passport!

GETTING THERE AND AROUND *By car:* Houlton, the terminus of I-95 and of Rt. 1, is The County's prime gateway (see *Guidance*). Head north on Rt. 1 through the Acadian heart of the St. John Valley or veer off to lakes and sights along Rt. 161; either way takes little more than two hours to reach Fort Kent and "America's First Mile" (of Rt. 1). But The County demands at least two days. Cross the border, at least from Madawaska to Edmundston, NB. The way south from Fort Kent, down wooded Rt. 11 (watch for moose), is again little more than two hours, 107 miles to I-95 at Sherman Mills.

By plane: **Northern Maine Regional Airport** (flypresqueisle.com) is served by **Pen Air** (penair.com). *By bus:* **Cyr Bus Line** (207-827-2335 or 1-800-244-2335) operates daily between Fort Kent and Bangor.

Christina Tree

A TYPICAL ST. JOHN VALLEY BARN

WHEN TO COME Winter offers dependable snow cover on no less than 2,300 miles of maintained **snowmobile** trails! **Dogsled races** are held annually in Fort Kent, and competitive skiers come to train on cross-country trails. Spring is **fishing** season at The County's many sporting camps, and summer, with cooler temperatures than downstate, attracts hikers, cyclists, and visitors to the many small museums. In early July the potato fields are a spread of pink and white blossoms. Fall colors include the red of buckwheat fields.

✱ To See

SOUTHERN/CENTRAL AROOSTOOK

Houlton (population 4,856) is the primary gateway to Aroostook's junction of Rt. 1, I-95, and Rt. 2A (the old high road south) with The County's big Maine Visitors Information Center. Turn off Rt. 1 and down Main Street to find the **Market Square Historic District**, with its brick commercial blocks, built after a 1902 fire, that reflect wealth from logging and potatoes. The site of a lively Sat. (9–1) farmers' market, the square offers a mix of shops and restaurants, plus the Temple Theater (films) and the Gateway Crossing suspension bridge across the Meduxnekeag River. T**he Aroostook County Historical and Art Museum** (207-532-4216), 109 Main St., is a must-see. Open Memorial Day–Labor Day, Mon.–Sat. 1–4. Housed in one of the town's boom period mansions, this large collection of local memorabilia includes artifacts from the German POW camp at Houlton's airport during World War II. The staffed Houlton chamber office (see *Guidance*) is here and helpful.

    The Maine Solar System Model. Pluto, just an inch in diameter, can be seen on a wall of the Maine Visitors Information Center in Houlton (see *Guidance*), the place to pick up a descriptive brochure about the eight planets that can be spotted (most on poles), heading

GATEWAY CROSSING BRIDGE IN HOULTON

NEW SWEDEN HISTORICAL SOCIETY MUSEUM

The community's reconstructed Kapitoleum (meetinghouse) includes a bust of William Widgery Thomas, the Portland man sent by President Lincoln to Sweden in 1863 to halt the sale of iron to the Confederacy. Thomas devoted his sizable energies to establishing a colony of Swedish farmers in Maine. A pink granite memorial in a pine grove behind the museum complex commemorates the arrival and hardships of those who settled here between 1870 and 1875. Despite the severe climate and thin soil, New Sweden prospered, with 689 buildings, including three churches, seven general stores, and two railroad stations by 1895.

The three-day "Midsommar Festival," the traditional Swedish celebration of midsummer, is a homecoming weekend for Swedes living throughout the Northeast. It includes dancing, community suppers, and concerts in nearby hilltop Thomas Park, an outdoor amphitheater with exceptional acoustics. On any day this is a special place. Don't miss the collections of incredible long wooden skis upstairs in the museum (this community is credited with introducing cross-country skiing to America) or the other historic buildings out back. Even if the museum is closed, the gravestones in the neighboring cemetery tell a moving story. ✐ (in-season, 207-896-5200), 116 Station Rd. just east of Rt. 161, New Sweden, also posted from Rt. 1. Open late May–Labor Day, Mon.–Fri. noon-4, weekends 1-4.

north along a 40-mile stretch of Rt. 1—they correspond in size and spacing to a scale of 1 to 93 million miles. The sun is in the Northern Maine Museum of Science (Folsom Hall) on the University of Maine's campus, 181 Main St. (Rt. 1), Presque Isle. The project continues to expand.

More museums, geographically south to north:

Oakfield Railroad Museum (207-757-8575), Station St., Oakfield, Houlton, off I-95 Exit 286, 17 miles west of Houlton. Open Memorial Day–Labor Day, Sat., Sun., and holidays 1-4. A 1910 Bangor & Aroostook Railroad station displays photographs from the early RR days, vintage signs, maps, newspapers, a rail motorcar, and a C-66 caboose.

Southern Aroostook Agricultural Museum (207-538-9300), 1664 Rt. 1, Littletown. Open mid-June–Sept., Thu.–Sat. 1-4. Milk and cream got around on a sled, and individual farms created their own potato bags—these facts are part of the local agricultural history depicted here. Public suppers are held through summer and fall.

✐ **Nylander Museum** (207-493-4209; nylandermuseum.org), 657 Main St., Caribou. Open year-round, 9–noon, 1:30–4:30. Housed with the chamber of commerce, displays fossils, minerals and rocks, shells and other marine life, butterflies and moths, birds, animals, and early human artifacts, most collected by Swedish-born Olof Nylander; also a medicinal herb garden in the back with traditional Native American plants.

Caribou Historical Center (207-498-2556), Rt. 1, Caribou. Open June–Aug., Wed.–Sat. 11–5. A log building filled with local memorabilia from the mid-19th century to the 1930s, also a replica of an 1860s one-room school with a bell in the cupola.

ST. JOHN VALLEY

The St. John Valley is a place apart, a totally bilingual but preferably French-speaking area suffused with a pride in Acadian culture. Acadians trace their lineage to French settlers who came to farm and fish in what is now Nova Scotia in the early 1600s, but were forcibly deported in 1775 by an English governor. This "Grand Dérangement," which dispersed a population of some 10,000 Acadians, brutally divided families (a tale told by Longfellow in "Evangeline"). Many were resettled in New Brunswick, from which they were once more dislodged after the American Revolution when the British government gave their land to loyalists from the former colonies.

In a meadow overlooking the St. John River behind Madawaska's Tante Blanche Museum (named for an 18th-century local Acadian folk heroine), a large marble cross and an outsized wooden sculpture of a voyageur in his canoe mark the spot on which several hundred of these displaced Acadians landed in 1785. They settled both sides of the St. John River, an area the Maliseet tribal members called "Mattawaska."

Not too long ago children could be punished for speaking French anywhere on public school grounds, but despite intense pressure to assimilate, Acadians have stubbornly preserved their traditions and distinctive "Valley French," a blend of old Acadian and Quebec dialects. Today bilingual signage is common in the valley, schools offer French immersion programs, Catholic churches have Masses in both French and English, and the University of Maine at Fort Kent offers a bicultural studies program and also maintains an extensive collection of Acadian historical materials. In 2014 the World Congress of Acadians was held in the St. John Valley, infusing new energy into a scattering of Acadian sites and small museums.

Christina Tree

ALONG RT. 1

Acadian Village (207-868-5042; acadian village.mainerec.com), 859 Main St., north of Van Buren. Open mid-June–Labor Day, daily noon–5. The 17 buildings, many moved here from around the valley, include a school and store, barbershop, train station, buckwheat mill, old homesteads, a jail, reconstructed 18th-century log church, art museum, and gift shop. $6 adults, $3 children.

Acadian heritage is visible in the very shape of St. John Valley towns, with wooden houses strung out along roads that stretch like arms from the cathedral-sized Catholic churches. The most striking example

MUSÉE CULTUREL DU MONT-CARMEL

is farther up Rt. 1 in the tiny village of Lille. Gilded angels trumpet from the twin towers of this splendid, olive green wooden church, built in 1910 but long since deactivated. It's now the **Musée Culturel du Mont-Carmel** (207-868-2691; museeculturel.org), and its high, many-arched interior is open June 15–Labor Day, daily 1–4. Artist Don Cyr, the curator and moving force behind the restoration and programs (check the website), is usually on-hand.

Seven miles up Rt. 1 the imposing brick church of **St. David's Church** (1911) forms the centerpiece for the village of the same name. The neighboring **Tante Blanche Acadia Museum** (207-728-4762), open June–mid-Sept., Wed.–Sun. 11–4, is a trove of Acadian information and memorabilia. Follow the dirt road behind the museum to the river where a cross and voyageur sculpture mark the 1785 landing spot of the Acadians.

Nowhere is the river border less of a divide than between the towns of **Madawaska** and **Edmunston**, NB (tourismedmunston.com). The chief employer for both is Twin Rivers Paper Mill; the pulp, produced in Edmunston, travels through a mile-long, high-pressure pipeline across the river to Madawaska, where it is turned into specialty papers. French is the primary language for 83 percent of Madawaska's 4,035 residents and for 93 percent of Edmunston's 16,032 people. Edmunston's visitors center, housed in an old rail station, is across from a park with walking trails to downtown shops and restaurants. Check out the nearby **New Brunswick Botanical Garden** (jardinnbgarden.com) and Madawaska's **Acadian Festival** (acadianfestival.com).

At Frenchville (some seven miles beyond Madawaska), Rt. 162 veers south to St. Agathe on Long Lake. Here the **St. Agathe Historical Society Museum** (207-543-6911), 534 Main St., is open late June–early Sept., Tue.–Sun. 1–4. **The Pelletier-Marquis House** (1854) offers a sense of the town's ethnic history, and **The Preservation Center** displays religious, domestic, and military artifacts along with an extensive photo collection.

Note: For more about Acadian sites and cultural sources visit **maineacadian.org**.

MORE ST. JOHN VALLEY SITES

✪ **Fort Kent Blockhouse Museum**, off Rt. 1, Fort Kent. Open Memorial Day–Labor Day, 9–7:30, a Maine State Historic Site maintained by the Bureau of Parks and Lands and the local Boy Scout troop. This symbol of the northern terminus of Rt. 1 is a convincingly ancient, much-restored, two-story 1830s blockhouse with its original foundation and walls. Documents and mementos from the Aroostook Bloodless War are exhibited inside. Be sure to wander down to the Fish River behind the blockhouse, a pleasant walk to picnic and tenting sites. This is the terminus of the **Northern Forest Canoe Trail**, which begins in Old Forge, NY. A granite marker farther along Main St. beside the bridge to Clair, NB now formally marks "America's First Mile," as in the 2,390 miles of Rt. 1 connecting Fort Kent with Key West. This fine old riverside blockhouse and its peaceful grounds still seem a much more fitting end-of-a journey icon.

Christina Tree

BLOCKHOUSE, FORT KENT

✳ To Do

BICYCLING The topography lends itself to long touring loops. For suggestions contact **The Bike Shop** (207-834-7000) in Fort

Million Dollar View Scenic Highway: At the southeastern corner of The County the 7.9 miles of Rt. 1 from the Danforth–Orient town line north offer long views west to Mount Katahdin.

Fish River Scenic Byway: 38 rolling, heavily wooded miles of Rt. 11 south from Fort Kent follow the Fish River and Eagle Lake.

Limestone Road (Rt. 1A) from Fort Fairfield north is great for long vistas.

Rt. 2 has been replaced by I-95 as the quick way to Houlton, but the stretch of this historic road along the Golden Ridge between Island Falls and Oakfield offers splendid views across this agricultural landscape. Note signs of the Amish community in Smyrna (see *Selective Shopping*).

Kent, **Daigle Sport Center** (207-728-3881) in Madawaska, **Aroostook Bicycle** (207-764-0202) in Presque Isle, and **The Ski Shop** (207-868-2737) in Van Buren.

CANOEING AND KAYAKING The **Allagash Wilderness Waterway** is considered *the* canoe trip in Maine (see *What's Where*). The entire 92 miles of lake and river canoeing begins in the Katahdin Area, but it's possible to put in at Round Pond and paddle the final 32 miles of the north-flowing Allagash River to its confluence with the St. John River in Allagash Village. We recommend using a shuttle service. **Peletier's Campground** (207-398-3187) in St. Francis is a good base, with canoe rentals and shuttle service to Round Pond. **Allagash Guide Service** (207-398-3418; allagashguideservice.com) in Allagash also rents canoes and offers transport and pickup as well as guided tours here and on the St. John.

Perception of Aroostook (207-764-5506; perceptionofaroostook.com), based in Presque Isle, offers kayak sales, rentals, and guided tours on the Aroostook River and Presque Isle Stream.

Christina Tree

RIDEOUTS

Note: The 740-mile **Northern Forest Canoe Trail** (northernforestcanoetrail.org) ends at the blockhouse in Fort Kent.

FISHING The catch in remote lakes here in the North Maine Woods (see *Lodging/Sporting Camps*) is so rich and varied that it's recognized throughout the country. Salmon grow to unusual size, and trout are also large and numerous. Contact the **Maine Department of Inland Fisheries and Wildlife** in Ashland (207-435-3231; in-state, 1-800-353-6334). The 80-mile Fish River chain of lakes (**Eagle, Long**, and **Square Lakes**) is in fishing circles. Fish strike longer in the season than they do farther south, and fall fishing begins earlier. East Grand Lake in the southeastern corner of The County (*Lodging*/**Rideouts**) also offers a serious catch.

GOLF The County's topography lends itself to golf, and the sport is so popular that most towns maintain at least a nine-hole course. The most famous course, with 18 holes, is **Aroostook Valley Country Club** (207-476-8083; avcc.ca), Fort Fairfield; its tees are split between Canada and Maine. The 18-hole **Va-Jo-Wa Golf Course** (207-463-2128; vajowa .com) in Island Falls and the **Presque Isle Country Club** (207-764-0439; picountryclub.com) are also considered above par. **Caribou Country Club** (207-493-3933; caribougolf.com), Rt. 161, Caribou, is a nine-hole course designed by Geoffrey Cornish. **Mars Hill Country Club** (207-425-4802; golfmhcc.com), 75 Country Club Rd., Mars Hill, has 18 holes. **The Houlton Community Golf Club** (207-532-2662) borders Nickerson Lake.

HIKING **Fish River Falls**. Ask locally for directions to the trail that leads from the former Fort Kent airport down along the river, an unusually beautiful footway through pines. Note the **swimming holes** below the falls. **The Dike in Fort Kent** is also worth finding: a 0.5-mile walk along the Fish River. The trail up **Mount Carmel** (views up and down the river valley) begins on Rt. 1 at the state rest area near the Madawaska–Grand Isle town line.
   Also see: **Deboullie Management Unit** and **Aroostook State Park** (*Green Space*).

✳ Winter Sports

CROSS-COUNTRY SKIING/SNOWSHOEING The same reliable snow that serves snow mobilers allows residents to take advantage of hundreds of miles of trails maintained exclusively for cross-country skiing by local towns and clubs. Any town office or chamber of commerce will steer you to local trails.
   10th Mountain Division Center (207-834-6203) in Fort Kent includes a biathlon range, links to recreational ski trails, and a handsome lodge. The **Nordic Heritage Center** (207-328-0991) is a similar facility in Presque Isle, and in Madawaska **Four Seasons Lodge** is a nonprofit cross-country and snowshoeing center.

DOWNHILL SKIING **Bigrock Mountain** (207-425-6711; bigrockmaine.com), 37 Graves Rd., Mars Hill. Downhill and cross-country; call to check open times/events.

SNOWMOBILING is the single biggest reason visitors come to The County. It's the easiest way to see some of the more remote sporting camps and wilderness areas, because riding over well-maintained trails is often smoother than bumping down logging roads in summer. Call any Aroostook County chamber of commerce for a *Trail Map to Northern Maine*, detailing 2,300 miles of trails maintained by The County's 40-plus snowmobile clubs and including locations of clubhouses, warming huts, and service areas.

✴ Green Space

Deboullie Public Reserved Lands (parksandlands.com) is a 23,461-acre pond-spotted preserve managed jointly by the state and **North Maine Woods** (see *Guidance*), accessible by gated logging roads from St. Francis and Portage. Campsites are clustered around ponds (good for trout) and near hiking trails leading to the distinctive summit of Deboullie Mountain.

Aroostook State Park (207-768-8341; fws.gov/northeast/Aroostook), marked from Rt. 1, 4 miles south of Presque Isle. Open May 15–Oct. 15. A 600-acre park with swimming and picnicking at Echo Lake; also 30 campsites (June 15–Labor Day only) at 1,213-foot Quaggy Joe Mountain—which offers hiking trails with views from the north peak across a sea of woodland to Mount Katahdin. In the small **Maxie Anderson Memorial Park** next door, a tin replica of the *Double Eagle II* commemorates the 1978 liftoff of the first hot-air balloon to successfully cross the Atlantic.

Aroostook National Wildlife Refuge (207-328-4634), Loring Commerce Center (formerly Loring Air Force Base), 97 Refuge Rd., Limestone. At 5,252 acres, this former airfield's grasslands welcome migrating birds; 6.5 miles of trails allow visitors glimpses of the birds—including the American black duck—along with 10 ponds and many streams and brooks. The refuge is 8 miles from Caribou. Buildings have been demolished to clear the area for wildlife, and wetlands are under restoration. The visitors center has limited summer hours listed at friendsofaroostooknwr.org.

Aroostook Valley and Bangor Aroostook Trails (207-493-4224). This 75-mile trail system, with a packed gravel surface good for mountain bikes and ATVs, connects Caribou, Woodland, New Sweden, Washburn, Perham, Stockholm, and Van Buren. Many bogs, marshes, wetlands, and streams lie along these trails, which are owned by the Maine Bureau of Parks and Lands. There are several parking lots and rest areas on the trails as well. Used in winter primarily by snowmobilers.

✴ Lodging

SOUTH AROOSTOOK

((ɪ)) 🏕 **Rideouts** (207-448-2440 or 1-800-594-5391; rideouts.com), 6 Waterfront Dr., Weston. Open May–Oct. Just a mile off Rt. 1, this classic sporting camp consists of a central lodge and a cluster of a dozen cabins on 22-mile-long East Grand Lake. The lure here is fishing for landlocked salmon, lake trout, and smallmouth bass. Jim Brown's well-kept cabins range from studios to four bedrooms ($125–160 per day), most with kitchen facilities. The waterside dining room offers three home-style daily meals. Dinner, served promptly at 6, is open to the public Wed.–Sun ($16.95–21.95). Guides and rental boats available. Dogs are $50.

((ɪ)) **First Settler's Lodge** (207-448-3000; firstsettlerslodge.com), 341 Rt. 1, Weston.

Stephen and Sue Mine's open-beamed lodge faces Mount Katahdin, some 50 miles west but still a magnificent presence. Facilities include four comfortable queen rooms ($125), a loft suite with kitchen ($150), a full guest kitchen, and a spacious common room with books, a big stone hearth, and the many-windowed view. A full breakfast is included in rates and other meals are available; the dining room is open to the public Fri., Sat.

((ɪ)) ♿ **Ivey's Motor Lodge** (207-448-3000; iveysmotorlodge.com), 241 North Rd. (jct. I-95/Rt. 1), Houlton. Comfortable and convenient, rooms with double queens, a king, or an efficiency. $112–125 includes a buffet breakfast, and there's an Irish pub on the premises.

Also see **Mountain Glory Farm** in Patten in the Katahdin chapter. Just over the county line but very much a part of it in feel. The farmhouse commands a spectacular view of Mount Katahdin, and the 170-acre farm is worked by an Amish family.

CENTRAL AROOSTOOK

(📶) **The Northeastland Hotel** (207-768-5321 or 1-800-244-5321; northeastlandhotel.com), 436 Main St., Presque Isle. This vintage-1934, three-story hotel is the heart of downtown Presque Isle. The 51 elevator-accessed rooms, ranging from two queens to a king suite, are spacious, nicely furnished, quiet (request one in the back), and spotless ($115–131). The high end is for an efficiency suite. The totally indoor **Sidewalk Café,** serving all three meals, fills with locals as well as guests. **Coppers Lounge** features a wide-screen TV and live music on weekends.

✪ (📶) **Old Iron Inn** (207-492-4766; old ironinn.com), 155 High St., Caribou 04736. Kate and Kevin McCartney offer three rooms in their comfortable Arts and Crafts cottage-style home. The name refers to Kevin's collection of 19th- and 20th-century irons arranged decoratively around the common rooms. Each of the three guest rooms also includes a decorative, gem-like piece of volcanic rock that Kevin (a geology professor) will tell you is called a geode. All are furnished with antiques; private baths and outlets where you need them. $89–99 includes a bountiful breakfast. Inquire about apartment rentals.

Presque Isle Hampton Inn (207-760-9292; presqueisle.hamptoninn.com), 768 Main St., Presque Isle 04769. A 93-room facility. Indoor heated pool, fitness center, and a hot breakfast included in the rates. $124–169.

☀ (📶) **Caribou Inn and Convention Center** (207-498-3733 or 1-800-235-0466; caribouinn .com), junction of Rts. 1 and 164, Caribou 04736. This is a sprawling 73-room motor inn with an indoor pool, hot tub, fitness center, and the full-service **Greenhouse Restaurant**. Rooms are large, suites have kitchenettes, and it fills a need. This is snowmobiler central, the guests mostly male. From $115.

☀ (📶) **Presque Isle Inn and Convention Center** (207-764-3321 or 1-800-533-3971; presqueisleinn.com), 116 Main St. (Rt. 1), Presque Isle 04769. With 151 guest rooms and suites, handy to the airport and the University of Maine, Presque Isle. Amenities include an Italian restaurant, bar and lounge, heated indoor pool, and full fitness center. From $98.

ST. JOHN VALLEY

(📶) **Inn at Acadia** (207-728-3402; innofacadia .com), 384 St. Thomas St., Madawaska. A boutique inn in a former 1950s convent? Yes! No two of the 20 rooms are alike, but all share an uncluttered European feel and attention to detail. The view from the **Voyageur Lounge** (*Where to Eat*) and many rooms is off across the St. John River to New Brunswick. Breakfast, featuring fruit-stuffed ployes (Acadian whole wheat crêpes), is included in the $96–139 rates. Owner J. J. Roy was manning the front desk on the morning we asked for help repairing a broken bag. We were referred to a friend of a friend who repaired it beautifully and refused to charge. Acadian hospitality! Renovated as well as owned and managed by the Roy family, this is a special place. Amenities include an elevator and fitness center, room fridges, Keurig coffeemakers, and flat-screen TVs.

☀ (📶) **Northern Door Inn** ("La Porte du Nord") (207-834-3133; northerndoorinn .com), 356 W. Main St., Fort Kent. A pleasant and comfortable 43-unit property located directly across from the international bridge to Canada and drawing guests (including many snowmobilers in winter) from both sides of the border. $80 for a single, $88 double, $96 triple, $104 for four people includes continental breakfast with doughnuts.

Four Seasons Inn of Soldier Pond (207-834-4722; fourseasonsinnofsoldierpond.com), 13 Church St., Wallagrass. Seven miles from Fort Kent, this inn has six guest rooms, each with private bath. Three rooms have double Jacuzzi and one has a single Jacuzzi bath. This inn is on the snowmobile trail. Breakfast is made to order, with eggs and Belgian waffles always available. $99–149.

✪ **Long Lake Motor Inn** (207-543-5006; longlakemotorinn.com), Rt. 162, St. Agatha 04772. Open year-round. Ken and Arlene Lerman pride themselves on the cleanliness and friendliness of this two-story motel. There is a lounge, and continental breakfast is included in $68 double for a standard room. The honeymoon suite ($83) has a whirlpool. Two efficiency units ($73-98). The motel is across the way from the lake but offers access and a dock.

NORTH WOODS SPORTING CAMPS

✪ ☀ **Libby Sporting Camps** (207-435-8274; libbycamps.com), P.O. Box 810, Ashland 04732. Open ice-out through Nov. Owned and operated by Matt and Jess Libby (it's been in the family since 1890), this is one of Maine's premier sporting camps, seriously dedicated to fishing. Guides and floatplanes stand ready to take you to 40 lakes and ponds. The eight peeled spruce cabins overlook 6-mile-long Northern Millinocket Lake and are lighted with propane; handmade quilts cover the beds. There are also 10 outpost cabins. Meals are served in the central lodge, decorated with bobcat, lynx, and golden eagle, to name a few of its trophies. $235 per person per night, less for kids under 15, includes all meals and boats: motor, kayaks, sailboats, and canoes. Pets welcome, $10 fee.

♿ **Bradford Camps** (207-746-7777; bradfordcamps.com), P.O. Box 729, Ashland 04732. Open following ice-out through Nov. Sited on Munsungan Lake, 50 miles over woods roads from Ashland, accessible by floatplane from Millinocket. This is a century-old, classic sporting camp with a lodge set amid well-tended lawns. Eight hand-hewn log, lakeside cabins all have full private bath. Depending on the season, this is all about fly-fishing (landlocked salmon and brook trout) or hunting, but you can also enjoy canoeing and kayaking, swimming, and fly-out day trips. $185 per person per night includes meals; kid and weekly rates; packages. Guides, boats, and fly-out trips are extra. Family rates in July and Aug. Inquire about two remote outpost cabins. Your hosts are Karen and Igor Sikorsky—and yes, Igor is the grandson of the pioneer aviator best known for developing the helicopter.

Red River Sporting Camps (207-435-6207; redrivercamps.com), P.O. Box 320, Portage 04768; 26 miles from Portage. Open late May–early Oct. Cabins sit next to Island Pond at this remote camp with a reputation for good cooking, run by Jen Brophy. There's a new central log lodge, two small cabins and three larger, with one that holds as many as eight people. Rates are $130 per person American Plan, with housekeeping service, linens, towels, and use of boats, canoes, and more. $70 per person for three housekeeping cabins includes linens, wood-burning stove, and gas lamps; the private island cabin is $75.

✳ Where to Eat

IN SOUTH AROOSTOOK

The Courtyard Café (207-532-0787; the courtyardcafe.biz), 61 Main St. (in the Fishman Mall), Houlton. Lunch Mon.–Fri. and dinner Tue.–Sat. Chef-owner Joyce Transue is known for making everything here from scratch with imagination and local ingredients. Reservations suggested for dinner, maybe salmon in a bourbon brown sugar glaze.

The Vault Restaurant (207-532-2222), 64 Main St., Houlton. Open Tue.–Fri. 11–10, Sat. 4–10. Reservations recommended for dinner. Housed in an old bank building with some seats inside the vault. Varied menu. At dinner you might begin with stuffed clams, then dine on pesto chicken and sun-dried tomatoes over penne ($14).

✪ 🍴 **Elm Tree Diner** (207-532-3777), 146 Bangor Rd., Houlton. Open 5:30 AM–dinner. A longtime local favorite. Owner Gary Dwyer has weathered the fire that reduced the previous building to ashes and rebuilt a sun-filled space with many booths. Breakfast all day with house-made bread and muffins, great salads and sandwiches, dinner staples like Maine shrimp with spiral sweet potato fries, pies. Beer and wine.

🍴 **Granny's Country Inn** (207-532-7808), 1689 Bangor Rd., Linneus. Open 6 AM–9 PM. Six miles south of Houlton, this place is known for its legendary portions, reasonable prices, and fresh ingredients. Surrounded by potato fields, it's the place for house-made fries, also all things fried, from clams to fiddleheads.

🍴 ♿ **Brookside Restaurant** (207-757-8456), 2277 Rt. 2, Smyrna Mills (at Exit 291 off I-95). Welcome back to the '50s. Go for the homemade pies, meat loaf, and lobster rolls. Everyone raves about this place, but beware what you order. Our salmon loaf and creamed corn both tasted off their cans. The biscuits were superb.

IN CENTRAL AROOSTOOK

🍴 **Boondock's Grille** (207-472-6074), 294 Main St., Fort Fairfield. Closed Mon.–Tue. Open for lunch and dinner Wed.–Sat., for breakfast and dinner Sun. Good, honest home cooking with a woodsy decor. Hand-cut steaks and fried seafood, lots of choices, including poutine with gravy, meat loaf, and fish chowder; pizza and burgers are mainstays. Entrées $10–26.

Café Sorpreso (207-764-1854; cafe sorpreso.com), 415 Main St., Presque Isle. Open Mon.–Sat. for lunch and dinner. Sophisticated dining, vegetarian options—check the website for a weekly changing, locally sourced menu. Entrées $20–28.

Napoli's (207-492-1102), 6 Center St., Caribou. Open for lunch and dinner. A friendly Italian red-sauce restaurant with good spaghetti and sausage. The feel is an old neighborhood standby, but the neighborhood itself has disappeared thanks to urban renewal. Comfortable booths, friendly staff; pizza, pasta, and generous, fresh salads. Try the house Chianti and marinara. Entrées $7–16.

Cindy's Sub Shop (207-498-6021), 264 Sweden St. (Rt. 161), Caribou. Open daily 7:30 AM–9 PM, 9–7 on Sun.; closed Sun. between Christmas and Easter. Turkey and bacon sub, great lobster rolls, homemade soups like chicken stew and fish chowder. Homemade pies, "Swirl Delight" squares, and whoopie pies, too.

Frederick's Southside Restaurant (207-498-3464), 507 Main St., Caribou. Open for lunch and dinner, closed Mon. Great pizzas and poutine. Big portions and reasonable prices.

Canterbury Royale Gourmet Dining Rooms (207-472-4910), 182 Sam Everett Rd., Fort Fairfield. Open year-round, daily by reservation for dinner, also for lunch and tea by reservation. Deep in the woods, this is destination dining, five courses served in one of two elegant rooms with hand-carved paneling. Guests choose elaborate entrées well in advance.

IN THE ST. JOHN VALLEY

✪ **Long Lake Sporting Club** (207-543-7584 or 1-800-431-7584; longlakesportingclub.com), Rt. 162, Sinclair. Open daily from 4:30 for dinner year-round. Right on Long Lake, this is destination dining for many. Patrons are seated in the lounge and their order is taken (no prices on the menu), then they're ushered to a table when their meal is ready. Specialties

ORDER PLOYES AT DORIS'S CAFÉ   Christina Tree

include appetizer platters (wings, mozzarella sticks, ribs, and shrimp), steaks, seafood, jumbo lobsters (3½-pound hardshells), and BBQ ribs. Huge portions. Plan to spend $50 per person. The lounge is open in-season from 11, and we were able to snag a bowl of onion soup with a side of ployes as well as a table on the deck.

✿ **Lakeview Restaurant** (207-543-6331; lakeviewrestaurant.biz), Lakeview Dr., St. Agatha. Open daily 11–9; breakfast weekends, daily during winter. Set on a hilltop with views across the lake and valley, this is a big, cheerful family restaurant. Specialties include steak, seafood, and BBQ baby back ribs. Entrées $11–29.

✿ **Mill Bridge Restaurant** (207-834-9117), 271 Market St., Fort Kent. Open 10:30–9; from 8:30 Sun. Nicely sited south of town, overlooking the Fish River, this is a great spot for lunch or for dinner ranging from chicken wing dings to surf and turf. ($8.99–25.99).

✪ **Doris's Café** (207-834-6262), Fort Kent Mills. Open 5 AM–2 PM. What's for breakfast? "Anything you'd like, ma'am," the friendly waitress said. Funny thing is that ployes, the crêpe-like buckwheat pancake for which the St. John Valley is famed, aren't on the menu. "You have to stop somewhere," Linda, the restaurant's owner, told us. Turns out that Linda prides herself on her fluffy blueberry pancakes, but I did breakfast on delicious ployes with local syrup, watching a round table fill with men speaking French, followed by an English-speaking group.

☼ **The Swamp Buck Restaurant & Lounge** (207-834-3055), 250 W. Main St., Fort Kent. Open Mon.–Sat. for lunch and dinner, Sun. 9–9. A big, cheerful, middle-of-town restaurant with a North Woods feel. Beef is cut in-house and veggies are al dente. Specialties include BBQ ribs and wings, along with pan-fried trout—but it's a big menu with dishes such as chicken breast sautéed with shallots, wine, ham, and cheese in a sage cream sauce. All this and friendly service.

✳ Selective Shopping

IN SOUTH/CENTRAL AROOSTOOK

Amish Pioneer Place General Store, Rt. 2 west of I-95 Exit 291, Smyrna. Not your usual general store. Lit only by skylights, shelves lined with basic (healthy) food, staples like well-made work boots, gizmos for generating energy without electricity, a large hardware section, also toolsheds and outhouses. Warning: We opened what we thought was a toolshed, but it turned out to be a working outhouse.

Bradbury Barrel Co. (207-429-8141 or 1-800-332-6021; bradburybarrel.com), 479 Main Rd. (Rt. 1), Bridgewater. Showroom of white cedar barrels—which used to be the way potatoes traveled around the country—as well as other wood products.

IN THE ST. JOHN VALLEY

☼ **Bouchard Family Farms** (207-834-3237; ployes.com), 3 Strip Rd. (at Rt. 161), Fort Kent. Look for the big red field of buckwheat several miles south of town. The farm store across the road is open Tue.–Fri. 10–5:30, Sat. 9–4. Having switched from growing potatoes to buckwheat in the 1980s (a move they credit with saving the farm), the Bouchard family is nationally known for their ploye mixes. Ployes are traditional Acadian fare, crêpe-like pancakes made with buckwheat flour (no eggs, no milk, no sugar, no oil, no cholesterol, no fat). Fresh produce, local specialty foods, and crafts also sold.

✳ Special Events

January: **Long Lake Ice Fishing Derby** (207-534-7805), St. Agatha.

Early March: The **Can Am Sled Dog Race** (207-444-5439), Triple Crown 60- and 250-mile races, starting and ending in downtown Fort Kent.

June:. **Midsommar** (weekend nearest June 21) is celebrated at Thomas Park in New Sweden and at the New Sweden Historical Society Museum with Swedish music, dancing, and food.

July 4th weekend: **Houlton State Fair** (houltonfair.com) is a colorful agricultural fair. **Acadian Festival** in Madawaska (acadianfestival.com). Parade, traditional Acadian supper, and talent revue.

Mid-July: **Maine Potato Blossom Festival**, Fort Fairfield (potatoblossom.org), a week of activities including mashed-potato wrestling, Potato Blossom Queen pageant, parade, entertainment, dancing, industry dinner, and fireworks.

August: **Northern Maine Fair, Presque Isle** (207-764-1884; first week). Animals, a music festival, an agricultural museum, and exhibits with a lumberjack roundup. **Ployes Festival and Muskie Fishing Derby** (1-800-733-3563; second weekend), Fort Kent—a celebration of the buckwheat crêpe and other traditional Acadian dishes. **Crown of Maine Balloon Festival, Presque Isle** (crownofmaineballoonfest.org; last weekend).

INDEX